The Case for
CLOSING
the UN

International Human Rights
A Study in Hypocrisy

JACOB DOLINGER

gefen גפן
publishing house בית הוצאה לאור
JERUSALEM • NEW YORK   Est. 1981

Scripture quotations based on *The Holy Scriptures According to the
Masoretic Text*, published by the Jewish Publication Society in 1917.

Quotations from the *Jerusalem Post* reprinted by gracious permission of the publisher.
Cover Design: Miriam Grunhaus, GreenHouse Design, Inc.
Typesetting: Raphaël Freeman, Renana Typesetting

ISBN: 978-965-229-857-7

1 3 5 7 9 8 6 4 2

Gefen Publishing House Ltd.
6 Hatzvi Street
Jerusalem 94386, Israel
972-2-538-0247
orders@gefenpublishing.com

Gefen Books
11 Edison Place
Springfield, NJ 07081
516-593-1234
orders@gefenpublishing.com

www.gefenpublishing.com

Printed in Israel

*   *   *

Library of Congress Cataloging-in-Publication Data

Names: Dolinger, Jacob, author.
Title: The case for closing the UN : international human rights : a study in
  hypocrisy / Jacob Dolinger.
Other titles: Case for closing the United Nations
Description: Jerusalem, Israel : Gefen Publishing House Ltd., 2016. |
  Includes bibliographical references and index.
Identifiers: LCCN 2016011708 | ISBN 9789652298577
Subjects: LCSH: United Nations. | Human rights. | Genocide--History.
Classification: LCC JZ4974 .D65 2016 | DDC 341.4/8--DC23 LC
record available at http://lccn.loc.gov/2016011708

▌Contents

Remembrances and Acknowledgments

On that morning – May 10, 1940 – everything changed. Antwerp, my hometown, was bombed by the Luftwaffe as Hitler opened his war against Western Europe, five months after he invaded Poland.

My family left Belgium, proceeded through France, and reached Portugal, where refugees were being treated humanely. Brazil accepted us, despite its strict rules against Jewish immigration – following the bad example of the United States. In Brazil we were treated as equals. On the beaches, in parks, in schools, and finally in the university one did not feel any discrimination, any difference between the Christian majority and the tiny Jewish minority. It was all dignified and very respectful. A relief from centuries in Europe!

There is a certain tendency in Latin American countries for law professors, upon reaching retirement age, to turn to other fields – philosophy, poetry, art – away from the legal matters to which they dedicated the better part of their lives.

With the present author the move was of another sort. I had written an article on the forgotten, practically unknown Armenian Genocide, a long piece on human rights from the perspectives of Brazilian and international law, and two articles on international terrorism, one of them foreseeing the destruction of the United Nations, all published in Brazilian law journals. These articles opened a new field of interest beyond my long dedication to private international law.

The Zionist ideal, which was a constant inspiration in the Dolinger and Zweig families, brought the author and his wife to Israel seven decades after that sad day in May 1940. In Israel my research was drawn to the subjects dealt with in those articles. And I came to better understand the connection between the genocide of the Christian Armenians and the genocide of the European Jews. There were foreign accomplices to the Turks in their mad annihilation of the Armenians, just as it was easy to detect a worldwide range of accomplices to the murderous Nazi hysteria against the Jews. After the catastrophes of 1915 and 1945, a lack of accountability prevailed. This stimulated a rich variety of dictators and cruel regimes to perpetrate the most unimaginable violent atrocities and actual genocides throughout the last sixty-five years. And so we have come to witness a hundred years of maddening perversities around the world.

Today, sitting comfortably in New York and in Geneva, the people who run the United Nations have become accomplices to terrorism and genocide and guarantors of impunity. And the eminences who sit in the Hague submissively acquiesce to the international injustices.

This book is a call to close that false, malicious, hypocritical organization and work toward a completely different way of organizing protection for human rights, security, and peace in the world.

To this end, the author had the privilege to count on the help of people in three continents.

In Brazil, my former student, today law professor Raphael Vasconcellos read various parts of the manuscript and offered advice. Doctoral candidate Felipe Albuquerque has been a researcher of the highest caliber from the beginning to the end of the present work.

Keith Rosenn, professor at the School of Law of the University of Miami, has been a steady friend for the last thirty years. He gave me valuable support for this book.

Our daughter Miriam Grunhaus, in Florida, understood the book's ultimate message, as very well portrayed in the cover she designed.

And here in Israel I received kind help from Mauricio Zalcberg, who searched and found a publisher for the book.

Gefen Publishing House accepted the challenge to undertake a project that deals with many polemic issues, formulated in nondiplomatic parlance. Editors Kezia Raffel Pride and Tziporah Levine very diligently took care of my "Latin English," checked all my sources, and corrected them whenever necessary, significantly contributing to the end result.

To all, the author extends his sincere gratitude.

In addition to people who directly contributed to this book, I am grateful to all those who helped me along my life's path.

During high school years in New York at Mesivta Torah Vodaas, where I was introduced to the treasures of the Talmud, I was inspired by the ethical personalities of Rabbi Avraham Pam and Rabbi Gedalia Schorr.

While at law school at Rio de Janeiro State University, I was privileged to receive the support of Professor Oscar Tenório, whom I eventually followed as head of the private international law department and whose classic book on the subject I reviewed. Two generations later it was my turn to be succeeded by Professor Carmen Tiburcio, a longtime coauthor of various publications, who has been reviewing my books for further editions. This is the gratifying academic chain that connects one generation to the next.

Luis Roberto Barroso, another former student, sits today on the Brazilian Supreme Court. He is an outstanding justice and a nationally respected authority on constitutional law, and maintains a close relationship with his former teacher.

I owe much to a variety of doctors both in Brazil and in Israel – too many to enumerate. But I cannot abstain from honoring Dr. Alex Saukhat, who saved my life, and Dr. Avigdor Abrahams, who kept me alive and fit for work. I am deeply grateful for their professional competence and extreme dedication.

Our three daughters, Rebeca, Iona, and Miriam, have followed the ways of their parents and succeeded in bringing up their children with dedication to learning, to the delight of the grandparents.

And above all, I would like to acknowledge the support and patience of my wife, Rachelle Zweig Dolinger, who renounced the comfortable position of companion to a retired professor and instead stimulated me to continue studying and working. She read the manuscript, gave me sound advice, and has stood at my side in the most difficult moments.

May we see the opening of a new era of peace, respect for human dignity, and protection of human rights on the national and international levels.

Preface

Akira Iriye and Petra Goedde wrote in the introduction to their book on human rights, "Legal and political experts, as well as human rights activists, have begun to recognize the importance of placing their work in historical perspective."[1] The dignity of a human being and the inherent human rights that derive from this concept were the central inspiration of the fundamental documents of the United Nations: the charter of the organization and the Universal Declaration of Human Rights. The preamble of the United Nations Charter, signed in San Francisco, California, on June 26, 1945, states that "We the peoples of the United Nations determined to save succeeding generations from the scourge of war, which twice in our lifetime has brought untold sorrow to mankind, and to reaffirm faith in fundamental human rights, in the dignity and worth of the human person, in the equal rights of men and women and of nations large and small...." This statement sets the two World Wars (1914–18 and 1939–45) center stage in the creation of the United Nations.

Universal peace, and respect for human rights and fundamental freedoms, have been established as the basic purposes for the creation of the United Nations. The same goes for the Universal Declaration of Human Rights (UDHR), approved in 1948,[2] which contains a beautiful preamble, inspired by the hope of its drafters that after the "barbarous acts which have outraged the conscience of mankind" (referring to the war that had just ended), a new

1. Akira Iriye and Petra Goedde, "Introduction: Human Rights as History," in Akira Iriye, Petra Goedde, and William I. Hitchcock, *The Human Rights Revolution: An International History* (New York: Oxford University Press, 2012), 6.
2. Proclaimed by the General Assembly Resolution 217 (III) of December 10, 1948.

era demanded the "recognition of the inherent dignity and of the equal and inalienable rights of all members of the human family [as] the foundation of freedom, justice and peace in the world." The authors of the declaration, like the drafters of the United Nations Charter, were convinced that human rights and peace in the world were two interconnected concepts.[3]

It should be noted that there is no article in the declaration regarding antisemitism or hateful incitement against other peoples, no rule in favor of tolerance and respect for other religions or races. Rather, the declaration only proclaims freedom of religion for the individual.

The next step was the approval, in December 1948, of the Convention on the Prevention and Punishment for the Crime of Genocide, "in order to liberate mankind from such an odious scourge."[4] The contracting parties undertook to prevent and to punish the crime of genocide, which is defined in article 2 as a series of acts "committed with intent to destroy, in whole or in part, a national, ethnical, racial or religious group."[5]

The UN endeavors for the universalization of human rights spread to various other areas, among them the Declaration on the Granting of Independence to Colonial Countries and Peoples, of 1960,[6] the International Convention on the Elimination of All Forms of Racial Discrimination of 1966,[7] the Convention against Torture and Other Cruel, Inhuman or Degrading Treatment or Punishment of 1984,[8] declarations and conventions that include the defense of the interests of women, children, disabled persons, right of development, human duties and responsibilities, cultural diversity,

---

3. The preamble of the UDHR proceeds to refer to the United Nations Charter, in which the peoples that joined the organization reaffirmed their faith in fundamental human rights and pledged to achieve the promotion of universal respect for and observance of these rights and fundamental freedoms in cooperation with the United Nations. A common understanding of these rights becomes of the greatest importance, this being the reason to produce the Universal Declaration of Human Rights "as a common standard of achievement for all peoples and all nations."

4. Convention on the Prevention and Punishment of the Crime of Genocide, General Assembly (GA) Resolution 260 A (III), December 9, 1948.

5. Ibid., article 2.

6. GA Resolution 1514 (XV), December 14, 1960.

7. GA Resolution 2.106, December 21, 1965.

8. GA Resolution 39/46 Annex, December 10, 1984.

indigenous peoples, defense of sexual orientation and gender identity, apartheid, refugees, and migrant workers.

And so, starting from the United Nations Charter and the Universal Declaration of Human Rights and going through a series of conventions and declarations, the international community has developed a wide and rich system with the purpose of protection from the most varied dangers, discriminations, sufferings, and persecutions, envisioning a world of peace and security.

The results of all these initiatives have been very poor at best and terribly disastrous at worst.

Two phenomena characterize the century from 1915 to 2015: complicity and impunity. Nations of the world have been accomplices to the evils of other nations, complicit in the worst crimes, cruel atrocities, and the most severe violations of human rights. Millions could have been saved, but were not, due to apathy in the best cases, economic and strategic interests in the worst instances – all inexcusable, all unforgivable.

And after the most serious violations of human rights, after unimaginable atrocities and actual genocides, there has been no punishment, no justice.

Before analyzing the post–World War II documents and their implementation, we turn in chapter 1 to the events that occurred during World War I in Turkey when the Muslim majority persecuted, tortured, and murdered approximately one and a half million Christian Armenians with terrible inhumanity, while the world looked on, then promised to take care of the survivors and provide them with compensation that never materialized. Important democracies have abstained till today from recognizing the genocide of the Armenian people, which causes a continuous suffering for the survivors' descendants. And so starts what we call the twentieth-century hypocrisy. The indifference of the world community regarding the Armenian tragedy strengthened Hitler's courage to go ahead with his murderous plan against European Jewry.

From the Armenian disaster the book turns to the Second World War, to the Holocaust of the Jewish people, focusing mainly on the complicity of the American and British governments, the main culprits being President Franklin Delano Roosevelt and his friends at the State Department. The utilization of the immigration quotas for Germany and Austria remained far below their maximum limits, causing the deaths of hundreds of thousands of Jews who could have entered legally into the United States. All possibilities and actual plans to absorb Jewish refugees in African and Latin American countries were torpedoed by the US government, which caused hundreds of thousands of Jews who could have been saved to perish instead in concentration camps. Moreover, Roosevelt refused to come out and accuse Germany for its genocidal plans, which gave Hitler the conviction that he could do with Jews as he wished, as clearly stated by the Fuehrer's declarations.

The State Department's behavior was so atrocious that the Treasury Department presented to President Roosevelt in 1944 a vehement and detailed accusation of the cruel attitudes of that other sector of the same government, but that happened late in the war, when most of the victims had already been murdered. Still, many hundreds of thousands of Hungarian Jews could have been saved, but Roosevelt's people made sure that no real help materialized.

The State Department and the White House received appeals from Christian leaders, from various members of Congress, from innumerable newspapers, from distinguished journalists, from the most important American intellectuals, but nothing moved the leaders of the government to change their evil policies toward the disaster of the Jewish people in Europe.

Roosevelt and his friends at the State Department stand accused of open complicity with Hitler and, according to principle 7 of the Principles of International Law Recognized in the Charter of the Nuremberg Tribunal, "Complicity in the commission of a crime against peace, a war crime, or a crime against humanity as set forth in Principle VI is a crime under international law." Therefore some members of the American government should have sat at the Nuremberg trial together with the Nazi criminals. The Nuremberg trial was not "victor's justice," as critics of that time proclaimed, but – much worse – it was the trial of the criminals conducted by their accomplices.

The accusations contained in this book cover the period that preceded the war (chapter 2), the years when the war was being waged (chapter 3), and the postwar behavior of the Allied countries (chapter 4).

The historical background of the UDHR – the three great documents, the English, American and French precedents – is described in chapter 5, which analyses critically the various rules contained in the declaration, some of them repetitious and others incongruent. The chapter contains a historical overview of the manifestos of great philosophers, theologians, and historians throughout time, on liberty, freedom, and all the other expressions reflecting human dignity, followed by a classification of the different categories of principles in the realm of law in general.

Chapter 6 is dedicated to a critique of the basic misconception of the Universal Declaration of Human Rights text, which the drafters proclaimed as a result of the Nazi atrocities against the Jews, whereas the provisions of the declaration are set to protect the individual and not persecuted minorities. Moreover, the chapter discusses the fact that the declaration remained a mere document – not a ratified agreement – and most member states of the UN do not abide by the protective measures proclaimed by the declaration.

All the resolutions of the United Nations, starting from the Universal Declaration of Human Rights, proceeding with the two basic covenants, and continuing through the various conventions approved during the following decades, concentrated on statements of principles, legal concepts, general rules, and multiple obligations, but did nothing about saving innocent people doomed by the powers of evil. The only exception is the 1948 Convention on the Prevention and Punishment for the Crime of Genocide, which prescribes prevention and punishment, but concentrates on punishment and leaves the prevention aspect undefined and inoperative.

Chapter 7 discusses the fact that saving people under persecution and suffering atrocities requires intervention, which might be considered as violating the state's sovereignty. The UN charter contains precepts in favor of both sides of the coin – the state's sovereign independence and the recourse to force to avoid human catastrophes. In recent times people are conscious of a new concept, the "responsibility to protect," which makes it easier to admit humanitarian interventions. But as chapter 7 concludes, the United Nations is ruled by political interests, which restricts the compliance of its conventions and covenants and the functioning of its committees.

Chapter 8 deals with the deadly subject of genocide, born out of the "Final Solution" that the Nazi regime applied to the "Jewish problem," which inspired the United Nations to create a convention exclusively dedicated to this international crime. Before describing the innumerable genocides that occurred after the Holocaust, this chapter criticizes the convention for having dealt only with one of its two objectives – punishment – while nothing was provided for the very important other goal of prevention.

In the development of the dozens of atrocities that took place after World

War II, the UN either remained paralyzed or intervened through ineffective operations which practically never brought any remedy to the disastrous situations. The genocides in Cambodia, Congo, Rwanda, the former Yugoslavia, and in many other countries were induced or aggravated by the complicity of the most important liberal democracies, a shameful inhumanity by nations that claim to be the leaders of the international human rights revolution. The convention also does not include universal jurisdiction as a means of bringing the authors of genocides to trial in any country where they are found. And the international courts that were created have achieved minimal results. As chapter 8 reveals, the great criminals of the last decades have remained free and unpunished.

Genocide and terrorism – the two great dangers that befell the world – are being neither punished nor prevented and are growing exponentially. Chapter 9 addresses the challenge of terrorism in the modern world. Whether Islam is a religion of peace is a difficult subject in view of the contradictions found in the Koran. But this is a theological subject and not what should really matter to the governments of Europe and the United States. For them and for the Western world in general, what is important is to realize that a certain number of Islamic leaders have managed to attract a considerable number of Muslim youths to dedicate themselves to murderous terrorism, which is growing from day to day and spreading all over the world, in some parts dedicated to eliminating the Christian minorities. The European governments are reacting with total blindness to this growing danger, and as of 2016 the president of the United States is supporting this policy.

The UN has never bothered to avoid the entrance of the worst totalitarian and terrorist-abiding states into its organization. Instead of coordinating a defensive war against terrorism, the UN has been busy defending the "human rights of the terrorist" in the spirit of Kofi Annan's frequent credulous manifestos. Terrorists face cowardice and naïveté, which only serve to help them in their murderous campaigns. The West (the UN and Europe, and eventually the United States), due to its cowardice, faces the danger of a world holocaust. This is the essence of chapter 9.

We next turn to the International Court of Justice, the judicial organ of the United Nations, to discover that it has declined to a level in which it does not conduct its activities as a court of law, but rather as an adjunct of the Security Council in its bigoted approach to certain international political situations. Rendering decisions without any basis in the authentic sources of public international law and without examining the factual data of the matters with which it is confronted, the International Court of Justice is dedicated to political interests and to the policies of the countries from which each individual judge is a national. The central case discussed in chapter 10 is the fence that Israel built to defend its population from the murderous terrorist infiltrations.

Former president of the Supreme Court of Israel Judge Barak and prominent American judge Posner discuss how democracy should face terrorism, the first one advocating a careful approach that fights this dangerous murderous movement with certain restrictions respecting the principles of human rights, whereas the second one advocates the sacrifice of these principles in order to fight terrorism with both hands, as otherwise democracies would be committing suicide.

The chapter narrates how the Israel Supreme Court has dealt with the problems caused by the fence, rejecting the decision of the International Court of Justice, but taking into consideration expertise that shows that the fence could move here and there, in order to facilitate the life of the Arab population without endangering the Israeli people.

The discrimination with which Israel is treated by the organs of the United Nations, which give more importance to construction of new Israeli homes in Jerusalem than to the systematic murder of hundreds of thousands of people and the displacement of millions – policies that are described in detail and accompanied by the critique of the most illustrious journalists and legal authorities – comprises chapter 11 under the title of "The UN in the Footsteps of Hitler."

The book closes in its last chapter with the proposal to abandon the United Nations and create a new world organization, indicating the principles that it would have to follow and some of its characteristics, totally distinguished from those that rule the United Nations. To wake up the world community, the book creates a fictitious resuscitation of Emile Zola, who directs a vehement *J'accuse* at the entirety of Western civilization.

Chapter One
The Armenian Genocide

The Armenian Genocide – The Beginning of the Twentieth Century's Hypocrisy

After the Treaty of Versailles, which ended the First World War, the feeling of "never again" prevailed throughout the world. The same feeling inspired the makers of the Universal Declaration of Human Rights after the Second World War and gave hope to the survivors and to the world at large.

From one "never again" to the next, the world witnessed a century of successive genocides. It started with the Armenians in 1915.

With the genocide of the Armenian people in 1915 begins the twentieth century's criminal silence in the face of unspeakable atrocities committed against millions of human beings in different corners of the earth. There had been massacres of Armenians by the Ottomans in the years 1895 to 1896, especially in Sason and in Constantinople. In 1909 the Turks again turned against their Armenian nationals and slaughtered tens of thousands of them in Cilicia,[1] but none of these tragic events can be equated to what took place during the First World War in the towns and villages where the Armenians had lived for centuries.

In 1915–16 the Turkish government eliminated approximately 1.5 million Armenian civilians – men and women, old and young – in unimaginably horrific and cruel massacres.[2]

---

1. Hilmar Kaiser, "Genocide at the Twilight of the Ottoman Empire," in *The Oxford Handbook of Genocide Studies*, ed. Donald Bloxham and A. Dirk Moses (New York: Oxford University Press, 2013), 368–69.

2. The exact number of Armenian losses is not clear and is open to different estimates. See ibid., 382; and Tribunal permanent des peuples, *Le crime de silence: Le génocide des Arméniens* (Paris: Flammarion, 1984), 187.

The execution of the massacres was planned and ordered by a group of three members of the Young Turks political party who composed a triumvirate that governed Turkey at the time: War Minister Ismail Enver Pasha, Interior Minister Mehmed Talaat Pasha, and Ahmed Djemal Pasha, the military governor of Constantinople and later on minister of the navy.

In early January 1915 the Armenian members of the national army were disarmed and taken away from their homes in small groups to be shot to death.

The Turkish government alleged that the Armenians had contact with fellow Armenians in Russia and that they were preparing themselves to betray Turkey in favor of the Russian enemy, with whom Turkey was at war. Based on this suspicion (real or fabricated), they organized a program of mass deportations and executions of the Armenian population, not only from the Turkish regions that bordered Russia, but from regions that were very distant from the battleground.

Dr. Clarence D. Ussher, an American doctor and envoy of the Episcopal Church who lived many years in Turkey, built and directed a hospital in the city of Van, where he also built a few schools. He was there when the atrocities started. Once back in the United States, he published a book, *An American Physician in Turkey*, in which he gives a testimony of what he saw. In one of his reports he tells how the massacres began in various provinces in May 1915: "In Bitlis and Mush the Government officials, solemnly swearing that innocent men should not be molested, succeeded in deceiving the Armenians and in making them surrender whatever arms they had for self-defense, entrapped the leaders, slaughtered the men first, then, after indescribable outrages, the women."[3]

In the college town of Marsovan, 1,216 men – professors, teachers, preachers, students, and others – were imprisoned for three days, then tied together in groups of four, marched out to a lonely gorge at midnight, and there slaughtered with axes by gendarmes and Kurds. Of one group of five thousand Armenians from the location of Harput, only 213 reached Aleppo, their supposed destination.[4]

Dr. Ussher tells how four of his old friends, college professors, "were most

---

3. Clarence D. Ussher, *An American Physician in Turkey: A Narrative of Adventures in Peace and War* (1917; repr., London: Sterndale Classics, 2002), 175.
4. Ibid., 175–76.

horribly tortured and done to death. The able-bodied men were thrown into the larger rivers on the way. Those who swam were shot. The pretty girls were sold as slaves. The gendarmes stole the clothing and food of the rest. They were driven naked over mountains and across the scorching plains for days and weeks, and taken in open cars like cattle through Aleppo, exposed to the jeers of the populace."[5]

The *New York Times* in its edition of October 7, 1915, quoted a report by the British ambassador, Viscount Bryce, who reported that the Turks would gather the whole population of a town and take them out of the city limits, where men were separated from women and children. The men were then executed. The women and children were marched away, many dying of hunger as they were given no food. Many were forced to undress and march naked under the burning sun. Women lost their minds. The road was full of dead bodies.[6]

The massacre of Trebizond was reported by the Italian consul: all the Christians of the town were taken to the beach, put on boats, brought out to sea, and thrown into the water. "The whole Armenian population, numbering 10,000, was thus destroyed in one afternoon."[7]

Another most important source on the Armenian genocide by the Turks is *Ambassador Morgenthau's Story*, in which the American diplomat Henry Morgenthau narrates in its most horrible details the massacres that the Turkish forces perpetrated on the Armenians.

When the Turkish authorities suspected that an Armenian had hidden weapons, they would torture him by pulling out the eyebrows and beard of their victim, "almost hair by hair; they would extract his finger nails and toe nails; they would apply red-hot irons to his breast, tear off his flesh with red-hot pincers, and then pour boiled butter into the wounds. In some cases the gendarmes would nail hands and feet to pieces of wood – evidently in

---

5. Ibid., 176.
6. "800,000 Armenians Counted Destroyed," *New York Times*, October 7, 1915, http://www.armeniapedia.org/index.php?title=800%2C000_Armenians_Counted_Destroyed_-nyt19151007.
7. Ibid. See also Clarence D. Ussher, *An American Physician in Turkey: A Narrative of Adventures in Peace and War* (1917; repr., London: Sterndale Classics, 2002), 175.

imitation of the Crucifixion, and then, while the sufferer writhed in his agony, they would cry, 'Now let your Christ come and help you.'"[8]

The ambassador reports that between April and October 1915, approximately 1.2 million people were forced to march under the most terrible conditions toward the Syrian desert. Whoever would stop walking to get a little rest or whoever fell on the road was forced, with all brutality, to get up and continue marching. Even pregnant women were forced to proceed. If a woman gave birth on the road, she was forced to continue the march immediately.[9]

Commenting on the defense that was many times expressed by the Turkish government, the ambassador wrote: "It is absurd for the Turkish Government to assert that it ever seriously intended to 'deport the Armenians to new homes'; the treatment which was given the convoys clearly shows that extermination was the real purpose of Enver and Talaat."[10] Morgenthau details how a convoy ultimately consisting of eighteen thousand Armenians left Harput, accompanied by seventy gendarmes. After seventy days only 150 women and children arrived at the supposed destination of Aleppo. A few additional women were still alive, enslaved by Turks or Kurds. The rest of the eighteen thousand people were all dead.[11]

In another dramatic passage, the ambassador writes that his only reason to report these terrible events was that without the details, the world would not understand what happened. He adds that he did not report the most horrible details, as a complete report of the "sadistic orgies of which these Armenian men and women were the victims can never be printed in an American publication. Whatever crimes the most perverted instincts of the human mind can devise, and whatever refinements of persecution and injustice the most debased imagination can conceive, became the daily misfortunes of this devoted people."[12]

On January 15, 1916, Talaat sent instructions to the governor of Aleppo – where a reduced number of Armenian survivors had arrived – in the following terms:

---

8. Henry Morgenthau, *Ambassador Morgenthau's Story: A Personal Account of the Armenian Genocide* (1918; repr., New York: Cosimo, 2010), 210–11.
9. Ibid., 216.
10. Ibid., 219.
11. Ibid., 119–21.
12. Ibid., 221.

To the Government of Aleppo:

We are informed that certain orphanages which have opened also admitted the children of the Armenians.

Should this be done through ignorance of our real purpose, or because of contempt of it, the Government will view the feeding of such children or any effort to prolong their lives as an act completely opposite to its purpose, since it regards the survival of these children as detrimental.

I recommend the orphanages not to receive such children; and no attempts are to be made to establish special orphanages for them.

Minister of the Interior,

Talaat[13]

Dr. Ussher makes a point of emphasizing that the majority of the Turkish population was opposed to the deportations and the massacres, and that in some places "petitions of protest" were presented, "stating that the Armenians were useful and loyal citizens and that it would be an injury to the country to send them away."[14]

The Promises of the Democracies

Throughout the whole time that the Armenians were being persecuted and murdered, some governments protested or appealed, but nothing concrete was undertaken to save the victims.

A short while before the end of the First World War, Lloyd George, premier of England, told an Armenian delegation, "Great Britain will not forsake its responsibility towards your suffering race."[15]

Aristide Briand, premier and foreign minister of France, declared in November 1916, "At the hour of legitimate reparations, France will not forget the atrocious sufferings of the Armenians and, in agreement with its Allies, will take the necessary measures to guarantee for Armenia a life of peace and progress."[16] His successor, Georges Clemenceau, wrote to an Armenian leader in July 1918: "I have the pleasure to confirm to you that the government of the Republic, as well as of Great Britain, never left the Armenians out of the group

13. Available at http://www.firstworldwar.com/source/armenia_talaatorders.htm.
14. Ussher, *An American Physician in Turkey*, 177.
15. Tribunal permanent des peuples, *Le crime de silence*, 49.
16. Ibid.

of nations, the destiny of which shall be settled by the Allies, in conformity with the supreme laws of Humanity and Justice."[17] And the prime minister of Italy said, "Tell the Armenian people that their cause is my cause."[18]

After the war, the leaders of the Turkish government ran away, and in July 1919 they were tried by a martial court that condemned Enver, Djemal, and Talaat in absentia to death, but the great number of criminals who led the genocide were not touched.[19]

At the Peace Conference in 1919, the Turkish representative admitted that "horrible acts were executed, which will shake forever the conscience of humanity."[20]

In 1920 the Treaty of Sèvres was imposed on the Ottoman Empire and signed by representatives of the sultan, according to which all rights of the Armenians would be returned, all forced conversions would be annulled, the towns of Van, Bitlis, Erzurum, and Trebizond would be integrated in the new Armenian republic, the Turkish government would help in the recuperation of the women and children who had been enslaved by the Muslims, and the law on the so-called abandoned goods that enriched Young Turks with the property of Armenians would be canceled.

This treaty was totally ineffective: it was never ratified. The Allies got busy with Syria, Palestine, Egypt, Mesopotamia, and parts of Anatolia and did nothing in favor of the Armenians. Mustafa Kemal Atatürk, the first president of modern Turkey, rejected the treaty, which had recognized the Armenian state.

In July 1923 the Lausanne Treaty was signed between the great powers and the new Turkish republic, without any mention of Armenia or the rights of the Armenian people. For this important treaty the Armenians did not exist, never even existed! The new Turkish borders and annexations were recognized.[21]

---

17. Ibid.

18. Ibid., 50.

19. "Verdict ("Kararname") of the Turkish Military Tribunal," Armenian National Institute, http://www.armenian-genocide.org/Affirmation.237/current_category.50/affirmation_detail.html.

20. Tribunal permanent des peuples, Le crime de silence, 53.

21. William Schabas, "Le génocide," in Droit international pénal, ed. Hervé Ascensio, Emmanuel Decaux, and Alain Pellet (Paris: Pedone, 2000), 319–32; M. Cherif Bassiouni, "L'Expérience des premières juridictions pénales internationale," in Droit international pénal, ed. Ascensio et al., 635–59; United Nations Economic and Social Council

The world assisted quietly the genocide of the Armenians during the war, and after the war accepted the results obtained by Turkey with the destruction of their Armenian minority. Thus the "crime of silence," as described by the Permanent People's Tribunal on the Armenian Genocide that assembled together in Paris in 1984.

This indifference toward the suffering of the Armenians during the war and the lack of persecution of the Ottoman criminals after the war repeated itself two and a half decades later when Jews were being gassed and burned by the Nazis while the "Allies" looked on and did nothing to save them, as well as after the conflict, when the majority of Nazi criminals were left untouched (see chapters 3 and 4, "Complicity during the War" and "Complicity after the War").

The Crime of Silence

The Permanent People's Tribunal on the Armenian Genocide was established by a group of eminent intellectuals and jurists from Europe, America, Australia, and Africa. They heard witnesses, examined documents and the existing literature regarding the events that took place in Turkey during the Great War, and came to the conclusion that, despite all the denials of successive Turkish governments, indeed a genocide had been committed against the Armenian people in Turkey, by initiative and under the leadership of the government led by the Young Turks.

The decision of the Permanent People's Tribunal stresses that the Turkish government was continuing, at the time of this trial (1984), with its anti-Armenian policies through the destruction or abandonment of Armenian cultural monuments and religious temples, with the purpose of eliminating any Armenian presence from the country.[22]

The judgment of this court resulted in the book *Le crime de silence: Le génocide des Arméniens*, containing contributions of many intellectuals who participated in the trial.

The court included the following personalities:

Commission on Human Rights, Report Prepared by the United Nations War Crimes Commission E/CN.4W.20, May 28, 1948, http://www.armenian-genocide.org/Affirmation.168 /current_category.6/affirmation_detail.html.
22. Tribunal permanent des peuples, *Le crime de silence*, 326.

- Madjid Benchick, professor of international law at the University of Alger
- Georges Casalis, French theologian
- Harald Edelstam, former ambassador of Sweden in Chili and in Algeria
- Richard Falk, professor of international law at Princeton University
- Ken Fry, member of the Australian parliament
- Andrea Giardina, professor of international law at the University of Rome
- Seán MacBride, Irish jurist, president of the International Peace Bureau, recipient of the Nobel and Lenin Peace Prizes and of the American Medal of Justice
- Leo Matarasso, French attorney
- Adolfo Perez Esquivel, Argentinian Nobel Peace Prize laureate
- James Petras, professor of sociology at New York University
- François Rigaux, professor of private international law at the Belgian University of Louvain
- Ajit Roy, Indian economist and journalist
- Georges Wald, emeritus professor of biology of Harvard University, Nobel Biology laureate

The court understood that the Genocide Convention has a declaratory character, therefore it is admissible to characterize the commission of the crime in relation to acts practiced before the convention went into force (1951) and independently of the accused state's ratification of the international agreement (which Turkey did in 1952).

The declaratory character of the convention, proceeds the Tribunal Permanent des Peuples, is characterized in its preamble, in which the contracting states "recognize that in all periods of history, genocide has inflicted great losses on humanity," and in article 1, which states that "the contracting parties confirm that genocide, whether committed in time of peace or in time of war, is a crime under international law." This confirms that the crime existed before December 9, 1948, when the convention was signed.

Actually, in addition to the declaratory argument, the Genocide Convention can be applied retroactively because in international criminal law – as opposed to domestic criminal law – retroactivity is accepted, so that rules established at a certain time may be applied to crimes committed earlier.[23]

More recently, a declaration was signed in March 2000 by 126 experts

23. Paul Guggenheim, *Traité de Droit International Public*, vol. 2 (Geneva: Georg, 1954),

on the Holocaust, under the leadership of Nobel Peace Prize laureate Elie Wiesel, which affirms that the genocide done against the Armenians during the First World War is an incontestable historic fact, calling on the Western democracies to recognize this reality.[24]

From the international law standpoint, genocide is a crime independently of the convention. The International Court of Justice issued an advisory opinion shortly after the convention was adopted that said:

> The origins of the Convention show that it was the intention of the United Nations to condemn and punish genocide as "a crime under international law" involving a denial of the right of existence to entire human groups, a denial which shocks the conscience of mankind and results in great losses to humanity and which is contrary to moral law and to the spirit and aims of the United Nations. The first consequence arising from this conception is that the principles underlying the convention are principles which are recognized by civilized nations as binding on States, even without any conventional obligation.[25]

In other words, genocide is a crime under customary public international law and therefore it is correct to classify the atrocities committed by the Turkish government on the Armenians in the second decade of the twentieth century as the crime of genocide.

German Participation in the Armenian Genocide

An important historic point is the role played by German agents in the tragic events that took place in Turkey in 1915.

Ambassador Morgenthau records the influence of Germany in the Turkish policy of deporting the Armenians. He affirms:

> I have also said that Admiral Usedom, one of the big German naval experts in Turkey, told me that the Germans had suggested this deportation to the

34; Stanislaw Plawski, *Étude des principes fondamentaux du droit international pénal* (Paris: Librairie Générale de Droit et de Jurisprudence, 1972), 147.

24. Deborah E. Lipstadt and Wole Soyinka, "Armenian Genocide Not Debatable," Letters, *Emory Magazine* 76, no. 3 (autumn 2000), http://www.emory.edu/EMORY_MAGAZINE/autumn2000/letters.html.

25. "Reservations to the Convention on the Prevention and Punishment of the Crime of Genocide (Advisory Opinion)," *International Court of Justice Reports* 16 (1951): 23.

Turks. But the all-important point is that this idea of deporting peoples *en masse* is, in modern times, exclusively Germanic. Any one who reads the literature of Pan-Germany constantly meets it. These enthusiasts for a German world have deliberately planned, as part of their programme, the ousting of the French from certain parts of France, of Belgians from Belgium, of Poles from Poland, of Slavs from Russia, and other indigenous peoples from the territories which they have inhabited for thousands of years, and the establishment in the vacated lands of solid, honest Germans.[26]

Dr. Clarence D. Ussher also reports on the German participation in the atrocities:

That the deportations were planned by the Prussian Government cannot be doubted by any one who has had first-hand knowledge concerning them. If Germany was to rule Turkey in the end, she would avoid trouble with the progressive and nationalistic Armenians by scattering them among the Turks. She followed the policy she had followed in France in the early days of the war and which she has since followed in Belgium: any territory occupied by her must be rid of its original inhabitants, or they must be so scattered as to form no longer a homogeneous population.[27]

Dr. Ussher further relates how "German missionaries were instructed to turn the Armenian orphans under their care out into the streets. The head of one such orphanage tried to save from this fate her Armenian teachers," which brought about a telegram from the German Consul ordering her to "give them up at once." The head of the institution undertook a difficult and dangerous journey to Constantinople to plead with the ambassador, to no avail. In the end she was forced to turn the young women over to the Turkish soldiers.[28]

26. Morgenthau, *Ambassador Morgenthau's Story*, 251.
27. Ussher, *An American Physician in Turkey*, 112. Vakahn N. Dadrian is the author of *German Responsibility in the Armenian Genocide: A Review of the Historical Evidence of German Complicity* (Watertown, MA: Blue Crane Books, 1996). A book of historical fiction on the Armenian genocide is Franz Werfel's *The Forty Days of Musa Dagh*, published in Vienna in 1933 as the Nazis were preparing themselves for the Holocaust of the Jews. Franklin Delano Roosevelt had the same idea regarding the need to scatter the Jews in the United States in order to weaken any influence they might acquire, as we shall see in chapter 3.
28. Ussher, *An American Physician in Turkey*, 113.

Dr. Ussher adds that German missionaries in Turkey were persecuted by their own government in response to their efforts on behalf of Armenian women and children.[29]

Efforts to Save the Armenians

Ambassador Morgenthau reports on his various meetings with the all-powerful German ambassador Hans Freiherr von Wangenheim and his efforts to convince him to use his influence over the Turkish governing group to stop the deportations and atrocities that were being committed on the Armenians.

In one of his meetings with his German colleague, the American ambassador told him that he did "not claim that Germany was responsible for these massacres in the sense that she instigated them. But she is responsible in the sense that she had the power to stop them and did not use it. And it is not only America and your present enemies that will hold you responsible. The German people will some day call your government to account. You are a Christian people and the time will come when Germans will realize that you have let a Mohammedan people destroy another Christian nation."[30]

Ambassador Morgenthau reports that the German ambassador was never moved by his pleas that, as the representative of the Turkish ally, he should endeavor to use his influence over the Turkish rulers to stop the deportations.

From scholarly analysis of old documents many decades after the fact as well as the testimony of illustrious and trustworthy personalities who were eyewitnesses to the atrocities, it is to be concluded that the cooperation of the German authorities with the Turkish government in the deportation and genocide of the Armenians is a proven fact.

The American diplomat invested enormous efforts to stop the genocide in innumerable meetings with Enver and with Talaat. He got nowhere. In one of those encounters with Talaat, an interesting dialogue about different religions took place. The Turk asked the American ambassador: "Why are you so interested in the Armenians, anyway? You are a Jew; these people are Christians. The Mohammedans and the Jews always get on harmoniously.

29. Ibid.
30. Morgenthau, *Ambassador Morgenthau's Story*, 261.

We are treating the Jews here all right. What have you to complain of? Why can't you let us do with these Christians as we please?"[31]

Morgenthau explains that in the Turkish mentality "the fact that, above all considerations of race and religion, there are such things as humanity and civilization, never for a moment enters their mind. They can understand a Christian fighting for a Christian and a Jew fighting for a Jew, but such abstractions as justice and decency form no part of their conception of things."[32]

Morgenthau told Talaat that in his capacity as ambassador of the United States, he was 97 percent Christian. But, he continued, "I do not appeal to you in the name of any race or any religion, but merely as a human being. You have told me many times that you want to make Turkey a part of the modern progressive world. The way you are treating the Armenians will not help you to realize that ambition; it puts you in the class of backward, reactionary peoples."[33]

And till our days the "crime of silence" prevails. The United States refers to the Armenian tragedy as a massacre, but avoids classifying it as genocide. The interest in maintaining good relations with Turkey and the terrible obsession of the Turks not to recognize that they committed a genocide against the Armenian people has prevented this recognition by a great part of the democratic nations. The European Union has never demanded from Turkey an admission of its attempted genocide. In 2004 President Jacques Chirac was strongly pressed to demand Turkey's acknowledgment of its crime, to no avail.

The Connection between the Two Genocides

An important point in Ambassador Morgenthau's book deals with the influence the German officials exercised over the Turkish government, their ally in the world war. Among other aspects, as seen above, is the revelation that German officials were the ones who suggested to the Turks to deport the Armenians.[34]

There are different approaches in matters of comparison between two different genocides, between one tragedy and another, as there are different

31. Ibid., 229.
32. Ibid.
33. Ibid.
34. Ibid., 251.

ways of comparing the misery of one and another person. Usually historians of the Holocaust stress the uniqueness of this event, showing how the Nazis industrialized death, how they went after the last Jew they could find in Germany and in the rest of Europe, to what degree of atrociousness their cold cruelty reached, and how the majority of the German people not only knew but supported what Hitler was doing to his chosen victims, themes that will be dealt with in the coming chapters.

A completely different view appears in the work of a historian who deals with the Holocaust uniqueness claim in a distorted and somehow cruel way. He says that "the assertion that the Holocaust is unique – like the claim that it is singularly incomprehensible or un-representable – is, in practice, deeply offensive. What else can all of this possibly mean except 'your catastrophe, unlike ours, is ordinary; unlike ours is comprehensible, unlike ours is representable.'"[35]

Nothing of the sort is meant by the "uniqueness." Besides Goldhagen's argument in his *Hitler's Willing Executioners* regarding the differences between the Holocaust and other genocides, one should keep in mind that Hitler succeeded not only in conquering the German people's willingness and the participation of a great portion of his people in the execution of his "Final Solution," but that he also succeeded in obtaining the participation of many European states' governments and even their peoples in the execution of the genocide of the Jews of the continent.

In the Armenian genocide, there was no cooperation of the Turkish population; much to the contrary there were many instances in which the people made efforts to help the Armenians and save them from the Turkish genocidal intentions. It is also important to stress that the Holocaust of the Jews of Europe followed a meticulous plan, philosophically prepared many years before and practically planned in advance, and included the participation of Germany's industry and technology. This, besides being the crowning chapter of a succession of persecutions, expulsions, and atrocities of all kinds that the Jewish people suffered throughout more than a millennia and a half on the European continent, was the crowning chapter of Europe's ferocious antisemitism. Its racial aspect was directly influenced by the Catholic Church, as James Carroll so strongly stresses in his *Constantine's Sword: The Church*

---

35. Peter Novick, *The Holocaust in American Life* (New York: Houghton Mifflin, 2000), 9.

and the Jews, which we shall see in chapter 3. All this makes the Holocaust undeniably unique.

Another aspect of uniqueness of the Holocaust is that the Universal Declaration of Human Rights and the covenants that followed as well as the Genocide Convention were all prepared by the UN as an answer to what happened in World War II, which was considered by the framers of these international documents as the greatest violation of human rights ever.

The Armenian genocide may have been on the minds of the framers of the UN charter when, in the first item of the preamble, it refers to "the scourge of war, which twice in our lifetime has brought untold sorrow to mankind." And yet whereas the nations of the world took into consideration the suffering of the Jewish people under the barbarism of Nazi Germany, among other things through the UN decision to make possible the creation of the State of Israel, the Armenians were totally forgotten by the Allies. The Turks came out as victorious from their murderous campaign. So, historically, socially, politically, and legally, the Holocaust indeed stands as unique.

On the other hand, there is undoubtedly a connection between what happened in Turkey in 1915 and what occurred in Germany twenty-five years later. Elie Wiesel, with his profound knowledge of the Holocaust and his unabated dedication to human rights, tells us something that has to do with the heart of international human rights: "I am haunted by the tragedy of the Armenians, which inspired Hitler to remark, speaking of the Jews: 'Who will remember them? Who still remembers the massacre of the Armenians?'"[36]

In another instance Wiesel commented on the denial of the Armenian

---

36. Elie Wiesel, *And the Sea Is Never Full: Memoirs, 1969–* (New York: Alfred A. Knopf, 1999), 186. Hannibal Travis published an essay titled "Did the Armenian Genocide Inspire Hitler? Turkey, Past and Future" in the *Middle East Quarterly* 20, no. 1 (winter 2013): 27–35, in which he writes:

> A number of clues point to the possibility that Hitler's "final solution" was inspired by the Turkish massacre of its Armenian population in 1915. His infamous 1939 question, "Who speaks today of the extermination of the Armenians?" although hotly debated concerning its authenticity, is only one indication leading to that conclusion.

And in his conclusion, the author writes:

> Numerous ideological and political influences led from the Armenian genocide to the rape of Poland and the Holocaust.... Subsequent efforts to discredit the speech by defenders of the Ottoman Empire should not, however, blind us to the manifold connections between the Armenian genocide and that perpetrated by the Nazis.

genocide by the Turkish people that "it's an insult, it's an offense to memory, it's an offense to dignity, it's an offense to humanity, to the humanity of Armenians!"[37]

The Mayor of Lodz to *Le Monde*

The city of Lodz, Poland, was occupied in 1939 by the Nazis, who closed the entire large Jewish community into a ghetto, the second largest after the Warsaw ghetto. From Lodz they were transferred to Auschwitz and Chelmno concentration camps.

In 2004, the mayor of Lodz was interviewed by *Le Monde* about the Holocaust, which was carried out in his city with great cruelty. He told the journalist, "*Si l'on ne crie pas avec les victimes, alors on se tait avec les criminels*" (If one does not cry with the victims, then one is silent with the criminals [in other words, complicit]).[38]

The very enthusiastic defender of human rights known as the European Court of Justice ruled in 2013 that denying that the mass killings of Armenians in Ottoman Turkey in 1915 was a genocide is not a criminal offense. According to the court, a Swiss law against genocide denial violates the principle of freedom of expression. A Swiss court had fined the leader of the leftist Turkish Workers' Party, Doğu Perinçek, for having branded talk on an Armenian genocide "an international lie" during a 2007 lecture tour in Switzerland.

The European Court of Justice said that genocide is a very narrowly defined legal notion that is difficult to prove, and Mr. Perinçek was making a speech of a historical, legal, and political nature in a contradictory debate.[39]

The judges cited a 2012 ruling by France's Constitutional Council which struck down a law enacted by then president Nicolas Sarkozy's government as an unconstitutional violation of the right to freedom of speech and communication.[40]

---

37. Interview in Andrew Goldberg, *The Armenians: A Story of Survival* (Two Cats Productions, 2002), documentary film broadcast on PBS.

38. Christophe Châtelot, "En Pologne, Lodz tente de sortir de l'oubli la liquidation d'un des plus grands ghettos," *Le Monde*, April 29, 2004, 22.

39. Preliminary Chamber judgment of the European Court of Human Rights in the case of Perinçek v. Switzerland (application no. 27510/08), described in a press release issued by the Registrar of the Court, ECHR 370 (2013), December 17, 2013 (final judgment in the case confirming Perinçek's right to free speech was rendered on October 15, 2015).

40. Judgment of European Court of Human Rights, case of Perinçek v. Switzerland

The "crime of silence" proceeds, now with the aid of the European Court of Justice and the French Constitutional Council.

Unfortunate are the grandchildren of the victims, as are the grandchildren of the executioners. And also unfortunate are all those who cooperated and continue cooperating through their silence, allies to cruel indifference, to criminal ex post facto complicity. Even more unfortunate are those European judges who protect the deniers of the Armenian genocide.

Chapter Two
Hitler's Accomplices before the War

The All-Too-Passive United States

It is indeed very sad and very difficult to return to those terrible days of the 1930s when the devilish Hitler was preparing his war against the Jews, against Europe, against the harmonious existence of nations, against every value of civilization, against all conquests of the human spirit, against humankind.

Even more painful is to recognize our own complicity. As David S. Wyman wrote, "The Nazis were the murderers, but we were the all too passive accomplices."[1]

The pattern of denial and inaction began quite early. Had there been any overt reaction to Nazi extremism when the first signs were being seen, perhaps there would have been a chance of preventing the atrocities. Yet the US administration's policy of noninterference was firmly established in the years leading up to the Holocaust. Secretary of State Cordell Hull wrote to the American ambassador in Berlin in March 1933:

> Unfortunate incidents have indeed occurred and the whole world joins in regretting them. But without minimizing or condoning what has taken place, I have reason to believe that many of the accounts of acts of terror and atrocities which have reached this country have been exaggerated, and I fear that the continued dissemination of exaggerated reports may

---

1. David S. Wyman, *The Abandonment of the Jews: America and the Holocaust, 1941–1945* (1984; repr., New York: The New Press, 2007), xix.

prejudice the friendly feelings between the peoples of the two countries and be of doubtful service to anyone.[2]

It must be stressed that the policy of denial continued to be followed by the State Department until the second half of 1942, when it became impossible to maintain this hypocritical stand.

Arthur Morse goes so far as to say that the American character and its ostensible value system were gravely compromised in these years, as America in effect aided and abetted Hitler's genocidal plans: "In the years between 1933 and 1944 the American tradition of sanctuary for the oppressed was uprooted and despoiled. It was replaced by a combination of political expediency, diplomatic evasion, isolationism, indifference and raw bigotry, which played directly into the hands of Adolf Hitler even as he set in motion the final plans for the greatest mass murder in history."[3]

There are some who dispute this view. I am well aware of Peter Novick's argument in his *The Holocaust in American Life* (2000), in which he practically denies all accusations against the US government regarding not doing what could have been done to save Jews from the Holocaust, and the few authors he quotes to strengthen his position. Notwithstanding his efforts, the fact is that the majority of the historians and other scholars who have studied the reaction of Franklin Delano Roosevelt and documents from the State Department and Treasury Department (accusing the State Department of omission and even commission in halting any initiative to give assistance to European Jews) arrive at the irrefutable conclusion that there was unforgiveable inertia in the highest echelons of the US government regarding the dangers to and the suffering and disappearance of millions of Jews.

Walter Laqueur, William Morse, David Wyman, Rafael Medoff, and many

---

2. Tony Bayfield, *Churban: The Murder of the Jews of Europe* (Germany: Michael Goulston Educational Foundation, 1981), 41. Cordell Hull was trying to deny the veracity of reports the State Department had received early in 1933 from US ambassador Frederic M. Sacket in Berlin, from Consul General Messersmith, also in Berlin, and from Consul General Leon Dominian in Stuttgart, as well as reports that appeared in English and American media, detailing stories of all kinds of violence, including of Nazis invading Jewish residences and murdering the heads of the families and about bodies that were frequently found in the woods, as reported by Arthur D. Morse, *While Six Million Died: A Chronicle of American Apathy* (1967; repr., New York: Overlook Press, 1998), 107–11.

3. Morse, *While Six Million Died*, 99.

other scholars demonstrate how many Jewish refugees were denied entrance into the US though the immigration quotas had not been fulfilled, how the US adhered to and strengthened the English policy against Jewish immigration into Palestine, and how the American government denied any help to transfer Jewish refugees to various possible safe havens in Africa, South America, and other continents.

Hitler's *Mein Kampf*

The drafters of the Universal Declaration of Human Rights and the literature on international law that followed – specifically on the subject of the "internationalization of human rights" – described this instrument as a reaction to Hitler's perversions. We must examine how and why the dictator in Berlin and his criminal organizations dared to plan, prepare, and execute the murder of millions of a particular human group that was never militarized and that as a community of people had no political standing and certainly no military capacity or aspiration whatsoever.

In his basic written agenda, *Mein Kampf*, Adolf Hitler exposes violent bias against the Jewish people, blaming them for all the world's problems. As time passed, his ideas about what to do with the Jews developed and emerged clearly. In his speeches between 1922 and 1939, the German people – and whoever in the world cared to listen – heard the following threats, among many others:

> The result [of war] will not be the bolshevization of the earth, and thus the victory of Jewry, but the annihilation of the Jewish race in Europe.[4]

> ...and we say that the war will not end as the Jews imagine it will, namely with the uprooting of the Aryans, but the result of this war will be the complete annihilation of the Jews.

> Now for the first time they will not bleed other people to death, but for the first time the old Jewish law of an eye for an eye, a tooth for a tooth will be applied.

> And the further this war spreads, the further will spread this fight against the world of the [Jew], and they will be used as food for every

---

4. Norman H. Baynes, ed., *The Speeches of Adolph Hitler, April 1922–August 1939*, vol. 1 (London: Oxford University Press, 1942), 741.

prison camp, and in every family which will have it explained to it why, the hour will come when the enemy of all times, or at least of the last thousand years, will have played his part to the end.[5]

The Singularity of the Holocaust

The lesson that we must apprehend from the Holocaust is the psychological preparations that made it possible – what former member of the Canadian parliament Irwin Cotler calls "the state-sanctioned ideology of hate" and "demonizing of the other."[6] Cotler was commenting on the Supreme Court of Canada's ruling upholding the constitutionality of anti-hate legislation, recognizing, in Cotler's formulation, that "the Holocaust did not begin in the gas chambers – it began with words."[7] This theory will be further discussed when we reach the subject matter of Holocaust denial legislation.

Among the various historical reports on the factors that contributed to Hitler's daring to go ahead with his diabolical plan regarding the Jews, one stands out: Arthur D. Morse's book *While Six Million Died: A Chronicle of American Apathy.*[8]

In his introduction, the author explains what distinguishes the Holocaust of the Jews from the other millions who died in the Second World War:

---

5. Cited in Franklin Watts, ed., *Voices of History 1942–43* (New York: Gramercy, 1943), 121.
6. Irwin Cotler, "The Universal Lessons of the Holocaust," *Jerusalem Post*, January 24, 2014.
7. Ibid.
8. This book was originally published in 1967 and then, in 1968, by Ace Publishing Corporation, New York. A new edition was published in 1998 by the Overlook Press, New York. The author had a long and distinguished career in television journalism, serving as reporter-director for Edward R. Murrow's *See It Now* television series and executive producer of *CBS Reports*. Morse resigned from CBS to write this book.

Herbert Mitgang, book critic and columnist for the *New York Times*, author of numerous books in the field of history, wrote a preface for the 1998 edition of Morse's *While Six Million Died*, in which he states:

In...such essential books as *While Six Million Died*, the story of the Holocaust must be told and retold. Time fades, but the facts about the Third Reich's death camps – and the indifference of the United States and other countries – should be inscribed in history forever.

On the cover of the 1998 edition we read: "This pioneering classic revealed – for the first time – the untold story about the deliberate obstruction placed in the way of attempts to save the Jewish people from Hitler's 'Final Solution.'"

But Jewish destruction was to be total. Hitler's indiscriminate attack began the moment he assumed power in 1933. The subsequent social and economic debasement of the Jews was unique and therefore the world's response was unique. In contrast to the selective murder of members of other ethnic, religious and racial groups, the Nazis' blatant announcement that they intended to destroy every Jew in Europe presented the United States and its allies with a clear-cut challenge. How this challenge was met is the subject of this report.

If genocide is to be prevented in the future, we must understand how it happened in the past – not only in terms of the killers and the killed but of the bystanders.[9]

The Sins of Roosevelt's Administration

The reaction of the democracies to Hitler's announced scheme against the Jews helps to clarify what has happened in this tragic chapter of world history throughout the postwar years and decades, from 1946 to 2015. The bystanders, the nations of the world, the United Nations, its Security Council, the biased Commission and then Council on Human Rights, all of us are well informed about the successive genocides that have been occurring on various points of the earth and yet passive, inert, paralyzed accomplices, as will be analyzed in another chapter.

The basic sin of the United States under the leadership of President Franklin Delano Roosevelt was the immigration policy of his government, which did everything to keep the entrance of Jews – in mortal danger – at an absolute minimum.

Statistics of the Immigration and Naturalization Service reveal that between July 1, 1933, and June 30, 1943, 165,756 Jews entered the United States (out of a total of 476,930 aliens), whereas during this ten-year period United States immigration quotas could have permitted the entry of over 1.5 million people. So the number of Jews entering the US during this period was approximately 10 percent of the total number of immigrants permissible under the law.[10] This is without considering the possibility of increasing the immigration quotas for Germans, Austrians, and other nationalities in light

9. Morse, *While Six Million Died*, x.
10. Ibid., 94.

of the tragic situation of European Jewry. Another important detail is that in 1933–34 only 4,839 of the 63,000 Jews who fled Germany in that period entered the US. The majority moved to European countries such as the Netherlands, Belgium, and France, from where most of them were ultimately deported to the concentration camps.

President Roosevelt did not obey the immigration law: his administration went far above and beyond the law, by imposing on would-be immigrants a long list of additional requirements that reduced the number of qualifying immigrants as much as possible. A maximum of 25,957 Germans citizens were permitted to enter each year, but the actual number admitted was just 1,324 in 1933; 3,515 in 1934; 4,891 in 1935; 6,073 in 1936; and 11,127 in 1937. The only year in which the entire German quota was filled was 1939. That year members of Congress introduced legislation – the Wagner-Rogers Bill – to permit the non-quota admission of 20,000 Jewish refugee children, considering that because of their age they would pose no competition to America's labor force and would be supported entirely by private sources. The president declined to support the measure, but the following year he supported bringing British children to the United States to escape the German bombing of London.

Sir Nicholas Winton, a London-born son of German Jews who became known as the "British Schindler" for his successful efforts in 1938–39 to rescue hundreds of Czech children, most of them Jews, wrote a letter in 1939 to President Roosevelt, asking the United States to accept some of the children. Roosevelt handed the letter to the State Department, which instructed the US embassy in London to inform Winton that "the United States Government is unable…to permit immigration in excess of that provided for by existing immigration laws."[11]

The application for a visa that was given to hopeful Jewish émigrés consisted of onerous forms and a requirement to produce dozens of documents attesting to a lack of criminal record and clean bill of health. In addition, a US resident had to certify a willingness to offer financial assistance to the prospective immigrant as a guarantee that he or she would not require public

---

11. Rafael Medoff, "Long-Lost Plea to FDR Revives Question: How Could Europe's Jews Have Been Saved?" *Tablet*, May 24, 2014, http://www.tabletmag.com/jewish-news-and -politics/173617/long-lost-letter-to-fdr.

support. Failure to provide even one of the numerous required documents would result in rejection.[12]

One keen observer of America's lack of enthusiasm for Jewish refugees was Hitler himself. Shortly after he was elected, he commented, "The American people were the first to draw the practical political consequences from the inequality in the difference of races. Through immigration laws it barred undesirables from other races. Nor is America now ready to open its doors to Jews fleeing from Germany."[13]

Throughout the critical years when an open refugee policy could have saved so many hundreds of thousands of lives, President Roosevelt insisted that his hands were tied; he would not be able to pass any reforms to immigration law because there were too many in Congress with the power to block them.[14] But a vastly larger number of refugees could have been let in even within the existing immigration law, without any reforms at all. The strictest interpretation of the laws did not have to be enforced.[15] In other words, the quotas for Germans and Austrians remained unfulfilled, as seen above, and this was a direct consequence of State Department bureaucratic policies.

The government's policy was clearly one of disinterest regarding the future of those condemned by the Nazi barbarity.

The United States had already shown its willingness to cooperate with Nazi propaganda schemes when it sent athletes to participate in the 1936 Munich Olympics, legitimizing what essentially amounted to a German propaganda

12. Rafael Medoff, *FDR and the Holocaust: A Breach of Faith* (Washington: The David S. Wyman Institute for Holocaust Studies, 2013), 2–5, from where the above data were taken. This author reports (page 64) that "the Bergson group [which worked incessantly to save more Jews from the Nazis] were convinced that as long as the refugee policy was in the hands of the State Department there was little chance that any meaningful steps would ever be taken. Deeply entrenched anti-immigration sentiment and anti-Semitism throughout the State Department would inevitably serve as an effective counterweight to refugee advocates' pleas to the White House."
13. Cited in Louis P. Lochner, Associated Press correspondent, "Hitler Explains Removal of Jews: Points to America's Exclusion Act against Yellow Race as a Precedent," *Newport Daily News*, April 6, 1933.
14. Wyman, *The Abandonment of the Jews*, 7, writes: "The anti-immigration forces wielded substantial political power. Moreover, a large number of congressmen were staunchly restrictionist, a reflection of their own views as well as of attitudes that were popular in their home districts."
15. Morse, *While Six Million Died*, 148.

fest.[16] The US was even willing to put up with Hitler's demeaning treatment of African American athletes.[17] Hitler well understood his audience. From the very beginning of his cruel reign, he watched very carefully the policy of the "liberal" nations and used their apathy and their refusal to accept Jewish immigration to support his deadly plans.

Positive but Ineffective Reactions

Some American newspapers displayed a vigorous reaction to Nazi policy. The Syracuse *Post-Standard* wrote in 1933 that "the whole weight of world disapproval should be summoned to stop this tragic situation, to impress upon the present rulers of Germany that the world will not permit a return to the dark ages."[18] The Providence *Journal* concurred: "If there ever was a time in recent history for marshaling world public opinion against such brutality, such a time is now."[19] And the Oklahoma City *Daily Oklahoman* opined: "Humanity, to say nothing of Christian duty, would call insistently for an American protest."[20]

Many other newspapers across the nation followed this line.

American organizations and private citizens as well attempted to prod their government to respond to outrages of Nazi policy. As far back as March 20, 1933, representatives of the American Jewish Committee and of the B'nai B'rith organization called on Secretary of State Cordell Hull with a plea for some official action or even a mere statement by the US government on behalf of persecuted German Jews.[21] A proposal had been made by the US chargé d'affaires in Berlin, based on the advice of a German industrialist, that if the United States would show to Hitler "in a friendly way the serious concern with which developments in Germany were being viewed in our country...it might have a favorable effect." Secretary Hull decided not to take any step.[22]

Communications by American diplomats in Germany kept coming in

---

16. Ibid., 186.
17. Ibid.
18. Cited in Edward Jewitt Wheeler et al., *The Literary Digest*, vol. 115 (New York: Funk and Wagnalls, 1933), 29.
19. Ibid.
20. Ibid.
21. Morse, *While Six Million Died*, 109.
22. Ibid., 111.

with reports about the atrocities, but the State Department maintained its policy of passivity.

Various meetings organized by the Jewish community started taking place, the largest at Madison Square Garden in March 1933, drawing some fifty-five thousand people, with the participation of distinguished public figures such as Governor Alfred E. Smith and Senator Robert Wagner of New York. Other important speakers were Catholic bishop Francis J. McConnell and Protestant bishop William T. Manning.[23]

The White House kept silent.

Arthur Morse reproduces a text from the diary of United States Ambassador to Germany William E. Dodd, entered on June 16, 1933, according to which Roosevelt summed up the situation in the following words:

> The German authorities are treating the Jews shamefully, and the Jews in this country are greatly excited. But this is also not a government affair. We can do nothing except for American citizens who happen to be made victims. We must protect them, and whatever we can do to moderate the general persecution by unofficial and personal influence, ought to be done.[24]

Dr. Jonah B. Wise, an officer of the Joint Distribution Committee, called bluntly for some sign of life from the White House "in the face of one of the great human disasters of our time. The tragic and needless sufferings of the Jews in Germany are such that it should have been impossible for the President of the United States not to have spoken a word of warning and condemnation to the German government."[25]

The president of the American Jewish Committee – the very prominent intellectual Cyrus Adler, distinguished scholar from Johns Hopkins University, of the Smithsonian Institute and later president of the Jewish Theological Seminary – was one of the members of a delegation that urged Secretary of State Cordell Hull in the March meeting to file a formal protest with the German authorities. In May Adler tried again, calling Hull's attention to a

23. Ibid., 113.
24. William E. Dodd Jr. and Martha Dodd, eds., *Ambassador Dodd's Diary, 1933–1938* (New York, 1941), 5.
25. David Morrison, *Heroes, Antiheroes, and the Holocaust: American Jewry and Historical Choice* (Jerusalem: Gefen Publishing House, 1999), 32.

memorandum prepared by his committee on the various interventions of the US against persecution of Jews in different places and times: in 1840 Damascus, 1857 Switzerland, 1863 Tangier, 1881 Russia, 1903 Rumania, and in 1915 in favor of the Armenians in Turkey.

The State Department did not react. The United States government would neither officially protest Germany's persecution of the Jews nor offer the victims asylum.

On January 1, 1936, James G. McDonald resigned from his post as League of Nations High Commissioner for Refugees (Jewish and other). To his letter of resignation he attached rich documentation on the actual situation of Jews in Nazi Germany. When McDonald was high commissioner, he invested a great deal of energy in trying to find ways to get Jews out of harm's way. One of his efforts was to write to Felix Moritz Warburg, an American Jewish banker who had been born in Germany and thus had a personal connection to the plight of Germany's Jews. He also was the president of the Joint Distribution Committee, a leading humanitarian assistance organization that had the power to make a difference. McDonald asked Warburg to try to arrange for fifteen to twenty thousand young Jews to leave Germany annually.[26] "There can be no future for Jews in Germany," McDonald stressed.[27]

Warburg sent the letter to Governor Herbert Lehman of New York, who forwarded it to President Roosevelt with a plea that the immigration quota of Jews from Germany be increased. Roosevelt turned the letter over to the State Department.

The reply of the State Department to Governor Lehman informed that

26. Morse, *While Six Million Died*, 188–89.
27. Richard Breitman, Barbara McDonald Stewart, Severin Hochberg, eds, *Refugees and Rescue: The Diaries and Papers of James G. McDonald, 1935–1945* (Bloomington and Indianapolis, Indiana University Press, 2009), 45. Nathan Feinberg, *Studies in International Law with Special Reference to the Arab-Israel Conflict* (Jerusalem: Magnes Press, Hebrew University, 1979), 359, reports on the attitude of the Great Powers in the 1930s regarding the discriminatory policies of the Nazi regime against the Jews. Note how this legal scholar follows the historians, an uncommon phenomenon in legal literature: "The Great Powers, of themselves, were not prepared to take firm decisive steps against Hitler's machinations – either within the League of Nations or outside it…. With regard to the Jews, not only did they fail to come to the defense of German Jewry but they even acquiesced in the application of the Third Reich's discriminatory legislation to their own Jewish citizens in Germany. Countries such as the United States and Great Britain did no more in fulfillment of their duty to protect their citizens abroad than send letters of protest to Berlin."

there was no Jewish quota, but only a German quota, and that a maximum of 25,957 Germans could be admitted annually to the United States, without reference to their religious beliefs. The letter went on to reveal that 14,202 Germans of all faiths had entered the US from 1932 to 1935, an average of 3,550 per year, a clear recognition of its perverse policy.

On October 28, 1936, Roosevelt was to address a gathering for the fiftieth anniversary of the Statute of Liberty. Professor John Dewey, a noted intellectual and educator, wrote to the president in advance of the ceremony to request that he make some meaningful gesture in honor of the symbol of liberty and freedom that was to be celebrated:

> Fifty years ago, at the dedication of the Statue, this country was spoken of as an asylum of the oppressed, a haven for political refugees who had been driven from their homelands. Today this tradition is in danger of being completely discarded. The gates have been closed to immigrants and, for the last five years, more people have been leaving the United States than have been entering it.... We urge you to declare ... that this country will live up to its promise of equal opportunity for the immigrants within its borders and that it will re-establish the proud principle it once maintained as an asylum for political and religious refugees.[28]

Roosevelt did not respond. Nor did his speech at the ceremony refer to the great problem that was afflicting so many Americans, and especially so many intellectuals and clergypeople.[29]

It was October 1937 before President Roosevelt addressed the subject of "quarantining aggressors."[30] Even this vague threat proved too much for the more radical isolationist and pacifist crowd, who were anything but pacifistic in their horror at the mere suggestion, however nebulous, of American action. With open opposition on the one hand and a distinct lack of enthusiasm from his own Democratic colleagues on the other, Roosevelt hastened to clarify that he had no intention of getting involved in European affairs.

28. Cited in Father Divine, *The Spoken Word* 3, nos. 1–20 (1936): 9.
29. Morse, *While Six Million Died*, 195.
30. Elmer Plischke, *U.S. Department of State: A Reference History* (Westport, CT: Greenwood, 1999), 344.

The Diabolic Évian Conference

The German-Jewish refugee problem continued to mount, and pressure on Roosevelt was sufficient to finally impel him to devote some attention to the issue. In March 1938 he hit upon the idea of organizing an international conference to address the problem of the massive numbers of German Jews who wanted desperately to leave Germany and Austria and had nowhere to go. Thirty-two countries from Europe to South America to Australia, New Zealand, and South Africa were to be invited to attend.

Roosevelt announced the conference would take place in July in the French town of Évian-les-Bains. At a press conference announcing the historic meeting, he indicated that the United States remained committed to sheltering asylum seekers the world over, but he also made clear that US immigration quotas and policy would not be changed. In other words, the result (or rather, non-result) of the conference was a foregone conclusion even before it happened.[31]

Chancellor Hitler reacted to the announcement of the conference with irony in a March 25, 1938, speech at Koenigsberg, saying: "I can only hope and expect that the other world, which has such deep sympathy for these criminals, will at least be generous enough to convert this sympathy into practical aid. We, on our part, are ready to put all these criminals at the disposal of these countries, for all I care, even on luxury ships."[32]

There was a hidden motive behind the invitation for the conference in accordance with what is revealed in an internal State Department memorandum prepared later, which unveils the origins of the Évian Conference with cold detachment. The Nazi absorption of Austria had brought about increased public demand for State Department action in behalf of refugees. The memo identifies "Dorothy Thompson and a few Congressmen with metropolitan constituencies" as the main concerned parties.[33] Secretary Hull and his subordinates advocated a proactive approach, stating the department should

31. Morse, *While Six Million Died*, 202.
32. "National Affairs: Refugee Committee," *Time* 31, no. 14 (April 4, 1938).
33. National Archives 840.48, Division of European Affairs, Memo on Refugee Problems, November 18, 1938, cited in William R. Perl, *The Holocaust Conspiracy: An International Policy of Genocide* (New York: Shapolsky, 1989), 42.

"get out in front and attempt to guide their pressure, primarily with a view towards forestalling attempts to have the immigration laws liberalized."[34]

According to this revelation it was Sumner Welles who had come up with the idea of an international conference, which the president approved. The Évian Conference was apparently conceived for the purpose of deflecting pressure, giving the appearance of action during extensive planning for an event that was essentially intended to shunt the refugee problem over onto other nations. The United States clearly had no intention of taking in the desperate refugees itself.[35]

The conference delegates were to be entertained in style; Évian-les-Bains was (and remains) a high-end spa resort in the French Alps. Twenty-nine nations had confirmed their attendance. Italy, despite its proximity to the site, declined to participate. A number of private organizations – primarily Jewish and highly interested in the topic under discussion – also were to send representatives. The press was to be in full attendance with more than two hundred credentialed journalists on site.[36] The world was watching.

Two days before the Évian Conference opened, the *New York Times* published a column signed by Anne O'Hare McCormick, in which she expressed the hopes of so many:

> It is heartbreaking to think of the queues of desperate human beings around our consulates in Vienna and other cities waiting in suspense for what happens at Évian. But the question they underline is not simply humanitarian. It is not a question of how many unemployed this country can safely add to its own unemployed millions. It is a test of civilization. Whatever other nations do, can America live with itself if it lets Germany get away with this policy of extermination, allows the fanaticism of one man to triumph over reason, refuses to take up this gage of battle against barbarism?[37]

---

34. Ibid., 43.
35. Morse, *While Six Million Died*, 203–4.
36. The journalist Hans Habe appended a full list of the participating journalists to his 1966 fictionalized account of the conference, *Die Mission* (The Mission).
37. Anne O'Hare McCormick, "The Refugee Question as a Test of Civilization," *New York Times*, July 4, 1938.

The answer to the journalist's question would come very soon. Yes, America could live in tranquility while millions of men, women, and children, innocent civilians, would be systematically murdered after untold sufferings.

This is how two Canadian history professors describe the Évian Conference:

> [Humphrey Hume] Wrong [the Canadian delegate to the Conference] realized as soon as the conference began that Canadian worries had been groundless. The chief American delegate, Myron Taylor, was the first speaker. Instead of the magnanimous gesture many of the representatives expected – and feared – the contribution of the United States government to solving the refugee crisis would be to fill its entire German-Austrian quota, rather than let part of it remain unfilled as might have been done in years past. The delegates sat stunned: the nations of the world had been mobilized for this? A collective sigh of relief from the assembly was almost audible as Taylor sat down. For the Jews of Europe, Taylor's speech was a cruel letdown; for everyone at Évian, it was a reprieve. It was clear that the Americans saw Évian as an exercise in public relations; they had no concrete proposals to solve – or even to alleviate – the crisis. And, if the Americans were going to do nothing significant, it was hardly likely that anything would be expected of the other countries assembled.[38]

And indeed, the delegations were greatly inspired to follow the United States' lead. One after another they announced their countries' positions, nearly all of them essentially refusing to do anything. They specified onerous conditions (Brazil would require a certificate of baptism, Canada would take only experienced farmers, and so on) and cited their own limited resources and difficult straits. Britain would take some nine thousand children (which did ultimately transpire, as the famous Kindertransports), but not their parents. Some nations, such as Australia, Switzerland, and France, essentially stated that they had enough Jews already and did not need any more.[39] The Dominican Republic alone among all the nations present pledged to accept a significant number of refugees.

38. Cited in Irving Abella and Harold Troper, *None Is Too Many: Canada and the Jews of Europe, 1933–1948* (Toronto: Lester and Orpen Dennys, 1983), 31.
39. Ervin Birnbaum, "Évian: The Most Fateful Conference of All Times in Jewish History," part 2, *Nativ* (February 2009).

A natural solution might have been Palestine. Many Jews would have been pleased to go there. However, the British, who then controlled Mandate Palestine, had other interests in the area. Up until 1936 the British did allow a certain amount of Jewish immigration to Palestine, but a desire to placate significant Arab displeasure had led to restrictions. In 1939 Britain's White Paper set a strict upper limit of seventy-five thousand Jewish immigrants over the coming five years, to be followed by a policy of allowing Jewish immigration to Palestine "only with Arab consent."[40] Various schemes were produced, developed, and discussed with foreign authorities by the British Ministry of Economic Warfare, most especially a plan to save thousands of Jewish children from Germany and occupied countries, with the support of Switzerland, negotiations sometimes prolonging for months and years. No results were ever achieved.[41]

The Netherlands and Denmark claimed to be overpopulated and to have already received large numbers of Germans; they proclaimed their willingness to help, but in a limited fashion.[42] Switzerland's delegate was categorically negative, complaining about the threatening refugee "inundation" after the German occupation of Austria, which brought about a few thousand refugees crossing the border into Switzerland.[43]

The United States, which had taken the initiative for the conference and agreed to accept its full, legal quota of 27,370 immigrants annually from Germany and Austria, never fulfilled this promise.

The Dominican Republic received a few hundred refugees, a far cry from the hundred thousand it had promised to receive, but then it had conditioned this on obtaining the necessary financing, which never materialized. The Roosevelt administration was against the acceptance of refugees by the Caribbean, whose proximity to the United States might lead to some refugees managing to eventually enter the United States.[44]

---

40. Louise London, *Whitehall and the Jews 1933–1948: British Immigration Policy and the Holocaust* (Cambridge: Cambridge University Press, 2000), 9.
41. Ibid., chapter 8.
42. Morse, *While Six Million Died*, 213.
43. Nora Levin, *The Holocaust: The Destruction of European Jewry, 1933–1945* (New York: Schocken, 1973), 77.
44. Medoff, *FDR and the Holocaust*, 47. Medoff also relates that some US officials were worried about German Jewish refugees becoming spies for the Nazis and wanted to keep them out of the region for this reason. Ibid., 255.

The Canadian historians comment:

> Évian had clearly shown that no one wanted Jews. The Jews were now
> solely Germany's problem, and having turned their backs, the nations of
> the world could hardly in conscience object to Germany's solution. In the
> eyes of the Nazis the world had given them carte blanche to solve their
> Jewish problem their way.[45]

For the German press, the result of the Évian Conference was a party.
The July 12, 1938, edition of the *Danziger Verposten* gloated:

> We see that one likes to pity the Jews as long as one can use this pity for
> a wicked agitation against Germany, but that no state is prepared to fight
> the cultural disgrace of central Europe by accepting a few thousand Jews.
> Thus the conference serves to justify Germany's policy against Jewry.[46]

Propaganda Minister Goebbels challenged the democracies: "If there is any
country that believes it has not enough Jews, I shall gladly turn over to it all
our Jews."[47] No answer from any quarter.

Countries like Argentina, Chile, Uruguay, and Mexico introduced more
restrictive immigration regulations after the Évian Conference. No help came
from the French, English, or Dutch colonies.[48]

The Jews were doomed, not only because no haven was found for them,
but because Nazi Germany felt that it could go ahead with its annihilation
program because nobody would have the moral authority to condemn the
murderer, as no nation was ready to receive the victims.[49]

It is clear that the Évian Conference was a propaganda trick of Roosevelt's
government to quiet down the wave of protests coming from different sectors

45. Abella and Troper, *None Is Too Many*, 32.

46. Cited in *The Wiener Library Bulletin*, vols. 13–18 (London: The Wiener Library for the
Study of the Holocaust and Genocide, 1959), 44.

47. Nora Levin, *The Holocaust Years: The Nazi Destruction of European Jewry, 1933–1945*
(Malabar, FL: Krieger Publishing Company, 1990), 30.

48. Morse, *While Six Million Died*, 229.

49. Martin Gilbert, *The Holocaust: A History of the Jews of Europe during the Second World
War 65* (New York: Henry Holt and Company, 1987), 65, writes: "For five years his [Hit-
ler's] anti-Jewish actions, although always severe, had been tempered with moments of
caution. Since the annexation of Austria, and the Évian conference, he seemed to have
thrown caution to the winds."

of the American population. A discrete action in partnership with a few governments would have produced concrete results, not in great numbers, but still good enough to save a considerable number of refugees. But that was not the policy of the White House or of the State Department. Évian had in fact been counterproductive, as new and more restrictive immigration regulations were adopted by conference participants.

The Holocaust's First Steps

The great test came on November 9, 1938 – Kristallnacht – when a government-sponsored wave of attacks against the Jewish population in Germany took place, resulting in the burning of 195 synagogues and the destruction and looting of over seven thousand establishments owned by Jews. Twenty thousand Jews were arrested and taken to concentration camps. Official German figures listed thirty-six Jews killed, but newsmen and diplomatic observers counted many more deaths. The pretext for the pogrom was the assassination of Ernst vom Rath, the third secretary of the German embassy in Paris, by a young Jewish boy of seventeen years whose parents had been expelled from Germany and were going through terrible hardships at the Polish border.

At the same time news had been arriving to the outside world about the daily deaths occurring in the Buchenwald concentration camp and how relatives of the victims were required to pay three marks for their ashes. In Dachau concentration camp, deaths occurred both of Jews and of anti-Nazi Christians.

American diplomats sent dispatches to Washington about the gravity of the situation and the dangers looming over the Jews of Germany and Austria. The ambassador to Germany was summoned to Washington for consultation.

On November 15, President Roosevelt gave a collective interview to two hundred correspondents.

The president read the following statement:

The news of the past few days from Germany has deeply shocked public opinion in the United States. Such news from any part of the world would inevitably produce a similar profound reaction among American people in every part of the nation. I myself could scarcely believe that such things could occur in a twentieth century civilization. With a view to gaining a first-hand picture of the situation in Germany, I have asked the Secretary of State to order our Ambassador in Berlin to return at once for report and consultation.[50]

Had the president considered where the refugees might go? asked one of the correspondents. He answered that he had given a great deal of thought to it but was not yet ready to make any announcements.

Another correspondent asked whether Mr. Roosevelt would recommend to Congress that immigration laws be modified to permit the entry of more refugees to the United States. The president replied in the negative. No modifications were contemplated.[51] Besides the meanness of not considering a change in the quota system, either by lifting the limits or by allowing German Jews to be accepted under the quota of other nations whose residents did not care to immigrate, there was the presidential hypocrisy, as he knew very well that his people at the State Department were by far not even fulfilling the immigration quota of Germans (nor of Austrians and other nationalities), despite the agonizing lines of thousands of Jews standing day and night in front of the American consulates in Europe.

The symbolic withdrawal of Ambassador Wilson and the president's brief verbal chastisement of Germany comprised the total American response to the major Kristallnacht pogrom. The United States continued its trade relations with the Third Reich, which impelled thirty-six of the most prominent American writers to send a telegram to Roosevelt on November 16, 1938, in which they said:

> We feel we no longer have any right to remain silent, we feel that the American people and the American government have no right to remain silent.... Thirty five years ago a horrified America rose to its feet to protest against the Kishinev pogroms in Tsarist Russia. God help us if we have grown so indifferent to human suffering that we cannot rise now in protest against pogroms in Nazi Germany.... We feel that it is deeply immoral for

---

50. Cordell Hull, *The Memoirs of Cordell Hull*, vol. 1, ed. Andrew Henry Thomas Berding (New York: Macmillan Co., 1948), 599.
51. Morse, *While Six Million Died*, 149.

the American people to continue having economic relations with a country that avowedly uses mass murder to solve its economic problems.... [52]

That was an authentic plea for collective human rights from a group of prominent intellectuals to an indifferent government that, with its silence, its continuing normal relations with Germany and its refusal to open its doors to the entrance of refugees, was aiding and abetting the beginning of the most horrific chapter of human history.

Signers of the telegram included Eugene O'Neil, Robert Sherwood, John Steinbeck, Pearl Buck, John Gunther, Edna Ferber, Sidney Howard, Lillian Hellman, George S. Kaufman, Robinson Jeffers, Van Wyck Brooks, Marc Connelly, Clifford Odets, Thornton Wilder, and Dorothy Thompson.[53]

The ambassador of the United States to Poland, Anthony Drexel Biddle Jr. notified Secretary Hull that according to reliable informants in Germany, "Nazi officialdom considered world opinion bankrupt. They believed people abroad would do nothing about it.... I consider these recent Nazi excesses in addition to those recently perpetrated against the Catholic clergy in Vienna and subsequently the Protestant clergy as nothing short of a challenge to modern civilization." The ambassador described the dangers looming over 3.5 million Jews in Poland, 900,000 Jews in Rumania, and 445,000 Jews in Hungary.[54]

As the United States would not give the good example of receiving refugees, as they did not even allow the entrance of the numbers set in the immigration law quotas, but kept them way below those quotas, it is not surprising that other countries followed America's attitude.

A suggestion was presented by Jewish organizations to the US government to let in 82,000 Jews from Germany, equivalent to the quota of the following three years. Secretary of Labor Frances Perkins discussed this possibility with Roosevelt on November 17, 1938. No result.

The English offered to the United States to use their immigration quota in favor of German refugees (allowing German and Austrian citizens to emigrate in place of British citizens who would otherwise have been permitted entry),

---

52. Shaun Usher, ed., *Letters of Note: Correspondence Deserving of a Wider Audience* (London: Canongate, 2013), letter 83.
53. Ibid.
54. Morse, *While Six Million Died*, 232.

which would allow around sixty thousand Jews to enter the United States in 1939. Mr. Sumner Welles told the British ambassador who had called upon him with the proposition that immigration quotas were established under law and were not the property of the nations to whom they were granted.[55] Technically correct. The discrimination of the German government against the Jews was equally correct in legal terms, based on the Nuremberg Laws that had established said discrimination.

False Trials to Save the Doomed

At Évian, an agency called the Intergovernmental Committee on Political Refugees had been created, to be housed in London. Roosevelt sent Myron Taylor there as his emissary. The British, together with Roosevelt, were exploring the idea of trying to send Jews to remote colonial areas such as Northern Rhodesia, British Guiana, Kenya, and Tanganyika.[56]

In the meantime hundreds of thousands of Jews were desperately seeking US visas at American consulates all over Europe. The Stuttgart consulate was bombarded with 110,000 applications for the 850 visas it had available. The number of those who actually received the visas was insignificant, and as already reported above, always below the official immigration quotas per nationality.

In their efforts to block and impede immigration, United States consulate officials did their best to impose the strictest interpretation of the laws, even to the point of inventing new ones. Immigration laws imposed no qualifications on the relationship between the prospective immigrant and the sponsor who signed his affidavit of support. But consuls turned people away when they deemed the relationship insufficiently close – even a brother and sister were at times deemed overly distant when it suited official purposes.[57] In Hamburg the consulate was accepting affidavits of support from parent, child, uncle, or aunt of a prospective immigrant, but objected to affidavits from brothers- and sisters-in-law and rejected outright those from distant relatives.[58]

Early in 1939 a delegation of Roman Catholic and Protestant clergymen presented a petition to the White House calling upon the United States to open its doors to German children.

55. Ibid., 234.
56. Ibid., 237.
57. Ibid., 192.
58. Ibid., 193.

Senator Robert Wagner of New York and Representative Edith Rogers of Massachusetts introduced bills in the Senate and in the House to implement the clergymen's proposal. Known as the Wagner-Rogers Bill or Child Refugee Bill, it proposed immigration of up to ten thousand children (no older than fourteen) in 1939 and again in 1940, above and beyond the regular German quota.[59] Various organizations volunteered to work on the details of moving the twenty thousand children to the United States. Thousands of families immediately offered to adopt the children. Mrs. Eleanor Roosevelt supported the Wagner-Rogers Bill, consistent with her permanent commitment to help refugees. The popular comedian and singer Eddie Cantor worked seriously for the approval of the bill.

At the end the bill was withdrawn by Senator Wagner, as he saw no chance of it being approved. Roosevelt remained silent despite his wife's endeavors. The children remained in Germany, and the official immigration quota from Germany was only partially fulfilled.

An interesting moment in this sad chapter was Mrs. Eleanor Roosevelt's persistence in her efforts to awaken her husband's interest in the Wagner-Rogers legislation. Morse tells us that while the president was vacationing aboard the USS *Houston*, she sent him a telegram: "Are you willing I should talk to Sumner and say we approve passage of Child Refugee Bill. Hope you are having grand time. Much love. Eleanor."[60]

It did not work. Morse speculates that perhaps the president was inhibited by the sixty anti-alien bills before the seventy-sixth Congress. The author adds that Roosevelt was very well aware of the impending new disasters facing the Jews of Europe as documented in a cable he sent to Myron Taylor on January 14, 1939, which said that for a human group of some seven million persons the future is "exceedingly dark."[61]

For Eleanor Roosevelt, the inability to convince her powerful husband to allow in more refugees "remained, her son Jimmy later said, 'her deepest regret at the end of her life.'"[62]

---

59. Ibid., 253.
60. Ibid., 256.
61. Ibid., 255–56.
62. Doris Kearns Goodwin, *No Ordinary Time: Franklin and Eleanor Roosevelt; The Home Front in World War II* (New York: Simon and Schuster, 1994), 176.

The Tragedy of the *St. Louis* Passengers

The climax of US cruelty toward the Jews persecuted by Hitler in the prewar period was reached in May 1939, in the chapter of the *St. Louis* transatlantic, of the Hamburg-American Line, which sailed from Germany bound for Havana, Cuba, with 936 passengers, 930 of them Jewish refugees, among the last to escape from Nazi Germany. They held official landing certificates signed by Colonel Manuel Benites, Cuba's director general of immigration.

Of the 930 refugees, 734 had fulfilled US immigration requirements, holding quota numbers that would allow them to enter the United States from three months to three years after their arrival in Cuba. Unknown to them, the Cuban president had invalidated all their landing certificates, new requirements being established for the concession of entrance documents. Long and painful negotiations to have the Cuban government allow the refugees to land were fruitless.

Captain Gustav Schroeder, the good German who was trying to save close to a thousand Jews on his ship,[63] sailed for the coast of Florida. A Coast Guard cutter was sent out to the scene to make sure that the *St. Louis* did not get any closer to America's shore.

Bishop James Cannon Jr. of Richmond, Virginia, wrote a letter to the *Richmond Times-Dispatch*, in which he said that the press reported that the ship came close enough to Miami for the refugees to see the lights of the city, but was sent away. The bishop concludes that "the failure to take any steps whatever to assist these distressed, persecuted Jews in their hour of extremity was one of the most disgraceful things which has happened in American history and leaves a stain and brand of shame upon the record of our nation."[64]

A committee of passengers addressed a telegram to Franklin Delano Roosevelt asking help for 907 passengers, of whom more than four hundred were women and children. There was no reply. Cuba was closed, the US was closed. On June 6, 1939, the *St. Louis* finally ended her idle cruising and set her course back to Europe. After negotiations with various European countries, England received 287; Holland, 181; France, 224.

The only passengers protected from Nazi terror were those received by

---

63. Morse, *While Six Million Died*, 273: "The passengers...were led on this unusual voyage by an unusual German. Captain Schroeder was making amends on this one journey for the entire German nation."

64. Ibid., 280.

England. Most of the others ended up in concentration camps, following the German invasion of Holland, Belgium, and France.

The *New York Times* of June 6, 1939, closed its editorial on the event by saying: "The cruise of the *St. Louis* cries to high heaven of man's inhumanity to man."

Meanwhile Hitler himself noticed the inhumanity as well and was thereby reassured that the United States clearly had no intention of stopping him. The German newspaper *Der Weltkampf* commented in August 1939: "We are saying openly that we do not want the Jews while the democracies keep on claiming that they are willing to receive them – and then leave the guests out in the cold. Aren't we savages better men after all?"[65]

The English, though they received a few thousand Jewish children (via the Kindertransports), mainly from Czechoslovakia, and a few hundred of the *St. Louis* passengers, kept her doors closed to refugees and maintained rigidly the prohibition against the entrance of Jews into Palestine above the minimum number that they had established in the White Paper of 1939.

Professor Talia Einhorn summarizes the British appeasement of the Arabs regarding Jewish immigration to Mandate Palestine: "They did so by restricting Jewish immigration to Palestine on the one hand, while, on the other hand, permitting the entry of Arabs from neighboring countries who sought to settle in Palestine following its development by the Zionist movement and the ensuing work opportunities; by restricting the sale of land to anyone who was not an Arab resident of Palestine; and by the poor administration of state lands, allowing the Arab population to seize them freely."[66]

The lengths to which Franklin Delano Roosevelt went in order to torpedo any plan devised to somehow help the persecuted Jews in Europe is illustrated by his negative intervention against an informative initiative. The Office of War Information (OWI) had authorized the establishment of a radio station out of US territorial waters that would broadcast to Europe news about the ongoing Holocaust in Yiddish, Russian, and Polish via London; full knowledge could sometimes orientate the persecuted about where to try to run to, where and how to hide. The plan was stopped by President Roosevelt himself,

65. Bayfield, *Churban*, 75.
66. Talia Einhorn, "The Status of Judea and Samaria (the West Bank) and Gaza and the Settlements in International Law" (Jerusalem Center for Public Affairs, 2014), http://jcpa.org/article/status-of-settlements-in-international-law/.

who according to Dr. Alex Raphaeli (coordinator of the initiative), overrode the powers of the OWI, which had authorized the station.[67]

With Nazi air attacks on England imminent, the American public demanded that English children be sheltered in the United States. Roosevelt did not move. Journalist Raymond Clapper advocated that the US and Canada shelter at least seventy thousand children, and addressing the president he asked why the great humanitarian did not do anything, not even asking Congress.

Journalist Joseph Alsop complained to the president that efforts to save English children were being smothered by State Department red tape. Finally the State and Justice Departments announced simplified procedures. The English children would be admitted on visitors' visas, a measure that was accomplished by the dedication and energy of private organizations rather than by the US government. The same applies to the saving of some European professors.

On October 8, 1940, former League of Nations high commissioner for refugees James G. McDonald, now serving as chair of the president's Advisory Committee on Political Refugees, handed President Roosevelt a stiff memorandum: 567 names had been forwarded to the State Department in August and September, but fewer than forty visas had been issued. McDonald protested vehemently and finally succeeded, but only in part.

By allowing the full quotas of German and Austrian immigrants to enter the US from 1933 to 1945, by providing shelter to refugees in Central American countries such as the Dominican Republic and others (a project that only needed financial support, which would in any event have been coming from private organizations), by actualizing all or some of the planned solutions for refugee acceptance in countries of Africa, the government of Franklin Delano Roosevelt could have saved many hundreds of thousands – perhaps even millions – of persecuted Jews and eventually weakened the courage and determination of the Nazis to go ahead with the "Final Solution," which was unquestionably stimulated by the Allied apathy and inertia.

By denying all these measures, Roosevelt and some of his aides in the government became Hitler's accomplices before the war.

This is what should be considered as the prewar complicity of the

---

67. Joanna M. Saidel, "A Thwarted Plan," *Jerusalem Post*, January 18, 2013, 19.

democracies – mainly American and English – with the crimes of Hitler and Nazi Germany. And then came about the complicity of the same powers, as well as of others, during the war proper.

Article VII of the "Principles of International Law Recognized in the Charter of the Nurnberg Tribunal and in the Judgment of the Tribunal" states: "Complicity in the commission of a crime against peace, a war crime or a crime against humanity as set forth in Principle VI is a crime under international law."[68]

Hitler's Desiderata

There is a general idea that the Universal Declaration of Human Rights and the Charter of the United Nations are tuned to the idea that the persecution of the Jews and the war Hitler waged against Europe were intertwined, as if belonging to one single great plan, and, as a consequence, that human rights instruments are related to individual rights and to the peace and security of the world. This was not so.

Rather, the two tragedies – the war against Europe and the persecution of the Jews that led to the Holocaust – were two different, independent desiderata of Hitler and of the German people. Hitler hated the Jews and considered them a danger for the Aryans and for Germany. And so he wrote in *Mein Kampf*:

> There is no such thing as coming to an understanding with the Jews. It must be the hard-and-fast 'Either-Or'.[69]

> The Jew offers the most striking contrast to the Aryan.[70]

Independently of his hate and his project to eliminate the Jew, Hitler wished for Germany to become a world power. This is what he wrote in *Mein Kampf*:

68. The text of the principles was adopted by the International Law Commission in 1950 and submitted to the General Assembly of the United Nations, *Yearbook of the International Law Commission*, vol. 2 (1950), para. 97. One may discuss whether the principle can be applied retroactively as a legal principle, but as a statement that also contains a moral principle, it can very well be applied to events that occurred years before.
69. Hitler's *Mein Kampf*, trans. James Murphy (London: Hurst and Blackett Ltd., 1939), 166.
70. Ibid., 234.

Thus the German nation could assure its own future only by being a World Power.[71]

At an epoch in which the world is being gradually portioned out among states many of whom almost embrace whole Continents, one cannot speak of World Power in the case of a State whose political motherland is confined to a territorial area of barely five hundred thousand square miles.[72]

For the future of the German national, the 1914 frontiers are of no significance. They did not serve to protect us in the past, nor do they offer any guarantee for our defense in the future. With these frontiers the German people cannot maintain themselves as a compact unit, nor can they be assured of their maintenance. From the military viewpoint these frontiers are not advantageous or even such as not to cause anxiety. And while we are bound to such frontiers it will not be possible to improve our present position in relation to the other World Powers, or rather in relation to the real World Powers. We shall not lessen the discrepancy between our territory and that of Great Britain, nor shall we reach the magnitude of the United States of America. Not only that, but we cannot substantially lessen the importance of France in international politics.[73]

Germany will either become a World Power or will not continue to exist at all. But in order to become a World Power it needs that territorial magnitude which gives it the necessary importance to day and assures the existence of its citizens.[74]

Therefore we National Socialists have purposely drawn a line through the line of conduct followed by pre-War Germany in foreign policy. We put an end to the perpetual Germanic march toward the South and West of Europe and turn our eyes towards the lands of the East. We finally put a stop to the colonial and trade policy of pre-War times and pass over to the territorial policy of the future. But when we speak of new territory in Europe to-day we must principally think of Russia and the border States subject to her.[75]

71. Ibid., 491.
72. Ibid., 492.
73. Ibid., 498.
74. Ibid., 500.
75. Ibid.

The independence of these two goals – annihilation of the Jew in the Aryan territories of Germany and Austria and the conquest of "World Power" status – is very clearly put by Paul Johnson, in his *Modern Times: The World from the Twenties to the Eighties.*

In this classic oeuvre of the great historian we read:

> Hitler's full programme, therefore, was as follows. First gain control of Germany itself and begin the cleansing process at home. Second, destroy the Versailles settlement and establish Germany as the dominant power in Central Europe. All this could be achieved without war. Third, on this power basis, destroy the Soviet Union (by war) to rid the 'breeding-ground' of the 'bacillus' and, by colonization, create a solid economic and strategic power-base from which to establish a continental empire, in which France and Italy would be mere satellites. In the fourth stage Germany would acquire a large colonial empire in Africa, plus a big ocean navy, to make her one of the four superpowers, in addition to Britain, Japan and the United States. Finally, in the generation after his death, Hitler envisaged a decisive struggle between Germany and the United States for world domination.[76]

One should not argue that since Hitler proceeded with the liquidation of Jews throughout Europe, wherever his armies reached, that his war on Europe was motivated by the desire to exterminate the Jews of the continent. No. The murder of Jews all over Europe was an independent objective, not a cause for the war. They are clearly two distinctive projects – destroy the Jews who endanger the Aryans (what Paul Johnson refers to as "the cleansing process at home") and then conquer the world. The fact that as he waged his war in Central Europe, he took advantage of the situation to proceed with the extermination of Jews in no way indicates that the war – which he undertook to lead him to world conquest – was motivated by the "Final Solution" for the "Jewish problem."

Actually, as the first important steps of Hitler's war against Europe were being consummated, the Jews were still free to leave Germany. So it was in 1933 when the Fuehrer started to build Germany's army and weapons, in

---

76. Paul Johnson, *Modern Times: The World from the Twenties to the Eighties* (New York: HarperCollins, 1983), 343.

1934 when he increased the size of the army and began to build warships and created an air force, while compulsory military service was introduced, in 1936 when German troops entered the Rhineland, and even in 1938 when German troops marched into Austria, which led to the Anschluss – the union of Austria with Germany – in the same year when Hitler demanded the Sudetenland region of Czechoslovakia and in March 1939, when Nazi Germany invaded the rest of Czechoslovakia.

Throughout these years, while some Jews were being jailed, tortured, and murdered, Hitler was telling them to emigrate to the countries that would be willing to accept them, a willingness that did not materialize, with the exception of the German Jews who were lucky to obtain an entrance visa to the United States or were allowed to cross the border into Belgium, or who one way or another were successful in reaching Switzerland, England, or Palestine. In these years, from 1933 to 1939, German Jews were being cruelly persecuted, lost the right to exercise their professions, had their businesses boycotted, and the danger of being incarcerated in Dachau concentration camp loomed over every adult Jewish man, but still the systematic murder and the total restriction to emigrate had not begun while the war had started, even if not officially.

An internal Nazi report in 1938 related that "in consequence of the steady anti-Semitic barrage, German Jews can scarcely stay in the smaller provincial localities. More and more, localities announce themselves to be 'Jew free.'"[77] Jews were fleeing rural areas, but also sought to leave Germany altogether. Life was not pleasant for Jews in Nazi Germany, already before the war, and Jews began to emigrate in greater numbers.[78]

Daniel Jonah Goldhagen reports that 525,000 Jews lived in Germany at the beginning of 1933. Over the course of the ensuing five years, a quarter of them left Germany: "By 1938, even the most self-delusionary of Jews had to admit to themselves that Jews could not live in Germany."[79] Within the next year, another quarter of Germany's Jews had fled to other countries. (Unfortunately, many of these countries were not ultimately havens; German Jews who had managed to get to Belgium or France, for example, generally ended

77. Cited in Daniel Jonah Goldhagen, *Hitler's Willing Executioners: Ordinary German and the Holocaust* (New York: Vintage, 1997), 98–99.
78. Ibid.
79. Ibid., 139.

up in concentration camps and did not live to tell the tale.) And once the war started, another 30,000 or so got out. "The Germans thus succeeded," points out Goldhagen, "in forcing over half of the Jews of Germany to leave – usually forfeiting virtually all of their property, belongings, and wealth – what had been to them a beloved homeland."[80]

The purpose of the war waged by Nazi Germany was defined by the indictment of the Nuremberg trial, which states the following:

> From the beginning, the National Socialist movement claimed that its object was to unite the German people in the consciousness of their mission and destiny, based on inherent qualities of race, and under the guidance of the Fuehrer. For its achievement, two things were deemed to be essential: the disruption of the European order as it had existed since the Treaty of Versailles, and the creation of a Greater Germany beyond the frontiers of 1914. This necessarily involved the seizure of foreign territories.
>
> War was seen to be inevitable, or at the very least, highly probable, if these purposes were to be accomplished. The German people, therefore, with all their resources, were to be organized as a great political-military army schooled to obey without question any policy decreed by the State.[81]

Parallel to and independently of this project, the Nazi regime expanded Hitler's plan to cleanse Germany from Jews into all the countries it invaded during the years the war lasted and into some non-occupied states that had submitted to the Nazi command.

As pointed out, the Nazi regime concentrated its hate policy on the Jewish people as people, or rather as a race, and not on Jews individually. The Holocaust was not the denial of liberty, equality, and freedom of individual human beings, it was the execution of a policy of total annihilation of a human group, the extermination of a race, in accordance with Adolf Hitler's lunatic hate, in which he was followed by the majority of German people.

---

80. Ibid.

81. Judgment of the Nuremberg International Military Tribunal, September 30, 1946, reprinted in 41 AJIL 186–218 (1946), as reproduced in Louis Henkin et al., *International Law: Cases and Materials* (St. Paul, MN: West Publishing, 1993), 880–81.

Goldhagen exposes the spirit of the German people and how they were ready to follow Hitler's genocidal intentions:

> The Germans sought to uncover and kill Jews everywhere that they could, outside their country and the territories that they controlled, ultimately throughout the world. Not just its spatial reach but the comprehensiveness of the Germans' extermination of the Jews is also distinctive. Every last Jew, every Jewish child had to die…. [82]
>
> These distinctive features of the Holocaust grew organically from the demonizing German racial antisemitism, an antisemitism that produced the will for *comprehensive* killing of Jews *in all lands* despite the absence of any *objective prior conflict* with Jews…. [83]

Inspired by his two desiderata – conquest of the world and murder of the Jews – Hitler's army marched into Poland on September 1, 1939.

Roosevelt's government did not react to the war until its navy was hit by the Japanese in Pearl Harbor on December 7, 1941. But the indifference to Jewish suffering proceeded throughout the whole war, as we shall see in the next chapter.

---

82. Goldhagen, *Hitler's Willing Executioners*, 412.

83. Ibid., 414. Nazism was accepted by all classes of the German people, law professors as well as philosophers. A special illustration is the case of Martin Heidegger, considered the greatest German philosopher of the twentieth century, who joined the Nazi Party in 1933, becoming shortly after that the rector of the University of Freiburg. He declared that "the Führer alone *is* the present and future German reality and its law." Cited in Jonathan Sacks, *The Great Partnership: God, Science and the Search for Meaning* (London: Hodder and Stoughton, 2012), 87.

Chapter Three
Complicity during the War

Introduction

If the attitudes of the US government as well as of the British cabinet during the years that preceded the war were ominously cruel, the policies followed by these two leaders of the so-called free world during the years of the war were staggeringly perverse and actually quasi-incomprehensible. In this chapter we will come to understand the truth of Jean-Paul Sartre's scathing indictment: "In this situation there is not one of us who is not totally guilty and even criminal; the Jewish blood that the Nazis shed falls on all our heads."[1]

The State Department set newer, complicated procedures for refugees to obtain entrance visas into the United States, by which their immigrations became extremely difficult, and in many cases impossible.

In July 1940, after the Nazis had occupied the Netherlands, Belgium, Luxembourg, and the north of France, Albert Einstein sent a letter to Mrs. Roosevelt in which he wrote:

> I have noted with great satisfaction that you always stand for the rights and humaneness even when it is hard. Therefore in my deep concern I know of no one else to whom to turn for help. A policy is now being pursued in the State Department which makes it all but impossible to give refuge in America to many worthy persons who are the victims of Fascist cruelty in Europe. Of course, this is not openly avowed by those responsible for it. The method which is being used, however, is to make immigration impossible by erecting a wall of bureaucratic measures alleged to be

---

1. Jean-Paul Sartre, *Anti-Semite and Jew: An Exploration of the Etiology of Hate* (New York: Schocken Books, 1948), 136.

necessary to protect America against subversive, dangerous elements. I would suggest that you talk about this question to some well-informed and right-minded person such as Mr. Hamilton Fish Armstrong. If then you become convinced that a truly grave injustice is under way, I know that you will find it possible to bring the matter to the attention of your heavily burdened husband in order that it may be remedied.[2]

Mrs. Roosevelt informed Professor Einstein that she would bring his letter to the president's attention "at once," but there is no indication in the presidential record that Mr. Roosevelt investigated the complaint.

Following its cruel policy, in June 1941 the State Department established even harsher regulations which made it virtually impossible for refugees in Europe to enter the United States. It was a major triumph for those like Assistant Secretary of State Breckinridge Long, Hitler's major accomplice in the US government, who pretended to see subversion entering the land of liberty cloaked in the shabby garment of a refugee.

The visa procedures and restrictive policies, such as the requirement that "enemy aliens" must pass security screenings, led to absurd situations. For instance, one woman became stranded in Vichy France with her twelve-year-old daughter. The father, an Austrian, was in Cairo with the Allied military forces. The mother was an American citizen and wanted to take the daughter to safety in the United States. But the girl could not obtain a visa because her Austrian birth made her an "enemy alien."[3]

The State Department succeeded in persuading Latin American governments to halt nearly all immigration from Europe. The reason given was the need to safeguard hemispheric security. Yet the department's information sources had no reports of Nazi agents or subversive activities among refugees in Latin America.[4]

2. Morse, *While Six Million Died*, 303–4.
3. Wyman, *The Abandonment of the Jews*, 126.
4. Ibid. The author also reports that years later, South American countries were willing to issue passports to Jews in order to save them. But for the plan to work, the State Department had to send a telegram to the German authorities advising them that Jews with Latin American documents were entitled to protection and were eligible for exchange. The State Department delayed sending the telegram for nearly seven weeks – thereby causing the deportation, almost certainly to Auschwitz, of at least 214 Polish Jews (ibid., 279–80).

The "Final Solution" and the *Struma* Tragedy

On December 7, 1941, the Nazi leadership met at Wannsee and formalized the decision to go ahead with the "final solution for the Jews."[5] The combination of the German extermination program and the American-British inhospitality to refugees drove many Jews to suicide. Others sailed on unseaworthy ships toward forbidden harbors. The most tragic of those episodes involved the *Struma*, a 180-ton Rumanian vessel that normally carried a hundred passengers on coastal runs. On December 16, 1941, the *Struma* picked up 769 refugees from the Rumanian port of Constanza and, though none of its passengers possessed British permits, began a slow voyage to Haifa, Palestine. Critically overloaded and endangered by a leaking hull and defective engines, it broke down off Istanbul. Turkish authorities would not permit the passengers to land unless they obtained British certificates for Palestine. The British refused to authorize the certificates.

The *Struma* remained at anchor for ten weeks. Finally, on February 24, in spite of protests by the captain that his ship was not seaworthy, the Turks towed the *Struma* to sea. Before the vessel faded from view, the people ashore read the large banner made by the passengers which said "SAVE US!"

Six miles from shore the *Struma* sank. It is not known whether it capsized, struck a mine, or was hit by a torpedo. Seventy children, 269 women, and 428 men drowned. Two passengers swam to safety. Immediately after the *Struma's* departure, local British officials received authorization from their superiors to issue Palestine certificates to the seventy children.[6] As usual during these terrible years, help came too late.

Suppression of the Truth

A very important report on what went on in the early forties and how the US government made incredible efforts to hide the tragic news from the public is contained in Walter Laqueur's *The Terrible Secret: Suppression of the Truth about Hitler's "Final Solution."* Originally published in 1980 and again in 1998, the book contains a great amount of information regarding the evolution of the Holocaust and mainly the State Department's incredible gymnastics to

5. Jonathan Sacks (*The Great Partnership*, 86) reports that more than half of the participants at the Wannsee Conference carried the title "doctor." They either had doctorates or were medical practitioners.
6. Morse, *While Six Million Died*, 308–9.

keep the situation under cover. Laqueur shows how the English government was well aware of the evolution of the murderous campaign of the German *Einsatzgruppen* against the Jewish populations of Poland and Russia. The same is found in David S. Wyman's *The Abandonment of the Jews.*[7] The accounts of Laqueur, Morse, Wyman, and Medoff coincide in so many details and refer to so many common sources that they reinforce each other, each one showing how carefully the other book's narrative has been constructed in its minute details. There are also other books that deal with the war of the Nazis and/or the Nuremberg trial that confirm what these four Holocaust-dedicated books report.

A very valuable source is the Tusas' book on the Nuremberg trial, in which they stress the cooperation that the bestial *Einsatzgruppen* received from the German army. The Tusas refer to the testimony of SS General Ohlendorff, who stated that the *Einsatzgruppen* had been totally dependent on army backup for their ghastly work of extermination: according to Counsel for the Prosecution Telford Taylor, "the idea that the extermination squads flitted through Russia, murdering Jews and Communists on a large scale but secretly and unbeknown to the Army is utterly preposterous."[8]

It is incredible that even though the war started in September 1939, with the German invasion of Poland and the SS following the Wehrmacht to "take care of" the Jewish populations in the conquered territories, it was not until the autumn of 1941 that clear news about the mass murders began to surface. Laqueur relates that until that time the information was sporadic; in late autumn the news came from all quarters.[9] Even the International Red Cross delegate in Washington reported that the State Department had been informed that Jews were killed in great numbers and speculated whether the IRC should make public what it knew.

A draft prepared by Professor Huber of the IRC committee, while mentioning no names and condemning no one in particular, simply said that civilians should be humanely treated. Two ladies on the committee demanded stronger language in the face of an unprecedented catastrophe. But the majority of

---

7. In his preface, xxii, Wyman writes the following: "I have written not as an insider. I am a Christian, a Protestant, of Yankee and Swedish descent." William Morse was also not a Jew.
8. Ann Tusa and John Tusa, *The Nuremberg Trial* (New York: Atheneum, 1986), 438.
9. In his introduction (9), Laqueur affirms that the first report of massacres was dated August 30, 1941. Page references refer to the 1998 edition (New York: Henry Holt Books).

the executive did not believe in appeals, which it considered emotional and futile, so they supported Huber's draft. The decisive meeting took place on October 14, 1942, and the final decision of the IRC was not to put out any statement at all concerning the murder of the Jews. And so the International Red Cross topped the list of silent witnesses to the greatest genocide known to mankind. Because of this decision and its further inertia throughout the whole war, the IRC, as an institution, should be considered one of Hitler's major accomplices.

But if leading members of the IRC did not believe in the value of public appeals, they were at least willing to pass on what they knew in their capacity as private citizens. At least, some did so.[10]

Detailed news about the murder of great numbers of Jews had been revealed in the early months of 1942. The *Grenzbote* of Bratislava announced in April that deportations from Slovakia had taken place and the Belgrade *Donauzeitung* wrote in June that no Jews were left in Kishinev. In April 1942 the correspondent in Turkey of the London *Sunday Times* reported that 120,000 Rumanian Jews had been killed, a figure that was remarkably accurate. On May 15, Polish sources in London provided figures on Vilna – the murder of 40,000 Jews.[11] But all these were minor items as far as the world press was concerned, overshadowed by the news of the great battles on the war fronts.

The correspondent of the London *Evening Standard* in Stockholm reported that the number at Vilna was even higher: sixty thousand Jews had been killed in that city. The news was published on the authority of a man who had escaped from the city and had just arrived after a dramatic escape via Warsaw and the port of Gdynia. The report was quite specific: it mentioned Ponary, the railway station outside Vilna, as the place where most of the killing had occurred. The item was picked up by some American and Jewish newspapers. Two months later, the US ambassador to Poland reported it to Washington.

In the same month, May 1942, the Jewish Labor Bund in Poland wrote a report detailing verified massacres which they managed to get into the hands of the Polish government in exile in London. In their message, the Jews of Poland traced the path of murder through their country, city by city, region by

---

10. Walter Laqueur, *The Terrible Secret: Suppression of the Truth about Hitler's "Final Solution"* (New York: Henry Holt/Owl Books, 1998), 63.
11. Ibid., 72.

region, month by month. They described the Chelmno killing center, including the gas vans: "For gassing a special vehicle was used in which 90 people were loaded at a time.... On the average, 1,000 people were gassed every day." They estimated the number of Polish Jewish victims to be seven hundred thousand at that point. Their conclusions: Germany had set out to "annihilate all the Jews in Europe" and millions of Polish Jews faced imminent death.[12]

On June 2 the BBC broadcast excerpts from various reports received from Eastern Europe which confirmed that indeed seven hundred thousand Jews had been killed. This, actually, only referred to Polish Jews, as it was based on information coming from this same Jewish Labor Bund. The Polish Bund did not know what was going on in the Soviet Union and in the Baltic countries.

Szmul Zygielbojm, the representative of the Bund on the Polish National Council in England, spoke at a September 2 protest rally in Caxton Hall. He said that "crimes had been committed that had no precedent in human history – crimes so monstrous, compared to which the most barbaric acts of the past ages appeared as mere trivialities."[13]

Brendan Bracken, the British Minister of Information, declared that when the war ended the "united nations" would bring to speedy and severe punishment the persons responsible for the war crimes committed in Poland against Jews and against other Poles. The term "united nations" was beginning to be used by early 1942 to refer to the countries allied in the war against the Axis.[14] As a matter of fact, on January 1, 1942, the "united nations" made a declaration regarding the ideals for which they were fighting against the Axis powers, which referred to "human rights."[15]

On September 30, 1942, Hitler gave a speech in the Berlin Sportpalast arena in which he said: "Once upon a time the Jews in Germany were laughing about my prophecies. I don't know whether they still laugh or whether they no longer feel like laughing. I can only assure them they will stop laughing everywhere and I shall be right also with these prophecies."[16]

12. Wyman, *The Abandonment of the Jews*, 21.
13. Laqueur, *Terrible Secret*, 76.
14. Ibid., 23; Mary Ann Glendon, *A World Made New: Eleanor Roosevelt and the Universal Declaration of Human Rights* (New York: Random House, 2002), 10.
15. *American Journal of International Law* 36, supp. 191, as referred to by David John Harris, *Cases and Materials on International Law*, 5th ed. (London: Sweet and Maxwell, 1998), 624.
16. Cited in Laqueur, *Terrible Secret*, 44.

The Swiss *Turgauer Zeitung* gave the following analysis of this speech: "There is no room for doubt any more: Hitler's word can be interpreted only in the sense that the extermination of the Jews remains one of the points which will be carried out irrespective of the outcome of the war. Hitler had destroyed all illusions which still existed on the fate of the Jews."[17]

All these reports, plus what individual members of the International Red Cross had revealed, must have been enough for the free world to realize the depth of the tragic end that was going to reach practically all the Jews of Europe. Inertia at this point amounted to nothing less than aiding and abetting the criminal acts of the Germans.

But regarding the reaction of the world to the developing news, the worst was yet to come.

Gerhard Riegner, a thirty-year-old Jewish lawyer, was the representative of the World Jewish Congress in Geneva. He was the first Jew to receive the news that Hitler had actually ordered the extermination of European Jewry by gassing. The news reached him from a German industrialist in July 1942.

Riegner sent the following cable to London and Washington:

Received alarming report that in Fuhrer's headquarters plan discussed and under consideration according to which all Jews in countries occupied or controlled by Germany numbering 3 and half–4 million should after deportation and concentration in East be exterminated at one blow to resolve once for all the Jewish Question in Europe stop the action reported planned for autumn methods under discussion including prussic acid stop we transmit information with all reservation as exactitude cannot be confirmed stop informant stated to have close connections with highest German authorities and his reports generally speaking reliable.[18]

In a covering memorandum to the State Department, US vice consul Elting wrote that when he mentioned that this report seemed fantastic, Riegner said that it had struck him in the same way – but that from the fact that mass deportations had been taking place since July 16 (as confirmed by reports received by him from Paris, Holland, Berlin, Vienna, and Prague), it was conceivable that such a diabolic plan was actually being considered by Hitler.

17. Ibid.
18. Ibid., 77.

Elting closed his message with a strong endorsement of Riegner: "For what it is worth, my personal opinion is that Riegner is a serious and balanced individual and that he would never have come to the Consulate with the above report if he had not had confidence in his informant's reliability and if he did not seriously consider that the report might well contain an element of truth."[19]

Some of Riegner's information was already known and some was incorrect: The plan was not "under consideration" but had been adopted many months earlier. Nor was it intended to kill all the Jews at one blow, which would have presented insurmountable technical difficulties. But it was true that Hitler had made a decision and now a German source had made it clear that this did not refer to widespread pogroms but to a "final solution."[20]

The reaction to Riegner's cable in London and Washington marks the beginning of the second phase of the Allies' complicity with Hitler's crimes, now during the war proper.

The British Foreign Office understood that the Nazis were subjecting Jews to harsh treatment, but the idea that there was a genocidal plan in place was viewed as improbable at best. Although the British government declined to publicize Riegner's message and offered nothing in the way of practical reaction to it, it did not object to passing the information on to others.[21]

The State Department, by contrast, would not even do that much. Howard Elting, US vice consul in Geneva, wanted to pass Riegner's cable on to Rabbi Stephen Wise, apparently the most prominent US Jewish leader he was aware of, but was denied permission by the State Department's Division on European Affairs, who called the message "fantastic" and considered it unsubstantiated.[22] Wise in fact did eventually receive the cable, via the British Foreign Office. Wise then contacted Undersecretary of State Sumner Welles, but the latter advised that no announcements of Hitler's supposed genocidal order should be made since the information was unconfirmed.[23]

During July, August, and September of 1942, additional evidence reached

---

19. Morse, *While Six Million Died*, 8; Wyman, *The Abandonment of the Jews*, 42–43.
20. Laqueur, *Terrible Secret*, 79.
21. Ibid., 80.
22. Ibid.
23. Ibid.

Washington through Carl Burckhardt, one of the few members of the Red Cross who decided to reveal the information the organization had received.

On July 1, for example, the Polish government in exile released a report from underground sources to the Allied governments and the press detailing the massacre of the seven hundred thousand Jews since the German invasion in September 1939.

In London, an eyewitness confirmation had been provided by Szmul Zygielbojm, a member of the Polish Jewish Socialist Bund whose wife and two small children had been murdered by the Nazis and who had fought the Nazi takeover of Warsaw until his capture. Incredibly, he had escaped the Nazis and made his way to England, where he was dedicating himself to spreading the news of the horrific events in Europe from his place on the Polish National Council in the Polish government in exile in London.[24]

Riegner's information also was lent independent confirmation by official news coming out of Berlin. On July 17, a Berlin radio report stated that the previous day, more than eighteen thousand Jews had been detained in Paris and that "all will be deported to the East, as previously announced."[25]

On July 22 the Germans began shipping the remaining 380,000 Jews in the Warsaw ghetto to Treblinka to be gassed with carbon monoxide, a move euphemistically referred to as "resettlement." The Polish government in exile informed the United States and Great Britain of these developments. At the same time word was received by mid-July that deportation trains were moving Jews daily from Belgium, Holland, and France.[26]

As if that weren't enough, the US government's own representatives were forwarding similar information. On August 26, Anthony J. Drexel Biddle, US ambassador to several governments in exile, sent directly to the White House a memo from Czechoslovak State Councilman Ernest Frischer, describing the fate of the Jews of Central Europe: "There is no precedent," Frischer had opined, "for such organized wholesale murder in all Jewish history, nor indeed in the whole history of mankind."[27]

And the warning:

---

24. Morse, *While Six Million Died*, 5–6.
25. Ibid., 6.
26. Ibid., 6–7.
27. Ibid., 10.

> This war is not being waged with bombs and guns alone, nor will the nature of the coming world be determined only by the outcome of battle. The victory of morality is an issue in this war. Should we succeed in no more than mitigating the enemy's foul design against his most hated victim, it would amount to partial victory.... Once again we have arrived at a juncture when we are threatened by grave sins of omission.... It is a case of putting a stop to boundless, unscrupulous destruction.[28]

What the Prague gentleman understood in mid-1942 was not understood by the powerful in London and Washington in mid-1944, not even after the war and perhaps not even till today. Or they very well understood it, but actually did not care. For the English and the Americans, the main, actually only, desideratum was winning the war. Nothing should distract the Allies from this objective, not even saving hundreds of thousands, nay, millions of human lives. Mr. Ernest Frischer is an important witness for the case against the Allied leadership.

On September 3, Jacob Rosenheim of New York, president of the Agudath Israel World Organization, received a telegram from Isaac Sternbuch, the Orthodox group's representative in Switzerland. The telegram read:

> According to numerous authenticated informations from Poland, German authorities have recently evacuated Warsaw ghetto and bestially murdered about one hundred thousand Jews. These mass murders are continuing. The corpses of the murdered victims are used for the manufacturing of soap and artificial fertilizers. Similar fate is awaiting the Jews deported to Poland from other occupied territories. Suppose that only energetic steps from America may stop these persecutions. Do whatever you can to cause an American reaction to halt these persecutions.[29]

Still another confirmed eyewitness account came from Dr. Donald A. Lowrie, an American in Europe as a representative of the World Alliance of the Young Men's Christian Association. On assignment in unoccupied southern

---

28. Ibid., 10–11.

29. Wyman, *The Abandonment of the Jews*, 45. According to Wyman, Sumner Welles, undersecretary of state, received a group of Jewish leaders on September 10 and agreed to have an investigation made. Within a few weeks, most of Sternbuch's disclosures were authenticated by further reports from Poland.

France, he had seen Jews in concentration camps established by the Vichy government. Vice consul Elting received Lowrie's report in Geneva and passed on the information to the State Department. Lowrie described in his report how Jews were being deported from France to Poland, backing up what Riegner had said.

The French Jewish community – both from unoccupied territory under the Vichy regime, as well as from the occupied zone – ended up in Auschwitz.

The deportations resulted in a barrage of denunciations. Several Roman Catholic prelates, including the archbishops of Paris, Lyon, and Toulouse, protested vigorously. The cardinals and archbishops of the Occupied Zone united in condemnation.

A statement by Bishop Pierre Theas of Montauban, which was read in all the churches of his diocese, was representative of the attitude of the Catholic leadership: "Hereby I make known to the world the indignant protest of Christian conscience, and I proclaim that all men, whether Aryan or non-Aryan, are brothers because they were created by the same God; and that all men, whatever their race or religion, have a right to respect from individuals as well as from states."[30]

In early October, Riegner forwarded the evidence of two young Jews who had crossed the Swiss border – one had been a witness to the Riga massacre, the other knew many details about the murder waves in Poland and Russia. A postcard from Warsaw was received by Isaac Sternbuch announcing the liquidation of the Warsaw ghetto.

In the same month, the Jewish Telegraphic Agency got hold of the Riegner cable and published it anonymously. In November, Undersecretary Sumner Welles summoned Rabbi Stephen Wise to a meeting in which the veracity of the ghastly events in Europe was confirmed. Wise was told he could now speak out about it, and he promptly gave a press conference to the effect that "he had learned through sources confirmed by the State Department that half the estimated four million Jews in Nazi-occupied Europe had been slain in an extermination campaign."[31]

On December 17, 1942, the eleven Allied governments together with de Gaulle's Free France committee published a declaration as "Members of the

---

30. Ibid., 34.
31. Laqueur, *Terrible Secret*, 93, quoting *The New York Herald Tribune* of November 25, 1942.

United Nations" that "the German authorities...are now carrying into effect Hitler's oft-repeated intention to exterminate the Jewish people in Europe."[32]

Finally, the reality began to filter into mainstream news and public discourse in the United States. Yet even then, government officials were reluctant to let the public know what was really going on. We refer in particular to the main Nazi collaborator in the State Department, one Breckinridge Long, assistant secretary in charge of the Special War Problems Division, a close friend of Franklin Delano Roosevelt. After the United States minister to Switzerland had forwarded yet another message from Riegner on the "Final Solution," Long asked the minister "not to accept and transmit any more such reports to private persons in the United States."[33] The prevailing sentiment in Washington was that such information "could have embarrassing repercussions."[34]

The fact is that since 1941, the US government was in possession of an untold number of reports, from both its own diplomats and other envoys, and all coincided about the fate that had befallen the Jews of various parts of Europe.

The 1942 reports, which were even more detailed, only confirmed what was already known. And yet the State Department employed all means at hand to hold back the information and even to stop it from arriving. This cover of silence by the United States over the mass genocide of a people in various countries of Europe by the Nazi power that had promised to execute such murderous policy cannot but be classified as complicity with the criminals.

A Messenger to Eden and to Roosevelt

The responsibility of the Allied powers regarding the murder of the Jewish people was expressed very clearly during the war in a dramatic meeting between Jan Karski, from the Polish Foreign Ministry, and two Jews in a ruined house in the suburbs of Warsaw. As Karski was preparing to travel to London for the third time since the war had begun, the two Jews told him that they were helpless, that the entire Jewish people would be destroyed. The

---

32. Joint Declaration by Members of the United Nations, December 17, 1942.

33. Laqueur, *Terrible Secret*, 93, quoting Henri L. Feingold, *The Politics of Rescue: The Roosevelt Administration and the Holocaust, 1938–1945* (New Brunswick, NJ: Rutgers University Press, 1970), 180.

34. Laqueur, *Terrible Secret*, 93.

Polish underground could save a few, but three million were doomed. And they added: "Place this responsibility on the shoulders of the Allies. Let not a single leader of the 'united nations' be able to say that they did not know that we were being murdered in Poland and could not be helped except from the outside."[35]

Karski traveled to London, where he met with British prime minister Anthony Eden and brought him the message from Warsaw. To no avail.

Karski then traveled to the United States and met President Roosevelt in the Oval Office on July 28, 1943. The meeting is described by Rafael Medoff:

> Karski began by describing the activities of the Polish underground, to which the president listened with fascination, asking questions and offering unsolicited advice, such as his idea of putting skis on small airplanes to fly underground messengers between England and Poland during the winter. But when Karski related details of the mass killings of the Jews, FDR had nothing to say. The president was, as Karski later put it, "rather noncommittal." As the meeting concluded, Karski asked FDR if there was any message he wanted him to bring back to the oppressed people of Europe. "Tell them that we shall win this war," Roosevelt replied.[36]

Karski also met Justice Felix Frankfurter and related to him everything he knew about the Jews. When he finished, the justice told him, "I can't believe you." Later he explained to someone: "I did not say this young man was lying. I said I cannot believe him. There is a difference."[37]

Zygielbojm, who had worked tirelessly to save Polish Jews, reached a point where he could no longer handle the situation and committed suicide in May 1943. His suicide note, addressed to the Polish president and prime minister in exile, condemned all humanity for its failure to stop these horrendous crimes, but he reserved special scorn for the Allied governments who had known about and done nothing to stop the travesty. He concluded:

> By passively watching the extermination of millions of defenseless, tortured to death children, women and men, those countries became accomplices of the murderers. I cannot remain silent. I cannot go on living when the

---

35. Laqueur, *Terrible Secret*, 119.
36. Medoff, *FDR and the Holocaust*, 9. See also Laqueur, *Terrible Secret*, 236.
37. Laqueur, *Terrible Secret*, 237.

remnant of the Jewish people of Poland of whom I am a representative is eliminated.... By my death I want to express my strongest protest against the extermination of the Jewish people.[38]

This represents a major accusation of the complicity of the Allied Powers with the heinous crimes that were committed by the German people under the Nazi regime and the leadership of Adolf Hitler. The last words of Zygielbojm received considerable attention at the time: the accusation of complicity was clearly stated during the war years.

After that tragic suicide, much could have still been done to save hundreds of thousands of Jews, perhaps more, but the policy remained the same – a perverse apathy, a cruel inertia, a barbarous silence, a criminal omission.

The main force behind maintaining silence was the US State Department, which took pains to keep all incoming news as secret as possible. The "defense" of the State Department's policy, as formulated by R. Borden Reams of the Division of European Affairs, a close assistant to Breckinridge Long, was that the possibility existed that the German government might agree to turn over to the United States and to Great Britain a large number of Jewish refugees. In the event of the Allies' admission that they could not take in the refugees, the onus for their continued persecution would have been largely transferred from the German government to the Allied nations.[39]

This was the official policy undertaken by the State Department since before the war and until after it ended. Naturally – as already pointed out – the United States could have taken up a part of the refugees and arranged for the remainder to be admitted in many of the countries over which America had definite influence. The State Department's explanation, however worded, amounted to a confession of complicity with the murderers.

The fundamental motivation of the State Department to raise all kinds of obstacles to Jewish immigration was pure antisemitism, not very different from the Nazi antisemitism.

Laqueur speculates about the reasons that caused the criminal attitude of the State Department officials, and concludes with the following statement:

38. Ibid., 121. See also Wyman, *The Abandonment of the Jews*, 123.
39. Laqueur, *Terrible Secret*, 228.

Did Reams, McDermott, Breckinridge Long and the others genuinely doubt the available information? This is difficult to believe. It is more likely that their second line of argument was decisive: if the State Department confirmed the news it would "come under the pressure to do something." But was the war effort their overriding concern? This makes sense only if one also assumes that the American diplomats were more single-mindedly and relentlessly devoted to the war effort than Churchill, Stalin and all the others, a supposition which stretches the powers of even a vivid imagination.[40]

Those who have studied the criminal silence that befell American society after the first news of annihilation arrived have equally blamed the Jewish leadership that knew and kept silent. The blame fell principally on Rabbi Stephen Wise and Dr. Nahum Goldmann, prestigious leaders of the American Jewish community.[41] Their defense was that they had been told by the State Department not to reveal the news, and they did not have (or perhaps incorrectly assumed that they did not have) the ways and means to reliably divulge that news to the American society.

The experience in America indicates that mass processions in several cities and especially a mass delegation to Washington would have brought the issue to the public's attention. So much so that the mere threat of a march on Washington by fifty to one hundred thousand African Americans in 1941 extracted an executive order from President Roosevelt that helped the employment situation of black Americans.[42]

The New Republic's criticism of the Allies became more pointed as the months wore on. An editorial in February 1943 asserted that if the Allies remained indifferent, "they will make themselves, morally, partners in Hitler's

---

40. Ibid.

41. Laqueur writes: "Much has been written about the suppression of the Riegner cable by the State Department. But out of ineptitude the news was suppressed by Jewish leaders in New York and London and even in Jerusalem for a considerably longer time. As Stephen Wise wrote to President Roosevelt in December 1942: 'I succeeded, together with the heads of other Jewish organizations, in keeping them [the cables about the systematic mass murder] out of the press.' There had been reliable accounts well before the Riegner cable but they had all been ignored. The Jewish Agency and the World Jewish Congress leaders were flooded with information by their own representatives" (ibid., 160).

42. Wyman, The Abandonment of the Jews, 78.

unspeakable crimes."[43] After the Bermuda Conference – which will be dealt with later on – produced no serious rescue plans, the *New Republic* editors wrote: "If the Anglo-Saxon nations continue on their present course, we shall have connived with Hitler in one of the most terrible episodes of history.... If we do not do what we can, our children's children will blush for us a hundred years hence."[44] Could there have been a stronger characterization of complicity?

The doubts and uncertainties repeatedly alleged by the State Department on the accuracy of the reports had been solved by a public speech given by Hitler at the Berlin Sportpalast on September 30, 1942, reported by German press and radio, which we referred to above, in which he expressed his criminal enthusiasm regarding the ongoing campaign against the Jews in Europe.

But the State Department and the White House did not budge.

Many years later, at the inauguration of the United States Holocaust Memorial Museum, in Washington, President Clinton referred to "America's lethargic response to the Holocaust as constituting complicity in what happened."[45]

We shall come back to this tragic chapter of the criminal silence that covered up the greatest tragedy of human history.

Indifference in the Face of Extermination

The first Jewish agent to send out information from Switzerland was Richard Lichtheim, the representative of the Jewish Agency in Switzerland. In November 1941 the mass deportations had not started and the death camps did not yet exist. But Lichtheim ended a dispatch on the following solemn note: "With regard to Germany, Austria and the Protectorate it must be said that the fate of the Jews is now sealed.... Generally speaking this whole chapter bears the title: 'Too late.' There was a time when the US and the other American states could have helped by granting visas. But this was obstructed by the usual inertia of the bureaucratic machine and by red tape."[46]

On October 22, 1942, eleven weeks after Riegner's original message, Riegner and Richard Lichtheim met with Leland Harrison, the US minister in Geneva. They gave him a three-page report on the atrocities, which stated:

43. Medoff, *FDR and the Holocaust*, 143.
44. Ibid.
45. Ibid., 165.
46. Laqueur, *Terrible Secret*, 174.

Four million Jews are on the verge of complete annihilation by a deliberate policy consisting of starvation, the ghetto system, slave labor, deportation under inhuman conditions and organized mass murders by shooting, poisoning and other methods. This policy of total destruction has been repeatedly proclaimed by Hitler and is now being carried out.[47]

Riegner and Lichtheim were asking for immediate help to save the lives of 1.3 million Jews in countries where there was still some hope for rescue (Hungary, Italy, Rumania, Bulgaria, and France). They wanted intervention by the Vatican, as well as official Allied denunciations and meaningful threats to nations that did not cooperate. In Rumania the situation was already dire: half of Rumania's nine hundred thousand Jews had been killed or deported to Transnistria in the Ukraine, a sorry development that might have been averted with active Allied intervention.[48]

Hungary, Rumania, Bulgaria, and Italy were not yet occupied by Germany, however, so the possibility of saving the Jews living in these countries was immensely higher than for the doomed Polish Jews.

The State Department refused to assist with a plan proposed by the Turkish minister in Bucharest that would have brought three hundred thousand Rumanian Jews via Turkey to Syria and then to Palestine.[49]

At about the same time of Riegner's endeavors, a key International Red Cross official who sought anonymity told Professor Paul Guggenheim – a famous Swiss authority in public international law – that he was aware of official extermination orders for Europe's Jews.[50]

Minister Harrison incorporated all this information from Riegner and Lichtheim and Guggenheim into a report. It would be reasonable to speculate that he did not anticipate a helpful response from the State Department's Division of European Affairs, but whatever the reason, Harrison sent his report personally to Sumner Welles, undersecretary of state.[51]

Thus, by November 1942, Secretary of State Cordell Hull, Undersecretary

---

47. Morse, *While Six Million Died*, 17.
48. Ibid., 18, 299.
49. Ibid., 299–300.
50. Ibid., 18.
51. Ibid. The author adds that this correspondence was discovered in the unpublished private papers of Sumner Welles.

Sumner Welles, and President Roosevelt had all been amply informed with reliable first-hand testimonies about the atrocities occurring in Europe.

A few months earlier, in June, Churchill and Roosevelt had held a meeting in Washington, at which time they had agreed upon the formation of a War Crimes Commission in order to compile evidence and to indict those accused of war crimes. De Gaulle had proclaimed that one of the Allies' principal war aims was the punishment of those guilty of war crimes, including all those who ordered, perpetrated, or participated in any way in those crimes. He appointed René Cassin as the French delegate to the commission. In April 1944 the commission received a list from each member nation of men who were known to be members of the SS, Gestapo, and other groups that committed atrocities in those nations under Nazi occupation. From these lists, the commission was to identify individuals to be given into Allied custody for potential prosecution for war crimes.[52]

However, though Roosevelt had suggested to Churchill the formation of the War Crimes Commission, he then delayed its implementation and at the end emphasized that only the leaders of Nazism would be punished. The official statement about the creation of the commission included this caveat.[53] This, of course, left the absolute majority of the executioners of the Jews at ease about their future, so there was nothing to stop them from proceeding with the extermination process. This exemption from guilt was driving complicity to the utmost extreme.

The American government remained quiet and inert. Even communications and requests from the British Foreign Office were ignored for weeks.

In early 1943, the *New York Times* published a dispatch from C.L. Sulzberger in London about a proposal by the Rumanian government to move seventy thousand Jews from Transnistria to any place of refuge chosen by the Allies. The Rumanians were no longer certain of the Axis victory and were attempting a gradual shift into the good graces of the Allies. Treasury Secretary Morgenthau brought the Sulzberger article to President Roosevelt, who sent him to speak to the Secretary of State. After a superficial investigation, the State Department ignored the proposition.

---

52. Jay Winter and Antoine Prost, *René Cassin and Human Rights: From the Great War to the Universal Declaration*, Human Rights in History (New York: Cambridge University Press, 2013), 147–49.
53. Morse, *While Six Million Died*, 26.

Wyman writes regarding this event that the main issue is not whether the plan might have worked. The critical point is that against a backdrop of full knowledge of the ongoing extermination program, the American and British governments almost cursorily dismissed this major potential rescue opportunity.[54]

The Nation published an editorial by Freda Kirchwey on March 15, 1943, entitled "While the Jews Die," which included some of the strongest words of condemnation of the Roosevelt administration to appear in print anywhere during this period. As Rafael Medoff transcribes:

> You and I and the President and the Congress and the State Department are accessories to the crime and share Hitler's guilt. If we had behaved like humane and generous people instead of complacent, cowardly ones, the two million Jews lying today in the earth of Poland and Hitler's other crowded graveyards would be alive and safe. And other millions yet to die would have found sanctuary. We had it in our power to rescue the doomed people and we did not lift a hand to do it – perhaps it would be fairer to say that we lifted just one cautious hand, encased in a tight-fitting glove of quotas and visas and affidavits, and a thick layer of prejudice.[55]

The accusation of complicity comes out so very clearly and in such strong words in this editorial. It is a perfect piece for the prosecution against the American government officials that aided and abetted Hitler's genocide of the Jewish people.

The Negativism of Franklin Delano Roosevelt

There are scholars who see Franklin Delano Roosevelt's connection with human rights from a positive perspective, stressing a speech he made in early 1941 that became known as the "Four Freedoms" speech in which he called for "a world founded upon four essential human freedoms," identified by him as "freedom of speech and expression," "freedom of every person to worship God in his own way," "freedom from want," and "freedom from fear."[56]

I hold that FDR's understanding of human rights was flawed. The first right,

54. Wyman, *The Abandonment of the Jews*, 83–84.
55. Medoff, *FDR and the Holocaust*, 144–45.
56. Thomas Buergenthal, *International Human Rights in a Nutshell*, Nutshell Series (St. Paul, MN: West Publishing, 1988), 17–18.

"freedom of speech and expression," is indeed a human right. The second right, however, concerning the freedom to worship God, does not reflect the complete human right. Religious freedom in its fullest form materializes in freedom to worship or not to worship, freedom to choose a religion or not to follow any religion, and freedom to accept the existence of God or follow the Greek philosophical atheistic schools of the Epicureans and others who throughout time did not accept the existence of a divinity.

The third right, "freedom from want," is conditioned by general economic circumstances, as well as by specific personal attitudes and capabilities – it cannot be guaranteed by social and/or political initiatives. Therefore it is not really a human right in the sense that has been established by the great documents of humanity and by the UDHR; it was left to be guided by the International Covenant on Economic, Social and Cultural Rights.[57] The fourth right, "freedom from fear," could be guaranteed by an organized political system in some cases, but in others it involves psychological and/or emotional characteristics, entirely divorced from state or international protection, so it is also not a human right in the political/constitutional/international sense.

And above all, Roosevelt did not refer to the fundamental human right – the right to life, which was being destroyed by the Nazis at that very same moment when he was speaking of his "four essential human freedoms." There is no freedom without life. Roosevelt was not only an accomplice to Hitler, he also pretended to ignore the sanctum sanctorum of the human freedoms – the human right to life. The widespread admiration that Roosevelt garnered corrupted people's minds to the point of elevating his "four freedoms" to the level of the most magnificent human statement, when it was actually an act of pure demagogy.

Thomas Buergenthal writes that "Roosevelt's vision of 'the moral order,' as he characterized it, became the clarion call of the nations that fought the Axis in the Second World War and founded the United Nations."[58] It could very well be that Roosevelt was an inspiration for his people, for the American

---

57. Article 7 of the covenant merely "recognizes" the right of everyone to the enjoyment of just and favorable conditions of work, which ensure remuneration, fair wages, a decent living, safe and healthy working conditions, opportunity of promotion in employment, rest leisure, and limitation of working hours.
58. Buergenthal, *International Human Rights in a Nutshell*, 18.

armed forces, and for America's allies in the common effort to destroy the invading German armies, demolish the Nazi organization, and liquidate Hitler and his gang. But on the other hand, the US president did not raise a finger to save the primary victims of Hitler's barbaric desideratum; their fundamental human right to life was not considered. The American president's philosophy and his behavior may have corrupted the so-called human-rights initiatives that kept the Allies busy after the war. As we shall see in chapter 6, the Allies drafted a Human Rights Declaration that contained absolutely nothing regarding the protection of persecuted minorities.

It is undeniable that Roosevelt could have done a lot during the war to save people from terrible suffering and agony that lasted, in many cases, almost the entire duration of the war. The president of the United States had the power to save an unimaginable number of lives but he did nothing. Roosevelt did not even exercise the powers that the law set for the executive power, which would have allowed him to bring hundreds of thousands of refugees in the ten years of the Nazi regime, without any support from Congress. Instead, his inertia gave more power, more animus to Hitler and to the executioners of Hitler's barbaric plan to proceed with the extermination of European Jewry, as well as providing a free ticket to the criminals at the State Department who helped the Nazis in many ways.

On November 24–25, 1942, after having kept silent during the months since Riegner's original alarming report, Rabbi Stephen Wise gave press conferences in Washington and New York about the murderous policy of the Nazis toward the Jewish populations in the occupied countries of Europe. The coverage of the press was insignificant.

Wise's revelation of mass killing on a scale previously unfamiliar to the human consciousness was greeted with a distinct lack of public interest, which Roosevelt did nothing to dispel. It took fully a year for the subject to even make its way into his biweekly press conferences. Both the president and the news reporters were equally eager to ignore the news, and major news outlets gave it short shrift.[59]

Rabbi Wise was a close friend of the president. On December 2, 1942, Wise wrote to him:

---

59. Wyman, *The Abandonment of the Jews*, 61–63.

Dear Boss. I do not wish to add an atom to the awful burden which you are bearing with magic and, as I believe, heaven-inspired strength at this time. But you do know that the most overwhelming disaster of Jewish history has befallen Jews in the form of the Hitler massacres... and it is indisputable that as many as two million civilian Jews have been slain.[60]

Wise asked if Roosevelt would meet a delegation of Jewish leaders representing organizations that had united to combat the Nazi threat, and he pointed out that the very day of his writing was being observed by Jewish people as a day of mourning all over the world.

A shocking aspect of Roosevelt's behavior was the audacity with which he tried to give his friends the wrong idea about what was going on with the Jews in Europe. One of those was Felix Frankfurter, Harvard professor and justice of the Supreme Court, who visited Roosevelt in December 1942 to express his grave concerns. The president poo-pooed him and said the deported Jews were merely being used as a labor force on the eastern frontier.[61] As Laqueur adds, Roosevelt was undoubtedly under no such illusion but rather had quite a clear picture of what had happened to those millions. After all, besides all the written reports that had reached the State Department, a month earlier Roosevelt had had an hour-long conversation with Jan Karski, who had related to him, in its most cruel details, the tragedy that had befallen the Jews in Poland.

On December 7, 1942, one year after the United States had entered the war, the *London Times* observed that it was uncertain whether the Allied governments, even now, could do anything to prevent Hitler's threat of extermination from being carried out.

The German-occupied countries were being given deadlines for the removal of Jews, and these dates were freely publicized on the Axis wireless or in reports from Berlin. In all parts of Europe the Germans were calling meetings or issuing orders, to bring about what they called the "Final Solution" of the Jewish problem.

The *Jewish Frontier* issue of November 1942 printed the following declaration:

---

60. Morse, *While Six Million Died*, 27.
61. Laqueur, *Terrible Secret*, 94.

In the occupied countries of Europe a policy is now being put into effect whose avowed object is the extermination of a whole people. It is a policy of systematic murder of innocent civilians which in its dimensions, its ferocity and its organization, is unique in the history of mankind.[62]

On December 8, Roosevelt received a Jewish delegation headed by Rabbi Wise. They handed the president a twenty-page document entitled "Blue Print for Extermination" – a country-by-country analysis of annihilation. Roosevelt told the delegation that he was "profoundly shocked" to learn that two million Jews had already perished, and that the Allies would do whatever they could to "save those who may yet be saved."[63] Wise emphasized at the meeting that the tide of war had turned and that Jews everywhere recognized that an Allied victory would end the Nazi terror. The question was whether any of them would be alive to see that great day.

The line of reasoning that led to the abandonment of the Jews had at its core the belief that rescue was incompatible with the Allies' principal war aims. The politicians, diplomats, and military leaders who shared this view brushed aside the question that Wise and his colleagues had gently raised with the president: What would victory mean to the dead?

Among many other possible solutions, Alaska had attracted attention already before the war as a possible site of refugees. At that point America was facing an aggressive Japan and attempting an alliance with the Soviet Union. Settling and developing Alaska coincided with America's strategic needs: a large labor force made up of European refugees could have served as a bulwark against potential attacks. In 1940 the Interior and the Labor Departments endorsed legislation, known as the King-Havenner Bill, to promote Alaskan development, partly through an influx of refugee workers. But the State Department was strongly opposed and FDR, who initially

---

62. Wyman, *The Abandonment of the Jews*, 49.

63. Ibid., 72. Wyman notes that FDR's reply proves that by December 1942 the president was fully aware of the Nazi's plans regarding the Jews. Wyman, ibid., also reports Adolf Held (Jewish Labor Committee) as quoting the president:

> The government of the United States is very well acquainted with most of the facts you are now bringing to our attention. Unfortunately we have received confirmation from many sources. Representatives of the United States government in Switzerland and other neutral countries have given us proof that confirm the horrors discussed by you.

was ready to support the plan provided that no more than 10 percent of the workers would be Jews, finally dropped the idea.[64]

Another shocking demonstration of FDR's negative attitude came about when Secretary of Interior Harold Ickes wrote to the president inquiring whether he would be willing to consider using the Virgin Islands, then under the administration of the US government, as a small-scale refuge. Roosevelt turned the request down.[65] This refusal of the White House came after the governor and the legislative assembly of the Virgin Islands declared their willingness to accept refugees. FDR claimed that granting the Jews shelter in that US territory would conceivably hurt the future of present American citizens since the immigrants might somehow find a way to reach the mainland United States.[66]

Another possible way of rescuing victims from Nazi persecution was through the educational system. Professor Stephen Norwood of the University of Oklahoma uncovered at least fifty scholarship offers made by American colleges to European Jewish refugee students that were stymied by visa refusals from the Roosevelt administration. Since the students could not prove they would return to Europe after their studies, claimed US officials, they posed a likely "risk" to become "financially dependent" on the United States government.[67]

Throughout those years, American Jews who wished that more direct action be taken to save their brethren in Europe were left in an awkward position. If they fought for more vigorous US policies toward their brethren, their own patriotism might be impugned.

American Jewry soon realized that their president was not willing to do anything to save those Jews in Europe who could still be helped. And in Europe, those who were willing to hide or in any way help Jews were disappointed by American inertia.

Beyond the issue of human survival lay other fundamental questions. What would the effect of Allied disinterest be on the captive peoples of

64. Medoff, FDR and the Holocaust, 52–53.
65. Wyman, The Abandonment of the Jews, 47.
66. Medoff, FDR and the Holocaust, 11.
67. Rafael Medoff, "Long-Lost Plea to FDR Revives Question: How Could Europe's Jews Have Been Saved?," at http://www.tabletmag.com/jewish-news-and-politics/173617/long-lost-letter-to-fdr?print=1.

Europe who might shelter the oppressed at the risk of their own lives – or on Axis troops weighing the commission of atrocities? The same question could be asked about churchmen in Nazi-occupied lands wrestling with their consciences, or on German commanders contemplating their own futures.[68]

Roosevelt's friends at the State Department, mainly Assistant Secretary of State Breckinridge Long, did everything to sabotage various memoranda initiated by the British government. One memorandum carried the following text:

> The attention of His Majesty's Government in the United Kingdom, of the Soviet Union and of the United States Government has been drawn to reports from Europe which leave no room for doubt that the German authorities, not content with denying to persons of Jewish origin in all the territories in Europe over which their barbarous rules has been extended, the most elementary human rights, are now carrying into effect Hitler's oft repeated intention to exterminate the Jewish people of Europe.

The document condemned "in the strongest possible terms this bestial policy of cold-blooded extermination." It affirmed that "the necessary practical measures" would be taken to ensure that those responsible for the crimes would be brought to retribution. Despite a State Department's weakening modification, it remained a forceful statement, the strongest concerning atrocities against Jews to be issued by the Allied powers during World War II. Furthermore, it committed the United States, Britain, and the Soviet Union for the first time to postwar prosecution of those responsible for crimes against the European Jews.

The declaration was greeted in the House of Commons with unanimous gravity.[69]

At the State Department everything was tried to weaken or, if possible, to avoid the publication of the memorandum, this time unsuccessfully. On December 17, 1942, the memorandum was released by the governments of Belgium, Czechoslovakia, Greece, Luxembourg, Netherlands, Norway, Poland, the Soviet Union, the United Kingdom, the United States, and Yugoslavia, as well as by the French National Committee.

---

68. Morse, *While Six Million Died*, 29.
69. Wyman, *The Abandonment of the Jews*, 75.

Around that time a letter was published in the *New York Times* by journalist and author Pierre Van Paasen, who had personally witnessed Nazi behavior. He wrote:

> To be silent in this hour when thousands of unarmed innocent Jewish human beings are murdered each day is not only a betrayal of elementary human solidarity, it is tantamount to giving the blood-thirsty Gestapo carte blanche to continue and speed its ghastly program of extermination.[70]

Van Paasen is another witness to the accusation of Allied – and principally American – complicity to the crimes of Nazi Germany.

Early in 1943, suggestions were again presented to Washington and London for the rescue of Jews. Among them was a new concerted Allied effort to convince the neutral countries to open their frontiers to all escaping Jews, which would include American guarantees for the maintenance and support of refugees until permanent homes could be found after the war. Funds for this purpose had been pledged by American Jews.

Another suggestion was to pressure the International Red Cross to provide the same safeguards for imprisoned Jews as for prisoners of war or interned civilians. These had been denied because the Germans had declared the Jews to be stateless common criminals, a designation that the IRC accepted – another of the great shames in the behavior of the Red Cross toward the Jewish tragedy during the war years.

And yet another suggestion was to renew the demand that the British revoke their White Paper of 1939, which limited Jewish immigration to Palestine to a total of seventy-five thousand within a five-year period ending in March 1944. As well, there was a call to lift American immigration quotas, at least temporarily.[71] These and other ideas were discussed by the citizenry, stated in petitions signed by hundreds of thousands of Americans, and floated in the halls of government.[72]

In the State Department sat a very good friend of Franklin Delano Roosevelt, who had contributed magnanimously to FDR's previous presidential campaign: Breckinridge Long, Assistant Secretary of State. The many

---

70. Morse, *While Six Million Died*, 34.
71. Morse, *While Six Million Died*, 37–38.
72. Ibid., 38.

divisions under his supervision included the Visa Division. Long's approach was to "delay and effectively stop for a temporary period of indefinite length the number of immigrants into the United States." He intended "to put every obstacle in the way and to require additional evidence and to resort to various administrative devices which would postpone and postpone and postpone the granting of the visas."[73]

As an example of the sometimes absurd lengths to which these obfuscations might run, the application for an immigration visa required someone who had evaded the Gestapo to produce a character reference from his local German police station.[74]

Roosevelt's administration accepted this with equanimity; the president never protested the bureaucratic blocking of refugee visas and thus made clear that this policy was not only acceptable but even desirable.[75]

Long's ostensible rationale for his obstructionist policy was to prevent enemy agents from getting into the country. But in fact only once did an enemy agent ever make his way in via this route. And he was not Jewish.[76]

Everything connected with possible relief for the Jews of Europe passed through divisions under Long's supervision – whether visas for visitors or immigrants, the dispatch of funds for food, clothing and medicine, or appeals to the International Red Cross for humane treatment of Jews, comparable to that prescribed for prisoners of war or interned civilians.

In the final chapter of his book *The Abandonment of the Jews*, Wyman writes the following about Roosevelt's policy:

> America's response to the Holocaust was the result of action and inaction on the part of many people. In the forefront was Franklin D. Roosevelt, whose steps to aid Europe's Jews were very limited. If he had wanted to, he could have aroused substantial public backing for a vital rescue effort by speaking out on the issue. If nothing else, a few forceful statements by the President would have brought the extermination news out of obscurity

73. Cited in Medoff, *FDR and the Holocaust*, 6.
74. Morse, *While Six Million Died*, 41.
75. Medoff, *FDR and the Holocaust*, 7.
76. Morse, *While Six Million Died*, 41–42.

and into the headlines. But he had little to say about the problem and gave no priority at all to rescue.[77]

In December 1942 the president had reluctantly agreed to Rabbi Wise's request to talk with Jewish leaders about the recently confirmed news of extermination. Thereafter he refused Jewish requests to discuss the problem; he even left the White House to avoid the march of four hundred Orthodox rabbis to the White House on October 6, 1943.[78] He dragged his feet on opening refugee camps in North Africa. He declined to question the State Department's arbitrary shutdown of refugee immigrations to the United States, even when pressed by the seven Jewish members of Congress.

After creating the War Refugee Board – which will be discussed below – the president took little interest in it. He never acted to strengthen it or provide it with adequate funding. He impeded its initial momentum by delaying the selection of a director and hindered its long-term effectiveness by ruining the plan to appoint a prominent public figure to the post. When the board needed help with the recalcitrant American ambassador to Spain (to save Jews by moving them to Portugal), Roosevelt maintained a hands-off approach. At the urging of the board, the president did issue a strong war crimes warning in March 1944. But he first diluted its emphasis on Jews.[79]

Wyman concludes:

> Years later, Emanuel Celler charged that Roosevelt, instead of providing even "some spark of courageous leadership" had been "silent, indifferent and insensitive to the plight of the Jews." In the end, the era's most

---

77. Wyman, *The Abandonment of the Jews*, 311.

78. The rabbis were met by presidential secretary Marvin McIntyre, who told them the president was unavailable "because of the pressure of other business." In fact the president's schedule was remarkably light that afternoon. His daily calendar listed nothing between a 1:00 p.m. lunch with Secretary of State Hull and a 4:00 p.m. departure for a ceremony at an airfield outside Washington.

Some claim that the real reason for the president's refusal to meet the rabbis was that Rabbi Stephen Wise (from the Reform movement) and Samuel Rosenman (the president's Jewish adviser and speechwriter) convinced Roosevelt to avoid the meeting. See Shimon Rosenberg and Yaakov Astor, "The Dark Side of FDR and the American Jewish 'Leaders' Who Advised Him," *Zman*, August 2011, 105.

79. Wyman, *The Abandonment of the Jews*, 311–12.

prominent symbol of humanitarianism turned away from one of history's most compelling moral challenges.[80]

On the First Lady, Wyman sums up that Eleanor Roosevelt cared deeply about the tragedy of Europe's Jews and took some limited steps to help. But she never urged vigorous government action. She saw almost no prospects for rescue and believed that winning the war as quickly as possible was the only answer.[81]

England tried on various occasions to get the United States to join in a common effort to help the victims of Nazism, but only after weeks of no response from the State Department, when the English prepared themselves to go it alone, did the United States jump in as the leader of the initiative.[82]

On January 21, 1943, another telegram from Riegner informed that the Germans were killing six thousand Jews per day in Poland. Riegner wrote about the terrible situation of the 130,000 Jews of Rumania who had been transferred to Transnistria. Sixty thousand had already died and the remaining were slowly starving to death.

Jewish organizations held a mass meeting in Madison Square Garden on March 1 under the slogan "Stop Hitler Now," at which speeches were delivered by New York mayor Fiorello La Guardia, AFL president William Green, and world-famous scientist and Zionist leader Chaim Weizmann. Messages were sent to the meeting by New York State governor Thomas Dewey, the archbishop of Canterbury and Cardinal Arthur Hinsley. Police estimated that seventy-five thousand came to the rally. A long list of proposals aimed at rescuing European Jewry was forwarded to the president.

The proposals composed an eleven-point program that called for:

1. Approaches through neutral channels to Germany and the satellite governments to secure agreements for the Jews to emigrate.
2. Swift establishment of havens of refuge by Allied and neutral nations.
3. Revision of US immigration procedures to permit full use of the quotas.
4. Agreement by Great Britain to take in a reasonable proportion of Jewish refugees.

---

80. Ibid., 313.
81. Ibid., 315.
82. Morse, *While Six Million Died*, 43.

5. Agreement by the Latin American nations to modify their extremely tight immigration regulations and provide temporary havens of refuge.
6. Consent by England to open the gates of Palestine to Jews.
7. A united-nations program to transfer Jewish refugees rapidly out of neutral countries bordering Nazi territory and to encourage those countries to accept more refugees by guaranteeing financial support and eventual evacuation.
8. Organization by the united nations, through neutral agencies such as the International Red Cross, of a system for feeding Jews remaining in Axis territory.
9. Provision by the united nations of the financial guarantees required to implement this rescue program.
10. Formation by the united nations of an agency empowered to carry out the program.
11. Appointment, without further delay, of a commission to assemble evidence for war-crimes trials and to determine the procedures for them.[83]

A *New York Times* editorial commended the rescue plans and asserted that the "united nations" governments had no right to spare any efforts that would save lives. Editorial support for the proposals also appeared in the *New York Post*, the *Sun*, the *Nation*, and the *Herald Tribune*.[84]

Rabbi Stephen Wise, seeking to utilize the momentum generated by the mass meeting, sent letters to the president, to the secretary of state, and to all members of the House and the Senate, describing the proceedings at the rally and listing the eleven rescue proposals. The White House shunted the letter to the State Department, where a reply was prepared, which was signed by the president, asserting vaguely that "this Government has moved and continues to move, so far as the burden of the war permits, to help the victims of the Nazi doctrines of racial, religious and political oppression."[85]

"We Will Never Die"

On March 9–10, 1943, a pageant entitled "We Will Never Die" took place in Madison Square Garden, each night with an attendance of twenty thousand

83. Wyman, *The Abandonment of the Jews*, 88–89.
84. Ibid., 89.
85. Ibid.

people. Organized by the Bergson group, it included some of Hollywood's most prominent Jews. The organizers tried to obtain a message from FDR to be read at the occasion, but the president was advised that such a message would raise a "political question."

Translated, this meant that publicizing the slaughter could raise the question of how America was going to respond to the Nazi genocide. And since Roosevelt had decided that the United States was not going to take any specific steps to aid the Jews, raising that question would be embarrassing.

The Bergson group worked very hard to raise the American people's awareness of what was happening in the war against the Jews and to pressure the US government, and specifically the president, to save as many Jews as possible. They ended up being persecuted by the IRS and the FBI, under suspicion of tax irregularities and Communist links. Neither of the two lengthy investigations, both very thorough, reached any result.[86]

The leader of the Bergson group was Hillel Kook, nephew of the former chief rabbi of Palestine, Abraham Isaac Kook. In the United States he adopted the name Peter H. Bergson. He was a dynamic speaker and had an extraordinary sense for public relations. The group called themselves the "Emergency Conference to Save the Jewish People of Europe." From time to time, they published full-page ads in the *New York Times* that attracted much attention. They also organized many rallies that brought together tens of thousands of people in order to impress upon the US government the need to save the persecuted Jews of Europe who could still be saved.

In early March 1943 a resolution was approved by the US Senate and then by the House of Representatives, which stated that "the American people view with indignation the atrocities inflicted upon the civilian population in the Nazi-occupied countries and especially the mass murder of Jewish men, women and children. These brutal and indefensible outrages are hereby condemned" and "it is the sense of this Congress that those guilty shall be held accountable and punished."

Despite all efforts by the Jewish organizations that the resolution should add a paragraph urging both the United States and the "united nations" to act immediately to rescue the Jews of Europe, the initiative did not succeed.[87]

---

86. Rafael Medoff, "Presidential Power," *Jerusalem Post*, May 31, 2013.
87. Wyman, *The Abandonment of the Jews*, 95.

At that time the British suggested that the twenty thousand Jews who were located in Spain should be transferred to North Africa in order to open more place in Spain for other refugees. Long disagreed because North Africa was under French administration, therefore beyond US jurisdiction. Ultimately, Long, Hull, and Roosevelt feared that such a move would annoy North Africa's Muslim population.[88]

And so, every practical proposition that was brought to the State Department, controlled by Roosevelt's friend, Assistant Secretary Long, was discarded, while the Holocaust was at its fullest tempo.

An appeal by Jewish sources was sent through Ambassador Myron Taylor to Long on March 26, 1943. Written in telegraph style, it read:

> Gravest possible news reaching London past week shows massacres now reaching catastrophic climax particularly [in] Poland also deportations [of] Bulgarian, Rumanian Jews already begun. European Jewry disappearing while no single organized rescue measure yet taken. Urge you energetically [to] take advantage [of the] presence [of] our visitor [Anthony Eden was then visiting the United States] [to] solemnly impress British-American authorities [of their] duty responsibility convoke immediately...conference for action not exploration otherwise too late to rescue a single Jew. We doing all possible but effective action now rests [with] America.[89]

Taylor received no response.

Back in 1942, when Wendell Wilkie confronted the British leadership with the need to admit large numbers of Jews into Palestine, the English high commissioner replied that since the United States was not taking Jews in even up to the quota limits, Americans were hardly in a position to criticize.[90]

The Hypocritical Bermuda Conference

Then, in April 1943, came the Bermuda Conference, an even greater bluff than the Évian Conference. The location was chosen because it would shield the conferees from public opinion, the press, and Jewish organizations, as wartime regulations restricted all access to the island. The Emergency Conference

---

88. Morse, *While Six Million Died*, 50.
89. Ibid., 51.
90. Wyman, *The Abandonment of the Jews*, 332.

requested permission to send a delegation to the conference, which was rejected. Then it presented to Undersecretary Welles a list of proposals for rescue action. The proposals were ignored.[91] Instructions given to the US delegation to the Bermuda Conference practically constrained it from doing anything. The instructions stated:

- not to limit the discussions to Jewish refugees;
- not to raise questions of religious faith or race in appealing for public support or promising US funds;
- not to make commitments regarding shipping program space for refugees;
- not to delay the wartime shipping program by suggesting that homeward-bound, empty transport pick up refugees en route;
- not to bring refugees across the ocean if any space for their settlement was available in Europe;
- not to pledge funds, since this was the prerogative of Congress and the president;
- not to ignore the needs either of the war effort or of the American civilian population for food and money; and
- not to establish new agencies for the relief of refugees, since the Intergovernmental Committee already existed for that purpose.[92]

The lone action the American delegates were empowered to accomplish was to offer financial assistance to other nations that would take in refugees.

The Bermuda Conference started on April 19, 1943. The opening speeches already showed that there would be no productive conclusions. The conference did not even consider transporting Jewish refugees to Angola, claiming that the Portuguese would not agree. The conference authorized the removal of twenty-one thousand refugees from Spain to North Africa, which never materialized. At that time, Adolf Berle suggested Cyrenaica (the eastern lump of Libya) as a sanctuary for as many as one hundred thousand Jews for the rest of the war. Nothing came of it. Britain's Palestine policy did not come up during the conference, in accordance with the English wish. The only concrete result was the decision to move five thousand Jewish refugees

---

91. Medoff, *FDR and the Holocaust*, 56.
92. Wyman (*The Abandonment of the Jews*, 141) notes that after the war, Welles evaluated the Intergovernmental Committee: "The final results amounted to little more than zero. The Government of the United States itself permitted the committee to become a nullity."

from Spain, but actually only two thousand were evacuated, most of them not until a year after the Bermuda Conference.

At least one person publicly called out the American diplomatic corps while the Bermuda Conference was still going on. Rabbi Israel Goldstein said: "The job of the Bermuda Conference apparently was not to rescue victims of Nazi terror, but to rescue our State Department and the British Foreign Office" from the pressure of Jewish groups and Christian prelates.[93]

On the very day that the Bermuda Conference opened, the Germans launched the final assault on the Warsaw ghetto and its Jewish population. Nobody helped them, not even the Polish resistance.

At about that time, President Roosevelt received a petition signed by 282 leading scholars and scientists, calling upon him to speak and to act. They appealed to the president to let every German know what was being perpetrated by its rulers and to warn them that for generations this guilt would rest upon them unless the hands of the murderers were stayed. The appeal continued by asking the president to apply methods so far unused to save the millions of European Jews doomed to death by the enemy of civilization.[94]

Regarding the move to North Africa, Roosevelt wrote to his secretary of state that "I know that there is plenty of place for them in North Africa, but I raise the question of sending large number of Jews there. That would be extremely unwise."[95] Fear of Muslim reaction in North Africa, of Arab reaction in Palestine and, alas, Christian reaction in the United States – these were the hallmarks of Franklin Delano Roosevelt's policy toward Jewish refugees.

Three days after the Bermuda Conference ended, the Emergency Conference to Save the Jewish People of Europe (Peter Bergson's group) published an ad in the *New York Times* headlined "To 5,000,000 Jews in the Nazi Death-Trap, Bermuda was a Cruel Mockery."[96]

Isaiah Bowman, a prominent geographer and president of Johns Hopkins University from 1935 to 1948, was Roosevelt's adviser on matters of land settlement and migratory policies. Among Bowman's theories was the notion that Palestine had limited ability to absorb Jewish refugees, due to the danger of angering the Arab world and the risks of America being drawn into a Mideast

93. Ibid., 122.
94. Morse, *While Six Million Died*, 52–53.
95. Wyman, *The Abandonment of the Jews*, 117.
96. Medoff, *FDR and the Holocaust*, 60.

conflict. Bowman went so far as to characterize Zionism as no different from Hitler's *Lebensraum* (Nazi territorial expansion). His warning to FDR about Arab opposition was a factor that sabotaged the British proposal to the United States in 1943 to temporarily settle some European Jewish refugees in Allied-occupied Libya.[97]

Libya became again a possible refuge in 1944, when the War Refugee Board pressed the matter, but this time it met with British opposition. In June 1944 the British finally agreed to one camp, with a capacity of fifteen hundred, but they managed by procrastination to avoid even that small step.[98]

Arab Participation in the Holocaust

A presidential report submitted to Congress in March 1, 1945, regarding the Yalta Conference and other recent overseas meetings, included a session with Ibn Saud, the king of Saudi Arabia. Ibn Saud told Roosevelt that he "objected violently" to proposals to create a temporary haven in Libya for Jews fleeing the Nazis. Saud even spurned FDR's talk of international aid to develop Arab countries, on the grounds that the benefits of such development might be "inherited by the Jews" since Jewish immigrants to Palestine were, in his view, secretly planning to conquer the entire Mideast.

Instead, Ibn Saud recommended settling the Holocaust survivors in Europe after the war, all consistent with the advice FDR had received from Isaiah Bowman, the president's expert on refugee settlement.[99]

In his address to Congress, FDR remarked that "I learned more about the whole problem, the Muslim problem, the Jewish problem, by talking with Ibn Saud for five minutes than I could have learned in the exchange of two or three dozen letters."

Apparently Roosevelt's meeting with Saud strengthened his totally

97. Ibid., 31.
98. Wyman, *The Abandonment of the Jews*, 260.
99. Medoff, *FDR and the Holocaust*, 68. The *Jerusalem Post* of October 24, 2012, French edition, published an article by Joanna Seidel, in which she reports on the meeting of FDR with Ibn Saud on February 14, 1945, to close an agreement regarding the airport of Dharhan. When the president touched on the Jewish problem, the king responded that he wanted the Jewish survivors to return to their countries of origin, affirming that the Arabs would not cooperate with the Jews anywhere – not in Palestine, nor anywhere else. The president then assured the king that he would do nothing to support the Jews against the Arabs and would never act in a hostile manner toward the Arabs.

unfavorable policy regarding the creation of a Jewish state. When Rabbi Stephen Wise came to the White House for reassurance, FDR told him: "You are a minister of religion. Do you want me to encourage five or six hundred thousand Jews to die?" – a reference to the Jewish population in Palestine at that time.[100]

Arab opposition to allow Jews into Palestine or into any corner of the Middle East, typified by Ibn Saud's remarks, must be reckoned with when we hear the Arabs complaining that they do not have responsibility for what the Europeans did to the Jews during the war and therefore do not have to "suffer" the Jewish presence in their midst. The truth is just the opposite. Among the many enemies of the Jewish people during those fatal years, starting from Hitler and going through the State Department officials, the White House, the British Foreign Service, and the Nazi collaborators of various nationalities, the Arabs have to be included – from the grand mufti of Jerusalem to the king of Saudi Arabia.

FDR Is Deaf to Christian leadership, to Congress, and to the Media

Roosevelt's statement sparked a barrage of criticism from members of Congress. "The choice of the desert king as expert on the Jewish question is nothing short of amazing," US Senator Edwin Johnson exclaimed. "I imagine that even Fala [the president's dog] would be more of an expert."[101]

The records show magnanimous attitudes from the Christian churches in the United States toward the European Jews and their suffering.[102] And yet Roosevelt maintained his attitude to throw the responsibility for his inaction on Congress, on the American people, on the Christians... The leader of

---

100. Medoff, *FDR and the Holocaust*, 69.

101. Ibid., 68–69.

102. In Cincinnati, Ohio, a group of more than one hundred Protestant ministers endorsed a statement to the Jews of their community, which said: "We of the Christian ministry cannot and will not remain silent before the spectacle of mass murder suffered by Jews in Nazi-controlled Europe." And then, as Wyman comments (*The Abandonment of the Jews*, 26), they expressed insights that should have been obvious but which seem to have gone widely unrecognized in American Christian circles during World War II, pointing out that:

> This is the tragedy of your European Jewish brethren but it is also our Christian tragedy. This is an evil suffered by those of Jewish faith but it is also an evil perpetrated by men of Christian names and Christian pretension.

so many battles, of so many reforms and changes in the US economy, was suddenly paralyzed.

In July 1943, an editorial by Max Lerner appeared in *PM* under the title "What About the Jews, FDR?" Lerner outlined some recommendations that had been proposed by the Emergency Conference, charged that the State Department and Downing Street "avert their eyes from the slaughter" and challenged Roosevelt: "You, Mr. President, must take the lead.... The methods are clear. Neither conscience nor policy can afford to leave them unused. And the time is now."[103]

The *New Republic* of August 30, 1943, included a fifteen-page section entitled "The Jews of Europe: How to Help Them." Its editors indicted the Western Allies:

> The failure of the democratic powers to make any sustained and determined effort to stay the tide of slaughter constitutes one of the major tragedies in the history of civilization; and the moral weakness which has palsied the hands of our statesmen is nowhere more vividly disclosed than in the now conventional formula, so often on their lips, that only victory will save the Jews of Europe. Will any of these Jews survive to celebrate victory?[104]

In Congress there were some members highly sensitive to what was going on in Europe, with whom Roosevelt could have established a common working program coupled with a radical change of the people running the State Department's divisions on immigration and the war in Europe.

The American Congress usually listens to the specialists of each area. All they knew definitively regarding saving Jews from extermination came from analyses produced by the sick, evil, antisemitic minds of Breckinridge Long and his colleagues.

A few days after the Bermuda Conference, William Langer, senator from North Dakota, warned the Senate that "2,000,000 Jews in Europe have been killed off already and another 5,000,000 are awaiting the same fate unless they are saved immediately. Every day, every hour, every minute that passes, thousands of them are being exterminated." He called on his colleagues to

---

103. Wyman, *The Abandonment of the Jews*, 147.
104. Ibid., 150.

press for action or ultimately face "the moral responsibility of being passive bystanders."[105] But, of course, any initiative had to come from the executive power, and that never came.

One of the most devilish attitudes of the State Department was connected to Sweden's offer to save twenty thousand Jewish children by petitioning Germany for their release, and asking England to help provide the needed food for the children. The Foreign Office contacted the State Department, which dragged its feet for eight long months with all kinds of silly bureaucratic and political considerations; by then Sweden was occupied with giving sanctuary to the eight thousand Jews that had been saved by a heroic deed of the Danes, which transported the Jews to Sweden in one night.[106] The State Department came up with the strange, devilish argument that saving only Jewish children would antagonize the Germans.[107]

Following the saving of the eight thousand Danish Jews, the Emergency Conference published a provocative advertisement which said that Denmark and Sweden had "destroyed completely the legend that 'nothing else can be done.'" The Emergency Conference sponsored a "Salute to Sweden and Denmark" mass meeting that overflowed Carnegie Hall in New York. Speaking there, Leon Henderson, former head of the Office of Price Administration, accused the Allied governments, and especially Roosevelt and Churchill, of "moral cowardice" for failing to counter the extermination of the Jews. He charged that the problem had been "avoided, submerged, postponed, played down and resisted with all the forms of political force available to powerful governments."[108]

105. Ibid., 143.
106. As Wyman (*The Abandonment of the Jews*, 153) writes: "Something was done that October for Jews trapped in Europe – but not by the United States, Britain, or the Intergovernmental Committee. The eight thousand Jews in Denmark escaped to life and freedom because Danes were willing to risk their lives for them and the Swedish government was willing to incur Germany's wrath to give them sanctuary."
107. Morse, *While Six Million Died*, 65–67.
108. Wyman, *The Abandonment of the Jews*, 154. A sad aspect of those terrible days is the opposition that Peter Bergson's activities suffered from certain prestigious Jewish leaders, such as Rabbi Stephen Wise (from the Reform movement) and Nahum Goldmann (president of the World Jewish Congress): following an old Jewish trait, they voiced the worry that going all out in favor of Jewish interests would inflame antisemitism and could be more harmful than beneficial. They were entirely wrong, and this should serve as a lesson to contemporary Jewish leadership.

In other words, the State Department and the White House would in no way antagonize the Germans – that is, the Nazis – and thus confirmed the American government's position as an accomplice to the crimes that were being executed against the Jewish people, thereby becoming real partners to the Holocaust.

One of many instances of the State Department's criminal negligence concerns Jewish children in France. Jews in France, especially children, were being cared for by Catholic and Protestant organizations. However, there was a shortage of money for food and medicine. No funds arrived from the United States.[109] A plan to save Rumanian Jews and French Jewish children – a total of one hundred thousand people – was transmitted in all its details to the State Department, which once again delayed its execution, dragging the plan along for eight months until it was no longer doable.[110]

The State Department's refusal to help the Jews reached a climax in 1943. Minister Harrison, in Switzerland, had detailed the terrible and ongoing suffering and murdering of Jews in various countries. In response, the State Department sent Cable 354, instructing the minister that private messages (from Riegner) should not come through the American system of communications.[111] In other words, the American government established total censorship of any and all news about the ongoing Holocaust.

Treasury Department Denounces State Department

In January 1944, the secretary of the Treasury, Henry Morgenthau, received an eighteen-page memorandum on State Department obstruction. Prepared by the Treasury staff members, the document was entitled "Report to the Secretary on the Acquiescence of This Government in the Murder of the Jews."[112] One passage in the "Report to the Secretary" accused State Department officials of "kicking the rescue matter around for over a year without producing results."

Treasury staff member Josiah E. DuBois, the main author of the report, exposed the State Department's obstruction of rescue:

---

109. Morse, *While Six Million Died*, 67–71.
110. Ibid., pp. 71–86.
111. Ibid., 87–88.
112. Wyman, *The Abandonment of the Jews*, 187.

I am convinced on the basis of the information which is available to me that certain officials in our State Department, which is charged with carrying out this policy, have been guilty not only of gross procrastinations and willful failure to act, but even of willful attempts to prevent action from being taken to rescue Jews from Hitler.

State Department officials have not only failed to use the Governmental machinery at their disposal to rescue the Jews from Hitler, but have even gone as far as to use this governmental machinery to prevent the rescue of these Jews.

On the practical aspects of rescue the report had the following to say:

Without any change in our legislation statutes we could receive a reasonable number of those who are fortunate enough to escape the Nazi hellhole, receive them as visitors, the immigration quotas notwithstanding. They could be placed in camps or cantonments and held here in such havens until after the war. Private charitable agencies would be willing to pay the entire cost thereof. They would be no expense to the Government whatsoever. These agencies would even pay for transportation by ships to and from this country.[113]

Randolph Paul, a Treasury official and a non-Jewish lawyer, described the group led by Assistant Secretary Breckinridge Long as an American "underground movement to let the Jews be killed." Paul reacted to the State Department policy with the following statement: "I don't know how we can blame the Germans for killing them when we are doing this. The law calls it *para-delicto*, of equal guilt."[114] It is difficult to imagine a stronger accusation of complicity.

In a discussion with his staff, Morgenthau asserted that the State Department's obstruction of rescue meant that "we find ourselves aiding and abetting Hitler."[115]

Nahum Goldmann presented Long with a plan to help in providing food and medicines to Jews still alive in Poland, Czechoslovakia, and the Balkans. It meant a few million dollars. Nothing came of it. The Treasury Department

---

113. As reproduced by Medoff, *FDR and the Holocaust*, 110ff.
114. Wyman, *The Abandonment of the Jews*, 183.
115. Medoff, *FDR and the Holocaust*, 96.

described the State Department's handling of the Goldmann plan: "Long first tossed it into the waste paper basket, namely the Inter-Governmental Committee." Asked about the plan a few months later, Long replied that the committee had approved the plan but no funds were currently available. This was an outrageous lie, as a Treasury Department inquiry confirmed that eighty million dollars remained available in the most obvious account for such undertakings, the president's Emergency Fund, which earlier in 1943 had allotted three million dollars for the transportation to Mexico and maintenance of up to twenty-eight thousand non-Jewish Polish refugees.[116]

The Treasury's memorandum continued:

> The State Department officials have not only failed to facilitate the obtaining of information concerning Hitler's plans to exterminate the Jews of Europe but in their official capacity have gone so far as to surreptitiously attempt to stop the obtaining of information concerning the murder of the Jewish population of Europe.[117]

Josiah DuBois added the following accusation:

> On the basis of the cold facts contained for the most part in State Department documents (which we have finally managed to obtain despite the strenuous opposition of certain State Department officials, including what appears to have been a deliberate falsification of one of the documents)… it appears that certain responsible officials of the Government were so fearful that this Government might act to save the Jews of Europe if the gruesome facts relating to Hitler's plans to exterminate them became known, that they not only attempted to suppress the facts but, in addition, they used the powers of their official position to secretly countermand the instructions of the Acting Secretary of State ordering such facts to be reported.[118]

More accusation followed in the memorandum, such as:

> They [State Department officials] have tried to cover up their guilt by:
>   a) concealment and misrepresentation;

---

116. Wyman, *The Abandonment of the Jews,* 188.
117. Laqueur, *Terrible Secret,* 223–24.
118. Medoff, *FDR and the Holocaust,* 98–99.

b) giving false and misleading explanations for their failures to act and their attempts to prevent action; and

c) issuance of false and misleading statements concerning the "action" which they have taken to date.

The report pointed out that while the State Department had been thus "exploring" the whole refugee problem, without distinguishing between those who were in imminent danger of death and those who were not, hundreds of thousands of Jews had been allowed to perish.[119]

The Treasury document assailed the cumbersome procedures of obtaining visas to the United States and quoted from a speech by Congressman Emanuel Celler of New York, who stated that according to Earl G. Harrison, Commissioner of the Immigration and Naturalization Service, not since 1862 had there been fewer aliens entering the United States. "Frankly, Breckinridge Long, in my humble opinion, is the least sympathetic to refugees in all the State Department. I attribute to him the tragic bottleneck in the granting of visas.... It takes months and months to grant the visa and then it usually applies to a corpse."[120]

David Wyman writes that when Treasury Department lawyers covertly looked into State Department immigration procedures during 1943, they came to the following conclusions:

Under the pretext of security reasons so many difficulties have been placed in the way of refugees obtaining visas that it is no wonder that the admission of refugees to this country does not come anywhere near the quota....

If anyone were to attempt to work out a set of restrictions specifically designed to prevent Jewish refugees from entering this country it is difficult to conceive of how more effective restrictions could have been imposed than have already been imposed on grounds of "security."

These restrictions are not essential for security reasons. Thus refugees upon arriving in this country could be placed in internment camps similar to those used for the Japanese on the West Coast and released only after a satisfactory investigation. Furthermore, even if we took these refuges

119. Morse, *While Six Million Died*, 89.
120. Ibid., 90.

and treated them as prisoners of war it would be better than letting them die.[121]

One cannot think of a stronger and more reliable witness for the accusation of the State Department's complicity with the Nazis than the detailed report produced by the Treasury Department – a witness from within the same government administration that gained access to the official archives of the state.

The report addressed to Secretary Morgenthau contained the following challenge:

> We leave it to your judgment whether this action made such officials *the accomplices of Hitler* in this program and whether or not these officials are not *war criminals* in every sense of the term.[122]

Morgenthau shortened the report and took it to Roosevelt on January 16, 1944. He was accompanied by two of his assistants, Randolph Paul, the Treasury Department's general counsel, and John Pehle, from the Foreign Funds Control Division. At the meeting both men vigorously attacked Assistant Secretary of State Long (Roosevelt's friend and campaign financier) and the whole department up to Secretary Sumner Welles. It was a powerful accusation directed to the people nearest to Franklin Delano Roosevelt – the war criminals at the State Department. No one more qualified than the Treasury Department officials could have stood at the Nuremberg International Court to depose against Hitler's accomplices at the State Department.

Moreover, Morgenthau saw German industry as the source of that country's capacity for evil. German industrialists had backed Hitler enthusiastically and joined the Nazi party, providing the material for the war. Therefore, Morgenthau recommended that German industry be destroyed forever. Germany must be pastoralized – the country would have to be stripped of its industrial plant and reduced to a nation of farmers. But Morgenthau's plan was not considered.[123]

The Extent of Long's Audacity

Just a few weeks before, on November 26, 1943, Long's testimony before the House Foreign Affairs Committee had been released. The testimony was full

---

121. Wyman, *The Abandonment of the Jews*, 133.
122. Medoff, *FDR and the Holocaust*, 98–99. Emphasis mine.
123. Tusa and Tusa, *Nuremberg Trial*, 51.

of misrepresentations, especially his declaration that since the beginning of Hitler's regime, the United States had taken in 580,000 Jewish refugees. As we have seen already, the official annual reports of the Immigration and Naturalization Service reveal that of the total 476,930 aliens of all religions from all countries who entered the United States between July 1, 1933, and June 30, 1943, only 165,756 were Jews. Of these, about 138,000 had escaped persecution. (For example, if a Jew escaped Germany in the thirties and settled in Belgium, France, or the Netherlands, then fled from these countries when the Nazis invaded them in 1940 and managed to arrive to Portugal and from there obtained a visa to enter the United States, US immigration would not consider him to have escaped from imminent danger). As already noted, during those ten years the United States immigration quotas could have permitted the entry of over 1.5 million aliens. Thus the number of Jews entering the United States during this period approximated 10 percent of the total number of immigrants permissible under law.

Long's testimony was presented to oppose the Gillette-Rogers Resolution, which "recommended and urged the creation by the president of a commission of diplomatic, economic and military experts to formulate and effectuate a plan of immediate action designed to save the surviving Jewish people of Europe from extinction at the hands of Nazi Germany." Long's argument was that since the United States was already rescuing Jews, a resolution demanding the creation of a rescue agency would be a repudiation of the lifesaving work that was already underway.

Long had the audacity and the cynicism to close his testimony with the following declaration:

> Everybody that I know, everybody in the Department of State, and everybody that I have come in contact with is interested and a lot have been active in endeavoring to save the Jewish people from the terrorism of the Nazis.... Your committee will want to consider whether you should take a step which might be construed as a repudiation of the act of the executive branch of your own Government, whether any action on your part would be interpreted as a repudiation of the cause of the Jews.[124]

---

124. Medoff, *FDR and the Holocaust*, 90.

And so the government rejected a resolution from the House of Representatives urging the creation of a commission to formulate and effectuate a plan of immediate action designed to save the surviving Jewish people of Europe from extinction.

Creation of the War Refugee Board

On January 22, 1944, six days after he received the report from the Treasury Department containing the heavy accusations against the State Department, Franklin Delano Roosevelt announced the establishment of the War Refugee Board, to which John Pehle was named acting executive director.

Three days later a cable drafted by John Pehle was sent over the signature of Cordell Hull to all US embassies, consulates and other diplomatic missions. It ordered that action be taken to forestall the plot of the Nazis to exterminate the Jews and other persecuted minorities in Europe; the instruction helped to save some Jews from Rumania, from the camps of Transnistria, and from Bulgaria, but many others who could have been saved were again caught by the obstructionist policies of the State Department.[125]

The War Refugee Board was hampered by a meager budget and the ongoing obstructionism of the State Department, which displayed a monumental disinterest in the problem.[126] Some federal agencies often refused to cooperate with the board, withholding critical information and assistance that badly stymied the rescue efforts.[127]

After the War Refugee Board started its work, Franklin Delano Roosevelt condemned the Nazi atrocities and promised that "none who participate in these acts of savagery shall go unpunished," a warning that Secretary of State Cordell Hull reemphasized twice in a three-week period.

125. Morse, *While Six Million Died*, 313–24.
126. Ibid., 98. Gerhart Riegner, who sent the famous August 1942 cable alerting the West to the Nazis' plans for the "Final Solution," would many years later write in his autobiography *Ne Jamais Desesperer* that many of the six million Jews killed in Nazi concentration camps could have been saved if the United States and Britain had acted when he sounded the alarm. "Never," he wrote, "had I so strongly felt the sense of abandonment, of powerlessness and solitude as when I sent the Free World those messages of disaster and horror, when no one believed me, and I waited for a reaction and help from the Allies" (*Never Despair: Sixty Years in the Service of the Jewish People and the Cause of Human Rights*, trans. William Sayers [Chicago: Ivan R. Dee, 2006], 127).
127. Rosenberg and Astor, "The Dark Side of FDR," 109.

A note sent from Josiah DuBois to Pehle, the War Refugee Board executive director, reminded him that the nations of the world had noted the hypocrisy of the United States. The government of Nicaragua, replying to a War Refugee Board appeal to open its doors, had observed sarcastically that it would permit the entry of war refugees under the same conditions as the United States and in a number proportionate to the population of both countries.[128]

On April 5, 1944, *New York Post* columnist Samuel Grafton suggested the designation of free ports for refugees within the United States – a few reservations where it would be possible for those who could not satisfy the requirements of law to rest a bit, without violating the law. He compared it to what was done in commercial free ports, for cases of beans, and argued that it would not be impossible to do the same for people.[129]

Grafton's idea caught the public's imagination and soon the White House was deluged with letters, telegrams, and petitions supporting the plan.

The War Refugee Board launched a campaign that America should allow temporary asylum for "all oppressed peoples escaping from Hitler." At a press conference, the president said that it would not be necessary to establish havens in the United States because there were many countries to which the refugees could go. Then, due to persistent pressure from the War Refugee Board, Roosevelt reluctantly consented to the establishment of a temporary refugee shelter in an abandoned army camp in Oswego, New York, to where fewer than one thousand refugees were brought. And in reality they were not really saved from danger, as most of them came from southern Italy, which was under Allied occupation.

The president's limited offer undermined the WRB's basic plan. The single camp failed to open any other doors. Charles Joy of the Unitarian Service Committee pointed out that "the smallness of the offer destroys the value of the gesture. If the United States with all its resources can take only one thousand of these people, what can we expect other countries to do?"[130]

Morse concludes this part of America's tragic collaboration with Hitler by stating that "between 1933 and 1944 the American tradition of sanctuary for the oppressed was uprooted and despoiled. It was replaced by a combination

128. Morse, *While Six Million Died*, 341–42.
129. Ibid.
130. Wyman, *The Abandonment of the Jews*, 267.

of political expediency, diplomatic evasion, isolationism, indifference, and raw bigotry which played directly into the hands of Adolf Hitler even as he set in motion the final plans for the greatest mass murder in history."[131]

Wyman sums up the quantitative results of America's wartime immigration policy by noting:

> Between Pearl Harbor and the end of the war in Europe, approximately 21,000 refugees, most of them Jewish, entered the United States. That number constituted 10 percent of the quota places legally available to people from Axis-controlled European countries in those years. Thus 90 percent of those quotas – nearly 190,000 openings – went unused while the mass murder of European Jewry ran its course. The quota limits were mandated by law. But the severe restrictions that the State Department clamped on immigration were not. They took the form of administrative regulations and, at times, purely arbitrary State Department innovations. President Roosevelt had the legal power at any time to modify the restrictions and open the quotas to full use. He did not do so, possibly out of concern that restrictionists in Congress might lash back and enact the restrictions into law. More likely, he was just not interested and found it convenient to leave immigration policy to Breckinridge Long and his associates.[132]

Late in 1945, a *New York Times* writer summarized the effect of America's wartime immigration policies: "The United States, once the haven of refuge for the oppressed peoples of Europe, has been almost as inaccessible as Tibet."[133]

An American Ambassador Refuses to Save Refugees

The US ambassador to Spain, one Carlton J.H. Hayes, refused to permit the assignment of a representative of the War Refugee Board to his embassy and deflected every board suggestion that he influence the Franco government to adopt more liberal refugee policies. The board put together a plan to expedite the transfer of refugees from France into Portugal, via Spain. Hayes refused to do anything to explain the policy on the subject to the Spanish government. Hayes countered with the argument that German agents might

---

131. Morse, *While Six Million Died*, 99.
132. Wyman, *The Abandonment of the Jews*, 136.
133. Ibid., 137.

slip thorough if border controls were eased, an argument he learned from Long. Congressman Emanuel Celler urged that the ambassador be recalled. But Hayes was not recalled and thousands who could have been saved out of France, via Spain/Portugal, were deported to their deaths.[134] In the earlier years of the war, refugees from Belgium, France, and other countries managed to cross the Spanish territory (despite the negative policy of Franco's dictatorial government) and reach Portugal, where they were received with cordiality. The author is a witness to this, as he and his family arrived at the French-Spanish border (with visas to Portugal) sometime in 1940. After initial obstacles raised by the Spanish authorities, they were finally allowed to embark on a train that took them directly to a small village in the north of Portugal. There they were greeted kindly and treated with dignity. The family lived peacefully in Portugal until the arrival of immigration visas to Brazil.

The Despicable Inertia of the International Red Cross

And then came the tragic events in Hungary, home to eight hundred thousand Jews, where the International Red Cross displayed its infamous inertia. Suffice it to say that the IRC kept only one delegate in Budapest, despite the requests from the War Refugee Board that it increase the number of its observers. The IRC's President Huber replied that "under the present circumstances such a mission might be considered as unrelated to the Committee's traditional and conventional competence." The mission of the Red Cross was to help war victims "without intruding into the domestic policy of any of those states," added the IRC. The board responded: "It is difficult to believe that measures designed to check such slaughter directly or indirectly can be considered as 'intruding into domestic policy.' . . . If the measure is unprecedented, so is the emergency."[135]

The Red Cross only changed its policies when Germany's defeat seemed inevitable and under strong pressure from the War Refugee Board.[136]

---

134. Morse, *While Six Million Died*, 332–35. This cruel sabotage of the War Refugee Board work by the American ambassador in Spain and the refusal to recall him is a clear demonstration of how the negative policy toward saving Jews continued till the very last days of the war.
135. Ibid., 325–29.
136. Ibid., 328.

Bombing Auschwitz

Serious and detailed requests were presented to the US government to bomb the railway lines from Hungary to Auschwitz and to bomb the camp's extermination chambers themselves. All propositions in this respect were blocked by the State Department, which claimed that the War Department had given serious consideration to the propositions, but found military reasons to justify the refusal of both requests.

The Allies were bombing at that very same time synthetic oil factories in Poland, one of them less than five kilometers from the gas chambers. One of the pilots of the American Air Force was a young man by the name of George McGovern, who became a member of the US Senate and in 1972 was candidate to the White House. In 2004, for the first time, he spoke to the press about his experience during the war years and said that the justification given by the US government for not bombing the gas chambers of the camp was not based on reality. There was no need to take the planes out of their route, as the chambers were exactly within their route; he added that there would have been many volunteers to execute the destruction of the killing chambers. McGovern also said that there is no question that "we should have attempted . . . to go after Auschwitz. There was a pretty good chance we could have blasted those rail lines off the face of the earth, which would have interrupted the flow of people to those death chambers, and we had a pretty good chance of knocking out those gas ovens."[137]

On bombing the Auschwitz gas chambers, Paul Johnson has the following to say:

> The question of bombing the gas chambers was raised in the early summer of 1944, when the destruction of the Hungarian Jews got under way. Churchill in particular was horrified and keen to act. The killing, he minutes, "is probably the greatest and most horrible crime ever committed in the whole history of the world." He instructed Eden in 7 July 1944: "Get anything out of the Air Force you can and invoke me, if necessary." An operation was feasible. An oil-refining complex 47 miles from Auschwitz was attacked no less than ten times between 7 July and 20 November 1944. On 20 August 127 Flying Fortresses bombed the Auschwitz factory area less than five miles to the east of the gas chambers. Whether bombing

137. Medoff, *FDR and the Holocaust*, 182.

would have saved Jewish lives cannot be proved. The SS were fanatically persistent in killing Jews, whatever the physical and military obstacles. It was certainly worth trying. But Churchill was its only real supporter in either government. Both air forces hated military operations not directed to destroying enemy forces or war potential. The US War Department rejected the plan without even examining its feasibility.[138]

With small variations, the historians of the Holocaust coincide in their reports on the Auschwitz bombing. David S. Wyman writes that in the very months that the State Department was ignoring the pleas to bomb the gas chambers, numerous massive American bombing raids were taking place within fifty miles of Auschwitz. Twice during that time large fleets of American heavy bombers struck industrial targets in the Auschwitz complex itself, not five miles from the gas chambers.[139]

Rafael Medoff reports that on August 7, US bombers attacked the Trzebinia oil refineries, just thirteen miles from Auschwitz. Likewise, on August 20, a squadron of 127 US bombers accompanied by one hundred Mustangs, piloted by the African-American unit known as the Tuskegee Airmen, struck oil factories less than five miles from the gas chambers.[140]

Beginning in May 1944, the State Department received innumerable requests to bomb the railroads to Auschwitz, the gas chambers, and the crematoria. Wyman calculates that if these requests had been heeded, the lives of hundreds of thousands of Jews might have been saved.[141]

The US War Department refused all appeals to go ahead with the attack on the murder factory, declaring:

> It is not contemplated that units of the armed forces will be employed for the purpose of rescuing victims of enemy oppression unless such rescues are the direct result of military operations conducted with the objective of defeating the armed forces of the enemy.[142]

138. Paul Johnson, *A History of the Jews* (New York: Harper and Row, 1988), 505.
139. Wyman, *The Abandonment of the Jews*, xxii.
140. Medoff, *FDR and the Holocaust*, 180.
141. Wyman, *The Abandonment of the Jews*, 288–307, especially 304. Also see Leni Yahil, *The Holocaust: The Fate of European Jewry* (Oxford: Oxford University Press, 1990), 638–39.
142. Wyman, *The Abandonment of the Jews*, 291. Also see John Loftus and Mark Aarons, *The Secret War against the Jews: How Western Espionage Betrayed the Jewish People*, 129 (New

The sad irony is that the Germans would delay military operations in order to annihilate the Jews, whereas the Allies put fighting the war before saving its victims. The Germans frequently gave priority to the transportation of the persecuted to the concentration camps, over the transportation of troops and/or military necessities to the front.

Destroying the gas chambers of Auschwitz and/or the railroad leading to the camp would not have required a millionth or perhaps even a billionth of the bombs that were employed in the Allied air-force bombing of the German city of Dresden. The Allies destroyed Dresden completely and killed tens of thousands of civilians in an operation that involved many air attacks without any strategic advantage whatsoever. But when it came to saving Jews, any excuse was good enough to avoid executing a simple operation that could have saved so many.

The British Complicity

Wyman reports on the visit of the British foreign minister, Anthony Eden, to Washington in the end of March 1943, a short while before the Bermuda Conference. Ambassador Taylor arranged for Rabbi Wise and Judge Joseph Proskauer to meet Eden.[143]

The meeting is described as most discouraging and presaged the outcome of the Bermuda Conference. Opening the discussion, Proskauer stressed the request that Britain and the United States call on Germany to permit the Jews to leave occupied Europe. Eden rejected the plan outright, declaring it "fantastically impossible." When asked to assist in moving Jews from Bulgaria to Turkey, Eden demurred: "Turkey does not want any more of your people." All in all, Eden offered no reasonable hope of action.

Later that day, Eden met with Roosevelt, Cordell Hull, Sumner Welles and the British ambassador to the United States, Lord Halifax. When Hull raised the issue of the sixty-to-seventy thousand Jews in Bulgaria who were threatened with extermination unless the British and Americans could get them out, Eden replied that "the whole problem of the Jews in Europe is very

York: St. Martin's Press, 1994). They write that "bombing the gas chambers at just three death camps – Sobibor, Treblinka and Auschwitz – might have shut down the killing system for months, sparing hundreds of thousands of lives. For the price of a few American bombs, however, the death camps remained open."

143. Wyman, *The Abandonment of the Jews*, 96–97.

difficult and we should move very cautiously about offering to take all Jews out of a country like Bulgaria. If we do that, then the Jews of the world will want us to make similar offers in Poland and Germany. Hitler might well take us up on any such offer and there simply are not enough ships and means of transportation in the world to handle them." These notes were taken by Harry Hopkins, Roosevelt's special assistant.[144]

Hopkins's notes give no indication that Eden's caution and his warning that Hitler mustn't be encouraged to actually release the Jews dropped any jaws among this distinguished group of statesmen.[145]

After this report, Wyman explains that Eden's adamant opposition to any initiative to rescue any number of Jews from the danger of annihilation had nothing to do with ships. It was – as we saw already – the immense pressure that the release of thousands of Jews from Europe would place on the British policy of placating the Arabs by strictly limiting Jewish immigration into Palestine. Placed in its broader context, Eden was reacting to the fundamental problem of where Jews could be put if they were rescued. No country wanted to take them in, as had been proved between 1933 and 1941 when persecuted Jews had been free to leave Nazi Europe. Unwillingness to offer refuge was a major cause of the Western world's inadequate response to the Holocaust.[146]

The French Complicity

On July 16–17, 1942, the French police arrested 13,152 Jewish men, women, and children from Paris and its suburbs and confined them to the city's Vélodrome d'Hiver (bicycle stadium). They were later deported to German concentration camps. Out of this entire group, 811 survived the war. A total of 76,000 French Jews were deported to the death camps. Only 2,500 returned.[147] The largest part of these deportations was executed with the help of the French police.

Jean-Paul Sartre reports that the Pétain government initiated antisemitic measures and the "Pétainists" did not protest.[148]

On July 22, 2012 – seventy years later – French president François Hollande

144. Ibid., 97.
145. Ibid., 98.
146. Ibid.
147. Numbers vary in the different sources on the Holocaust. But the main point is the voluntary collaboration of the French authorities with the Nazi criminals.
148. Sartre, *Anti-Semite and Jew*, 70.

presided at a commemoration of the seventieth anniversary of the Vel d'Hiver roundup. Among other statements President Hollande made on that occasion was the following:

> The truth is that French police – on the basis of the lists they had themselves drawn up – undertook to arrest the thousands of innocent people trapped on July 16, 1942. And that the French gendarmerie escorted them to the internment camps....
>
> The Republic's schools – in which I hereby voice my confidence – have a mission: to instruct, educate, teach about the past, make it known and understood in all its dimensions. The Holocaust is on the curriculum of the final primary and junior school years and the second *lycée* year....
>
> The Shoah was not created from a vacuum and did not emerge from nowhere.... It was also made possible by centuries of blindness, stupidity, lies and hatred. It was preceded by many warning signs, which failed to alert people's consciences....
>
> Conscious of this history, the Republic will pursue all anti-Semitic acts with the utmost determination, even remarks that may lead France's Jews to feel uneasy in their own country....
>
> Anti-Semitism is not an opinion, it is an abhorrence. For that reason, it must first of all be faced directly. It must be named and recognized for what it is. Wherever it manifests itself, it will be unmasked and punished....
>
> To tirelessly teach historical truth, to scrupulously ensure respect for the values of the Republic, to constantly recall the demand for religious tolerance, within the frame of our secular laws, never to give way on the principle of freedom and human dignity, always to further the promise of equality and emancipation. Those are the measures we must collectively assign ourselves.[149]

The sad reality, however is that the ingrained antisemitism in the French soul plus the malignant campaigning exercised by the Muslims against Israel and the French Jewish community result in a panorama very far from President François Hollande's beautiful vision.

Less than a year after the president's noble words, terrorist acts perpetrated

---

149. François Hollande, "The 'Crime Committed in France, by France,'" *New York Review of Books*, August 18, 2012.

by fanatic Muslims in the heart of Paris targeted a newspaper (where journalists were murdered for having exercised free speech) and then two days later a Jewish grocery store (where Jews were murdered as they shopped for the Sabbath meals).

The Swiss Complicity

The Swiss closed their borders to Jewish refugees; with very few exceptions Jews trying to cross the French-Swiss border into safety were returned by the local police to the Nazis stationed at the frontier. A few Swiss Jews, most especially Mrs. Recha Sternbuch and her husband, refused to be deterred and succeeded in smuggling thousands of Jewish refugees into Swiss territories.[150] It was the Swiss police who suggested to Germany to mark passports belonging to Jews with a red J sign, to make the Jew easily identifiable to the Swiss border police.[151]

Many years after the war, Swiss economic historian Jean-François Bergier explored and reported on widespread Swiss involvement with Axis interests: Switzerland was a financier of German armaments, a client for forced labor, and a harbor for gold and art objects looted during the German conquests of Belgium and the Netherlands. The report also condemned the Swiss government's adoption of racist restrictions on Jewish refugees before and during the war, as well as the repatriation of thousands of refugees to Nazi-occupied countries, where they faced almost certain extermination.[152]

The Vatican's Complicity

The Vatican's behavior was not merely of disinterest: it reached the level of the highest hypocrisy, as can be seen in an address by Cardinal Salotti entitled "The Historical Mission of Pius XII," which included the following "jewel":

> But at Rome there is a great Pope who, though navigating with extreme difficulty through the raging tempest, has given unmistakable proofs of a great and undiscriminating affection for all peoples and who has, moreover,

150. Joseph Friedenson and David Kranzler, *Heroine of Rescue: The Incredible Story of Recha Sternbuch Who Saved Thousands from the Holocaust* (New York: Mesorah Publications, 1984), xii, 20, and 100.
151. Ibid., 30.
152. Allen Pusey, "Aug. 12, 1998: Swiss Banks Settle Holocaust Claims," *American Bar Association Journal* 100, no. 8 (August 2014): 72.

in order to avoid the slightest appearance of partiality, imposed upon himself, in word and deed, the most delicate reserve.[153]

Commenting on the cardinal's declaration, Harold Tittman, Myron Taylor's colleague at the US mission in Rome, wrote to the State Department that "the continued silence of the Pope on the moral issues of the day, especially in the face of one notorious Nazi atrocity after another, has alarmed many loyal Catholics and has led them to question whether the Holy See is not rapidly being reduced thereby to the status of a minor Italian state and the Pope's functions to those of an Italian patriarch."[154]

The American diplomat chose to focus his critique on the leader of one billion Catholics. Actually, what cried out to the skies was that a prince of the Catholic Church was defending the pope's neutrality between evil and good, between murderers and their victims. And this is what took place in the Vatican throughout the whole war.

No greater authority on the complicity of the Vatican exists than James Carroll. A former priest of the Catholic Church and a man of the highest knowledge of Catholicism and of the history of the Catholic Church's antisemitism, Carroll authored the *New York Times* bestseller *Constantine's Sword: The Church and the Jews*, a book dedicated to the Church's antisemitism throughout seventeen centuries. Carroll reports on the charges against Pope Pius XII, including his eagerness in 1933 to negotiate the Nazi-legitimizing *Reichskonkordat*; his indifference to the fate of unbaptized Jews; the 1939 cancellation of his predecessor's encyclical condemnation of Nazi antisemitism; his refusal to condemn the brutal German invasion of Catholic Poland; his tacit acceptance of Nazi and fascist anti-Jewish legislation; and his failure to mention the Jews, or even the Nazis, by name in his Christmas message of 1942. As well, the pope repeatedly met with Croatian Ustashi leaders – including Ante Pavelic, a mini-Hitler who found refuge in the Vatican after the war. And finally, the pope declined to excommunicate Hitler, Himmler, Bormann, Goebbels, and other Catholic Nazis[155] – this despite the fact that after the war, in 1949, he excommunicated all Communist members throughout the

153. Morse, *While Six Million Died*, 13.
154. Ibid., 13–14.
155. James Carroll, *Constantine's Sword: The Church and the Jews* (Boston: Mariner, 2001), 523–24.

world, without regard for the consequences to the privileges of the Church, or even to the safety of Catholics behind the Iron Curtain.[156]

Carroll goes back to the dramatic events that led to the destruction of the Jewish community of Rome, describing the details of what occurred:

> The Germans had occupied Rome in September 1943. Until then Jews had been relatively safe, but at 5:30 A.M. on October 16, the noise of gunfire broke the night silence of the ghetto. By then it was home to about four thousand Jews. The streets leading out of the quarter were blocked. SS officers drove residents from their homes, and in a few hours the Germans had arrested more than twelve hundred people. The Jews were taken to a temporary jail in the Italian Military College, which stood a few hundred yards from Vatican City. Yet from the Vatican no voice was raised in public support of the Jews. Two days later the prisoners were put on trucks, taken to the railroad station, and loaded into boxcars. Again, no voice was raised in protest. The arrested Jews were gone. Five days later, this entry appears in the meticulously kept log at Auschwitz: "Transport, Jews from Rome. After the selection 149 men and 47 women have been admitted to the detention camp. The rest have been gassed."[157]

Carroll comes back many times to two statements from the Vatican on its role during World War II: the 1998 statement "We Remember: A Reflection on the Shoah" and the 2000 statement "Memory and Reconciliation: The Church and the Faults of the Past." Carroll characterizes both of these as "defensive and self-exonerating." He claims that the behavior of a relatively few number of heroes is highlighted, and the hierarchy's choice of pragmatic, behind-the-scenes diplomacy over moral confrontation is presented in the most favorable way. For example, in both documents "many" Christians are credited with assisting persecuted Jews, while some "others" are faulted for not doing so. The truth requires a reversal of that construction: "many" did nothing, while "others," a few, gave assistance.[158]

The fundamental critique of the author is summed up with the claim that "the Vatican issues 'We Remember: A Reflection on the Shoah' as an 'act of

---

156. Ibid., 437.
157. Ibid., 524.
158. Ibid., 27.

repentance', yet puts responsibility for failure on the Church's children, not the Church; it praises the diplomacy of Pius XII. Pope John Paul II offers a millennial mea culpa early in the year 2000, and while there was a profound significance in that apology, as far as it went, it revealed how far is the distance that must be traveled yet."[159]

Carroll claims that Pope Pius XII, without violating his tactic of diplomatic prudence, could have quietly instructed parish priests throughout Europe to destroy baptismal records which were being applied by the Nazis to discover Jewish ancestry of members of the Catholic Church, but he never did.[160] Carroll opposes the campaign to canonize the wartime pope – an act that represents a step toward sainthood.

The attitude of the Vatican is well illustrated by the exchange between the American ambassador and the secretary of the Holy See regarding the persecutions that the Jews were undergoing in Poland and in other European countries. On September 26, 1942, Myron Taylor, who had become the US representative to the Vatican, inquired of Cardinal Maglione, the secretary of the Holy See, whether they had information that would confirm the news contained in the various reports that were arriving from East Europe. "If so," said Taylor, "I should like to know whether the Holy Father has any suggestions as to any practical manner in which the forces of civilized public opinion could be utilized in order to prevent a continuation of these barbarities."

Two weeks later the cardinal handed Ambassador Taylor's deputy an informal, unsigned response that said that reports of severe measures against the Jews had also reached the Vatican but that it had not been possible to check their accuracy.[161] This response characterizes the coldness, the distance, the apathy with which the Vatican responded to the Jewish Holocaust.[162]

---

159. Ibid., 599.
160. Ibid., 533. Goldhagen (*Hitler's Willing Executioners*, 164) includes among the perpetrators of the Shoah "any Church officials who knew that their participation in the identification of Jews as non-Christians would lead to the deaths of the Jews."
161. Morse, *While Six Million Died*, 12–13.
162. Rolph Hochhuth, a German Protestant, authored in 1965 the play *The Deputy*, which exposed the pope's refusal to openly condemn the Nazi anti-Jewish genocide. John Cornwell, in his book *Hitler's Pope: The Secret History of Pius XII*, writes of "the moral abyss into which Pacelli, the future Pontiff, had led the once great and proud German Catholic Church" (as quoted by Carroll, *Constantine's Sword*, 500). Cornwell, a Catholic who got access to the Vatican archives, narrates the details of the 1933 concordat between the

John Morley was a member of a joint Jewish-Catholic commission established to examine the Vatican archives concerning the Holocaust. He concludes his book, *Vatican Diplomacy and the Jews during the Holocaust, 1939–1945,* with the following statement:

> It must be concluded that Vatican diplomacy failed the Jews during the Holocaust by not doing all that was possible for it to do on their behalf. It also failed itself because in neglecting the needs of the Jews, and pursuing a goal of reserve rather than humanitarian concern, it betrayed the ideals that it had set for itself. The nuncios, the secretary of state, and most of all, the Pope share the responsibility for this dual failure.[163]

Though Morley employed diplomatic parlance, he clearly states that the Vatican and its leader were disloyal to authentic religious values.

Another historian who delved into Vatican documentation, David I. Kertzer, relates the indifference of the Vatican to the atrocities committed by the Nazi regime in Germany and then all over Europe, and shows the strong antisemitic tradition of the Catholic Church from time immemorial.[164]

However, not all Church leaders copied the pope's callousness. An outstanding example was Monsignor Angelo Roncalli, the Vatican's apostolic delegate to Turkey, who exploited the Church's function as a racial-certification agent to provide false identity documents to Jews, saving thousands of lives.[165] In 1958, Roncalli was elevated to the papacy as John XXIII, in substitution of Pius XII. The appointment opened a new era in Christian history, especially regarding the Jews.

Catholic Church and Hitler's regime. The concordat was negotiated and signed by Eugenio Pacelli – future Pope Pius XII – when he was the Vatican's representative in Germany. The historian Yehuda Bauer ("God's Deputy Sheriff," *Jerusalem Post,* March 3, 2000) writes that this concordat was the cause of the destruction and disintegration of Catholic resistance to the Nazis, led by the Catholic Center Party. Bauer notes that "Pacelli knowingly sacrificed Germany's Catholics and suppressed those bishops who disagreed with the surrender to Nazism." Bauer adds that Pius XII helped Hitler consolidate his rule over Germany, paralyzed Catholic reaction to the horrors that the Nazis unleashed all over Europe, and rendered the Church politically impotent.

163. As quoted by Carroll, ibid., 528.

164. David I. Kertzer, *The Popes against the Jews: The Vatican's Role in the Rise of Modern Anti-Semitism* (New York: Alfred A. Knopf, 2001).

165. Carroll, *Constantine's Sword*, 532.

James Carroll, who was inspired by John XXIII to enter a seminary,[166] describes the changes that took place in the Vatican under the new pope:

> The Church's failure in relation to Adolf Hitler was only a symptom of the ecclesiastical cancer Pope John was attempting to treat. The long tradition of Christian Jew-hatred, on which Hitler had so efficiently built, was the malignant tumor that had metastasized in the mystical body. John XXIII had instinctively grasped this. Hence his open-hearted response to Jewish historian Jules Isaac (in June 1960), who traced the Church's anti-Semitism to the Gospels, and John's subsequent charge (in September) to those preparing for the council that it take up the Church's relations with Judaism as a matter of priority. Hence his elimination from the Good Friday liturgy of the modifiers "faithless" and "perfidious" as applied to Jews, an implicit rejection of supersessionism. Hence his greeting to a first Jewish delegation at the Vatican: "I am Joseph, your brother," he said, then came down from his throne to sit with them in a simple chair.[167]

As I once wrote on that meeting of the pope with the Jewish delegation, "this was an extraordinary moment, full of drama and of the highest significance, an electrifying manifestation of the most elevated and noblest human dignity, inspired in the true love that crosses all frontiers, races and religions, a hope for all men and women that live on this planet."[168]

In his acceptance speech for the Nobel Prize, René Cassin saluted Pope John XXIII as his brother in the defense of human rights and in the effort to make international law superior to the sovereignty of states.[169]

Complicity of the Press

As far as complicity is concerned, the press should not be forgotten. The majority of the important US newspapers, most especially the *New York*

166. Ibid., 37: "When the pope embraced me, I let myself fall for the first time into a sure trust in God's love, an experience that led to my entering a seminary less than two years later."
167. Ibid., 550.
168. Jacob Dolinger, "Dignidade:o mais antigo valor da humanidade. Os mitos em torno da Declaração Universal dos Direitos do Homem e da Constituição brasileira de 1988. As ilusões do Pós-Modernismo/Pós Positivismo. A visão judaica," *Revista de Direito Constitucional e Internacional* 70 (January–March 2010): 90.
169. Winter and Prost, *René Cassin*, 339.

Times, kept the Holocaust as hidden as possible.[170] The most important tragic events were kept in the very inside pages of the paper, which only a minority of readers would open.[171] This policy kept the majority of the American people practically in the dark about the atrocities that were being committed against millions of Jews. The ignorance of the people was reflected in the disinterest of Congress and consequently supported the inertia of the executive power.

American Policy

As late as 1944 a few hundred Jews were detained in Vittel, France. Swiss intervention could have saved their lives, but for that to happen the State Department had to request it of the Swiss government. The War Refugee Board drafted the request, but the State Department refused to send the message because it imposed excessive pressure upon the Swiss. The board submitted a more restrained version of the cable, which was equally rejected. When the State Department finally sent the cable and the Swiss tried to do their part, it was too late – the refugees had been deported. And so, 238 Jews

---

170. Wyman (*The Abandonment of the Jews,* 73) refers to an important meeting between FDR and a Jewish delegation, in which the president made one or two positive remarks. Wyman notes that "the coverage of this event was spotty, and most newspapers that did report it gave it little prominence. The *New York Times,* for instance, provided a very thorough account, but it appeared on page 20, unusually deep in the paper for any news directly concerning the President. The *Washington Post* printed only a small report and placed it far inside the paper." William Randolph Hearst was an exception in the realm of the American press. All his thirty-four newspapers were always ready to publish, as they indeed did, any material in favor of helping the Jews of Europe.

171. Novick (*The Holocaust in American Life,* 23) claims that "there were only secondhand and third-hand reports of problematic authenticity." Given the coinciding reports that the State Department received of different sources, the witnesses who escaped the concentration camps and reported what they had seen, the reports of the Polish government in exile, and all the sources that were referred to in this chapter, Novick's comparison of what went on in the 1940s to the propaganda on atrocities that occurred during the First World War is indeed very strange. In a footnote on page 65, Novick maintains that the war correspondents would refer to Jews by their nationalities rather than their religion because to refer to a French Jew as a Jew, rather than a Frenchman, seemed to be buying into Hitler's categories, and American correspondents' usage was "anti-fascist." This borders on maliciousness, because Novick knew very well – as did the war correspondents – that the French police cooperated with the Nazis to deport French Jews, so for France they were Jews rather than Frenchmen. By referring to the victims as French, American correspondents avoided publicity about what the Nazis and their collaborators were doing to the Jews.

of Vittel, among them the distinguished Yiddish and Hebrew writer Itzak Katznelson, were sent to their deaths. If the State Department had not held up its cable to Switzerland for three weeks, Katznelson and the Jews of Vittel might have survived.[172]

Wyman makes a short analysis of the American government's behavior:

> During those months [the winter of 1943] the patterns of the American government's response to the ongoing annihilation of the Jews became evident. The State Department had shown itself to be entirely callous. Most members of Congress seemed to know little and care less. And the President, who was well aware of the catastrophic situation, was indifferent, even to the point of unwillingness to talk about the issue with the leader of five million Jewish Americans.[173]

And then Wyman comes back to the English fear of the Arabs:

> The war strengthened British determination to minimize Jewish immigration to Palestine. Unrest there or elsewhere in the Moslem world could hamper military operations, threaten supply lines, and drain off British troops to maintain order. The British realized that the Jews could not turn against them. The Arabs might. So British policy called for appeasing the Arabs, even though that meant excluding imperiled Jews from the national home the British had promised them in the Balfour Declaration of 1917.
>
> To avoid risking Arab animosity and to make the 75,000 openings last as long as possible, the British intentionally kept the White Paper quota undersubscribed. By October 1943 (four and one-half years into the White Paper's five-year tenure), 31,000 places (over 40 percent) remained unused.[174]

It seems that submission to Muslim terrorism is not a twenty-first-century phenomenon. It was there during the war; British cowardice was the same then as today.

So, again, the Arabs' claim that they have no responsibility for the Holocaust has no basis in the actual facts.

---

172. Morse, *While Six Million Died*, 345–47.
173. Wyman, *The Abandonment of the Jews*, 103.
174. Ibid., 157–58. See also Medoff, *FDR and the Holocaust*, 66.

Rafael Medoff analyzes the mental process of FDR before and during World War II regarding the Jews. In an attempt to understand the president's stance, he explores Roosevelt's personal views on the Jews:

> FDR's statements indicate he regarded "Jewish blood" with some disdain. He believed that if Jewish immigrants were allowed to live near one another in significant numbers, they would never assimilate into American society and become fully loyal, trustworthy citizens. He was also convinced that if too many Jews were permitted in various professions, they would exercise undue influence over major aspects of society. In Roosevelt's view, the number of Jewish residents of the United States should be sharply limited through tight restriction on immigration, and the nation would be best served if those who were admitted were 'distributed' to remote locales where, because they were "spread thin" they would be "digestible."[175]

This analysis does not explain why the US president did not accept sending Jewish refugees to Alaska, to the Virgin Islands, to Latin America, and to other locales where American society would not be affected. It does not explain the lack of pressure from the American government on South American and Central American states to accept the refugees, with US participation in the financial burden. It does not explain why FDR supported the British policy of closing the doors of Palestine to the refugees. It does not explain the alleged fear of Arab reaction to Jewish immigration to North Africa. It does not explain the weakness of FDR's pronunciations about the Nazi crimes, and the omissions of the Jewish victims in most of his declarations and interviews to the press.

Simply put, FDR's insensitivity to the suffering of the Jews went much further than just opposing their immigration into the United States.

Regarding the claim of the Americans and the English that there were no available ships to transport Jewish refugees to different places out of Europe, Wyman refers to innumerable shipping actions that brought food to starving populations; to three Portuguese liners, with a combined capacity of two thousand passengers, that sailed regularly between Lisbon and US

---

175. Medoff, *FDR and the Holocaust*, 31–32. This may remind us of the orientation the Germans gave to the Turks about spreading the Armenians among the Turkish population, following their general policy regarding the populations of occupied territories. (See chapter 1 for Dr. Clarence Ussher's explanation of this policy.)

ports, carrying only fractions of their potential loads; and to the American troopships and other cargo vessels, which could have carried refugees on their returning voyages to the United States. Shipping availabilities were ignored when it came to saving Jews.[176] Conversely, hundreds of thousands of non-Jewish Poles, Yugoslavs, and Greeks were moved to different parts of the world with the help of the American and British governments.[177]

And as before the war started, so also throughout the whole war and the tragic murder of six million Jews, no measure was taken to stop the murderers or to save the Jews.

The Tragedy of Hungarian Jewry

At the beginning of 1944, when more than seven hundred thousand Jews were still alive in Hungary, the Jewish Agency proposed to the British authorities to take hundreds of Palestinian Jews and drop them by parachute into Hungary. According to the considered judgment of British military circles, this could have helped the Allies militarily and could have also helped prevent the extermination of the greater part of Hungarian Jewry. The program had been approved by all military authorized bodies. But as arrangements were being made to carry out the plan, the Colonial and Foreign Offices intervened and, because of political considerations, ordered the military authorities to refrain from implementing the program.[178]

And so, the last and most tragic chapter of the Holocaust was the deportation of Hungarian Jews to Auschwitz: in less than two months, between May 15 and July 7, 437,000 Jews were shipped to the extermination camp. Within a forty-six-day period, between 250,000 and 300,000 of the Jews from Hungary were gassed or shot. The extent of the maddening urge to annihilate the Jewish people went against any logic, as at that time the invasion of the Allied armies in France was well advanced and the Russians were nearing German territory. Germany was about to lose the war, but continued with its murderous campaign of eliminating Jewish lives.

176. Wyman, *The Abandonment of the Jews*, 336.
177. Ibid., 338–89.
178. Morse, *While Six Million Died*, 361.

The War Hero Wallenberg

During the last months of the war, things in Budapest changed, as the War Refugee Board began to force the mobilization of world opinion. Help came from the Nuncio Apostolico, a little from the Vatican, and above all from a young Swedish diplomat, Raoul Wallenberg, who, through all kinds of courageous and elaborate plans, saved the lives of about one hundred thousand Jews.[179]

Wallenberg was absolutely heroic in his use of any and all tactics to save Jews from deportation. He distributed thousands of life-saving passports (often forged) and also directly negotiated with, bribed, and threatened Nazi officials such as Adolf Eichmann and Major General Gerhard Schmidthuber, in so doing preventing a Nazi plan that would have blown up the ghetto and killed seventy thousand Jews. To Schmidthuber, Wallenberg wrote: "I will personally see to it that you will be hanged for war crimes if the planned massacre in the ghetto takes place." The letter found its mark and Schmidthuber canceled the plans.[180]

One man did more and better than the International Red Cross, the United States, the British Empire, the "united nations," the whole twentieth-century "civilized world." Raoul Wallenberg's actions form an important point in the indictment of Hitler's accomplices.

The ineptitude, the indecisiveness, the negativism of the Allied governments was the direct cause of the deaths of hundreds of thousands of Hungarian Jews in the very last months of the war.

Morse concludes his masterful, detailed report on the apathy of the Allies and especially of the United States by stating: "The holocaust has ended. What about the future. Who are the potential victims? Who are the bystanders?"[181]

I ask again whether Breckinridge Long, Cordell Hull, Sumner Welles, and some of their colleagues at the State Department should not have sat at the Nuremberg trial next to the leaders of the Nazi murderous organization, under the accusation of complicity in the crimes of the Nazis.

What about Anthony Eden and some gentlemen from the Foreign Office? And finally, Franklin Delano Roosevelt?

179. Wyman (*The Abandonment of the Jews*, 241–42) writes that Wallenberg saved at least twenty thousand Jews directly, and that indirectly he was involved in the saving of practically one hundred thousand Jews.
180. Deborah Danan, "Hero or Victim," *The Jerusalem Post*, December 28, 2012.
181. Morse, *While Six Million Died*, 384.

The Authority of a Great Historian

Paul Johnson, the recognized authority on the history of the twentieth century and renowned historian, dedicated a book to the history of the Jews, in which he presents an important analysis of the events of the Second World War that brought about disaster to the Jewish world. He writes:

> The British and American governments were in theory sympathetic to the Jews, but in practice were terrified that any aggressively pro-Jewish policy would provoke Hitler into a mass expulsion of Jews whom they would then be morally obliged to absorb. For the Nazis, emigration was always one element in the Final Solution, and although the balance of evidence seems to show that Hitler was determined to murder Jews rather than export them, he was quite capable of modifying his policy to embarrass the Allies if they gave him the opportunity. Goebbels wrote in his diary on 13 December 1942: "I believe both the British and the Americans are happy that we are exterminating the Jewish riff-raff." This was not true, but neither power was prepared to save Jewish lives by accepting large numbers of refugees.[182]

And on Franklin Delano Roosevelt, Paul Johnson writes:

> A major obstacle to action was F.D. Roosevelt himself. He was both anti-Semitic, in a mild way, and ill informed. When the topic came up at the Casablanca Conference, he spoke of "the understandable complaints which the Germans bore towards the Jews in Germany, namely that while they represented a small part of the population, over 50 per cent of the lawyers, doctors, schoolteachers, college professors in Germany were Jews" (the actual figures were 16.3, 10.9, 2.6 and 0.5 per cent). Roosevelt seems to have been guided purely by domestic political considerations. He had nearly 90 per cent of the Jewish vote anyway and felt no spur to act. Even after the full facts of systematic extermination became available, the President did nothing for fourteen months. A belated Anglo-American conference on the issue was held in Bermuda in April 1943, but Roosevelt took no interest in it and it decided that nothing of consequence could be done.[183]

---

182. Johnson, *A History of the Jews*, 503.
183. Ibid., 503–4.

An Irish Diplomat Connects the Shoah to Israel's Fate

Conor Cruise O'Brien was the ambassador of Ireland to the United Nations. Since seating was dictated by alphabetical order, he sat between the ambassadors of Iraq and of Israel. After many conversations with each of them, he started studying the Middle East problems and ended up writing an eight-hundred-page book on the subject.

O'Brien writes:

> Israel is obliged, by the nature of its predicament, to remain on its guard, and to be the judge of its own security. And those who condemn Israel should reflect that Israel's predicament is not the creation of Israelis only, but is also the creation of all the rest of us – those who attacked and destroyed the Jews in Europe and those in Europe and America who just quietly closed our doors.[184]

O'Brien's indictment is an elegant way of reminding the world of the Allied powers' complicity with Nazi Germany.

And the ambassador continues:

> Against that background, the statesmen of Europe might have the grace to be more sparing in their admonitions addressed to Israel, bearing in mind that so many of the people those statesmen represent did so much over so many years, and in so many ways, to impress upon Jews the necessity of creating the Jewish state.[185]

O'Brien here subtly refers to the vicious antisemitism that prevailed in Europe throughout the centuries and which brought about the idea of Zionism and finally the creation of the State of Israel. He calls upon the governments of that continent to be more mindful of the dangers that loom over Israel before teaching her how to defend herself against modern Arab terrorism.

The war ended. The Holocaust was over. But the betrayal of the Allied powers against all those who suffered during those horrible years – Jews, Poles, Gypsies, war prisoners and others – continued. This is what we will see in chapter 4.

---

184. Conor Cruise O'Brien, *The Siege: The Saga of Israel and Zionism* (New York: Simon and Schuster, 1986), 661.
185. Ibid.

Chapter Four
Complicity after the War

Warnings during the War

On August 14, 1941, Roosevelt and Churchill signed the Atlantic Charter, which stated that a new world order had to emerge after the Nazis' defeat, in which all nations would be afforded "the means of dwelling in safety within their own boundaries [and the] assurance that all the men in all lands may live out their lives in freedom from fear and want."[1]

In October 1941, still before the United States entered the war, President Roosevelt and Prime Minister Churchill declared:

> The massacres of the French are an example of what Hitler's Nazis are doing in many other countries under their yoke. The atrocities committed in Poland, Yugoslavia, Norway, Holland, Belgium and particularly behind the German front in Russia, exceed anything that has been known since the darkest and most bestial ages of humanity. The punishment of these crimes should now be counted among the major goals of the war.[2]

On January 1, 1942, twenty-five nations, among them England and the United States, signed the "United Nations Declaration," affirming their commitment to the destruction of the Nazi regime. At the same time, the governments in exile of the occupied countries of Europe declared that among the principal aims of the Second World War should be the punishment, through the

---

1. Atlantic Charter, article 6. *Foreign Relations of the United States: Diplomatic Papers 1941*, vol. 1, *General: The Soviet Union* (Washington, DC: Government Printing Office, 1958).
2. Tusa and Tusa (*Nuremberg Trial*, 21), quoting from the transcript of the Nuremberg trial, IMT, vol. 5.

channel of organized justice, of those guilty and responsible for these crimes, whether they have ordered them or in any way participated in them.

In mid-1942, a letter from Roosevelt was read at a Jewish rally in Madison Square Garden. It stated: "The Nazis will not succeed.... The American People not only sympathize with all victims of Nazi crimes but will hold the perpetrators of these crimes to strict accountability in a day of reckoning which will surely come."[3]

Not a word about the persecution and annihilation of Jews.

In October 1943 the Big Three Allies followed suit, proclaiming that any German soldiers or Nazi party members guilty of atrocities, massacres, and executions would be sent back to the countries in which their abominable deeds were done in order that they may be judged and punished according to the law of these liberated countries.[4]

And again in November 1, 1943, during the Moscow Conference, Roosevelt, Churchill, and Stalin published a "Declaration on German Atrocities in Occupied Europe" which gave a "full warning" that when the Nazis were defeated, the Allies would "pursue them to the uttermost ends of the earth...in order that justice may be done." The declaration referred to "Germans who take part in the wholesale shooting of Italian officers or the execution of French, Dutch, Belgian or Norwegian hostages, or of Cretan peasants, or who have shared in slaughters inflicted on the people of Poland or in the territories of the Soviet Union which are now being swept clear of the enemy, will know that they will be brought back to the scene of their crimes and judged on the spot by the peoples whom they have outraged."[5] No reference whatsoever in the Moscow Declaration to the Jewish victims of the Nazis. The same omission had occurred in the Quebec Conference of August 1943.[6]

Despite the strong demand by the World Jewish Congress that a new specific statement regarding the Jews be pronounced, the British opposed the statement on the grounds that similar declarations had been ineffective and had proved "embarrassing" to the Allies.[7] In the War Refugee Board

3. Morse, *While Six Million Died*, 309.
4. Donald Bloxham and Devin O. Pendas, "Punishment as Prevention? The Politics of Punishing Génocidaires," in Bloxham and Moses, *Oxford Handbook of Genocide Studies*, 619.
5. Morse, *While Six Million Died*, 335.
6. Wyman, *The Abandonment of the Jews*, 256.
7. Morse, *While Six Million Died*, 336.

there was justified concern that the Nazis had concluded that the Allies did not care if they went on slaughtering Jews.[8]

Finally, on March 24, 1944, Roosevelt issued a strong statement drafted by the War Refugee Board, which was widely circulated all over Europe. It read:

> In one of the blackest crimes of all history – begun by the Nazis in the days of peace and multiplied by them a hundred times in time of war – the wholesale systematic murder of the Jews of Europe goes on unabated every hour.... That these innocent people, who have already survived a decade of Hitler's fury, should perish on the very eve of triumph over the barbarism which their persecution symbolizes, would be a major tragedy.
>
> It is therefore fitting that we should again proclaim our determination that none who participate in these acts of savagery shall go unpunished.... That warning applies not only to the leaders but also to their functionaries and subordinates in Germany and in the satellite countries. All who knowingly take part in the deportation of Jews to their death in Poland or Norwegians and French to their death in Germany are equally guilty with the executioner. All who share the guilt shall have the punishment.
>
> Hitler is committing these crimes against humanity in the name of the German people. I ask every German and every man everywhere under Nazi domination to show the world by his action that in his heart he does not share these insane criminal desires. Let him hide these pursued victims, help them to get over their borders, and do what he can to save them from the Nazi hangman. I ask him also to keep watch and to record the evidence that will one day be used to convict the guilty.[9]

Roosevelt's declaration came a few years too late. Millions had perished, only thousands could be saved. The collective expression of Allied indignation over known Nazi brutality in due time might have stimulated greater resistance to their German masters within the Nazi satellite countries. It might also have strengthened what little internal opposition existed in Germany.[10] Let's add that it might have weakened the enthusiasm with which the murderous Nazi organizations proceeded in their program of annihilation. Members of those

8. Wyman, *The Abandonment of the Jews*, 256.
9. Morse, *While Six Million Died*, 337–38.
10. Ibid., 338.

organizations might have even established contact with the Allies, seeking an exchange of victims for a guarantee of non-prosecution; others may have simply chosen to be transferred from murdering unarmed civilians to fighting at the front, sacrificing their security in order to be left in peace after the war.

The Shameful Postwar Realities

Shamefully, the day of reckoning never arrived. The perpetrators of the Holocaust, with very few exceptions, were never brought to trial, never suffered any consequence for their barbaric acts. On the contrary, many of them went back to important positions in post–World War II Germany. Some were allowed to enter the United States and live peacefully;[11] some – such as Eichmann, Mengele, Roschmann, Stangl, and Wagner – were transferred by the Vatican to South American countries by "Operation Odessa";[12] and some ended up in Arab countries, mainly Egypt, and collaborated in attacks against the State of Israel. The majority remained in Germany and benefited from the social security system of postwar Germany.

And all those high government functionaries of the Allied countries who aided and abetted the Nazi atrocities in many different ways, most especially in the United States and England, were never even reminded of their perverse collaboration with Hitler.

Rafael Medoff reports on the evolution of the American policy regarding the punishment of the Nazi criminals. In June 1943 the United Nations Crimes Commission was established, and President Roosevelt named former ambassador Herbert C. Pell, an old friend and campaign contributor, to represent the United States on that body.

The State Department delayed Pell's departure to London for many

---

11. See Novick, *The Holocaust in American Life*, 88–89, on the entry of ex-SS men into the United States in the years following the war and the organizations that supported that policy.

12. See Loftus and Aarons, *Secret War against the Jews*, 112: "By 1947 the Vatican 'Ratline' as it was called by US intelligence, was the single largest smuggling route for Nazi war criminals. Nearly all the major war criminals, from Adolf Eichman to Pavelic, ended up following Dulles's money route from the Vatican to Argentina. The lower-level Nazis wound up in a variety of countries, including Syria, Egypt, the United States, Britain, Canada and Australia, although several big-time criminals emigrated to those countries too." And: "The State Department actually agreed in writing to use the Vatican to smuggle Nazis out of Italy to Argentina, before they could be identified as wanted war criminals."

months. At a certain point, Secretary of State Cordell Hull warned Pell that as far as the department was concerned, the purpose of the commission was simply to gather facts, not to prepare war crimes trials. The legal experts of the department believed the Allies had a legal right to prosecute only those Nazis or Nazi collaborators who had committed crimes against citizens of Allied countries. Under that definition, Nazi killers of Germans, Poles, Russians, Belgians, Dutch, Rumanians, Hungarians, Gypsies, and Jews of other nationalities would have gone free. In general, the State Department preferred to limit postwar trials to the most prominent and notorious war criminals, out of concern that prosecuting large numbers of Germans could harm America's relations with Germany after the war. Pell favored prosecuting all war criminals. The State Department fired him.[13]

Pell met with Peter Bergson of the Emergency Conference, who advised him to go public with the story. Thus, at a New York press conference in January 1945, Pell declared:

> If we are not tough and hard toward the war criminals it will encourage other tyrants to try the same thing – to murder, persecute and loot from minorities. Conviction and punishment of Axis war criminals is not a matter of revenge. It is justice.[14]

It sounds as if Pell envisioned the future atrocities in Cambodia, Congo, Uganda, Libya, Iraq, Rwanda, Bosnia-Herzegovina, Kosovo, Sudan, Syria, and all the other countries where persecutions and mass executions of millions of human beings took place.

The Pell declaration appeared on the front page of the *New York Times* and throughout the American press. Embarrassed by the avalanche of negative publicity, the State Department adopted a different attitude. Within days, acting secretary of state Joseph Grew announced a reversal of its previous position: the State Department now agreed that Nazi murderers of European Jews should be prosecuted. And so the Nuremberg trial came about.

13. Medoff, *FDR and the Holocaust*, 154–56.
14. Ibid., 157.

The International Military Tribunal

On August 8, 1945, the governments of France, the United Kingdom, the United States, and the USSR, "acting in the interests of all the United Nations and by their representative duly authorized thereto," signed an agreement for the establishment of an International Military Tribunal "for the trial of war criminals whose offences have no particular geographical location."[15] The tribunal was to operate in accordance with the charter annexed to the agreement.

Robert H. Jackson, associate justice of the US Supreme Court, was nominated head of the US prosecution team for the trial of twenty-three members of the political and military hierarchy of Nazi Germany. On November 21, 1945, Jackson gave an opening statement in which he described the International Military Tribunal, which included the United States, United Kingdom, France, and the Soviet Union, as

> the first trial in history for crimes against the peace of the world.... The wrongs which we seek to condemn and punish have been so calculated, so malignant and so devastating that civilization cannot tolerate their being ignored, because it cannot survive their being repeated. That four great nations, flushed with victory and stung with injury, stay the hand of vengeance and voluntarily submit their captive enemies to the judgment of the law is one of the most significant tributes that power has paid to reason.[16]

These were inspiring words, but in reality the trial was only for a few of the most prominent criminals. In addition to this Nuremberg trial of the Nazi leaders, twelve more trials of lesser-known criminals were held between 1946 and 1949. In total, 185 Nazis were tried, and 142 of them were convicted.[17]

And so those who wanted to go easy on war criminals had the last laugh, as the majority of the leading Nazi criminals were either not prosecuted or were given sentences "light enough to please a chicken thief," as one Nuremberg prosecutor put it.[18] The near totality of the SS and the *Einsatzgruppen* officers

---

15. Article 1 of the London Agreement, *United Nations Treaty Series* 5, 251.
16. James Podgers, "1985–1994: The Legacy of Nuremberg," *American Bar Association Journal* 101, no. 1 (January 2015): 55.
17. Medoff, *FDR and the Holocaust*, 157.
18. Johnson, *Modern Times*, 422.

and soldiers who humiliated, tortured, starved, and killed millions of Jews, as well as many thousands of Gypsies and people from other ethnic groups, were never punished, never touched, never bothered.

Many of those who were convicted and jailed were soon set free, thanks to former assistant secretary of war John McCloy, who became US high commissioner for Germany in 1949. One hundred four German industrialists had been convicted of war crimes, of whom eighty-four were still in jail when McCloy arrived in Germany. Of those eighty-four, McCloy reduced the sentences of seventy-four to time already served, setting them free immediately.[19] According to Bloxham and Pendas, the need to placate German national sentiment amid the burgeoning political conflict with the USSR led to the ending of the war crimes trials in all western occupation zones in the late 1940s, within the context of a general easing of occupation policy. Later it resulted in a series of increasingly politicized sentence reviews which ultimately developed the simple aim of releasing all war criminals, most of them prematurely. The final four war criminals in US custody were released by 1958: the number incarcerated at the beginning of 1955 had been forty-one. Jails in the erstwhile British zone of Germany were empty by 1957. Among those released after serving only a few years of life sentences and commuted death sentences were some of the worst Nazi offenders, including commanders of the *Einsatzgruppen* (SS killing squads) and senior members of the concentration camp hierarchy. Rejection of the legal validity of the trials was subtly built into articles 6 and 7 of the 1952 Bonn Treaty ending the Allied occupation.[20]

Since Nuremberg, the international system of punishing war criminals has failed miserably. And the same has been happening with all those who practice crimes against humanity, crimes against peace, crimes of genocide, and crimes of terrorism – despite all the international tribunals, with their

19. Loftus and Aarons (*Secret War against the Jews*, 101) write about "several multibillionaires who had been prominent members of Hitler's inner circle. A few even had served time in the Allied prisons as Nazi war criminals, but they all were released quickly. The bottom line is that the Nazi businessmen survived the war with their fortunes intact and rebuilt their industrial empires to become the richest men in the world."

20. Bloxham and Pendas, "Punishment as Prevention?" in Bloxham and Moses, *Oxford Handbook of Genocide Studies*, 624. Johnson (*Modern Times*, 422) reports on the early releases and refers to executives of the Buna plant in Auschwitz who got prison terms from eight years to eighteen months.

magnificent compositions, multimillion-dollar budgets, and excellent PR and propaganda machines.

Looking back and forward, the trials conducted after World War II were a disaster and helped to encourage evil for decades to come. As we read in the introduction to the Tusas' *Nuremberg Trial*:

> Forty-five years later, it is necessary to ask whether, on balance, the Nuremberg trials did more good than harm. By convicting and executing a tiny number of the most flagrant criminals, the Nuremberg court permitted the world to go on with business as usual. The German economy was quickly rebuilt.... The tribunal asked for too little when it implicitly expiated the guilt of thousands of hands-on murderers by focusing culpability on a small number of leaders who could never have carried out their wholesale slaughter without the enthusiastic assistance of an army, both military and civil, of retail butchers.[21]

The other reason for the atrocious genocides of the last seven decades is the lack of prevention, the abhorrence to intervene in foreign soils, the idolatry of sovereignty at any price, even at the cost of millions of lives, as we shall see in the following chapters.

When the General Assembly of the UN was discussing the Universal Declaration of Human Rights and the Soviet delegate criticized it as an incursion on national sovereignty, René Cassin reminded him that in 1933 Hitler's representative had used the same argument in the League of Nations to oppose any interference with Germany's actions against its own countrymen. Yet the reality of the UN is the same as that of the League of Nations, despite all the grandiloquent resolutions and declarations and the sophisticated structure of commissions and committees.

A Witness to the Hypocrisy of the "Internationalization of Human Rights"

In the rich literature on human rights, one book stands out very impressively. It is not a theoretical work, nor a laudatory essay, nor a wishful-thinking appreciation of the so-called "internationalization of human rights"; it is a down-to-earth report on the catastrophic inertia and the falsities that have

---

21. Introduction by Alan M. Dershowitz to Tusa and Tusa, *Nuremberg Trial*.

characterized the world community's reactions to the most atrocious events that took place in the last sixty-plus years.

The reference is to David Scheffer's *All the Missing Souls*,[22] a heartbreaking report by one who was involved in the battle against various genocides. Scheffer tried heroically to prevent the genocides, to combat them, and to punish the responsible criminals. Yet at the end of many years of work, Scheffer recognizes how little was done. Though he did all he could, Scheffer cannot forgive himself for his inability to end the death and destruction.

This book is a witness to the weaknesses of the United States, to the unreliability of the British, to the falsity of the French – the three peoples who created the three monumental historic documents for the protection of human life: the English Magna Carta, the French Declaration of the Rights of Man, and the American Bill of Rights.

Scheffer was adviser and counsel to Dr. Madeleine Albright, America's ambassador to the United Nations from 1993 to 1996. In 1997, when Albright became secretary of state, Scheffer was nominated by President Bill Clinton and confirmed by the Senate as the first-ever US ambassador-at-large for war crimes issues. In his book he demonstrates the absolute inefficiency and unreliability of the United Nations.

Scheffer writes on his special ambassadorship:

> On the one hand, this initiative marked a sad commentary on the state of the world at the close of the twentieth century – fifty years or so after the Holocaust and the Nuremberg and Tokyo tribunals and two decades after the atrocity crimes that devastated Cambodia during the rule of Pol Pot. On the other hand, my ambassadorship demonstrated that the United States recognized the gravity of the situation and rose to the challenge. No other nation had seen fit to designate anyone as an ambassador to cover atrocity crimes.[23]

Scheffer affirms:

> The futile slogan of "never again" after World War II collapsed under the weight of atrocity crimes occurring again and again. The challenges were

22. *All the Missing Souls: A Personal History of the War Crimes Tribunals* (Princeton and Oxford: Princeton University Press, 2012).
23. Scheffer, *All the Missing Souls*, 3.

colossal in those years, as hundreds of thousands of individuals participated in the murder and ethnic cleansing of millions.[24]

The book relates the origin and ostensible purpose of the various war crimes
tribunals – the International Criminal Tribunals for the former Yugoslavia
and Rwanda, the Special Court for Sierra Leone, the Extraordinary Chambers
in the Courts of Cambodia, and the International Criminal Court – which
"were conceived and built to end the impunity of political and military leaders."[25] The author affirms that during the eight years that he served as US
ambassador-at-large for war crimes issues (1993–2001), "failures far exceeded
successes."[26]

In his introductory remarks Scheffer so describes the twentieth century:

> …a bloody century that had experienced the extinction of countless
> Congolese, the atrocities against the Armenians, the Stalinist purges, the
> Nanking massacre, the Holocaust, Chairman Mao's Cultural Revolution,
> Pol Pot's harvest of death, Uganda's suicide under Idi Amin, the Ethiopian
> nightmare under Mengistu, disappearances in Honduras, Chile and
> Argentina, Saddam Hussein's genocidal assault on the Kurds, large-scale
> atrocities in the Balkans, including Kosovo, in Rwanda, Burundi, Sudan,
> Congo, Sierra Leone, Liberia, Ethiopia, Eritrea, Angola, East Timor, Iraq,
> Afghanistan, Burma and Chechnya.… Despite the information revolution,
> the economic prosperity, the military superiority of modern armies and
> the enlightened diplomacy of the new world order following the Cold War,
> the killing, mutilating and wanton destruction proliferated. Only a few
> atrocities met a rapid response from diplomats and civilized warriors.[27]

Scheffer tries to teach the bitter truth to the world community of jurists, politicians, diplomats, international organizations, and democratic governments:
tribunals cannot end atrocities. In other words, what justice is capable of doing
within national communities (in a relative, partial way) is totally inoperative
in the international arena.

Theodor Meron refers to the succession of genocides "from the brutal

24. Ibid., 2.
25. Ibid., 3–4.
26. Ibid., 4.
27. Ibid.

regime of Pol Pot to Saddam Hussein's extermination of ethnic Kurds; from the genocide in Rwanda to the massacres in Darfur; from the ethnic cleansing in Bosnia and the Srebrenica enclave to the attacks on Kosovo Albanians; and from Sierra Leone to Uganda; the world has continued to witness malevolent deeds that surpass understanding."[28]

But Judge Meron, former president of the International Criminal Tribunal for the former Yugoslavia (ICTY) and then appeals judge, also tries to show a brighter side in the reality of modern international criminal law. He claims that the ICTY has brought justice to the peoples of former Yugoslavia by helping the return of refugees across ethnic boundaries. In his view, "because of the Tribunal, international humanitarian law and human rights law today enjoy greater currency and are better understood throughout the world than just a decade ago. The existence of the International Criminal Court may prompt more extensive prosecution of war criminals and their ilk in the courts of the countries within its jurisdiction."[29] He also claims that the "reference of the Darfur case to the International Criminal Court has created a great opportunity and an immense challenge for the Court."[30]

Unfortunately, the ten years that have passed since Judge Meron's essay was published have not confirmed his optimistic forecast.

Germany: First Murderer, Then Accomplice

In the First World War Germans and Turks were allies. Germany did not move to stop the genocide of the Armenians; on the contrary, it advised the Turkish military on deportation matters, becoming an accomplice to the first genocide of the twentieth century.

As we saw in chapter 1, the indifference of the Allies regarding the suffering of the Armenian people at the hands of the Turks has gone as far as denial – many democracies refuse up to the present day to recognize that genocide was executed by the Muslim Ottomans against the Christian Armenians.

After the Second World War, it was impossible not to recognize the horror that had taken place, the barbarity to which Germany had fallen. The terrible reality was inescapable, due to the American press coverage during the war years;

---

28. Theodor Meron, "Reflection on the Prosecution of War Crimes by International Tribunals," *American Journal of International Law* 100, no. 3 (July 2006): 577.
29. Ibid., 577–78.
30. Ibid., 579.

the testimonies of the American soldiers who entered the concentration camps; the enormous number of displaced persons in Western Europe; and the war that the Nazis had waged against England, North America, and other democracies. Then West Germany agreed to "compensate" the war victims, and in later years Holocaust monuments and museums were built around the world.

And yet, denial of the Holocaust began to surface just a few decades after the war, and it has spread through the work of various authors who present themselves as historians. Some countries have legislated that it is a crime to deny the Holocaust, but this has not prevented the cruel, distorted "historical theory" from being proclaimed and published in other countries and sometimes even in the countries that passed anti-denial laws.

Undoubtedly, the impunity of the majority of the Nazi criminals has made the denial possible. And besides the Allies' betrayal of what they had proclaimed time and again regarding the punishment that would be meted out to all the participants in the persecution of minorities and the atrocities perpetrated against them, Germany itself is most responsible for this impunity, for not cleaning itself of the organizers and executors of the Holocaust.

When the first denials of the Holocaust began to appear, it was up to Germany to proclaim to the world that it was proven beyond any doubt that the Holocaust, in its minutest details, had occurred. Germany should have reported the number of Jews murdered, classified by nationalities and prewar domiciles, and should have made accessible all the available proofs. The report should have covered all the atrocities committed against the Jews – the complete detailing of the most barbarous crimes ever committed by a people throughout the history of mankind. The proclamation should have been followed by a book that provided full details of the Holocaust, with reference to all the documents that were contained in the country's state archives. The book should then have been distributed throughout the world in many languages.

By this proclamation and comprehensive book, Germany would have officially and openly recognized the crime of the Nazi regime, and the world would not now be hearing from these sick "historians."

Germany did nothing of the sort, but on the contrary has become a nest of terrorists. Some of the murderers of the three thousand New Yorkers on 9/11 had lived and studied in German schools and various members of the terrorist organizations that are active in Afghanistan carry German passports.

Germany would have to undertake leadership in the European Union in favor of the State of Israel and against the insulting Arab propaganda and Islamic terror – the heirs of the Muslims who pressured Great Britain not to allow Jews into Palestine during the war years. But Germany has been intimidated, becoming submissive – as the rest of Western Europe – to the terror of the Islamic leadership, allowing the growth of a terrible danger in its midst. German companies develop business in the worth of billions with Iran, thereby financing the war effort of the Nazis' heirs.

In the twentieth century, Germany committed the greatest crime in the history of mankind. Yet it remains silent and inert in the face of the growing antisemitic campaign, which could lead to a new genocide in the twenty-first century.

Germany – the murderer of yesterday – is the accomplice of tomorrow.

No Apology Forthcoming

On December 22, 1945, seven months after the war ended, the "Truman Directive" was issued to expedite the admission of displaced persons to the United States. For the first time since the 1930s, the US immigration quotas were open for full use. Concerning the refugees at the Oswego camp – described in chapter 2 – President Harry Truman called it "inhumane and wasteful" to send them back to Europe in order to receive visas that would allow them to immigrate to the United States.[31] But the United States government offered no apology for not allowing the entrance of Jews even to fill the existing immigration quotas during the war years.

The lack of apology stands in stark contrast to another episode in American history. In the last quarter of the nineteenth century, after the Civil War, the US economy struggled and jobs declined. Immigration – legal and illegal – skyrocketed, and the new immigrants accepted jobs at low pay, resulting in the unemployment of many citizens. By 1880, more than 9 percent of California's population was Asian. This unstable state of affairs led to the Chinese Exclusion Act, which closed America's borders to people of Chinese heritage. That was May 6, 1882.

In June 2012 – 130 years later – the US House of Representatives unanimously approved an official apology for the Chinese Exclusion Act.

---

31. Wyman, *The Abandonment of the Jews*, 274.

The Exclusion Act was a matter of economic policy that did not cause Chinese people to die or suffer torment. There has been no initiative by the United States regarding the Jewish people who disappeared in the Holocaust, when a great part of them could have been saved by being allowed into the United States, Latin America, North Africa, other countries of the African continent, and Palestine, if the United States had taken the initiative and led the world in the right path.

It is true that the United States has been a constant supporter of the State of Israel since its founding in 1948, and that it came to its aid in many decisive moments, but the recognition of its cruel policy during the Second World War and the leniency practiced toward a huge number of Nazi murderers after the war must still be recognized officially, for the benefit of the American people and especially for the education of its younger generations.

The Swiss Banks' Robbery

Between 1933 and 1945, nearly 6.9 million foreign accounts were opened in the Swiss banks. Those who survived the war and the children of those who perished tried to locate the accounts that their families owned and found the doors of the banks closed to them. In many cases, heirs brought evidence that a certain account had belonged to their parents together with documentation proving the family relationship – yet the banks demanded death certificates. Auschwitz and the other extermination camps did not issue death certificates for their victims. These stolen accounts, deemed "heirless assets" because of the impossible conditions set for claiming them, were fiercely protected by the secretive Swiss banking system. Searches undertaken at the behest of the Swiss government uncovered a mere 775 accounts acknowledged to be those of Holocaust victims.[32]

By 1996, when the Swiss had proved themselves unwilling to undertake a serious investigation without outside compulsion, class action lawsuits began to be launched and a concerted effort was made to force a serious search. Paul Volcker, formerly the Federal Reserve chairman, headed up an international commission that employed 650 forensic accountants to comb through records for 4.1 million foreign-owned accounts in 254 Swiss banks. Then, comparing

32. Allen Pusey, "Aug. 12, 1998: Swiss Banks Settle Holocaust Claims," 72.

the account information to Israeli and US records on Holocaust victims, the accounts were exhaustively scrutinized for matches.[33]

This investigation and another similar one undertaken simultaneously had a persuasive effect, and the Swiss banks undertook to come to settlement terms. They established a fund of 1.25 billion dollars to compensate victims for un-claimable deposit balances as well as for "Swiss participation in slave labor, the trafficking of looted assets, and race-based refugee policies."[34]

British Cruelty

After the war, thousands of survivors were placed in internment camps in occupied Germany. Many of the survivors desired to go to Palestine – yet to the horror of every decent human being, the British kept the doors of the Holy Land closed to the holy survivors of the Holocaust. Until their relinquishing of Palestine in 1948, the British consistently refused entry to survivors; those who dared the voyage were sent back to Europe or interned on the island of Cyprus. The tragedy was fictionally narrated in the famous movie *Exodus*, based on Leon Uris's book of the same title.

As they approached Palestine, the survivors, broken in body and spirit, saw the lights of the Jewish homes in Haifa and rejoiced to come back after two thousand years of exile and suffering to the Promised Land – the land that their ancestors had prayed for throughout the centuries, the land they had dreamed of in the inferno of Auschwitz. Suddenly, their entrance was blocked by British soldiers. The British, who were occupied at that very same time in drafting the Universal Declaration of Human Rights, who were writing beautiful pages about the dignity of the human being, showed themselves to be Hitler's accomplices even after the war.

The State Department's "Tradition"

Throughout the State of Israel's turbulent history, the United States government has maintained a position of support to the only democratic state in the Middle East.

The State Department, however, has not followed a consistent policy, with various secretaries of state expressing themselves in prejudicial terms about

33. Ibid.
34. Ibid.

the Jewish state. The statements made by President Obama's secretary John Kerry are probably the most antagonistic to the State of Israel in the approximately seven decades of its history. For instance, in May 2014, in the midst of peace negotiations between Israel and the PLO, Kerry had the audacity to say that if Israel would not cut a deal with the Palestinians, it would either cease to be a Jewish state or it would become "an apartheid state."

The only possible defense for Kerry is that he does not know the meaning of an apartheid state, or that he is totally uninformed about the positions of both parties: Israel, a state with one and a half million Arab citizens, with full rights, and on the other hand, the Palestinians, who have declared time and again that they would not admit one single Jew in their desired future state.

Kerry also warned Israel that if it would not come to terms with the Palestinians, it would be the victim of a new Intifada – a wave of organized, murderous terrorist attacks. This sounds like an anticipated justification for the Palestinian recourse to violence against the Israeli population. That would amount to complicity before the crime. So seventy years after World War II, it seems we are again facing the State Department's complicity with Israel's enemies.

This attitude of Kerry's, taken at face value, puts him in the position of some kind of follower of Roosevelt's State Department officials, who maintained a negative attitude toward any step to help the persecuted Jews of Europe. The present secretary of state resuscitates this approach when he justifies the persecution of Israeli citizens and residents by an Arab population that is educated from childhood to hate the Israelis and the Jews in general and that is ruled by a regime that officially declares its desideratum to destroy the Jewish state. Did the secretary of state not read the PLO Charter, in which the final objective of the organization is stated as being the total destruction and disappearance of the Jewish state?

The New Face of Antisemitism

Antisemitism has many sources: racial, social, religious, theological, and political. Modern antisemitism has gained a new face: international. Pilar Rahola, a Spanish politician, journalist, activist and member of the far left, is a staunch defender of the State of Israel, a cause that has taken her to many countries where she proclaims her severe critique of the European leftist circles and the press around the world, demonstrating the hypocrisy of those who pretend to defend human rights. Why, she asks, do we not see demonstrations against Islamic dictatorships, against the Burmese dictatorship, the enslavement of millions of women who live without any legal protection, against the use of children as human bombs, against the suffering of the people in Sudan, as well as manifestations in favor of Israel's right to exist?

The new Left, claims Rahola, is never concerned with the people of Syria, or Yemen, or Iran, or Sudan, or other such nations. They are never preoccupied when Hamas destroys freedom for the Palestinians. They are only concerned with using the concept of Palestinian freedom as a weapon against Israeli freedom.

Regarding the international press, she claims that on the Israeli-Palestinian issue they do not inform, they propagandize. Any act of self-defense by the Israelis becomes a massacre and any confrontation turns into a genocide.

Pilar Rahola denounces the antisemitism of the twenty-first century, which has dressed itself in the efficient disguise of anti-Israelism, or its synonym, anti-Zionism. Not all criticism of Israel is antisemitism, but all present-day antisemitism has turned into prejudice and the demonization of the Jewish state. And Rahola censures the United Nations, which instead of defending human rights, has become a broken puppet in the hands of despots. She claims that the United Nations is only useful to Islamo-fascists like Ahmadinejad, or dangerous demagogues like the deceased Hugo Chavez, offering them a planetary loudspeaker where they can spit their hatred. She concludes that the United Nations exists to systematically attack Israel.[35]

In chapter 11, "The UN in the Footsteps of Hitler," we shall see how far the complicity after the war has reached and we will further examine the contemporary globalized antisemitism.

The Courageous Standing of José María Aznar

It is critical that the international community hear José María Aznar, the former Spanish prime minister. Aznar published a powerful editorial in the *Times of London*,[36] in which he analyzes and criticizes the policies of the West toward Israel – which he describes as "a nation with deeply rooted democratic

---

35. "La izquierda lunática," PorIsrael, July 5, 2011, http://www/porisrael.org/2011/07/05/la-izquierda-lunatica.
36. José María Aznar, "Support Israel: If It Goes Down, We All Go Down," *Times of London*, June 17, 2010.

institutions... a dynamic and open society that has repeatedly excelled in culture, science, and technology." And yet, argues Aznar, Israel is the only democracy whose right to exist has been debated and attacked from day one. First it was invaded by the neighboring nations in a conventional war, then it suffered from terrorism and suicide attacks (still ongoing today), and now it must also confront an international chorus of continual protest against its every move via sanitized channels of "international law and diplomacy." The dangers Israel faces are manifold – a hail of missiles from multiple directions, radical Islamism which sees the destruction of Israel as its religious destiny, and threats from a nuclear-aspirant Iran.

Aznar proclaims that Israel "is our first line of defense in a turbulent region that is constantly at risk of descending into chaos." Indeed, "if Israel goes down," claims the former Spanish prime minister, "we all go down." Aznar criticizes what he diagnoses as the West's "masochistic self-doubt over our own identity." Aznar notes that the West suffers from a "multiculturalism that forces us to our knees before others" and from a secularism that "blinds us even when we are confronted by jihadis promoting the most fanatical incarnation of their faith."

Aznar proclaims that he decided to promote a new Friends of Israel initiative with the help of other prominent politicians and personalities. What binds the group together, affirms Aznar, is their unyielding support for Israel's right to exist and to defend itself. He concludes his article by saying that Israel is a fundamental part of the West. The West is what it is thanks to its Judeo-Christian roots. If the Jewish element of those roots is upturned and Israel is lost, "then we are lost too." Israel and the West are inextricably intertwined.

The positions taken by Pilar Rahola and by José María Aznar demonstrate that the campaign against the Jews as a nation-state is finally beginning to meet with significant resistance.

Rupert Murdoch: "The War against the Jews"

A few months after Aznar's article appeared in the *London Times*, Rupert Murdoch, the controversial newspaper magnate, spoke at the annual banquet of the Anti-Defamation League in New York on modern antisemitism, which he called the "ongoing war against the Jews." Murdoch declared that the new phase of the war is "the soft war that seeks to isolate Israel by delegitimizing it." Its success is evident in today's inconceivable reality: "Israel becomes increasingly ostracized, while Iran – a nation that has made no secret of wishing Israel's destruction – pursued nuclear weapons loudly, proudly, and without apparent fear or rebuke."[37]

The manifestations of antisemitism reported here illustrate the international community's complicity with the Holocaust after the war's end, which has turned antisemitism into a policy of demonization of the State of Israel. We will return to modern antisemitism in chapters 8 and 12.

The demonization of the Jewish state has infected most international organizations, the greatest part of the international media, and a considerable part of the intelligentsia of the democracies of the world. Strangely, though, the State of Israel and her friends around the world have yet to build a massive counterpropaganda effort against the constant Arab incitement.

In truth, the delegitimization of Israel would be more effectively fought by non-Jewish personalities and organizations, Christians as well as Muslims. They should make known their support of one of the outstanding democracies of the West, a small country that has been contributing to the progress of civilization in all fields of culture, science, technology, and medicine. Let it be known that Israel has raised the legal, social, and economic status of its Arab citizens way above what is enjoyed by the populations of any of the Arab states.

37. "Murdoch on Anti-Semitism," *New York Sun*, October 14, 2010, http://www.nysun .com/editorials/murdoch-on-antisemitism/87113/.

Chapter Five
The Universal Declaration's Origins and Principles

Origins of the Universal Declaration of Human Rights

Thomas Buergenthal writes:

> The Universal Declaration is the first comprehensive human rights instrument to be proclaimed by a universal international organization. Because of its moral status and the legal and political importance it has acquired over the years, the Declaration ranks with the Magna Carta, the French Declaration of the Rights of Man and the American Declaration of Independence as a milestone in mankind's struggle for freedom and human dignity. Its debt to these great historical documents is unmistakable.[1]

The Magna Carta states:

> No bailiff on his own bare word without credible witnesses is to send a man to the ordeal. No free man shall be taken or imprisoned, or disseised, or outlawed, or exiled, or in any way destroyed, nor will we go upon him, nor will we send upon him, except by the lawful judgment of his peers or by the law of the land. To no one will we sell, deny or delay right of justice. All persons are to be free to come and go and stay in the land in time of peace except outlaws, prisoners and enemy aliens.[2]

---

1. Thomas Buergenthal, *International Human Rights in a Nutshell*, 25–26.
2. Free adaptation from clauses 38, 39, 40, and 42. See Nicholas Vincent, *Magna Carta: A Very Short Introduction* (Oxford: Oxford University Press, 2012).

These clauses are reflected in various provisions of the Universal Declaration, such as the following:

> Article 8 – Everyone has the right to an effective remedy by the competent national tribunals for acts violating the fundamental rights granted him by the constitution or by law.

> Article 9 – No one shall be subjected to arbitrary arrest, detention or exile.

> Article 10 – Everyone is entitled in full equality to a fair and public hearing by an independent and impartial tribunal, in the determination of his rights and obligations and of any criminal charge against him.

> Article 11 – Everyone charged with a penal offence has the right to be presumed innocent until proved guilty according to law in a public trial at which he has had all the guarantees necessary for his defense.

> No one shall be held guilty of any penal offence on account of any act or omission which did not constitute a penal offence, under national or international law, at the time when it was committed. Nor shall a heavier penalty be imposed than the one that was applicable at the time the penal offence was committed.

> Article 12 – No one shall be subjected to arbitrary interference with his privacy, family, home or correspondence, nor to attacks upon his honor and reputation. Everyone has the right to the protection of the law against such interference or attacks.

> Article 13 – Everyone has the right to freedom of movement and residence within the borders of each State.

> Everyone has the right to leave any country, including his own, and to return to his country.

The American Declaration of Independence proclaims the "self-evident truths that all men are created equal. That they are endowed by their Creator with certain unalienable rights, that among these are Life, Liberty and the pursuit of Happiness."

This is reflected in article 3 of the Universal Declaration, which states: "Everyone has the right to life, liberty and security of person."

The pursuit of happiness is found in various articles of the Universal

Declaration, such as the ones that provide for the rights of marriage (16), social security (22), work with favorable conditions (23), and rest and leisure (24).

Multiple parallels exist between the Universal Declaration and the French Declaration of the Rights of Man. This is evidenced in the very beginning of the French declaration, which states:

> Article 1 – Men are born and remain free and equal in rights. Social distinction may be founded only upon the general good.

> Article 2 – The aim of all political association is the preservation of the natural and imprescriptible rights of man. These rights are liberty, property, security and resistance to oppression.

Other articles of the French Declaration are similarly mirrored in the UDHR:

> Article 7 – No person shall be accused, arrested or imprisoned except in the cases and according to the forms prescribed by law. . . .

> Article 8 – The law shall provide for such punishments only as are strictly and obviously necessary and no one shall suffer punishment except it be legally inflicted in virtue of a law passed and promulgated before the commission of the offense.

> Article 9 – All persons are held innocent until they shall have been declared guilty; if arrest shall be deemed indispensable, all harshness not essential to the securing of the prisoner's person shall be severely repressed by law.

As King Solomon said: there is nothing new under the sun.[3]

Yet despite the similarity in ideals, the UDHR deviates from the other declarations with regard to its effectiveness. While the English, French, and American peoples built societies that realized their ideals as established in their fundamental documents, recent history demonstrates that the United Nations has been unsuccessful in realizing the UDHR's ideals internationally.

An Analysis of Some of the Statements and Principles of the UDHR

The declaration is made up of a preamble that contains seven considerations, one proclamation, and thirty articles. It resulted from almost two years'

---

3. "The thing that has been, it is that which shall be; and that which is done is that which shall be done; and there is no new thing under the sun" (Ecclesiastes 1:9).

deliberations in various bodies of the United Nations, mainly in the Human Rights Commission. It was preceded by six drafts.[4] In the ensuing paragraphs we will reveal the problematic nature of many of the UDHR's statements.

The first consideration of the preamble states:

> Whereas recognition of the inherent dignity and of the equal and inalienable rights of all members of the human family is the foundation of freedom, justice and peace in the world.

It is hard, if at all possible, to expect equality of rights on the world scenario ("all members of the human family"). What *can* be realistically considered is the equality of rights of all members of each particular nation, in accordance with the particular state's political regime and with the level of its economy.

The preamble also states that respect of the individual rights of all members of the human family, which indeed can be considered the foundation of freedom and justice, also supports "peace in the world." Such a statement displays flawed logic; equality should not be considered a requisite for the maintenance of "peace in the world." Countries with different levels of human rights policies can coexist peacefully.

The fifth consideration of the declaration proclaims:

> Whereas the peoples of the United Nations have in the Charter reaffirmed their faith in fundamental human rights, in the dignity and worth of the human person, and in *the equal rights of men and women*[5] and have determined to promote social progress and better standards of life in larger freedom.

The charter of the United Nations had already proclaimed in its preamble its intention to

> reaffirm faith in fundamental human rights, in the dignity and worth of the human person, in *the equal rights of men and women* and of nations large and small.

---

4. The Humphrey Draft, the Cassin Draft, the June 1947 Human Rights Commission Draft, the Geneva Draft, the Lake Success Draft, and the Third Committee Draft.
5. Emphasis mine.

"Fundamental human rights," "dignity and worth of the human person," "social progress," "better standards of life in larger freedom," "equal rights of nations large and small" – these are all ideals central to the political systems of the nations of the world. But "equal rights of men and women" is a matter of domestic, substantive, concrete legal provisions. Either a legal system concedes this equality or discriminates against women. It is not a subject regarding which one proclaims one's faith.[6] In 1945 when the UN's charter was approved, and in 1948 when the Universal Declaration of Human Rights was proclaimed, many of the member states of the international organization maintained more or less severe restrictions to women's rights, especially to married women. And this lasted for many years. In some states it prevails till today.

The declaration often uses the expression "human rights." In the fifth consideration of the declaration, however, the term "fundamental human rights" appears, in keeping with the wording of the UN charter – yet there is no distinction between "human rights" and "fundamental human rights."

The UDHR also suffers from hyperbolic and hypocritical language. Article 1 of the declaration proclaims:

> All human beings are born free and equal in dignity and rights. They are endowed with reason and conscience and should act towards one another in a spirit of brotherhood.

There is a difference between what should be and what is. All human beings should be born free and equal in dignity and rights. But they are not. The reality is that millions of children are born into slavery or quasi-slavery, never attain freedom, and consequently never achieve human dignity. The statement of article 1 – affirming the equality of all human beings at birth – is at best hyperbolic, and at worst, hypocritical.

The call for brotherhood reminds us of the French motto *liberté, égalité, fraternité* and of various biblical proclamations. In reality, brotherhood has never been achieved within any nation, nor within any organized community, in any period of history. How will it ever be achieved on the international level? This is one of the declaration's various extreme, hyperbolic statements, which certainly does not add to its force, even on the moral plane.

6. See my comment on article 16 below.

In addition, the declaration is unduly repetitive. Article 2 of the declaration establishes:

Everyone is entitled to all the rights and freedoms set forth in the Declaration, without distinction of any kind, such as race, color, sex, language, religion, political or other opinion, national or social origin, property, birth or other status. Furthermore, no distinction shall be made on the basis of the political, jurisdictional or international status of the country or territory to which a person belongs, whether it be independent, trust, non-self-governing or under any other limitation of sovereignty.

And article 3 adds:

Everyone has the right to life, liberty and security of person.

In light of article 1, the first part of article 2, and article 3, one may wonder what articles 6 and 7 came to add, when they provide:

Article 6 – Everyone has the right to recognition everywhere as a person before the law.

Article 7 – All are equal before the law and are entitled without any discrimination to equal protection of the law. All are entitled to equal protection against any discrimination in violation of this Declaration and against any incitement to such discrimination.

Does being "recognized as a person" in article 6 add anything to the general principle that recognizes all human beings as "free and equal in dignity and rights" in article 1? Does it add anything to article 2, which guarantees for everyone "all the rights and freedoms without distinction," and to article 3 which proclaims to everyone "the rights to life, liberty and security of person"?

Do the first two times that article 7 speaks of equality add anything to the principle of equality established in article 1, and does forbidding discrimination add anything to the second article's provision against "distinction of any kind"?

In truth, article 7 is repetitive in itself: if one is equal before the law, one automatically benefits from equal protection of the law and consequently one is protected against any discrimination. But the text repeats equality three times.

Article 8 mandates:

Everyone has the right to an effective remedy by the competent national tribunals for acts violating the fundamental rights granted him by the constitution or by law.

Who does this article address? If a state has a constitution and is ruled by laws, the right for effective remedy is built into the system. The declaration can add nothing to that. And if, on the other hand, the state is not ruled by a constitutional legal system, what does the reference to the constitution and the law address?

Article 9's provision that "no one shall be subjected to arbitrary arrest, detention or exile" is perfectly covered by article 8 when it refers to effective remedy granted by the state's constitution or its law. And if a certain legal system guarantees against arbitrary arrest and detention, but has no rule against exile, can the UDHR be of help?

There are other instances of repetitions in the declaration. For instance article 8, already transcribed, is practically repeated in article 10 when it declares that

everyone is entitled in full equality to a fair and public hearing by an independent and impartial tribunal, in the determination of his rights and obligations and of any criminal charge against him.

The final part of this article – "and of any criminal charge against him" – is fully covered by article 11:

Everyone charged with a penal offence has the right to be presumed innocent until proved guilty according to law in a public trial at which he has had all the guarantees necessary for his defence.

And article 14 states:

Everyone has the right to seek and to enjoy in other countries asylum from persecution.

The declaration can establish the right to seek asylum, though it may be considered unnecessary, but the right to enjoy it in another country is a matter of that country's policies: the declaration cannot interfere with the sovereign right of any state to grant or deny an asylum request.[7]

Article 15 proclaims that "everyone has the right to a nationality," and

7. Hersch Lauterpacht considered it "artificial to the point of flippancy." "The Universal Declaration of Human Rights," *British Yearbook of International Law* 25 (1948): 373.

proceeds to say that "no one shall be arbitrarily deprived of his nationality." The natural consequence of the first part of the article would be the prohibition of deprivation – arbitrarily or otherwise. Yet the second part only protects the person from arbitrary deprivation, which means that in some cases the right to nationality might be taken away and lead to statelessness. This weakens the first statement's assertion that everyone has the (absolute) right to a nationality.

The article continues by declaring that "no one should be denied the right to change his nationality." That goes against the basic principle that no state has an obligation to concede its nationality to anyone. Therefore, we must conclude that there is no absolute right to change nationality. The American Declaration of the Rights and Duties of Man[8] has a more rational provision in article 19, which states that "every person has the right to the nationality to which he is entitled by law and to change it, if he so wishes, for the nationality of any other country that is willing to grant it to him."

A number of the UDHR provisions deal with matters that should have been left to the covenants that the United Nations later approved, especially the International Covenant on Economic, Social and Cultural Rights. Examples include the rights to property ownership, social security, work, just remuneration, joining trade unions, rest and leisure, adequate standard of living, and education. All these rights, as important as they are, are not as fundamental as the rights contained in the earlier articles of the declaration. Including economic, social, and cultural rights weakened the declaration and subverted its position as the fundamental constitution for mankind.

Article 16 equates the rights of men and women with regard to marriage. At the time the UDHR was proclaimed, some of the democratic state members of the UN had legislation that discriminated against women in their rights within marriage.[9] So this pronouncement went against national legislative enactments and weakened the declaration's value. This is true even if the document is taken only as a moral beacon, as proclaimed by so many of those who participated in its making and by later scholarly commentaries. In fact, some of the states that voted to approve the Universal Declaration in 1948

8. The American Declaration of the Rights and Duties of Man, O.A.S. Res. xxx, adopted by the Ninth International Conference of American States (1948).
9. Brazilian law, for instance, maintained married women as partially incompetent until 1962, when legislation altered the civil code on this subject.

did not respect the fundamental principles inscribed therein. Can we build moral obligations on lies and contradictions?

In our days, the world panorama has become such that the majority of the state members of the United Nations do not respect the majority of the provisions of the Universal Declaration of Human Rights. That says everything about the course followed by humankind in matters of human rights. A study by Freedom House counted 90 "free countries" out of 194 in 2013, where a free country is "one where there is open political competition, a climate of respect for civil liberties, significant independent civic life and independent media." The other countries perpetrate a range of human-rights abuses.

The Philosophical Underpinnings of Human Dignity

The preamble to the Charter of the United Nations "reaffirms faith in the fundamental human rights, in the dignity and worth of the human person...." The idea of the dignity of the human person and the resulting legal concept of human rights appears, one way or another, in the writings of a series of great thinkers. One of the first thinkers to write about this topic was Augustine (354–430 CE). This famous Catholic theologian believed that human dignity was expressed in the urge to live, the fight to keep alive, which we detect in illness and suffering, among all peoples, throughout the history of mankind.[10]

Philosophers and theologians throughout the ages continued to discuss this topic, as can be seen from the following statements:

- PICO DELLA MIRANDOLA (1463–1494). In "Oration on the Dignity of Man," he imagines how God addressed the first human:

   We have made you neither of heavenly nor of earthly stuff, neither mortal nor immortal, so that with free choice and dignity, you may fashion yourself into whatever form you choose. To you is granted the power of degrading yourself into the lower forms of life, the beasts, and to you is

---

10. Augustine, *The City of God*, 11:27. Hugo Grotius quotes Cicero's repeated notion of a first principle of self-preservation: "The first business of each is to preserve himself in the state of nature; the next, to retain what is according to nature, and to reject what is contrary to it." *The Rights of War and Peace*, 1:2n1, ed. Richard Tuck, based on the French edition by Jean Barbeyrac (Indianapolis, IN: Liberty Fund, 2005).

granted the power, contained in your intellect and judgment, to be reborn into the higher forms, the divine.[11]

- HUGO GROTIUS (1583–1645):

Add to this that sacred History, besides the Precepts it contains to this Purpose, affords no inconsiderable Motive to social affection, since it teaches us that all Men are descended from the same first Parents. So that in this respect also may be truly affirmed what Florentinus said in another sense. That Nature has made us all akin: Whence it follows, that it is a Crime for one Man to act to the Prejudice of another.[12]

- THOMAS HOBBES (1588–1679):

The public worth of a man, which is the value set on him by the Commonwealth, is that which men commonly call *dignity*.[13]

- SAMUEL VON PUFENDORF (1632–1694):

Whence this also is a universal Duty of the Law Natural. That no Man, who has not a peculiar Right, ought to arrogate more to himself than he is ready to allow to his Fellows, but that he permit other Men to enjoy Equal Privilege with himself.

The same *Equality* also shews what every Man's behavior ought to be, when his business is to *distribute Justice* (originally *jus*, which might here be better translated as "right") among others, to wit, *that he treat them as Equals, and indulge not that, unless the Merits of the Cause require it, to one, which he denies to another.* For if he do otherwise, he who is discountenanced is at the same time affronted and wronged, and loses somewhat of the *Dignity* which Nature bestowed upon him.[14]

---

11. Sacks, *The Great Partnership*, 112. Rabbi Sacks observes that "Pico understood that one of the driving themes of the Hebrew Bible is that it is precisely in our freedom that the human person most resembles God." Rabbi Sacks holds that "human dignity never received a higher expression." Pico, according to the author, developed a "religious humanism that was to have an extraordinary influence on the artists of the Renaissance."
12. Grotius, *The Rights of War and Peace*, preliminary discourse, n. 14.
13. Thomas Hobbes, *Leviathan*, in vol. 23 of Robert Hutchins and Robert Maynard, eds., *Great Books of the Western World* (Chicago: Encyclopedia Britannica, 1952), chapter x, 73.
14. Samuel von Pufendorf, *The Whole Duty of Man According to the Law of Nature*, trans. Andrew Tooke (Indianapolis, IN: Liberty Fund, 2003), 102.

- BARUCH SPINOZA (1632–1677):

This doctrine contributes to the welfare of our social existence, since it teaches us to hate no one, to despise no one, to mock no one, to be angry with no one, and to envy no one. It teaches every one, moreover, to be content with his own, and to be helpful to his neighbor, not from any womanish pity, from partiality, or superstition, but by the guidance of reason alone, according to the demand of time and circumstances, as I shall show in the Third Part. This doctrine contributes not a little to the advantage of common society, in so far as it teaches us by what means citizens are to be governed and led: not in order that they may be slaves, but that they may freely do those things which are best.[15]

- JOHN LOCKE (1632–1704):

Foreigners, and such as were strangers to the commonwealth of Israel, were not compelled by force to observe the rites of the Mosaical law, but, on the contrary, in the very same place where it is ordered that an Israelite that was an idolater should be put to death, there it is provided that strangers should not be vexed nor oppressed....[16]

If we may openly speak the truth, and as becomes one man to another, neither Pagan nor Mahometan, nor Jew, ought to be excluded from the civil rights of the commonwealth because of his religion. The Gospel commands no such thing. The Church, which "judgeth not those that are without," wants it not.[17]

- CHARLES DE SECONDAT, BARON DE MONTESQUIEU (1689–1755):

Philosophic liberty consists in the free exercise of the will.... Political liberty consists in security....[18]

- JEAN JACQUES ROUSSEAU (1712–1778):

Man receives the same impulsion, but at the same time knows himself at

---

15. Baruch Spinoza, *Ethics*, trans. W.H. White, in vol. 31 of Hutchins, *Great Books*, 394.
16. John Locke, "A Letter Concerning Tolerance," in vol. 35 of Hutchins, *Great Books*, 14.
17. Ibid., 20.
18. Montesquieu, *The Spirit of Laws*, chapter 12, trans. Thomas Nugent, in vol. 38 of Hutchins, *Great Books*, 85n2.

liberty to acquiesce or resist: and it is particularly in his consciousness of this liberty that the spirituality of his soul is displayed.[19]

Even if each man could alienate himself, he could not alienate his children: they are born men and free; their liberty belongs to them, and no one but they has the right to dispose of it. Before they come to years of discretion, the father can, in their name, lay down conditions for their preservation and well-being, but he cannot give them irrevocably and without conditions; such a gift is contrary to the ends of nature, and exceeds the rights of paternity....[20]

We might, over and above all this, add, to what man acquires in the civil state, moral liberty, which alone makes him truly master of himself: for the mere impulse of appetite is slavery, while obedience to a law which we prescribe to ourselves is liberty.[21]

· IMMANUEL KANT (1724–1804):

Now I say: man and generally any rational being exists as an end in himself, not merely as a means to be arbitrarily used by this or that will, but in all his actions, whether they concern himself or other rational beings, must be always regarded at the same time as an end.

For all rational beings come under the law that each of them must treat itself and all others never merely as means, but in every case at the same time as ends in themselves. Hence results a systematic union of rational beings by common objective laws, i.e., a kingdom which may be called a kingdom of ends, since what these laws have in view is just the relation of these beings to one another as ends and means. It is certainly only an ideal....

And this not on account of any other practical motive or any future advantage, but from the idea of the *dignity* of a rational being, obeying no law but that which he himself also gives.

In the kingdom of ends everything has either value or *dignity*. Whatever has a value can be replaced by something else which is equivalent;

19. Jean Jacques Rousseau, *On the Origin of Inequality*, first part, trans. G.D.H. Cole, in vol. 38 of Hutchins, *Great Books*, 338.

20. Jean Jacques Rousseau, *The Social Contract* I:4, trans. G.D.H. Cole, in vol. 38 of Hutchins, *Great Books*, 389.

21. Ibid., I:8.

whatever, on the other hand, is above all value, and therefore admits of no equivalent, has a *dignity*.

Now morality is the condition under which alone a rational being can be an end in himself, since by this alone is it possible that he should be a legislating member in the kingdom of ends. Thus morality and humanity as capable of it, is that which alone has *dignity*.

This estimation therefore shows that the worth of such a disposition is *dignity*, and places it infinitely above all value, with which it cannot for a moment be brought into comparison or competition without as it were violating its sanctity....

Now the legislation itself which assigns the worth of everything must for that very reason possess *dignity*.... Autonomy then is the basis of the *dignity* of human and of every rational nature....

It is easy to see how it happens that although the conception of duty implies subjection to the law, we yet ascribe a certain *dignity* and sublimity to the person who fulfills all his duties....

And the *dignity of humanity* consists just in this capacity of being universally legislative, though with the condition that it is itself subject to this same legislation.[22]

Love God above everything and thy neighbor as thyself...is he not sustained by the consciousness that he has maintained humanity in its proper *dignity* in his own person and honored it, that he has no reason to be ashamed of himself in his own sight, or to dread the inward glance of self-examination.[23]

• GEORG WILHELM FRIEDRICH HEGEL (1770–1831):

...Because what this amounts to is that even philosophic science itself, plunged in self-despair and extreme exhaustion, is taking as its principle barbarity and absence of thought, and would do its best to rob mankind of all truth, worth and *dignity*....[24]

22. Immanuel Kant, *Fundamental Principles of the Metaphysic of Morals*, second section, trans. Thomas Kingsmill Abbott, in vol. 42 of Hutchins, *Great Books*, 271, 274–75, 277.
23. Immanuel Kant, *Critique of Practical Reason*, chapter 3, trans. Thomas Kingsmill Abbott, in vol. 42 of Hutchins, *Great Books*, 326, 328.
24. Georg Wilhelm Friedrich Hegel, *Philosophy of Right*, paragraph 21, trans. T.M. Knox, in vol. 46 of Hutchins, *Great Books*, 17.

Hence, the imperative of right is: "Be a person and respect others as persons."[25]

That is to say, man is an object of existence in himself only in virtue of the divine that is in him – that which was designated at the outset as *reason*, which in view of its activity and power of self-determination, was called *freedom*.[26]

This is the sense in which we must understand the state to be based on religion. States and laws are nothing else than religion manifesting itself in the relations of the actual world. This is the essence of the Reformation: man is in his very nature destined to be free.[27]

- JOHN STUART MILL (1806–73). In his famous essay *On Liberty*, Mill advocates unlimited freedom till he comes to the point of discussing the possibility of a person selling himself into serfdom. Regarding this, he writes:

But by selling himself for a slave, he abdicates his liberty, he foregoes any future use of it beyond that single act. He therefore defeats, in his own case, the very purpose which is the justification of allowing him to dispose of himself. He is no longer free; but is thenceforth in a position which has no longer the presumption in its favor, that would be afforded by his voluntarily remaining in it. The principle of freedom cannot require that he should be free not to be free. It is not freedom to be allowed to alienate his freedom.[28]

The common thread in the thoughts of philosophers and theologians throughout history is the connection between morality and liberty. Taken together, we arrive at humanity's most noble characteristic: the *dignity* of every human being. And it is this dignity that serves as the fundamental value, that lays the foundation for human rights. In truth, human dignity establishes the right to have rights.

---

25. Ibid., paragraph 36. 46:21.
26. Georg Wilhelm Friedrich Hegel: *Philosophy of History*, introduction, III, trans. J. Sibree, in vol. 46 of Hutchins, *Great Books*, 168.
27. Ibid., "The German World," section III, 350.
28. John Stuart Mill, *On Liberty*, chapter 5, "Applications," in vol. 43 of Hutchins, *Great Books*, 316.

Writing on the history of law, Sir Henry Sumner Maine reveals the advanced state of human rights in Roman times, at least on a theoretical level. So we learn from his classic *Ancient Law*.

Maine notes that Roman jurisconsults of the Antonine era established that "*Quod ad jus naturale attinet, omnes homines aequales sunt*" (As for the natural law, all men are equal). Assuming a law of nature, and assuming that man-made law bears – at least in some aspects – a direct relationship to natural law, then, the separation of various categories of people into different classes with varying statuses is not a legal reality. Maine explains that this axiom bore great significance to the Roman legal system, for it established that in situations in which Roman law was taken to be in accord with natural law, all classes of Roman residents had equal legal status, whether citizens or foreigners, freemen or slaves.

Maine points out that when the Roman jurisconsults wrote "*aequales sunt*" (all men are equal), they meant exactly that. Modern civilians, on the other hand, employ the same words "in the sense of 'all men ought to be equal.'"[29]

In Roman law, moral and legal principles were frequently interconnected, sometimes superposed. As we find in Roman sources, *Juris praecepta sunt haec: Honeste vivere, alterum non laedere, suum cuique tribuere,* meaning that the basic principles of law are to live honorably, not to harm any other person, and to render to each his own.[30] Roman law demanded that each person respect these principles as society's fundamental norms. In light of the obligations to refrain from harming others and to render to each his own, the first precept – to live honorably – could seem superfluous. In fact, however, it was meant to cover those acts that are not determined by laws, but are expected as part of a moral code.[31] And so we have in Roman law the intertwinement of the principles of morality and law. The principles that command not to harm any other person and render to each his own recognize the equality of every human being, thereby establishing human *dignity*.

But the idea of human dignity goes back even farther – to humanity's earliest source, to the biblical narrative of the creation of man in the image of

---

29. Henry Sumner Maine, *Ancient Law* (London: Oxford University Press, 1959), 76–77.
30. Ulpianus, *Libro primo regularum*, dig. 1.1.10.
31. Jose Carlos de Matos Peixoto, *Curso de Direito Romano*, 2nd ed. (Rio de Janeiro: Fortaleza, 1950), 1:177.

God.[32] This account stresses the idea that Homo sapiens was implanted and inspired with nobility and dignity. From this followed the idea of fraternity, as described by the prophet Malachi: "Have we not all one father? Hath not one God created us? Why do we deal treacherously every man against his brother, profaning the covenant of our fathers?"[33] The notion of equality of all men is further symbolized in the Talmudic passage that tells us that the clay with which Adam was created had been gathered in all corners of the earth.[34]

In his *Rights of Man* (1791), Thomas Paine notes that even if the biblical narrative about man's creation does not have divine authority, it at least has historic authority. The account shows that the equality of men, far from being a modern doctrine, is the oldest registered idea.[35]

Nathan Feinberg reflects on the strangeness that "those engaged in the history of human rights only rarely mention the fact that ancient Hebrew religious thought is concerned with the inherent *dignity* of Man and gives special prominence to the principle that all who are created in the image of God are equal – a principle clearly reflected in the status which the law of Moses assigns to 'the stranger that sojourns among you' and in the liberal attitude of that law towards the slave, as compared with that of other peoples."[36]

Sadly there has been – and continues to be – a tendency to ascribe the origins of the cardinal principle of human dignity to Christianity, with total disregard for Christianity's origins in the Old Testament.

One characteristic example is Josef L. Kunz's claim that the idea of the "rights of man" has its origin in Christianity, that the Catholic natural law as expressed by St. Thomas of Aquinas and by the Spaniards Francisco de Vitoria and Suarez teaches the equality of all men. Kunz writes that "it is the Catholic natural law which emphasizes the *dignity* of man as a rational creature, participating in the *lex externa*, made to the image of God and having

---

32. Genesis 1:26–7. In his commentary to the Pentateuch, J.H. Hertz, former chief rabbi of the United Kingdom, calls Genesis's declaration of man as the image of God "the Magna Carta of Humanity." See Sacks, *The Great Partnership*, 366.
33. Malachi 2:10.
34. Babylonian Talmud, *Sanhedrin* 38a; *Pirkei d'Rabbi Eliezer* 11.
35. Haim Cohn, *Human Rights in Jewish Law* (Hoboken, NJ: Ktav, 1984), 149.
36. Feinberg, *Studies in International Law*, 293.

an eternal destiny." He adds that it is the Catholic natural law that knows no discriminations as to race and color.[37]

As demonstrated above, the principle of equality was firmly established in the Law of Moses, as the better informed Catholic theologians and historians have recognized. One of the great historians of the law and of the Catholic Church, Jean Gaudemet, stresses the influence of the Old Testament as a source of canon law.[38]

Jonathan Sacks, an influential modern Jewish thinker, carried the idea of the will of the people to the highest degree: the need for the people's willing acceptance of the Law of God, as symbolized in the Sinaitic transmission of the commandments in the form of a covenant.[39]

These fundamental ideas concerning human dignity and equality are the philosophical and theological values that have guided human thinking throughout millennia and that have led to the legal principles enshrined in our modern documents.

In the Words of American Presidents

Three American presidents wrote on liberty, freedom, and the rights of man:

> God who gave us life gave us *liberty*. And can the liberties of a nation be thought secure when we have removed their only firm basis, a conviction in the minds of the people that these liberties are of the Gift of God? (Thomas Jefferson, *Notes on the State of Virginia*, Query XVIII, p. 237)

---

37. Josef L. Kunz, "The United Nations Declaration of Human Rights," *American Journal of International Law* 43, no. 2 (April 1949): 316. The tendency to attribute to Christianity the origin of human dignity is found in many scholarly works. Eric Posner, for instance, in his *The Twilight of Human Rights Law* (Inalienable Rights Series [Oxford: Oxford University Press, 2014], 20), states: "These ideas can be found in one form or another throughout recorded history, including in the major religions, and especially Christianity, with its radical notion that all humans are equal in the eyes of God."

38. Jean Gaudemet, *Les sources du droit de l'église en occident du IIe au VIIe siècle* (Paris: Cerf, 1985), 15–16. See also Adolphe Tardif, *Histoire des sources du droit canonique* (Aalen: Scientia Verlag, 1974), 21, 27, 40; and David Flusser, *Jewish Sources in Early Christianity*, trans. John Glucker (Tel Aviv: Mod Books, 1993).

39. Jonathan Sacks, *A Letter in the Scroll: Understanding Our Jewish Identity and Exploring the Legacy of the World's Oldest Religion* (New York: Free Press, 2000), 24, 118.

Those who deny *freedom* to others, deserve it not for themselves; and, under a just God, cannot long retain it. (Abraham Lincoln, Letter to Henry Pierce, April 6, 1859)

The *rights of man* come not from the generosity of the state but from the hand of God. (John F. Kennedy, Inaugural Address, January 20, 1961)[40]

Concept and Hierarchical Position of Principles

In every realm of the law we deal with principles as distinguished from rules. The former have the higher position, carry more weight, and are fundamental in orientating the legislator and the courts. Human rights, as set in the UDHR and in every constitutional system, form the basic principles on which the whole legal order is built and its rules established.

Different classifications have been employed in the use of the word *principles.*

- FUNDAMENTAL PRINCIPLES. In its Strasbourg Declaration, the Council of Europe referred to the organization's *fundamental principles.*[41] Likewise, a commentator on the UNIDROIT Principles of International Commercial Contracts referred to the *"fundamental principles* or basic ideas that are expressly stated in the UNIDROIT Principles."[42]

- FIRST PRINCIPLES. In some sources, both old and more recent, we find the concept of *first principles.*

  In the seventeenth century, Blaise Pascal stated that "we know the truth, not only by the reason, but also by the heart, and it is in this last way that we know *first principles.* ... And it is ... useless and absurd for reason to demand from the heart proofs of her *first principles."*[43]

---

40. Cited in Sacks, *The Great Partnership*, 128.

41. "We, Heads of State and Governments of the Member States of the Council of Europe ... solemnly reaffirm our attachment to the *fundamental principles* of the Council of Europe – pluralist democracy, respect for human rights, the rule of law. ... " "Basle Committee on Banking Supervision: Basle Core Principles for Effective Banking Supervision," September 22, 1997, *International Legal Materials* 37, no. 2 (March 1998): 435. The emphasis is my own in quotations throughout this section.

42. M.J. Bonell, *An International Restatement of Contract Law*, 2nd ed. (New York: Transnational, 1997), 58.

43. Blaise Pascal, *Pensés*, trans. W.F. Trotter, in vol. 33 of Hutchins, *Great Books*, 223n282.

Moses Mendelssohn wrote that "in order to place this in a proper light, I may be allowed to ascend to *first principles* and to examine more closely the origin of the rights of coercion and the validity of contracts among men."[44]

In the field of private international law we find Antoine Pillet, who wrote about the "*premiers principles*."[45] And in the realm of court decisions, Justice Holmes, of the US Supreme Court, closed one of his important opinions saying, "the Constitution and the *first principles* of legal thinking allow the law of the place where a contract is made to determine the validity and consequences of the act."[46]

GENERAL PRINCIPLES OF LAW OR GENERAL PRINCIPLES. In legal literature and in judicial decisions appears the concept of *general principles of law* or *general principles*. In the Guardianship Convention case between Netherlands and Sweden, decided by the International Court of Justice, Judge Lauterpacht stated that public policy is a *general principle of law* in the field of conflicts of law (private international law).[47] One of the earlier authorities on this field of law, Josephus Jitta, referred to "the system of the *general principles* of private international law."[48]

The Institut de Droit International at its 1989 session in Santiago de Compostela approved a resolution on arbitration between states, state enterprises, and state entities and foreign enterprises. Article 6 of the resolution stated that in determining the law applicable to the substance of the dispute, the parties may choose principles and rules "from different national legal systems as well as from non-national sources such as principles of international law, *general principles of law*, and the usages of international commerce," and also "*general principles* of public and private international law, as well as *general principles* of international arbitration."

44. Moses Mendelssohn, *Jerusalem, or On Religious Power and Judaism*, trans. Allan Arkush (Hanover: Brandeis University Press, 1983), 45.

45. Antoine Pillet, *Principes de droit international privé* (Paris: Pedone, 1903), vii, x, 18, 375.

46. Mutual Life Insurance Co v. Liebing, 259 US 209 (1922).

47. *Dicey and Morris on the Conflict of Laws*, ed. Lawrence Collins, 12th ed. (London: Sweet and Maxwell, 1993), 88n2.

48. Josephus Jitta, *Metodo del Derecho Internacional Privado*, trans. J.F. Prida (Madrid: La Espana Moderna), 132.

The most important demonstration of the relevance of the *general principles* is article 38 of the statute of the International Court of Justice. When listing the sources that the court will resort to, the statute includes "the *general principles of law* recognized by civilized nations."

• OTHER PRINCIPLES. We find in the literature on law, philosophy of law, and legal theory a great variety of adjectives for principles, such as *guiding principles, great principles, underlying general principles, logical principles, universal principles, universally accepted principles, generally accepted principles, historical principles, directing principles, leading principles, established principles, principles of legal thinking,* and *superior principles.*

• OTHER TERMS. These include principles of law recognized as normative by civilized nations, principles of law normally recognized by civilized nations in general, leading principles of modern civilization, and relevant principles of international law. The French Cour de Cassation referred to "*principes de justice universelle… considérés dans l'opinion publique comme doués de valeur international absolue*" (principles of universal justice considered by public opinion as having absolute international value).[49]

The Relativity of Principles in Time and Space

There are different categories of principles, distinguished in accordance with various classifications. Firstly, there are general philosophical/natural/moral/legal principles that derive from logical speculation, from natural law, and from the deeply held values of human morality that have prevailed in the minds of men from time immemorial. These include the Decalogue's respect for human life, Aristotle's non-contradiction, Cicero's self-preservation, the Romans' golden triple rule, and Locke's tenderness for one's offspring. These principles are absolute; they do not change across time and space.

Other principles have evolved as a result of men's and women's learning and suffering. Though they are not yet accepted universally, they are expected to become absolute someday. An obvious example of this category is the right of every human being to liberty and equality. Similar principles exist in each and every field of law – theoretical foundations for the good functioning of

---

49. Lautour v. veuve Guiraud, Bertrand Ancel and Yves Lequette, *Grands arrêts de la jurisprudence française de droit international privé*, 3rd ed. (Paris: Dalloz, 1998), 147.

society and of human relations and transactions. Some are millenary, some are recent; most have not been committed to codes or statutes but have still been respected by legislators, judges, and people in general. In private law and in the field of business transactions, the principle of good faith and fair dealing – translated in some but not all European civil codes – has been the ideal norm among peoples across space and time.

There are other principles that are specific to certain periods or places. The Universal Declaration of Human Rights, for example, contains rights of different categories, which may bring us to establish a scale of priorities and a notion of hierarchy, an analysis that may differ from one nation to another, and from one epoch to another.

But what presumably will get unanimous acceptance is the one principle that rises above all other principles: the right to life, which concentrates the essence of human dignity.

With relation to this theme we shall see in another chapter the debate between the great jurists Richard Posner and Aharon Barak, as well as a legal opinion delivered by the International Court of Justice, concerning certain measures that succeeded in keeping Israeli lives protected and avoiding new wars. These measures may indeed sacrifice certain rights of the Palestinians for a certain period of time, but they may lead to peace and the future return of all human rights to all the affected people. On the other hand, the loss of life on one side leads to the elimination of all, or of most, human rights on both sides.

Terrorism comes to destroy life and to cause war. Should one fight against it with one hand tied behind one's back – by having to respect the human rights of the terrorists – or with both hands free? This was the debate between the two jurists.

Everything should be endeavored, all rights must be sacrificed when needed, in order to save human lives, to save minorities, to guarantee the future of humankind.

Human dignity, liberty, freedom – in fact, all human rights – depend on the right to life.

Nobel Peace laureate Elie Wiesel and Judge Thomas Buergenthal are two great fighters for human rights. They both suffered in concentration camps; they saw death surrounding them day and night; they lost their liberty, their human dignity. They survived. They rose from the ashes of the Holocaust and reconquered their dignity and their human rights. And they became beacons for our civilization. Irwin Cotler describes Holocaust survivors as "the true heroes of humanity [who] witnessed and endured the worst of inhumanity, but somehow found, in the depths of their own humanity, the courage to go on, to rebuild their lives as they helped build our communities."[50]

There is only one "fundamental human right" – the one that guarantees life. The other human rights protect this life from all kinds of suffering and evil and guarantee a decent existence.

This distinction of the right to life as a separate, higher class of human right, standing above all other human rights, is not commonly accepted in legal literature. Theodor Meron, in an essay that discusses the hierarchy of human rights, states:

> But except in a few cases (e.g., the right to life or to freedom from torture), to choose which rights are more important than other rights is exceedingly difficult. It is fraught with personal, cultural and political bias and, to make matters worse, has not been addressed by the international community as a whole, perhaps because of the improbability of reaching a meaningful consensus.[51]

As seen in this text, Judge Meron equates the right to life with the right to freedom from torture.

Carmen Tiburcio, a Brazilian scholar of international law, references Meron's point that international human rights instruments use the terms "human rights," "freedoms," "fundamental human rights," and "fundamental freedoms" interchangeably. This leads Tiburcio to the conclusion that "fundamental rights" and "human rights" are the same. She introduces her study on the human rights of aliens by establishing that

> these fundamental rights, for the purposes of this work, comprise the right to life, the right to personal freedom (not to be subjected to torture, slavery or illegal arrest), right not to be discriminated against (equality before the law) and right not to be incriminated under *ex post facto* laws.[52]

50. Irwin Cotler, "Universal Lessons of the Holocaust," *Jerusalem Post*, January 24, 2014.
51. Theodor Meron, "On a Hierarchy of International Human Rights," *American Journal of International Law* 80, no. 1 (January 1986): 4.
52. Carmen Tiburcio, *The Human Rights of Aliens under International and Comparative Law* (The Hague, Netherlands: Martinus Nijhoff, 2001), 75.

The Universal Declaration of Human Rights in its article 3 equally prioritizes the "rights to life, liberty and security of person."

Similarly, the American Law Institute's Restatement of the Foreign Relations Law of the United States provides in its section 702, under "Customary International Law of Human Rights," that "a state violates international law if, as a matter of state policy, it practices, encourages, or condones (a) genocide, (b) slavery or slave trade, (c) the murder or causing the disappearance of individuals, (d) torture or other cruel, inhuman, or degrading treatment or punishment, (e) prolonged arbitrary detention, (f) systematic racial discrimination, or (g) a consistent pattern of gross violations of internationally recognized human rights."

Indeed, the tendency is to equate the right to life with other fundamental human rights and not to distinguish it as a separate class, standing above all other human rights.

However, the Covenant on Civil and Political Rights provides in article 6 that "every human being has the inherent right to life. This right shall be protected by law. No one shall be arbitrarily deprived of his life."

Though the international community is hesitant to ascribe a hierarchy to human rights, in truth the establishment of the right to life as the one and only "fundamental" human right provides a clear lens with which to view the complicated tangle of human rights.

Chapter Six
The Misconceived Universal Declaration of Human Rights

The Strange Origins of the Universal Declaration of Human Rights

The supposedly basic inspiration for drafting a Universal Declaration of Human Rights was the cruel persecution, the horrors, the atrocities perpetrated by the Nazi regime against the Jews of Europe – the Holocaust. The most thorough report on the origins, drafting, and intent of the declaration was written by Johannes Morsink, who read all the minutes of the hundreds of meetings of different UN bodies – the collective work that resulted in the final document, based on which he affirms that the pivotal inspirational motivation was the Holocaust, as "without the delegates' shared moral revulsion against that event, the Declaration would never have been written."[1] He refers to the statement in the declaration's preamble that "disregard and contempt for human rights have resulted in barbarous acts which have outraged the conscience of mankind" and affirms that "this shared outrage explains why the declaration has found such widespread support."[2]

The drafting of the declaration lasted almost two years. It occupied various commissions, subcommissions, committees, and a few permanent organs

---

1. Johannes Morsink, *The Universal Declaration of Human Rights: Origins, Drafting and Intent* (Philadelphia: University of Pennsylvania Press, 1999), xiii–xiv.
2. Ibid., 91.

of the United Nations,[3] and involved the participation of dozens of country delegations holding UN membership, who discussed all aspects related to the dignity of the human being and his fundamental rights, always returning to the tragic events of the Second World War. In his meticulous report, Morsink states that the drafters were aware of how far the nazification of the German legal system had gone, and they evidently felt that only a clear statement of the separate issues involved could set the record straight. This meant delineating all the legal rights that by the middle of the twentieth century had become part of the jurisprudential systems of all civilized nations.

And yet, the declaration did not do anything toward securing peoples of the world against genocide, against systematic atrocities. No clear empowerment was given to the United Nations and/or to any group of member states to interfere immediately in order to save populations under physical persecution.

All the resolutions of the United Nations – starting with the Universal Declaration of Human Rights, proceeding with the two basic covenants, and continuing with the various conventions approved during the following decades – concentrated on statements of principles, legal concepts, general rules, and multiple obligations. They were all focused on protecting individual persons; they said nothing about saving collectivities doomed by the powers of evil. The only exception is the Genocide Convention, which prescribes protection of human groups through prevention and punishment. However, the failure of this fundamental convention is that it concentrated on punishment, leaving the prevention aspect undefined and inoperative, and consequently ineffective.

Three points should be taken into consideration. Firstly, even after Hitler's racial theories and plans became known, the nations that had inscribed in their constitutions and other fundamental documents most of the principles that years later were set in the Universal Declaration remained totally passive. The United States, England, the South American countries, and many other

---

3. The Nuclear Committee, consisting of eight members, held eighteen meetings in May 1946. At its suggestion, an eighteen-member commission was created that held eighty-one meetings. At the same time, a drafting committee, consisting of eight members, held forty-four meetings. Then the Third Committee on Social, Humanitarian and Cultural Affairs had one hundred fifty meetings. Finally, the General Assembly adopted the declaration. See ibid., 28.

nations could have saved the Jews whom the Nazis were persecuting and murdering, but they refused to extend any help.

Secondly, the very people who were drafting the declaration – some of the UN's most important members – were committing atrocities against innocent civilians even as they worked on the declaration. We refer to the English policy toward the Jewish survivors who were trying to reach Palestine, which involved sending the Jews back to Europe and its camps or interning them in Cyprus; and the Batang Kali massacre by British troops on December 12, 1948, during the Malayan Emergency, which killed twenty-four unarmed villagers. As well, history registers the cruel Belgian policies in the Congo, the atrocious measures of the French in North Africa, the Russians' murderous treatment of dissenters, and the Americans' severe discrimination against African Americans. And yet, the delegates of these countries were among the most vocal in meetings on the declaration's wording.

And thirdly, it is much easier to transport evil theories into practice than to implement bona fide, idealistic values, as the development of modern, post–World War II history abundantly proves.

Based on the official registries of the Commission on Human Rights, Morsink shows how the various articles of the declaration were produced as a response to Hitler's racist theories and how this purpose was stressed by delegates to the different committees that worked on the declaration.

The Nazi policy against the Jews could only succeed because of the hate inherent in the German soul, explained by some as stemming from jealousy of the Jews due to their success in medicine, law, journalism, art, and other fields of human creativity. In a word, the German citizen was profoundly antisemitic, which made it possible for Hitler to implement his diabolic plan. This accounts for the immediate, positive response to Hitler's theories and programs by practically all classes of the German people, including the legal society.

In a conference of German law professors, "it was the consensus of the assembled jurists that 'the concept of race is closely linked to the concept of law.'"[4]

And yet, there is not a single article in the declaration regarding antisemitism or hate incitement toward other peoples. There are no rules in favor of

4. Ibid., 45.

tolerance and respect for other religions and other races, only a guarantee of freedom of religion as a right of each individual. Everything in the declaration is set in the singular; there is not a word about the communal perspective.

I do not claim that the plural approach would necessarily have helped to avoid all the genocides and atrocities that followed. But at least it would have been a more exact demonstration of the repudiation of the Nazi bestiality. Eventually, it could have contributed to an effective application of the Genocide Convention, as far as prevention is concerned.

Simple questions arise: In what measure does the Universal Declaration carry more authority, more enforceability, than the legal system of each country, as far as the behavior of their people and the policies of their governments in the internal matters of that nation are concerned? And further than that, did the civilized nations respect the principles of their legal systems beyond their own territories, such as France in her North African colonies, England in India and other colonies, Belgium in the Congo, Italy in Libya, and so on? If not, would the UDHR have any stronger effect than the principles enshrined in the national constitutional systems? Perhaps this was the hope of the drafters, but it turned out to be mere wishful thinking.

On the other hand, for nations that had not inscribed these principles in their legal systems, would the Universal Declaration have any effect?

From the discussions that went on in the various commissions of the UN on the specific articles of the declaration, it comes out very clearly that the declaration is a direct result of the Fuehrer's plans and the Nazi party's legal system.[5] Because Hitler said this or that, because the Nazis did this or that, because a Nazi court decided this or that, we, the UN, must create an article that contradicts those statements and those policies. Rarely would a rule, constitutional or otherwise, of one or more of the state members of the world organization serve as a model. The model was always to contradict, to oppose Hitler and his Nazi regime.

When a delegate in the Third Committee observed that the principles set in the declaration were too well known and did not need to be stated again, Cassin responded that the argument "was invalid in light of recent events. Within the preceding years millions of men had lost their lives, precisely because those principles had been ruthlessly flouted, therefore it was essential

5. Ibid., 43–45.

that the UN should again proclaim to mankind those principles which had come so close to extinction and should refute the abominable doctrine of fascism."[6] The belief in the power of a mere proclamation was indeed the tonic of the assembled delegates.

The extent to which the declaration has been interpreted as connected to Nazi Germany's atrocities has reached the point that we read, with reference to articles 3, 4, and 5,[7] that these rules "are not simply Enlightenment reflexes, but profound reactions to what went on in the concentration camps."[8] These rights had been established by the Western world on different occasions and in different ways long before Hitler's perversities, so it is not very plausible to connect them with the events of the war that had just ended.

Another such grandiloquent but equally equivocal statement is made by analysts of the declaration who comment that the nazification of the German legal system taught the drafters that the strongest protection against systematic human rights violations is the kind of legal system articles 6–12 prescribe. These are the articles that deal with the guarantees of legal protection, inclusive in courts of law. The German constitution carried all these guarantees; yet the German leadership, followed by the majority of its people and mainly by the legal circles, accepted the total corruption of its juridical system and the systematic violation of all human rights.

Other illustrations of the ostensible influence of Hitler's crimes on the drafters of the UDHR are offered as follows:

- Article 9 ("No one shall be subjected to arbitrary arrest, detention or exile") derived from what had occurred in Nazi Germany, which Ingo Muller classifies as "the readiness of the Nazi courts to bow to the wishes of their political masters."[9]
- Article 10 ("Everyone is entitled in full equality to a fair and public hearing by an independent and impartial tribunal in the determination of his

---

6. Glendon, *A World Made New*, 38–39.
7. Article 3: "Everyone has the right to life, liberty and security of person."
Article 4: "No one should be held in slavery or servitude; slavery and the slave trade shall be prohibited in all their forms."
Article 5: "No one shall be subjected to torture or to cruel, inhuman or degrading treatment or punishment."
8. Morsink, *Universal Declaration*, 331.
9. Ibid., 49.

rights and obligations and of any criminal charge against him") was drafted precisely to counteract the lack of independence of Nazi courts.[10]
- Article 11 (no punishment based on retroactivity of the law) was included because this principle was constantly violated by the Nazis.[11]

And so, it is claimed, Hitler and the Nazi regime were the guidelines of the drafting and redrafting of the Universal Declaration. As Morsink comments on the declaration's preamble ("Whereas disregard and contempt for human rights have resulted in barbarous acts which have outraged the conscience of mankind . . ."), this outrage was the drafters' main motivation for proclaiming the declaration.[12]

In reality, the connection between the declaration and Hitler's program is very weak. Whereas the declaration proclaims that all human beings are born free and equal in dignity and rights, Hitler's campaign was based on the extravagant contention that Jews were subhumans. And if a future Hitler will so declare, what influence can the declaration have? What about those Muslims who consider Jews as pigs, quoting their holy sources? The declaration does not define who is a human being, and so it does not prohibit the return to the Nazis' absurdities, nor does it affect the radical Muslim view of the Jew, and perhaps of those whom they call "infidels" in general.

In defense of the UDHR, one could claim that these extravagances would be barred by article 6, which states that "everyone has the right to recognition everywhere as a person before the law." And article 16 of the International Covenant on Civil and Political Rights includes a similar statement.

Articles 13 and 14 assert the freedom of movement and residence, the right to leave any country, and the right to asylum. Morsink claims that the adoption of these rights can also be traced directly to the experience of the Second World War. "For many Jews, gypsies and others hunted down by the Nazis, to be able to leave Germany and be granted asylum elsewhere was a matter of life or death and therefore a question of their human rights."[13]

However, if we go back to the historical development of World War II, the denial of asylum to the Jews persecuted by the Nazis was the policy followed

10. Ibid., 51.
11. Ibid., 53.
12. Ibid., 329.
13. Ibid., 332.

by the United States, Canada, and all the other countries of the American continent, while Great Britain had closed the doors of Palestine to the Jews. So the need to establish an international right to asylum has much less connection to Nazi Germany than to the so-called "Allies."

Similar to Morsink, Daniel Cohen relates several articles of the declaration to what happened to the Jews during the Nazi regime. He points to article 7, which guarantees universal equality before the law, article 13 on the right to leave a country, article 14 on the right to seek asylum from persecution, and article 15 on the right to a nationality – all rights that had been denied the Jews by Germany.[14] In spite of all this, it is important to emphasize that there is not one paragraph, not one line in the whole declaration that guarantees that in the future, a persecuted people, a racial tribe, or a religious or ethnic group will be protected by the United Nations.

The causal relationship between the atrocities committed during the Second World War and the Universal Declaration of Human Rights came out again very clearly during the final UN General Assembly debate in December 1948. This is the way various delegates expressed themselves on that occasion:

- Charles Malik (Lebanon): "The document was inspired by opposition to the barbarous doctrines of Nazism and fascism."
- Lakshimi Menon (India): "The Declaration was born from the need to reaffirm those rights after their violation during the war."
- Bodil Begtrup (Denmark): "The drafters wanted to avoid the horrors of a new war."
- Jorge Carrera Andrade (Ecuador): "From the ruins of destruction wrought by the Second World War, man had once again fanned the immortal flame of civilization, freedom and law."
- Count Henri Carton (Belgium): "The essential merit of the Declaration was to emphasize the high dignity of the human person after the outrages to which men and women had been exposed during the recent war."

14. G. Daniel Cohen, "The Holocaust and the 'Human Rights Revolution,'" in Iriye, Goedde, Hitchcock, *Human Rights Revolution*, 60–61. Cohen refers to the websites of the United Nations and the European Union as propagators of this foundational narrative and notes that numerous historians of human rights have also contended that the first international guarantees aimed at sheltering individuals from abusive states stemmed predominantly from Holocaust awareness (ibid., 53–54).

- René Cassin (France): "The last war had taken on the character of a crusade for human rights," and the Declaration "was the most vigorous and the most urgently needed of humanity's protest against oppression."
- Geoffrey Wilson (UK): "The historical situation in which the Committee met...was one [in which] Germany and other enemy countries during the war had completely ignored what mankind had regarded as fundamental human rights and freedoms. The Committee met as a first step toward providing the maximum possible safeguard against that sort of thing in the future."[15]

The records of the first meeting of the Commission on Human Rights of the Economic and Social Council, held on Monday, April 29, 1946, registers the presentation of Mr. Henri Laugier, assistant secretary-general of the UN in charge of social affairs, who said the following:

> You will have to look for a basis for a fundamental declaration on human rights acceptable to all the United Nations, the acceptance of which will become the essential condition of the admission in the international community. You will have before you the difficult but essential problem to define the violation of human rights within a nation, which would constitute a menace to the security and peace of the world and the existence of which is sufficient to put in movement the mechanism of the United Nations for the maintenance of peace and security. You will have to suggest the establishment of machinery of observation which will find and denounce the violations of the rights of man all over the world. Let us remember that if this machinery had existed a few years ago, if it had been powerful and if the universal support of public opinion had given it authority, international action would have been mobilized immediately against the first authors and supporters of fascism and nazism. The human community would have been able to stop those who started the war at the moment when they were still weak and the world catastrophe would have been avoided."[16]

15. Morsink, *Universal Declaration*, 36–37.
16. Cited in Morsink, *Universal Declaration*, 14.

The various drafts that were composed in the different stages of the preparatory work of the declaration[17] never got near the point of formulating a structure that would observe, detect, and denounce violations of human rights and subsequently mobilize immediate action in order to stop the warmongers and avoid human catastrophe. Excepting a reference in the preamble of the final text to "peace in the world" and "development of friendly relations between nations," nothing in the actual text of the declaration relates in any way to "peace and security," as proposed in the initial conception.

In a more realistic analysis, Mary Ann Glendon maintains that a cool look at the document leads to the consideration that as far as the great powers of the day were concerned, the main purpose of the United Nations was to establish and maintain collective security in the years after the war. The human rights project was peripheral, launched as a concession to small countries and in response to the demands of numerous religious and humanitarian associations that the Allies live up to their war rhetoric by providing assurances that the community of nations would never again countenance such massive violations of human dignity. But Britain, China, France, the United States, and the Soviet Union did not expect these assurances to interfere with their national sovereignty.[18]

History has proven that the great powers were right in their skepticism and that the idealists never got what they had hoped for.

And yet, the connection of the Universal Declaration with Nazism and its crimes was generally accepted by the scholarly community. The analysis of various authors demonstrates the generalization of the theory.

1. Shigeru Oda:

   The cruelties and oppression of the Nazi regime in Europe brought the conviction both during and after the Second World War that the international recognition and protection of human rights for people throughout the world is essential to the maintenance of international peace and order.[19]

17. Glendon (*A World Made New*, 271–314) reproduces the seven drafts.
18. Ibid., xv–xvi.
19. "The Individual in International Law" in *Manual of Public International Law*, ed. Max Sorensen (New York: St. Martin's Press, 1968), 497.

2. A textbook on public international law, written specifically for students in the British law schools:

> However, the Second World War and the suffering inflicted under the Nazi regime gave new impetus to those demanding international recognition and enforcement of fundamental human rights and freedom.[20]

3. Paul G. Loren:

> What ultimately tipped the scale in favor of human rights after the Second World War was the unimagined destruction of human life in the genocide of the Holocaust's Final Solution that exceeded all previously known bounds.[21]

4. Daniel Levy and Natan Sznaider:

> The horrors of the Holocaust formed the background against which human rights norms and a host of other UN conventions initially established their legitimacy.[22]

5. Micheline R. Ishay:

> The horror of the Holocaust would shape now international humanitarian law for decades to come.[23]

---

20. Lord Templeman and Robert Maclean, *Public International Law* (London: Old Bailey, 1997), 192.

21. Paul Gordon Lauren, *The Evolution of International Human Rights: Visions Seen* (Philadelphia: University of Pennsylvania Press, 1998), 291, quoted in Iriye, Goedde, and Hitchcock, *Human Rights Revolution*, 54.

22. "The Institutionalization of Cosmopolitan Morality," 149, as quoted by Cohen, "The Holocaust and the 'Human Rights Revolution,'" in Iriye, Goedde, and Hitchcock, *Humans Rights Revolution*, 55. Cohen refers to the opinion of certain historians that the human-rights movement after the Second World War intentionally moved away from minority rights in favor of individual human rights, and there was little that the Holocaust had to do with this revolution. Cohen considers that "the turn to individual rights characteristic of the 1940s may well have served to hinder third party interference in the Great Powers' affairs, legitimate ethnic cleansing and population transfers, or prevent self-determination of the colonies" (ibid., 57). This view strengthens the critique raised in this chapter that the declaration deals with the rights of individuals but does nothing to protect minorities, which were the real victims of Nazism.

23. *The History of Human Rights: From Ancient Times to the Globalization Era* (Berkeley: University of California Press, 2004), 241. Cited in Cohen, ibid., 55.

A strange analysis of the modern conscience of human rights appears in the work of eminent American scholars, who write, for example, that "concededly, a major reason for this favorable turn of events, partly catalyzed by the Nazi slaughter of six million Jews and the persistent victimization of *apartheid*-controlled black Africans, has been a growing recognition that major denials of sociopolitical and economic justice provoke violence, even war."[24]

The juxtaposition of the Holocaust and South African apartheid is not acceptable. And why mention the African apartheid and not the discrimination that the people of African heritage in the southern states of America were suffering at the same time?

The mistaken view that the protection of individual human rights is to be connected to the Holocaust is accepted even by Thomas Buergenthal, a survivor of Auschwitz who became a world authority on the subject of human rights. He writes:

> Modern international human rights law's development can be attributed to the monstrous violations of human rights of the Hitler era and to the belief that some of these violations might have been prevented had an effective international system for the protection of human rights existed in the days of the League of Nations.[25]

He also states:

> Since the late 1960s, however, the central place occupied by the Holocaust in the remembrance of the Second World War has reshaped our perception of the origins of modern human rights. Now elevated to the rank of iconic "breach of civilization," the Holocaust is today equally portrayed as "civilizer of nations": the epitome of twentieth-century suffering that purportedly fostered the internationalization of human rights and the humanization of international law.[26]

24. Burns H. Weston, Richard A. Falk, Anthony D'Amato, *International Law and World Order: A Problem-Oriented Course*. 2nd ed. (St. Paul, MN: West Publishing, 1990), 628.
25. Buergenthal, *International Human Rights in a Nutshell*, 17.
26. Thomas Buergenthal, "International Law and the Holocaust," in *Holocaust Restitution: Perspectives of the Litigation and Its Legacy*, as quoted by Cohen, "The Holocaust and the 'Human Rights Revolution,'" in Iriye, Goedde, and Hitchcock, *Humans Rights Revolution*, 54.

The author restricts his retroactive optimism on prevention of World War II atrocities to "some of these violations" and stresses that this could only have happened if an effective system of protection of human rights existed, which does not reflect the reality of the system that was approved in 1948 and has been in effect since then.

The fundamental claim I make in the present chapter is that the alleged connection between the Holocaust and the Universal Declaration of Human Rights, as described in so many quoted sources and as proclaimed by the drafters of the UDHR, is totally erroneous.

The drafting of the declaration lasted almost three years, from April 1946 to December 1948. It went through seven drafting stages, occupied hundreds of meetings, received hundreds of amendments and more than a thousand votes in discussions about all kinds of matters, but nothing appears in its text regarding how to secure peoples of the world against genocide or against systematic atrocities. No empowerments are granted to the United Nations and/or to any group of member states to interfere immediately in order to save populations from being persecuted and murdered.

The two basic covenants – the International Covenant on Civil and Political Rights and the International Covenant on Economic, Social and Cultural Rights – were followed by innumerable UN conventions and resolutions, focused on statements of principles, legal concepts, general rules, and multiple obligations. Yet none of them contained anything about saving the doomed by the powers of evil.[27]

The UN charter's chapter 7 foresees action by the United Nations "with respect to threats to the peace, breaches of the peace and acts of aggression," including military measures. However, these have not been put efficiently to use for the benefit of the victims of the most serious human rights violations, as we shall be seeing in chapter 7.

---

27. Morsink (*Universal Declaration*, 20) states that "there are today around two hundred assorted declarations, conventions, protocols, treaties, charters and agreements, all dealing with the realization of human rights in the world. Of these postwar instruments, no fewer than 65 mention in their prefaces or preambles the Universal Declaration of Human Rights as a source of authority and inspiration." This was written in 1999. After that the volume of international documents only grew. The failure of the UDHR, which will be analyzed further on, applies to all of those documents. Eric Posner refers to the existence of three hundred human rights set in the multiple international documents; he enumerates them one by one (*Twilight of Human Rights Law*, 92, 151–61).

The Characterization of the Universal Declaration

Josef L. Kunz declared: "No talk about natural law has saved the Jews from Hitler."[28] With this statement, the author expressed his disagreement with the philosophical school that ties human rights to natural rights. Kunz held that human rights can only be achieved through positivism, by express legal rules. This would have been the basic purpose of the Universal Declaration of Human Rights. And so he goes against the statement of Alfred Verdross that "human rights stand and fall with the recognition of natural law."[29] Kunz proceeds to say that "to us it is exactly to the contrary, they stand and fall with positive law guaranteeing them and giving an effective remedy against their violation in independent and impartial courts."[30]

Now, almost seven decades after the approval of the Universal Declaration of Human Rights, we know that even if we were to attach to the declaration any legal, positivistic character, above natural law, it still did not help the millions who were tortured and murdered by the innumerable dictators who converted the second half of the twentieth century into rivers of blood, or the millions of women and children who have been and continue to be sold out to slavery and sex, or the millions of women cruelly discriminated against in the Muslim countries, or the hundreds of thousands of Christians harassed and persecuted in those countries.

In a judgment by the civil tribunal of Brussels, the Universal Declaration of Human Rights was characterized for what it really is – a mere declaration, without force of law. The court declared:

---

28. Kunz, "The United Nations Declaration of Human Rights," 319.

29. In 1989, in a course delivered at the Hague Academy of International Law, Louis Henkin also maintained that both international law and domestic legal norms in the Christian world had roots in an accepted morality in natural law and had common intellectual progenitors, such as Grotius, Locke, and Vattel ("International Law: Politics, Values, and Functions," *Hague Academy of International Law* 216 [1989]: 208–9). Eric Posner (*Twilight of Human Rights Law*, 11–12), referring to the American Declaration of Independence and the French Declaration of the Rights of Man, reports that at those times people often used the term "natural rights" rather than "human rights," and adds that the terms "meant the same thing."

30. Kunz proceeds to say that "the whole dispute about 'natural law' seems to this writer to be only a terminological quarrel. We men of the Christian Western culture firmly believe in the basic dignity of the human person. These ethical and religious convictions are sources which contribute to the contents of the positive, man-made law: but natural law is not law, but ethics."

However, the Universal Declaration does not have the force of law. Its sole aim is to express the common ideal to be attained by all peoples and all nations in order that by instruction and education, respect for these rights and freedoms may be developed and that measures may be taken progressively to ensure that they are recognized and universally and effectively applied in the future.[31]

This opinion that the UDHR is not a legal instrument has been expressed by various authorities,[32] foremost among them Arthur J. Goldberg, the supreme court justice and United States ambassador to the United Nations:

The Universal Declaration has received universal recognition, but it remains just that, a declaration. In these two words thus are reflected both the hope and the tragedy of human rights in our day. We agree all too often on principles, but practice and enforcement have not kept pace with pronouncements.[33]

The authors of the declaration recognized that it would be relatively easy to reach agreement on the text of a hortatory declaration, but that acceptance of the wording for a legally binding treaty would prove much more difficult to obtain. Therefore the UN Commission on Human Rights decided to work on a declaration and prepare one or more draft treaties thereafter. This resulted in the Universal Declaration of Human Rights in 1948, and many years later in the two covenants – on civil and political rights and on economic, social,

---

31. *M. v. United Nations and Belgium*, Civil Tribunal of Brussels (1966) 45 I.L.R., 446, referred to in Leslie C. Green, *International Law through the Cases*, 4th ed. (Toronto: Carswell, 1978), 157.

32. Ian Brownlie quotes the Corfu Channel case as saying, "The Declaration is not a legal instrument, and some of its provisions, for example the reference to a right of asylum, could hardly be said to represent legal rules. On the other hand, some of its provisions either constitute general principles of law or represent elementary considerations of humanity." *Principles of Public International Law*, 2nd ed. (Oxford: Clarendon Press, 1973), 554. That is a far cry from the proclaimed original intentions of the Commission of Human Rights when it began to draft the declaration, pretending to create a document that would not allow history to repeat the human suffering caused by the Nazi regime.

33. Arthur J. Goldberg, "Our Concerns for Human Rights," *Congress Bi-Weekly* 32, no. 13 (November 15, 1965): 9, as quoted by Weston et al., *International Law and World Order*, 629, who consider Ambassador Goldberg's dictum as "somewhat exaggerated." History has proven how right the ambassador was.

and cultural rights. The covenants entered into force in 1976,[34] yet they too brought about no positive results for the protection of persecuted minorities of all kinds.

The declaration was seen as having only moral force, as binding only in the sphere of conscience. Accordingly, every state was entitled to interpret its provisions in accordance with its own understanding as to the ethical rights and wrongs of any given situation.[35]

As a tendency developed to upgrade the meaning and value of the declaration, international scholars have warned about the need to exercise restraint in describing it as a legally binding instrument.[36]

Actually, denial of its legal character appeared from the very moment of its approval by the General Assembly of the United Nations on November 10, 1948. At that point, the US representative, Mrs. Eleanor Roosevelt, said:

> In giving our approval to the declaration today, it is of primary importance that we keep clearly in mind the basic character of the document. It is not a treaty, it is not an international agreement. It is not and does not purport to be a statement of law or of legal obligation. It is a declaration of basic principles of human rights and freedoms, to be stamped with the approval of the General Assembly by formal vote of its members, and to serve as a common standard of achievement for all peoples of all nations.[37]

34. Buergenthal, *International Human Rights in a Nutshell*, 24–25.

35. Lauterpacht, "The Universal Declaration of Human Rights," 370.

36. In Oppenheim's *International Law*, we read the following careful analysis:

> The Declaration has been of considerable value as supplying a standard of action and of moral obligation. It has been frequently referred to in official drafts and pronouncements, in national constitutions and legislation, and occasionally – with differing results – in judicial decisions. These consequences of the Declaration may be of significance so long as restraint is exercised in describing it as a legally binding instrument. However, in the years since its adoption, the widespread acceptance of the authority of the Declaration has led some to the opinion that while the Declaration as an instrument is not a treaty, its provisions may have come to be the embodiment of new rules of customary international law in the matter. (L.F.L. Oppenheim, *International Law*, 9th ed., vol. 1, *Peace*, ed. Sir Robert Jennings and Sir Arthur Watts [London: Longman, 1997], 1002)

37. *Department of State Bulletin* 19 (1948): 751, as quoted by Henkin et al. in *International Law: Cases and Materials*, 606, and Joseph Modeste Sweeney, T. Oliver Covey, and E. Leech Noyes, *The International Legal System: Cases and Materials*, 3rd ed. (Westbury, NY: Foundation Press, 1988), 629.

On another occasion, at a meeting of the Third Committee, which preceded the UN General Assembly meeting that approved the declaration, Mrs. Roosevelt made an enthusiastic statement about the document, in which she said:

> This Declaration may well become the international Magna Carta of all men everywhere. We hope its proclamation by the General Assembly will be an event comparable to the proclamation of the Declaration of the Rights of Man by the French people in 1789, the adoption of the Bill of Rights by the people of the United States and the adoption of comparable declarations at different times in other countries.[38]

The two quoted statements by Mrs. Roosevelt are not necessarily conflicting. In 1948, still under the impact of the catastrophic consequences of the war, there was a deep urge to create conditions for a better world. But at the same time, there was a careful approach to respect the sovereignty of state members of the UN and not to interfere with their basic legal principles. So while diplomats wished that the declaration would bring about a world of peace and security, they also desired that each state establish through its constitution and

---

In the course of the drafting of the declaration by the Commission on Human Rights in June 1948, Mrs. Roosevelt had said:
> The Declaration should not be in any sense a legislative document. The General Assembly was not a legislative body. . . . It was clear that the Declaration, as envisaged, did not create legal remedies or procedures to ensure respect for the rights and freedoms it proposed to the world; that ideal would have to be achieved by further steps taken in accordance with international and domestic law. The Declaration would have moral, not mandatory, force. (Reproduced by Lauterpacht, "The Universal Declaration of Human Rights," 358n4)

Sweeney et al. (630) quote Humphrey (as a publicist's view), who wrote the following wishful text:
> Even more remarkable than the performance of the United Nations in adopting the Declaration has been its impact and the role which it almost immediately began to play both within and outside the United Nations – an impact and a role which probably exceed the more sanguine hopes of its authors. No other act of the United Nations has had anything like the same impact on the thinking of our time, the best aspirations of which it incorporates and proclaims. It may well be that it will live in history chiefly as a statement of great moral principles. As such its influence is deeper and more lasting than any political document or legal instrument.

I would comment on this statement that from thinking and aspiring to acting there is a considerable distance.

38. Lauterpacht, "The Universal Declaration of Human Rights," 354.

legal system the necessary guarantees for reaching that goal. Mrs. Roosevelt was addressing one and the other position in each of her remarks.

When the declaration was approved, the president of the General Assembly made a statement that expressed both aspects. He began saying that the document was simply a "declaration of rights that does not provide by international convention for States being bound to carry out and give effect to these rights, nor does it provide for enforcement." On the other hand the president of the General Assembly believed the declaration to be

> a first step in a great evolutionary process. It is the first occasion on which the organized community of nations has made a declaration on human rights and fundamental freedoms, and it has the authority of the body of the United Nations as a whole, and millions of people – men, women and children all over the world, many miles from Paris and New York, will turn for help, guidance and inspiration to this document.[39]

A delegate from Australia said:

> For the first time, the international community of nations considered and declared what, in its opinion, are those human rights and fundamental freedoms which every human being, without exception, is entitled to enjoy.... The rights in the Declaration will go forth to the world immeasurably strengthened by the fact that the international community of nations has agreed upon and approved them.... The collective authority of the present Declaration of Human Rights gives the declaration very great weight.[40]

Syria's delegate likewise sang the praises of the ostensible accomplishment: "To-night we can proclaim to the peoples of the world that their goal and their aims have been reached by the United Nations." The representative of Paraguay felt the declaration was "certainly the most harmonious and comprehensive structure yet erected in this field, a flaming force which will lead all mankind toward felicity."[41]

---

39. Ibid. Lauterpacht further wrote: "The practical unanimity of the Members of the United Nation in stressing the importance of the Declaration was accompanied by an equally general repudiation of the idea that the Declaration imposed upon them a legal obligation to respect the human rights and fundamental freedoms which it proclaimed" (ibid., 356).
40. Ibid., 355.
41. Ibid.

Perhaps the most enthusiastic appraisal came from the Belgian representative, who said:

> It seems to us, finally, that very frequent objection has been made to this document by many who pointed out that this was just a statement of platonic wishes, just one more scrap of paper. This is an erroneous statement. In this Declaration, voted by the virtual unanimity of all the Members of the United Nations, there is a moral value and authority which is without precedent in the history of the world, and there is the beginning of a system of international law. The man in the street will claim that he is entitled to the rights proclaimed in this Declaration, and his claims will be supported by the decisions which were taken by the Third Committee and which will subsequently be taken by the General Assembly. There will be, therefore, very great moral prestige and moral authority attaching to this Declaration. Therefore the man in the street claiming certain rights would not simply be an isolated voice crying in the wilderness; it will be a voice upheld by all the peoples of the world represented at this Assembly.[42]

The secretary-general of the United Nations enlightened the General Assembly regarding his estimation of the importance of the document. "This declaration," he claimed, "the first attempt in history to write a 'Bill of Rights' for the whole world, is an important first step in the direction of implementing the general pledges of the Charter concerning human rights."[43]

The intellectual level of the declaration was well defined by comments made at the time of its adoption, to the tune that the "Universal Declaration was written for ordinary men and women, for people of all walks of life and in all the different cultures of the world."[44] Eleanor Roosevelt put this idea very bluntly when she declared that the declaration "was not intended for philosophers and jurists but for the ordinary people."[45]

The history of the declaration's title supposedly helps to clarify the real nature of the document. René Cassin proposed that the original title, "International Declaration," be changed to "Universal Declaration," explaining that "universal" meant that the declaration was morally binding on everyone,

---

42. Ibid.
43. Cited in ibid., 356.
44. Morsink, *Universal Declaration*, 33.
45. Ibid., 34.

not only on the governments that voted for its adoption, as it "was not an 'international' or 'intergovernmental' document, but was addressed to all humanity and founded on a unified conception of the human being."[46] This statement at the same time enhances the moral value of the document and recognizes its nonlegal nature.

Hersch Lauterpacht was diametrically opposed to these optimistic analyses of the declaration. In an extremely legal-logical argumentation, he showed that the document in no way posed a legal constraint on states. Attempting to establish rights for individuals unaccompanied by corresponding duties on the part of states was, in Lauterpacht's eyes, "a juridical heresy."[47] Individual rights, he points out, can only exist "as a counterpart and a product of the duties of the state. There are no rights unless accompanied by remedies. That correlation," he affirmed, "is not only an inescapable principle of juridical logic. Its absence connotes a fundamental and decisive ethical flaw in the structure and conception of the Declaration."[48]

The development of the United Nations' history has never shown any international moral opprobrium toward the states that do not abide by the human rights principles, let alone any substantial legal consequences to their constant, atrocious violations of the principles set both in the declaration and in the covenants.

Pope John XIII, the great prince of the Catholic Church, the pope of peace, fraternity, and reconciliation, praised the declaration in his encyclical Peace on Earth, as "an act of the highest importance."[49] That could be so, provided it developed into concrete legal measures and international action, an aspect outside of the Church's jurisdiction.

The international situation immediately following World War II, with the "iron curtain" formed by Soviet Russia around her satellites and the consequent tension that it caused, brought about the gradual vanishing of

---

46. Glendon, A World Made New, 161, quoting from Cassin, La Pensée et l'Action, 114. Years later, the International Covenant on Civil and Political Rights, approved in 1966 and in force since 1976, established the obligations of each state party to "respect and ensure to all individuals within its territory and subject to its jurisdiction the rights recognized by the present Covenant" (article 2.1).
47. Lauterpacht, "The Universal Declaration of Human Rights," 372.
48. Ibid., 373.
49. Glendon, A World Made New, 132.

the wartime alliance. This made it difficult, if not impossible, to create an enforceable charter of human rights, even if such an ideal might have materialized under normal circumstances.

A weighty reason for the unenforceable terms in which the declaration was approved is exposed by the biographers of René Cassin:

> Among the most powerful opponents of the Universal Declaration were the imperial powers of the time, Great Britain, France, the Netherlands, Portugal and Belgium. These states had absolutely no interest in helping colonized people to turn the Universal Declaration into a weapon to be used against their own supremacy. France opposed measures advanced by Cassin himself: the point at issue was the right of individual petition, which the Quai d'Orsay anticipated would produce an avalanche of claims from colonized people. Cassin made every effort to make the rights of petition acceptable to French diplomats, but to no avail. Manifestly, the Universal Declaration was framed in such a way as to enable the colonial powers to sign it, but once signed, the fight for realizing the aspiration stated in it had just begun.[50]

Interestingly enough, Louis Henkin includes the United Nations Charter, the Universal Declaration of Human Rights, and the two covenants in the section of his book on international law devoted to "International Human Rights Law."[51]

He quotes Sohn and Buergenthal:

> The duty to "observe faithfully and strictly" not only the provisions of the Charter but also of Universal Declaration was proclaimed by the General Assembly in the 1960 Declaration on the Granting of Independence to Colonial Countries and Peoples. Similarly, the 1963 Declaration on the Elimination of All Forms of Racial Discrimination recognized that every State shall "fully and faithfully observe the provisions of... the Universal Declaration of Human Rights." Both declarations were adopted unanimously.

---

50. Winter and Prost, *René Cassin*, 349.
51. Henkin et al., *International Law: Cases and Materials*, 599. This is a far cry from the position of Hersch Lauterpacht, who wrote that "not being a legal instrument, the Declaration would appear to be outside international law. Its provisions cannot properly be the subject-matter of legal interpretation" ("The Universal Declaration of Human Rights," 369).

Taking the above-mentioned developments into account, the unofficial Assembly for Human Rights, which met in Montreal in March 1968, stated that the "Universal Declaration of Human Rights constitutes an authoritative interpretation of the Charter of the highest order, and has over the years become a part of customary international law." The Declaration of Teheran, the official International Conference, which met in Iran's capital in April–May 1968, reached a similar conclusion and proclaimed that the "Universal Declaration of Human Rights states a common understanding of the peoples of the world concerning the inalienable and inviolable rights of all members of the human family and constitutes an obligation of the members of the international community."... The General Assembly of the United Nations in December 1968 endorsed the Proclamation of Tehran "as an important and timely reaffirmation of the principles embodied in the Universal Declaration of Human Rights."[52]

Concluding their view of the declaration, Henkin et al., on a relatively positive note, state the following:

It has been suggested that the Universal Declaration, after the UN charter, is the most influential instrument of the second half of the twentieth century. It underlies the entire international law of human rights, but, as the Declaration itself contemplated, its principal influence may have been to secure the recognition of human rights by states and instill the idea and the principles of human rights into the national constitutions and laws of virtually all states. The Universal Declaration has been copied or incorporated in numerous constitutions of new states.[53]

This is the sweet illusion in which many legal scholars have lived throughout the second part of the twentieth century. The declaration as well as the covenants and the various conventions on different aspects of human rights

52. Louis B. Sohn and Thomas Buergenthal, eds., The International Protection of Human Rights (Indianapolis, IN: Bobbs Merrill, 1972), 518–19, 522, as reproduced in Henkin et al., International Law: Cases and Materials, 606–7.

53. Henkin et al., International Law: Cases and Materials, 608. Theodor Meron (*Human Rights Law-Making in the United Nations: A Critique of Instruments and Process* [Oxford: Clarendon Press, 1986], 276) refers to the Universal Declaration of Human Rights as "a truly remarkable instrument" but does not substantiate or explain in what way the document is remarkable.

suffer from a basic failure: a sizable portion of the member states of the United Nations – more than half – live under dictatorial regimes, some of them with intolerant religious legal systems that do not abide by the most elementary principles and values contained in these international instruments.

Despite the opinion of a few eminent scholars and the proclamations heard in a few UN meetings, in reality, the UDHR and the documents that followed it are not practiced in the larger number of states and so do not protect the majority of humankind.

A classical example is Saudi Arabia, which abstained from the General Assembly vote that approved the declaration because of the article that proclaims equal the rights of men and women to marry and the article that refers to the right to change one's religion (articles 16 and 18). Previously, when the declaration was being discussed in the Third Committee, the Saudi delegate Jamil Boroody accused the drafters of considering "only the standards recognized by Western civilization and ignoring more ancient civilizations which were past the experimental stage, and the institutions of which, for example marriage, had proved their wisdom through the centuries. It was not for the Committee to proclaim the superiority of one civilization over all the others or to establish uniform standards for all the countries in the world."[54] This was an honest position taken by a state that did not, and still does not, respect human rights and makes no secret of it.[55] Similar charges of ethnocentrism were raised by other members of the UN, such as states that made up the Soviet bloc as well as the Union of South Africa.

Morsink, writing at the end of the twentieth century, affirmed that the "document enjoys unprecedented prestige," and that "it has high moral visibility both in courts of law and in the trenches." He refers to a few dozen court decisions that mention the declaration and various constitutions that do the

---

54. Morsink, *Universal Declaration*, 24.
55. Saudi Arabia is not so honest anymore. In 2007 it ratified the treaty banning discrimination against women, whereas by law it subordinates women to men in all legal areas. Punishments meted out in this country follow medieval patterns: "amputation of a hand for theft, stoning for adultery, one hundred lashes of a whip for sexual relations before marriage, death by decapitation for apostasy, etc." (Gilles Cuniberti, *Grands Systèmes de droit contemporains*, according to a book review by Vivian Grosswald Curran, *American Journal of Comparative Law* [2013]: 724).

same. Yet, he adds that "it is still living with the suspicion, nurtured in many intellectual circles, that something went wrong way back at the beginning."[56]

Even if nothing went wrong in the beginning, it is undeniable that as the United Nations tripled in size since 1948, the declaration became a real ethnocentric document, as witnessed by the relative – actually diminutive – application of human rights in the great, ever-growing number of nondemocratic states that became members of the United Nations. It is important to take into consideration that in 1948, at the time the declaration was approved, UN membership was composed of twenty-one countries from North and South America, sixteen European countries, fourteen Asian countries, four African countries, and three South Sea Island countries, a total of fifty-eight member states. In 2013–14 (as registered by the Freedom House study[57]), the United Nations was composed of 194 members, the majority of which were ruled by regimes that were nondemocratic and did not respect human rights. Therefore, despite its title, the Universal Declaration can only have limited applicability, and attempts to enforce it globally are bound to fail.

Wolfgang Friedmann wrote that while in theory the declaration reflects "a universal concern of mankind, in fact, the disparity of standards, systems and values is too great to make an effective international organization possible in this field."[58] This was written in 1964: the fifty years that have gone by have proven the correctness of the Columbia University professor's foresight.

In 2012 we had a clear manifestation of the Universal Declaration's lack of universality – not only de facto, but also de jure. During that year, the Association of Southeast Asian Nations (ASEAN) adopted a human rights declaration at a meeting of the heads of state of the countries belonging to the association.

Articles 6 and 7 of the ASEAN declaration proclaim:

6. The enjoyment of human rights and fundamental freedoms must be balanced with the performance of corresponding duties as every person

---

56. Morsink, *Universal Declaration*, xii–xiii.
57. See above, "An Analysis of Some of the Statements and Principles of the UDHR," in chapter 5.
58. Wolfgang Friedmann, *The Changing Structure of International Law* (New York: Columbia University Press, 1964), 63.

has responsibilities to all other individuals, the community and the society where one lives.

7. All human rights are universal, indivisible, interdependent and inter-related. All human rights and fundamental freedoms in this Declaration must be treated in a fair and equal manner, on the same footing and with the same emphasis. At the same time, the realization of human rights must be considered in the regional and national context bearing in mind different political, economic, legal, social, cultural, historical and religious backgrounds.

The US State Department issued a statement expressing concern at the limitations and qualifications of the ASEAN text, which "could weaken and erode universal human rights and fundamental freedoms as contained in the UDHR."[59]

In a later manifestation, a deputy assistant secretary of state explained US concerns, saying that "the Declaration [of ASEAN] subordinates respect for fundamental freedoms to an assumed cultural context. Yet universal human rights are just that – universal. These rights are not Western, or Eastern. These rights are not subject to regional and national limitation. These rights do not bear in mind political, economic, legal, social, cultural, historical, or religious backgrounds.... Subordinating universal rights to domestic law is a departure from more than 50 years of established international practice of human rights, going back to the UN Declaration."[60]

---

59. John R. Crook, ed., "Contemporary Practice of the United States Relating to International Law: United States Criticizes ASEAN Human Rights Declaration," *American Journal of International Law* 107, no. 1 (January 2013): 238. The State Department's statement includes the following wording: "While part of the ASEAN Declaration adopted November 18 tracks the UDHR, we are deeply concerned that many of the ASEAN Declaration's principles and articles could weaken and erode universal human rights and fundamental freedoms as contained in the UDHR. Concerning aspects include the use of the concept of 'cultural relativism' to suggest that rights in the UDHR do not apply everywhere; stipulating that domestic laws can trump universal human rights; incomplete descriptions of rights that are memorialized elsewhere; introducing novel limits to rights; and language that could be read to suggest that individual rights are subject to group veto."

60. Deputy Assistant Secretary for Bureau of Democracy, Human Rights, and Labor Daniel Baer, U.S.-ASEAN Symposium on the ASEAN Human Rights Declaration, November 29, 2012, http://www.humanrights.gov/dyn/u.s.-asean-symposium-on-the-asean-human -rights-declaration.

The concerns and the critique of the State Department are naive, if not hypocritical, as the ASEAN declaration does nothing more than honestly proclaim what has been known and practiced from the very beginning by the nondemocratic states – either total or at least partial rejection of the fundamental principles of human rights proclaimed in the various UN documents.

In 1983, the review of the International Commission of Jurists published an analysis of the declaration, under the heading "The Universal Declaration at 35." Authored by Philip Alston, the review notes:

> It is sometimes suggested that the doctrines of human rights as embodied in the Universal Declaration of Human Rights may not be relevant to societies with a non-Western cultural tradition or a socialist ideology. In its extreme form such an approach would thoroughly undermine the existing system for the international protection of human rights and create a "free for all" situation in which each dictator and each military junta, as well as each democratically elected but embattled government could design its own bill of rights to suit not only local traditions but also its own self-interest.[61]

Alston and the State Department personnel would do well to go back to the classic commentaries on the UDHR and to the declarations of the drafters of the document – as referred to above – in order to better comprehend that the Universal Declaration is neither universal nor enforceable.

Besides, what is preferable – a simple hypocritical adhesion to the UDHR by a state or group of states that manifestly do not respect its principles, or an honest declaration that restricts human rights, so that the rest of the world knows exactly where a state or a group of states stands on the matter?

Another wishful text proclaims the following:

> It is sometimes suggested that there can be no fully universal concept of human rights, for it is necessary to take into account the diverse cultures and political systems of the world. In my view this is a point advanced mostly by states, and by liberal scholars anxious not to impose the Western view of things on others. It is rarely advanced by the oppressed, only too

---

61. Alston, "The Universal Declaration at 35," *Review of the International Commission of Jurists* 31 (1983): 60, reproduced in Henry J. Steiner and Detlev F. Vagts, *Transnational Legal Problems*, 3rd ed. (New York: Foundation Press, 1986), 445.

anxious to benefit from perceived universal standards. The non-universal, relativist view of human rights is in fact a very state-centred view and loses sight of the fact that human rights are human rights and not dependent on the fact that states, or groupings of states, may behave differently from each other so far as their political, economic policy, and culture are concerned. I believe, profoundly, in the universality of the human spirit. Individuals everywhere want the same essential things: to have sufficient food and shelter, to be able to speak freely, to practice their own religion or to abstain from religious belief; to feel that their person is not threatened by the state: to know that they will not be tortured, or detained without charge, and that, if charged, they will have a fair trial. I believe that there is nothing in these aspirations that is dependent upon culture, or religion, or stage of development. They are as keenly felt by the African tribesman as by the European city-dweller, by the inhabitant of a Latin American shanty-town as by the resident of a Manhattan apartment.[62]

The text reveals the hope of humanity but does not reflect the position of a great part of the member states of the United Nations, which are the ones that decide who will live and who will die; who will have a secure life and who will live in torment; who will enjoy the benefits of state security and who will be discriminated against; who will go around free and who will lose his liberty and suffer torture; who will practice freely his religion and who will be imprisoned, tortured, and even killed for daring to stay loyal to his faith.

Yet another optimistic tendency in certain sectors leads some to accept a paradoxical situation, as described by the biographers of René Cassin:

The normative character of the Universal Declaration is reflected in the fact that its wording has been incorporated in scores of constitutions of new states. Even when such states do not practice human rights, they need to pretend to do so, as least in principle, and thereby, vice pays tribute to virtue.[63]

The major problem, however, lies elsewhere. As pointed out in the beginning of this chapter, the Universal Declaration of Human Rights, as well as the two following covenants, have a basic, fundamental deficiency: the declaration in

62. Harris, *Cases and Materials*, 626, who attributes the text to Higgins.
63. Winter and Prost, *René Cassin*, 351.

its entirety as well as the covenants, aside from very brief dispositions regarding the needs of the state parties, are directed exclusively to natural persons,[64] without considering the protection of communities, of peoples, the collective in general, whereas the reasons for the creation of these documents as well as the history of the sixty-seven years since the approval of the declaration consist of transgressions of catastrophic dimensions against human groups. Taking aside the atrocities committed during the Second World War, human rights were never so vilified, human life was never so cheapened, there was never so much suffering of collectivities caused by other collectivities or by tyrants as after the approval of the Declaration of Human Rights, despite all the subsequent treaties, conventions, resolutions, declarations, commissions, councils, conferences, international and regional courts' decisions, and other initiatives of the society of nations in the last seven decades, all pretending to protect peoples and individuals.

The idealistic view of Harris, that every human being on earth is entitled to be protected, could never materialize based on a document that directs itself to the individual, because the member states of the United Nations – the states that approved the UDHR – have different policies toward their citizens, as a result of their cultures, religions, and political systems. What is needed is a document that would clearly authorize the world community to intervene whenever any state committed atrocities against its own people. The African tribesman and the Latin American shanty-town resident would

64. Henkin et al., *International Law: Cases and Materials*, 598: "International Human Rights generally, the Universal Declaration, and, notably, the International Covenant on Civil and Political Rights, address the rights of natural persons only." A historical analysis of the UDHR by Hilary Charlesworth reports that John Humphrey, of the UN secretariat, charged with preparing the first draft of the UDHR, borrowed a provision relating to the rights of people belonging to ethnic, linguistic, and religious minorities from a draft bill of rights drawn up by Hersch Lauterpacht in 1945. The draft provided for the rights of these groups to their own schools and to their own cultural and religious organizations, as well as to the use of their language in public institutions. Supported by states such as Denmark, the Soviet Union, and Yugoslavia, it was strongly opposed by Eleanor Roosevelt, who observed that there were different ethnic and linguistic groups in the United States, and insisted that there were "no minority problems." In the Third Committee doubts were raised about the provision from countries with significant immigrant populations such as Australia, Brazil, Canada, and Uruguay, as they were concerned that it would discourage assimilation. Most probably this was also the concern of the US delegation. The provision did not survive to the final wording of the declaration.

still not reach the standard of the European city dweller and the Manhattan apartment resident, but at least he would have a good chance of being saved from the worst persecutions, from atrocious behavior by his government or the majority of his compatriots. If the UN would practice intervention, states that do not respect their citizens would slowly but surely begin to consider the need to move to a policy that would avoid outside interventions. This would eventually lead them to a better, softer, kinder way of treating their people.

In other words, by avoiding the worst, the leaders of the African tribesmen and of the Latin American shanty-town dwellers would get nearer and nearer to treating their people on a basis of human dignity and eventually reach the full recognition of human rights. Strong intervention by the world community, practiced with careful strategy and respectful techniques, could perhaps change the "other side" of the globe.

The UDHR was drafted and approved in a time when human rights were being violated by the states that were working on the document: the Soviet Union had the gulag; the United States its de jure[65] racial discrimination; France and Great Britain, their colonial empires. It was therefore not in their interests to draft a charter that established an effective international system for the protection of human rights, which is what some nations advocated.[66] On more than one occasion the Russians delegates attacked the British colonial policies and made reference to the lynching of African Americans in the United States, to which an English delegate responded with a long statement about the Russian concentration camps set up by Stalin, about which the Russian government was keeping absolute silence.[67]

---

65. Actually de facto discrimination as well, as black people still sat in the back of the buses, among various other forms of differentiation based on race. The *American Bar Association Journal* of February 2014 reports on the civil rights sit-ins that took place in various states of the South in 1960 as a protest against store owners' refusal to serve black people at store lunch counters. Allen Pusey, "Students Spark Civil Rights Sit-Ins," *American Bar Association Journal* 100, no. 2 (February 2014): 72. Acting secretary of state Dean Acheson wrote in 1946 that "the existence of discrimination against minority groups in this country has an adverse effect upon our relations with other countries." David Sloss, review of *Socializing States: Promoting Human Rights through International Law*, by Ryan Goodman and Derek Jinks, *American Journal of International Law* 108, no. 3 (July 2014): 578.
66. Buergenthal, *International Human Rights in a Nutshell*, 18.
67. Morsink, *Universal Declaration*, 40. Actually there is only one reference to human rights in the UN charter. The UDHR is the one that carries the various references.

Unfortunately, both sides were right. However, these reciprocal accusations did not prevent the parties from moving forward with finalizing a text that could be accepted by the members of the Human Rights Commission.

French atrocities in the North African colonies persisted throughout the 1950s, most especially in Algeria, where torture was the main policy of the French forces. They lasted until 1962 – including during the presidency of Charles de Gaulle. The French air force bombarded the border town of Sakiet Sidi Youssef in Tunisia.[68]

On the occasion of the one hundredth anniversary of the American Society of International Law's *American Journal of International Law*, the journal published a series of centennial essays. One of the essays, on the topic of international human rights, was authored by Thomas Buergenthal, a steadfast fighter for human rights in the regional and international arenas.[69]

In this essay, the author's belief in the internationalization of human rights and his optimism for what has been and continues to be done for this ideal is balanced by his recognition of the difficulties, the obstacles, and the setbacks that it suffers.

On the one hand, the author expresses his optimism with the number of states that have ratified the hundreds of human rights treaties that the United Nations and its specialized agencies have adopted,[70] which "not only have internationalized the subject of human rights as between the parties to them, but also to the same extent have internationalized the individual human rights these treaties guarantee."[71] He manifests his optimism regarding the establishment of international criminal tribunals,[72] as well as the powerful pressure group of the NGOs in the service of international human rights.[73]

On the other hand, Buergenthal admits that the Charter of the United Nations has adopted intentionally vague provisions on human rights (referring to articles 55 and 56). He comments on the ambivalence of the Security

68. Winter and Prost, *René Cassin*, 277.
69. Thomas Buergenthal, "The Evolving International Human Rights System," *American Journal of International Law* 100, no. 4 (October 2006): 783–807.
70. Ibid., 789.
71. Ibid., 789–90.
72. Ibid., 802.
73. Ibid., 804.

Council regarding the "human tragedy being played out in Darfur"[74] (but at the same time praises the "gradual emergence of a modern version of collective humanitarian intervention") and recognizes the "many violations of human rights that are still victimizing millions of human beings in different parts of the world."[75]

Failed Attempts to Strengthen the Declaration

In the Sub-Commission on Prevention of Discrimination and Protection of Minorities, the Russian delegate Alexander Borisov proposed an addition to article 7, which deals with discrimination ("All are entitled to equal protection against any discrimination..."). The addition would state that any advocacy of national, racial, or religious hostility or of national exclusiveness or hatred and contempt, as well as any action establishing a privilege or a discrimination based on distinction of race, nationality, or religion, constituted a crime and would be punishable under the law of the state.

On a later occasion, the Russian delegate A.E. Bogomolov added an important analysis by saying that "the affirmation of the equality of individuals before the law should be accompanied by the establishment of equal human rights in political, social, cultural and economic life" and that "in terms of practical reality, this meant that one could not allow advocacy of hatred or racial, national or religious contempt."[76] He added that "without such a prohibition, any declaration would be useless." He did not accept the argument that "to forbid the advocacy of racial, national, or religious hatred constituted a violation of the freedom of the press or of free speech," as "between Hitlerian racial propaganda and any other propaganda designed to stir up racial, national, or religious hatred and incitement to war, there was but a short step. Freedom of the press and free speech could not serve as a pretext for propagating views which poisoned public opinion. Propaganda in favor of racial or national exclusiveness or superiority merely served as an ideological mask for imperialist aggression. That was how German imperialists had attempted to justify by racial considerations their plan for destruction

74. Ibid., 790.
75. Ibid., 806.
76. Morsink, *Universal Declaration*, 70.

and pillage in Europe and Asia."[77] The Russian delegate was condemning what became known years later as "hate speech."

The Russian delegation insisted that the proposal "was a test of whether or not the United Nations Organization was to be effective in its protection of minorities."[78] On a later occasion, Pavlov, another Soviet delegate, brought up his colleagues' proposition again, but it was not accepted.[79] The final draft of article 7 merely states that "all are equal before the law and are entitled without any discrimination to equal protection of the law. All are entitled to equal protection against any discrimination in violation of this Declaration and against any incitement to such discrimination."

Morsink distinguishes the Russian proposal from the final redaction by "one crucial difference": the proposal calls for the outright prohibition of advocacy or incitement to hostility, hatred, and contempt, while the final text only guarantees protection against incitement.[80] Prohibition versus protection.

I see a much wider distinction between the two formulations, which differ in two very important aspects: 1) the Russian proposal was directed to minorities as a collective group of human beings. The final text of the declaration, on the other hand, merely protects individuals. It begins with the word "all" – meaning everyone. 2) The Russian proposal characterized the violation of its precept as a crime, to be punished by the law of the state, whereas no such provision is found in the final text of the declaration.

While the acts of the cruel, criminal Russian regime of that time must be viewed with horror, it should be recognized that its delegation at the Human Rights Commission suggested a much better and more adequate proposition – historically, politically, and legally – than the formula that was finally approved.

Some authors recognize that the efforts to establish human rights on an international plane reflected a widespread international desire "to finish off the moribund interwar system of minority rights in favor of more expedient

77. Ibid.
78. Ibid.
79. Ibid., 71.
80. Ibid., 72.

individual rights."[81] For this reason, the UN established a framework that blocked the full-fledged recognition of self-determination and only offered weak protections to endangered minority groups while reinforcing the sovereign prerogatives of nation-states.[82] This is a sad description of the results reached by the movement for the "internationalization of human rights," but it is the correct analysis of what resulted from the UDHR.

The much-praised "internationalization of human rights" was actually empty of any real meaning, as it did not confront the great catastrophe that occurred during World War II, it added nothing to what the constitutional democracies already guaranteed, and it did not influence the states that did not respect human rights in their internal legislations.

Regarding the second affirmation of the declaration's preamble – twice quoted above – I have two remarks. The affirmation states:

> Whereas disregard and contempt for human rights have resulted in barbarous acts which have outraged the conscience of mankind and the advent of a world in which human beings shall enjoy freedom of speech and belief and freedom from fear and want has been proclaimed as the highest aspiration of the common people…

Firstly, the "barbarous acts that outraged the conscience of mankind" did not stem from disregard for human rights. The unspeakable atrocities committed by Nazi Germany go far beyond the simple disregard of human rights. A state can disregard human rights and still not commit a mega-genocide. Thus, there is no real connection between the barbarity of World War II and the Declaration of Human Rights.

Secondly, "freedom of speech and belief and freedom from fear and want" are indeed great ideals, for which individuals and governments have to extend all possible efforts. But these ideals still do not constitute "the highest aspiration of the common people." The highest, strongest aspiration of the "common people," as well as the not-so-common people, is the right to life (provided for in article 3 of the declaration). Yet this right, which was so wildly disrespected in both world wars, found no reference in the preamble,

---

81. Cohen, "The Holocaust and the 'Human Rights Revolution,'" in Iriye, Goedde, Hitchcock, *Human Rights Revolution*, 56.
82. Ibid.

which establishes the declaration's fundamental philosophical, historical, social, political, and, in a certain sense, legal desiderata.[83]

We saw in chapter 5 that the concept of human rights is a very old conquest of civilization, as expressed in theology, philosophy, all religions, and political literature. Its origin is in the very first chapter of Genesis, the oldest book known to humanity – and still a best seller. This long history of conceptual respect for human rights has always been a matter of international recognition. Yet what comes out from the work of the commission that prepared the declaration – as well as from the subsequent literature – is that Hitler is the cause of the human rights instruments, most especially of the Universal Declaration. That amounts to a horrific view of history, a preposterous historical and legal analysis of recent facts.

Moreover, as we saw in chapters 2 and 3, the drafters of the Universal Declaration of Human Rights had no moral authority to respond to Nazism, as they represented countries that could have, but did not, save a great part of the victims. In fact, we saw that Hitler could not have actualized his perversion against the Jews were it not for the policy of the United States, followed by the other Allied countries, of refusing entrance to the Jews when they could have escaped from Europe, a policy that gave the maniac in Berlin a green light to proceed with his barbarous objective, which he realized in carrying out his "Final Solution" against the majority of the Jews who lived in the European continent.

Regarding the objectives of the UDHR, its preamble proclaims that the

---

83. One of the drafts for the declaration, called the "Lake Success Draft" (see Glendon, *A World Made New*, 294), went even further. It stated:

> Whereas disregard and contempt for human rights resulted, before and during the Second World War, in barbarous acts which outraged the conscience of mankind and made it apparent that the fundamental freedoms were one of the supreme issues of the conflict...

There is a long way between not respecting the fundamental freedoms and organizing the methodical, scientific, atrocious murder of an entire people or race or religion – any human group – dispersed all over a continent. The same critique applies to the Cassin Draft, which stated in the very beginning of its preamble that

> ignorance and contempt of human rights have been among the principal causes of the suffering of humanity and particularly of the massacres which have polluted the earth in two world wars.

There is no correspondence between disrespect of human rights and organized, systematic massacres, as the former does not necessarily lead to the later.

"recognition of the inherent dignity and the equal and inalienable rights of all members of the human family is the foundation of freedom, justice and peace in the world." Actually "freedom" and "justice" are human rights as well, so it would have been more precise to enumerate these two principles together with dignity and equality without conditioning the ones on the others.

As already noted, it is not easy to understand the relationship between individual human rights with peace in the world, or as the preamble further adds, between human rights and the essentiality of promoting the development of friendly relations between nations.[84]

At the ceremony awarding the Nobel Peace Prize to René Cassin, Mrs. Aase Lionaes, chairman of the Nobel Prize Committee, who had been Norway's representative at the UN from 1946 to 1965, stated that "today, where there is no respect for human rights and freedom, there is no peace either."[85]

What is really the connection between individual human rights and world peace? Where is the evidence that governments that abuse their people's human rights pose a greater threat to international peace than those that respect such rights? During the twentieth century, various South and Central American countries went through shorter or longer periods of dictatorial regimes, which restricted the rights of their citizens and violated fundamental human rights, and yet they did not present a threat to world peace. The same goes for Portugal, during the long regime of President Salazar. Did Franco's Spain threaten peace beyond its borders, even in the years of the internal war that was waged there in the 1930s?

Iraq, Cuba, and Vietnam are often brought as examples to demonstrate that states violating human rights are likely to go to war. This does not prove the point, as there are dozens of states that do not respect human rights, yet never go to war. On the other hand, states that observe human rights do sometimes go to war, but never against another such state. It should be taken into consideration that interventions to reestablish human rights many times lead to war, as will be discussed in chapter 7.

---

84. As Charles R. Beitz puts it in his *The Idea of Human Rights* (Oxford: Oxford University Press, 2009), 19: "Broadly speaking, there are two distinguishable themes in the characterization given in the preamble of the declaration's justifying aims: that international recognition of human rights is necessary to protect the equal dignity of all persons and that respect of human rights is a condition of friendly relations among states."
85. Winter and Prost, *René Cassin*, 261.

The Genocide Convention

The only possible connection between the Holocaust and the international legislation on human rights is the Convention on the Prevention and Punishment of the Crime of Genocide.

The term *genocide* says it all – it is the crime against the group, not the individual. The war criminals were condemned by the Nuremberg Military Tribunal for crimes against peace, crimes against humanity, and war crimes, the last two together adding up to what has been established as the crime of genocide.

The General Assembly of the United Nations adopted the Genocide Convention on December 9, 1948, one day before their adoption of the Universal Declaration of Human Rights. Aimed at addressing the horrors of the Holocaust, the Genocide Convention decrees that "genocide is a crime under international law which the contracting states undertake to prevent and punish."

Here lies the connection of the Holocaust with an international instrument that established a pact to prevent the recurrence of such an event.

The president of the General Assembly, Australia's Herbert Evatt, addressed the member states and requested that they ratify the convention urgently, for it was, he said, "an epoch-making development in international law." And he further proclaimed that

> intervention of the United Nations and other organs which will have to supervise application of the convention will be made according to international law and not according to unilateral political considerations. In this field relating to the sacred right of existence of human groups we are proclaiming today the supremacy of international law once and forever.[86]

Indeed, the convention focuses attention on the protection of national, racial, ethnic, and religious minorities from threats to their very existence. In that sense, it is in keeping with the goals of both the United Nations and the modern human rights movement, aimed at the eradication of racism and xenophobia.

We shall be analyzing the Genocide Convention and the long succession

---

86. Glendon, *A World Made New*, 163–64, quoting the *New York Times* of the day after the convention's approval, December 10, 1948.

of genocides in chapter 8. There we shall examine whether the convention really created an organized system of prevention and how the convention has functioned over the almost seven decades that have gone by since that day in December 1948. But before considering the actual implementation of this instrument, we must hear what the classic Oppenheim's *International Law* says about it:

> It is apparent that to a considerable extent, the Convention amounts to a registration of protest against past misdeeds of individual or collective savagery rather than to an effective instrument of their prevention or repression in the future.[87]

The Genocide Convention is a source of international law, containing rules on prevention and punishment, but classifying it as a "registration of protest" against what took place in the years of the Second World War is an adequate historical analysis of the convention's essence. As a "registration of protest" it did much better than the Universal Declaration of Human Rights and the two covenants that followed. And as it unfortunately remained very far from its ostensible purposes of prevention and punishment (as we shall see below), its ultimate effect remained the "registration of protest."

International Conferences after 1948

In Teheran, between April 22 and May 13, 1968, the United Nations held an international conference that dealt with all aspects of human rights, with special attention given to matters of racial discrimination and apartheid. Other subjects that were dealt with include the independence of colonial countries, women's rights, scientific and technological developments, refugees, detained persons, the Children's Fund, disarmament, family planning, legal aid, armed conflicts, and the so-called Israeli "occupation" of the West Bank (a constant preoccupation of the United Nations).

Teheran was then under the command of Emperor Reza Pahlavi, who kept control over his people through the Savak, the Iranian secret police agency known for torturing opponents of the government – not exactly a regime that observed human rights.

The Vienna Declaration and Program of Action on Human Rights adopted

---

87. Oppenheim's *International Law*, 994.

in the World Conference, in 1993, proclaimed, among other points, the following:

1. The World Conference on Human Rights reaffirms the solemn commitment of all States to fulfill their obligations to promote universal respect for and observance and protection of all human rights and fundamental freedoms for all in accordance with the Charter of the United Nations, other instruments relating to human rights, and international law. The universal nature of these rights and freedoms is beyond question....

4. The promotion and protection of all human rights and fundamental freedoms must be considered as a priority objective of the United Nations in accordance with its purposes and principles, in particular the purpose of international cooperation. In the framework of these purposes and principles, the promotion and protection of all human rights is a legitimate concern of the international community....

5. All human rights are universal, indivisible and interdependent and interrelated. The international community must treat human rights globally in a fair and equal manner, on the same footing, and with the same emphasis. While the significance of national and regional particularities and various historical, cultural and religious backgrounds must be borne in mind, it is the duty of States, regardless of their political, economic and cultural systems, to promote and protect all human rights and fundamental freedoms.

The *New York Times* described the atmosphere of the conference as "strangely removed from reality."[88] The proceedings were to be strictly limited to discussion of situations that were not then current. No actual, ongoing abuses of human rights were to be mentioned. Thus hothouses of persecution, maltreatment, and even atrocity – such as China, Cuba, Angola and Liberia, and even Bosnia-Herzegovina (where, a short plane-ride away from the conference, people were actively being massacred) – were strictly off the

---

88. Alan Riding, "A Rights Meeting, But Don't Mention the Wronged," *New York Times*, June 14, 1993, http://www.nytimes.com/1993/06/14/world/a-rights-meeting-but-don-t -mention-the-wronged.html.

table. This was ostensibly to avoid politicization, but the effect was rather stunningly out of touch.[89]

The Vienna World Conference and its beautiful message took place on June 14–25, 1993. The resulting document was a "well crafted but empty exhortation."[90] Ten months later, in April–July 1994, eight hundred thousand human beings were atrociously murdered in Rwanda. None of the signatories of the Vienna Declaration lifted a finger to save even a few Rwandan children.

In September 2005, the United Nation General Assembly held a plenary meeting in New York. The meeting adopted the "2005 World Summit Outcome," with 178 paragraphs containing hortatory resolutions. Regarding genocide, paragraphs 138 and 139 are of the utmost interest. They read as follows:

> 138. Each individual State has the responsibility to protect its populations from genocide, war crimes, ethnic cleansing and crimes against humanity. This responsibility entails the prevention of such crimes, including their incitement, through appropriate and necessary means. We accept that responsibility and will act in accordance with it. The international community should, as appropriate, encourage and help States to exercise this responsibility and support the United Nations in establishing an early warning capability.

> 139. The international community, through the United Nations, also has the responsibility to use appropriate diplomatic, humanitarian and other peaceful means, in accordance with Chapters VI and VII of the Charter, to help protect populations from genocide, war crimes, ethnic cleansing and crimes against humanity. In this context, we are prepared to take collective action in a timely and decisive manner, through the Security Council, in accordance with the Charter, including Chapter VII, on a case-by-case basis and in cooperation with relevant regional organizations as appropriate, should peaceful means be inadequate and national authorities manifestly fail to protect their populations from genocide, war crimes, ethnic cleansing and crimes against humanity. We stress the need for the General Assembly to continue consideration of the responsibility

---

89. Kevin Boyle, "Stock Taking on Human Rights: The World Conference on Human Rights, Vienna 1993," *Political Studies* 43, no. 1 (August 1995): 80–81.
90. Ibid., 81.

to protect populations from genocide, war crimes, ethnic cleansing and crimes against humanity and its implications, bearing in mind the principles of the Charter and international law. We also intend to commit ourselves, as necessary and appropriate, to helping States build capacity to protect their populations from genocide, war crimes, ethnic cleansing and crimes against humanity and to assisting those which are under stress before crises and conflicts break out.[91]

After this emphatic, enthusiastic, specifically formulated, and convincing resolution was approved in 2005, how many mass atrocities, crimes against humanity and, yes, genocides have taken place? And what has the United Nations, through its General Assembly, its Security Council and the Commission (followed by the Council) on Human Rights done to save millions of human beings from stress, hunger, persecution, rape, ethnic cleansing, torture, and death?

On this occasion the UN finally recognized – mildly and diplomatically, it is true – that human rights are conditional on the culture and the civilization existing in the different member states. So much so that after setting in paragraph 13 a reaffirmation of the "universality, indivisibility, interdependence and interrelatedness of all human rights," the 2005 World Summit acknowledged, in paragraph 14, the "diversity of the world," recognized that "all cultures and civilizations contribute to the enrichment of humankind," and acknowledged the "importance of respect and understanding for religious and cultural diversity throughout the world." The document committed the member states to "encourage tolerance, respect, dialogue and cooperation among different cultures, civilizations and peoples."

In other words, human rights are not necessarily conceived the same way in different places of the world, or, as Aristotle said, "the things which are just not by nature but by human enactment are not everywhere the same, since constitutions also are not the same."[92]

But in paragraphs 119 and 120, the hyperbolic and fanciful document states that human rights "belong to the universal and indivisible core values

91. A/RES/60/1 – UN General Assembly 24/X/2005, sixtieth session, agenda items no. 46 and 120.
92. Aristotle, *Nicomachean Ethics*, book 5, chapter 7, trans. W.D. Ross, in vol. 9 of Hutchins, *Great Books*, 382.

and principles of the United Nations" and that "the universal nature of these rights and freedoms is beyond question." And paragraph 121 reaffirms that "all human rights are universal, indivisible, interrelated, interdependent and mutually reinforcing." The contradictions are "pacified" with a new contradictory statement in this same paragraph, which reads:

> While the significance of national and regional particularities and various historical, cultural and religious backgrounds must be borne in mind, all States, regardless of their political, economic and cultural systems, have the duty to promote and protect all human rights and fundamental freedoms.

The same is repeated in the subsequent paragraph (122):

> We emphasize the responsibilities of all States, in conformity with the Charter, to respect human rights and fundamental freedoms for all, without distinction of any kind as to race, color, sex, language or religion, political or other opinion, national or social origin, property, birth or other status.[93]

Among the member states signing this document were those that forbid women to drive and obligate them by law to cover themselves from head to toe, and to suffer honor execution in the case of any perceived sexual transgression or even simply unaccepted social interaction. In these states, Catholics may not have a church and Jews may not keep a synagogue; homosexuals are executed; people are imprisoned, tortured, and executed for expressing their opposition to the regime; there are no elections; there is no free press. In sum, these states have absolutely no respect for the most elementary human rights.

Actually, states have no difficulties in signing and ratifying human rights conventions and proclamations, as their violation entails essentially no consequences.[94] Nor do such treaties and declarations imply any need for non–rights abusers to modify their policies; they already fall within the parameters of the treaties' conditions anyway.[95]

---

93. A/RES/60/1 – UN General Assembly 24/X/2005, sixtieth session, agenda items no. 46 and 120.

94. Jack L. Goldsmith and Eric A. Posner, *The Limits of International Law* (Oxford: Oxford University Press, 2005), 120.

95. Ibid. On page 121 the authors add that "there is no evidence that ratification of human

A more general view of the relationship of states to human rights treaties was given by Eric Posner in the following terms:

> Thus, while states are willing to enter into human rights treaties and hope that they will exert positive pressure on human rights violators, they are not willing to put significant resources into enforcing those treaties. More to the point, they tolerate the treaty regime because the ambiguities and conflicts in and among the treaties provide countries with plenty of freedom of action – permitting Western countries both to restrict human rights domestically when necessary, and to refrain, without appearing to repudiate their treaty obligations, from putting too much pressure on foreign rights violators. The key move was to enter into these treaties without providing for strong international organizations to enforce them, so that – unlike in domestic law – countries can work around the treaties without defying specific legal orders.[96]

This shows us the relativity and flexibility of what the idealists have welcomed as the "internationalization of human rights," as human rights on the international plateau stand at a much lower and more relative level than national human rights.

The Colonies

As we have already observed, in the debates over the drafting of the Universal Declaration, constant tension prevailed regarding the colonies of the European powers – Great Britain, Belgium, France, Italy, and the Netherlands.

The British were determined to resist the erosion of their imperial power and therefore were not ready to champion human rights. The future of the colonial territories was a point of dispute with the United States, which (perhaps naturally, given its own origins) assumed the eventual independent status of British colonies – not at all what Great Britain desired.[97] When the United States suggested the establishment of UN trusteeships in the colonies,

---

rights treaties affects human rights practices. By contrast, empirical studies do find statistical relationships between democracy, peace and economic development, on the one hand, and protection of human rights, on the other (Poe and Tate, 1994; Poe 2004)."
96. Posner, *Twilight of Human Rights Law*, 106.
97. Glendon, *A World Made New*, 6.

Churchill vehemently vowed that "not one scrap of British territory" would ever be included in such an arrangement if he could prevent it.[98]

The Russian delegation persisted in their critique regarding the treatment of black people in the United States, of Indians in South Africa, and of the peoples in the British colonies of the Gold Coast, Nigeria, and Rhodesia.[99]

After long discussions in UN meetings, and against English and French opposition, the final text in article 2 (second paragraph) reads:

> Furthermore, no distinction shall be made on the basis of the political, jurisdictional or international status of the country or territory to which the person belongs, whether it be independent, trust, non-self-governing or under any other limitation of sovereignty.

Again the preoccupation was with the individual, but nothing was established to protect the groups that made up the hundreds of millions of human beings who were going to be freed from foreign hegemony. The transition from colonies to independent states was left entirely in the hands of the colonial powers without any outside support for the peoples who were going to become self-governing nations. The United Nations, through its Commission on Human Rights – which worked two long years to formulate the UDHR – took no initiative to prepare or protect the colonized people in their upgrade to independent statehood. Ultimately, the tribal rivalries, the internal rifts, and the lack of culture and of civilized principles led to the tragedies that befell over tens of millions of human beings in the African civil wars. The persecutions and the atrocities that occurred after independence were results of the sudden change from colonial to sovereign status.[100]

Important documents produced by the United Nations did not consider the necessity and means to prepare colonized people for independence. The Declaration on the Granting of Independence to Colonial Countries and Peoples, adopted by the UN General Assembly in 1960,[101] makes the following statements:

98. Ibid., 9.

99. Morsink, *Universal Declaration*, 95.

100. Contrary to Glendon (*A World Made New*, 12), there is no reference in the UN charter's preamble to "self-determination of peoples"; this concept only appears in article 1.2 of the charter itself.

101. UNGA Res. 1514 (xv).

Immediate steps shall be taken, in Trust and Non-Self-Governing Territories or all other territories which have not yet attained independence, to transfer all powers to the peoples of those territories, without any conditions or reservations, in accordance with their freely expressed will and desire, without any distinction as to race, creed or color, in order to enable them to enjoy complete independence and freedom (number 5).

The other statement of the declaration, under number 3, says:

Inadequacy of political, economic, social or educational preparedness should never serve as a pretext for delaying independence.

The UN did nothing, however, to help those peoples prepare themselves for independence, democracy, or respect for human rights, which they did not experience under the control of the colonial powers. This help could have been provided before and/or after the attainment of independence. In some cases it could have prevented the deaths of millions and the continued endangering of populations, decades after the conquest of their independence.

And so we have, on the one hand, a rich collection of international documents on human rights. And on the other hand, as we shall see in other chapters, we have a catastrophic panorama of continuous suffering, internal wars, persecutions of minorities, crimes against humanity, genocides – an unfortunate succession of failures, which have proven the total inoperativeness of those documents.

The Universal Declaration of Human Rights has not brought any improvement to the situation of humanity. It is a total failure.

Chapter Seven
The Ineffectiveness of the UN Organization

The Tension between Intervention and Sovereignty

Hugo Grotius and Emmerich de Vattel – both seventeenth-century jurists – recognized the right of intervention to save another nation from atrocities.[1]

A classic example occurred in 1860, when the French army intervened in Lebanon to save Christian Maronites.[2] And at the end of the nineteenth

---

1. Jacques Dumas, "La Sauvegarde internationale des droits de l'homme," *Recueil des cours de l'Académie de droit international à la Haye* 59 (1937). In reference to these two jurists, he writes: "they taught that a sovereign has the right to take up arms in order to punish the nations that commit grave offenses against natural law" (my translation).

Thomas Buergenthal (*International Human Rights in a Nutshell*, 3) says that

the doctrine of humanitarian intervention, as expounded by Hugo Grotius in the 17th century and other early international lawyers, recognizes as lawful the use of force by one or more states to stop the maltreatment by a state of its own nationals when that conduct was so brutal and large scale as to shock the conscience of the community of nations.

Intervention has been dealt with by many modern authors. Buergenthal refers to E.C. Stowell, L. Sohn and Buergenthal, Brownlie, J.N. Moore, Lillich, and Franck and Rodley.

2. Dominique Carreau, *Droit international*, 5th ed. (Paris: Pedone, 1997), 395. Feinberg (*Studies in International Law*, 294), writes that

according to the accepted definition of "humanitarian intervention" a State may interfere in the internal affairs of another if that State conducts itself inhumanly towards its subjects, in breach of the fundamental principles of civilized government and shocking the conscience of mankind. In other words, the general prohibition against intervention in the domestic affairs of a State does not hold good where flagrant injustices or despicable atrocities have been committed in it.

century, the United States invaded Cuba in order to stop atrocities being committed there by the Spanish.[3]

In modern times, humanitarian intervention has been a subject of debate. Hersch Lauterpacht's view was that the doctrine of humanitarian intervention never became a fully acknowledged part of positive international law, while Leo Strisower, Charles de Visscher, and probably P. Guggenheim, too, hold otherwise, as summarized by Nathan Feinberg.[4]

Intervention has been on the minds and souls of historians, international law scholars, international relations specialists, theologians, and philosophers. The great humanitarian and valiant fighter for human rights Professor Elie Wiesel has taken to heart all human sufferings of the last decades. He has traveled to the sites of persecution in order to bring the warring sides together, or – when that was impossible – to simply show his solidarity to the suffering masses. Regarding the Balkans war, he notes that "for at least five centuries Sarajevo was an example of urban coexistence. There was cooperation among its Jews, Christians, and Muslims, a harmony marred by not a single racial, ethnic, or religious incident."[5] And he asks, "What provoked the abrupt change?"[6]

And then the fundamental question, the painful dilemma:

> What can one do? Intervene? How? With arms? Make war on war? The debate divides America. A few months after my visit to Sarajevo, I am in Washington for the inauguration of the Holocaust Museum. I interrupt my speech, turn to President Clinton and urge him to do something – anything – to stop the bloodshed over there.... Charles Krauthammer, the *Time* editorialist, reproaches me for it. A Jew, he says, should not get involved in the Balkan war. According to him, I should not have launched my appeal from the "sacred place" that is the Holocaust Museum. I don't agree, Mr. Krauthammer. First of all, no museum is sacred. Secondly, when

3. Alex J. Bellamy, "Military Intervention," in Bloxham and Moses, *Oxford Handbook of Genocide Studies*, 597.
4. Feinberg, *Studies in International Law*, 298. The Third Restatement of US Foreign Relation Law, which rules American public international law, provides in section 703 (2) that "any state may pursue international remedies against any other state for a violation of the customary international law of human rights."
5. Wiesel, *And the Sea Is Never Full*, 394.
6. Ibid.

men are dying, when innocent people are subjected to rape and torture, when cities are being transformed into cemeteries, Jews do not have to right to be silent.[7]

And then Wiesel turns to the next chapter of that European tragedy of the 1990s – the intervention of NATO in Kosovo:

> Was NATO's decision to intervene correct? Was Washington right to push for it? The answer to both questions is yes. Faced with Milosevic's stubborn policy of ethnic cleansing, no self-respecting government or nation could knowingly violate the Biblical injunction "Thou shall not stand idly by."
>
> Surely, when human lives are involved, indifference is not an answer. Not to choose is also a choice, said the French philosopher Albert Camus. Neutrality helps the aggressor, not his victims. If NATO had been created only to protect the weak and defenseless, it would be enough to justify its existence.
>
> Critics of the attacks on Milosevic say that sending our army to the former Yugoslavia is not in America's national interest. From an economic or geopolitical viewpoint, the critics may have a point. But a nation is great not because of its wealth or its military might; its greatness is measured by the way it uses or abuses its wealth and power. In other words: its greatness derives from its commitment to moral principle.[8]

The idea that intervention conflicts with the principle of sovereignty continues to appear very frequently in legal literature. Advocates of sovereignty even raised a consideration that the Convention on the Prevention and Punishment of the Crime of Genocide would threaten geopolitical stability "by introducing a countervailing principle of humanitarian intervention."[9]

A characteristic demonstration of the conflict between intervention and sovereignty already occurred in the Human Rights Commission as it was working on a draft of the Universal Declaration of Human Rights. Vladimir Koretsky, a delegate of the Soviet Union, had raised objections to the right of foreign intervention in internal matters of a sovereign state, to which René

7. Ibid., 395.
8. Ibid., 398.
9. Bloxham and Pendas, "Punishment as Prevention?" in Bloxham and Moses, *Oxford Handbook of Genocide Studies*, 621–22.

Cassin responded that he was very much struck by the statement of the delegate from the Union of Soviet Socialist Republics, who several times used the word *interference*. Cassin stated:

> I must state my thoughts very frankly. The right of interference is here; it is here in the [UN] charter.... Why? Because we do not want a repetition of what happened in 1933, when Germany began to massacre its own nationals, and everybody... bowed, saying "Thou art sovereign and master in thine own house."[10]

There is a school that defends the right, and even the duty, to intervene in a third country when its population is suffering atrocities, provided that the circumstances indicate that the intervention will do more good than harm. Underlying this policy is the notion that human beings matter more than sovereignty. Others, however, claim that when foreign nations send troops, they rarely act without personal interest. Military intervention in the name of human rights could potentially serve as "a thinly veiled justification for a coercive form of Western hegemony or neo-imperialism." States empowered to intervene in other states' affairs on humanitarian grounds, critics fear, could "wage wars to protect and violently export their own cultural preferences."[11]

James Pattison, in *Humanitarian Intervention and Responsibility to Protect: Who Should Intervene?*[12] examines intervention from legal and practical perspectives and shows that interventions of the past have been unsuccessful – as exemplified by what occurred in Liberia and in Côte d'Ivoire. He further notes that other major humanitarian crises have not been averted – such as in Darfur, Somalia, and Congo. Pattison discusses who should intervene and how interventions should be tackled.

Who should intervene – the United Nations, NATO, a regional or subregional organization (such as the African Union), a state, a group of states, or someone else? The issue is complex and difficult. Who has the right to intervene and who has the duty to intervene?[13]

---

10. Glendon, *A World Made New*, 60.
11. Bellamy, "Military Intervention," in Bloxham and Moses, *Oxford Handbook of Genocide Studies*, 602–3, 607.
12. Oxford University Press, 2012.
13. Pattison, *Humanitarian Intervention*, 6–8.

The Challenges of the UN Charter

Human Rights are mentioned numerous times in the Charter of the United Nations: in the opening paragraph, and in articles 1.3, 13, 55, 56, 62, 68, and 76. The basic rules are found in article 1, par. 3 and articles 55–56. Article 2.7, mentioned in an earlier chapter, though not referring to human rights, is an important factor in the charter's general analysis of this subject.

In article 1.3 the charter calls for achieving

> international cooperation in solving international problems of an economic, social, cultural or humanitarian character and in promoting and encouraging respect for human rights and for fundamental freedoms for all without distinction as to race, sex, language or religion.

Articles 13, 62, 68, and 76 refer to assisting, promoting, and encouraging the realization, observance, and respect of human rights.

Various provisions of the charter are connected to the dilemma between sovereignty and intervention. First we have article 2.7 of the charter, which states the following:

> Nothing contained in the present Charter shall authorize the United Nations to intervene in matters which are essentially within the domestic jurisdiction of any state or shall require the Members to submit such matters to settlement under the present Charter, but this principle shall not prejudice the application of enforcement measures under Chapter VII.

Article 2.7 mandates respect for a state's sovereignty, but leaves the door open to chapter 7's provisions.

The measures provided for in chapter 7 concerning the objective to "maintain or restore international peace and security" include military actions, as prescribed in articles 42–50. First the charter recommends that the Security Council decide upon measures not involving the use of armed forces (article 41) and then it deals with "action by air, sea or land forces as may be necessary to maintain or restore international peace and security" (article 42). The subsequent articles, from 43 to 50, detail the military measures to be employed, the procedures to be taken by the Security Council, and the cooperation to be given by the state members of the international organization.

The whole chapter is concerned with the purpose of maintaining or restoring international peace and security as detailed in articles 39, 42–43,

47–48, and 51, but nothing is expressly foreseen regarding military intervention to save endangered human groups, though sometimes the UN documents identify human rights observance with peace and security.

To maintain equilibrium between the principle enshrined in article 2.7 and the measures prescribed in chapter 7 has been, and continues to be, a major legal and political challenge.

Article 2.7 has also been analyzed in light of articles 55 and 56. This juxtaposition also focuses the debate regarding when intervention in a member state is acceptable and should be implemented.

Article 55 of the charter states the following wishful expressions:

> With a view to the creation of conditions of stability and well-being which are necessary for peaceful and friendly relations among nations based on respect for the principle of equal rights and self-determination of peoples, the United Nations shall promote:
>
>   a) higher standards of living, full employment, and conditions of economic and social progress and development;
>
>   b) solutions of international economic, social, health and related problems; and international cultural and educational cooperation; and
>
>   c) universal respect for, and observance of human rights and fundamental freedoms for all without distinction as to race, sex, language or religion.

And article 56 provides that all members pledge themselves to take joint and separate action in cooperation with the organization for the achievement of the purposes set forth in article 55.

So on the one hand we have article 2.7, strongly in defense of state sovereignty, and on the other hand we have chapter 7 and articles 55–56, which foresee the possibilities of intervention.

Article 55 connects the "observance of human rights and fundamental freedoms for all" with the "attainment of peaceful and friendly relations among nations." The idea was expressed by René Cassin in 1941 when he spoke at the inter-Allied conference on September 24, saying that "we the French believe that in order to establish a real peace it is essential to ratify and to put into practice fundamental human rights."[14]

---

14. Winter and Prost, *René Cassin*, 146. The connection between human rights and

Some authors hold that it is not illegal under article 2.7 for the UN to take appropriate measures designed to compel that a state not engage in gross violations of human rights. Commenting on Resolution 2144, which established the concept of "gross violations," these authors admit that the "required magnitude of the concept of 'massive' or 'gross' violations may change with time as the international community becomes less tolerant of what is lawful behavior under the Charter. They conclude that viewed in this light, the human rights provisions of the Charter are 'elastic clauses' whose expansion is tied to the evolving standards of international legality and decency."[15]

Historically, world peace and respect for human rights have at times coincided. We see this in René Cassin's biography in the following terms:

> The heart and soul of this earlier twentieth-century history is the linkage between the defense of peace and the defense of human rights. It is too simple to say that the defense of peace arose out of the First World War and human rights arose out of the Shoah (Holocaust) and other atrocities of the Second World War. The key point is that the very same generation that struggled for peace after 1918 fought for human rights after 1945. It was the same struggle against what Cassin termed the Leviathan state. Both imply the necessity of limiting state sovereignty, in terms of the state's power to make war on its neighbors, as well as in terms of its treatment of its own citizens.[16]

I would propose that though peace and human rights are two ideals that have been tied together by the UN charter, historically they have not been necessarily connected to each other.

In the case of Nazi Germany, it was held by some scholars that the persecution of the Jews brought about the Second World War, but, as was seen in an earlier chapter, this theory does not correspond to the actual historical facts.

---

international peace and order has been accepted by the literature of International Law. Shigeru Oda states: "The cruelties and oppression of the Nazi regime in Europe brought the conviction both during and after the Second World War that the international recognition and protection of human rights for people throughout the world is essential to the maintenance of international peace and order" ("The Individual in International Law," in Sorensen, *Manual of Public International Law*, 497).

15. Buergenthal, *International Human Rights in a Nutshell*, 77–78, quoting Sohn and Buergenthal, *International Protection of Human Rights*, 947.

16. Winter and Prost, *René Cassin*, 348.

Germany's drive to "conquer the world" was already manifest in the Great War (1914–18), and after Germany's downfall, it returned with Hitler, who had no difficulty in convincing the German people to go back to the original plan. Aside from and independently of that goal, the Fuehrer exploited the deeply ingrained antisemitism of the Aryans to get their support in his specific war against the Jews.

Hitler waged two wars, one against Europe and another against the Jews of Germany and of Europe. He strategically combined the two, but they were essentially two independent objectives. At certain periods of the war the fanatical desire to eliminate the Jews disturbed Germany's war effort, as documented in innumerable sources that deal with the trans-European transportation strategy of the German Reich during the war years. Moreover, as already stressed before, what Nazi Germany did to the Jews was the great historical persecution and genocide of an entire people, which is not connected to human rights as proposed in the UN documents, directed to the individual person and not to the collectivity.[17]

Some authors hold that "major denials of sociopolitical and economic justice provoke violence, even war." They quote former president John F. Kennedy, who once said, "Is not peace in the last analysis, basically a matter of human rights?"[18] Modern history has proven that major denials of justice, policies of discrimination, and serious disregards of human rights do not necessarily bring about external violence or war. South Africa and the United States, in their disregard for the human rights of people of color, did not occasion any disturbance to world peace.

We have seen above that among the purposes of creating the UN, its charter proclaims its mission to "achieve international cooperation in solving

---

17. After stressing that Hitler waged two independent wars, I found the same opinion in Alan Dershowitz. In his introduction to the Tusas' book on the Nuremberg trial he expresses exactly the same understanding: "Document after document proved beyond any doubt that the Nazis had conducted two wars: one was its aggressive war against Europe (and eventually America) for military, political, geographic and economic domination. The other was its genocidal war to destroy 'inferior' races, primarily the Jews, and gypsies. Its war aim was eventually crushed by the combined might of the Americans and the Russians. Its genocidal aim came very close to succeeding. Nearly the entire Jewish and gypsy populations within the control of the Third Reich were systematically murdered while the rest of the world turned a blind eye." Tusa and Tusa, *Nuremberg Trial*.

18. Weston et al., *International Law and World Order*, 628.

international problems of an economic, social, cultural or humanitarian character, and in promoting and encouraging respect for human rights and for fundamental freedoms for all, without distinction as to race, sex, language or religion." International cooperation in the economic, sociocultural areas has been endeavored and, to a certain degree, met with success, but what has the UN accomplished in the humanitarian camp? Whereas at the time of the creation of the organization, the majority of the member states were run by democratic governments that basically respected human rights, today, with the enormous increase in state membership, the majority of the UN state members are run by regimes that have no consideration for the dignity of the human being, deny elementary human rights, and disrespect all humanitarian international conventions.

Regarding article 55, Buergenthal very rightly points out that the UN charter does not define what is meant by "human rights and fundamental freedoms."[19] Then comes article 56 of the charter, which, as already seen above, provides that "all members pledge themselves to take joint and separate action in cooperation with the organization for the achievement of the purposes set forth in Article 55." The lack of definition of human rights and fundamental freedoms of article 55 causes the inoperativeness of article 56 and consequently makes it impossible to achieve article 55's purposes, whatever they are meant to be.

The apparent conflict between article 2.7 and articles 55–56 was a matter of intensive debate in the case of South African discrimination against its black population. The UN Ad Hoc Political Committee on the apartheid policy conducted by the government of South Africa, which met in 1953, concluded that the exercise of the powers and functions devolving on the assembly in such matters did not constitute an intervention within the meaning of article 2.7. This understanding was diametrically opposed to the theory exposed by the South African delegation, which expressed its faith in article 2.7 as a protection against any interference in matters within the domestic jurisdiction of states. The delegation therefore did not recognize the United Nations as having any right to take action which would amount to such interference.

19. Buergenthal, *International Human Rights in a Nutshell*, 20. In the same vein, Shigeru Oda writes that "the Charter does not provide for or indicate machinery to secure the observance of human rights and fundamental freedoms" ("The Individual in International Law," in Sorensen, *Manual of Public International Law*, 498).

The South African delegation drew attention to the matters to which the conflict related: legislation on land tenure, conditions of employment in public services, regulation of transport, suppression of communism, combat service in the armed forces, nationality, the franchise movement of population, residence, immigration, the work and practice of the professions, social security, education, public health, criminal law, taxation, housing, regulation of the liquor traffic, regulation of labor and wages, marriage, food subsidies, local government, and pensions and workmen's compensation. In short, the delegation insisted that all matters within the domestic jurisdiction of the Union of South Africa were immune from UN interference. Furthermore, they argued that to accept the thesis that the United Nations was entitled to intervene in such matters was tantamount to denying the principle and attributes of national sovereignty and to repudiating the provisions of article 2.7; it would signal the end of the United Nations as an organization of sovereign states.

There were voices in the UN who had attempted to justify UN intervention by alleging that the racial policy of the government of the Union of South Africa (1910–1961, the precursor to the current Republic of South Africa) constituted a threat to international peace. The delegation of South Africa regarded those allegations as preposterous and mischievous. A threat to international peace could exist only if and when the territorial integrity or political independence of a state was threatened, directly or indirectly. It could hardly be charged that the domestic laws of a state constituted such a treat.

The delegation of the United Kingdom agreed, expressing the view that the item under discussion was outside the competence of the General Assembly for it concerned domestic policies of the government of the Union of South Africa, a view "borne out by the provisions of Article 2, paragraph 7, of the Charter which should prevail over all other Articles of the Charter."[20]

The UK delegation went so far as to express the thought that the commission appointed to study the racial situation in the Union of South Africa,

---

20. Sweeney et al., *International Legal System*, 615. According to this position, the states that practice all sorts of discrimination, whether against women, against ethnic or religious minorities or any other minority, can perfectly well maintain that, as long as they do not export their policies, they may not be considered as liable to intervention, provided no atrocities are exercised against the minorities.

whose report the Ad Hoc Political Committee was discussing, had been established illegally and that all its activities were therefore illegal.[21]

The strong international reaction to the discrimination against the black population in South Africa has not been followed by any reaction of the world community or of the United Nations to the shocking discriminatory policies followed in many Muslim countries against women and against members of other religions, to the point that both women and members of other religions have been submitted to the worst imaginable "punishments" for trying to live their lives in accordance with their understanding and/or conscience.

In certain instances, when the policies of a state endangered the lives of its citizens, the attitude was different, as some cases of grave violations occupied organs of the United Nations and led to resolutions of intervention. Security Council Resolution 688 of 1991, based on chapter 7 of the UN charter, authorized an intervention in Iraq with the aim of protecting the Kurdish population of that country.

Similar resolutions were taken in the cases of Bosnia-Herzegovina, Somalia, Haiti, Rwanda, and Albania (respectively, Resolutions 770 of 1992, 794 of the same year, 841 of 1993, 940 of 1994, and 1101 of 1997, all of the Security Council). The resolutions authorized all the state parties that were ready to cooperate to utilize all the necessary measures to guarantee humanitarian help to the populations of these countries.[22] In reality, not much humanitarian help was effectively extended to the suffering populations of these countries.

Dominique Carreau refers to authorities who view the humanitarian measures prescribed by chapter 7 of the charter as a right, or rather, as an obligation (*droit-devoir*), which leads to the involvement of the international community when its most fundamental norms are violated.[23] Other authors point to sources that indicate the opposite, such as General Assembly Resolution 2131, of December 21, 1965. Adopted by 109 votes against none, with the only abstention being Great Britain, the resolution forbade any form of armed intervention in interstate relations. No exceptions were foreseen in this interdiction, not even an armed intervention for the purpose of guaranteeing respect for the most fundamental norms of international law, as

21. Ibid.
22. Carreau, *Droit International*, 83.
23. Ibid.

those that belong to *jus cogens*. But the French author concludes, in spite of that resolution, that in certain circumstances (such as the danger of massive extermination of aliens), military intervention is to be accepted.[24]

At the same time, Carreau has difficulties with the possibility of intervention, as its implementation is actually applicable only to the stronger states with higher military prowess. This brings him, in a note of slight irony, to ask: How can we not recognize that this type of preoccupation, as altruistic as it may be, was often invoked in the past to justify colonization in the name of "a civilizing mission"?[25]

What attitude should the UN take in the occurrence of a civil war? Hans Kelsen deals with such a possibility:

> In accordance with the second part of Article 2, paragraph 7, of the Charter, the United Nations may intervene in a matter of domestic jurisdiction by applying enforcement measures under chapter vii. This is of particular importance in case of a civil war taking place within a state, whether a member or not of the United Nations. But such intervention is possible only if the Security Council, under Article 39 of the Charter, has previously decided that the civil war constitutes a threat to international peace.[26]

Some attitudes of the United Nations have contradicted the basic principles for protection of human rights. When Vietnam invaded Cambodia in 1979, it ousted the murderous Khmer Rouge regime, responsible for the death of some two million Cambodians. Yet the invasion was done without the Security Council's authorization, and Vietnam was condemned for violating Cambodian sovereignty.[27]

Sometimes political interests prevented interventions. For instance,

24. Ibid., 542–43.

25. Ibid., 84.

26. Hans Kelsen, *Principles of International Law*, 2nd ed., rev. and ed. Robert W. Tucker (New York: Holt, Rinehart and Winston, 1966), 299–300. The civil war going on in Syria from 2012 most certainly constituted a threat to international peace, but the Security Council, together with the whole system of the United Nations, does not abide by Hans Kelsen or by any of the major authorities in international law.

27. Bellamy, "Military Intervention," in Bloxham and Moses, *Oxford Handbook of Genocide Studies*, 610.

America did not help the Darfur population partly because Sudan constituted an important source of information about Islamic extremism.[28]

A Critique of the Security Council

The Security Council has been criticized by the scholarly world. A severe analysis was presented by Marco Roscini on whether the Security Council really functions as an international humanitarian law enforcer. Based on a rich assortment of scholarly sources, he demonstrates that the most important body of the United Nations fails in achieving the UN's uppermost mission – to work for peace and security in the world and to heal gross humanitarian violations:

> In spite of its broad powers, the role the Security Council has in fact played in the enforcement of international humanitarian law can be criticized from several points of view. First, the Council has acted in a selective and opportunistic manner. It has dealt with certain conflicts, but in others it has kept a very low profile or has not adopted any measure at all: divisions within the Council or lack of political interest have often constrained action. Furthermore, the Council has tried to enforce certain *jus in bello* [rules of war] provisions and instruments but not others, has condemned the violations committed by only one belligerent (e.g., in Iraq and Afghanistan), has adopted coercive measures in certain cases but milder measures in other comparable circumstances without this being justified by the situation on the ground. In the end, this "ad hoc-ism" must be ascribed to the fact that the Council is a political organ, which the Charter does not require to be consistent or impartial. In practice, this means that the Council acts only when it is in the interest of its members: no obligation to take action exists, not even in the case of massive violations of international humanitarian law amounting to a threat to the peace. As has been observed, to establish such obligation "the UN charter would have to be rewritten, and even then it would be difficult in practice to force the Security Council to live up to its presumed obligation to intervene" [Österdahl]. This selective and opportunistic approach of the Security Council with regard to, inter alia, the enforcement of international humanitarian law could in the end affect its legitimacy: even though "[n]o system of collective

28. Ibid., 614.

security can be realistically expected to respond to every transgression of the prevailing order or effectively respond to every breach of the public peace[,] ... [it must nonetheless] show a reasonable degree of coherence, consistency and effectiveness" [Gill].[29]

In the conclusions to his essay, Roscini writes:

> Fifteen years ago, Judge Schwebel observed that "criticizing the United Nations Security Council has been a popular sport since 1946." Some of this criticism is undoubtedly fair and is still valid today, at least with regard to the role that the Council has been playing in securing compliance with international humanitarian law. Indeed, the Security Council was not conceived as a law enforcer but as peacekeeper that acts on political grounds: a lot depends on the interests of the permanent members and the reasons for acting or not acting are often not explained. The political nature of the Council tends then to enforcement *à la carte* where certain situations are addressed but others are ignored.[30]

The resolutions of the Security Council qualifying certain acts of member states as "illegal" can hardly have any real juridical value in light of the political nature of this body of the UN, which approves resolutions in accordance with the interests and the ideologies of its members. This manifests itself very strongly in the council's insistence on condemning the State of Israel while ignoring the constant aggressions it has suffered from its Arab enemies.

Similarly, the Security Council's authorization of measures to help persecuted people has been hindered by the veto power of the permanent members. This was seen in the decision not to authorize NATO's 1999 intervention in Kosovo due to Russia's veto, which maintained ties with the murderous Milosevic regime.[31]

Where there are no political interests, the Security Council may choose to intervene. In the period of July–August 2012, for example, the council approved Resolutions 2.062/3/4/6, which decided to extend mandates of international or regional operations in Côte d'Ivoire, Sudan, Lebanon, and

29. Marco Roscini, "The United Nations Security Council and the Enforcement of International Humanitarian Law," *Israel Law Review* 43 (2010): 352–53.
30. Ibid., 357–58.
31. Pattison, *Humanitarian Intervention*, 6. NATO ended up intervening anyhow.

Liberia, as the situations in these countries "continues to pose a threat to international peace and security."[32] Yet most of these and other interventions were not successful as the intervening party tends to end up siding with one of the parties in the conflict.

Likewise, in the following period of October–November 2012, the Security Council approved Resolutions 2071/2/3/6/8 regarding Mali, Somalia, and Congo, where situations existed that "pose a threat to international peace and security." The result of these resolutions was close to nill.

UN Paper Resolutions

As we have seen, the UN has recurrently argued that human suffering may have repercussions on international peace and security, since the eruption of grave violence in one state brings about violations of international humanitarian law. This brings us to the development of human rights in the field of armed conflicts. This amplification of the concept of human rights was introduced at the 1968 UN International Conference on Human Rights in Teheran, which contains a chapter on "Human Rights in Armed Conflicts." It is further stated in Resolution 9/9 of the Human Rights Council of 2008, which emphasizes in its article 1 that "conduct that violates international humanitarian law, including grave breaches of the Geneva Convention of 12 August 1949, or of the Protocol Additional thereto of 8 June 1977 relating to the Protection of Victims of International Armed Conflicts (Protocol 1) may also constitute a gross violation of human rights."

The repercussion of the violation of international humanitarian law on peace and security was formulated in the Security Council's Resolutions 808 (1993) and 955 (1994), respectively on Yugoslavia and Rwanda. When a state is "manifestly failing" to protect its population from four specified crimes, the heads of state and government confirmed that the international community was prepared to take collective action, through the Security Council and in accordance with the Charter of the United Nations.

In the early 2000s, discussions started about what became known as the "responsibility to protect." According to this principle, a state has the responsibility to uphold its citizens' human rights. However, if it is unable or

---

32. "United Nations Security Council Resolutions," *International Legal Materials* 51, no. 4 (2012): 922.

unwilling to fulfill this responsibility, as in cases of mass killing, its sovereignty is temporarily suspended and the responsibility to protect the citizens of that state is transferred to the international community. The three pillars of the responsibility to protect, as stipulated in the Outcome Document of the 2005 United Nations World Summit,[33] are:

1. The State carries the primary responsibility for protecting populations from genocide, war crimes, crimes against humanity and ethnic cleansing, and their incitement;
2. The international community has a responsibility to encourage and assist States in fulfilling this responsibility;
3. The international community has a responsibility to use appropriate diplomatic, humanitarian and other means to protect populations from these crimes. If a State is manifestly failing to protect its populations, the international community must be prepared to take collective action to protect populations, in accordance with the Charter of the United Nations.

The international community's responsibility to protect involves the "responsibility to prevent" the crisis, the "responsibility to react" to it and the "responsibility to rebuild" after it is over. What was known originally as "the right to intervene" of any state turned into the "responsibility to protect" of every state.

The 2005 World Summit was the occasion of the High Level Plenary Meeting of the sixtieth session of the United Nations General Assembly, with over 160 heads of state and government in attendance. There it was agreed that there exists a universal responsibility to protect populations – including to undertake action should peaceful means be inadequate – when national authorities are manifestly failing to protect their populations from genocide, war crimes, ethnic cleansing, and crimes against humanity.

In paragraph 139 of the General Assembly's resolution (mentioned above), it was decided that:

We stress the need for the General Assembly to continue consideration of the responsibility to protect populations from genocide, war crimes,

---

33. (A/RES/60/1, para. 138–140) and formulated in the Secretary-General's 2009 Report (A/63/677) on Implementing the Responsibility to Protect.

ethnic cleansing and crimes against humanity and its implications, bearing in mind the principles of the Charter and international law. We also intend to commit ourselves, as necessary and appropriate, to helping States build capacity to protect their populations from genocide, war crimes, ethnic cleansing and crimes against humanity and to assisting those which are under stress before crises and conflicts break out.

In July 2008, the secretary-general of the UN, Ban Ki-moon, made a pronouncement that practically repeated what had been agreed to by world leaders, stressing that the responsibility to protect rests on three pillars:

1. The responsibility of the state to protect its own populations from genocide, war crimes, ethnic cleansing and crimes against humanity;
2. The international community's duty to assist states in meeting these obligations;
3. The international community's responsibility to respond in a timely and decisive manner when a state is manifestly failing to protect its population using Chapter VI (peaceful means), Chapter VII (coercive means authorized by the UN Security Council) and Chapter VIII (regional arrangements) of the UN charter.[34]

All these resolutions are hardly worth the paper they were printed on, as we shall see in chapter 8 when describing the succession of genocides that have been taking place in the decades since the end of World War II and the creation of the United Nations.

Mild Interventions

The majority of the tragic internal events that occurred since World War II were not attended by the United Nations in due time or were not treated effectively. It is true that the many references in the Charter of the United Nations to the "maintenance or restoration of international peace and security" could be interpreted as not necessarily applying to internal conflicts, as violent and murderous as they might become. And yet, the common understanding of chapter 7 of the charter – which is titled "Action with respect to threats to the

34. Bellamy, "Military Intervention," in Bloxham and Moses, *Oxford Handbook of Genocide Studies*, 604–5.

peace, breaches of the peace and acts of aggression" – has been understood
to relate to internal conflicts as well.

A sequence of interventions took place since 1989, some of which related
to the specific genocides that are described in chapter 8. The following are
some of those interventions:

- The Economic Community of West African States (ECOWAS) intervention in Liberia in 1990, to restore law and order.
- The French, British, and American intervention in northern Iraq in 1991,
  to create safe havens and to implement no-fly zones to protect thousands
  of endangered Kurds.
- The US-led intervention in Somalia in 1992 to open up humanitarian
  corridors.
- The US-led intervention in Haiti in 1994 to restore the democratically
  elected president, Jean-Bertrand Aristide.
- NATO's bombing of Bosnian Serb positions in 1995 to end the civil war
  in the former Yugoslavia.
- The ECOWAS intervention in Sierra Leone in 1997 to restore peace and
  stability after heavy fighting.
- NATO's intervention in Kosovo in 1999 to protect the Kosovan Albanians
  from ethnic cleansing.
- The Australian-led intervention in East Timor in 1999 after Indonesian
  brutality.
- UN actions (including European Union forces) in eastern parts of the
  Democratic Republic of Congo, since 1999.
- The UK intervention in Sierra Leone in 2000 to strengthen the faltering
  United Nations Mission (UNAMSIL).
- The ECOWAS, UN, and US intervention in Liberia in 2003 after the
  renewal of fighting.
- The French and UN intervention in Côte d'Ivoire in 2003.[35]

In most cases the intervention could have taken place much earlier and would
have saved many of the lives that were sacrificed on the altar of barbarous

---

35. Pattison, *Humanitarian Intervention*, 1–2.

terrorism. The interventions were also not very successful.[36] They should be classified as mild interventions.[37]

The Incapacity of the United Nations

The sad reality is that despite the need to be able to move quickly to prevent genocides and crimes against humanity, the United Nations has no capacity to avert such catastrophes, even when prompt action could save hundreds of thousands of lives. The international community's failure to stop genocide in Rwanda in 1994 and to avert the ongoing ethnic cleansing occurring in the Darfur region of Sudan are the classic illustrations of this incapacity, besides other massive killings of civilians in Cambodia, East Timor, Sierra Leone, the Democratic Republic of Congo, the former Yugoslavia, and many other locations, as detailed in chapter 8.

In recent years, huge atrocities have killed millions of innocent people, wounded millions more, forced tens of millions from their homes, destroyed economies, and wasted hundreds of billions of dollars.[38]

And then came the post–Arab Spring Syrian tragedy, causing hundreds of thousands of deaths and millions of displaced persons, while the international community looks on, passive, inert, paralyzed by disagreements amongst the maestros of the international orchestra that plays its cruel tricks in an imposing building located in Manhattan, New York.

The idea that sovereignty is an obstacle to intervention may be reflected in the Genocide Convention, which occupies itself with punishment, but does not tackle intervention's other objective: prevention.

A recent demonstration of the impotence of the United Nations was the declaration of Secretary-General Ban Ki-moon in July 2012, when the killing in Syria started: "The United Nations is doing all that we can. But action – meaningful action will take the concerted efforts of the international community.

---

36. Pattison reports that in the 1990 intervention in Liberia, after successfully pushing back the rebel advances and restoring law and order in Monrovia, ECOWAS became more like a party in the conflict and was unable to establish authority in the interior (ibid., 206).

37. The data described above should be compared with the sequence of genocides described in chapter 8.

38. Robert C. Johansen, "A United Nations Emergency Peace Service to Prevent Genocide and Crimes against Humanity," www.responsibilitytoprotect.org/files/UNEPS _PUBLICATIONS.

Without unity, there will be more bloodshed. Without unity, more innocents will die."[39] The lack of unity he was referring to was connected to the division in the Security Council between the Western powers on one side and Russia and China on the other.

The UN's incapacity is a consequence of the lack of a reliable and effective coercive system to enforce the wide collection of human rights international documents. The Universal Declaration of Human Rights is an enunciation of principles and values of different categories and diversified levels, the more important of which had been recognized (even if not always respected) by the liberal democracies for centuries before the declaration's approval by the UN General Assembly, but have not as yet been accepted by the majority of the UN's state members. The declaration was wrongly conceived, as it equates the most important conquests of political science and constitutional law with values of social and economic characteristics of various levels, a mixture that does not fit in any legal document. As far as application is concerned, the document has proved itself to be a total failure in protecting human collectivities.

Actually, the history of the declaration's creation itself reveals that it is totally devoid of any kind of implementation device. The Economic and Social Council established the Commission of Human Rights on June 21, 1946, and requested it to "submit suggestions regarding ways and means for the effective implementation of human rights and fundamental freedoms."[40] At the very first session, the representative from Australia, Colonel William Hodgson, asked why the question of implementation was not among the list of items on the agenda, to which the US representative, Mrs. Eleanor Roosevelt, answered that "the Commission needed to agree on what should be included in the Bill in the way of rights and then the question of implementation might be taken up and considered very carefully."[41] The Australian delegate was not satisfied and insisted that "the Commission's task was to draft a bill of human rights, not a declaration, which, he felt, entailed no legal obligations and would not in any way affect the lives of men and women unless translated into concrete action."[42] In the same vein Fernand Dehousse, the Belgian

39. Reuters, "Recalling Srebrenica, Ban Urges Action on Syria," *Jerusalem Post*, July 26, 2012, internet edition, http://www.jpost.com/printarticle.aspx?id=278899.
40. Morsink, *Universal Declaration*, 14.
41. Ibid., 16.
42. Ibid., 17.

delegate, argued against a mere declaration, which "would cause immense disappointment to a world that was awaiting positive solutions capable of influencing human destiny."[43] We have covered this fundamental weakness of the UDHR in chapter 6.

"When the Declaration was adopted," notes Glendon, "many regarded it as a milestone in the history of freedom, but to others it seemed to be just a collection of pious phrases – meaningless without courts, policemen, and armies to back them up."[44]

As for the Charter of the United Nations, the discussions around articles 55 and 56, the difficulties in making them work in view of article 2.7 of the same instrument, and the experience of almost seven decades all indicate the same problem: the charter has no legal power to guarantee protection in the face of the worst atrocities committed throughout the last three generations. The same goes for the Covenant on Civil and Political Rights as well as for the Covenant on Economic, Social, and Cultural Rights and for the succession of human rights conventions that have been approved by the United Nations General Assembly.

There is a very rich literature on the "internationalization of human rights," to the point that the state parties to the UN charter recognize that the "human rights" discussed in it are a subject of international concern and no longer within their exclusive domestic jurisdiction. This is very fine in theory, but has never had any real positive effect regarding the human rights of collectivities, of ethnic/religious groups and of minorities in general.

The same goes for the Universal Declaration of Human Rights, which is supposed to work hand in hand with the charter, but has been equally unsuccessful in avoiding the most serious offenses to the dignity of the human person, as the General Assembly of the United Nations has recognized on various occasions. For instance, Resolution 2144A (XXI) of October 26, 1966, expressed the conviction of the General Assembly that "gross violations of the rights and fundamental freedoms set forth in the Universal Declaration of Human Rights continue to occur in certain countries." The same resolution called on ECOSOC and the Commission of Human Rights "to give urgent consideration to ways and means of improving the capacity of the United

43. Ibid.
44. Glendon, *A World Made New*, 235.

Nations to put a stop to violations of human rights wherever they may occur."[45] Summing up, the innumerable UN resolutions regarding the need to implement the two major documents – the charter and the declaration – have not avoided the growing violations of collective human rights.

The same goes for the specific human rights treaties – they increased from 20 in 1975 to 100 in 1980, 175 in 1990, and 300 in 2013. These treaties cover so many areas of collective life that they end up rendering each other meaningless.[46]

The Performance of the Human Rights Council

The partiality and political orientation of the Security Council are blatantly reflected in the performance of the Human Rights Council, as before in its antecessor, the Human Rights Commission.

The former commission was known for concentrating most of its time on criticizing Israel. Throughout the years, one third of its resolutions criticizing a specific state were directed to Israel. The commission oversaw various committees dedicated to civil and political rights, children's rights, and protection from torture. There is only one committee without a generic theme and that is the Committee on Israeli Practices Affecting the Human Rights of the Palestinian People and Other Arabs of the Occupied Territories, created in 1968. The only division of the UN Secretariat devoted to the claims of a single people champions Palestinians and is based on an explicitly anti-Israel historical and political narrative.[47]

In 2006, in light of the severe critiques raised against the absurdly discriminatory policies of the commission, the UN General Assembly replaced the commission with the council. The "reform" of the UN's top human rights body was fundamentally flawed, since America's proposal to condition membership in the new council on some degree of actual respect for the human rights of their own populations was categorically rejected.

With the abolition of the commission and the creation of the council, statistics remained the same: about one-third of all critical resolutions concerning human rights situations are directed at Israel. The situation has

45. See www.un.org/documents/ga/res/21/ares21.htm.
46. Posner, *Twilight of Human Rights Law*, 92–93.
47. Anne Bayefsky, "Neither Redeemable nor Reformable," *Justice: The International Association of Jewish Lawyers and Jurists* 45 (spring 2008): 29.

reached the point that the only subject matter that appears on the agenda on every single session of the council is Israel.

A State Department press release of March 2011 stated that the United States will continue to work hard to diminish the council's biased, disproportionate focus on Israel. "The U.S. maintains a vocal, principled stand against this focus, and will continue its robust efforts to end it."[48] Unfortunately, one member cannot change the orientation of an organ composed of forty-seven states.

When the United States was reelected to the council in November 2012, the State Department issued a press statement expressing satisfaction with the reelection and reviewed the more recent activities of the council, which it summarized through the following specific situations:

- Syria – Condemnation of the atrocities occurring in this country and establishing an independent International Commission of Inquiry.
- Libya – Establishment of a Commission of Inquiry on the dire human rights situation.
- Iran – A Special Rapporteur nominated to highlight Iran's deterioration of the human rights situation.
- Belarus – A Special Rapporteur nominated to highlight human rights abuses.
- Côte d'Ivoire – A Commission of Inquiry established to investigate human rights abuses.
- Burma – In a period of three years, four resolutions taken that addressed the human rights situation.

These resolutions, commissions of inquiry, and nominations of special rapporteurs are hardly known in the world community. They are rarely referred to by the international press and lead to absolutely no results.

The irony of what goes on in the United Nations can be exemplified by the facts that Libya and Côte d'Ivoire were members of the council while the

---

48. John R. Crook, "Contemporary Practice of the United States Relating to International Law," *American Journal of International Law* 106, no. 4 (October 2012): 843–44; Crook, "Contemporary Practice of the United States Relating to International Law: State Department Hails U.S. Accomplishments in UN Human Rights Council; United States to Seek Election to Another Council Term," *American Journal of International Law* 105, no. 3 (July 2011): 592–93.

commissions of inquiry on their abuses of human rights were being established, and Iran and Syria were elected to other human rights panels – Iran on the women's rights commission and Syria on UNESCO's human rights committee. The satisfaction and apparent optimism of the State Department with the US election to the council was merely wishful thinking, a formal diplomatic declaration, rather than a serious appreciation of the council's work. The council achieves no effective, practical results whatsoever and perseveres in its discrimination against one single state. The international institution with the mission to discover and condemn all kinds of discrimination is itself the champion of discrimination!

As of 2013, the following states were members of the Human Rights Council: Algeria, Argentina, Austria, Benin, Botswana, Brazil, Burkina Faso, Chile, China, Congo, Costa Rica, Côte d'Ivoire, Cuba, Czech Republic, Estonia, Ethiopia, France, Gabon, Germany, India, Indonesia, Ireland, Italy, Japan, Kazakhstan, Kenya, Kuwait, Maldives, Mexico, Montenegro, Morocco, Namibia, Pakistan, Peru, the Philippines, Republic of Korea, Republic of Macedonia, Rumania, Russian Federation, Saudi Arabia, Sierra Leone, South Africa, United Arab Emirates, United Kingdom, United States, Venezuela, and Vietnam.

Fewer than half of those states are fully free democracies.

Many states have violated human rights in the most atrocious ways and yet were never condemned: Angola, Saudi Arabia, Bahrain, Bangladesh, Burkina-Faso, Cameron, Cuba, Egypt, Gabon, Ghana, Indonesia, Qatar, Madagascar, Mauritius, Nicaragua, Nigeria, Pakistan, Zambia.

On November 13, 2013, the president of the Human Rights Council, Remigiusz Henczel, presented a report to the UN General Assembly in which he stated that in the past year the council had achieved significant progress, adopting a total of 107 resolutions, decisions, and president's statements. Unfortunately, this is the measure of accomplishments in the UN: high-level panels, commissions of inquiry, nomination of rapporteurs and, above all, resolutions. Words, empty words.

For many years, the council based its campaign against Israel on the reports of Special Investigator Richard Falk, who excelled in demonizing Israel without ever referring to the constant incitement and the manifold murderous terrorist acts conducted by the Palestinians against civilians in the State of Israel.

Actually, the mandate of the rapporteur is in and of itself totally biased. It reads: "To investigate Israel's violations of the principles and bases of international law, international humanitarian law and the Geneva Convention relative to the Protection of Civilian Persons in Time of War...." Not a word about investigating the possible motives that would characterize Israel's actions as defensive measures against terrorist activities. The wording of the mandate is itself a condemnation. Therefore, there should have been no need to investigate. It is a contradiction in terms!

Falk's bigoted pronouncements reached the point of accusing Israel of "genocidal" intentions against the Palestinians in a brief English-language interview on Russian television. This led the Canadian government to call on the council to dismiss Falk. John Baird, Canada's foreign minister, announced:

> Canada has previously called for Falk to be fired for his numerous outrageous and anti-Semitic statements and these comments underscore once more the complete and total absurdity of his service as a UN Special Rapporteur. I call on the United Nations Human Rights Council – once again – to remove Falk from this position immediately.[49]

A symptomatic event is the Universal Periodic Review (UPR), which takes place every four years. In the review, the council spends a few hours dealing with the human rights record of each UN member state. The country under consideration sends representatives to deliver a statement about its human rights situation. The other states are given two minutes each to comment and make recommendations for improvement of the status of human rights in the state under review, which voices its acceptance or rejection of those recommendations. NGOs are allotted a limited time to make comments. And then all of this material is put into a report.

An interesting description of the procedure of the UPR by Anne Bayefsky, an expert on human rights, shows the following hilarious panorama:

> In practice, the UPR looks like this. A very large number of friends of each rights-abusing country line up to praise its human rights record and

---

49. Tovah Lazaroff, Canada Calls for Dismissal of Richard Falk for Accusing Israel of 'Genocidal' Intentions," *Jerusalem Post*, December 19, 2013, http://www.jpost.com /Diplomacy-and-Politics/Canada-calls-for-dismissal-of-Richard-Falk-for-accusing-Israel -of-genocidal-intentions-335446.

generate a long list of false congratulatory recommendations which can be easily "accepted." The favor is repaid when their pals' turns come along. These states then announce that serious recommendations "do not enjoy their support." The praise and the rejections all get included in a report that contains no findings and no conclusions, and there are no decisions to take action.

The UPR has recently faced the acid test of dealing with a country committing crimes against humanity, namely Syria. The spectacle of the Syrian UPR included Burma saying it "congratulates Syria for its successful efforts to create advanced health care for its people." While Venezuela "wished to reiterate its unambiguous support to the significant effort that President Assad is making to preserve his country's stability when faced with the onset of greedy imperialism."

... By contrast, during the UPR of the United States in 2010, Iran told the US to "combat violence against women." Nicaragua told the US to redress the wrongs "caused by capitalism." North Korea told the US to "prohibit and punish brutality by law enforcement officials." And China complained that the US limited citizens' freedom of expression and the right to free internet access.

On October 21, 2013, Saudi Arabia sent two female representatives to its UPR who addressed the Council shrouded entirely in black but for the slits of their eyes. In that condition, one said: "I would like to underline that the system in Saudi Arabia doesn't make a distinction between men and women." And the other defended the rape of children: "our country has prohibited marriage of any persons who have not reached the age of puberty." As the 2012 State Department human rights report on Saudi Arabia points out, in practice "girls as young as 10 may be married."

And Bayefsky's description of the UPR concludes by saying, "It is little wonder, therefore, that the world's worst human rights violators are delighted by the grotesque moral relativism of the UPR and repeatedly applaud its 'universality.'"[50]

50. Anne Bayefsky, "Europe, US Pressuring Israel to Endure Discrimination at UN Human Rights Council," *Jerusalem Post*, October 27, 2013, http://www.jpost.com/Opinion /Op-Ed-Contributors/Europe-US-pressuring-Israel-to-endure-discrimination-at-UN -Human-Rights-Council-329832.

The president of the Human Rights Council, in his statement to the General Assembly on November 13, 2013, said that he wished

> to acknowledge the fact that the constructive, consensual and non-politicized approach maintained by the Council throughout this year has encouraged Israel to re-engage with the UPR (Universal Periodic Review). And I welcome Israel's reengagement as it upholds the integrity and the universality of this important process.
>
> Furthermore, it is my firm conviction that by applying all existing practices and rules in a consistent manner to all States under review, we will contribute to strengthening the UPR's credibility and to the successful second cycle of the UPR, taking into account one of its principles, which is that of an equal treatment of all States under review.[51]

This is hypocrisy reaching the absolutely grotesque, or perhaps the absolutely obscene.

Crowning all these falsities and probably the most important negative factor is the politicization of the former Human Rights Commission, today the Human Rights Council. Thomas Buergenthal, in an attempt to justify the behavior of the Human Rights Commission, ended up demonstrating the failure that it represents:

> The Commission has been frequently criticized for its ineffectiveness and for tending to politicize the UN human rights program. Although some of the criticism is justified, much of it overlooks the fact that the Commission can do no more than the states comprising it are willing to do.... Since the Commission is a political body, it should surprise no one, regrettable as this may be, that it tends to politicize the issues before it.[52]

This politicization of the Human Rights Council follows the spirit and practice of the Security Council which we described above.

51. Ibid.
52. Buergenthal, *International Human Rights in a Nutshell*, 63–64. Then the author proceeds with praises on the contribution the commission has brought to the "broadening of the human rights agenda of the UN, for transforming human rights into a major item on the agenda of the international community and for significantly broadening the legal scope and application of the human rights provisions of the UN charter." This is mere wishful thinking coming from a person who has sincerely dedicated his life to the improvement of human rights.

At the origin, René Cassin wanted members of the Human Rights Commission to be independent representatives, but that was a lost battle. As his biographers write: "That was not to be and today they are still appointed by states, whatever their record of violation or respect for human rights."[53]

Eleanor Roosevelt, René Cassin, and other idealists of the postwar era toiled to establish respect for human rights the world over. One can easily imagine how they would feel were they to see how their work has been degraded and practically nullified.

The Observance of Human Rights for State Interests

In the rich literature on human rights in the international arena, we find the view that "some states have an interest in improving the way other states treat their citizens in order to expand trade, minimize war and promote international stability. This was a primary impetus for the human rights movement which followed World War II."[54] According to this view, "most states' foreign aid reflects mixed humanitarian/economic/strategic concerns, and a concern for people in other states tends to translate into humanitarian intervention only when it dovetails with a state's economic or security interests."

Regarding measures applied by democracy A to stop grave human rights transgressions by dictatorship B, the following story illustrates the policy of the liberal democracies: President Clinton organized five banquets to celebrate the incoming year 2000 (as the start of the new millennium), and for each occasion an illustrious personality was invited to speak to the guests. In one of these banquets Nobel Peace Prize laureate Professor Elie Wiesel was the guest speaker. As he had just returned from the former Yugoslavia, where he had sat for days and nights with the representatives of the enemy peoples, he reported on his efforts to stop the fighting and killing, unfortunately without success. NATO, with strong American backing, had to employ severe military measures to bring the killing to a halt.

When Wiesel finished the narrative of his heroic fight to stop the atrocities and of NATO's mighty intervention, a guest got up and asked him: "Professor Wiesel, if so much was invested to stop the murdering in Central Europe, why was nothing done, especially by the United States, to stop the genocide

53. Winter and Prost, *René Cassin*, 349.
54. Goldsmith and Posner, *Limits of International Law*, 110.

in Rwanda?" The honorable guest answered that the question should not be addressed to him but to the host, the president of the United States. President Clinton got up and confessed that Rwanda had been a grave mistake, pledging that in the future the United States would act differently.[55]

President Clinton's response was in the same spirit as his speech to survivors at the Genocide Convention in Kigali, Rwanda, on March 25, 1998:

> We did not immediately call these crimes by their rightful name: genocide.... It may seem strange to you here, especially the many of you who lost members of your family, but all over the world there were people like me sitting in offices day after day after day, who did not fully appreciate the depth and speed with which you were being engulfed by this unimaginable terror.[56]

Charles Beitz explains the basic policy in a nutshell:

> Even when powerful actors have been authentically concerned to protect human rights, their attention has usually been directed at regions where they have strategic interests and diverted from those where they do not.[57]

Peter Novick joins the critique of the US government:

> There was not the slightest will in American political circles for any U.S. intervention. Indeed, the principal action of the Clinton administration while the killing was going on was to issue a directive cutting back the American commitment to peacekeeping operations and stressing that there would be no U.S. involvement in such operations when our national security wasn't directly threatened.... The administration instructed officials to avoid calling what was going on in Rwanda genocide. (To acknowledge that it was genocide would, in principle, oblige the United States, along with other signers of the UN Genocide Convention, to take action).[58]

---

55. Oral report by Professor Wiesel to the author on May 10, 1999, in Rio de Janeiro, where he came to receive the local state university's "doctor honoris causae," the one-hundredth university honor that the illustrious fighter for human rights had received thus far.
56. Scheffer, *All the Missing Souls*, 45.
57. Beitz, *The Idea of Human Rights*, 6.
58. Novick, *The Holocaust in American Life*, 250.

This coincides with what Goldsmith and Posner describe:

> Consider the patterns of US human rights enforcement. The United
> States committed significant military and economic resources to redress
> human rights violations in Yugoslavia (where it had a strategic interest
> in preventing central European conflict and resolving NATO's crises of
> credibility and purpose), Haiti (where turmoil was threatening a domestic
> crisis in Florida) and Iraq (where it had obvious strategic interests). But
> the United States had done relatively little in the face of human rights
> abuses in Africa, where it lacks a strong strategic interest, or in Saudi Arabia,
> China and Russia, where its strategic interests conflict with enforcement
> of a human rights agenda, and where in any event the costs of enforcement
> are significantly higher.[59]

The restatement of the Foreign Relations Law of the United States has adopted
this approach as a general policy on the treatment that may be provided to
states that violate human rights. Section 703 provides that "any state may
pursue international remedies against any other state for violation of the
customary international law of human rights." It then adds in comment f:

> *State sanctions for human rights violations by another state.* A state may crit-
> icize another state for failure to abide by recognized international human
> rights standards, and may shape its trade, aid or other national policies
> so as to dissociate itself from the violating state or to influence that state
> to discontinue the violations.

As part of the United Nations weak preventative system, the Genocide Convention has justly been blamed for failing to protect minorities from massive
violence during and after the Cold War.[60]

---

59. Goldsmith and Posner, *Limits of International Law*, 117. At 124 the authors add: "The
case studies always focus on human rights change in small or weak states that are most
susceptible to coercion or economic bribes; they do not focus on larger states like China,
Saudi Arabia, or Russia, where human rights progress has been slow and where coercion
and bribes are less efficacious." The authors also inform that the United States has consistently threatened to withhold hundreds of millions of dollars in US and International
Monetary Fund monies unless the successor regimes in Yugoslavia continue to send war
criminals to the International Criminal Tribunal for the former Yugoslavia (ibid., 116).
60. Cohen, "The Holocaust and the Human Rights Revolution," in Iriye, Goedde, and
Hitchcock, *Humans Rights Revolution*, 62–63.

The strongest accusation regarding the Genocide Convention comes from Novick:

> Despite the broad scope of the language adopted, over the next fifty years, which saw tens of millions die in actions, that were, by the UN definition, clearly genocidal, the United Nations has never invoked the procedure for charging the crime of genocide. From the outset, "genocide" was a rhetorical rather than a juridical device, employed for purely propagandistic purposes.[61]

The Covenants and Their Committees

The 1996 Resolution 2200 of the UN General Assembly approved the International Covenant on Civil and Political Rights; the International Covenant on Economic, Social, and Cultural Rights; and the Optional Protocol to the International Covenant on Civil and Political Rights, all in line with the Universal Declaration of Human Rights.[62]

The International Covenant on Civil and Political Rights is directed mainly to individuals. Most of its articles refer to "individuals," "persons," "human beings," "everyone," "anyone," "no one," "family," "child," and "citizen," in the spirit of the Universal Declaration. The reference it contains to the collective is found in article 4, which allows, in cases of "public emergency which threatens the life of the nation, to derogate from its obligations under the Covenant to the extent strictly required by the exigencies of the situation." The collectivization of one right is found in article 27, which forbids "the denial to persons belonging to ethnic, religious or linguistic minorities in community with the other members of their group, to enjoy their own culture, to profess and practice their own religion or to use their own language."[63] Article 20, which

---

61. Novick, *The Holocaust in American Life*, 100–101.

62. UNGA done at New York, December 16, 1966, UN Doc. A/6316 (1967).

63. Buergenthal (*International Human Rights in a Nutshell*, 34) points out that the covenants have a number of common substantive provisions which "deal with what might be described as 'peoples' or 'collective' rights." He refers to article 1(1) of both covenants, which proclaims that "all peoples have the right of self-determination" and article 1(2) that "all peoples" have the right to freely dispose of their natural resources and that "in no case may a people be deprived of its own means of subsistence." Those provisions refer to established old principles of public international law. The specificities and the basic philosophy of both covenants revolve around the individual, as demonstrated in the text above.

provides that "any advocacy of national, racial or religious hatred that constitutes incitement to discrimination, hostility or violence shall be prohibited by law," does not constitute a protection by force of the international document, as it merely delegates to the member states to legislate on the matter.

Part IV of the covenant establishes a Human Rights Committee, to which the states' parties undertake to submit reports on the measures they have adopted and on the progress made in the enjoyment of these rights. State parties may recognize the competence of the committee to receive and consider communications by one state party claiming that another state party is not fulfilling its obligations under the covenant. A state party may also bring to the attention of another state party that it is not respecting the provisions of the covenant; the receiving state party should respond with an explanation within three months. If the matter is not settled between the two states, it will be dealt with by the committee, which shall make available its good offices to the states' parties concerned with a view to a friendly solution of the matter on the basis of respect for human rights and fundamental freedoms, as recognized in the covenant.

And then follows a series of rules on further developments that should take place if disagreement between the two involved states has not been settled.

The Optional Protocol also allows the committee to receive and consider communications from individuals subject to the jurisdiction of a state that becomes a party to the protocol, who claim to be victims of a violation by that state party of any of the rights set forth in the covenant.[64] The committee shall bring the individual's claim to the attention of the state party and after receiving from it the explanations or statements clarifying the matter and the remedy it may have been taking, the committee shall forward its views to the state party and to the individual.[65]

The reports that are prescribed in these modern human rights documents have no effective or reliable coercive enforcement mechanism and there is a very large number of overdue reports. Regarding individual complaints, it is interesting to note that although 1.4 billion people have the formal right under these treaties to file complaints against their governments, there are only about sixty complaints per year.[66]

64. Article 1 of the protocol.
65. Articles 4 and 5 of the protocol.
66. Goldsmith and Posner, *Limits of International Law*, 120; see different numbers in Buergenthal, *International Human Rights in a Nutshell*, 67–68, but he refers to a decision

The various committees created by the UN have produced insignificant results, including the important Human Rights Committee. As there is no credibility to the whole system, few people or countries recur to them, and even when they do, the decisions are not respected by the states involved.

taken in 1947 by the UN Human Rights Commission, "logically the most appropriate body within the Organization to deal with these petitions, that decided that it had 'no power to take any action in regard to any complaints concerning human rights.'"

Chapter Eight
The Modern Succession of Genocides

Genocide: Defining the Problem

The inertia of the Allies during the Second World War regarding the systematic murder of the Jewish populations in occupied Europe – a continuation of the inertia that prevailed during the genocide of the Armenians in 1915 – is reflected in a similar attitude by the democracies and by the United Nations throughout all the genocides, mass atrocities, and crimes against humanity committed in the last seventy years, which sacrificed many tens of millions of human beings. The American Bar Association refers to more than three hundred smaller conflicts in various parts of the world, resulting in some one hundred million deaths, most of them civilians.[1] As UN secretary-general Kofi Anan said in a statement to the International Bar Association in March 1998, during the celebration of half a century of the UDHR and the Genocide Convention, "Many thought, no doubt, that the horrors of the Second World War – the camps, the cruelty, the exterminations, the Holocaust – could never happen again. And yet they have. In Cambodia, in Bosnia-Herzegovina, in Rwanda. Our time – this decade even – has shown us that men's capacity for evil knows no limit."

As we have already noted, the only postwar international document that has an actual connection with the events that took place during the Nazi regime is the Convention on the Prevention and Punishment of the Crime of Genocide. In contrast to all the other human rights documents, it does not

---

1. Podgers, "1985–1994: The Legacy of Nuremberg," 55.

refer to individuals but instead deals with human groups, be they national, ethnic, racial, or religious.

The convention was considered to be the centerpiece of international law regarding the protection of human groups.[2] However, the convention has very rarely been applied because it only protects cases where a specific intent has been characterized – "the intent to destroy, in whole or in part, a national, ethnical, racial or religious group."[3] Most cases of large-scale destruction of communities do not involve such specific intent. This has been very well established by David Scheffer in the dramatic account he published on his mission as US ambassador-at-large for war crimes issues,[4] in which he shows that most major collective atrocities have not met the criteria stipulated by the convention on genocide.

In Resolution 96(1) of December 11, 1946, by which the General Assembly of the United Nations recommended the drafting of a convention on genocide, this crime was defined as the "denial of the right of existence of entire human groups, as homicide is the denial of the right to live of individual human beings."

And the resolution tied the need for such a document to the "many instances of such crimes of genocide that have occurred when racial, religious, political and other groups have been destroyed, entirely or in part." The intent to destroy entire human groups or parts thereof was already present in the resolution that led to the convention, approved two years later.

The term *genocide* was born out of the execution of the "Final Solution" on the Jewish people. Therefore, the convention does not merely set the objective of punishment but very clearly establishes the obligation to prevent genocide. Prevention is the key to the materialization of the "internationalization of human rights" in its highest degree – the protection, the survival of human groups. And yet it is the convention that has the lowest degree of compliance, to the point that governments and international organizations have been unwilling to recognize and name genocide when it takes place.

The definition of the crime of genocide contained in the convention is not

---

2. Yoram Dinstein, "Collective Human Rights of Peoples and Minorities" in *International and Comparative Law Quarterly* 25, no. 1 (1976): 102, 105, as cited by Buergenthal, *International Human Rights in a Nutshell*, 49.
3. Article II.
4. Scheffer, *All the Missing Souls*.

perfectly clear. Its language is subject to various interpretations, so much so that the national laws that incorporated the crime in their legal systems have imposed their own views on the term, some of them varying slightly, others considerably, from the established international definition. As a result, there are many definitions or interpretations of the concept of genocide.[5] And the characterization of the crime of genocide is difficult because, as was noted, it is nearly impossible to prove that there is "intent to destroy."

The International Court of Justice in the Bosnia Genocide case demonstrated the complicated nature of the "intent" requirement in its finding that only the atrocities in Srebrenica were genocidal. The court based its views on the lack of a concerted plan or of a consistent pattern of conduct evincing the necessary intent.[6] Coinciding with this decision, the International Criminal Tribunal for the former Yugoslavia found genocidal intent in the decisions of the Bosnian Serb leadership to kill all men and many boys in Srebrenica, and to forcibly transfer other elements of the population.[7]

In 2005, the UN Security Council commissioned a study to determine whether genocide was being committed in Darfur. The resulting report concluded that the Sudanese government had not pursued a policy of genocide, as "the policy of attacking, killing and forcibly displacing members of some tribes does not evince a specific intent to annihilate, in whole or in part, a group distinguished on racial ethnic, national or religious grounds."[8]

Another problem with the text of the convention is that it refers exclusively

---

5. William A. Schabas, "The Law and Genocide," in Bloxham and Moses, *Oxford Handbook of Genocide Studies*, 123.

6. Steven R. Ratner, Jaspon S. Abrams, and James L. Bischoff, *Accountability for Human Rights Atrocities in International Law: Beyond the Nuremberg Legacy*, 3rd ed. (Oxford: Oxford University Press, 2009), 37, referring to paragraphs 277, 295, 319, 354, and 370–76 of the court's decision in Bosnia-Herzegovina v. Serbia and Montenegro. Paragraph 354 deserves to be quoted. It states that "on the basis of the element presented to it, the Court considers that there is convincing and persuasive evidence that terrible conditions were inflicted upon detainees of the camps. However, the evidence presented has not enabled the Court to find that those acts were accompanied by specific intent (*dolus specialis*) to destroy the protected group in whole or in part. In this regard, the Court observes that in none of the ICTY cases concerning camps cited above, has the Tribunal found that the accused acted with such specific intent (*dolus specialis*)."

7. Ibid., 38.

8. Schabas, "The Law and Genocide," in Bloxham and Moses, *Oxford Handbook of Genocide Studies*, 138–39, also referred to by Ratner, Abrams, and Bischoff, 39.

to the commission of the crime by "persons,"[9] whereas in many cases in the history of genocide the intent and its execution was an act of the state. While it is true that even in such cases, prosecution would be moved against the state representatives involved in the act, still the convention should have described the crime to cover all possibilities – genocide organized by private people and genocide resulting from state planning.

Scholars disagree with the view of the International Criminal Court for the former Yugoslavia that an individual, acting alone, can commit the crime of genocide if he or she engages in killing with a genocidal intent. They claim that this view "loses sight of the importance of the plan or policy of a state or analogous entity, that in practice, genocide within the framework of international law is not the crime of a lone deviant but the act of a state."[10] And they add that it is "the organizers and instigators of genocide who bear the greatest responsibility, the physical acts themselves are committed by individuals who are low in the hierarchy and who may well be ignorant of the genocidal intent."[11]

As mentioned, the convention establishes a condition for the occurrence of genocide – it must result from the intention to destroy in full or in part a certain human group. That may mean a national, ethnical, racial, or religious group. What if a dictator organizes and executes the murder of all the people who live in a certain province of his country, without any distinction between the different national, ethnical, racial, and religious groups who live in that particular place? According to the accepted legal doctrine, that would be a crime against humanity, but not the crime of genocide. So, as far as the Genocide Convention is concerned, there would be no justification for intervention, as the occurrence does not fit into the convention's definition. And the following month, when it becomes known that the dictator is about to execute the same murderous scheme in another of the provinces of his state, there will be nothing that the world community can do to save those people, at least not based on the Genocide Convention.

Was the tragedy of Cambodia really a case of genocide within the parameters established by the convention? The arch-criminal Pol Pot transferred

---

9. Articles 4 and 6.
10. Schabas, "The Law and Genocide," 138.
11. Ibid., 139.

and murdered those he considered his political enemies. And so he killed millions of human beings. It was a terrible crime against humanity, but it did not reflect a genocidal intention. The ideal of world human solidarity – the survival of persecuted collectivities, without consideration of the murderers' motivation – is missing protection. Where is the responsibility to protect?

This is the major problem that the world community faces – that the right (actually the obligation) to exercise prevention, which may lead to intervention, is only foreseen for the crime of genocide, but not for crimes against humanity. David Luban is absolutely right when he advocates that the concept of genocide must extend beyond group destruction to include all large-scale massacres that are currently proscribed by the crime against humanity.[12]

The preamble to the Genocide Convention states: "*Being convinced* that, in order to liberate mankind from such an odious scourge, international cooperation is required." Unfortunately, however, the convention is inoperative regarding efforts to liberate mankind from the odious scourge. This derives from the convention's text itself. Though article 1 classifies genocide as a crime under international law and establishes the obligation of the contracting parties to prevent it and punish it,[13] the provisions that follow are confined to a discussion of punishment, while not a word appears thereafter about stopping the act in the first place. Article 2 defines the crime of genocide and enumerates the different acts in which it can materialize; article 3 proceeds with a criminal-law categorization of punishability stating that "the following acts shall be punishable: (a) genocide; (b) conspiracy to commit genocide; (c) direct and public incitement to commit genocide; (d) attempt to commit genocide; (e) complicity in genocide."

So the convention made sure to cover all possible events connected to the crime of genocide as far as punishment is concerned, but did not establish one single rule regarding the inhibition of the crime.

Article 4 provides that persons committing genocide or any of the other

---

12. David Luban, "Calling Genocide by Its Rightful Name: Lemkin's Word, Darfur, and the UN Report," *Chicago Journal of International Law* 7, no. 1 (summer 2006), as cited by Alexander K.A. Greenawalt, review of *Genocide: A Normative Account*, by Larry May, *American Journal of International Law* 105, no. 4 (October 2011): 858.
13. "The Contracting Parties confirm that genocide, whether committed in time of peace or in time of war, is a crime under international law which they undertake to prevent and to punish."

acts enumerated in article 3 shall be punished, whether they are constitutionally responsible rulers, public officials, or private individuals (as provided by Resolution 96 (1) which referred to "private individuals, public officials or statesmen"). The details enumerated regarding the punishment side of the convention and the absence of rules on preventive measures empties the convention of its most important objective. The resolution of 1946 had established the need of relevant legislation and recommended "cooperation with a view to facilitating the speedy prevention and punishment of the crime of genocide." The convention did not implement the resolution, however, as it left out any mechanism for thwarting the crime it ostensibly targeted.

In the same vein, article 5 provides that the contracting parties undertake "to enact . . . the necessary legislation to give effect to the provisions of the present convention and, in particular, to provide effective penalties for persons guilty of genocide, or any of the other acts enumerated in Article III." So the actual undertaking of the contracting parties was restricted to providing effective penalties for the persons who have committed genocide or the other acts related to genocide. No undertakings were specified regarding halting genocide in progress or keeping aggressions from reaching such a level.

Articles 6 and 7 deal with jurisdictional and procedural aspects of the trials of those charged with genocide: competent tribunals and extradition. Again, only punishment is addressed.

The only practical reference to prevention appears in article 8:

> Any Contracting Party may call upon the competent organs of the United Nations to take such action under the Charter of the United Nations as they consider appropriate for the prevention and suppression of acts of genocide or any of the other acts enumerated in article III.

This provision, however, is clearly of an optional character ("may call . . . to take action"), and not obligatory. Besides, the convention is absolutely silent on what measures could be undertaken.

And so the convention does not provide ways to prevent and also does not oblige the United Nations or the contracting parties to any concrete measures. It simply "allows" contracting parties to take an initiative by calling on the UN organs to suppress genocide, under the authority of the Charter of the United Nations. The charter is silent on this specific matter.

What was the purpose of the convention?

Scholars who have dealt with the Genocide Convention have reasoned that no government would have ratified the Genocide Convention if the intent of its article 1 were to legally obligate state parties to deploy their military forces onto foreign territory to stop genocide whenever and wherever it occurs; therefore nothing in the negotiating history of the convention speaks of precisely what is expected as measures of prevention. A state party's action could be diplomatic, economic, juridical or military in character.[14] The lack of specific preventive rules resulted in a weak agreement that did not attain its main purpose – to save human groups from destruction.

To go after the "widest possible adherence to the convention" was not the ideal approach. What is better – to have a good, working convention with fewer ratifications, or an agreement with wide acceptance, which lacks any power of implementation? If only a majority of the UN member states in 1948 had approved a convention containing strict measures and a specific system of prevention and punishment, any crime under the category of genocide committed by a person as an official of a state that did not approve the convention could at least have resulted in the application of severe sanctions against that state. That would have produced a different kind of convention, foreseeing concrete measures and severe sanctions. As a matter of fact, there are voices that advocate the need for a new formulation of the definition of genocide.[15]

So we see that from its very birth, the convention was primed for failure as far as prevention is concerned. Should we say that the concern with sovereignty prevailed above the concern for the life of human groups? The international tribunals formed by the UN were meant to prosecute atrocities, including genocide. This is the punishment part. But even after these international tribunals were formed, acts of mass murder continued to occur in the same territories – and so we witness the disaster that stems from the lack of deterrence.

We conclude that as far as international statutory law is concerned, prosecution is very feasible. But if no real system of prevention exists, lives will be sacrificed when they could have been saved.

Another great failure of the Genocide Convention –as we shall see further

14. Scheffer, *All the Missing Souls*, 64. See also Ratner, Abrams, and Bischoff, *Accountability for Human Rights Atrocities*, 30.
15. Ratner, Abrams, and Bischoff, *Accountability for Human Rights Atrocities*, 47.

down – is the omission of universal jurisdiction, which would have established that perpetrators of genocides could be prosecuted and tried in any jurisdiction where they would be found. So the weakness of the convention regarding prevention is coupled with the difficulties of prosecuting the violators of this horrific crime, once they escape from the original competent jurisdictions – the place where they committed the crime and the place where a special criminal tribunal has been established.

The nonintervention attitude was well exposed in the judicial sphere years before the convention was approved. Robert Jackson, justice of the US Supreme Court and head of the US delegation to the London Conference of 1945, made the following statement on July 23, 1945:

> It has been a general principle of foreign policy of our Government from time immemorial that the internal affairs of another government are not ordinarily our business, that is to say, the way Germany treats its inhabitants, or any other country treats its inhabitants is not our affair any more than it is the affair of some other government to interpose itself in our problems. The reason that this program of extermination of Jews and destruction of the rights of minorities becomes an international concern is this: it was a part of a plan for making an illegal war. Unless we have a war connection as a basis for reaching them, I would think we have no basis for dealing with atrocities. They were a part of the preparation for war or for the conduct of the war in so far as they occurred inside of Germany and this makes them our concern.
>
> Ordinarily we do not consider that the acts of a government toward its own citizens warrant our interference. We have some regrettable circumstance at times in our own country in which minorities are unfairly treated. We think it is justifiable that we interfere or attempt to bring retribution to individual or to states only because the concentration camps and the deportations were in pursuance of a common plan or enterprise of making an unjust or illegal war in which we became involved. We see no other basis on which we are justified in reaching the atrocities which were committed inside Germany, under German law or even in violation of German law, by authorities of the German state.[16]

16. Minutes of Conference Session of 23 July 1945 in Report of Jackson, US Representative,

Jackson's statement contains an honest, if indirect, recognition of US racial discrimination. And yet the comparison is not easily acceptable – racial discrimination by the Americans versus racial elimination by the Germans. In the United States there were no concentration camps and no annihilation program as in Germany.

Jackson was entirely wrong on another point – the persecution, torture, and murder of German Jews as well as the Jews in Poland and the other occupied countries was not related to the German war against Europe, as we have explained previously. Hitler waged two wars simultaneously – the war against Europe and the war against the Jews – and they were unrelated. So, according to Jackson's basic position – no interference with the internal affairs of another state – the Nuremberg trial was not established to deal with what happened to the German Jews.

As a matter of fact, the Nuremberg Court, after recognizing the persecution of the Jews by the Nazis between 1933 and 1939, decided that to constitute crimes against humanity, the acts must have been in execution of, or in connection with, any crime within the jurisdiction of the tribunal. It therefore only considered those crimes that were executed from the beginning of the war in 1939 and were in execution or connection with war crimes, to be crimes against humanity.[17]

So we have the following situation: all the persecutions, tortures, atrocities, and murder of thousands of Jews during the years 1933 to 1939 in Germany were not considered by the court as crimes against humanity, and yet those were the crimes that inspired the UN Human Rights Commission to draft and approve the Universal Declaration of Human Rights. This only proves, once again, that the declaration was not a document of a legal nature, as we have demonstrated in chapter 6.

And so Jackson launched – immediately after World War II – the idea that no intervention should be allowed regarding the manner in which states treat their own citizens – not even if it includes the worst kind of atrocities. That

331–33, as reproduced by Schabas, "The Law and Genocide," in Bloxham and Moses, *Oxford Handbook of Genocide Studies*, 126.

17. Weston et al., *International Law and World Order*, 163. The Nuremberg Court decision was based on the International Military Charter approved by the Allied Powers, which established the jurisdiction of the court regarding crimes against peace, war crimes, and crimes against humanity.

makes the United States the initiator of the policy of no intervention and no prevention – a policy that has been followed for over seven decades.

On the other hand, there is a minority opinion that the Genocide Convention does allow for intervention:

> With regard to the latter (the United Nations) the result of the provision in question (on prevention) is that acts of commission or omission in respect of genocide are no longer, on any interpretation of the Charter, considered to be a matter exclusively within the domestic jurisdiction of the states concerned, for the parties expressly concede to the United Nations the right of intervention in this sphere.[18]

Summing up, the Genocide Convention was born with various deficiencies. It lacks rules on deterrence, and its requirement of intent is difficult to satisfy. In practice, courts have had doubts about characterizing mass killings as corresponding to the crime of genocide, which leads to David Scheffer's conclusion that the best way to deal with mass atrocities is to call them just that – the "atrocity crimes," ruled by "atrocity law."[19]

International Criminal Tribunals

Scholars in the field of international criminal law are not in agreement about the efficacy of the various international criminal tribunals that have been formed in the last years. In a book dedicated to the subject of human rights atrocities, we first read a positive analysis on the topic:

> The United Nations tribunals for the former Yugoslavia and Rwanda established in 1993 and 1994 have gained custody over and tried a large number of defendants; their lengthy judgments accompanying each verdict have yielded an important international criminal jurisprudence. States concluded a treaty establishing the International Criminal Court, which has itself begun proceedings associated with several bloody conflicts, and have created hybrid domestic/international courts to try offenders as well. The experiences of these international and internationalized courts offer important lessons on the possibilities for justice at the global level.[20]

18. Oppenheim's *International Law*, 995.
19. Scheffer, *All the Missing Souls*, 432.
20. Ratner, Abrams, and Bischoff, *Accountability for Human Rights Atrocities*, xlvi. But see

The situation is far from what the authors describe. There was no "large number of defendants," as we will see in the sections that deal with the atrocities in the former Yugoslavia and Rwanda, and the "important international criminal jurisprudence" may have great value on a theoretical plane, but has not had any impact on the criminals who have brought about and continue causing unimaginable suffering. While the International Tribunal of Yugoslavia was in full session, the atrocities in Bosnia-Herzegovina, and later on in Kosovo, were not affected. Criminal justice is to be valued according to results on the ground and here lies the question: Has there been any impact on potential and actual mass murderers? Is any potential genocidaire worried about the ICC?

In fact, the same optimistic authors agree with this skepticism, as a little later they say that "it seems premature to speak of revolution in favor of accountability. Atrocities by governmental and non-governmental forces continue with impunity in many parts of the world."[21] The International Criminal Tribunal for the former Yugoslavia has issued opinions in only a small number of cases, not always resulting in convictions, and the International Criminal Tribunal for Rwanda has issued "some two dozen convictions."[22]

The question of which genocides are prosecuted and which are not has been a subject of analysis by scholars, who arrived at a very cynical panorama. Donald Bloxham and Devin O. Pendas concluded that geopolitics is the barometer by which genocides or cases of large-scale crimes against humanity are either prosecuted or ignored. On the one hand, there is a proliferation of International Criminal Court cases against politically relatively marginal states in Africa, and on the other hand it seems highly unlikely that there will be any indictments brought against perpetrators from close strategic allies of the United States. As remarked by Eric Posner, a scholar on human rights, the ICC has taken jurisdiction only over African countries, which has led to accusations of bias even though several of those countries sought ICC intervention.[23]

---

next note and accompanying text with reference to the same authors regarding general impunity.

21. Ibid., xlviii.

22. Ibid., 27. The authors admit that "the treaty has clearly not prevented genocide in the post–World War II era, to which tragic events in such varied places as Rwanda, Yugoslavia and Sudan attest."

23. Posner, *Twilight of Human Rights Law*, 24.

The numbers are revealing. The International Criminal Tribunal for the former Yugoslavia (ICTY) had yielded sixty-four convictions by the end of 2012, out of thousands of criminals who had conducted mass killings and atrocities of all kinds. The International Criminal Court yielded only one conviction in the first decade of its existence.[24] The court runs a yearly budget of roughly 150 million US dollars.[25] The ICTY runs a similar budget.[26]

The naïveté of the American legal circles is well illustrated by a statement contained in the American Bar Association's journal, which asserts that "more than a decade after its birth, the ICC is one of the most notable achievements in law – and politics – in recent decades."[27]

As with terrorism, the pedantic approach of many jurists and the international criminal courts to the crime of genocide has been complicating

24. The only conviction was of Thomas Lubanga Dillo, sentenced to fourteen years of imprisonment. It took the ICC six years to render a trial verdict in a case involving a single defendant accused only of the war crime of child soldiering. The nearly six-hundred-page verdict was criticized "for having failed to paint a complete picture of the Ituri region, its size, its economy and the causes of its conflict," and also because "the accused remained obscure...nowhere stating the place and date of the birth of the defendant, his background, the languages he understands, what led him to leadership of the militia at issue, whether he himself had been a soldier," and so did not meet "the bar of a fully reliable record so that future generations can remember and be made fully cognizant of what happened." Diane Marie Amann, "International Decisions: Prosecutor v. Lubanga," *American Journal of International Law* 106, no. 4 (October 2012): 815–17.
25. Alexandra Huneeus, "International Criminal Law by Other Means: The Quasi-Criminal Jurisdiction of the Human Rights Courts," *American Journal of International Law* 107, no. 1 (January 2013): 2.
26. Ibid. A review of David Scheffer's book by Doug Cassel presents a more optimistic report by stating that the ICTY (former Yugoslavia) has indicted more than 160 suspected war criminals and completed proceedings against most of them, the ICTR (Rwanda) has indicted 93 persons and completed proceedings for all but 10, the Special Court for Sierra Leone has indicted 13 senior leaders and convicted 9, and the ICC has opened full investigation in seven situations: Central African Republic, Côte D'Ivoire, Darfur, Democratic Republic of Congo, Kenya, Libya, and Uganda. *American Journal of International Law* 107, no. 1 (January 2013): 252. It should be understood that there is a difference between "indictment" and "completing proceedings" versus "convictions." In the case of the Special Court for Sierra Leone, Charles Ghankay Taylor, the former president of Liberia, was convicted to a fifty-year sentence for aiding and abetting rebel forces that perpetrated brutal crimes during the civil war in Sierra Leone. Erin Louise Palmer, "Introductory Note to Prosecutor v. Charles Ghankay Taylor (SCSL)," *International Legal Materials* 53, no. 1 (2014). He remains free.
27. Podgers, "1985–1994: The Legacy of Nuremburg," 55.

its definition and hindering proceedings against mass murderers, justly called genocidaires. David Scheffer's accounts of his efforts to pin on the ex-Yugoslavian politicians and generals the crime of genocide,[28] as well as the descriptions of Larry May in his book *Genocide: A Normative Account*,[29] reveal the unfortunate kind of legal sophistication that goes on in the academic circles. The exaggerated legal speculations regarding the definition of an international crime such as genocide has been one of the great allies of the mass murderers of the last decade. As David Luban puts it, "the concept of genocide must extend beyond group destruction to include all large-scale massacres that are currently proscribed by the crime against humanity of extermination."[30] Crimes against humanity and the crime of genocide keep being confused one with the other, to the advantage of the perpetrators of the worst mass murders.

As Scheffer cries out: "Atrocities do not wait for well briefed discussions in regularly scheduled meetings of high level officials.... Atrocities, or the imminent launch of such atrocities, scream out for immediate, imaginative bold actions tailored to the unique threat. *Timing is everything*."[31]

Unfortunately, this view is not shared widely, as Doug Cassel states in his review of Scheffer's book.[32]

The same respect Hitler received from England, France, the United States, and other nations in the 1930s – as the untouchable leader of a sovereign country – continued to prevail after the war of the 1940s regarding cruel dictators, as seen during and after all genocides that followed throughout the last decades.

The impunity of the major criminals has been focused on time and again. In a statement to the Assembly of State Parties to the Statute of the International Criminal Court in mid-December 2011, Ambassador-at-Large for War Crimes Issues Stephen J. Rapp described US views on international criminal justice and the ICC. Among other statements, this is what he stressed:

28. *All the Missing Souls.*
29. As described in a review by Alexander K.A. Greenawalt, *American Journal of International Law* 105, no. 4 (October 2011): 852–59.
30. Ibid., 858.
31. Scheffer, *All the Missing Souls*, 68.
32. Doug Cassel, book review of Scheffer's *All the Missing Souls* in *American Journal of International Law* 107, no. 1 (January 2013): 254.

It is a persistent and serious cause for concern that eight individuals who are the subject of existing ICC arrest warrants remain at large.... Years after their warrants were issued, these suspects who currently remain at large all too often remain free to continue to commit serious human rights violations, which contribute to the cycle of impunity and persistent instability. The international community must demonstrate its respect for accountability, and should bring diplomatic pressure to bear on States that would invite or host these individuals.[33]

The same conclusion had been established in the detailed reports of the previous US ambassador who lived through ten years of atrocities watch: the majority of the great violators of human rights and humanitarian principles have never been brought to face justice.[34]

The great humanitarian and moralizing objectives of the convention on genocide cannot be denied. Its ineffectiveness and inoperativeness are equally undeniable. As David Scheffer laments, "The futile slogan of 'never again' after World War II collapsed under the weight of atrocity crimes occurring again and again."[35] The International Criminal Tribunals for the former Yugoslavia and Rwanda, the Special Court for Sierra Leone, the Extraordinary Chambers in the Courts of Cambodia, and finally the International Criminal Tribunal have so far had no real effect of avoiding new waves of mass atrocities in different parts of the world. Scheffer holds that "thrusting the burden of ending all atrocities on the backs of the tribunals is naïve at best and dangerous at worst."[36]

Charles Beitz deals throughout his *The Idea of Human Rights* with the problematic nature of enforcement/interference/intervention to protect the various human rights, the lack of its regulation, and the skepticism that derives from this. He justifies the interventions in Bosnia, Haiti, Somalia, Kosovo, and East Timor,[37] but decries the inertia of the "international community to act decisively where genocide has been an imminent threat."[38]

33. John R. Crook, ed., "Contemporary Practice of the United States Relating to International Law: U.S. Official Describes U.S. Policy toward International Criminal Court," *American Journal of International Law* 106, no. 2 (April 2012): 385.
34. Scheffer, *All the Missing Souls*.
35. Ibid., 2.
36. Ibid., 6.
37. Beitz, *The Idea of Human Rights*, 39.
38. Ibid., 81.

The Responsibility to Protect

Since the United Nations usually abstains from intervening in instances of mass murder, the idea has come up – despite the inexistence of any international legal rule in that sense – that a state or a group of states should be allowed to take the initiative and intervene in a third state where genocide is being committed against neighboring nationals or against its own people, under the motto "Intervention to Protect" or "Responsibility to Protect."[39]

Donald Francis Donovan, when president of the American Society of International Law, summed up the tragic consequences of the Security Council's inertia. Due to political considerations, the veto rights of the permanent members very often obstruct the UN from acting in circumstances where the imperative to prevent widespread human rights violations calls for vigorous action. Thus, the collective wellbeing that the charter was intended to protect is overpowered. According to the critics of the system, the responsibility to protect constitutes a freestanding norm. In the face of gross human rights violations, it may trump or operate outside of the strictures on the use of force imposed by the charter. The emphasis lies on the core purpose of the charter to recognize and protect the fundamental rights of all human beings, the necessary corollary of which is the right of states to act in order to deter the widespread violation of those rights. The contention is that in these circumstances the proportionate use of force targeted at preventing gross human rights violations is consistent with international law. According to this proposition, the intervention in Kosovo by NATO provides a good example of the legitimacy and utility of the norm.[40]

A possible alternative is to content ourselves with the idea that some actions will be "illegal but legitimate," as the Independent Commission on Kosovo concluded on the nature of NATO's intervention. In the same spirit can be classified the UN Security Council's authorization of military operations in Libya on humanitarian grounds, when Gaddafi threatened to massacre civilians in a rebel stronghold.

---

39. The delicate topic of intervention was dealt with in more detail in chapter 7.
40. "Responding to Mass Atrocities: The Challenge and Promise of International Law," *American Society of International Law Newsletter*, January–March 2014, 1.

Universal Jurisdiction

Regarding the punishment of people guilty of genocide – the only real subject of the convention, as we saw above – the convention only sets the jurisdiction of the state in the territory in which the act was committed, or by such international penal tribunal as may have jurisdiction with respect to those contracting parties that shall have accepted its jurisdiction. The convention contains not a word about universal jurisdiction for the *hostis humani generis* – the enemy of humankind that committed genocide.[41]

The Nuremberg trial was a perfect precedent. Michael Musmanno, of the Supreme Court of Pennsylvania, participated in the Nuremberg trial. He wrote that if a nation may only judge crimes that occurred in its own territory, than he had no right to be a member of a court that tried the members of the *Einsatzgruppen* who were not Americans and did not commit their crimes on US territory. So he invoked the seventeenth-century philosopher and jurist Hugo Grotius in his *De Jure Belli et Pacis* (*On the Law of War and Peace*), where he wrote that kings and those with similar authority are to punish brutal violation of the law of nature or the law of the nations committed against anyone, anywhere.

Musmanno proceeded to invoke Blackstone, who wrote that since the pirate is *hostis humani generis* (an enemy of humankind), all humankind has the right to punish him, just as any individual – in the state of nature – would have the right to defend himself.[42]

Manuel A. Vieira, an Uruguayan international legal scholar, goes back to Roman law, quoting from the Justinian Code (c. 3.15) that *ubide criminibus agi oportet*, which established the criminal jurisdiction of the governors of the Roman Empire by force of the location where the accused was arrested.[43]

In modern times, universal jurisdiction received considerable prestige from a thorough study prepared by the Harvard University School of Law

41. Carroll, *Constantine's Sword*, 347. This expression was used with reference to the pirates of earlier times. In the literature on the Holocaust, specifically on the anti-Jewish measures of the Catholic Church, we find the expression *Humani Generis Inimicus*, which carries the same meaning as *Hostis Humani Generis*.

42. Michael Musmanno, "The Objections in Limine to the Eichmann Trial," *Temple Law Quarterly* 35, no. 1 (fall 1961): 1–22.

43. Manuel A. Vieira, *Derecho Penal Internacional y derecho internacional penal* (Montevideo, Uruguay: Fundacion de Cultura Universitaria, 1969), 145. He also invokes the authority of Hugo Grotius, for whom there exists a *societatis generis humani*, the society of the humans.

on the competent jurisdictions to try war crimes. The conclusion of the study related to five different possible jurisdictions, the widest of all being universal jurisdiction, based on the principle of universality by which any state may exercise its jurisdiction over an international criminal, without any consideration as to nationality or place of commitment of the crime and independently of any connection between the state and the criminal.[44]

Universal jurisdiction was consecrated by the four Geneva Conventions of 1949, with the following provision:

> Each Contracting Party will have the obligation to search for the persons accused of having committed or of having ordered the commitment of any of these grave infractions and hand them to their own courts, whatever their nationalities.[45]

Though the Genocide Convention does not provide for universal jurisdiction, as article 6 restricts competence to the jurisdiction where the crime was committed and to an international tribunal that will have been recognized by the parties, some authors maintain that this may be amplified in accordance with customary international law.[46]

44. Report of the Harvard University School of Law, supplement of the *American Journal of International Law* 29 (1935).

45. Author's translation from the French. This provision is found in articles 49, 50, 129, and 146, respectively, of the four 1949 Geneva Conventions. See Stefan Glaser, *Droit international pénal conventionnel* (Brussels: Établissements Émile Bruylant, 1970), 24n17.

46. A.R. Carnegie, "Jurisdiction over Violations of the Laws and Customs of War," *British Yearbook of International Law* 39 (1963): 402–24.

Some states have amplified the competent jurisdiction in their legislation on genocide – such as the United States, which has established universal jurisdiction, and France, which provides for jurisdiction based on nationality and passive personality. Spain and Belgium have also had experiences with universal jurisdiction (Ratner et al., *Accountability for Human Rights Atrocities*, 198–202). A Special Rapporteur of the Sub-Commission on Discrimination and Minorities (of the International Commission of Jurists) submitted a report in 1985 proposing that the Genocide Convention be amended in various aspects, among them to make the crime of genocide a matter of universal jurisdiction (*Review of the International Commission of Jurists* 35 [1985]: 12, as reproduced in Sweeney et al., *International Legal System*, 625–26.

Passive Personality Jurisdiction

In the Eichmann case, involving one of the principal executioners of Hitler's "Final Solution" during World War II, Israel relied on universal jurisdiction, but even more on the principle of passive personality.[47]

The attorney general of the government of Israel, in his presentation in favor of Israel's jurisdiction, stated:

> Let us take an extreme example and assume that the Gypsy survivors, an ethnic group or a nation who were also, like the Jewish people, victims of the "crime of genocide," would have gathered after the War and established a sovereign State in any part of the world. It seems to us that no principle of international law could have denied the new State the natural power to put on trial all those killers of their people who fell into their hands. The right of the "hurt" group to punish offenders derives directly, as Grotius explained, from the crime committed against them by the offender, and it was only want of sovereignty that denied them the power to try and punish the offender. If the injured group or people thereafter reaches political sovereignty in any territory, it may make use of such sovereignty for the enforcement of the natural rights to punish the offender who hurt them.[48]

And the attorney general proceeded:

> All this holds good in respect to the crime of genocide (including the crime against the Jewish people) which, it is true, is committed by the killing of the individuals, but is intended to exterminate the nation as a group. According to Hitler's murderous racialism, the Nazis singled out Jews from all other citizens in all the countries of their domination, and carried the Jews to their death solely because of their racial origin. Even as the Jewish people constituted the object against which the crime was directed, so it is now the competent subject to place on trial those who assailed their existence. The fact that that people has become after the catastrophe a subject, where it had hitherto been an object, and has turned from the

47. Restatement of the Foreign Relations Law of the United States, section 404, reporter's note 1.
48. Cited in Myres S. McDougal and W. Michael Reisman, *International Law in Contemporary Perspective: The Public Order of the World Community* (Mineola, NY: Foundation Press, 1981), 1392.

victim of a racial crime to the wielder of authority to punish the criminals is a great historic right that cannot be dismissed. The State of Israel, the sovereign State of the Jewish people, performs through its legislation the task of carrying into effect the right of the Jewish people to punish the criminals who killed their sons with intent to put an end to the survival of this people. We are convinced that this power conforms to the principles of the law of nations in force. For these reasons we have dismissed the first contention of Counsel against the jurisdiction of the Court.[49]

This argumentation is based on the principle of passive personality, by which a state is entitled to bring to judgment the criminal that harmed its nationals. In general, scholars and courts have preferred to invoke the principle of universal jurisdiction.

A United States court approved a request by Israel for the extradition of John (Ivan) Demjanjuk, charged with murder, manslaughter, and related offenses committed in Nazi concentration camps. Although none of the crimes were committed in the territory of the requesting state, the court held that Israel had jurisdiction to try the person sought, since "international law provides that certain offenses may be punished by any state because the offenders are 'common enemies of all mankind' (*hostis humani generis*) and all nations have an equal interest in their apprehension and punishment."[50]

A Failed American Attempt to Stop Impunity

In August 2011 President Barack Obama issued a directive regarding the prevention of mass atrocities and genocide. An excerpt from a White House fact sheet states:

> Today, President Obama is directing a comprehensive review to strengthen the United States' ability to prevent mass atrocities. The President's directive creates an important new tool in this effort, establishing a standing interagency, Atrocities Prevention Board, with the authority to develop prevention strategies and ensure that concerns are elevated for senior decision-making, so that we are better able to work with our allies and partners to be responsive to early warning signs and prevent potential

49. Ibid.
50. 612 F. Supp. 544 (N.D. Ohio, 1985) and 776 F.2d 571 (6th. Circ. 1985).

atrocities. Today he is also issuing a proclamation that, for the first time, explicitly bars entry into the United States of persons who organize or participate in war crimes, crimes against humanity and serious violations of human rights.[51]

The Atrocities Prevention Board has remained inactive regarding the events going on in Syria and in Darfur.

Impunity is a major reason why the fight for human rights in the international arena has been largely unsuccessful from the beginnings in 1945. The Nazis were granted total impunity, as the few who were indicted and condemned represented an insignificant proportion of the tens and tens of thousands of cruel violators of the most elementary human right – the right to life. This impunity was reflected years later, when antisemitic manifestations and demonstrations began to appear on the German panorama, a phenomenon that is becoming graver as time passes. What could be more impressive than Chancellor Merkel warning the German people to be vigilant to the dangers of antisemitism, as she wrote in her weekly podcast, ahead of the seventy-fifth anniversary of the Kristallnacht pogrom? She lamented that it was "almost inexplicable but also the reality that no Jewish institution can be left without police protection."[52] Merkel may be unaware of the unforgiveable impunity in which the murderers of the Jewish people and of other peoples were left after the war by her country. Impunity is a stimulating factor for crime renewal.

The international system of punishing war criminals failed miserably in

51. John R. Crook, ed., "Contemporary Practice of the United States Relating to International Law: U.S. Presidential Initiative Aimed at Preventing Mass Atrocities, Sanctioning Perpetrators," *American Journal of International Law* 105, no. 4 (October 2011): 805.

52. "Merkel Laments Need to Protect Jewish Sites in Modern Germany," *Jerusalem Post*, November 2, 2013, http://www.jpost.com/Jewish-World/Jewish-News/Merkel -urges-Germans-to-be-vigilant-to-dangers-of-anti-Semitism-330422. On September 14, 2014, Chancellor Merkel came to a landmark rally in Berlin, organized to protest a rise in antisemitism. Speaking to thousands, she said that Germany would do all it could to fight antisemitism. "That people in Germany are threatened and abused because of their Jewish appearance or their support for Israel is an outrageous scandal that we won't accept. Anyone who hits someone wearing a skullcap is hitting us all. Anyone who damages a Jewish gravestone is disgracing our culture. Anyone who attacks a synagogue is attacking the foundations of our free society," proclaimed Mrs. Merkel (Maya Shwayder and Benjamin Weinthal, "Merkel: Our Jewish Friends Are at Home in Germany," *Jerusalem Post*, September 15, 2014, http://www.jpost.com/Diaspora/Merkel-Our-Jewish-friends-are-at -home-in-Germany-375341).

the Nuremberg days. It has continued to fail with regard to all those who have committed crimes against humanity, crimes against peace, the crime of genocide, and the crime of terrorism, despite all the international tribunals, with their magnificent compositions, multimillionaire budgets, and extremely good public relations and propaganda machines.

But above the shame of impunity stands the unforgiveable lack of prevention, the abhorrence to intervene on foreign soils, the idolatry of sovereignty at the price of millions of lives.

A retrospective of the number of victims from the genocides and atrocities committed in the last hundred thirty years, starting from King Leopold II of Belgium (Congo, 1886–1908) and including those caused by Hitler, Stalin, and Mao Zedong of China, adds up to over one hundred million human beings.[53] More than half of these murders occurred during the seventy years of the United Nations' existence.

After the Second World War, we have assisted many countries in all sorts of atrocities, mass murders, and ethnic cleansings. Most of them – but not all – are here described. Some reached the level of genocide as technically conceived in the convention; the majority did not, but they certainly constitute what in the Nuremberg documents was conceived of as crimes against humanity. From a moral standpoint, it makes no difference whether an atrocity does or does not fit the legal definition of the crime of genocide. And so we shall be referring in the following narratives to many of the crimes perpetrated in different parts of the world as genocides, though technically by legal definition they cannot be labeled exactly as such. The long list of human suffering that follows in the coming pages is not completely comprehensive, nor does it necessarily follow a chronological order.

Russia

Stalin's targeted economic policies brought about dramatic famines that caused the deaths of millions.

Then came the purges ordered by the dictator, and the gulag (forced labor in distant parts of the USSR, mainly in Siberia) – each of these campaigns causing more millions of deaths.

---

53. Piero Scaruffi, "The Worst Genocides of the 20th and 21st Centuries," http://scaruffi .com/politics/dictat.html.

Stalin caused the deaths of at least twenty million of his own people, by execution, starvation, and enslavement to suit the regime's wishes.[54]

China

The rapid industrialization of China in the years 1958–61, which became known as the Great Leap Forward, redirected peasant labor into industrial production. It led to a famine in which millions died of starvation. The official death toll was fourteen million, but some observers suggested substantially higher numbers. Instead of considering it a deliberately engineered plan to destroy or weaken any social group, it has been seen as the blind confidence of party leaders in the capacity of the human will to achieve official goals and the unwillingness of officials to report anything except the abundant fulfilment of those goals.[55]

Besides this tragedy, the Chinese Communist Party led a series of savage purges in Chinese society to eliminate so-called "dangerous elements" from Chinese society (landlords and business owners), people politically associated with the previous regime, dissident intellectuals, followers of organized religion, and party members suspected of abuse of power. The fate of those purged varied from public executions to beating, jailing, or exile in the countryside, public humiliation, confiscation of possessions, and loss of career prospects. Estimates of the number of executions in this period range from four hundred thousand to two million.[56]

Then, in May 1966, Mao Zedong launched the Great Proletarian Cultural Revolution. He intended to do away with the "Four Olds": old customs, habits, culture, and traditional culture. All traditional Chinese religious culture fell under this rubric as well as Western thought and culture. People who had a Western education or connections with the West, or who practiced a traditional Chinese religion, and anyone who had books or artifacts connected with either of these orientations, was targeted. Those identified as rebels against the Maoist revolution would be summarily fired from their jobs, their possessions confiscated, their persons paraded into the streets and visited with sordid violence. Many were maimed or even beaten to death. Researchers

54. Sacks, *The Great Partnership*, 119.
55. Robert Cribb, "Political Genocides in Postcolonial Asia," in Bloxham and Moses, *Oxford Handbook of Genocide Studies*, 454–55.
56. Ibid., 455.

estimate that between 750,000 and 1.5 million people were killed in this manner during the early years of the Maoist revolution, and an equivalent number crippled.[57]

Dissident nationalists of the Mongol, Tibetan, and Uyghur minorities in China contend that China has committed physical and cultural genocide against their nationalities.[58]

An opinion has been expressed that China's participation in UN human rights venues is moving her to a more humane plateau. This does not seem likely, given the determination of the Chinese regime to stamp out opposition; the vacillating weakness of the UN Council on Human Rights; the strong desire in Europe, Japan, and the United States to have new markets in China; and the general lack of political will, international stature, and policy consistency in the United States. All of these factors contradict the view that the future will see a better record on human rights in China.[59]

The same sad analysis can be made regarding other states that have committed and that continue committing atrocities against parts of their population and/or the peoples of neighboring countries.

Vietnam

Jean-Paul Sartre articulated the tragic question regarding the post–World War II world:

> Are we then so innocent? Have there been no further war crimes since 1945? Since then, has nobody resorted to violence, or to aggression? Has there been no "genocide"? Has no strong country attempted to break by the use of force the sovereignty of a small nation?[60]

Sartre introduced the Russell International War Crimes Tribunal, which functioned in 1966–67. At the time, the governments of the United States, South Korea, Australia, and New Zealand had been accused of "war crimes" in

---

57. Ibid., 456–59.
58. Uradyn E. Bulag, "Twentieth-Century China: Ethnic Assimilation and Intergroup Violence," in Bloxham and Moses, *Oxford Handbook of Genocide Studies*, 426.
59. Iriye, Goedde, and Hitchcock, *Humans Rights Revolution*, 41.
60. Jean-Paul Sartre's inaugural statement to the Russell International War Crimes Tribunal, in John Duffett, ed., *Against the Crime of Silence: Proceedings of the Russell International War Crimes Tribunal* (New Jersey: O'Hare Books, 1968), 41.

connection with the war in Vietnam. In his opening remarks, Sartre explained that Bertrand Russell had taken the initiative to form the tribunal in order to determine whether those accusations were justified.[61]

The Russell Tribunal[62] set out its aims and objectives in a declaration that, among other items, established the following points:

We therefore constitute ourselves a Tribunal which, even if it has not the power to impose sanctions, will have to answer, amongst others, the following questions:

1. Has the United States Government (and the Governments of Australia, New Zealand and South Korea) committed acts of aggression according to international law?

2. Has the American Army made use of or experimented with new weapons or weapons forbidden by the laws of war?

3. Has there been bombardment of targets of a purely civilian character, for example hospitals, schools, sanatoria, dams, etc., and on what scale has this occurred?

4. Have Vietnamese prisoners been subjected to inhuman treatment, forbidden by the laws of war and, in particular, to torture or mutilation? Have there been unjustified reprisals against the civilian population, in particular, execution of hostages?

5. Have forced labor camps been created, has there been deportation of the population or other acts tending to the extermination of the population, and which can be characterized legally as acts of genocide?

The US war against Vietnam was the subject of many severe critiques. These were sometimes shrouded in careful interrogative remarks, such as asking "whether the U.S. forces, through their bombing and other attacks during the Vietnam war, intend to destroy the Vietnamese nation in part, or was the intent purely to achieve a military objective?"[63]

---

61. Ibid., 40.
62. The tribunal was composed of over twenty important personalities of various nationalities, including the writer Simone de Beauvoir; the former president of Mexico, Lazaro Cardenas; and the historian Isaac Deutscher. Bertrand Russell was the honorary president, Jean-Paul Sartre was the executive president, and Vladimir Dedier was the chairman and president of sessions.
63. Ratner, Abrams, and Bischoff, *Accountability for Human Rights Atrocities*, 44.

The drama of the Vietnam war, its extension to Laos and Cambodia, the accusations levelled against the US government, and the performance of the main figures of the Nixon government, most especially Secretary of State Henry Kissinger – all of these deserve an independent study, which could not be included in the limits of the present work.

Cambodia

As Elie Wiesel wrote in his moving account of the massacres perpetrated in Cambodia, "The atrocities committed by Pol Pot and his Khmer Rouge… reached new lows even in the bloody annals of Communism."[64]

Abby Seiff is an American journalist who lives in Cambodia, where she covers politics, foreign affairs, and the Khmer Rouge Tribunal. Seiff avers that when Sihanouk – who ruled the country for fifteen years – was overthrown in 1970 while out of the country, he was replaced by a "U.S. backed regime whose conduct ranged from inept to despotic."[65] This is one more instance of the classic ineptitude of the United States in foreign affairs, which stems –at best – from ignoring foreign languages, foreign cultures, and foreign realities.[66]

In 1975, the local Communists, under the label of Khmer Rouge and led by one who adopted the name Pol Pot, came to power with plans to remake Cambodian society following radical Maoist models. Private property was abolished and so were religion and schools. The cities were emptied as the regime sent almost the entire population to live in collectives in an effort to convert the country into an agrarian society.

The Khmer Rouge killed hundreds of thousands of people, and hundreds of thousands more died of overwork and malnutrition. An estimated 1.7 million Cambodians died during the three and a half years the Khmer Rouge terrorized the country. In early 1979 the regime was overthrown by the Vietnamese army, which occupied Cambodia for the next decade.[67]

64. Wiesel, *And the Sea Is Never Full*, 90.
65. Abby Seiff, "Seeking Justice in the Killing Fields: For a War Crimes Tribunal in Cambodia, Successful Prosecution of Khmer Rouge Leaders Is No Sure Thing," *American Bar Association Journal* 99, no. 3 (March 2013): 52.
66. For more on the ignorance guiding American policy, see "American Naïveté" in chapter 9.
67. The Khmer Rouge rule over Cambodia and its eventual fall as a consequence of the Vietnamese invasion is described in detail by Ratner, Abrams, and Bischoff, *Accountability for Human Rights Atrocities*, 305–18.

In an interview on National Public Radio in November 1978, Senator George McGovern condemned the mass killing in Cambodia and called for an international military intervention. His was a lone voice.[68] When Pol Pot's regime collapsed shortly thereafter, its horrors began to be revealed. It was too late to save any of the almost two million victims.

Before that, on May 3, 1977, the Subcommittee on International Organizations of the House Committee on International Relations heard a statement by John Barron, senior editor of the *Reader's Digest*, in which he narrated the atrocities that were going on in Cambodia.

Barron referred to orders given by the Khmer Rouge in the autumn of 1975 to field commanders to prepare for the extermination, after the forthcoming harvest, of all former government soldiers and civil servants regardless of rank, as well as their families. Barron added: "I will say here that it is no longer any secret. What goes on the airwaves is frequently heard. While I am not at liberty to discuss what has been heard, I suggest that a lot of governments know that these orders were issued."[69]

The United States and the rest of the democratic world did not take any initiative; no attempt was made to save some of the Cambodian people. They were left entirely in the hands of their tormentors and murderers. There was no prevention of genocide, no initiative against mass atrocities.

One version of the events of those years has it that the United States indirectly supported Pol Pot. Following a policy of restraining the Vietnamese, who were seen as the real threat to American interests, the United States kept Pol Pot in play as counterweight.

According to one source, Zbigniew Brzezinski, President Carter's national security adviser, said that "I encouraged the Chinese to support Pol Pot. Pol Pot was an abomination, we could never publicly support him, but China could. So the United States winked semipublicly at China's funneling arms to him via Thailand."[70]

After Pol Pot's fall, all efforts to apprehend him and hold him out of

68. Scheffer, *All the Missing Souls*, 341–42.
69. Reproduced in Sweeney et al., *International Legal System*, 624.
70. Novick, *The Holocaust in American Life*, 248, referring to Strobe Talbot, "America Abroad: Defanging the Beast," *Time* 133 (February 6, 1989), 40. The author adds in a note that "the policy of ambiguous support for the Khmer Rouge against the Vietnamese continued during the Reagan and Bush administrations."

Cambodia until a tribunal could be installed were unsuccessful. Various countries were asked to bring him to trial, under the theory of universal jurisdiction, but none of them accepted the responsibility. All kinds of legal arguments were raised against holding the mass murderer in US territories until a tribunal would be set up.

There was also an obstacle in transferring Pol Pot to an international tribunal, due to China's opposition. Beijing had supported and collaborated with the Pol Pot regime, so the Chinese had much to fear from the possible disclosure of their links with the criminal activities that went on in Cambodia.[71] Pol Pot died in 1998 without spending one day in a court of law.

After talks between Cambodia and the United Nations that lasted for a decade, a tribunal was eventually formed. Judges and prosecutors representing Cambodia and the international community were sworn into office in July 2006, around thirty years after the crimes had been committed. The new national court is of limited jurisdiction over specific crimes for a set period of time and over a small class of likely suspects.[72] Initially a list of about thirty possible trial defendants was considered, but that number decreased to between five and ten.[73]

The first case was limited to a single defendant, Kaing Guek Eav, who oversaw S21, a detention center where over 12,380 detainees were tortured and killed. The prosecution established how executions were carried out by smashing the victim at the base of the neck with a metal bar and then slitting the victim's neck or stomach. Pictures were taken of high-ranking detainee executions to prove to superiors that executions had been carried out. At least one hundred detainees were killed by having their blood completely drawn, in order to provide blood to soldiers wounded in battle against the Vietnamese. Eav was condemned to life in prison.[74]

Case number two involves three defendants who stood at the head of the atrocities, but it contains evidentiary complexities and the age of the defendants is a serious factor, as illness or death could catch up with them at any moment. For the next cases no suspects have been formally identified, and

71. Scheffer, *All the Missing Souls*, 349.
72. Ibid., 343.
73. Seiff, "Seeking Justice in the Killing Fields: For a War Crimes Tribunal in Cambodia, Successful Prosecution of Khmer Rouge Leaders Is No Sure Thing," 56.
74. *International Law News* 43, no. 3 (summer 2014), American Bar Association.

the Cambodian government has made it clear that it prefers not to see any more cases go forward. Many former Khmer Rouge cadre leaders are free and occupy positions in Cambodia. Remember Nazi Germany after the war?

For a genocide that murdered close to two million people, one defendant was condemned. There was no prevention. There was really no punishment. Some of those who got involved in later barbarities in other parts of the globe certainly knew that for decades the authors of one of the world's greatest genocides walked around freely in the country where they had committed their crimes.

What consequences will this and later evasions of responsibility, as well as earlier ones, have on future potential mass criminals?

Rwanda and Yugoslavia

The Tribunal for Yugoslavia left a great number of criminals untouched. As well, its extreme slowness allowed new atrocities to occur in the region even as the gathering of evidence of earlier crimes marched on. Regarding the Rwanda Tribunal, Scheffer affirms that American leadership in the building of the tribunal cannot be appreciated without first examining the American failure – shared with so many others – in confronting the genocide that Rwanda suffered.[75] The massacre of eight hundred thousand women, children, and men, most of Tutsi identity, commenced on April 6, 1994, and lasted about one hundred days – an average of eight thousand murders per day.

A UN-commissioned report on Rwanda characterized the 1994 genocide as "one of the most abhorrent events of the twentieth century." It condemned the failure to "prevent, and subsequently, to stop, the genocide in Rwanda" as "a failure by the United Nations system as a whole. There was a persistent lack of political will by Member States to act, or to act with enough assertiveness."[76]

Scheffer, who visited all the theaters of atrocities that occurred during the ten years in which he exercised his official functions, affirms that no

---

75. Scheffer, *All the Missing Souls*, 46.
76. Philip Alston and Ryan Goodman, *International Human Rights: The Successor to International Human Rights in Context* (Oxford: Oxford University Press, 2012), 747.

other atrocity zone quite compared with the intense savagery that occurred in Rwanda. And he adds this chilling remark, which reflects the spirit of his whole book: "For those of us in the policy rooms at the time, the memory of our vacillation over the horror is sickening and will never be extinguished. I owe the victims and their families my soul every day."[77]

After bitterly criticizing the Pentagon and the State Department for their hedging and their peacekeeping operations, he notes that Madeleine Albright finally recognized the truth in a speech in Addis Ababa on December 9, 1997 (three and a half years after the tragic events), in which she said that the international community should have been more active in the early stages of the atrocities in Rwanda "and called them what they were – genocide."[78]

Based on his knowledge of the African reality, Scheffer underlines that the previous slaughters of tens of thousands of Tutsi and Hutus in Burundi during the fall of 1993 was a sign of possible further violence next door in Rwanda. "The international community's collective detachment from the reality unfolding in Burundi sent a strong signal to the extremist Hutu in Rwanda that the shooting gallery was open, free of charge."[79]

At the United Nations, the policies toward Rwanda were criminally negligent. Before the outbreak of the atrocities there was a 2,500-strong UN peacekeeping force – the United Nations Assistance Mission for Rwanda (UNAMIR). In February 1994, UNAMIR's force commander, Major General Romeo Dallaire, obtained death lists with the names of Tutsi and moderate Hutu targets. It was clear that genocide was in the cards, but Dallaire was denied his request for permission to capture and destroy arms caches. Instead, in the middle of the crisis, the size of UNAMIR was decreased, leaving only a token force.[80] The retrieval of the UN force was ordered by Kofi Annan, at the time UN undersecretary for peacekeeping, who said he was acting under orders of the secretary-general, Boutrous Boutrous-Ghali. The termination of UNAMIR'S mission was executed despite General Dallaire's warning of an "anti-Tutsi extermination plot." In the Kigali Genocide Memorial, one can see

77. Scheffer, *All the Missing Souls*, 47.
78. Ibid.
79. Ibid., 48.
80. Pattison, *Humanitarian Intervention*, 5.

Kofi Annan's cables forbidding Dallaire from making any effort to stop the genocide.[81] The United States went along with the UN policy.[82]

Scheffer reports on the terrible accusation against France and Belgium as having been complicit in the Hutu-orchestrated genocide of the Tutsi. Rwandan president Paul Kagame implicated France repeatedly in policies and actions that allegedly facilitated the genocide (all attracting vehement denials by Paris).[83] Regarding the phase of detaining the suspects of the genocide, which took place years later, Scheffer refers to France's negative approach to apprehending them and asks:

> Was the explanation really so simple as the fact that the Hutu had been their favored clientele in Rwanda for so many years prior to the genocide? I recall leaning back at my desk in astonishment – how gullible do they think we are?[84] In two years I would be asking the same question regarding the mysteriously liberated status of fugitives indicted by the

81. Shmuley Boteach, "No Holds Barred: Susan Rice and the Politicization of Genocide," *Jerusalem Post*, February 27, 2015, 19. Boteach notes that Samantha Power, Pulitzer Prize–winning author, has referred to Susan Rice, former US ambassador to the UN, as a bystander to genocide. Power quotes Rice in her 2002 book as saying: "If we use the word 'genocide' and are seen as doing nothing, what will be the effect on the November congressional election?" Boteach's comment: "This is an astonishing statement. Here you have Rice hearing about the murder of 330 people every hour for three months and her response is – how will this affect us politically? That Rice would have brought up the midterm elections as a more important consideration than stopping the mass murder of so many men, women and children that their bodies were damming the rivers of Rwanda is one of the most heartbreaking pronouncements ever uttered by an American official."
82. Scheffer, *All the Missing Souls*, 55. Irwin Cotler writes: "The Rwandan genocide was particularly tragic not only due to the horror of the genocide itself, but to the fact that it was preventable. No one can say that we did not know; we knew, but we did not act.... Let there be no mistake about it: Indifference and inaction always mean coming down on the side of the victimizer, never the victim. In the face of evil, indifference is acquiescence" ("The Universal Lessons of the Holocaust," *Jerusalem Post*, January 24, 2014).
83. Scheffer, *All the Missing Souls*, 56.
84. Ibid., 110. On the Rwandan tragedy others have also written negatively about France's intervention. According to Alex J. Bellamy, the French government was primarily motivated by a concern to protect Hutu allies and Francophones in Rwanda, rather than a desire to end the genocide, choosing a strategy that did little to protect the victims ("Military Intervention," in Bloxham and Moses, *Oxford Handbook of Genocide Studies*, 609).

Yugoslav Tribunal, including Radovan Karadzic, living in the French sector of Bosnia.[85]

Scheffer relates that the United States government was fully behind the decision to withdraw UNAMIR soldiers from Rwanda. A cable from the State Department to the US mission at the UN stated that there was "an insufficient justification to retain a UN peace keeping operation in Rwanda and that the international community must give highest priority to full, orderly withdrawal of all UNAMIR personnel as soon as possible." The final judgment of Washington was that the "U.S. will oppose any effort at this time to preserve a UNAMIR presence in Rwanda. In the current environment, there is no role for UN peacekeeping. Our opposition is firm. It is based on our conviction that the Security Council has an obligation to ensure that peacekeeping operations are viable, that they are capable of fulfilling their mandate and that UN peacekeeping personnel are not placed or retained, knowingly, in an untenable position."[86]

Scheffer bitterly laments his share in the clearance of this instruction cable to Albright, the US ambassador to the United Nations. He mentions the justifying factors for that step and yet he says that "I cannot justify why I did not refuse clearance at that critical moment."[87]

The legal circles and the United Nations community have difficulties with the term *genocide*. After a few hundred thousand Tutsis had been hacked to death, many UN Security Council members refused to use the word "genocide" in their resolution, preferring to refer to "serious violations of international humanitarian law committed in Rwanda during the conflict."[88] Therefore Scheffer started using the term *atrocity crimes* in his propositions regarding the suspects of the mass murders.[89]

85. Ibid., 110. Scheffer adds: "One of our closest allies appeared determined to act as an accomplice in facilitating the genocidaires' freedom."
86. Ibid., 55.
87. Ibid., 54–55.
88. Ibid., 64. The term *genocide* eventually was accepted to define the events in Rwanda. See Ibid., 66.
89. The definitional difficulties with the term *genocide* are discussed by Ratner, Abrams, and Bischoff (*Accountability for Human Rights Atrocities*, 45): "The limitations and requirement of the Genocide Convention have also inevitably precipitated sterile debates over the definition of genocide that run the unfortunate risk of detracting from the enormity of the atrocities themselves." What comes out clearly from various jurisprudential sources

Actually, the international legal society also has difficulties with the term *terrorism*, insisting that as it lacks definition, no indictment can materialize against those responsible for terrorist acts. Somehow the two worst dangers the world faces – genocide and terrorism – are not covered by effective remedies.

The Rwanda Court had jurisdiction over events that occurred until 1994, so a massacre of hundreds of Tutsis that occurred in 1997 was beyond the court's jurisdiction. Again, legalities obstructed justice. Or as a jurist characterized another aspect of modern international realities: "legal conceptualism prevail[ed] over realism."[90]

Scheffer was also involved in Yugoslavia, regarding which he records an equally staggering panorama. The following appears in his introduction to the activities of the tribunal created to try the murderers of the Balkans:

> The Yugoslav Tribunal had to rely exclusively on the reluctant cooperation of governments and of NATO forces in Bosnia to take into physical custody indictees who could be officially arrested by tribunal prosecutors. The unbearable timidity of the United States and its European allies to rapidly strategize and then implement effective means of apprehending indicted fugitives from justice in the former Yugoslavia constituted an abdication of responsibility that will haunt the legacies of these governments and those who led them.[91]

Radovan Karadzic, who was sought on charges of perpetrating genocidal atrocities as the Bosnian Serb president, was a fugitive from justice for more than fifteen years until his capture in 2008, and Ratko Mladic, the Bosnian

---

is that "the part targeted must be significant enough to have an impact on the group as a whole (ICJ)," and as Ratner, Abrams, and Bischoff summarize, at 41, the ad hoc tribunals have focused on the destruction of a "substantial" part of the group, one whose elimination would threaten the group's existence as a whole, which includes evaluating the number of those targeted not just in absolute terms, but also in relation to the overall size of the group. The authors proceed with various considerations on the extension and limitations of the crime of genocide to "more closely reflect the values and political landscape of the twenty-first century" (ibid., 46–47).

90. F.A. Mann, "The Protection of Shareholder's Interests in the Light of the Barcelona Traction Case," *American Journal of International Law* 67, no. 2 (April 1973): 274, as quoted by Tiburcio, *Human Rights of Aliens*, 70.

91. Scheffer, *All the Missing Souls*, 124.

Serb general charged with the Srebrenica genocide, was only arrested in 2011.[92] President Slobodan Milosevic of Serbia was tried for atrocity crimes in Bosnia, Croatia, and Kosovo, in procedures that started in February 2001; he died in March 2006, a few months before the trial court was expected to render its judgment.

Ambassador Scheffer accuses a few very prominent members of the US governments of those years, some top generals, and the CIA director of having derailed viable apprehension strategies regarding the great criminals of former Yugoslavia. And he concludes by referring to the president of the United States: "I never saw Clinton enter the ring to grapple with the toughest problems that, if overcome with his personal engagement, might have led to rapid arrests of Karadzic and Mladic during his presidency."[93]

The author questions whether the governments of America and of its European allies were truly committed to the mission of apprehending the indicted war criminals, particularly Karadzic and Mladic.[94]

Louise Arbour, the prosecutor of the Yugoslav Tribunal, characterized America's policy as bureaucratic nonsense,[95] and declared her astonishment that military leaders were unwilling to promote the enforcement of laws of war.[96]

Scheffer puts it very bluntly: "Karadzic and Mladic were the most wanted men in Europe, responsible for ethnic cleansing, the siege of Sarajevo and the genocide of Srebrenica, and yet somehow the stars never aligned to hunt them down."[97]

Karadzic was hiding in the French part of the divided territory, and the French did not care to apprehend him. At the International Tribunal it was understood that the apprehension of Karadzic would send a strong message to Milosevic, who was busy with the conflict in Kosovo. This meant that the French were manifestly neglecting their duties as a state party of the Genocide

---

92. Ibid., 125. In March 2016, Karadzic was found guilty of genocide by the International Criminal Tribunal for the former Yugoslavia and sentenced to forty years in jail.
93. Ibid., 126.
94. Ibid., 142.
95. Ibid., 144.
96. Ibid., 149.
97. Ibid., 151.

Convention by not enabling the punishment of one genocide criminal and consequently allowing the continuation of another genocidal campaign.

At certain passages of his book, it seems that Scheffer himself was not really aware of the reasons for the French refusal to arrest those enemies of humankind and his own government's reluctance to take a step and detain Karadzic in French "territory." Scheffer relates that US secretary of defense Cohen clearly stated to the new Yugoslav Tribunal prosecutor, Carla Del Ponte, that he was against US troops occupying themselves with arresting indicted war criminals.[98] Remember the refusal to bomb Auschwitz?

It may be true that no evidence ever emerged pointing to a specific intent by Milosevic to destroy all or a substantial part of the Kosovar-Albanian population. There was thus no basis for a genocide indictment, and the prosecutor chose not to infer such intent. But this does not justify the international bureaucracy that oversaw the whole process of indicting and trying the responsible individuals for what came to be known as "atrocity crimes." Speaking to the State Department press corps, Scheffer described Kosovo as one of the worst atrocities in history:

> With the exception of Rwanda in 1994 and Cambodia in 1975, you would be hard pressed to find a crime scene anywhere in the world since World War II where a defenseless civilian population has been assaulted with such ferocity and criminal intent and suffered so many multiple violations of international humanitarian law in such a short period of time as in Kosovo since mid-March.... Kosovo represents a government planned campaign to eliminate, either through forced deportation or killing most of an ethnic population from its homes. The criminal character of such an enterprise – divorced in large part from any semblance of military necessity – cannot be ignored.[99]

In Kosovo, NATO air forces intervened with air strikes, but the atrocities proceeded with a great number of victims. The author describes how Serb forces used human shields to protect themselves from NATO's bombings, a primary reason why NATO restrained its use of air power in scores of situations.[100]

98. Ibid., 156.
99. Ibid., 282.
100. Ibid., 282–84.

The activities of the international tribunals created by the UN to bring to justice the great criminals of these two genocides are described very briefly as follows:

> As of July 2013, the Yugoslavia tribunal had indicted 161 persons, concluded proceedings for 115 and sentenced 56, and its trials on average lasted about a year. The Tribunal two-year budget for operating in 2012 and 2013 was $250,814,000. As of February 2013, the Rwanda tribunal had indicted 93 people and completed 75 cases. Of those, they had convicted 47. The budget for the Rwanda Tribunal was $174,320,000 for 2012 and 2013. In other words, the two tribunals spent several billion dollars over almost 20 years to convict less than half a dozen people per year on average, a tiny fraction of the thousands of perpetrators.[101]

Congo

In the years 1960–64, the United Nations was involved in peacekeeping operations in the Congo, with relative success.[102]

Years later, as a consequence of the Rwanda genocide and the Hutus' downfall, some two million of them entered the Congo.

There is a plethora of reports on the Congo tragedy. At certain points, various other African countries were involved in the conflict, in addition to Rwanda: Uganda, Angola, Burundi, Chad, Zimbabwe, and Namibia. And there are those who claim that the United States and the United Kingdom were behind Rwanda's and Uganda's belligerent actions in the Congo, arming and training them.[103]

And so in August 1998 a second Congo war erupted, which pitted at least seven African nations and numerous irregular groups against one another. The Democratic Republic of Congo brought a case before the International Court of Justice, which ruled that Uganda had violated both the prohibition

---

101. Posner, *Twilight of Human Rights Law*, 54.

102. See Henkin et al., *International Law: Cases and Materials*, 996.

103. Journalist Glen Ford accuses the United States of "having financed and given overall direction to the worst genocide since WWII in Democratic Republic of Congo." "16 Years of U.S. Genocide in Congo, Black Agenda Report, December 12, 2012, www.blackagendareport.com/content/16-years-us-genocide-congo.

on the use of force and the principle of nonintervention by engaging in military activities on Congolese territory.[104]

A United Nations peacekeeping mission has been in the Congo since 1999, with almost twenty thousand personnel, with a mandate to protect civilians and help with the reconstruction of the country.

Estimates put the death toll somewhere between 5 and 6 million people, making it the deadliest conflict since the end of World War II.[105] Various peace accords have been brokered starting in 2003, but the violence has persisted, especially in the eastern part of the country.[106]

A 2009 report by UN-commissioned experts said that UN involvement has done nothing to quell the violence – with rebels continuing to kill and plunder natural resources with impunity. The report claimed that the rebels are supported by an international crime network stretching through Africa to Western Europe and North America.[107]

Sudan's Genocide in Darfur

Probably the most flagrant case of the inoperativeness of the International Criminal Court is the procedure against Sudan's President Omar Hassan Ahmad al-Bashir, accused of war crimes, crimes against humanity, and genocide in Sudan's Darfur region. The International Criminal Court issued a warrant of arrest for Omar al-Bashir for war crimes and crimes against humanity,

---

104. *Armed Activities on the territory of the Congo (Dem. Republic Congo v. Uganda)* 2005 ICJ REP. 168.

105. Pattison (*Humanitarian Intervention*, 7) quotes sources that estimate 5.4 million deaths in the Congo since 1998. According to this author, the MONUC mission from the UN employed significant force against rebel factions (29), yet it was unable to halt the egregious violations of human rights (66).

106. As reported by Anna Stolley Persky in "The Capital of Rape: Fighting Widespread Sexual Violence in the Democratic Republic of the Congo," *American Bar Association Journal* 98, no. 2 (February 2012): 59.

107. "Q&A: DR Congo Conflict," November 20, 2012, www.bbc.co.uk/news/world -africa-11108589. Glen Ford accuses former American ambassador to the United Nation, Susan Rice, presently US national security adviser, of subverting the efforts to demand that Rwanda cease supporting the atrocities going on in the Congo (*Workers Action*, December 3, 2012). He claims that for sixteen years Uganda and Rwanda have done the bidding of their paymasters and arms suppliers, the American and British governments (*Black Agenda Report*, December 12, 2012).

but not for the crime of genocide.[108] Al-Bashir has been the president of Sudan since 1989. The Darfur tragedy has been going on for years, with attacks orchestrated by Bashir against the populations of Fur, Masalit, and Zaghawa, further aggravating the murderous situation in which Sudan was embroiled in the majority of the fifty-plus years since its independence in 1956.

The African Union has criticized the warrants for his arrest, maintaining that Bashir's head-of-state status entitles him to immunity from prosecution and that the charges interfere with ongoing efforts to negotiate peace in Sudan. The African Union has decided that its member states will not cooperate to arrest and surrender the president of Sudan. In 2010 and 2011, Chad, Kenya, Djibouti, and Malawi received Bashir on state visits without any move to arrest or extradite him, despite the court's request for assistance in his apprehension and despite their obligation under article 86 of the Rome Statute to "cooperate fully with the Court in its investigation and prosecution of crimes within the jurisdiction of the Court."

The International Criminal Court stated that the Republics of Chad and Malawi had failed to comply with their obligation to cooperate with the court with respect to the arrest and surrender of Omar Hassan Ahmad al-Bashir, thus preventing the court from exercising its functions and powers under the statute.[109] It referred the decision to the president of the court for transmission to the Security Council and the Assembly of States Parties, via the UN secretary-general.[110]

Article 27 of the Rome Statute, which created the International Criminal Court, provides that "official capacity as a Head of State or of Government,

---

108. *International Law News* 38, no. 3 (summer 2009): 23, American Bar Association.

109. The court's decision ends with the following statement: "Indeed, it is the view of the Chamber that when cooperating with this Court and therefore acting on its behalf, States Parties are instruments for the enforcement of the *jus puniendi* (punishing jurisdiction) of the international community whose exercise has been entrusted to this Court when States have failed to prosecute those responsible for the crimes within its jurisdiction" (Alston and Goodman, *International Human Rights*, 1223).

110. Alexander K.A. Greenawalt, "Introductory Note to the International Criminal Court: Decisions Pursuant to Article 87(7) of the Rome Statute on the Failure by the Republic of Malawi and the Republic of Chad to Comply with the Cooperation Requests Issued by the Court with Respect to the Arrest and Surrender of Omar Hassan Ahmad al-Bashir and African Union Response," December 2011–February 2012, *International Legal Materials* 51, no. 2 (2012): 393–417.

a member of a Government or parliament, an elected representative or a government official shall in no case exempt a person from criminal responsibility under this Statute."

And so one of the major genocidaires of our generation is escaping justice with the help of member states of the UN, while the official reaction consists solely of decisions, communications, and proclamations. It is yet further evidence of the inoperativeness of the whole international machinery structured to protect human rights.

Darfur is a sad example of how humanitarian crises go unchecked. According to the UN Department of Peacekeeping Operations (DPKO), an estimated three hundred thousand people have died and 2.5 million people have been displaced in Darfur since 2003.

The United States' relative inertia in this tragedy has been analyzed in light of various considerations. An armed intervention in Darfur is problematic given America's military commitments in Iraq and in Afghanistan, since the policy makers in Washington prioritize the war on terror being waged in Afghanistan and obtaining stability in Iraq over stopping the genocide in Darfur. Besides, the government in Sudan became an important source of intelligence information on Islamic terrorism, so American intelligence required a working relationship with the government of Sudan. Additionally, given the public-relations disaster that accompanied the US intervention in Iraq, the last thing America needed was to antagonize the Arab world further by intervening against Sudan's Arab government on behalf of Darfur's African population.[111]

There are, however, other considerations against an intervention in that region. Alex de Waal, a leading commentator on African affairs, spent time in Darfur trying unsuccessfully to bring the parties to a peace agreement. In 2006, Waal wrote:

> The knock-down argument against humanitarian invasion is that it won't work. The idea of foreign troops fighting their way into Darfur and disarming the Janjaweed militia by force is sheer fantasy. Practicality dictates that a peacekeeping force in Darfur cannot enforce its will on any resisting armed groups without entering into a protracted and unwinnable

111. Bellamy, "Military Intervention," in Bloxham and Moses, *Oxford Handbook of Genocide Studies*, 614.

counter-insurgency in which casualties are inevitable. The only way peace-keeping works is with consent: the agreement of the Sudan government and the support of the majority of the Darfurian populace.... Without this, UN troops will not only fail but will make the plight of Darfurians even worse.[112]

The Iraqi Genocide of the Kurds

Resolution 688 (1991) of the Security Council condemned "the repression of the Iraqi civilian population in many parts of Iraq, including most recently in Kurdish populated areas, the consequences of which threaten international peace and security in the region."[113] The resolution demanded that Iraq remove the threat by ending the repression, and allow immediate access of international humanitarian organizations to all those in need of assistance in all parts of Iraq.[114] The French foreign minister unrealistically classified this resolution as a new approach toward "humanitarian intervention in case of massive violations of human rights."[115]

Some authors have come to the conclusion that connecting chapter 7 of the UN charter with humanitarian initiatives created a right – actually an obligation – of the international community to involve itself in the affairs of individual nations when its most fundamental rules are violated,[116] a subject we dealt with in chapter 7.

The persecution of the Kurds by the Iraqi authorities has a long history. In the late 1980s, hundreds of thousands of men, women, and children were executed during a systematic attempt to exterminate the Kurdish population in Iraq in the Anfal operations. The actual genocide of the Kurds in Iraq began

---

112. Ibid., 613–14.
113. It is difficult to understand how an internal massacre of the Kurds by the Iraqis could threaten international peace and security. The Security Council was rigorously following the articles of chapter 7 of the charter which, as I said before, must be interpreted as referring to internal conflicts without necessary repercussions in the international arena.
114. Harris, *Cases and Materials in International Law*, 920.
115. Carreau, *Droit International*, 83. The author adds that this new approach regarding humanitarian aid was confirmed with Resolution 770 of 1992 regarding Bosnia-Herzegovina, Resolution 794 of 1992 regarding Somalia, Resolution 841 of 1993 about Haiti, Resolution 940 of 1993 about Rwanda, and Resolution 1101 of 1997 with reference to Albania.
116. Ibid.

in 1963; it is estimated that since then a million people have been murdered with chemical weapons.

The Iraqi High Tribunal tried and convicted six former members of the Saddam Hussein regime in connection with the 1986–89 Anfal campaign against Iraqi Kurds. During the Anfal operations, 90 percent of Kurdish villages and more than twenty small towns and cities were completely destroyed.[117] The Iraqi High Tribunal convicted them for the crime of genocide, as the genocidal intent was clearly demonstrated.[118] In 2006, Saddam Hussein was convicted and executed for crimes against humanity.[119]

Haiti

In March 1966, the International Commission of Jurists, seated in Geneva, published a report on the "dictatorship of Dr. Duvalier in Haiti" in which it revealed "flagrant violations of fundamental notions of democracy."[120] François Duvalier, also known as "Papa Doc," was the president of Haiti from 1957 until his death in 1971. Originally elected, he proclaimed himself in 1964 "president for life." His was a cruel dictatorship, which persecuted, tortured, and killed any opponent. The Duvalier regime worked for the enrichment of the family, while the Haitian people lived in misery. He was succeeded by his son Jean Claude Duvalier, or "Baby Doc," who continued the regime of his father.

In 1986, a popular uprising overthrew the second-generation dictatorship and Baby Doc found refuge in France.

His crimes against human rights and against humanity should have caused France to recognize her obligation to bring him to judgment under the accepted theory of universal jurisdiction, based on the axiom *delicta juris gentium* (crimes against the law of nations), to which applies another axiom, *ubi te invenero, ibi te judicabo* (wherever I find you, there I will try you). Yet France took no initiative in this sense and allowed the criminal to live peacefully in the land of liberty.

This old principle of international law, applied to the pirates of centuries

117. "What Happened in the Kurdish Genocide," KRG UK Representation London, http:// uk.gov.krd/genocide/pages/page.aspx?lngnr=12&pnr=37.
118. Ratner, Abrams, and Bischoff, *Accountability for Human Rights Atrocities*, 45.
119. Ibid., 186.
120. Bulletin no. 25 of the International Commission of Jurists, 5.

ago, has not been adopted by France even when dealing with the worst criminals against humanity.

In 1986 I wrote about Duvalier, after he found refuge in France:

> Duvalier is one more in a long list of *hostis humani generis* – enemies of the human race – and he should be taken to a court of law in a case that would represent the beginning of the end of murderers of their own people, because they would become aware that, once deposed, they would not have anywhere to run away to, as justice would always be done to them by the legitimate exercise of universal jurisdiction for the sake of the fundamental rights of the human being.[121]

India-Pakistan

India and Pakistan gained their independence in August 1947, while the Universal Declaration of Human Rights was being prepared. The separation resulted in sizeable ethnic minorities in both of the two new countries. Violence resulting from tensions over the split killed more than five hundred thousand people within a year.[122] It was not genocide in the strict sense of the crime's definition. But the tragedy could have been avoided if the colonial power had prepared and conducted the partition with care and consideration for human life.

Of the violence that accompanied the partition of India, historians Ian Talbot and Gurharpal Singh write:

> There are numerous eyewitness accounts of the maiming and mutilation of victims. The catalogue of horrors includes the disemboweling of pregnant women, the slamming of babies' heads against brick walls, the cutting off of victims' limbs and genitalia and the display of heads and corpses. While previous communal riots had been deadly, the scale and level of brutality was unprecedented. Although some scholars question the use of the term "genocide" with respect to the Partition massacres, much of the violence manifested as having genocidal tendencies. It was designed to cleanse an existing generation as well as prevent its future reproduction."[123]

121. Jacob Dolinger, "Jean Claude Duvalier: Hostis Humani Generis," *O Estado de São Paulo*, March 4, 1986.
122. Glendon, *A World Made New*, 75.
123. Ian Talbot and Gurharpal Singh, *The Partition of India* (Cambridge: Cambridge University Press, 2009), 67–68.

East Pakistan

Many years later, in 1971, East Pakistan became the site of widespread targeted violence that scholars and observers have described as genocide. The army, which was in power, launched a violent campaign against the Bengalis. Despite being the majority ethnic group, the latter were disadvantaged and sought independence. The violence left an estimated one million people dead and resulted in the mass exodus of between eight and ten million others to neighboring India. In December of that year, India intervened militarily and the Pakistani forces surrendered. East Pakistan became the independent state of Bangladesh.[124]

Geofrey Robinson maintains that the United States had no interest in drawing critical attention to the violence committed by its ally Pakistan "at the height of the cold war, a time when President Nixon and Henry Kissinger were engaged in the most cynical use of military force and secret diplomacy to achieve US political and strategic objectives." Robinson writes that "despite the internal assessment of US officials in Dhaka (East Pakistan) that the events constituted genocide, the Nixon administration publicly denied any knowledge of atrocities and provided Pakistan with assurances of its diplomatic and military support."[125]

East Timor

A Portuguese colony for more than three hundred years, East Timor was invaded by neighboring Indonesia in December 1975 and occupied until 1999. In these twenty-four years, some one hundred thousand people died due to Indonesian actions including forced displacement and relocation of civilian populations; deliberate destruction of villages, crops, and livestock; and the torture, rape, arbitrary imprisonment, and summary execution of suspected supporters of independence.

The United States, the UK, and Australia, among others, gave backing to Indonesia. US president Gerald Ford and Secretary of State Kissinger gave explicit support to the invasion, including economic and military aid. Indonesia withdrew from East Timor only when powerful nations finally took concrete steps to bring the situation to an end.[126]

124. Geoffrey Robinson, "State-Sponsored Violence and Secessionist Rebellions in Asia," in Bloxham and Moses, *Oxford Handbook of Genocide Studies*, 467–70.
125. Ibid., 470–71.
126. Ibid., 480–81. According to James Pattison (*Humanitarian Intervention*, 1), Australia

Uganda

Idi Amin toppled Obote in January 1971 and became the master and hang-man of Uganda, responsible for the deaths of two hundred thousand of his countrymen.

Paul Johnson writes:

> It could be argued that the UN power politics of the 1970s, the ugly consequences of the relativistic morality impressed on the organization by Hammarskjold and his school, were responsible for prolonging the Amin regime by six terrible years. According to one authority, the failure to take international action in 1972, when the nature of the regime was already glaringly apparent, cost the lives of 200,000 Ugandans. Britain bore a heavy responsibility.[127]

After Amin's downfall, he was received by Libya and then by Saudi Arabia and was protected till the end of his days.

North Africa

The end of the rule of North Africa by colonial powers was a tragic chapter of modern history. Events in Algeria were particularly appalling. After 120 years of colonial rule, the French pulled out but not before more than a million people were killed in a brutal war that ended the French Fourth Republic.[128]

Chad

Hissène Habré was president of Chad from 1982 to 1990. He has been accused of engaging in torture, war crimes, and crimes against humanity affecting thousands of victims during his term in office. Habré has lived in Senegal as a political refugee since the overthrow of his government.

---

led an intervention in East Timor, duly authorized by the Security Council, which has been considered a success.

127. Johnson, *Modern Times*, 535. The author reports (534) that Britain was shipping armored cars to Amin as late as December 1972. And he adds that "freighting of scarce luxuries to Uganda from Stansted airport, an important traffic which enabled Amin to keep up the morale of his soldiers, continued with British government approval almost to the end of the terror."

128. Paul Johnson, "The Answer to Terrorism? Colonialism," *Wall Street Journal*, October 10, 2001, 15.

Since 2000, Chadian nationals filed complaints against Habré, mainly in the courts of Senegal and Belgium. As Senegal did not prosecute Habré, Belgium requested his extradition from Senegal, which was refused.

The matter reached the International Court of Justice, where on July 2012 it confirmed the obligation of states to either prosecute alleged perpetrators or extradite them to another country with jurisdiction for prosecution, as per the UN Convention against Torture and Other Cruel, Inhuman or Degrading Treatment or Punishment. After this decision, Senegal decided to prosecute Habré.[129]

Côte d'Ivoire

A chamber of the International Criminal Court authorized the prosecutor's request to open investigation into crimes committed during post-election violence in the Republic of Côte d'Ivoire, starting in November 2010. The investigation led to an arrest warrant against Laurent Gbagbo, the former president of the country, who had refused to relinquish power despite an election loss, sparking massive violence and the deaths of more than three thousand people.[130] His wife Simone, president of the Parliamentary Group of the Ivorian Popular Front, was also arrested, accused of participation in crimes against humanity.[131] Mrs. Gbagbo was not extradited. Tried in a local court in Côte d'Ivoire, she was found guilty in March 2015 and sentenced to twenty years in prison.[132] Former president Gbagbo's ICC trial began on January 28, 2016, and was still ongoing as of this writing.

---

129. Cindy Galway Buys, "Introductory Note to the International Court of Justice: Obligation to Prosecute or Extradite (Belg. v. Sen.)," July 20, 2012, *International Legal Materials* 51, no. 4 (2012): 706.

130. Saskia de Rothschildjan, "Trial of Ivory Coast's Laurent Gbagbo Will Test International Criminal Court," *New York Times*, January 27, 2016, http://www.nytimes.com/2016/01/28/world/africa/ivory-coast-laurent-gbagbo-hague-trial.html.

131. Scott W. Lyons, "Decision Pursuant to Article 15 of the Rome Statute on the Authorisation of the Investigation Into the Situation in the Republic of Côte d'Ivoire (Int'l Crim. Ct.)," October 3, 2011, *International Legal Materials* 51, no. 2 (2012): 225.

132. Marilia Brocchetto, "Ivory Coast's Simone Gbagbo Sentenced to 20 Years in Prison," CNN, March 10, 2015, http://edition.cnn.com/2015/03/10/africa/ivory-coast-first-lady/index.html.

Kenya

After the results of the Kenyan elections of December 2007 were announced, serious ethnically driven violence erupted in the country. Within two months, 1220 Kenyans were killed, over 3560 injured, and about 350,000 displaced, and more than 900 acts of rape were documented.[133]

Sierra Leone

During the country's civil war of 1991–2002, rebels and pro-government forces murdered and mutilated civilians, brutally raped women, and forced children to fight. A Special Court for Sierra Leone was created in 2002, which tried only ten individuals.[134]

Somalia

In December 1992, the UN Security Council authorized intervention to provide humanitarian aid in the context of a civil war in Somalia. A multinational force was sent but did not succeed, and eventually the troops left the country. For the United States, Somalia was a sad experience, as American troops fell victim to the Somali warlords. This led many Americans to form a "never again" mentality regarding the intervention of US forces abroad. D.J. Harris holds that the Somalia case is an important precedent for UN action under chapter 7 of the charter for the provision of humanitarian aid in a purely civil-war situation in the absence of government consent. However, the operation itself is generally deemed to have been largely a failure due to the opposition of the competing warlords.[135]

According to the International Crisis Group, 1.1 million people have been displaced in Somalia since 2006.

Syria

While this book is being written, Syria is a country under constant fire and it is too early to comprehend the exact nature of the conflict and know the exact

---

133. Data referred to in a decision of the International Criminal Court on the situation in Kenya. See Charles Chernor Jalloh, "Situation in the Republic of Kenya," *American Journal of International Law* 105, no. 3 (July 2011): 540–41.
134. Sigal Horovitz, "How International Courts Shape Domestic Justice: Lessons from Rwanda and Sierra Leone," *Israel Law Review* 46, no. 3 (November 2013), 339–40.
135. Harris, *Cases and Materials*, 923.

figures of the dead, which unofficially is around two hundred thousand with millions of displaced people. There was an episode of chemical war, which apparently has not been repeated. It is the latest eruption of mass murder in our convoluted world.

Nigeria

An increasing number of young girls are donning explosive devices and blowing themselves up in public places of Nigeria – in the name of the Boko Haram terror organization. More than a dozen attacks had been carried out as of December 2014, with one attack claiming up to 78 victims.

Boko Haram killed more than 5,000 civilians between July 2009 and June 2014. Since 2009, Boko Haram abducted more than 500 women and children, including the kidnapping of 276 schoolgirls from Chibok in April 2014. An estimated 650,000 people fled the conflict zone.

The security forces and the military have been ineffective in countering the terror wave, hampered by an entrenched culture of official corruption.

Chile: An Example of American Support of Dictatorships

Political and economic interests have led the United States of America to cooperate with innumerable dictatorships in Asia, Africa, and South America. In some cases, America has supported revolutions and coups d'états that brought down democratically elected governments. In most of these cases, the political upheavals caused populations to suffer serious violations to their human rights. The classic case is Chile. The aborted coup to stop Salvador Allende from taking office as the democratically elected president of Chile, and the campaign against him during his years in government until he was killed (or committed suicide) in the presidential palace, were supported by the CIA, duly authorized by the White House according to Henry Kissinger's instructions. The government that followed Allende's, headed by General Augusto Pinochet, was an egregious violator of human rights.[136]

---

136. McDougal and Reisman, *International Law in Contemporary Perspective*, 1022–26. Daniel Feierstein ("National Security Doctrine in Latin America: The Genocide Question," in Bloxham and Moses, *Oxford Handbook of Genocide Studies*, 497) reports that officially during the Pinochet era more than a thousand people were murdered and another thousand political detainees disappeared, also presumably murdered. The National Commission for Truth and Reconciliation concluded that the real number of victims was probably greater

Arab Genocidal Terrorism

In 2007, this author delivered a conference paper at the University of Belo Horizonte, in the Brazilian state of Minas Gerais, under the title "O Terrorismo Internacional Derrota a ONU" (International terrorism defeats the United Nations). There he said the following:

> If Arafat yesterday, and his successors today, Hanieh of Hamas, and Nasralah from Hezbollah declare, proclaim, and leave it clearly documented that their purpose is to annihilate the Jewish people who live in Israel and in the rest of the world; and if they go ahead and launch rockets from Lebanon and from Gaza, come into Israeli territory and explode innocent civilians as they have done in thousands of cases throughout the years; if they invade a synagogue in Istanbul and kill the Jews during their sabbatical prayers; if they explode the central building of the Jewish community of Buenos Aires, killing tens of people; if they terrorize Jews in France, if they kidnap one of them and torture him to death; in short, if they undertake actions entirely consistent with their stated goals, as set in their charters and in accordance with what they advertise in their public manifestos, this amounts to genocide exactly as established in the convention, and should be taken to the International Criminal Tribunal to be tried.[137]

The Continuous Daily Genocide

The United Nations Children's Fund estimates, as of 1998, that more than twelve million children under the age of five die preventable deaths every year.[138]

Peter Novik writes regarding this ongoing tragedy:

> They are not targeted for death by an identifiable villain – a Hitler or a Pol Pot. Their deaths are not the result of any satanic, genocidal impulse, nor even the result of hatred. They die for the banal reason that they lack

and that many cases will never be reported. The same author relates that in Argentina between 1976 and 1983, under the dictatorship of General Jorge Rafael Videla, officially over thirteen thousand people disappeared or were murdered, whereas an Argentinean human rights organization put the total at between twenty and thirty thousand.

137. Jacob Dolinger, *Direito e Amor* (Rio de Janeiro: Editora Renovar, 2009), 98.
138. UNICEF webpage.

the food and minimal medical facilities that would keep them alive.... As concerns these children, each of us individually (via OXFAM, UNICEF, or other agencies) can save not just one life but many, not in some one-time crisis, but every year. And doing so does not involve, as it did in occupied Europe, risking our own lives and the lives of others; at most it's a matter of forgoing some luxury we'd hardly miss.[139]

The Universal Declaration of Human Rights, which is supposed to be a moral message to each and every one of us, citizens of the world, knocks on our doors every day, claiming the need to honor the holiest of human rights – the right to life. Yet most of us keep silent, just as our governments do, as the powerful states do. By doing so we associate ourselves with the ongoing human tragedies that afflict humanity.

The Contrast between Genocides and the Holocaust

I have criticized the theory that connects the so-called "internationalization of human rights" produced by the UDHR with the Holocaust, as proclaimed by the UN Commission on Human Rights, because individual rights and human groups' protection are two different phenomena. Moreover, to think that the Nazi atrocities against the Jews could inspire the world with the hope of "never again" is wishful thinking, as the seventy years since the end of the war has proven.

Besides these points, there is a fundamental distinction between the Holocaust of the Jews by Nazi Germany and the other genocides of the twentieth and twenty-first centuries. Whereas these occurred in the context of some preexisting realistic conflict (territorial, class, ethnic, or religious), the Jews in Germany wanted nothing more than to be good Germans. The Jews of Eastern Europe also felt no enmity toward Germany, but just the opposite. Jews all over Europe spoke Yiddish, a language heavily influenced by German, and some even identified themselves with German culture. With regard to religion, many German Jews were either secular or followers of the Orthodox school of Frankfurt, which produced a harmonious bridge connecting the observance of Jewish religious traditions with the study and exercise of all sciences and professions. And as throughout Jewish history, German Jews

---

139. Novick, *The Holocaust in American Life*, 255, 256–57.

respected all other religions and strictly followed the Jewish rule against any initiative to convert people of other religions to Judaism.

The Germans fabricated a totally false picture of the Jew – his thinking, his behavior, and his alleged enmity to Germany – out of profound antisemitism, originating from the racial theories of certain Catholic orders and of the Catholic Church as a whole.

James Carroll, who carefully analyzed the treatment of Jews by the Catholic Church throughout seventeen centuries of history, examined the thinking and attitudes of the Germans toward the Jewish people, showing that Hitler's genocidal assault on the Jews became the work of an entire people, and an entire civilization was prepared to let it happen. Caroll's report coincides with the analysis of Daniel Jonah Goldhagen in his *Hitler's Willing Executioners*, to which I referred in chapter 2.

Carroll notes that the Nazi policy of eliminating "undesirable" people elicited such a strong negative reaction from the German people that the program was stopped. In contrast, no reaction was expressed regarding the elimination program of the Jewish people. And he quotes Deborah E. Lipstadt, who wrote that "had the Nazi hierarchy encountered unambiguous and sustained revulsion by non-Jewish Germans at their anti-Semitic policies, there probably would have been no Final Solution."[140]

To produce a real response to the Holocaust, the UN should have created a convention against antisemitism, which would deal with both prevention and punishment. This was not considered and, if proposed, would have been opposed by many Christian and by all Muslim countries. UN secretary-general Kofi Annan, speaking in June 2004, linked the Holocaust to the emergence of modern human rights. He declared that "a human rights agenda that fails to address anti-Semitism denies its own history."[141] The problem is that antisemitism was never really addressed during all these years. On the contrary, the Western world accepts and participates in the propaganda war against Israel, the newest and most sophisticated expression of antisemitism, as we shall see in chapter 11.

---

140. Carroll, *Constantine's Sword*, 30.
141. Iriye, Goedde, and Hitchcock, *Humans Rights Revolution*, 53.

Twenty-First-Century Antisemitism

Antisemitism of the worst kind has returned to the streets of Europe, mainly in France, Belgium, Sweden, England, and Germany. We refer to street antisemitism: demonstrations in front of synagogues; the vandalizing of commercial establishments belonging to Jews; and murderous terrorist attacks in schools, museums, and stores. The need for constant vigilance in the protection of synagogues has been a reality all over the continent already since the 1990s.

The possibility of a new Holocaust has been the subject of many warnings by various personalities, among them journalists George Will and Charles Krauthammer, legal scholar Louis René Beres, historian Benny Morris, hero Natan Sharansky, Nobel laureate Robert J. Aumann, and Spanish statesman José María Aznar. Their worry centers on the possibility of a nuclear attack against the State of Israel. George Will commented that Zionism grew out of a profound pessimism about the possibility of European Jews having their survival guaranteed without a Jewish home. The State of Israel was finally born out of the Holocaust – the greatest lesson of pessimism in history, says Will. But he ends his article saying that today "pessimists are realists who worry that, for the portion of world Jewry gathered in Israel, history may have saved its worst for last."[142] And so all of the work involved in preparing the Universal Declaration of Human Rights – inspired, as the drafters proclaimed with insistence, by the Holocaust – has been for naught.

Renowned thinker and lecturer Nathan Lopes Cardozo has written on the connection between the ordeal imposed on Israel by Arab terrorism and the propaganda offensives promoting European antisemitism:

> With an increase in Arab hostility, terrorist attacks, more wars, more loss of life, many Israelis became convinced that the eternal condition of Jewish suffering could not be escaped. With the outbreak of the Intifada, with its continuous stream of suicide bombings, this feeling of hopelessness became even stronger. Simultaneously, Israel lost its credibility and admiration among large parts of the world community when it was forced to defend itself against the Palestinian populace, using last-resort tactics it had hoped to avoid. An outbreak of anti-Semitism in Europe came shortly after. As if it were just waiting for an opportunity to turn its back on the

142. George F. Will, "'Peace Psychosis' in the Mideast," *Newsweek*, January 8, 2001, http://europe.newsweek.com/peace-psychosis-mideast-150879?rm=eu.

Jews, Europe used Israel's self-defense as a provocation for anti-Semitic attacks on its own Jewish communities and on Israel. Comparing Israel's army to the Nazis, European countries accused Israel of stealing land from the Palestinians and managed to rewrite the history of the Middle East in radically anti-Semitic ways.[143]

As already pointed out in earlier chapters, human rights, as far as minorities are concerned, gained absolutely no protection from the UDHR and the other international diplomas produced by the UN. So the declaration represents no guarantee against a second Holocaust.

Iran: The Present-Day Major Genocidaire

The speeches of Iran's former president Mahmoud Ahmadinejad about the state's intention to erase Israel from the map, which are being followed by the present leaders of the country – Hassan Rouhani and Ali Khamenei – perfectly characterize the intention of destroying a people, exactly as foreseen in the Convention against Genocide.

The constant military help and support that Iran has been delivering to Hamas and to Hezbollah – participating in this way in their murderous terrorist campaigns against Israel's civil population – realizes the declared genocidal intentions of Iranian's leadership. Thus, Iran's behavior perfectly matches the legal definition of genocide: declared intention to destroy a people and the initiation of actual murderous acts against them (in this case, through third parties). Has there been any reaction from the West, from the democracies? Yes – they have welcomed Iranian leaders in the UN, listened to their murderous speeches, and allowed them to receive a standing ovation. They have received Iranian leaders in their universities and applauded them. They have ignored Iran's crimes against women, against homosexuals, against minorities – religious or other; they have ignored Iran's most flagrant violations against all human rights; they have conducted business with them, enriched them, allowed them to proceed with their nuclear ambitions...and to lead the world to terror and chaos, to genocide and a Holocaust.

---

143. Nathan Lopes Cardozo, *Crisis, Covenant and Creativity: Jewish Thoughts for a Complex World* (New York: Urim, 2005), 90–91. In chapters 11 and 12 we will analyze the attitudes of the Western world toward Israel through demonization, delegitimization, and double standards.

Chapter Nine
UN and European Cowardice

The Protection of Human Rights

Hersch Lauterpacht, the eminent professor of international law at Cambridge University and later judge of the International Court of Justice, spoke in 1948 to the Conference of the International Law Association. He proclaimed:

> A declaration emanating from Governments is not a substitute for a deed. What the conscience of mankind expects from Governments is not the proclamation of the idea of the rights of man or even the recognition of the rights of man. What the conscience of the world expects from that quarter is the active protection of human rights and the assumption for that purpose of true and enforceable obligations.[1]

Indeed, despite the covenants that followed the declaration, and despite the Genocide Convention which preceded the Human Rights Declaration by one day, the UN has not succeeded in stemming the continuous wave of mega-violations of all human rights and has remained inoperative at the sight of the most egregious genocides. An absolute failure.

Terrorism Leading Back to Colonialism?

The attack that the United States suffered on September 11, 2001, started a new chapter in the international arena. First Afghanistan, then Iraq, were occupied by American troops, under the reasoning that terrorist states or

---

1. Lauterpacht, "The Universal Declaration of Human Rights," 372.

states that habitually give aid to terrorists must be controlled from inside their territories.

Paul Johnson expressed a hopeful wish in the days that followed that major terrorist act by speculating that "America and her allies may find themselves, temporarily at least, not just occupying with troops but administering obdurate terrorist states."[2] He speculated that these might eventually include not only Afghanistan and Iraq, but also Sudan, Libya, Iran, and Syria. That was a look far into the future. And the historian suggested a return to the League of Nations mandate system:

> Countries that cannot live at peace with their neighbors and wage covert war against the international community cannot expect total independence. With all the permanent members of the Security Council now backing, in varying degrees, the American-led initiative [the Afghanistan occupation], it should not be difficult to devise a new form of United Nations mandate that places terrorist states under responsible supervision.[3]

Johnson even foresaw the possibility of implanting democratic regimes that would abide by international law into countries connected to terror.

However, the international panorama has changed since Johnson's vision. The UN Security Council is deeply divided, as illustrated by the divergence regarding how to stop the massacres going on in Syria. And the General Assembly has become more and more controlled by the Afro-Islam-Arab–Third World majority, composed almost entirely of undemocratic states that do not adhere to the principles established in the UDHR and the UN charter and that have no concern for international peace and security.

And so we have an international organization divided between a minority of states that function by democratic or semi-democratic regimes, most of which are usually willing to participate in efforts to achieve world peace, and a majority of states that have no interest in cooperating to improve the international scenario.

2. Paul Johnson, "The Answer to Terrorism? Colonialism," *Wall Street Journal*, October 10, 2001.
3. Ibid.

Discriminations of All Sorts

The declarations, covenants, conventions, and resolutions against discrimination of all sorts are inspiring initiatives of the United Nations, but unfortunately have no influence on the ground. The amount of discrimination prevailing in the world today and the cruelties involved are staggering. Gender and religious discriminations are perhaps the most evident.

Saudi Arabia, Iran, and over a dozen other countries exercise cruel policies toward any religion other than Islam.

In Saudi Arabia, a court sentenced a Lebanese man to six years in prison and three hundred lashes for assisting a Saudi woman in her effort to convert to Christianity; the same court sentenced a Saudi man to two years and two hundred lashes for helping the young woman flee Saudi Arabia. The woman, who escaped to Sweden and secured asylum, is referred to as the "girl of Khobar," a Saudi city on the Persian Gulf.[4]

Saeed Abedini was born in Iran and converted to Christianity as a teenager; he was ordained as a minister and married an American woman, becoming a US citizen. During a visit to Iran in September 2012, to see his family and build an orphanage in the city of Rasht, the local authorities arrested him for "undermining national security through Christian evangelical activities" and sentenced him to eight years in prison.[5] He was denied medical treatment for several serious health problems, including internal bleeding due to being severely beaten in prison. In a letter to his family, Pastor Abedini wrote that the Iranian authorities threatened him with death because of his belief in Christianity.[6]

A notorious manifestation of religious intolerance is the treatment of the Baha'i community in Iran, Egypt, and other Muslim countries. In 2012, the American Bar Association published a detailed report on the history and the situation of the Baha'is in Egypt, authored by Naseem Kourosh, a graduate of New York University School of Law, a member of the ABA Section of International Law, and a human rights policy advocate in Washington, DC.

4. Benjamin Weinthal, "Saudi Gov't Sentences Man to 6 Years for Christianity," *Jerusalem Post*, May 12, 2013.
5. Irwin Cotler and Mark Kirk, "Sounding the alarm on Iran's massive human rights violations," *Jerusalem Post*, June 14, 2003.
6. Ibid. Abedini was freed and returned to the United States on January 16, 2016, under a negotiated prisoner exchange.

According to this report, the freedom of religion established in Egypt's 1971 constitution does not actually protect the estimated five hundred to two thousand Egyptian followers of Baha'i. What really counts is Presidential Decree 263, which dissolved all Baha'i institutions, seized all its properties, and made engaging in public Baha'i activities a criminal act punishable by imprisonment.[7]

In the Egyptian legal system, matters of personal status are governed not by civil law, but by religious law – specifically the family law of the only three recognized religions: Christianity, Judaism, and Islam.

Many fatwas have declared the Baha'i faith to be heresy and blasphemy. In 2003, the Islamic Research Center of Al-Azhar University – one of the oldest and most respected centers of Islamic learning in the world – issued a fatwa stating that Baha'is are apostates and that the Baha'i faith is a "lethal spiritual epidemic" that the state must "annihilate."

As a result, Baha'i members are not accorded equal treatment under the law: their marriages are not recognized, their children are considered illegitimate, and they have no right to family allowances, pensions, inheritance, divorce, alimony, or custody of children.

In the field of religion, a supreme court decision held that the constitutional freedom of belief only protects the Baha'is' right to inwardly believe in their religion, but not the right to practice it. Bahai's are therefore unable to obtain ID cards and are consequently refused access to many essential government services. They are denied birth certificates and driver's licenses, attendance at public schools and universities, and immunizations and medical treatment in public hospitals. They cannot obtain employment nor engage in financial transactions, such as opening a bank account or acquiring title to property.

In 2009, the government issued the first ID cards to Baha'is with a dash in the religion field. But in the same year unfortunate events occurred, such as the vandalizing of several village homes of Baha'is; in 2011, in the same village, several Baha'i homes were torched.[8]

Egypt violates the principle established in the United Nations Charter

---

7. *International Law News* 41, no. 3 (summer 2012): 31–33, American Bar Association.
8. Ibid.

that guarantees human rights without distinction as to race, sex, language, and religion.[9]

The persecution of Christians in Muslim countries has been growing exponentially. According to Open Doors USA, an organization that seeks to prevent the persecution of Christians, the Islamic republics of Iran, Syria, Iraq, Saudi Arabia, and Yemen are among the top ten violators of Christianity. In terms of global persecution of Christians, Open Doors noted that hundreds of Christians are murdered each month simply for being Christians.[10] Dexter Van Zile, a Christian media analyst for the Committee for Accuracy in Middle East Reporting in America, said that "the efforts to help the Christians in the Middle East will look a lot like the choices the West was faced with when the Jews were being murdered in Europe. We'll have to get serious about providing permanent refuge to Christians from the region in our own countries, which ominously enough, did not happen with the Jews. I hope and pray we make a different choice this time. These people need homes, permanent homes in the West."[11]

The Inoperativeness of Human Rights Diplomas

One author referred to the Universal Declaration of Human Rights as an "extraordinary success."[12] In fact, it has never been a success – not immediately after its approval; not by 1999, when this praise was written; and certainly not now as we approach its seventieth anniversary.

There are really no enforced international human rights. The only real protection of citizens of any country comes from their own state; the persecuted do not receive effective protection from other states or from the world community. In the case of a totalitarian state, a dictatorship, or a nondemocratic regime, the persecuted person and/or the group have no one to appeal to.

9. In the Israeli city of Haifa, on top of a hill, there is a beautiful Baha'i Temple. Its members enjoy full liberty to practice their religion, and total equality with the rest of the citizens of the Jewish state, which recognizes and respects all religions and grants them full religious autonomy.

10. Benjamin Weinthal, "The Religious Cleansing of Middle East Christians," *Jerusalem Post*, December 28, 2014.

11. Ibid.

12. Morsink, *Universal Declaration*, xi. He writes: "Now, as the document passes its fiftieth anniversary, critics have to make their case against the background of the extraordinary success that the Universal Declaration has become."

The various UN commissions and committees supposedly charged with the protection of human rights have busied themselves with a few individual human rights offenses out of the long list of rights enumerated in the Universal Declaration and more specifically in the covenants.

Resolutions 1235 (1969) and 1503 (1970) of the Economic and Social Council (ECOSOC) established procedures for communications from states, individuals, and nongovernmental organizations. But these procedures have not resulted in saving people from persecution, from torture, from atrocities, from genocides. ECOSOC Resolution 1503 authorized the Sub-Commission on Prevention of Discrimination and Protection of Minorities (a body of twenty-six supposedly independent experts) to examine communications received by the UN secretary-general with a view to referring to the Commission on Human Rights "situations which appear to reveal a consistent pattern of gross and reliably attested violations of human rights." And subsequently, in 1993, as a result of the Vienna World Conference, the UN established the position of UN High Commissioner for Human Rights. All these measures have not produced any results, as bloc politics intervene and paralyze the whole system.[13]

Mary Ann Glendon, comparative law professor at Harvard University, closes her book on Eleanor Roosevelt by saying that "today's friends of human rights are in the process of building on the legacy of the Declaration's framers."[14] Unfortunately, realities do not confirm this optimistic view. The same critique goes for the rosy statements that the prominent professor makes in her preface, where she writes: "The Universal Declaration would become an instrument as well as the most prominent symbol of changes that would amplify the voices of the weak in the corridors of power."[15]

A different statement by Glendon is a little closer to reality:

The Declaration has come to be treated more like a monument to be venerated from a distance than a living document to be reappropriated by each generation. Rarely, in fact, has a text been so widely praised yet so little read or understood.[16]

13. Harris, *Cases and Materials*, 629–30.
14. Glendon, *A World Made New*, 241.
15. Ibid., xvi.
16. Ibid., xvii.

I would rather say that the declaration has been relatively well read, and considerably well understood, but it has not been effective because indeed it is just a monument that confirmed well-known principles for those nations that live democratically and was ignored by those other states that do not respect the rights of their peoples.

Joseph Bishop put it bluntly when he wrote:

> What, then, has the Magna Carta of international law done for the welfare of humanity since its promulgation? The answer is clear and simple: nothing. Since Nuremberg there have been at least eighty or ninety wars, some of them on a very large scale.... In none of these cases was an aggressor arrested and brought to the bar of international justice and none is likely to be. For all the good it has done, the doctrine that aggressive war is a crime might as well be relegated to the divinity schools.[17]

The UDHR and the Self-Aggrandizement of the UN

The United Nations never tires of elaborating self-congratulatory pronunciations regarding the great success of the UDHR and the progress of international human rights. In a UN documentary section we read that "the UDHR has inspired more than 80 international human rights treaties and declarations, a great number of regional human rights conventions, domestic human rights bills and constitutional provisions, which together constitute a comprehensive legally binding system for the promotion and protection of human rights."

The report relates that all UN member states have ratified at least one of the nine core international human rights treaties and 80 percent have ratified four or more, "giving concrete expression to the universality of the UDHR and international human rights."[18]

This trend of optimistic analysis has caught on in many institutions and among many scholarly studies. The American legal community reveals this trend in diverse fashion. For instance, the American Society of International

17. Joseph Warren Bishop, *Justice under Fire: A Study of Military Law*, 284, as quoted in Sweeney et al., *International Legal System*, 802. Bishop wrote this in 1974. Since then an infinite small number of aggressors has been brought to the "bar of international justice" but with proportionately minor, insignificant results.
18. "The Foundation of International Human Rights Law," http://www.un.org/en/sections /universal-declaration/foundation-international-human-rights-law/index.html.

Law has expressed a "balanced" analysis of the human rights situation around the world, as can be seen in various materials published in its quarterly newsletter. The fourth issue of 2013 published an analysis of the human rights situation around the world, signed by its president, Daniel Donovan, and the executive director, Elizabeth Anderson. It states the following:

> The annual December 10 celebration of Human Rights Day, marking the anniversary of the signing of the Universal Declaration of Human Rights, produces a ritualized glass half-full/glass half-empty debate about progress on human rights.
>
> On the one hand the rights agenda has made remarkable strides forward – in law, in politics, in institutions. Starting with just the bare-bones Declaration of 65 years ago, we now have a raft of regional and global treaties and conventions, specifying conditions for most aspects of human existence. The concept of human rights has also obtained widespread currency in politics the world over, with most leaders, in government and commerce alike, at least espousing a commitment to this agenda. Viewing the human rights landscape today through the eyes of Eleanor Roosevelt, perhaps most impressive would be the development of a vast array of international institutions dedicated to monitoring and adjudicating rights.[19]

This statement is immediately annulled by what follows in the text of the two leaders of the society, as they refer to modern-day slavery, widespread sexual violence against women, and the relatively small number of states that have fully implemented legislation to cooperate with the International Criminal Court. This is coupled with the fundamental challenges faced by the court; the draconian regulations, harassment, and state-sanctioned violence by which civil society is increasingly threatened; and the difficulties in accessing legal assistance. Even in the United States fewer than one in five low-income people can obtain legal assistance. The analysis concludes with the hope that policy options may be developed to "fill the gap between our values and our realities."[20]

Most of the tragic violations of human rights that occur in the world

---

19. Donald Donovan and Elizabeth Andersen, "Toward the Effectiveness of International Human Rights Law," ASIL Forum, December 10, 2013, https://www.asil.org/node/697.
20. Ibid.

today – as described in the present study – are not mentioned in the "half-empty glass" of the description. On the other hand, the half-full part of the glass has been illustrated by factors that have absolutely no value. The "raft of regional and global treaties and conventions specifying conditions for most aspects of human existence" is entirely meaningless, because, as anyone can see, the absolute majority – if not the totality – of these international diplomas are not worth the paper they have been printed on and the translation expenses accrued. When the exposition of the two directors of the ASIL refers to the leaders in government and commerce, they carefully note that they have "at least" espoused a commitment to the agenda of human rights. This is unfortunately the truth: it is only a commitment, with no real, dynamic action in favor of basic human rights. The "vast array" of international institutions dedicated to monitoring and adjudicating rights were not listed, as the authors probably had difficulty pinpointing which entities really obtain concrete results in fighting the terrible human rights violations that are practiced in all sectors of politics and business throughout the world.

Human rights of minorities, collectivities, and entire nationalities continue being violated in all ways, leading to unimaginable atrocities.[21] The few existing impartial institutions are unable to do more than point out the atrocities to an indifferent world.

American Naïveté

American scholars, especially in the field of legal science, are not inclined to learn foreign languages. In consequence, they ignore what is being published throughout the world; they are oblivious of the civil law system. This ignorance is mixed with a certain disdain, and the end result is arrogance, which covers up the lack of knowledge of the foreign systems. To a great extent, this also applies to political scientists.

The executive power of the US government has as its most important advisers scholars of the fields of law and of political science; this helps to understand the lack of comprehension that prevails in the White House and, to a large extent, also in the State Department, regarding what really

---

21. The preamble to the Rome Statute that created the International Criminal Court says: "Mindful that during this century millions of children, women and men have been victims of unimaginable atrocities that deeply shock the conscience of humanity."

goes on in the rest of the world. We are back to good old isolationism, which explains the innumerable fiascos that American policies have suffered in the realm of foreign relations since the Second World War. Important sectors of this failure are the relationships to the Arab states, the wider Islamic world, and terrorism.

The blindness of the American legal milieu goes hand in hand with the hypocrisy that prevails in the organs of the United Nations, as illustrated by comments given at the 2013 American Bar Association Day at the UN – an annual event organized by the International Law Section of this association. On that occasion Ban Ki-moon, the UN secretary-general, delivered a speech in which he highlighted the UN's growing emphasis on the rule of law as an important tool in overcoming poverty, hunger, and disease around the world, and in responding to serious violations of international criminal law. And addressing the American attorneys he said: "You may be here at UN headquarters for just this one day but I know you are our partners throughout the year on a full spectrum of issues of vital concern to all humankind."[22]

Laurel Bellows, former president of the association, said that "attending the meeting was a memorable experience. It was a celebration that brought chills to my spine. I anticipated it would be an extraordinary event, but it was delightful to see the passion of presidents of countries who came to speak in support of the Declaration of Human Rights given the tension in the Middle East and Korea. It was reassurance that peace is possible and global leaders can come together."[23]

These remarks reflect the traditional hypocrisy of the secretary-general and the total naïveté of the ABA's president.

A dramatic instance of this blindness occurred after 9/11 when President Bush invited Saudi crown prince Abdullah to his ranch in Texas and told him, "You are our ally in the war against terrorism." The reality is that Prince Abdullah contributed funds to the Muslim Brotherhood and to al-Qaeda.[24] It was no secret that fifteen out of the nineteen suicide terrorists that destroyed

22. Richard Acello, "Two Days' Agenda: International Law Section Launches a Lobbying Event to Complement Its Annual Visit to the U.N.," *American Bar Association Journal* 99, no. 9 (September 2013): 60.
23. Ibid., 60–61.
24. Melissa Radler, "Newsmaker: A Different Kind of Muslim," *Jerusalem Post*, internet edition, April 18, 2004.

the Twin Towers and attacked the Pentagon were Saudi citizens of middle-class families. The power of the oil companies in the Western world is such that the role of the House of Saud as the main supporter of extremism and international terrorism goes on being covered up.[25]

The Human Rights of Thy Neighbor

If human rights has been internationalized by the UDHR – as claimed by jurists, politicians, and statesmen – then no state should extend any kind of support to another state in instituting a regime that does not respect human rights.

But this has not been respected by some democracies, most notably the United States of America, which has exported terror and the violations of human rights to other states. As reported in chapter 8, it was the US government that supported the substitution of a democratically elected president by a cruel, despotic general.

This flagrant disrespect of international human rights is exposed by the eminent Yale professors Myres McDougal and Michael Reisman, who included in their *International Law in Contemporary Perspective* a few critical essays on the policies of the CIA and some of its covert operations. One of these essays was authored by Professor Daniel Halperin of Harvard University, who refers to Henry Kissinger's famous remark regarding Chile: ""I don't see why we need to stand by and permit a country to go Communist due to the irresponsibility of its own people."[26]

The events in Chile constitute perhaps the strongest example of this phenomenon of illegal US interference in the internal politics of a democratic state. During the Pinochet regime, which followed the coup d'état stimulated by Kissinger's policy, there was widespread torture, many disappearances, a great number of executions – grave violations of human rights that extinguished thousands of lives. During those years, the Chilean citizens did not live freely, could not express their ideas, and suffered constant fear. It was a dictatorship maintained by terror.

The United States cooperated with the Chilean army in the downfall of President Allende, which elevated Pinochet to the presidency of the country,

25. Ibid.
26. McDougal and Reisman, *International Law in Contemporary Perspective*, 1022–33.

and then Washington cooperated with a revolution that brought terror and horror to the Chilean people, cooperating with an evil that it would never allow to occur to its own people.

It goes without saying that there are no terms of comparison with the terror installed by the German Nazi and the Russian Communist regimes in various other countries, but still it cannot be denied that on several opportunities the United States has disrespected the democracy of other peoples; in its paranoid obsessions regarding communism and certain critical situations, it cooperated in bringing about death and misfortunes of all kinds to other peoples.[27] This is state terrorism and a profound violation of "international human rights."[28]

When democracies cooperate with dictatorial regimes, maintaining economic, political, and commercial relations with them, they are strengthening the hands of those who deny freedom and human rights to their peoples. To what extent those economic and political relations are unavoidable, in what measure they can be restricted – these are the most difficult questions in modern international relations. But not to think of this dilemma, not to search for a change of approach and attitudes, not to look for a balanced policy that will restrict cooperation to the absolutely necessary is forfeiting the human rights of a great part of humanity. To vote in the UN in accordance with the policies and interests of nondemocratic regimes is an unforgiveable sin in the bible of human rights.

It is an absolute obligation to support groups living under cruel regimes who are willing to change the ways of their state's policies by introducing democracy or at least more liberal rules. This was clearly stated at the first meeting of the Human Rights Commission, on April 29, 1946, when work on drafting a declaration of human rights was launched. On that occasion, Mr. Henri Laugier, assistant secretary-general in charge of social affairs, told the members of the commission:

> You will have before you the difficult but essential problem to define
> the violation of human rights within a nation, which would constitute a

27. In chapter 8 we report on the participation of the United States in the tragedies of Cambodia, East Timor, and other countries.

28. Jacob Dolinger, "State Terrorism in the Twentieth Century: Lessons for the Twenty-First Century," in *Direito e Amor*, 54–55.

menace to the security and peace of the world and the existence of which is sufficient to put in movement the mechanism of the United Nations for the maintenance of peace and security.[29]

But this, as we know, has never become a reality.

Mr. Laugier suggested the implementation of a machinery of observation that would find and denounce the violations of human rights all over the world, stressing that if such a system had existed "a few years ago," and if it had been powerful and if the universal support of public opinion had given it authority, international action would have been immediately mobilized against the first authors and supporters of fascism and Nazism. "The human community," he concluded, "would have been able to stop those who started the war at the moment when they were still weak and the world catastrophe would have been avoided."[30]

Naive idealism was the spirit of those postwar days. The aggression of the Nazi regime against the Allied nations was not a matter of human rights but an international political upheaval aimed at conquest and domination.

Those good people who composed the original Human Rights Commission were really being fooled, or perhaps were fooling themselves and the whole world, when they heard Laugier counsel to "look for a basis for a fundamental declaration of human rights, acceptable to all the United Nations, the acceptance of which will become the essential condition of the admission in the international community."[31] They did absolutely nothing to guarantee the enforcement of that "essential condition"; instead, they approved a declaration without any force of law and without establishing strict guarantees that the acceptance and observance of the document would become a *conditio sine qua non* for becoming a member of the United Nations.

And so any state wishing to become a member of the United Nations has been accepted without the slightest question about the regime in force in its territory, despite the express condition established in the Charter of the United Nations in 1945 that "membership in the United Nations is open to all other peace-loving states which accept the obligations contained in the present Charter and, in the judgment of this Organization, are able and willing

29. Conseil Economique et Social, E/HR/6, 1 May 1946.
30. Ibid.
31. Ibid.

to carry out these obligations"[32] The UDHR, which was approved in 1948, does not contain any means for strengthening the conditions established in the charter of the UN.

In the years that have followed, every tyrannous, dictatorial state has been accepted into the UN. And even in 1946, when work on the UDHR started, and in 1948, when it was approved by the General Assembly, a number of states that manifestly violated basic human rights were members of the "international community." Some of them, such as the United States, corrected their ways; others remained as they were – no race equality, no freedom of religion, no freedom of expression, no freedom for women, no right of defense, no human rights whatsoever. The hypocrisy may not have been manifest, but it existed in a dormant state at the very origin of the whole movement for the "internationalization of human rights."

This brings us back to the article of Professor Kunz, whose statement on "natural law versus positive law" regarding human rights was quoted at the opening of chapter 6. Kunz writes that "in the field of human rights, as in other actual problems of international law, it is necessary to avoid the Scylla of pessimistic cynicism and the Charybdis of mere wishful thinking and superficial optimism."[33]

Today, after all these years, the accumulation of human rights violations, the total inoperativeness of the United Nations, and its complicity in many atrocities demonstrate that whereas the illustrious members of the Human Rights Commission who worked on the drafting of the Universal Declaration were inspired by idealism and wishful thinking, their work did nothing to open a new era of peace and security, of respect for the dignity of every human person, recognition of the rights of every minority. Besides the weakness of the declaration itself, a significant factor – and perhaps the decisive one – was the cynicism, the hypocrisy of the very same Human Rights Commission in the years that followed the approval of the declaration, and then of its successor, the Council of Human Rights. These, as well as other organs of the United Nations, aided and abetted many of the human tragedies, and so the fundamental purposes of the United Nations – peace and human rights – have

---

32. Charter of the United Nations, article 4.
33. Kunz, "The United Nations Declaration of Human Rights," 320.

not been attained and are not foreseeable. Pessimism (not cynicism) is more than justified.

The hypocrisy that pervades the international community materializes in various ways and in all kinds of situations. In October 2013, Saudi Arabia, along with Chad and Nigeria, were elected to rotating seats on the United Nations Security Council. Besides violating practically all aspects of human rights, Saudi Arabia finances terrorism abroad and flagrantly disrespects the charter of the UN and practically all principles of the Declaration of Human Rights and both covenants. The election of Saudi Arabia to the most authoritative and powerful body of the world organization was an act of major hypocrisy.

For reasons of its own, Saudi Arabia did not accept the invitation to participate in the Security Council.

Slavery and Human Trafficking

The Slavery Convention was signed in Geneva on September 25, 1926, and entered into force on March 9, 1927. It was amended by the protocol drawn up at the United Nations headquarters on December 7, 1953; the amended convention entered into force in July 7, 1955.[34]

Parallel to the Slavery Convention, in 1950 the General Assembly of the United Nations approved Resolution 317, which became the Convention for the Suppression of the Traffic in Persons and of the Exploitation of the Prostitution of Others. By 2012, eighty-two states were parties to the convention, and thirteen states had signed the convention but had not ratified it.

The convention requires state signatories to punish any person who "procures, entices or leads away, for purpose of prostitution, another person, even with the consent of that person." It prescribes procedures for combating international traffic for the purpose of prostitution, including the extradition of offenders.

The preamble of the convention states:

---

34. In the Brussels Conference Act of 1890 the signatories declared that they were "equally animated by the firm intention of putting an end to the traffic in African slaves." This was supplemented and revised by the Convention of Saint-Germain-en-Laye signed by the Allied Powers of the First World War on September 10, 1919, in which the signatories undertook to "endeavor to secure the complete suppression of slavery in all its forms and of the slave trade by land and sea." See http:/en.wikipedia.org/wiki/1926_Slavery_Convention.

Whereas prostitution and the accompanying evil of the traffic in persons for the purpose of prostitution are incompatible with the dignity and worth of the human person and endanger the welfare of the individual, the family and the community.

In 2000, the United Nations General Assembly adopted the Protocol to Prevent, Suppress and Punish Trafficking in Persons, especially Women and Children. This protocol, known as the Palermo Protocol, came as a response to the critiques that the original convention concentrated on the punishment of the traffickers but did not sufficiently protect the victims. The protocol entered into force on December 25, 2003, and 150 nations are party to it.

In 2005, in Warsaw, the Council of Europe Convention on Action against Trafficking in Human Beings was opened for accession and has since been signed by forty-three member states of the Council of Europe. The convention established a group of experts on action against trafficking in human beings, which monitors the implementation of the convention through country reports. Complementary protection is ensured through the Council of Europe 2007 Convention on the Protection of Children against Sexual Exploitation and Sexual Abuse.

Yet despite this rich collection of international agreements, statistics compiled by various nongovernmental organizations reveal that millions of human beings fall victim to the forbidden trafficking every year.[35]

The International Labor Organization, an agency of the United Nations, released in 2012 an Estimate of Forced Labor, which states that some 20.9 million people around the world are victims of sex trafficking and other types of forced labor. The comparable number in the ILO's 2005 report was 12.9 million. (Other estimates put the 2012 number of forced labor victims as high as 27 million.)

According to the 2012 report, some 4.5 million people, or 22 percent of all enslaved workers, are victims of forced sexual exploitation; 14.2 million, or 68 percent, are victims of forced-labor exploitation in such economic activities as agriculture, construction, domestic work, and manufacturing. The remaining 2.2 million, or 10 percent, are victims of state-imposed forms of forced labor. The report states that no region of the world is free from

35. Melissa Holman, "The Modern-Day Slave Trade," *Texas International Law Journal* 44 (fall/winter 2008): 99 ff.

slavery. Geographically, it estimates that there are some 11.7 million victims of sexual exploitation, labor exploitation or state-imposed forced labor in China, India, and the rest of Asia (excluding Japan). There are another 3.7 million in Africa, 600,000 in the Middle East, 1.8 million in Eastern Europe and the former Soviet Union, and 1.5 million in the United States, Canada, Australia, Japan, New Zealand, and Western Europe.

Human trafficking is extremely profitable. It generates some $32 billion per year, making it the second largest criminal activity in the world, only behind drug dealing.[36]

According to a report by Steven Seidenberg, the numbers for the United States are disappointing. In federal fiscal year 2011, about 2,000 human trafficking cases were investigated by the Justice Department, the FBI and Immigration and Customs Enforcement. During the same year, the Justice Department prosecuted only 42 cases of forced labor or sex trafficking involving adult victims. That number increased to 125 when cases involving sex trafficking of minors were added in.

36. Ibid., 99, and Steven Seidenberg, "Of Human Bondage," *American Bar Association Journal* 99, no. 4 (April 2013): 51–57. See also same edition of the journal, 8, Laurel Bellows, "Intolerance for Inequities," and the September 2012 issue, 64, "Raising Awareness." See also the May 2013 edition of the journal, at 59, Rhonda McMillion, "Two for One: Congress Moves to Reauthorize Laws Targeting Domestic Violence, Human Trafficking." The *International Law News* of the Section of International Law of the American Bar Association published in its issue of summer 2013 (vol. 42, no. 3) an article by Corinne Lewis titled "Don't Overlook Human Rights Risks When Negotiating and Drafting International Commercial Transaction Agreements," which deals with those companies that have suppliers in countries like China, Uzbekistan, and other places, where forced labor and other violations of human rights are the norm. The next issue of the *International Law News*, fall 2013 (vol. 42, no. 4), has a number of lengthy articles on this subject: "The Modern Abolitionist Movement: How Lawyers, Litigation, and Legislation Can Combat Trafficking in Persons" by Laurel G. Bellows; "Joining the Fight against Human Trafficking" by Gabrielle M. Buckley; "Ending Impunity and Securing Justice: Criminal Justice Responses to Human Trafficking" by Anne T. Gallagher; "Advancing Access to Justice for Sex Trafficking Victims in Iraq" by Sherizaan Minwalla and William H. Pryor; "Soccer, Samba, and Sex: Preventing Human Trafficking from Attending Brazil's World Cup and Olympics" by Natalie Lamela; "Human Trafficking and the Private Sector" by Jonathan Trodes; "Human Trafficking of LGBT individuals" by Omar Martinez and Guadalupe Kelle; "European Judges Adopt Aggressive Policy on Human Trafficking" by Donald E. Shaver; and "Demand Reduction: Critical Next Step in the Fight against Sex Trafficking" by Abigail L. Kuzma. These articles demonstrate the manifold aspects of the problem and the dedication of American lawyers in the war against this evil.

Laurel G. Bellows, former president of the American Bar Association, wrote that the unfortunate reality is that many of the products that American consumers rely on every day – from cotton to coffee to cellphones to fish – arrive at the US markets via supply chains often tainted by forced labor. This problem touches the lives of all Americans; making headway toward a solution requires the commitments and contributions of private-sector leaders. The good news is that many companies have made commitments to address this problem and have started taking a look at their own supply chains.[37]

Another surprising and sad point that Laurel G. Bellows gives us is that in workplaces across America, women working side by side with men earn seventy-seven cents to every dollar that men earn.[38] One can imagine the proportion of earnings between men and women in Asian, African, and South American countries.

Human trafficking is one of the many mega-violations of human rights, a constant worldwide violation that is a shameful stain on the dignity of the human being. As with all other violations, it is not with conventions, resolutions, and declarations that this atrocious situation will be remedied. It requires action – dynamic, constant international cooperative action. But the United Nations is not prepared and not willing to undertake this, as it busies itself with political maneuvers, with submission to cruel dictatorships.

In another article, Steven Seidenberg relates that there are about a dozen US states with comprehensive laws against human trafficking. He reports on the project of a Uniform Act on Prevention of and Remedies for Human Trafficking. Presently many US states prosecute victims of sexual servitude as prostitutes, whereas the Uniform Act would change that, seeking to protect victims and enable them to start their lives anew. Proponents plan to initially push for enactment of the Uniform Act in about fifteen states.[39]

Laurel Bellows, when referring to the planned Uniform Act, writes that "getting rid of an embedded criminal enterprise such as human trafficking will not be easy. It will take time and discipline and continued persistence over the long term. But I trust in the American people to take this issue to heart

37. *International Law News* 42, no. 4 (fall 2013): 7, American Bar Association.
38. "Intolerance for Inequities: Law Day Reminds Us That We Must Continue to Fight Inequality in All Its Forms," *American Bar Association Journal* 99, no. 4 (April 2013): 8.
39. Steven Seidenberg, "A Law with Bite," *American Bar Association Journal* 99, no. 12 (December 2013): 58.

and help the victims who cannot help themselves. Slavery in the land of the free will not be tolerated."[40]

The Lack of a Definition of Terrorism Protects Terrorists

"I urge Member States to conclude, as soon as possible, a comprehensive convention on international terrorism" – so spoke Kofi Annan in his report as secretary-general of the United Nations to the General Assembly's sixtieth session, in 2006.[41]

It is true that in every theme of public international law, the legal and the political are closely intertwined, so that it is impossible to examine a subject from the juridical perspective without considering its political aspects. In the case of terrorism there is still another factor, usually absent in international law, namely the religious one. That explains the complexity of the problem, the difficulties in finding a solution, and the possibility of strong points of divergence.[42]

While the United Nations hardly paid attention to the monstrous atrocities perpetrated in different corners of the world by dictators and totalitarians, and also did nothing to help the billions of people living under oppressive regimes, it did turn its attention to the human rights of a specific class of people, to which it has been dedicating the utmost care and consideration: the international terrorist.

As paradoxical as it may seem, the care dedicated to the international terrorist is the reason that the community of nations has not succeeded in defining the crime of terrorism. This crime therefore remains out of the International Criminal Tribunal's jurisdiction. There are thirteen conventions on terrorism directed to specific areas, but no consensus has been reached on the definition of the generic crime.

José Cretella Neto, a Brazilian law professor, has summarized the difficulty of reaching a definition of the crime of terrorism by saying that all the violent, politically motivated attacks that have been occurring, including those perpetrated by Palestinian groups in Israel, are doubtlessly acts of terrorism and

40. Ibid.
41. United Nations General Assembly, A/60/825, April 27, 2006.
42. "International Terrorism Defeats the UN," in Dolinger, *Direito e Amor*, 63.

that it is the Islamic opposition to this conception that blocks the adoption of a universally accepted definition for international terrorism.[43]

Antonio Cassese, an Italian professor, presented another point of view. He claims that a definition of terrorism exists in international law, but there is disagreement about certain exceptions to this definition, such as the "freedom fighters." He adds that it is a logical error to say that because there is no consensus about the exception, we do not have a general notion. This would be equivalent to saying that since, in criminal law, there is a doubt whether coerced homicide can be justified, we have no definition for homicide.[44]

Palestinian attacks kill men, women, and children, in kindergartens, restaurants, markets, weddings, even the world Olympic games. Yet according to Cassese's position, the fact that there is no consensus over whether the perpetrators should be called "terrorists" or "freedom fighters" merely constitutes an exception; it does not affect the definition of terrorism.

Cassese is roundly mistaken for three reasons. Firstly, the exception he refers to is not an exception, but the rule. If we examine the number of terrorist attacks of the last few decades, we shall discover that the absolute majority, if not the totality, of terrorist acts are made under the claim of liberty for the Palestinian people or for a people connected to the Palestinians (such as the expulsion of American troops from Saudi Arabia).[45] The false "freedom fighter" acts are the rule, not the exception.

Secondly, the Palestinians who live in Gaza and the ones located on the left margin of the Jordan River (the "West Bank") are not freedom fighters – their objective is not the establishment of a state of their own, but the destruction of the State of Israel, as clearly established in the Palestinian National Charter. This document is rich in affirmations of the illegality of all international documents that led to the creation of the State of Israel, including the UN resolution on the partition of the land into two states, one Jewish and one Arab.[46]

---

43. José Cretella Neto, "Dos Fundamentos Jurídicos do Combate ao Terrorismo," São Paulo, 2006.

44. Karima Bennoune, review of *Enforcing International Law Norms against Terrorism*, ed. Andrea Bianchi, *American Journal of International Law* 100, no. 2 (April 2006): 511.

45. For more on the connection between the Palestinians and Saudi Arabia, see below in the chapter.

46. See below for the specific affirmations of the charter.

Thirdly, freedom fighters do not kill innocent children and civilians engaging in civilian activities. Freedom fighters attack an oppressing army, as the Israeli "terrorists" did in the years before the proclamation of the State of Israel (1945–48). At that time the British army's policy was entirely in favor of the Arab aggressors, and they imprisoned Jewish fighters who were trying to defend the Jewish population from Arab terrorists and help the survivors of the Holocaust to enter the land of Israel. Etzel (the acronym for the Irgun Tzva'i Leumi [national military organization], a militant resistance group) opposed the cruel policy of the British government, according to which survivors were sent back to camps in Europe or on the island of Cyprus. These freedom fighters fought exclusively against the British army and did not touch a civilian.

In order to qualify as freedom fighters, individuals must fulfill two requirements: just cause and just means.[47] The people who call themselves Palestinians (the term arose as a specific identification of the Arab population only in the 1960s, as will be discussed in greater detail below) are focused on the destruction of the Jewish state and the murder of all Jews living in this state, as is attested by their laws, their consistent speeches, and the incitement that occurs in their schools and mosques. They are not interested in the establishment of an Arab state in the territory designated to them by the UN Partition Plan of 1947 – which they repudiated as soon as it was approved and consistently thereafter throughout the last seven decades. On two occasions, after hard negotiations, two different Israeli governments offered the Palestinians 97 percent of their official demands (Prime Minister Ehud Barak to Arafat in Camp David, in the year 2000, and Prime Minister Ehud Olmert to Mahmoud Abbas in 2008); on both occasions no agreement came from the Arab side, not even a counterproposal. It is therefore manifestly clear that they do not pursue a "just cause."

The Palestine National Charter states:

The partition of Palestine in 1947 and the establishment of the State of Israel are entirely illegal, regardless of the passage of time, because they were contrary to the will of the Palestinian people and to their natural right in their homeland, and inconsistent with the principles embodied in the

47. Louis René Beres, "Terrorists are not 'Freedom Fighters,'" News with Views, March 13, 2002, http://www.newswithviews.com/israel/israel15.htm.

Charter of the United Nations, particularly the right to self-determination. (Article 19)

Article 20 proceeds to state that

the Balfour Declaration, the Mandate for Palestine, and everything that has been based upon them, are deemed null and void. Claims of historical or religious ties of Jews with Palestine are incompatible with the facts of history and the true conception of what constitutes statehood.... [48]

The denial of historical ties of the Jewish people with Palestine has been repeated by the Arab Palestinian leadership time and again. They deny the existence of the First and Second Temples in Jerusalem. By this denial of universally accepted historical facts, the people who identify themselves as Palestinians are also denying the birth of Christianity, as the New Testament is clear about the presence of Jesus Christ in Jewish Jerusalem and in its Temple.

The charter starts in article 1 with the claim that "Palestine is the homeland of the Arab Palestinian people; it is an indivisible part of the Arab homeland, and the Palestinian people are an integral part of the Arab nation." So we have "Arab Palestinian people," "Arab homeland," "Palestinian people," "Arab nation." This is a confusing set of loose denominations. The historical truth is that Palestine – a name given by the Romans which remained throughout millennia – became, under Ottoman rule and later under British rule, the homeland of all those who lived in the region – Jews, Muslims, and Christians. All of them carried Palestine identity cards and, when traveling abroad, Palestinian passports.

The use of the term "Palestinians" to refer to the Arabs is an artifice created by the Arabs in the mid-sixties and somehow accepted by the world – yet the term carries no historical background, nor any legal basis. Moreover, Palestine is not "Arab homeland": it is the ancient homeland of the Jewish people, the place where Christianity was born at the time when there was no Muslim religion in the world and an "Arab nation" was unknown. Article 1, therefore, establishes wrong premises. Article 2 claims that "Palestine, with the boundaries it had during the British Mandate, is an indivisible territorial unit."

48. Palestinian National Charter. See http://avalon.law.yale.edu/20th_century/plocov. asp.

The charter pretends to forget that when Great Britain assumed the mandate, Palestine included the territory which only later, in 1946, became the Kingdom of Jordan.[49] So if those who call themselves Palestinians consider illegal all the decisions of the League of Nations, including the mandate that was handed to Great Britain, they should be claiming Jordan as theirs, the same way they claim Israel's territory as belonging to them. (The truth of the matter is that Jordan's population is composed of a majority of those who call themselves Palestinians, which means that for those who accept the League of Nations and the UN resolutions, the so-called Palestinians already got their state.)

Article 9 of the Palestinian Charter is clear about the Palestinian Arab desideratum: "Armed struggle is the only way to liberate Palestine.... The Palestinian Arab people assert their absolute determination and firm resolution to continue their armed struggle and to work for an armed popular revolution for the liberation of their country and their return to it." The aggressive character of the charter is again established in article 15, which speaks of "the liberation of Palestine"; it attempts to "repel the Zionist and imperialist aggression against the Arab homeland and aims at the elimination of Zionism in Palestine." [50]

The "Zionism is racism" libel approved by the UN General Assembly stems from the charter, which declares in article 22 that "Zionism ... is racist and fanatic in its nature, aggressive, expansionist and colonial in its aims, and fascist in its methods." The same article proceeds to state that "liberation of Palestine will destroy the Zionist and imperialist presence and will contribute to the establishment of peace in the Middle East."

History has proven how peace in the Middle East is affected by the manifest, vicious hate that prevails between the many sects of the Muslim religion, which have been murdering each other in Iraq, Egypt, Syria, and other Arab countries. It is a phenomenon that is progressively aggravated as time goes by. The hate and cruelty prevailing between the different groups of the "Palestinian" people itself (those who live in the West Bank vs. the Gaza population under Hamas) is the best proof of the falsity of the charter's affirmations.

The hypocrisy of the Palestinian Charter comes out very clearly in article 24, which states that the "Palestinian people believe in the principles of justice,

---

49. *League of Nations Official Journal*, November 1922, 1188–89, 1390–91.
50. http://avalon.law.yale.edu/20th_century/plocov.asp.

freedom, sovereignty, self-determination, human dignity and the right of all peoples to exercise them." Among the Palestinian Arabs, as among all the Arab peoples, there is no justice, as people suspected of treason are executed without any court of law judgment; there is no freedom, as media is totally controlled by the governing forces; there is no human dignity, as women are dominated by men's and society's dictatorships, homosexuals are not allowed to live, and the whole population is submitted to the diktat of those who managed to get hold of internal power.

In 1974, the Palestinian Liberation Organization (PLO) adopted a "Phased Plan" in which it reaffirmed the aim of "the liberation of all Palestinian territory" (article 8). Interestingly enough, the plan repudiated Resolution 242 of the UN Security Council, which "obliterates the national right of our people.... Therefore [the PLO] refuses to have anything to do with this resolution at any level" (article 1). (This declaration should legally free the State of Israel of any commitment regarding this UN resolution, which orders the return of territories occupied during the Six-Day War.)[51]

As a consequence of the Oslo Accord and the exchange of letters between Chairman Yasser Arafat and Prime Minister Yitzhak Rabin, the PLO approved a statement that "nullifies" certain articles and parts of other articles that are inconsistent with the commitment to recognize Israel and live in peace side by side. But, as Talia Einhorn points out, "the problem is that to this day no new Charter has been drawn up, nor has a legal committee been set up to rewrite one. In fact on the contrary, statements by Arab leaders indicate that the PLO Charter remains in force."[52]

In 1975, Arafat's terror group Fatah defined its objectives in a founding document, which established the following principles:

---

51. "The PLO's 'Phased Plan,'" IRIS, http://www.iris.org.il/plophase.htm. In chapter 10 we shall come back to the Palestinian Charter and the Phased Plan; we shall quote other sources where they are published, analyze those documents from historical and legal perspectives, and demonstrate that Resolution 242 does not carry any obligation of Israel toward the "Palestinians."
52. Einhorn, "The Status of Judea and Samaria (the West Bank)." See also Khaled Abu Toameh, "Kaddoumi: PLO Charter Was Never Changed," *Jerusalem Post*, April 22, 2004, quoted by Caroline Glick, *The Israeli Solution: One-State Plan for Peace in the Middle East* (New York: Crown Forum, 2014), 18n10.

- •"The complete liberation of Palestine and eradication of Zionist economic, political, military and cultural existence" (article 12).
- •"Armed struggle is a strategy and not a tactic, and the Palestinian Arab people's armed revolution is a decisive factor in the liberation fight and in uprooting the Zionist entity and this struggle will not cease unless the Zionist state is demolished and Palestine is completely liberated" (article 19).
- • It is Fatah's obligation to "oppose any political solution offered as an alternative to demolishing the Zionist occupation in Palestine" (article 22).[53]

The attitude of the Palestinians toward the State of Israel frees her from withdrawing its armed forces from the so-called occupied territories, as the logical interpretation of United Nations Security Council Resolution 242 is that this withdrawal is dependent on what the resolution describes as "respect for and acknowledgment of the sovereignty, territorial integrity and political independence of every State in the area and their right to live in peace within secure and recognized boundaries free from threats or acts of force."

The Palestinian regime has continually denied Israel's right to "live in peace" – as is evident from its charter, as well as its schools, mosques, newspapers, television programs, and the honoring of its "martyrs," all of which stimulate more terrorism. Israel therefore had no obligation – and continues to have no obligation – to withdraw its armed forces from the "occupied territories," as the UN classifies Israel's presence in the West Bank.

Since the Arabs of the West Bank and of the Gaza Strip do not even come close to meeting the first requisite of "just cause," to discuss "just means" is a nonissue. But if "just means" may be judged independently, then the points raised above – the murder of civilians at all times, in all places, on any kind of occasion – is the best demonstration that there is also no "just means" in their fight. The violation of article 3 (1) of the four 1949 Geneva Conventions – which protects all those who are not militarily involved in the conflict – is clear and evident. Thus, even if there were a "just cause" – which there isn't – it would not justify "unjust means."

American and European supporters of a Palestinian state presume that

---

53. "Introduction to the Fatah Constitution: The Essential Principles of the Constitution," Ariel Center for Policy Research, http://bit.ly/16WvuNa, as quoted in Glick, *The Israeli Solution*, 54 and note 15.

it will be part of a "two-state solution" – that is, that the new Arab state will exist side-by-side with the existing Jewish state. Yet, this presumption is dismissed everywhere and every time in the Arab/Islamic world. Indeed, the "Map of Palestine" at the official website of the Palestinian National Authority includes all of Israel. There are no two states on this map – only one: "Palestine." Insurgents who resort to terrorism against Israel have never acknowledged that a Jewish state has any right to survive.

At any rate, Cassese's theory has been categorically destroyed by the chief terrorist of all times, the fanatically murderous Osama bin Laden, who proclaimed a jihad on October 12, 1996. He declared:

> The people of Islam have suffered from aggression, iniquity and injustice imposed by the Zionist Crusader alliance and their collaborators....
>
> It is the duty now on every tribe in the Arabian peninsula to fight jihad and cleanse the land from these Crusader occupiers. Their wealth is booty to those who kill them.
>
> My Muslim brothers: your brothers in Palestine and in the land of the two Holy Places [i.e., Saudi Arabia] are calling upon your help and asking you to take part in fighting against the enemy – the Americans and the Israelis. They are asking you to do whatever you can to expel the enemies out of the sanctities of Islam.[54]

In a later statement bin Laden claimed that "terrorising the American occupiers [of Islamic Holy Places] is a religious and logical obligation."[55]

Bin Laden's February 1998 fatwa proclaimed:

> The killing of Americans and their civilian and military allies is a religious duty for each and every Muslim to be carried out in whichever country they are until Al Aqsa mosque has been liberated from their grasp and until their armies have left Muslim lands.[56]

The same fatwa called for "an attack on the American soldiers of Satan" and proclaimed:

54. Sean D. Murphy, ed., "Contemporary Practice of the United States Relating to International Law: Terrorist Attacks on the World Trade Center and Pentagon," *American Journal of International Law* 96, no. 1 (January 2002): 239.
55. Ibid.
56. Ibid.

We – with God's help – call on every Muslim who believes in God and wishes to be rewarded to comply with God's orders to kill Americans and plunder their money whenever and wherever they find it. We also call on Muslims … to launch the raid on Satan's U.S. troops and the devil's supporters allying with them, and to displace those who are behind them.[57]

These statements were followed by innumerable fatwas and appeals by mullahs, sheikhs, and all kinds of religious leaders in the Muslim world to their people, urging them to participate in the "holy war" against the Western world. Bin Laden's fatwa is the fundamental source of what some jurists classify as "freedom fighters."

In a 2013 speech at an event marking the forty-ninth anniversary of the founding of the PLO, President Abbas made it clear that the original goal of the movement – the destruction of Israel – remains the movement's goal.[58] The West lives in total denial about the nature of Islam's jihad, its seriousness, its worldwide reach, and its murderous nature.

There is no sense in distinguishing the Islamic State from other no less barbaric organizations such as Hamas, Hezbollah, al-Qaeda, al-Shabaab, and Boko Haram. It is not only the Islamic State that beheads its victims. Daniel Pearl and Nick Berg were beheaded by al-Qaeda years before the Islamic State became known. The use of children as human bombs by Hamas and Hezbollah is just as depraved. And so is Boko Haram burning Christians alive in Nigerian churches, or kidnapping a few hundred Christian girls from an African institution, raping them, and selling them into slavery. The aim of these groups is the same: to kill and conquer "infidels" and ultimately to establish Islamic rule across the world.[59]

Obama and Cameron have denied that the Islamic State has anything to do with Islam. Obama declared: "ISIL is not Islamic. No religion condones the killing of innocents." Cameron stated: "Islam is a religion of peace. They are not Muslims. They are monsters."

57. Ibid., 240.
58. Evelyn Gordon, "Abbas: PLO Charter Reflects What Palestinians Want," *Commentary*, June 3, 2013, as quoted in Glick, *The Israeli Solution*, 248–49.
59. See Raymond Ibrahim, "U.S. Denies Visa to Victim of Boko Haram: Muslim Persecution of Christians, May 2014," http://www.gatestoneinstitute.org/4763/muslim-persecution -christian-may-2014.

Journalist Melanie Phillips, a columnist for the *Times* (UK), contests these claims:

> This is ridiculous. Does it follow that those who are slaughtering thousands of Christians in the name of Islam are not Muslims either? Islamist State and other jihadists were taught to wage war for Islam at mosques and madrassas funded by Saudi Arabia, Qatar and other Islamic states. So are Saudi and Qatar therefore un-Islamic?[60]

Phillips holds that there are various reasons for this state of denial. Western leaders are terrified of alienating the Islamic world, partly in fear of violent consequences and partly because they do not want to endanger their lucrative trade and financial dealings with Muslim states. They fear that recognizing that the terror in the name of Islam is really Islamic would demonize all Muslims. This, Phillips points out, is fallacious, as there are many Muslims who want to reform their religion and bring it to a peaceful coexistence with the world.

Phillips further notes:

> The fundamental goal of Islamic State is ... to establish a caliphate and force the world to submit to Islam. What Islamic State openly stands for is mass murder and barbarism in the name of God.
>
> Neither air strikes nor ground troops will defeat the religious idea for which Islamic State stands. ... To defeat Islamic terror, that idea has to be defeated. The free world needs to help truly reformist Muslims to purge it from their religion.[61]

In a symposium that took place at the United Nations on global antisemitism, Brigitte Gabriel, a Lebanese Arab who has been fighting for human rights and denouncing antisemitism, referred to Muslim terrorism in terms that should serve as a lesson to the world community. She stated:

> Remember, ladies and gentlemen, savagery is not merely their strategy. It is an article of their faith. They commit genocide in the name of Allah.
>
> Israel has been familiar with the concept, and the reality, of genocide in the name of Allah for a long time. The war that ISIS has declared on the

---

60. Melanie Phillips, "As I See It: If the West Denies What It's Up Against, It Will Lose," *Jerusalem Post*, September 19, 2014.
61. Ibid.

world is the same as the war that Hamas has been waging against Israel
for decades. The only difference, again, is focus. ISIS seeks a world-wide
caliphate. Hamas is focused on the destruction of Israel.

However their motivation, methods, and morals are the same....

Once the intentional mass murder of innocent civilians was legitimized
against Israel, it was legitimized *everywhere*, constrained by nothing more
than the strong-held beliefs of those who would become the mass murderers. Because the Palestinians were encouraged by most of the world to
believe that the murder of innocent Israeli civilians is a legitimate tactic to
advance the Palestinian nationalist cause, the Islamists believe that they
may commit mass murder anywhere in the world to advance their holy
cause. As a result, we suffer from a plague of Islamic terrorism, from Moscow to Madrid, from Bali to Beslan, from Nairobi to New York, authored
and perfected by the Palestinians. Israel and the United States are not
separate targets of Islamic terrorism. The whole world is their target.[62]

This is an important message to the leaders of the United States and the United
Kingdom as well as to the whole of Western civilization.

Terrorism and Genocide at the International Criminal Tribunal

The International Criminal Tribunal cannot judge the crime of terrorism
because it lacks a legal definition. On the other hand, the tribunal has jurisdiction over the crime of genocide, as established in articles 5 and 6 of the
Rome Statute which created the court. That leads to the rationale that I have
already exposed in chapter 8: given that Hamas and Hezbollah declare their
intent to annihilate the State of Israel and then go about killing Jews worldwide, their speeches and actions meet the definition of genocide as set forth
in the Genocide Convention, and their terrorist actions should be judged by
the International Criminal Court under the crime of genocide.

However, we know from the cases of Bosnia-Herzegovina, Kosovo, and
others that the sophisticated legal machinations of various factors involved
have resulted in a failure to indict international criminals for genocide, as
so well documented in David Scheffer's book *All the Missing Souls*. We may

62. Brigitte Gabriel, "Tolerating Hate Is Not an Option," *Frontpage Magazine*, September
10, 2014, http://www.frontpagemag.com/2014/brigitte-gabriel/tolerating-hate-is-not
-an-option.

conclude that the same would result from an attempt to prosecute Arab terrorists for that major crime.

So we are left with the impossibility of trying the Arab leadership for the crime of terrorism as well as for the crime of genocide. But we are still left with the possibility of trying them for crimes against humanity and eventually for war crimes.

But ironically, the Arabs are the ones approaching the International Criminal Tribunal with requests to indict Israeli soldiers and government leaders for the "crime" of defending the land of Israel against their constant terrorist attacks, involving thousands of missiles and suicide missions.

Internal Conflicts in the Muslim World

Nowadays any observer realizes that the murderous characteristics of the leading Muslim world are not directed only against the Western world, but extend to the religious conflicts between the different sects of Islam – such as the Sunnis, Shiites, and Alawites – and between the movements that have sprung up to fight the internal "holy wars," such as the Muslim Brotherhood, ISIS, and Boko Haram. Those who have had a chance to study Islam throughout the ages know that this has practically always been the case – decades ago, centuries ago.

A perfect illustration of this phenomenon in the modern age is the massacre ordered by Syrian president Hafez Assad of the population of the city of Hama, where in February 1982 between 25,000 and 38,000 people were murdered.[63] The massacres of the Kurds by the Iraqi authorities of the last decades is just another illustration of the tragic role the Islamic world is playing in contemporary history.

In Algeria, an armed Islamic group has been murdering great numbers of citizens of all classes, in a terrorist campaign for which no end is in sight. In Iraq and Syria the wave of mass murders has shocked the world. Boko Haram has been raping Christian girls and then selling them into slavery. ISIS is killing and decapitating their victims.

Today everyone is conscious of the danger that the fanatic minority of Islamic terrorists represents to the world and to the Muslim masses that they

63. Thomas L. Friedman, *From Beirut to Jerusalem* (New York: Doubleday, 1989), 76–105; O'Brien, *The Siege*, 619.

dominate and control. The horrible events going on in Iraq and in Syria have ended any illusions about the reliability of their leadership to cooperate in any way toward peaceful solutions of the problems that afflict the Middle East and that are extending into many European countries. President Obama and Prime Minister Cameron are only aggravating the situation with their naive and misleading declarations.

Worse still are the decisions of the European Court of Human Rights, which, in its urge to reaffirm and strengthen human rights practices, has decided against judgments of European domestic courts. Exemplifying this is the court's decision to block the deportation of the Islamist fanatic cleric Abu Qatada from Great Britain to Jordan.[64]

Peaceful Intellectual Muslims

In Rome there lives a great Islamic personality who has not been given the attention that he and his ideas deserve if we are to march toward peace and security. Sheikh Abdul Hadi Palazzi is a highly surprising voice of moderation in the present turbulent Islamic world. A student of Sheikh Muhammad Shaarawy (an Egyptian cleric who promoted Jewish-Muslim relations and backed Anwar Sadat's decision to make peace with Israel), he is professor and director of the Istituto Culturale della Comunità Islamica Italiana, in Rome.[65]

Responding to a question about how antisemitism entered mainstream Islam, Sheikh Palazzi stated:

> It's a consequence of Britain's foreign policy immediately after World War I. The original Weizmann-Feisal agreement was one of friendship and cooperation between the Zionist movement and the leaders of the Hashemite family, and the acceptance of the creation of two states – a Jewish state and an Arab kingdom, with the Jordan River as the natural border. Had that agreement been respected by the British, the Jewish state would have been born 30 years earlier, and the Arab and Zionist movements would have cooperated. Unfortunately, the Foreign Office

64. Nicholas Watt, "David Cameron Calls for Reform of European Court of Human Rights," *Guardian*, January 24, 2012.

65. Melissa Radler, "Newsmaker: A Different Kind of Muslim," *Jerusalem Post*, April 18, 2004, available at http://www.freerepublic.com/focus/f-news/1120851/posts.

empowered the House of Saud, which promotes cultural Wahhabism, a belief that has anti-Semitism as one of its defining features. Until today, Saudis are using their oil money to promote anti-Semitism in the Arab world and beyond....

When Emir Feisal declared in 1919 that he was welcoming the Jews home, no one used a religious argument against him. Maybe some said that from a political point of view we are not inclined to accept your idea of cooperating with the Zionist movement, but no one said that Islam forbids cooperating with the Zionists, or that Islam prevents us from accepting the existence of a Jewish state. That ideology, which is so widespread in the Arab world today, simply did not exist.[66]

On the final destiny of the West Bank, the Sheikh holds that the Palestinians who abide by Israeli law have the right to go on living in Judea and Samaria, exactly like the Israeli Arabs in the Galilee and the Bedouin Arabs in the Negev, but he strongly rejects the idea of an Arab state in that area, claiming that Palestine is already divided into a Jewish Palestinian state (Israel) and an Arab Palestinian state (Jordan). To create a third state for the Palestinian Liberation Organization is neither in the interests of Israel nor in the interests of Jordan, and even less in the interests of those Palestinian Arabs who would be compelled to live under a barbaric regime. Muslims, he declares, need democracy, and democracy for Muslims of Judea and Samaria can only be granted by the State of Israel.

Palazzi quotes various suras from the Koran that indicate Islam's full agreement with Jewish reinstatement in the Holy Land. Specifically, he quotes from sura 17 v. 104, which reads: "And thereafter We said to the Children of Israel: 'Dwell securely in the Promised Land.'" He also advocates that Jerusalem belongs to the Jews, for whom it plays the same role as Mecca for the Muslims. On this matter he wrote:

> If we consider ourselves as religious men, we must necessarily include justice among our qualities. As regards our argument, we have to admit that the same idea of justice requires that we treat Jews, Christians and Muslims equally. No community can demand for itself privileges that it is not ready to recognize to others. We know that Roman Catholics

66. Ibid.

consider Rome their own capital, and the fact that that city has the largest mosque in Europe and an ancient Jewish community does not alter its role as the center of Catholicism. Even more can be said of Mecca: it is the main religious center for Muslims the world over and is completely under Islamic administration. Respecting this principle of fair-mindedness, we necessarily conclude that the Israelis as a nation and the Jews as a religion must have their own political and ethical capital, under their sole administration, even though it contains certain places regarded as sacred by the other two Abrahamic faiths.[67]

Palazzi strongly objects to any division of Jerusalem, saying that "if everyone is happy to see the Berlin Wall destroyed, it was because the idea of forced separation within a single city is something offensive to human sensitivity. We cannot even think of creating another Berlin in the heart of the Middle East. Of course the idea of two Jerusalems, if ever realized, will by no means be a solution, but a source of new troubles and conflicts."[68]

Palazzi is not the only Muslim intellectual to advocate peace between Israel and Islam. Osman Zumrut, associate professor at the Faculty of Theology at Ondokuz Mayis University in Samsun, Turkey, teaches that Islam and Judaism share the same aims[69] and that Judaism, Christianity, and Islam are variations of the same system.[70] Most importantly, he establishes that "as God forbids quarrels, disputes and conflict among human beings forever, all our efforts must be aimed at the realization of peace, to halt wars and prevent conflicts among the descendants of Abraham. As religions, Judaism and Islam should never – theoretically speaking – clash with one another. Their Holy Books (the Bible and the Qur'ân) do not allow such a conflict; those conflicts that do arise are caused by the members of each religion claiming superiority."[71]

Many Muslim scholars, journalists, and politicians follow this line. They have published their thoughts on the problems of the Middle East, stressing

---

67. Abdul Hadi Palazzi, "Jerusalem: Three-Fold Religious Heritage for a Contemporary Single Administration," in Nahum Rakover, *Jerusalem: City of Law and Justice* (Jerusalem: Library of Jewish Law, 1998), 80–81.
68. Ibid., 81.
69. Osman Zumrut, "The Influence of Jewish Law on Islamic Legal Practice," in Rakover, *Jerusalem*, 476.
70. Ibid., 479.
71. Ibid., 481.

the absence of any fundamental conflict between Israel and Islam and advocating that the youngest of the Abrahamic religions can and must live in peace with the oldest one.

At the end of this chapter I quote Melanie Phillips's enumeration of Muslim authorities who express their total disagreement with the conduct of radical Islam and criticize Muslim society for their inaction. In chapter 12 we shall see the harmony that prevailed in the Iberian Peninsula in the Middle Ages, under the so-called "Convivencia."

The UN Position on Terrorism

The fact remains that the barbaric acts of terror that have plagued the world during the last decades have succeeded in avoiding a definition of terrorism, due to the political power of the Muslim states in the halls of the United Nations. The number of Muslim terrorist organizations and the spread of their activities over the world is staggering. In November 2014 the United Arab Emirates cabinet published a list of those organizations, in which the Muslim Brotherhood and its offshoots figure prominently. These offshoots are found in the Middle East, Africa, Asia, Europe, and the United States. Many of them pose as welfare associations for the defense of the Muslim minorities' rights. Other such organizations include al-Qaeda and its affiliates, Islamic State, Boko Haram, Ansar Bayt al-Maqdis, and many more.

The attitude of the United Nations toward terrorism and terrorists, which may one day engulf the world in total nuclear disaster, amounts to suicide. Specifically in the war against terrorism, the "sages" of the world organization, as well as leaders of the nations, have decided to be supercautious in their respect for human rights. No such caution is exercised with regard to the rights of women, children, refugees, or girls sold into slavery and prostitution. No such special care is taken concerning minorities, persecuted people in dozens of UN member states, and people living under totalitarian regimes. In sum, the UN demonstrates continuous disregard for the most elementary human rights in different aspects of life, but fanatic concern and respect for the human rights of terrorists – the great enemies of human rights, who pose the greatest danger to humankind.

This policy toward the terrorists has been expressed by various UN representatives. The words of Kofi Annan, the former UN secretary-general, are a precious illustration of it. Annan wrote the following in a report dated April

27, 2006, under the title "Uniting against Terrorism: Recommendations for a Global Counter-terrorism Strategy":

> At the same time, in the fight against terrorism, we must never sacrifice our values and lower our standards to those of the terrorists. International cooperation to fight terrorism must be conducted in full conformity with international law, including the Charter of the United Nations and relevant international conventions and protocols. It is an obligation of States to ensure that any measures taken to combat terrorism comply with their obligations under international law, in particular human rights law, refugee law and international humanitarian law.
>
> Only by placing counter-terrorism within a rule-of-law framework can we safeguard the internationally valued standard that outlaws terrorism, reduce conditions that may generate cycles of terrorist violence and address grievances and resentment that may be conducive to terrorist recruitment. To compromise on the protection of human rights would hand terrorists a victory they cannot achieve on their own. And when human rights are abused as part of a campaign against terrorism, terrorists exploit the abuse to mobilize recruits and seek to further justify their actions. To this end, States should ratify and implement the core international human rights instruments and accept the competence of international and national human rights monitoring bodies, including those entrusted with monitoring all places where people are deprived of their liberty.
>
> International human rights experts continue to express concern that many counter-terrorism measures infringe on human rights and fundamental freedoms. Pursuant to General Assembly Resolutions 57/219, 58/187 and 59/191, I have submitted reports on protection of human rights and fundamental freedoms while countering terrorism. The Office of the United Nations High Commissioner for Human Rights should continue to play a lead role in examining this question, make general recommendations on the obligation of States, and provide them with assistance and advice should they request it.[72]

72. United Nations General Assembly, sixtieth session, April 27, 2006, document A/60/825 and "United Nations Global Counter-Terrorism Strategy," http://www.un.org/en/terrorism/strategy-counter-terrorism.shtml.

Resolution 57/219 of December 18, 2002, referred to by the secretary-general above, states the following:

1. Affirms that States must ensure that any measure taken to combat terrorism complies with the obligations under international law, in particular international human rights, refugee and humanitarian law;

2. Encourages States, while countering terrorism, to take into account relevant United Nations resolutions and decisions on human rights, and encourages them to consider the recommendations of the special procedures and mechanisms of the Commission on Human Rights and the relevant comments and views of United Nations human rights treaty bodies.[73]

Resolution 58/187, also mentioned above, goes under the title of "Protection of human rights and fundament freedoms while countering terrorism." It states:

Reaffirming the fundamental importance, including in response to terrorism and the fear of terrorism, of respecting all human rights and fundamental freedoms and the rule of law;

Recalling that States are under the obligation to protect all human rights and fundamental freedoms of all persons;

The resolution repeats the need of "compatibility of counter-terrorism measures with human rights obligations," or very similar language, no fewer than eleven times.

And then appears the possibility of derogation, established in the International Covenant on Civil and Political Rights, article 4, which provides:

In time of public emergency which threatens the life of the nation and the existence of which is officially proclaimed, the States Parties to the present Covenant may take measures derogating from their obligations under the present Covenant, to the extent strictly required by the exigencies of the situation, provided that such measures are not inconsistent with their other obligations under international law, and do not involve discrimination solely on the ground of race, color, sex, language, religion or social origin.

73. Identical content to be found in Resolution 59/191.

For the purpose of interpreting article 4, in 2001 the Human Rights Committee produced a general comment under number 29 containing seventeen long paragraphs and accompanying notes that occupy eight pages. The comment is made up of continuous repetitions of the rule contained in article 4, and all kinds of exceptions, reservations, and reductive statements. Again, we must ask: Who is the committee talking to? Democracies know the limits of states of emergency, and are eager to return to normalcy as soon as possible; states that are not run by democratic principles are permanently living in the most stringent state of emergency, independent of any terrorist danger.

The UN, through its various bodies that deal with human rights, seems like a Mother Superior telling an audience of nuns and prostitutes how to behave. The first group does not need the advice; the second will have a good laugh at it.

Kofi Annan insists in his report that counterterrorism measures are to be conducted within a rule-of-law framework, because this way we "reduce the conditions that may generate cycles of terrorist violence and address grievances and resentment that may be conducive to terrorist recruitment" and that "when human rights are abused as part of a campaign against terrorism, terrorists exploit the abuse to mobilize recruits and seek to further justify their actions."

This philosophy was inserted in the 2005 World Summit Outcome, article 85, which declared:

> We recognize that international cooperation to fight terrorism must be conducted in conformity with international law, including the Charter, and relevant international conventions and protocols. States must ensure that any measures taken to combat terrorism comply with their obligations under international law, in particular human rights law, refugee law and international humanitarian law.

This is infantile. Terrorists do not care about human rights, one way or another. Their objective is to terrorize, to create panic, and thereby achieve total submission from their victims. They work incessantly to recruit more and more adherents to their criminal activity. Any benevolence shown by the victim is taken as a sign of weakness and stimulates them to proceed harder and stronger. They do not need to be stimulated by means of harsh measures against them. On the contrary, when measures established by one state create obstacles to their terrorist activity, the result may be that they will turn to another place to continue with their murderous activities. Treating terrorists in accordance with the strictest legalistic principles and procedures only invites them to proceed with the annihilation of the "enemy."

In another pronouncement, on March 10, 2005, Kofi Annan repeated his warning:

> By the same token, the United Nations must continue to insist that, in the fight against terrorism we cannot compromise the core values I have listed. In particular, human rights and the rule of law must always be respected. As I see it, terrorism is in itself a direct attack on human rights and rule of law. If we sacrifice them in our response, we will be handing victory to the terrorists.[74]

Kofi Annan's premises are totally misguided. The terrorist cares nothing for a rule of law and he assigns no importance to human rights, nor is he even conscious of this conquest of human dignity.

Terrorism is not a mere attack on human rights and the rule of law – it is an attack on the lives of the victims; it is an attack on all of our lives.

The terrorist, Kofi Annan should have known, lives, philosophically speaking, in medieval times, in the era of brute force, of merciless conquest. The more delicate and considerate the enemy, the more delicious for him to execute his nefarious mission.

It is not being proposed here that we come down to the level of the terrorist, or that we ignore the fundamental principles that rule international human rights. But it is important to understand that our ethical policies will not influence terrorists for good. We choose to uphold high moral standards because we believe in the sanctity of every human being, not because by behaving as such we diminish the danger of international terrorism.

In fact, those states that fight terrorism with terrorism have been much more successful than those that abide by the rules of international human rights. Saudi Arabia and Egypt have controlled and reduced internal terrorism, certainly not by respecting the rules of human rights.

---

74. Secretary-General's Keynote Address to the Closing Plenary of the International Summit on Democracy, Terrorism and Security: A Global Strategy for Fighting Terrorism, Madrid, March 10, 2005.

The cradles of international terrorism are concentrated in Saudi Arabia, Syria, Pakistan, and Afghanistan. From there they proceed, duly recruited, trained, and poisoned. For them it makes absolutely no difference how we behave regarding human rights. Besides internal activities, Saudi Arabia finances madrassas in foreign countries that teach fundamentalist Islamic doctrine, not human rights.

Instead of moralizing to us about how to behave toward the international terrorist, the UN bodies would do well to fight the sources from which he proceeds, by sanctioning those states that allow in their midst the organizations that prepare the terrorist to attack the Western world. This should be done by excluding these states from every organ of the United Nations, approving the most stringent sanctions against them, and blocking international trade with them. In sum, the UN should attempt to force their governments to eliminate the growth of this malignant movement that endangers us all.

The war on terrorism must be fought at its origin, not only where the consequences of its barbarism are felt.

Kofi Annan confuses internal with international terrorism. In the same statement about uniting against terrorism (A/60/825, April 27, 2004), he expressed his opinion that

> Terrorism often thrives in environments in which human rights are violated and where political and civil rights are curtailed. Indeed, terrorists may exploit human rights violations to gain support for their cause. Persecution and violent Government crackdowns often radicalize opposition movements. The absence of non-violent channels to express discontent and pursue alternate policies may lead some groups to resort to violent means and terrorism.
>
> Past cases show that Governments that resort to excessive use of force and indiscriminate repression when countering terrorism risk strengthening the support base for terrorists among the general population. Such measures generally invite counter-violence, undermine the legitimacy of counter-terrorism measures and play into the hands of terrorists. I therefore call on Governments to avoid excessive use of force and to comply with international human rights law.[75]

75. Ibid.

This discourse evidently deals with internal terrorism and has little, if any, connection to international terrorism and international human rights law.

And then Kofi Annan deals with discrimination in the same document in which he wants to teach the world about how to avoid the emergence of terrorist movements. He writes:

> Exclusion or discrimination on the basis of ethnic origin or religious belief, and the failure of many countries to integrate minorities or immigrants, create grievances that can be conducive to the recruitment of terrorists, including feelings of alienation and marginalization and an increased propensity to seek socialization in extremist groups. This seems to be particularly true of young people, especially second-generation immigrants, in some developed countries, who see themselves as outsiders lacking equal opportunities.
>
> Exclusion based on ethnic origin, religion or national origin is often compounded by political, as well as economic and social exclusion. On the social and economic side, particular attention should be paid to youth unemployment.... Taken together these various types of exclusion can combine to produce a volatile mix. Marginalization, alienation and the resulting sense of victimization can propel extremism, which can facilitate exploitation by terrorists.[76]

Who is Kofi Annan talking about? The Muslim immigrants in England, France, Belgium, Holland, Germany, Denmark, Sweden, and other advanced European countries? Never, nowhere was so much done in favor of immigrants as in these countries in the last decades. They exploit the social service benefits of these countries; a considerable percentage of them do not work, relying instead on government benefits as a result of their multiple wives and numerous children.

If there were a revolt of the suffering lower class, it would amount to internal terrorism – not to the earthshaking tragedy of international terrorism, which has no connection whatsoever with social or economic factors. International terrorism is built on highly sophisticated politico-religious fundamentalism, organized by fanatics consumed by hatred of the Western world,

---

76. Ibid.

who train and send young people whom they manage to convert to their "religion" to execute the most horrendous acts of terror in other countries.

Another aspect of international terrorism that Kofi Annan seemed to be unaware of is that the authors of the great terrorist attacks that have been identified were members of the middle class of their original societies; they were not the kind of miserable, lower-class rebel that Annan describes. This is true of the terrorists who brought down the Twin Towers and three thousand civilians on September 11, 2001 – they were all of the middle class (the majority Saudi Arabians), they all had gone through regular schooling, and some had even studied in European universities.[77]

The frustrated terrorist attack in London in 2007 was meant to be executed by British-born Muslims, among them one or more doctors. The Muslim immigrant to the West comes from societies where there is no respect for human rights – not at home, not in the wider society, not in relations between individuals and the state. Yet when he comes to France, England, Germany, and the other countries that have opened their doors and where he is respected in line with the principles of the UDHR, he suddenly becomes – in Kofi Annan's theory – a human rights expert and considers that he is not being treated in accordance with its rules!

We referred above to Kofi Annan's words in 2005, when he said that terrorism is a direct attack on human rights, and if we do not respect human rights in the fight against terrorism we hand victory to the terrorists.

This is a fundamental misconception. Terrorism is not an attack on human rights and the rule of law. It is an attack on Western civilization; it is a war against Christianity, against Judaism, against Buddhism, against Hinduism, against atheism, against everything and everybody that does not submit to the Muslim religion. It is a manifestation of Islam in its extreme, fanatic, fundamentalist conception, by which all infidels must convert or die. The jihad terrorism is a war against peace and security, against love and friendliness, against the state and the individual, against liberty and fraternity, against

77. In a *New York Times* op-ed of October 16, 2001, Thomas Friedman wrote: "To listen to Saudi officials, or read the Arab press, you would never know that most of the hijackers were young Saudis, or that the main financing for Osama bin Laden – a Saudi – has been coming from other wealthy Saudis, or that Saudi Arabia's government was the main funder of the Taliban." "Saudi Royals and Reality," http://www.nytimes.com/2001/10/16/opinion/16FRIE.html.

life and freedom, against men and women, against old and young. It is a war against humanity. In the Islamic jihad, terrorism and genocide go hand in hand. It is ridiculous to pretend that terrorism is an attack on human rights and the rule of law, since terrorists do not recognize these concepts, do not know what they mean, and do not care to understand them.

In her book *Londonistan*, journalist Melanie Phillips gives us a glimpse of what happens when a modern society submits itself to the false notion of human rights despite acts of terror.

> When Abu Hamza was finally jailed in February 2006 for soliciting murder and inciting racial hatred, an astounded British public suddenly discovered that for years he had been allowed to operate from his London mosque as a key figure in the global terrorist movement while the British authorities sat on their hands. Not only had he openly incited murder and racial hatred, but he had amassed inside his mosque a huge arsenal of weapons to be used in terrorist training camps in Britain. Worse still, through his preaching of *jihad*, he had radicalized an unquantifiable number of British Muslims, including three of the London bombers.[78]

Journalist Phillips reports that *Filisteen al-Muslima* (Muslim Palestine), the journal of the terrorist organization Hamas, is published and distributed from the North London district of Cricklewood. *Al-Sunnah*, the Islamist magazine that calls repeatedly for human-bomb terror operations against the United States, is published in London, as is *Risalat al-Ikhwan* (Message of the Brotherhood).[79]

After reporting about an extradition request for a Saudi extremist, which was not granted by the English courts, Phillips writes:

> For the judiciary and the so-called progressive intelligentsia, human rights law is an article of faith, the legal progenitor of a brave new world in which prejudice, discrimination and oppression are consigned to history. In fact, it has undermined Western society, eviscerated its values and helped create the conditions breeding Islamist extremism and terror in the U.K. and

---

78. Melanie Phillips, *Londonistan: How Britain Is Creating a Terror State Within* (New York: Encounter Books, 2006), xi, based on a report by John Steele and George Jones, printed in the *Daily Telegraph*, February 8, 2006.
79. Ibid., 3.

its export around the world. It lies at the very heart of the hollowing out of British society, which has all but destroyed Britain's internal defenses against the external threat it faces from Islamist aggression.[80]

Phillips quotes some Muslims who spoke out against the terrorist activities of their people. Sheikh Abd al-Hamid al-Asari, the former dean of the Faculty of Sharia at the University of Qatar, wrote in the London-based Arabic-language *Al Hayat* on August 2, 2004:

> Why won't we take the opportunity of the appearance of the 9/11 commission's report to ponder why destructive violence and a culture of destruction have taken root in our society? Why won't we take this opportunity to reconsider our educational system, our curricula, including the religious, media and cultural discourse that cause our youth to live in a constant tension with the world?[81]

And Mansour Ijaz wrote in the *Financial Times* on July 11, 2005, shortly after the first set of London attacks:

> It is hypocritical for Muslims living in western societies to demand civil rights enshrined by the state and then excuse their inaction against terrorists hiding among them on grounds of belonging to a borderless Islamic community. It is time to stand up and be counted as model citizens before the terror consumes us all.[82]

And so I come to the sad conclusion that the UN has failed miserably to save millions of victims from the atrocities conducted by cruel chiefs of state, in their wars against their own citizens and those of neighboring countries. The world organization has not only failed to prevent their crimes but also to punish them; it has not even been able to produce a generic definition for terrorism and, as a consequence, has not been able to include this mega-crime

---

80. Ibid., 23. The author adds:

    The Human Rights Convention (*sic*) was originally conceived in another era altogether. Drafted in the wake of World War II, it was an attempt to lay down a set of principles to ensure that totalitarianism would never deface Europe again. It has now mutated into something very different. Far from protecting European civilization, it has turned into its potential nemesis. (Ibid., 24)

81. Ibid., 185–6.

82. Ibid., 186.

in the Rome Statute that rules the International Criminal Court. At the same time it has wasted its time warning – nobody knows whom – about the care to be exercised for "the human rights of the terrorist." And so terrorism has become the road to genocides and both have been allowed a free hand due to UN paralysis.

Let us take a hypothetical example. A terrorist attempt against a very busy airport is discovered and the executors, who are holding remote-control equipment that can send their objective into the air, are hidden in a house in the neighborhood. The police, with the help of the army, close off the vicinity and operate a house-to-house investigation. Legally, the authorities would have to obtain a warrant from court, but there is no time because at any moment the terrorists may set their equipment into motion and destroy the whole neighborhood. From the human rights point of view, no invasion into "my home, my castle" without a court warrant should be allowed, but thousands of lives are in imminent danger, and there is no time to go for a court order. The terrorist is counting on UN assurances that human rights will be rigorously respected. What about the population living in that neighborhood?

Would not every sensible citizen immediately allow the authorities into his home? Is this not similar to the body search and the luggage search to which we willingly submit ourselves when boarding an airplane? But if so, what about human rights?

This question was asked by Professor Rosalyn Higgins, former president of the International Court of Justice, in her keynote address to the American Society of International Law's yearly meeting. So spoke the illustrious jurist:

> What does "justice" tell us about line drawing when the perceived demands of security apparently require limitations to be placed upon rights? Which rights may be qualified? And to what extent and with what checks and balances? And which may not?[83]

The bureaucrats at the United Nations, disciples of Kofi Annan – would they know how to answer? Would they know how to draw the line?

---

83. Rosalyn Higgins, "A Just World under Law" (Plenary Address at the Centennial Meeting of the American Society of International Law, March 31, 2006), in *Proceedings of the American Society of International Law Annual Meetings* 100 (2006): 388–95.

The question to be put is very simple. Whose life is more important – ours, our children's, the peaceful population of any region, or the life of the terrorist who endangers our survival? Whose human right to life should be sanctified?

Let it be said loud and clear that there is a right above certain rules stemming from the human rights doctrine: the right to life.

The extreme "orthodoxy" of the UN personnel in their care to protect terrorists reached its climax when the United States executed the super-terrorist Osama bin Laden. The UN special rapporteur on extrajudicial, summary, or arbitrary executions responded by calling for "the United States of America to disclose the supporting facts to allow an assessment, in terms of international human rights law standards. For instance, it will be particularly important to know if the planning of the mission allowed an effort to capture Bin Laden." The US State Department legal adviser took the time to give a lengthy response to the UN official about the readiness of the US Navy personnel "who were prepared to accept his surrender if offered in accordance with the laws of war."[84]

The defense of the human rights of terrorist Osama bin Laden is the most flagrant example of the corrupted philosophy of the UN organization toward guaranteeing international peace and security. In a word, the UN relates to terrorism with the utmost cowardice.

The same attitude has been taken in France, in Germany, and in all the European countries toward their Muslim minorities, within which have been erupting all kinds of troublesome events, at the most extreme end of which are outright acts of terrorism.

Why this constant denial? Why this fear of truth?

The answer has been given by Mathias Dopfner, CEO of Axel Springer, in an editorial for *Die Welt* way back in 2005. He wrote:

> What else has to happen before the European public and its political leadership get it: There is a sort of crusade underway, an especially perfidious crusade consisting of systematic attacks by fanatic Muslims, focused on civilians and directed against our free, open Western societies. It is a

---

84. John R. Crook, ed., "Contemporary Practice of the United States Relating to International Law: U.S. Special Operation Personnel Raid Compound in Pakistan, Kill Osama bin Laden," *American Journal of International Law* 105, no. 3 (July 2011): 602.

conflict that will most likely last longer than the great military conflicts of the last century – a conflict conducted by an enemy that cannot be tamed by tolerance and accommodation but only spurred on by such gestures, which will be mistaken for signs of weakness.

While the alleged capitalistic robber barons in America know their priorities, we timidly defend our social welfare systems. Stay out of it! It could get expensive. We'd rather discuss the 35-hour workweek or our dental health plan coverage. Or listen to TV pastors preach about "reaching out to murderers."[85]

The prestigious German journalist and enterpriser concludes his editorial with the title he gave to the article: "Europe, thy name is cowardice."[86]

According to Dopfner, it is not a matter of worrying about human rights, nor an exaggerated, suicidal tolerance behavior; it is simply cowardice, a similar attitude to the one the English and the French demonstrated in Munich in 1938, when, after meeting Adolf Hitler, they proclaimed "peace in our time."[87] The cowardice is reflected in the hysterical reaction by the Europeans to any accusation of "Islamic terrorism" by regarding it as "Islamophobic" – a very common attitude of people who wish to distance themselves from seeing the dangerous reality that the Islamists represent to the Western world.

Aisha Siddiqa Quereshi wrote in *Muslim World Today* that "radical Islam threatens to subjugate the world and murder, enslave or convert all non-Muslims." Radical Islam "share[s] Hitler's goal," according to Quereshi, yet liberals are "not willing to defend their own institutions against this threat."[88]

The European democracies, the leadership of the continent and of England, and the greater part of European intellectuals are blind and deaf to the reality surrounding them. And so they cooperate with the growth of a cancer that may one day destroy their entire civilization.

85. Mathias Dopfner, "Europe – Thy Name Is Cowardice," *Die Welt*, December 12, 2005, trans. Hartmut Lau, www.freerepublic.com/focus/f-news/1532876/posts.
86. Ibid.
87. Ibid.
88. Philips, *Londonistan*, 186.

Chapter Ten
The Demoralized World Court

A Politicized, Bigoted Court

It is a sad reality that the judges of the International Court of Justice rule in accordance with the interests and/or policies of the states of their citizenship. The politicization of the court is a reflex of the politicization of the Security Council, of the Council of Human Rights, of the whole structure of the United Nations.

As Professor Amichai Cohen observes, "the identity of the judges in international courts, their politics, values and independence from political control should become major issues in the debate over international law."[1]

The UN General Assembly requested an advisory opinion from the court about the fence erected by Israel in strategic areas to avoid infiltrations by terrorists intent on suicide missions, which had recently caused the deaths of approximately a thousand Israeli citizens and left thousands maimed for life.

In various places, the fence disturbed the life of Arab communities in the West Bank, the so-called "territories." On the other hand, the fence succeeded in ending the wave of infiltrations of terrorist attackers, bringing some peace and tranquility to the population of Israel. In a few especially strategic places the fence turns into a wall. But the UN General Assembly and the court referred only to the "wall."[2] When the advisory opinion was formulated, the

---

1. Amichai Cohen, "Rules and Applications of International Humanitarian Law," *Israel Law Review* 41, nos. 1–2 (2008): 67.
2. In the government of Israel's written statement it says that the reference to "wall" instead of "fence" "reflects a calculated media campaign to raise pejorative connotations in the mind of the Court of great concrete constructions of separation such as the Berlin Wall,

"wall" had already prevented many terrorist infiltrations. The court was not asked to opine about the defense policy of the State of Israel against terrorist infiltrations, about the assassination of a few terrorist leaders, about Israel's bombing terrorist's fortresses; it was asked only to discuss the "separation wall" erected beyond the line that was established in the cease-fire negotiations of 1949 – after the armies of five Arab countries attacked Israel as it proclaimed its statehood.

The fundamental error of the court's decision is that it did not have the necessary information regarding the situation to be able to give an opinion. This was stressed by Judge Buergenthal, who reminded the court of the *West Sahara* case, where it was decided that the critical question in giving an advisory opinion is "whether the Court has before it sufficient information and evidence to enable it to arrive at a judicial conclusion upon any disputed questions of fact, the determination of which is necessary for it to give an opinion in conditions compatible with its judicial character."[3] Therefore, Judge Buergenthal concluded, the absence of the requisite information and evidence regarding the "wall" vitiates the court's findings.

It is unthinkable that the legality or illegality of a fence erected to protect civilians from constant murderous terrorist attacks could be decided without the opinions of experts. Any court, in any country, would demand experts' reports when deciding a case that concerns military or security matters and that demands knowledge of the historical background and the land's geography. All the more so in a case such as this one, which was aimed at stopping the flow of terrorist attacks. How can such a case be decided without expertise? It is mind boggling that the International Court of Justice was satisfied with a report from highly politicized UN organs.

intended to stop people escaping from tyranny. The reality is however different. Along a 180 kilometer route of the completed or planned fence, 8.8 kilometers, or less than 5 percent, is made up of a concrete barrier, generally in areas where Palestinian population centers abut onto Israel." Quoted by Karin Calvo-Goller in "More Than a Huge Imbalance: The ICJ's Advisory Opinion on the Legal Consequences of the Construction of the Barrier," *Israel Law Review* 38, nos. 1–2 (winter/spring 2005): 166.

3. The declaration of Judge Buergenthal is found in *International Legal Materials* 43, no. 5 (September 2004): 1078–81. The full text of the court's advisory opinion, "Text of Decision Judicial and Similar Proceedings: International Court of Justice (ICJ): Legal Consequences of the Construction of a Wall in the Occupied Palestinian Territory," is in the same volume, at 1009–98.

Judge Buergenthal wrote a dissenting opinion. As a person who dedicated his entire professional life to human rights, as a strong pacifist, and as the extremely gentle human being that he is, Judge Buergenthal was extraordinarily careful and respectful in his declaration, of which I transcribe the following passage:

> It may well be, and I am prepared to assume it, that on a thorough analysis of all relevant facts, a finding could well be made that some or even all segments of the wall being constructed by Israel on the Occupied Palestinian Territory violate international law. But to reach that conclusion with regard to the wall as a whole without having before it or seeking to ascertain all relevant facts bearing directly on issues of Israel's legitimate right of self-defense, military necessity and security needs, given the repeated deadly terrorist attacks in and upon Israel proper coming from the Occupied Palestinian Territory to which Israel has been and continues to be subjected, cannot be justified as a matter of law. The nature of these cross–Green Line attacks and their impact on Israel and its population are never really seriously examined by the Court, and the dossier provided the Court by the United Nations on which the Court to a large extent bases its findings barely touches on that subject. I am not suggesting that such an examination would relieve Israel of the charge that the wall it is building violates international law, either in whole or in part, only that without this examination the findings made are not legally well founded. In my view, the humanitarian needs of the Palestinian people would have been better served had the Court taken these considerations into account, for that would have given the Opinion the credibility I believe it lacks.

Though Judge Buergenthal did not deal directly with the merits of the opinion, precisely because of the lack of evidence, he did advance the following comments:

> See article 21 of the International Law Commission's Articles on Responsibility of States for Wrongful Acts, which declares: "The wrongfulness of an act of a State is precluded if the act constitutes a lawful measure of self-defense taken in conformity with the Charter of the United Nations."
>
> Whether Israel's right of self-defense is in play in the instant case depends, in my opinion, on an examination of the nature and scope of

the deadly terrorist attacks to which Israel proper is being subjected from across the Green Line and the extent to which the construction of the wall, in whole or in part, is a necessary and proportionate response to these attacks. As a matter of law, it is not inconceivable to me that some segments of the wall being constructed on Palestinian territory meet that test and that others do not. But to reach a conclusion either way, one has to examine the facts bearing on that issue with regard to the specific segments of the wall, their defensive needs and related topographical considerations.

The universal problematic regarding terrorism and genocide, so well explained by David Scheffer in his book *All the Missing Souls*, comes out clearly in Judge Buergenthal's concise statement:

> The Court's formalistic approach to the right of self-defense enables it to avoid addressing the very issues that are at the heart of this case.

On the court's inattentiveness to Israel's position, Judge Buergenthal said the following:

> It is equally true, however, that the Court barely addresses the summaries of Israel's positions on this subject that are attached to the Secretary General's report and which contradict or cast doubt on the material the Court claims to rely on. Instead, all we have from the Court is a description of the harm the wall is causing and a discussion of various provisions of international humanitarian law and human rights instruments, followed by the conclusion that this law has been violated. Lacking is an examination of the facts that might show why the alleged defenses of military exigencies, national security or public order are not applicable to the wall as a whole or to the individual segments of its route. The Court says that it "is not convinced" but it fails to demonstrate why it is not convinced, and that is why these conclusions are not convincing.

These remarks from Judge Buergenthal should suffice to demonstrate the inaccuracy of the procedure followed, the lack of scientific demonstration, the lack of factual evidence, the lack of consideration for the arguments of one of the involved parties, the absolute one-sidedness of the consultation proposed by the secretary-general of the UN and consequently of the court's opinion, which relied exclusively on that consultation.

One of the court's arguments is that though article 51 of the UN charter recognizes the existence of an inherent right of self-defense in the case of armed attack by one state against another state, it so happened that Israel did not claim that the attacks against it were imputable to a foreign state; therefore article 51 has no relevance in the case.[4]

As Judge Buergenthal excellently argues, the charter does not make defense dependent on an armed attack by another state. Article 51 of the charter provides that "nothing in the present Charter shall impair the inherent right of individual or collective self-defense if an armed attack occurs against a Member of the United Nations...." And then Buergenthal refers to various resolutions of the Security Council that established the right of a state's self-defense against attacks by non-states, one of them being Resolution 1368, adopted the day after the 9/11 terrorist attack on the Twin Towers in New York, the Pentagon in Arlington County, Virginia, and other targets.[5]

So we have the International Court of Justice deciding *contra legem* – against international law as conceived by the United Nations. As a matter of fact, Resolution 1368 of the UN is absolutely correct, because it would be absurd that a state may defend itself from an attack by another state and not have the same right if the attack originates from an entity that is not a state. To exclude the right of self-defense when the attack does not originate from a state is the most vigorous encouragement to the war of terrorists against the civilized world.

Another judge who showed how the court did not live up to expectations was Rosalyn Higgins. Below are just a few critical statements of her separate opinion, which shed some light on the quality of the advisory opinion:

> 15. Addressing the reality that "the question of the construction of the wall was only one aspect of the Israeli-Palestinian conflict" the Court states that it "is indeed aware that the question of the wall is part of a greater whole and it would take this circumstance carefully into account in any opinion it might give."[6]

> 16. In fact, it never does so. There is nothing in the remainder of the Opinion that can be said to cover this point. Further, I find the "history"

---

4. Para. 139 of the court's advisory opinion, ibid., 1049–50.
5. Para. 6 of Judge Buergenthal's declaration, ibid., 1079.
6. Ibid., 1060.

as recounted by the Court in paragraphs 71–76 neither balanced nor satisfactory.

In paragraph 33, the judge says:

> I do not agree with all that the Court has to say on the question of the law of self-defense. In paragraph 139 the Court quotes Article 51 of the Charter and then continues: "Article 51 of the Charter thus recognizes the existence of an inherent right of self-defense in the case of armed attack by one State against another State." There is, with respect, nothing in the text of Article 51 that *thus* stipulates that self-defense is available only when an armed attack is made by a State.

And then Judge Higgins shows a flagrant contradiction made by the court:

> I also find unpersuasive the Court's contention that, as the uses of force emanate from occupied territory, it is not an armed attack "by one State against another." I fail to understand the Court's view that an occupying Power loses the right to defend its civilian citizens at home if the attack emanates from the occupied territory – a territory which it has found not to have been annexed and is certainly "other than" Israel. Further, Palestine cannot be sufficiently an international entity to be invited to these proceedings, and to benefit from humanitarian law, but not sufficiently an international entity for the prohibition of armed attack on others to be applicable. This is formalism of an uneven handed sort. The question is surely where responsibility lies for the sending of groups and persons who act against Israeli civilians and the cumulative severity of such action.[7]

The contradiction regarding the Palestinian position constitutes a steady characteristic of the UN bodies' resolutions – when it suits, the Palestinians are not an international entity; at other times, they are treated as a state.

Strangely, Judge Higgins voted with the court.

And now, let's analyze the court's advisory opinion. In its short historical review, the Court refers to the War of Independence of the State of Israel in the following terms:

---

7. Ibid., 1063.

Israel proclaimed its independence on the strength of the General Assembly resolution; armed conflict then broke out between Israel and a number of Arab States and the Plan of Partition was not implemented.[8]

"Conflict broke out." Why did the court feel the need to hide the universally known truth that five Arab states, unwilling to accept the reality of the proclamation of Israel's statehood, attacked and invaded the territory designated by the UN Partition Resolution to become the State of Israel?

The Court is part of the UN. When the conflict started, the secretary-general of the UN Trygve Lie stated: "The invasion of Palestine by the Arab States was the first armed aggression which the world has seen since the world war."[9] Referring to Friday, May 14, 1948, Paul Johnson tells it simply: "A provisional government [of Israel] was formed immediately. Egyptian air raids began that night. The next day, simultaneously, the last British left and the Arab armies invaded."[10]

Conor Cruise O'Brien was the Irish ambassador to the General Assembly of the United Nations. As already reported in an earlier chapter, in accordance with alphabetical order, on his left sat the ambassador of Iraq and on his right, the ambassador of Israel. The Irishman made a point to get well acquainted with both colleagues and hear their points of view, which brought him to study the conflict between Israel and the Arabs. The subject became his expertise, leading him to write an eight-hundred-page book, entitled *The Siege: The Saga of Israel and Zionism*.

O'Brien reports the preparations of the Arabs' chiefs of staff in April 1948 for a coordinated offensive against the State of Israel as soon as it would be proclaimed. The author describes in detail the Arab attacks and the territories occupied by the Syrians, Lebanese, and Iraqis. The Egyptians – the most successful of the invaders – were only halted in Ashdod, today the second most important port of the State of Israel. The Egyptian air force bombed Tel Aviv and other Jewish centers. The greatest losses to the new state occurred in Jerusalem, in the hands of the Arab Legion, known then as the army of Transjordan – Abdullah's forces, under General Glubb's command. On May

8. Ibid., 1030.
9. As quoted by Dore Gold, *The Fight for Jerusalem: Radical Islam, the West, and the Future of the Holy City* (Washington: Regnery Publishing, 2007), 135.
10. Johnson, *History of the Jews*, 527.

29, the Security Council adopted a resolution ordering a cease-fire, which came into effect on June 11. President Truman forced England to stop arming the Arabs.[11]

But soon the fighting broke out again. This is how O'Brien describes it:

> On July 9, the truce was due to expire, and the Egyptians, whatever their real intentions, sounded as if it would not be renewed. On the day before, July 8, fighting broke out in the Negev. It is now considered likely that the fighting was initiated by Israel, but those who had insisted that the war was not over were hardly in a position to complain when it was shown that they had inadvertently been telling the truth.[12]
>
> Cairo radio was the most powerful and the most active of the broadcasting stations whose competition in propaganda had helped to precipitate the two attacks by the Arab states on Israel.[13]

Cecil Roth closes his *Short History of the Jewish People* with a reference to the proclamation of the State of Israel and adds that "Arab states were already poised menacingly on the borders."[14] Joan Peters in *From Time Immemorial* quotes a passage from a press conference of Azzam Pasha, secretary-general of the Arab League, in which he proclaimed: "This will be a war of extermination and a momentous massacre ... like the Mongolian massacres and the Crusades."[15] The conference took place in Cairo on May 15, 1948, and was reported in the *New York Times* on the following day.

Gilbert Guillaume, professor of the Institut d'Études Politiques of Paris and former president of the International Court of Justice, states: "On the eve of the date [for the closing of the British mandate] Israel proclaimed its independence and the neighboring Arab states engaged in a military operation against Israel."[16]

The illustrious members of the International Court of Justice have at

11. O'Brien, *The Siege*, 291–300.

12. Ibid., 301.

13. Ibid., 304.

14. Cecil Roth, *A Short History of the Jewish People* (London: East and West Library, 1953), 449.

15. Joan Peters, *From Time Immemorial: The Origins of the Arab-Jewish Conflict over Palestine* (USA: Harper Torchbooks, 1988), 444n14.

16. Gilbert Guillaume, "O Estado de Israel e a Questão Palestina," in Leonardo Nemer Caldeira Brant, ed., *Terrorismo e direito: Os impactos do terrorismo na comunidade internacional*

their disposal a wonderful library and all the modern gadgets to access the newspapers of 1947–49 and other reliable sources of information. They could have easily become aware that the war was an exclusive initiative of the Arab nations; to state that "armed conflict broke out" does not bode well for the prestige of any court, let alone the ICJ.

A few more points of the opinion of the court that leave no doubt regarding its prejudice of Israel, in the tradition of the United Nations:

In paragraph 141 the court wrote:

> The fact remains that Israel has to face numerous indiscriminate and deadly acts of violence against its civilian population. It has the right, and indeed the duty, to respond in order to protect the life of the citizens. The measures taken are bound nonetheless to remain in conformity with applicable international law.

Why this indetermination? Why refer to "deadly acts of violence against its civilian population" without referring to the authors of those acts? Was the court attempting to whitewash the Palestinians? Why refer to Israel's acts and hide the Palestinians' terrorism?

And why does the court omit the nature of the "deadly acts"? An opinion with 162 paragraphs, occupying 90 pages of the American Society of International Law's *International Legal Materials*, could not specify the nature of these "deadly acts of violence"? Israel noted in its submission to the General Assembly of the UN that in the forty months immediately preceding the erection of the fence, Palestinian terror attacks had left 916 people dead and over 5,000 injured, many critically. Not a word about that in the General Assembly's request for an advisory opinion from the International Court of Justice. Israeli professor Talia Einhorn writes that "the fact that the resolution of the Emergency Special Session of the General Assembly requesting the advisory opinion is absolutely silent on the matter [of the calamitous nature of the Palestinian terrorist attacks] is a travesty, reflecting the gravest prejudice and imbalance within the General Assembly."[17] Despite the UN's

---

e no Brasil. Perspectivas politico-jurídicas (a Brazilian collection of essays on terrorism), 72. Translation mine.

17. Einhorn, "The Status of Judea and Samaria (The West Bank)," 33.

unforgiveable omission, the court could have very well discovered these facts on its own initiative, but did not really care to search for the truth.

As mentioned above, the court said that it is "aware that the question of the wall is part of a greater whole, and it would take this circumstance carefully into account in any opinion it might give."[18] The long advisory opinion does not take this into consideration at all; it bypasses the constant terrorism under which the State of Israel has lived throughout decades. The court did not adhere to its own agenda.

On the arguments raised that the court should decline to exercise its jurisdiction because it does not have at its disposal the requisite facts and evidence to enable it to reach its conclusion (para. 55), the court enumerates all the materials it received from the UN secretary-general and from other sources and states that it considers that it has sufficient information and evidence (para. 57 and 58).[19] However, as Judge Buergenthal noted, the court barely addresses the summaries of Israel's position that were attached to the secretary-general's report, which contradict or cast serious doubts on the material the court claims to relay on.

The court never stops to consider other measures that could have been taken by Israel to defend its population from the Palestinian "deadly acts."

The historical analysis of the court is amazingly one-sided. In paragraph 77 it refers to

> a number of agreements signed since 1993 between Israel and the Palestine Liberation Organization imposing various obligations on each party. Those agreements inter alia required Israel to transfer to Palestinian authorities certain powers and responsibilities exercised in the Occupied Palestinian Territory by its military authorities and civil administration. Such transfers have taken place.[20]

So far the court follows the events as they took place, but immediately after that it adds

18. Para. 6 of Judge Buergenthal's declaration.
19. "Text of Decision *Judicial and Similar Proceedings: International Court of Justice (ICJ): Legal Consequences of the Construction of a Wall in the Occupied Palestinian Territory,*" *International Legal Materials* 43, no. 5 (September 2004): 1027–28.
20. Ibid., 1031.

... but, as a result of subsequent events, they remained partial and limit-ed.[21]

Israel's limited compliance with the transfer agreements was a result of con-tinuous Palestinian terrorist attacks, which caused an enormous number of Israeli deaths. This was too difficult for the court – in such a long opinion – to point out. It restricted itself by referring to "subsequent events." One thousand assassinations of Israel civilians is, for the court, a mere bundle of "subsequent events." Judicial cruelty!

In paragraph 88 the court refers to the right of every people to self-determination, as prescribed in the covenants, and the obligation of state parties to promote the realization of that right and to respect it in conformity with the provisions of the United Nations charter. But the court, so careful about certain historical facts, neglected to mention that the Arabs of Pales-tine refused to accept the Partition Plan in 1947 and that in the period from 1948 to 1967, when they were under occupation by Jordan and Egypt, did absolutely nothing to reach self-determination. In fact, partition had already been suggested by the British Peel Commission in 1936, when it was accepted by the Jews. The Arabs, however, refused it and instead launched a revolt that lasted from 1936 to 1939, causing the deaths of many Jews.

Till the present day, the Palestinian Authority's charter establishes the objective of conquering the entire Palestinian territory and destroying the State of Israel. This is a declaration against a United Nations resolution (the 1947 Partition Plan) and against the 1993 Oslo Agreements between Israel and the PLO. This charter cannot be considered a proclamation of self-determination. It is a clear, vehement manifestation of genocidal intent.

Paragraph 137, which the court classified as a "sum[ming] up," is a jewel of uncertainty and self-contradiction, two factors that annul the opinion's legal value. The paragraph states:

> To sum up, the Court, from the material available to it, *is not convinced* that the specific course Israel has chosen for the wall was necessary to attain its security objectives.[22]

---

21. Ibid.
22. Ibid., 1049. Emphasis mine.

First, as already pointed out, the court did not discuss in its opinion the Israeli documents attached to the UN secretary-general's report, which explain the need of the course Israel followed with the erection of the fence/wall. So how can it judge whether the construction of this defense system is or is not necessary?

And, second, if the court is not convinced, it could ask the secretary-general of the UN for more information. What court decides based on lack of conviction? And assuming that the added data would convince the court, one way or another, how could it decide before getting the necessary information? Any arbitral institution would ask for complementary information in order to reach a decision based on conviction.

After all, article 65 of the court's statute, paragraph 2, provides that

> questions upon which the advisory opinion of the Court is asked shall be laid before the Court by means of a written request containing an exact statement of the question upon which an opinion is required, and accompanied by all documents likely to throw light upon the question.

Paragraph 137 of the court's advisory opinion proceeds with the following statement:

> The wall, along the route chosen, and its associated regime gravely infringe a number of rights of Palestinians residing in the territory occupied by Israel, and the infringements resulting from that route cannot be justified by military exigencies or by the requirement of national security or public order.[23]

But if the court starts that very paragraph by declaring that it is "not convinced that the specific course Israel has chosen for the wall was necessary to attain its security objectives," this means that the court is unsure. If so, how can the court say in the very same paragraph that the wall cannot be justified by military exigencies or by requirements of national security or public order? First the court does not know whether the measures taken by Israel were necessary to attain security and then it decides categorically that the measures are not justified by security needs. If you are not convinced, how can you give an opinion?

23. Ibid.

This paragraph 137 – almost the final paragraph of the opinion – constitutes a flagrant, incomprehensible contradiction in terms. It is totally illogical. But even more difficult than that is paragraph 140, *in fine*, which reads:

> In the light of the material before it, the Court is not convinced that the construction of the wall along the route chosen was the only means to safeguard the interest of Israel against the peril which it invoked as justification for that construction.[24]

If the court is not convinced that the wall was the only defense available, it means, logically interpreted, that the fence/wall is a means to safeguard, but not the only one. This being the case, the choice between different possible means of defense is up to the interested state and not the court – which does not refer to any other means that it could contrive.

The statements of the court are simply self-defeating.

Paragraph 149 states:

> The Court notes that Israel is first obliged to comply with the international obligations it has breached by the construction of the wall in the Occupied Palestinian Territory (see paragraphs 114–137). Consequently, Israel is bound to comply with its obligation to respect the right of the Palestinian people to self-determination and its obligations under international humanitarian law and human rights law. Furthermore, it must ensure freedom of access to the Holy Places that came under its control following the 1967 war (see paragraph 129 above).[25]

Let's examine the last sentence regarding the holy places.

In paragraph 129 the court refers to the various treaties of the past, starting from the Treaty of Berlin of 1878 and continuing through the British Mandate and a resolution from the UN, all demanding guarantees of freedom of access to the religious places to people of all faiths.

Between 1948 and 1967 no Jew had access to the Jewish holy places, including the Western Wall, as those places were in the hands of the Jordanians, who destroyed 90 percent of the Jewish cemetery on the Mount of Olives. This, the opinion of the ICJ does not even mention.

24. Ibid., 1050.
25. Ibid., 1051–52.

Members of the court seem to ignore everything related to the geography and the history of the holy places. From 1967 on, when the whole of Jerusalem returned to Jewish control, all religions, including the Muslims, enjoyed – and continue to enjoy – absolute, free access to their holy places. This the court also does not mention.

In 1967, Israel reconquered Jerusalem – the city that is referred to seven hundred times in the Bible and not once in the Koran, the city of King David, the city of King Solomon, the locus of the First and Second Holy Temples, the land Jesus Christ walked on and preached from centuries before Islam appeared on the map. After expelling the Arab armies, the Israeli army handed to the Muslim religious authorities the keys to the Al-Aqsa Mosque on the Temple Mount. Ironically and tragically, in consequence thereof, Jews have been forbidden to pray on the site of the Holy Temples. In banning this the Muslims prevented the free expression of Jewish religion, in absolute disrespect of the various treaties and resolutions of the past and with a cruel lack of recognition for Israel's gesture. This, the court also does not mention. It only reminds Israel of its interreligious obligations – instead of praising the Jewish state for its magnificent performance and criticizing the Jordanians, responsible for the Muslim holy places on the Temple Mount, for their stubborn perversity.[26]

If the court deviated from the consultation (which had nothing to do with the holy places), why not refer to the fact that when the Palestinians received control of the city of Jericho some years ago, they burned the tomb of Joseph to the ground? Why not refer to the fact that when the Palestinians received absolute control over Gaza, through a spontaneous gesture of the Israelis that forced many thousands of Jewish settlers to abandon the land, the Palestinians burned down all the synagogues they found? These are deeds perpetrated by people who have been educated since childhood to hate, to destroy, to practice terrorism and genocide. But the court (like the other bodies of the United

26. The cynicism of the court follows the hypocrisy of the Security Council, which never took any measure to repeal Jordanian laws restricting the rights of Christian institutions in Jerusalem, not to speak of the Jewish religious interests. Dore Gold (*The Fight for Jerusalem*, 267) writes that "the UN's most significant religious intervention during the years of Jordanian rule was a letter by the UN Truce Supervision Organization on November 30, 1964, demanding that Israel switch off Chanukkah lights that were lit on the Israel enclave on Mt. Scopus because they might offend the Jordanians."

Nations) does not take into consideration the atrocities of the Palestinians, only the defensive measures of the State of Israel.

It is difficult to imagine a more one-sided, prejudiced opinion than this, written by the International Court of Justice, the court of the United Nations, the world's supreme judicial entity.

It has become a common platitude to speak of "proportionality." I shall come back to this concept. But one question has to be put to the court and all those who think like it: The Palestinians claim that the fence disturbs their daily life – they have to travel farther to reach work and school – and that there was a disturbance of their commercial or agricultural activities. Israel built the fence to protect her citizens from the "deadly attacks" that cost in the preceding years a thousand victims. What is proportionally dearer – life or easy access to work and school?

In paragraph 73 the court says: "In the 1967 armed conflict Israel forces occupied *all the territories which had constituted Palestine under British Mandate* including those known as the West Bank, lying to the east of the Green Line."[27] Here the ICJ reveals an unforgiveable historic-geographic blunder, because "all the territories which had constituted Palestine under British Mandate" included (1) the territory of the State of Israel, (2) the territories it occupies east of the Green Line, and (3) the territory of what was then called Transjordan. Later, the British separated 70 percent of the whole territory of the Mandate and created the state of Jordan. Israeli forces did not occupy Jordan, which was part of the initial Palestine Mandate of the British, nor could Israel occupy its proper territory, the territory of the State of Israel, which had been part of Palestine till the partition decided upon by the UN General Assembly in 1947. The above statement is therefore based on total ignorance.

This statement shows once again the court's negligence in relating facts of geography and relatively recent history, in order to please the UN General Assembly, which in turn is bent on pleasing the Arabs.

The Six-Day War of 1967 – a vicious attack Israel suffered from Egypt, Syria, and Jordan – is referred to by the court as "an armed conflict." Yes, it was an armed conflict, but in such a detailed decision, it is only just to refer to what occurred in 1967 as the conflict resulting from a tridimensional attack against Israel (this will be analyzed in detail below). Yet there is not a word about

27. Ibid., 1030. Emphasis mine.

Egypt having closed the Straits of Tiran to Israeli navigation – a classic *casus belli*. The court refrains from noting that Egyptian dictator Nasser requested that the UN secretary-general withdraw the peacekeeping troops from the Sinai Peninsula, or that Nasser brought his army to the southern border of Israel and proclaimed his determination to attack Israel and throw all the Jews into the sea. There is not a word about the offensive of Jordan's and Syria's armies.

The much-criticized "occupation" of the land beyond the Green Line is a result of Israel's defense against the three foreign armies. The court pretends to ignore that, too.

The court is not interested in the legal background that the occupied land was supposed to have become the Arab state resulting from the partition approved by the United Nations in 1947, and that this did not materialize due to the Arab nonacceptance of the UN resolution, followed by the immediate attack by five Arab armies with the support of the Arabs who lived in the territories.

The court is also not interested in the legal background of Palestine. The Partition Plan did not supersede or replace the rights of the Jewish people, which were recognized by the League of Nations in the Mandate and preserved by the UN charter through article 80.[28] The Mandate for Palestine had been a binding legal document – an international treaty – while the UN General Assembly proposals were merely nonbinding recommendations that were rejected outright by one side. Of course, had the Partition Plan been accepted by both parties, it could have become an international binding agreement, but that did not occur.[29] And so, the previous legal status of Palestine, established by the League of Nations in accordance with the British Mandate over Palestine in favor of the Jewish people, stood and stands.

The ICJ likewise does not care that these so-called territories were occupied in 1948 by the Egyptians (Gaza) and by the Jordanians (West Bank) and that the Palestinian Arabs did not create their state and did not complain

---

28. Article 80 reads: "nothing in this Chapter shall be construed in or of itself to alter in any manner the rights whatsoever of any states or any peoples or the terms of existing international instruments to which Members of the United Nations may respectively be parties."
29. Dore Gold (*The Fight for Jerusalem*, 139–40 and elsewhere in the book) explains the legal status of Palestine according to the successive treaties that were approved before the creation of the United Nations, which was not altered by UN General Assembly resolutions.

about the illegal occupation by Jordan and Egypt. So this land that, till May 1948, was under British mandate, became illegally occupied territory by those two Arab countries, which only left in 1967, having lost their second war of aggression against Israel. The consequence of the Palestinians' refusal to accept partition of the land, the successive wars of aggression, and the illegal Egyptian/Jordanian occupation between 1948 and 1967 is that the territories were never under anyone's sovereignty. With their abandonment by Egypt and Jordan, they became no-man's-land, known in international law as "sovereignty vacuum" or "*territorium nullius*."[30] As explained above, the whole land (Israel and the territories of the West Bank) returned to the status awarded it by the British Mandate and the League of Nations.

Israel occupied a land that was not a state, but a territory that had no sovereign power over it, a land that the Palestinian Arabs did not accept when the UN decided on the partition and offered it to them. A land that they refuse till today, as their charter declares the illegality of Resolution 181 of the UN General Assembly, which approved the partition. And so it can very well be said that the land has gone back to the status it had when promised to the Jewish people by the Balfour Declaration, confirmed by the League of Nations and maintained by the UN charter's article 80.

Stephen Schwebel, former president of the International Court of Justice, wrote a short essay on the legal situation of these territories in which he states: "When the prior holder of territory had seized that territory illegally, the State that subsequently takes that territory in the lawful exercise of self-defense has, against that prior holder, better title."[31]

We saw in Judge Buergenthal's opinion about the statement the court makes in paragraph 139 of the advisory opinion that the right to self-defense established in article 51 of the UN charter only applies in relation to attacks coming from another state; since Israel does not claim that the attacks she

---

30. About *territorium nullius* or *terra nullius*, see Martin Dixon and Robert McCorquodale, *Cases and Materials on International Law* (London: Blackstone Press, 1995), 285 and 287. Elihu Lauterpacht (*Jerusalem and the Holy Places* [London: Anglo-Israel Association, 1968], 48) holds that Israel seized East Jerusalem legally and therefore had the right to fill the vacuum in sovereignty, as quoted by Moshe Hirsch, "The Legal Status of Jerusalem Following the ICJD Advisory Opinion on the Separation Barrier," *Israel Law Review* 38, nos. 1–2 (winter/spring 2005): 300.

31. Judge Schwebel's essay will be referred to in more detail below.

has been suffering come from another state, the defense provision does not apply. The court proceeds to say that the Security Council's resolutions that originated from the 9/11 attacks cannot be invoked by Israel for the same reason – those attacks originated from outside the United States, and Israel claims that she is being attacked from within. As we have already seen, the lack of logic in this argumentation is evident. If I may defend myself from attacks from abroad, why do I not have the same right if the attack comes from within? In both cases we are dealing with terrorist attacks, which, if not stopped by the strategic means available, will continue, always more dreadful and more murderous. I would say that we can apply the *ad majorem* argument: if I may defend myself from an enemy located abroad, all the more so may I defend myself from an enemy within my borders, or within an area under my control.

A legal curiosity: Why did the court consider 9/11 an attack from abroad, if the perpetrators were American residents and all their preparatory acts were processed in the territory of the United States?

The court should be consistent: since the court considers the territories of the West Bank as belonging to the Palestinians, then it is equivalent to an attack from outside, notwithstanding Israel's statements. Once more the court contradicts itself.

In paragraph 75 the ICJ refers to Resolution 298 of the Security Council of 1971 regarding Jerusalem, which states:

> Having considered the letter of the Permanent Representative of Jordan on the situation in Jerusalem;

> Reaffirming the principle that acquisition of territory by military conquest is inadmissible;

> Noting with concern the non-compliance by Israel with the above-mentioned resolutions;

> Noting with concern also that since the adoption of the above-mentioned resolutions Israel has taken further measures designed to change the status and character of the occupied section of Jerusalem;

> 1. Reaffirms its resolutions 252 (1968) and 267 (1969);

> 2. Deplores the failure of Israel to respect the previous resolutions adopted

by the United Nations concerning measures and actions by Israel purporting to affect the status of the City of Jerusalem;

3. Confirms in the clearest possible terms that all legislative and administrative actions taken by Israel to change the status of the City of Jerusalem, including expropriation of land and properties, transfer of populations and legislation aimed at the incorporation of the occupied section, are totally invalid and cannot change that status.

As usual, the Security Council takes resolutions without any regard to historical reality. This entity, which bows to the interests of the Arab states and the many states that, for one reason or another, support the Arab positions, did not look into the original UN resolutions on Jerusalem and in what measure they were respected or totally annulled.

Resolution 181 of the UN General Assembly of 1947 established a special status for the city of Jerusalem (a *corpus separatum*), with a governor to be appointed by the Trusteeship Council, who would not be a citizen of either state in Palestine. Among a long set of rules, the resolution guaranteed free access to holy places (article 13).

The Jordanians immediately expelled all the Jewish residents from East Jerusalem. All but one of the thirty-five synagogues in the Old City were destroyed over the course of the next nineteen years, either razed or used as stables and chicken coops. The ancient cemetery on the Mount of Olives was desecrated and the tombstones used for construction, paving roads, and lining latrines.

Between 1948 and 1967 the Old City of Jerusalem was in the hands of the Jordanians, and the New City was held and developed by Israel. The Jordanians, as seen above, did not allow the Jews access to their holy places. The United Nations did not undertake any measure, not even a resolution against the Jordanians for not keeping the freedom of access to the holy places of all religions and for the destruction of the Jewish synagogues. The Security Council thus referred to two of its former resolutions but totally ignored the basic Resolution 181 of the General Assembly and its flagrant violation by the Jordanians.

In 1967, during the war waged by the three Arab countries against Israel, the Jordanians tried to conquer the New City of Jerusalem. They failed and even lost control of the Old City, which was conquered by the Israeli army; Israel immediately opened free access to all religions to all holy places.

The facts on the ground between 1948 and 1967 and the new facts created by the war initiated by the Arabs against Israel overturned the circumstances that had led to Resolution 181 on the status of the City of Jerusalem.

Only then did the United Nations Security Council move with Resolutions 252/1968 and 267/1969 "concerning measures and actions by Israel designed to change the status of the Israeli-occupied section of Jerusalem" which were referred to in Resolution 298 of 1971, quoted above, that declared invalid a series of legislative and administrative acts of the Israeli government, which – claims the Security Council – changed the status of the city.

This claim that Israeli acts "changed the status" goes flagrantly against the real story that evolved since 1948, since Resolution 181 of the General Assembly. The Arabs, and most especially the Jordanian government of that time, are the ones that broke everything contained in that resolution, completely changing the status that had been set in Resolution 181 (the Partition Plan). Israel's acts were a natural consequence of that change of status.

The audacity of the UN regarding the status of Jerusalem following the Six-Day War started with Resolution 2253 of the General Assembly, of July 4, 1967, which reads as follows:

The General Assembly

Deeply concerned at the situation prevailing in Jerusalem as a result of the measures taken by Israel to change the status of the City,

1. Considers that these measures are invalid;

2. Calls upon Israel to rescind all measures already taken and to desist forthwith from taking action which would alter the status of Jerusalem.

Well, the status had already been changed by the Jordanians, who entirely disrespected Resolution 181.

When the events are contrary to the interests of Israel, when the Arabs disrespect rules established by the UN, no measures are taken, no resolutions are approved regarding their violations. But when Israel defends its security and its interests, a shower of resolutions rains down from the United Nations, proclaiming the illegality of the new situation created by the Jewish state.

This is political terrorism.

Considering that the United Nations is supposed to treat all state parties with equal justice and fairness, the inequality of its treatment of the two sides is highly unjust and illegal. So whereas the UN, through the Security Council, proclaims the invalidity of Israel's deeds and legal measures, I hereby propose that it is the council's resolutions that ought to be considered invalid. They are prejudiced and in total contradiction of the facts. Therefore they are *contra legem* – against the law and invalid.

As the International Court of Justice follows the United Nations General Assembly and the Security Council in their one-sidedness, in their absolute partiality regarding the conflict between Israel and the Arabs, their opinion – and not Israel's policies – is without any legal basis.

And regardless, we must remember that a political organ has no authority to decide on legal matters. Its decisions on legality or illegality, validity or invalidity of any measures taken by member states are therefore of no legal consequence.

One final point concerns the court's "moral lecture" in paragraph 162:

> The Court would emphasize that both Israel and Palestine are under an obligation scrupulously to observe the rules of international humanitarian law, one of the paramount purposes of which is to protect civilian life. Illegal actions and unilateral decisions have been taken on all sides.[32]

To equate Israel and "Palestine" regarding the protection of civilian life is utter hypocrisy, scandalous falsity. The court knows, or should have known, that the 1948 war, the 1967 war, and the 1973 war were wars of aggression by the Arabs against Israel. The court must have heard about the constant infiltrations into Israeli territory way back in the late forties, and throughout the fifties and the sixties, by Egyptians and Syrians, in operations that resulted in the loss of a great number of civilian Israeli lives; the court could not ignore the Intifada executed by the so-called Palestinian Arabs, which caused one thousand deaths and thousands of wounded Israelis; the court knows that Israel's policy has been a constant defensive policy. The court must have known of the constant aggressions of the Arab states and the Palestinian Arabs. The court must have known of the various peace talks held after 1993, including the Israeli

---

32. "Text of Decision *Judicial and Similar Proceedings: International Court of Justice (ICJ): Legal Consequences of the Construction of a Wall in the Occupied Palestinian Territory,*" *International Legal Materials* 43, no. 5 (September 2004): 1054.

prime minister's offer to Arafat in Camp David, in the presence of President Bill Clinton, to return the "occupied" lands, inclusive of most of the parts of Jerusalem as demanded by the Palestinian representatives, and that Arafat refused to come to an agreement, nor even to present a counterproposal.

The court knows, or should have known, that the Palestinian Charter proclaims its desideratum to destroy the State of Israel and only accept the permanence of Jews who were there before 1917; the court should have known of the incitement that goes on in the schools of the Palestinians and in their mosques against the State of Israel. As Caroline Glick reports:

> Since the inception of the Palestinian Authority in 1994, the PA-controlled media organs, school system, mosques, and governing ministries have carried out a massive, systematic campaign of incitement against Israelis. These institutions do not call for Israel's return to the 1949 armistice lines: they call for Israel's complete destruction. And they do not portray Israelis merely as citizens of an enemy state: they portray Israelis and Jews as satanic monsters, subhuman enemies of Allah. This campaign of incitement – which continues to this day – has encouraged Palestinians to make the destruction of Israel and the genocide of the Jewish people their highest goal in life.[33]

The court should have informed itself of the comfortable, free life that one and a half million Arabs enjoy in Israel and that not one of them would wish to live under any Arab sovereignty; the court should have informed itself of the help that Israeli hospitals have extended to Arabs living in the West Bank, saving the lives of hundreds or perhaps thousands of children.

And finally, the court should have understood that the war of aggression that the Arabs waged against Israel in 1967 forced Israel to occupy the West Bank in order to avoid another war of aggression and that these territories were not returned – though, as explained before, there is no international legal obligation to return these territories – because there has never been any guarantee of peace from the side of the Arabs. Therefore, again, the court should have known that Israel has respected the most important of the Security Council's resolutions, namely Resolution 242 which clearly conditioned the devolution of territories (not "the territories," but only "territories") to

---

33. Glick, *The Israeli Solution*, 8.

a guaranteed state of peace, and so, as long as there is no peace, there is no devolution of territories, and there is no "illegal occupation" as the United Nations proclaims *ad nauseam*.

The International Court of Justice follows the United Nations, its General Assembly, and its Security Council that have been declaring, deciding, and resolving, with obsessive insistence, that Israel occupies the West Bank and that this occupation is illegal. They proffer no explanation about the nature and the reason of this "illegality." There is not a word about the source in public international law upon which they base the statement of illegality.

I return to Stephen M. Schwebel, former judge and president of the International Court of Justice from 1981 to 2000. His short editorial comment in the *American Journal of International Law* has become a centerpiece in the field of international law regarding Israel's presence in the West Bank. Referring to a declaration by the then secretary of state William P. Rogers, Schwebel wrote that

> since the danger in response to which defensive action was taken remains, occupation – though not annexation – is justified, pending a peace settlement.

Referring to the conclusion reached by the secretary of state, that the United States does not support expansionism, Schwebel stated:

> It is submitted that the Secretary's conclusion is open to question on two grounds: first, that it fails to distinguish between aggressive conquest and defensive conquest; second, that it fails to distinguish between the taking of territory which the prior holder held lawfully and that which it held unlawfully....
>
> As a general principle of international law, as that law has been reformed since the League, particularly by the Charter, it is both vital and correct to say that there shall be no weight to conquest, that the acquisition of territory by war is inadmissible. But that principle must be read in particular cases together with other general principles, among them the still more general principle of which it is an application, namely that no legal right shall spring from a wrong, and the Charter principle that the Members of the United Nations shall refrain in their international relations from the threat of use of force against the territorial integrity or political

independence of any state. So read, the distinctions between aggressive conquest and defensive conquest, between the taking of territory legally held and the taking of territory illegally held, become no less vital and correct than the central principle itself.

And the former president of the International Court of Justice continues:

> It follows that the application of the doctrine of according no weight to conquest requires modification in double measure. In the first place, having regard to the consideration that, as between Israel, acting defensively in 1948 and 1967, on the one hand, and her Arab neighbors, acting aggressively in 1948 and 1967, on the other, Israel has better title in the territory of what was Palestine, including the whole of Jerusalem, than do Jordan and Egypt (the U.A.R. indeed has, unlike Jordan, not asserted sovereign title); it follows that modification of the 1949 armistice lines among those states, within former Palestinian territory are lawful (if not necessarily desirable).[34]

Did the International Court of Justice refer to this classic piece so well and clearly exposed by one of its former judges and presidents, published in the most important international law journal of the United States, if not of the whole world? Did the court refer to any other scholarly opinion about the subject matter it was dealing with? No, absolutely no, on both questions.

Another weighty point to be added to Judge Schwebel's argumentation: On June 5, 1967, at 10:00 A.M., Jordan opened artillery fire on Israel territory, moved ground troops across the previous armistice lines. Despite Israel's warning through the UN at 11:00 A.M., Jordanian attacks nonetheless persisted, and Israeli military action began at 12:45. Considering that Iraqi forces had crossed Jordanian territory and were poised to enter the West Bank, the temporary armistice boundaries of 1949 lost all validity. There is no legal sense in considering that Israel occupied foreign territory because, once the armistice boundaries were nullified, the West Bank went back to its original status of "Palestine." As the Arabs had not accepted the partition plan approved by the UN in 1947, the whole territory returned to its status of the land promised

---

34. Stephen Schwebel, "Editorial Comment: What Weight to Conquest?" *American Journal of International Law* 64, no. 2 (April 1970): 344–47.

to the Jews by the Balfour Declaration,[35] later approved by the League of Nations through the mandate given to Great Britain at the San Remo Peace Conference in 1920 with its resolution of April 25.

Following the establishment of the British Mandate, on July 24, 1922, in accordance with article 22 of the Covenant of the League of Nations, the League determined the conditions of the Mandate over Palestine and charged the Mandatory government with the responsibility of establishing a national home for the Jewish people in Palestine.

The preamble to the Mandate Document stated that it was based on international recognition of "the historical connection of the Jewish people with Palestine." The Mandate document made Britain responsible for placing the country under such political, administrative, and economic conditions as to secure the establishment of the Jewish national home (article 2), required the Mandatory Power to "facilitate Jewish immigration" (article 6), and made Britain responsible for enacting a nationality law framed so as to facilitate the acquisition of Palestinian citizenship by Jews who take up their permanent residence in Palestine (article 7).

The Palestine Mandate does not mention Arab national rights to Palestine and there is no reference to political rights of the non-Jewish population, since the object and purpose of the Mandate was exclusively to reconstitute the political ties of the Jewish people to their homeland. The document only provides that "nothing should be done which might prejudice the civil and religious rights of existing non-Jewish communities" (second paragraph of the preamble and article 2 of the Mandate document).

Above and beyond all of these critiques, we must remember that the court is simply not a judicial body. The sad truth is that the International Court of Justice is nothing more than a *longa manus* (long arm) of the General Assembly and the Security Council of the United Nations, and like these, it is a mere political body, which decides according to the political orientations

35. The declaration was delivered by British foreign secretary Lord Arthur Balfour to Lord Lionel Walter Rothschild on November 2, 1917, whereby "His Majesty's government view with favour the establishment in Palestine of a national home for the Jewish people, and will use their best endeavors to facilitate the achievement of this object, being clearly understood that nothing shall be done which may prejudice the civil and religious rights of existing non-Jewish communities in Palestine, or the rights and political status enjoyed by Jews in any other country."

of the other UN bodies and also in accordance with the policies of the states of which the judges are nationals.

In other words, all of the opinion's omissions were actually essential for the court, as they lead to the conclusion that Israel conquered the West Bank through an inadmissible use of force rather than in a most legitimate defensive war. Legal procedure's fundamental method commands that courts first examine the facts and then the law. The ICJ followed a different path and excelled in reaching an unjust, politicized, totally bigoted opinion without referring to the historical background of the situation and without recourse to the applicable law. It consolidated its position as an obedient branch of the General Assembly and of the Security Council. It demonstrated that it is not international, it is not a real court, and it does not perform justice.

The court undermined its own legitimacy by accepting the case at all, because the General Assembly's consultation was not a legal question, but rather a military, political question in legal garb, motivated by political considerations rather than a genuine uncertainty about the law. It was part of the political strategy to delegitimize Israel, which is pursued relentlessly in the General Assembly. Accepting jurisdiction involved the ICJ in a purely political dispute.[36]

As already noted in the beginning of this chapter, the Six-Day War, when three Arab countries attacked Israel, was described by the court in 2004 as the "the June 1967 hostilities" and the "outbreak of hostilities." No reference to the actual aggressive war waged by the Arab countries. In the International Conference on Human Rights that took place in Teheran in 1968, less than a year after the Six-Day War, the UN was already using this false description. The ICJ simply follows the cynical statements of the political organs of the international organization.

The hypocrisy of ignoring the facts of the Six-Day War has invaded the realm of scholarship. A good example is Otto Kranzbühler, a German attorney who enlisted voluntarily in 1937 into the Kriegsmarine. Throughout the war he served in various important positions of the Nazi Germany marine. After the war he was arrested by Allied Forces, along with other German Navy judges. After a few weeks he was freed and eventually served the British and the Americans in marine matters, in accordance with the complicity policies

36. "Jerusalem Viewpoints" of the Jerusalem Center for Public Affairs, February 15, 2004.

of the "Allies" before, during and after the war, as has been explained in earlier chapters. At the International Military Trial he served as defense counsel for Grand Admiral Karl Donitz, commander and chief of the German Navy and Fuehrer of Germany after Adolf Hitler's suicide. Donitz had requested Kranzbühler, a fellow navy man in the Kriegsmarine, to represent him in his defense. In 1965 Kranzbühler published an article in an American law journal, under the title "Nuremberg, Eighteen Years Afterwards,"[37] in which, with reference to the Six-Day War, he had the audacity to state that "in Israel even now, there is a state of war. No one so far has had the courage to state who is the aggressor in that war, much less to attempt to call that aggressor to account." Only a Nazi official could produce such a perverse lie! Sadly, one of the most respected American books on international law reproduced part of Kranzbühler's article, inclusive of the false statement on the Six-Day War.[38]

The same book, however reproduces Judge Stephen Schwebel's article, parts of which we quoted above, where the author states that

the facts of the June 1967 'Six Day War' demonstrate that Israel reacted defensively against the threat and use of force against her by her Arab neighbors. This is indicated by the fact that Israel responded to Egypt's prior closure of the Straits of Tiran, its proclamation of a blockade of the Israeli port of Eilat, and the manifest threat of the United Arab Republic's [UAR, composed of the fusion of Egypt and Syria] use of force inherent in its massing of troops in Sinai, coupled with its ejection of UNEF [United Nations Emergency Force]. It is indicated by the fact that, upon Israeli responsive action against the U.A.R., Jordan initiated hostilities against Israel. It is suggested as well by the fact that, despite the most intense efforts by the Arab States and their supporters, led by the Premier of the Soviet Union, to gain condemnation of Israel as an aggressor by the hospitable organs of the United Nations, those efforts were decisively defeated. The conclusion to which these facts lead is that the Israeli conquest of Arab and Arab-held territory was defensive rather than aggressive conquest.[39]

37. Otto Kranzbühler, "Nuremberg, Eighteen Years Afterwards," *De Paul Law Review* 14 (1965): 333.
38. McDougal and Reisman, *International Law in Contemporary Perspective*, 1002–3.
39. Ibid., 1063–64, reproduced from Schwebel, "Editorial Comment: What Weight to Conquest?" 344.

Another piece reproduced in McDougal and Reisman's book is by Malawer, "Anticipatory Self-Defense under Article 51 of the United Nations Charter," which closes by saying that

> both the Security Council and the General Assembly refused to censure Israel for its 1967 attack against the Arabs. This failure to censure Israel evidences an acceptance by the international community of the Israeli case. Unlike the censure of Israel in 1956, the United Nations implicitly approved the Israeli unilateral use of force. This evidences a development of United Nations practice which allows a state to exercise under Article 51 anticipatory self-defense.[40]

The same understanding of the Six-Day War is found in English legal literature, as seen in D.W. Greig's *International Law*. He writes:

> The pre-emptive attack launched by Israel principally against the United Arab Republic in June, 1967, is an excellent illustration of the circumstances in which a right of anticipatory self-defense might still be claimed. It had long been the stated objective of most of the Arab states to 'liberate' the areas of Palestine under the sovereignty of the State of Israel. In their opinion Israel did not exist as a state. Right of passage for its vessels through the Suez Canal was denied, and more recently a passage through the Strait of Tiran had been obstructed. On the eve of Israel's attack, a propaganda campaign threatening annihilation of Israel reached a peak and the Egyptian President Gamal Abdel Nasser demanded the withdrawal of the small contingent of U.N.E.F. that was supervising the 1957 Egypt/Israel cease fire line. To all outward appearances an invasion of Israel was imminent.[41]

The International Court of Justice's opinion, needless to say, contradicts the views of all of these highly respected authorities on public international law.

Journalist Charles Krauthammer of the *Washington Post* made a number

---

40. Ibid., 988, 991, reproduced from *Studies in International Law* (1977), 191.

41. Donald W. Greig, *International Law* (London: Butterworths, 1970), 681. For a critical analysis of the UN secretary-general U Thant's decision to withdraw the UN force, see Rosalyn Higgins, "The June War: The United Nations and Legal Background" in *Journal of Contemporary History* 3 (1968): 253, reprinted in J.N. Moore, ed., *The Arab-Israeli Conflict* (Princeton University Press, 1977) 535, 544ff., as referred to by Einhorn, "The Status of Judea and Samaria (The West Bank)," 14.

of important remarks in the edition of July 16, 2004, a few days after the ICJ opinion was pronounced:

> The fence is only one-quarter built and yet it has already resulted in an astonishing reduction in suicide attacks in Israel. In the past four months, two Israelis have died in suicide attacks, compared with 166 killed in the same time frame at the height of the terrorism. But what are 164 dead Jews to this court? Israel finally finds a way to stop terrorism and 14 eminences sitting in the Hague rule it illegal – in a 64-page opinion in which the word terrorism appears not once (except when citing Israeli claims).
>
> Yes, the fence causes some hardship to Palestinians. Some are separated from their fields, some schoolchildren have to walk much farther to class. This is unfortunate. On any scale of human decency, however, it is far more unfortunate that 1,000 Israelis are dead from Palestinian terrorists, and thousand more horribly maimed, including Israeli schoolchildren with nails and bolts and shrapnel lodged in their brains and spines who will never be walking to school again.
>
> What makes the travesty complete is that the denial of Israel's right to defend itself because doing so might violate "humanitarian" rights was read in open court by the chief judge representing China, whose government massacred hundreds of its own citizens demonstrating peacefully in Tiananmen Square. Not since Libya was made chairman of the Commission on Human Rights has the UN system put on such a shameless display of hypocrisy.
>
> It must be noted that one of the signatories of this attempt to force Israel to tear down its most effective means of preventing the slaughter of innocent Jews was the judge from Germany. The work continues.

This advisory opinion demonstrates that the world has no International Court of Justice.

This case is not the only one in which the court decided without fact-finding. On February 26, 2007, the court decided on the "Application of the Convention on the Prevention and Punishment of the Crime of Genocide (Bosnia and Herzegovina v. Serbia and Montenegro)." In response, Jose E. Alvarez, then president of the American Society of International Law, published a "note from the president" in the organization's newsletter, in which he launched a severe critique against the court for having failed to engage in independent fact-finding. He claims that the decision will be seen as one of the court's greatest self-inflicted wounds. And he adds:

> Even those who might be inclined to accept the central conclusion on the merits reached by the Court – that except for the massacre at Srebrenica, the mass killing of Bosnian Muslims after the breakup of the former Yugoslavia did not constitute genocide, that Serbia was not responsible for Srebrenica, and was only guilty of failing to prevent and to punish genocide – are not likely to be persuaded by an opinion whose factual underpinnings are so weakly supported.[42]
>
> Missing from the Bosnia proceedings – as with respect to other ICJ fact-finding that has come under fire [Professor Alvarez refers in a footnote to the construction of a wall in the "Occupied Palestinian Territory" in 2004] is a fact-finding process that generates the kind of confidence that is generated either by civilian investigatory judges or common law adversarial processes, including the energetic cross examination of witnesses.[43]

And Professor Alvarez concludes with an ironic note:

> Just like some U.S. journalists, the majority of the ICJ's judges appear in need of a basic course in Fact-Finding 101.[44]

In the same issue of the ASIL newsletter appear two strong critiques of the court's decision. Makau Mutua, of the State University of New York, Buffalo Law School, wrote that in this "remarkably contorted decision, the ICJ has done lasting damage to itself and the development of international criminal law" and "the ICJ has retarded decades of lawmaking in the area of accountability for mass atrocities. Regrettably, this opinion suggests, for example, that it would be very difficult to hold Sudan accountable for the genocide

---

42. The ICJ based its view on the lack of a concerted plan or of a consistent pattern of conduct evincing the necessary intent, whereas in Srebrenica, the decision of the Bosnian Serb leadership to kill all men and many boys and the forcible transfer of other elements of the population was cited to show the intent to eliminate the group from Srebrenica. As summed up by Ratner, Abrams, and Bischoff, *Accountability for Human Rights Atrocities*, 37–38.

43. *American Society of International Law Newsletter* 23, no. 2 (spring 2007): 1.

44. Ibid.

committed by the state-supported Janjaweed militias." Mutua concludes: "It is a sad day for international law."

And Siegfried Wiessner, of St. Thomas University School of Law, writes that "lamentably the Court, on the basis of incomplete facts, failed to fully grasp and legally sanction a centerpiece of the horrendous atrocities committed in Europe at the end of the twentieth century."

The failure of the whole procedure of advisory opinions has been pointed out in a book titled *Evidence Before the International Court of Justice*, authored by Anna Riedel and Brendan Plant. The book was reviewed by John R. Crook, who reports the following:

> Chapter 10 deals with fact-finding in advisory opinion proceedings. The authors express substantial reservations about the Court's fact-finding in these cases. There are no parties bearing a burden of proof and no adversarial testing of evidence, creating the risk that the Court may surmise facts "on the basis of information which has not been fully tested in adversarial litigation, and so may be biased, incomplete, misleading and/or erroneous."[45]

In the case of the fence built by Israel, the court refrained from any fact-finding, and so constructed a totally false narrative, consequently reaching an opinion flagrantly in conflict with elementary principles and rules of international law.

Benjamin Netanyahu, then finance minister of Israel, published an article in the *New York Times* four days after the ICJ pronounced the advisory opinion, to which he reacted as follows:

> The obstacle to peace is not the fence but Palestinian leaders who, unlike past leaders like Anwar Sadat of Egypt and King Hussein of Jordan, have yet to abandon terrorism and the illegitimate goal of destroying Israel. Should Israel reach a compromise with a future Palestinian leadership committed to peace that requires adjustments to the fence, those changes will be made. And if that peace proves genuine and lasting, there will be no reason for a fence at all....
>
> The Palestinians complain that their children are late to school because of the fence. But too many of our children never get to school – they are

---

45. *American Journal of International Law* 107, no. 1 (January 2013): 263.

blown to pieces by terrorists who pass into Israel where there is still no fence.…

Because the court's decision makes a mockery of Israel's right to defend itself, the government of Israel will ignore it. Israel will never sacrifice Jewish life on the debased altar of "international justice."[46]

In an article published in the *Washington Post*, George Will reported:

In the Intifada that began in 2000, Palestinian terrorism killed more than 1,000 Israelis.… Israeli parents sending two children to a school would put them on separate buses to decrease the chance that neither would return to dinner.

But the Judges of the World Court developed their Opinion around a series of International conventions and UN resolutions, so that the facts on the ground, the reality, the background, the behavior of the other side, could be totally ignored.[47]

Caroline Glick set the tragic consequences of Palestinian terrorism more precisely: between September 2000 and the end of 2009, Palestinians killed some 1,200 Israelis in terrorist attacks and more than 8,100 Israelis were wounded during that period, of whom over 70 percent were civilians.[48]

Professor Alan Dershowitz, in his tireless defense of the State of Israel, commented on the ICJ opinion:

No Israeli judge may serve on that court as a permanent member, while sworn enemies of Israel serve among its judges, several of whom represent countries that do not abide by the rule of law. Virtually every democracy voted against that court's taking jurisdiction over the fence case, while nearly every country that voted to take jurisdiction was a tyranny. Israel owes the International Court absolutely no deference. It is under neither a moral nor a legal obligation to give any weight to its predetermined decision.

The International Court of Justice is much like a Mississippi court in the

46. Benjamin Netanyahu, "Why Israel Needs a Fence," *New York Times*, July 13, 2004, http://www.nytimes.com/2004/07/13/opinion/why-israel-needs-a-fence.html?_r=0.
47. George Will, "Skip the Lecture on Israel's 'Risks for Peace,'" *Washington Post*, August 19, 2010.
48. Glick, *The Israeli Solution*, xxiv.

1930s. The all-white Mississippi court, which excluded blacks from serving on it, could do justice in disputes between whites, but it was incapable of doing justice in cases between a white and a black. It would always favor white litigants. So, too, the International Court. It is perfectly capable of resolving disputes between Sweden and Norway, but it is incapable of doing justice where Israel is involved, because Israel is the excluded black when it comes to that court – indeed when it comes to most United Nations organs.…

If the International Court of Justice were itself to apply the rule of law instead of the calculus of politics, it might deserve respect. Now – like the general assembly of which it's a creation and the Mississippi courts of the 1930s, of which it's a clone – all it deserves is the contempt of decent people for its bigoted processes and its predetermined partisan result.[49]

As the Israeli ambassador to the UN at the time, Dan Gillerman, said, "We will point to the great hypocrisy in the fact that the court has actually put the people who are trying to prevent terror and the victims of terror in the dock, rather than the terrorists themselves."[50]

Above all arguments exposed and above everything that has been written critically by the quoted jurists and journalists about the merits of the court's opinion, hovers the question of why the court accepted in the first place to give an opinion it had no obligation to contemplate. Considering that the court has the power not to exercise jurisdiction and further considering that the problem between Israel and the Palestinians could only be settled through negotiations, and that the problem was of a political and not a legal nature, various European states questioned why the court insisted on going ahead and emitting such a heavily one-sided opinion, without any examination of the rich background of the conflict. I can only think of one answer: the court is totally committed to demonizing the State of Israel, in exactly the same spirit as the General Assembly of the United Nations, its Security Council, the Council of Human Rights, and all the other organs of the international organizations, and in line with the bulk of the international media.

49. Alan Dershowitz, "Israel Follows Its Own Law, Not Bigoted Hague Decision," *Jerusalem Post*, July 11, 2004, internet edition.
50. Melissa Radler and Tovah Lazaroff, "Gillerman: Dark Day for the United Nations," *Jerusalem Post*, July 15, 2004, internet edition.

"A Court of UN Law" is the title of an essay by Professor Michla Pomerance of the Hebrew University of Jerusalem, in which she shows that the ICJ, instead of a court of law, has become a court of the United Nations.[51] She writes:

> It would make a mockery of the independence of the Court if it could never "reach conclusions at variance with the conclusions stated by the General Assembly."... It would also render the Court largely useless as an organ for giving legal advice to the Assembly.[52]

Further in her essay, Pomerance quotes Yale professor Michael Reisman, who noted in 1986 that "the Court appears to have sensed that its major constituency had become the transformed General Assembly, both for election of its members and for budget purposes and thereafter moved much more sharply in the direction of the political preferences of the Assembly."[53]

The essay closes with the following statement:

> The more the Court's pronouncements are perceived as weakening rather than strengthening the rights of those who would deter aggression and combat the scourge of terrorism, the more widely accepted will be the conclusion that "there is no necessary connection between world law (and one might add, world order) and the particular institutions that is housed in the Peace Palace in the Hague."[54]

In the introduction to the volume of the *Israel Law Review* dedicated to the ICJ opinion on the "wall," Professor David Kretzmer writes that

> rather than relying solely on these sources of law (enumerated in article 38 of its Statute), the ICJ relied heavily on resolutions by UN bodies, including those of the General Assembly. This approach is challenged by Michla Pomerance, who argues that the trend of the Court to resort to

---

51. Michla Pomerance, "A Court of UN Law," *Israel Law Review* 38 (2005): 134.

52. Ibid., quoting D.H.N. Johnson, "The Case Concerning the Northern Cameroons," *International and Comparative Law Quarterly* 13 (1964): 1176–77.

53. Ibid., 161.

54. Ibid., 164, quoting Anthony D'Amato and Mary Ellen O'Connell, "United States Experience at the International Court of Justice," in Lori Fisler Damrosch, ed., *The International Court of Justice at a Crossroads* (Dobbs Ferry, NY: Transnational, 1987), 422.

"UN Law" rather than the consensual international law may further its demise as a judicial body.[55]

In 1999 the *American Journal of International Law* published an agora[56] in which nine scholars participated. Four of them were critical of the court's decision,[57] three supported the court,[58] one had varied positions on different aspects of the opinion,[59] and one was restricted to an analytical report.[60]

The International Organization and International Law

I have stressed the political nature of the resolutions of the various organs of the United Nations – not only of the General Assembly, but also of the Security Council and of the Council of Human Rights, and up to the supposedly prestigious International Court of Justice. But do these entities not have a legal advisory board composed of lawyers – *international* lawyers – to orientate them and show them what the law says, what the great authorities in public international law of the different member states have published? And to advise on precedents, on customary international law? How can a situation be considered internationally legal or illegal, without the advice of experts, the scholars in the field? After all, the Charter of the United Nations provides in its first article that the organization will act "in conformity with the principles of justice and international law."[61]

55. David Kretzmer, Introduction, *Israel Law Review* 38, nos. 1–2 (winter/spring 2005): 13.
56. *The American Journal of International Law* 99, no. 1 (January 2005).
57. Michla Pomerance, "The ICJ's Advisory Jurisdiction and the Crumbling Wall between the Political and the Judicial," ibid., 26–42; Ruth Wedgwood, "The ICJ Advisory Opinion on the Israeli Security Fence and the Limits of Self-Defense," ibid., 52–61; Sean Murphy, "Self-Defense and the Israeli Wall Advisory Opinion: An *Ipse Dixit* from the ICJ?" ibid., 62–76; Michael J. Dennis, "Application of Human Rights Treaties Extraterritorially in Times of Armed Conflict and Military Occupation," ibid., 119–141.
58. Richard Falk, "Toward Authoritativeness: The ICJ Ruling on Israel's Security Wall," 42–52; Ian Scobbie, "Words My Mother Never Taught Me: 'In Defense of the International Court,'" 76–88; Ardi Imseis, "Critical Reflections on the International Humanitarian Law Aspects of the ICJ Wall Advisory Opinion," 102–18.
59. David Kretzmer, "The Advisory Opinion: The Light Treatment of International Humanitarian Law," *American Journal of International Law* 99, no. 1 (January 2005): 88–102.
60. Geoffrey R. Watson, "The 'Wall' Decisions in Legal and Political Context," 6–26.
61. Article 1: "The Purposes of the United Nations are: 1. To maintain international peace and security and to that end: to take effective collective measures for the prevention and removal of threats to the peace, and for the suppression of acts of aggression or other

This question has been dealt with in a book by Ralph Zacklin, a former United Nations assistant secretary-general for legal affairs, which was reviewed in the *American Journal of International Law*.[62] From this book we learn that the United Nations functions practically without any legal assistance. Zacklin informs that the Security Council does not seek the advice of lawyers in the UN secretariat – "instead, the individual members of the Council normally rely on their own legal advisers, if they rely on legal advice at all." He adds that the secretary-general does listen to the in-house lawyers. Lawyers of the member states of the Security Council as well as the in-house lawyers can be very useful for administrative matters, for UN procedural matters and, in general, for basic legal advice, but when it comes to complicated issues of international peace and security, when it comes to defining the legality (or illegality) of international situations, it is evident that the works of the most prestigious and authoritative international law scholars would have to be consulted.

Regarding the International Court of Justice, its statute is very clear about the sources to be applied, as provided in article 38:

> The Court, whose function is to decide in accordance with international law such disputes as are submitted to it, shall apply:
>
> a. International conventions, whether general or particular, establishing rules expressly recognized by the contesting states;
>
> b. International custom, as evidence of a general practice accepted as law;
>
> c. The general principles of law recognized by civilized nations;
>
> d. Subject to the provisions of Article 59, judicial decisions and the teachings of the most highly qualified publicists of the various nations, as subsidiary means for the determination of rules of law.[63]

breaches of the peace, and to bring about by peaceful means, and *in conformity with the principles of justice and international law*, adjustment or settlement of international disputes or situations which might lead to a breach of the peace." (Translation mine.)

62. Frederic L. Kirgis, review of *The United Nations Secretariat and the Use of Force in a Unipolar World: Power v. Principle*, by Ralph Zacklin, *American Journal of International Law* 105, no. 3 (July 2011): 619.

63. Article 59 of the statute of the International Court of Justice provides: "The decision of

It should be understood that to recur to the sources in the first three categories, one needs the support of the experts in the field. The interpretation of a convention (a), the exact content of an international custom (b), and the general principles of law recognized by civilized nations (c) can only be clearly and correctly understood through the writings of the eminent scholars of the field and judicial decisions of prestigious and respected jurisdictions (d).

It is a logical proposition that when other organs of the UN, such as the Security Council and the Council of Human Rights, confront the need to decide on a matter of international law, when they are about to approve a resolution on the legality or illegality of a situation, they would consult the sources determined for the International Court of Justice. Otherwise we could end up with an international law resolution by the Security Council that contradicts a decision of the court. If the charter commands application of international law in article 1, it cannot be a different international law than the one ordered by the court's statute.

Thus one sees how ridiculous are the Security Council's decisions regarding the policies of the State of Israel in the territories and in Jerusalem, qualifying them as "illegal" without any recourse to authoritative sources of public international law. The authoritative sources tell us one thing: the Security Council decrees the opposite of the truth. The illegalities rest with the Security Council and the larger United Nations, not with the State of Israel.[64]

The Israeli Supreme Court on the Wall/Fence

In Beit Sourik Village Council v. The Government of Israel, the Supreme Court of Israel had to decide on the harm that the fence the government was erecting would cause to the life of the inhabitants of the Beit Sourik village.

The court received detailed analyses from experts on military matters and based on humanitarian principles and the principle of proportionality, decided that the fence – which in itself the court considered perfectly legal, demonstrating the error of the ICJ opinion – should change its route in order to ease the life of the inhabitants of that particular village, a change that,

the Court has no binding force except between the parties and in respect of that particular case."

64. As Posner (*Twilight of Human Rights Law*, 17) writes: "The U.N. Charter did not give the General Assembly the power to make international law." The same goes for the Security Council.

according to the expert assessments received, would still protect the safety of the Israeli population. Considering all the evidence and the expert opinions that were presented, the court decided which segments of the fence illegally violated the rights of the local population according to international law, and which fence segments were legal.

Aharon Barak, the president of the court, referred to another case – *Ajuri v. IDF Commander*. There he had described the security situation prevalent in Israel:

> Israel's fight is complex. Together with other means, the Palestinians use guided human bombs. These suicide bombers reach every place where Israelis can be found (within the boundaries of the State of Israel and in the Jewish communities in Judea and Samaria and the Gaza Strip). They sow destruction and spill blood in the cities and towns. The forces fighting against Israel are terrorists: they are not members of a regular army; they do not wear uniforms; they hide among the Palestinian population in the territories, including inside holy sites; they are supported by part of the civilian population, and by their families and relatives.[65]

In this decision the Israel Supreme Court described the systematic, careful procedures followed by the Israeli authorities for the erection of the fence, which illustrate the respect and consideration of the Israeli authorities to the Arab populations of the left side of the Jordan, known as the West Bank:

> Parts of the separation fence are being erected on land which is not privately owned. Other parts are being erected on private land. In such circumstances – and in light of the security necessities – an order of seizure is issued by the Commander of the IDF forces in the area of Judea and Samaria. Pursuant to standard procedure, every land owner whose land is seized will receive compensation for the use of his land. After the order of seizure is signed, it is brought to the attention of the public, and the proper liaison body of the Palestinian Authority is contacted. An announcement is relayed to the residents, and each interested party is invited to participate in a survey of the area affected by the order of seizure, in order to present the planned location of the fence. A few days after the order is issued, a

---

65. *Beit Sourik Village Council v. The Government of Israel*, HCJ 2056/04, Israel: Supreme Court, 30 May 2004, in *Israel Law Review* 38, nos. 1–2 (winter/spring 2005): 84.

survey is taken of the area, with the participation of the landowners, in order to point out the land which is about to be seized.

After the survey, a one-week leave is granted to the landowners, so that they may submit an appeal to the military commander. The substance of the appeal is examined. Where it is possible, an attempt is made to reach understanding with the landowner. If the appeal is denied, leave of one additional week is given to the landowner, so that he may petition the High Court of Justice.... [66]

As the various cases that were brought to the High Court of Justice demonstrate, the arguments of the Arab owners are taken into due consideration, experts' advice is accepted and duly examined, and finally the court decides whether the direction of the planned fence should be modified. In some cases this is exactly what happened: the court ordered the military authorities to modify the direction of the fence.

It would be very difficult – if at all possible – to indicate a similar respectful attitude to the people of occupied land by any occupying authority and by any court in the world at any time in history.

The concluding paragraph of this decision is an important contribution to the major modern legal problem – democracy versus terrorism. It reads:

Our task is difficult. We are members of Israeli society. Although we are sometimes in an ivory tower, that tower is in the heart of Jerusalem, which is not infrequently hit by ruthless terror. We are aware of the killing and destruction wrought by the terror against the state and its citizens. As any other Israelis, we too recognize the need to defend the country and its citizens against the wounds inflicted by terror. We are aware that in the short term, this judgment will not make the state's struggle against those rising up against it easier. But we are judges. When we sit in judgment, we are subject to judgment. We act according to our best conscience and understanding. Regarding the state's struggle against the terror that rises against it, we are convinced that at the end of the day, a struggle according to the law will strengthen her power and her spirit. There is no security

66. Ibid., 88.

without law. Satisfying the provisions of the law is an aspect of national security.[67]

Ma'arabe v. the Prime Minister of Israel, also with reference to the fence, was decided upon the same principles as the *Beit Sourik* case, considering the scope of the danger and the proportionality of the injury to the local residents. In this decision the Israeli justices showed how flawed the International Court of Justice's advisory opinion was, totally lacking in the factual motives that led the State of Israel to defend its population from terrorist activities, which had caused thousands of deaths and injuries in recent years.

Among the various observations of the Israel Supreme Court on the ICJ's opinion figures the following:

> We find this approach of the ICJ hard to come to terms with. It is not called for by the language of paragraph 51 of the Charter of the United Nations. It is doubtful whether it fits the needs of democracy in its struggle against terrorism. From the point of view of a state's rights to self-defense, what difference does it make if a terrorist attack against it comes from another country or from territory external to it which is under belligerent occupation?[68]

The Israeli Supreme Court points out how the opinion of the ICJ lacks any consideration regarding the security aspect of the fence's construction, stating in paragraph 63:

> The security-military necessity is mentioned only most minimally in the sources upon which the ICJ based its opinion. Only one line is devoted to it in the Secretary General's report, stating that the decision to erect the fence was made due to a new rise in Palestinian terrorism in the spring of 2002. In his written statement, the security consideration is not mentioned at all. In the Dugard report and the Zeigler report there are no data on this issue at all. In Israel's written statement to the ICJ on jurisdiction and discretion, data regarding the terrorism and its repercussions were

67. Ibid., 132. This is the essence of Justice Barak's legal philosophy regarding the need to conciliate democracy and human rights with the defense of the state and its citizens from terrorism, as we shall see at the end of this chapter.
68. "Supreme Court of Israel: Mara'abe v. the Prime Minister of Israel," September 15, 2005, *International Legal Materials* 45, no. 1 (January 2006): 213.

presented, but these did not find their way to the opinion itself. It contains no real mention of the security-military aspect. In one of the paragraphs the opinion notes that Israel argues that the objective of the wall is to allow an effective struggle against the terrorist attacks emanating from the West Bank. That's it.[69]

And so the Supreme Court's position on the ICJ opinion was set in the following terms:

> Our answer is as follows: the Supreme Court of Israel shall give the full appropriate weight to the norms of international law, as developed and interpreted by the ICJ in its Advisory Opinion. However, the ICJ's conclusion, based upon a factual basis different than the one before us, is not *res judicata*, and does not obligate the Supreme Court of Israel to rule that each and every segment of the fence violates international law. The Israeli Court shall continue to examine each of the segments of the fence, as they are brought for its decision and according to its customary model of proceedings; it shall ask itself, regarding each and every segment, whether it represents a proportional balance between the security-military need and the rights of the local population. If its answer regarding a particular segment of the fence is positive, it shall hold that that segment is legal. If its answer is negative, it shall hold that that segment is not legal.[70]

Judge M. Cheshin, vice president of the court at the time, wrote a separate opinion in which he dealt with the ICJ opinion, expressing the following thoughts:

> And if all that is not enough, there is the ICJ's almost complete ignoring of the horrible terrorism and security problems which have plagued Israel – a silence that the reader cannot help noticing – a foreign and strange silence. I can only agree with Judge Buergenthal, and partly with Judges Higgins, Judge Kooijmans and Judge Owada, that the factual basis upon which the judgment was built is inadequate to the point that it is inappropriate to pass judgment upon it, even by way of opinion. . . . I am sorry, but the decision of the ICJ cannot light my path. Its light is too dim for me to

69. Ibid., 227.
70. Ibid., 232.

guide myself by it to law, truth and justice in the way a judge does, as I learned from those who preceded me and from my father's household.[71]

Security Council Resolution 242/1967

Regarding the repetitious references to UN Security Council Resolution 242 present in practically all official statements of the United Nations that deal with the Arab-Israeli conflict, I contend that based on a careful reading of its contents and a simple analysis of the historical background, it could seriously be questioned whether the territories occupied by Israel – the so-called West Bank – are affected by that resolution.

Resolution 242 reads as follows:

The Security Council,

Expressing its continuing concern with the grave situation in the Middle East,

Emphasizing the inadmissibility of the acquisition of territory by war and the need to work for a just and lasting peace in which *every State in the area*[72] can live in security,

Emphasizing further that all *Member States* in their acceptance of the Charter of the United Nations have undertaken a commitment to act in accordance with Article 2 of the Charter,

1. Affirms that the fulfilment of Charter principles requires the establishment of a just and lasting peace in the Middle East which should include the application of both the following principles:
    a) Withdrawal of Israel armed forces from territories occupied in the recent conflict;
    b) Termination of all claims or states of belligerency and respect for and acknowledgment of the sovereignty, territorial integrity and political independence of *every State in the area* and their right to live in peace within secure and recognized boundaries free from threats of acts of force;

---

71. Ibid., 245.
72. The emphasis is my own throughout this source.

2. Affirms further the necessity
   a) For guaranteeing freedom of navigation through international waterways in the area;
   b) For achieving a just settlement of the refugee problem;
   c) For guaranteeing the territorial inviolability and political independence of *every State in the area*, through measures including the establishment of demilitarized zones;

3. Requests the Secretary General to designate a Special Representative to proceed to the Middle East to establish and maintain contacts with the *States concerned* in order to promote agreement and assist efforts to achieve a peaceful and accepted settlement in accordance with the provisions and principles in this resolution;

4. Requests the Secretary General to report to the Security Council on the progress of the efforts of the Special Representative as soon as possible.

As can easily be seen from its text, the resolution deals with "Member States," the "States in the area," "every State in the area," the "States concerned." These references address *Egypt, Syria* and *Jordan* – which started the war – and *Israel*, which defended itself successfully. How does Resolution 242 apply to the so-called West Bank territory which is not a *state*?

Once peace was signed with Egypt, Israel returned the Sinai Peninsula. And once peace was signed between Israel and Jordan, the latter withdrew from the territories it had occupied illegally. Resolution 242 thus accomplished its desideratum regarding the conflict between Israel and these two Arab states.

Israel and Egypt signed a "Framework for Peace in the Middle East," which included a project to achieve a solution for the West Bank and Gaza, which would be reached by negotiations between Israel, Egypt, and Jordan – negotiations that never materialized.

The negotiations that did take place between Israel and the Arabs of the West Bank had no direct connection with Security Council Resolution 242 as – besides Israel – no other state was involved.[73] Israel voluntarily initiated negotiations with the Arabs living in the West Bank, but these attempts always

---

73. As Dore Gold (*The Fight for Jerusalem*, 260) points out, neither Jerusalem nor the Palestinians are even mentioned in 242.

failed due to lack of cooperation from the entities that represent these Arabs, which instead resorted continuously to terrorist acts.

The resolution's reference to a "settlement of the refugee problem" (2b) does not clarify which refugees it refers to (the Arabs who had lived in the part of Palestine that became Israel, or the Jewish refugees who were forced to leave various Arab countries, or both of them). Since two of the three Arab states involved did not present any claim or any plan regarding this item, nor did Israel suggest any kind of solution, the refugee matter became a nonissue.

The third invading state in the Six-Day War was Syria. All attempts to bring about an Israel-Syria agreement have failed because Syria has maintained its aggressive policy toward the State of Israel. During the war Israel annexed the Golan Heights in order to prevent infiltrations and missile attacks from Syria – activities that Syria continuously engaged in during the period 1948–67. The Golan Heights had become part of Syria due to an act of the British colonial power that gave this territory to France's Syrian colony in 1923, in a trade-off agreement with that country. Before that the region was part of the old land of Israel.

Three days after the Golan's annexation, the Security Council, in its traditional clumsiness, passed a unanimous resolution, under number 497, stating that the Israeli decision to impose its laws, jurisdiction, and administration in the occupied Syrian Golan Heights is null and void and without international legal effect, and calling upon Israel to rescind the law.[74] But the Security Council has no legal authority to decide on the legality or illegality of a sovereign state's laws.

In sum, a thorough analysis of the issue must consider that

    a) the Arab States and the Arabs living in the so-called territories refused to accept Resolution 181 of 1947, which decided on the partition of Palestine into a Jewish state and an Arab state;

    b) from 1948 – when the Jewish state was proclaimed and recognized by the international community of nations – until 1967, no initiative was taken by the Arabs of the territories to proclaim their state, and instead they submitted themselves to Jordan's illegal occupation of the territory in which they lived;

    c) Jordan made peace with Israel, retreated from the territories – though

74. UN Security Council Resolution 497, December 17, 1981, http://bit.ly/1a1vQIO.

they did not belong to any state – and gave up any claim concerning the same;

d) Egypt obtained Israel's total return of the Sinai Peninsula and renounced sovereignty over the Gaza Strip;

e) the Golan Heights, even if the historical demonstration that it belonged to Israel were not accepted, still could not be returned to Syria due to the lack of a peace treaty, a condition established by the resolution for the return of territories – the "withdrawal of Israel armed forces from territories occupied in the recent conflict" was attached and connected to the "establishment of a just and lasting peace in the Middle East" – and as Syria maintained a continuous belligerent policy and continuously attacked the northern Israeli population, Resolution 242's item on return of territories did not apply to the Golan Heights;

f) Resolution 242 did not recommend devolution of *all* territories, but merely "territories";

g) Israel – although not obliged by the resolution – has returned the Gaza territory (which did not belong to any state) to its Arab inhabitants;

h) Egypt did not proceed with the initiative regarding peace between Israel and the inhabitants of the West Bank (the so-called "Framework for Peace in the Middle East");

i) the West Bank Arab representatives and organizations have persisted in their consistent belligerency against the Israeli population, characterized by constant invasions and suicide attacks that culminated in two murderous Intifadas;

The above points demonstrate that, excepting the lack of peace with Syria, as this state refused to negotiate a settlement, Israel made and remained in peace with Egypt and Jordan. The peace signed with Jordan brought about its retreat from the territories it had occupied since 1948; the peace signed with Egypt resulted in the retreat of Israel from the Sinai Peninsula, which it had occupied during the Six-Day War, and the return of this territory to Egypt. Resolution 242 has thus been implemented, and no claim can be put to Israel based on this UN document.

As a consequence of all the above, there is no "belligerent occupation" (as the Israeli Supreme Court characterized the situation) because it concerns an occupation of a no-state's-land, which Israel conquered in a defensive war against the Arab states. Jordan – the former occupier of that land – has signed a peace agreement with Israel and presented no claim concerning said land, and Egypt also signed a peace agreement with Israel, and as a result received the land that Israel had occupied during the war. As peace treaties were signed between Israel and Egypt and between Israel and Jordan, all demands of Resolution 242 were accomplished, excepting peace between Israel and Syria – so far proven to be unattainable. There are thus no more *state* territories to be withdrawn from through peace agreements.

And considering that a "just settlement of the refugee problem" (2b of the resolution) is inapplicable after the passing of half a century (two generations), the people classified in 1967 as refugees cannot anymore be considered as such according to customary international law, which applies to Arab refugees who left the territory of Israel and Jewish refugees who left the territories of various Arab states, including Egypt and Syria.

All this leads to the conclusion that Resolution 242 has been implemented by all concerned state parties (with the exception of Syria, as explained above).

To all the above should be added that United Nations resolutions are nonbinding recommendations and their legal validity is conditional on the acceptance by the parties. Going back to the General Assembly's Partition Plan of 1947, Israel declared its willingness to accept the obligations embedded in the resolution, whereas the Arab nations, as well as the Arabs living in territory the UN attributed to them, rejected it outright. The United Nations did nothing to enforce it. Consequently the Partition Plan remained devoid of validity, and Israel was accepted to the UN without being required to accept the boundaries proposed in that resolution. Security Council Resolution 242 does not mandate the establishment of a separate Palestinian state in Jerusalem, Judea and Samaria, and the Gaza Strip.[75] Moreover, the Arabs living on the West Bank, known as "Palestinians," have clearly rejected Resolution 242 in their Palestinian 1974 Political Program which states the following:

Article 1 – To reaffirm the Palestine Liberation Organization's previous attitude to Resolution 242, which obliterates the national right of our

75. Einhorn, "The Status of Judea and Samaria (The West Bank)," 68.

people and deals with the cause of our people as a problem of refugees. The Council therefore refuses to have anything to do with this resolution at any level, Arab or international, including the Geneva Conference.[76]

All these considerations and arguments lead to the conclusion that Israel's presence in the territories of Judea and Samaria (the "territories" or the "West Bank," in UN parlance) is not an illegal occupation – as the organs of the UN do not tire themselves of repeating. It is not even an occupation, as it is land that was illegally occupied by Jordan, which was never an independent state but is part of the Palestine that the Balfour Declaration and the League of Nations' mandate included in the Jewish state in formation. Therefore Israel is entitled to establish its sovereignty on the whole of those territories.

According to Israel's Ministry of Foreign Affairs, the West Bank and Gaza should not be viewed as "occupied" because of the following distinction:

> The West Bank and Gaza Strip are disputed territories whose status can only be determined through negotiations. Occupied territories are territories captured in war from an established and recognized sovereign. As the West Bank and Gaza Strip were not under the legitimate and recognized sovereignty of any state prior to the Six Day War, they should not be considered occupied territories.[77]

This position of the Israeli government has never been taken into consideration by the United Nations. The General Assembly and Security Council insist, in innumerable resolutions, on classifying Israel's presence in the territories as an "illegal occupation." But the subject of the ownership of these territories goes back to a much earlier time. Law and history are interdependent. When a question of public international law arises concerning such matters as occupation and sovereignty, one must consider history.

S.Y. Agnon, Nobel laureate in literature, spoke about this matter in his 1966 acceptance speech of the prize: "As a result of the historic catastrophe in which Titus of Rome destroyed Jerusalem and Israel was exiled from its

---

76. "The PLO's 'Phased Plan,'" IRIS, http://www.iris.org.il/plophase.htm.

77. As quoted from a document of the Israeli Ministry of Foreign Affairs written by Grant T. Harris, "Human Rights, Israel and the Political Realities of Occupation," in *Israel Law Review* 41 (2008): 92.

land, I was born in one of the cities of the exile. But always I regarded myself as one who was born in Jerusalem."[78]

It is also important to read the synopsis of Jewish history given by Prime Minister Benjamin Netanyahu to the US Congress:

> In Judea and Samaria, the Jewish people are not foreign occupiers. We are not the British in India, we are not the Belgians in the Congo. This is the land of our forefathers, the Land of Israel, to which Abraham brought the idea of one God, where David set out to confront Goliath, and where Isaiah saw a vision of eternal peace. No distortion of history can deny the 4,000-year-old bond between the Jewish people and the Jewish land.
>
> Two thousand years ago, the Jews were exiled from their land. The violent ethnic cleansing of the area that took place long ago could have been forgotten by history. However, history remembered the Jews, since the Jews never forgot their homeland. And almost 2,000 years later, historic justice was achieved, when the Jews returned to the Land of Israel and reestablished their own independent state.
>
> The establishment of the State of Israel is nothing less than a symbol of historic justice. No amount of delegitimization, revisionist history or "alternative narratives" will change this plain fact.[79]

The Settlements

The enemies of the State of Israel employ various weapons, among them factual lies, the falsification of history, and the misrepresentation of legal principles and rules.

The classic case in which these three weapons are employed is the settlements. The accusation and the defense on the settlements occupies thousands of pages. A good illustration is the fiery encounter between Prime Minister Margaret Thatcher and her foreign secretary, Lord Carrington, versus Israeli prime minister Menachem Begin, as narrated by the meticulous biographer of the most outstanding Israeli prime ministers, Yehuda Avner.

Lord Carrington told Begin that "Israeli settlement policy is expansionist. It is intemperate. It is a barrier to peace." "The settlements," proceeded the

---

78. Cited in Dan Illouz, "Why You Should Be Proud Zionists," *Jerusalem Post Magazine,* January 31, 2014, 38.
79. Ibid.

British foreign secretary, "are built on occupied Arab soil. They rob Palestinians of their land. They unnecessarily arouse the animosity of the moderate Arabs. They are contrary to international law. They are inconsistent with British interests."

Thatcher intervened to say that the "foreign secretary is speaking on behalf of Her Majesty's government in this matter."

Avner relates that Begin chose to fight the secretary, rather than the prime minister. Begin told Carrington:

> The settlements are not an obstacle to peace. No Palestinian Arab sovereignty had ever existed in the biblical provinces of Judea and Samaria. The Geneva Convention did not apply. The Arabs had refused to make peace before there was a single settlement anywhere. The settlements were built on state-owned, not Arab-owned land. Their construction was an assertion of basic Jewish historic rights. The settlement enterprise was critical to Israel's national security.[80]

Then Begin turned to face Margaret Thatcher.

> Madam Prime Minister, your foreign secretary dismisses my country's historic rights. He pooh-poohs our vital security needs. So, I shall tell you why the settlements are vital: because I speak of Eretz Yisrael, a land redeemed, not occupied; because without these settlements Israel could be at the mercy of a Palestinian state astride the commanding heights of Judea and Samaria. We would be living on borrowed time. And whenever we Jews are attacked we are always alone. Remember in 1944 how we came begging for our lives – begging at this very door?[81]

The conversation continued about the refusal of the British (and the Americans) to bomb the road to Auschwitz, but by then Begin had revealed the lie about settlements being on private Arab-owned land, the historical falsity about the land being Arab land, and the perversion of the settlements' supposed illegality.

80. Yehuda Avner, "When Begin Met Thatcher," *Jerusalem Post Magazine*, April 19, 2013, 7.
81. Ibid.

The Conflict between State Safety and Human Rights

In 2006, Aharon Barak, former chief justice of Israel's Supreme Court, published in the United States a book entitled *The Judge in a Democracy*. Many reviews of this book were published, the most critical of which was written by Richard Posner, judge on the US Court of Appeals for the Seventh Circuit and professor at the University of Chicago Law School.

Barak's position comes out clearly from various statements. In one of them he declared: "We, the judges in modern democracies, are responsible for protecting democracy both from terrorism and from the means the state wants to use to fight terrorism."[82]

Posner states that Barak formulated a judicial power undreamed of even by the most aggressive US Supreme Court justices, putting Marshall in the shade. Among the many judicial principles that Barak established in his Supreme Court, Posner refers critically to the decision that any government act that is "unreasonable" is illegal, and that a court can countermand military orders, decide whether to prevent the release of a terrorist within the framework of a political "package deal," and direct the government to move the security wall that keeps suicide bombers from entering Israel from the West Bank. "Only in Israel (as far as I know) do judges confer the power of abstract review on themselves, without benefit of a constitutional or legislative provision. One is reminded of Napoleon's taking the crown out of the pope's hands and putting it on his own head."

Posner maintains that Barak takes for granted that judges have inherent authority to override statutes, an approach which, according to the American judge, can be accurately described as usurpative. In Barak's conception of the separation of powers, the judicial power is unlimited and the legislature cannot remove judges (and in Israel, judges participate in the selection of judges). In a Barak-dominated court, says Posner, it would be very difficult to tell whether a judgment of unconstitutionality was anything more than the judges' opinion that it was a dumb statute, something they would not have voted for if they were legislators. And such an opinion would have no significance at all for the question of constitutionality.

In the end of his review, Posner states that whatever the weaknesses of

---

82. *Jerusalem Post*, May 6, 2005.

the book, "Barak himself is by all accounts brilliant, as well as austere and high-minded – Israel's Cato."

"Israel," says Posner, "is an immature democracy, poorly governed; its political class is mediocre and corrupt; it floats precariously in a lethally hostile Muslim sea; and it really could use a constitution. Barak stepped into a political and legal vacuum and with dash and ingenuity orchestrated a series of... 'surprisingly agreeable outcomes.'"[83]

In December 2007, the Hebrew University organized a debate between Posner and Barak, attended by over a thousand academics, jurists, and journalists. The event was titled "The Power of the Judiciary – How Far?" Barak said that even in times of war, it is possible and indeed even essential for the court to intervene in issues involving human rights. Posner differed with this and argued that in times of war the judiciary must permit the executive branch to carry out its work and only afterward to take up judicial issues connected with the events. For US president Lincoln, he said, it was more important to protect the nation than to protect civil rights during the Civil War. After the war, the situation returned to normal and democracy continued to evolve in the United States.[84]

Barak's position is that it is the duty of the courts to uphold human rights as much during wartime as during peace, because once civil liberties are curbed, restoring them is problematic, if not impossible – like in Nazi Germany. "In Israel we have not only an 11th of September, but rather also a 10th and a 12th." Despite this situation, Barak holds that there is a line that democracy cannot permit itself to cross. Only a strong democracy can fight for human rights.

For the American judge, the greater the danger, the more justified is the provisory suspension of human rights; for the Israeli judge, the greater the danger, the greater is the need to protect human rights. Barak maintains that "sometimes a democracy must fight with one hand tied behind its back," while Posner holds that in the defense of security, both hands have to be free.[85]

Daniel Doron, director of the Israel Center for Social and Economic Progress, reports that an activist Supreme Court that was led by Barak habitually constrained the military from taking effective measures to protect innocent

83. Richard A. Posner, "Enlightened Despot," *The New Republic*, April 23, 2007.
84. The Hebrew University of Jerusalem, News Release, December 24, 2007.
85. Daniel Doron, "Elena Kagan, Terrorism and the Law" *Jerusalem Post*, August 5, 2010, internet edition.

lives. It feared impairing Palestinian Arab rights to free movement or to a decent quality of life. Changes dictated by the Supreme Court in the security fence cost hundreds of millions of shekels. Judicial interference in military operational details such as the positioning of roadblocks resulted in fatalities, while insistence on freedom of movement for Palestinian Arabs facilitated the penetration of suicide bombers.

Doron distinguishes between the two existing schools through their positions on the human rights of terrorists versus the right to security. On one side, judicial activists like Barak believe that human rights are God's – or nature's – given rights. Such rights must be defined and strictly enforced by the judiciary even in times of war. The pragmatists argue that the right to life of potential victims is no less sacred than the human rights of their assassins. They believe that even human rights must be weighed against other rights and adjudicated case by case.

For Posner, judges lack qualification in military matters. They base their judgments on their values and their ideology, on their personal and professional experience. Casting their decisions in terms of human rights is often an excuse to impose their ideology and personal bias under the guise of lofty principles. The rigid application of human rights at almost any cost sacrifices innocent lives to protect abstract principles.

This is also Posner's philosophy regarding internal American problems with terrorism versus human rights. As he writes in *Not a Suicide Pact: The Constitution in a Time of National Emergency*, "In times of danger, the weight of concerns for public safety increases relative to that of liberty concerns and civil liberties are narrowed."[86]

The author elaborates on his theory:

> One would like to locate the point at which a slight expansion in the scope of the right would subtract more from public safety than it would add to personal liberty and a slight contraction would subtract more from personal liberty than it would add to public safety. That is the point of balance, and determines the optimal scope of the right. The point shifts continuously as threats to liberty and safety wax and wane. At no time can the exact point be located. Yet to imagine it the object of our quest is

86. Richard A. Posner, *Not a Suicide Pact: The Constitution in a Time of National Emergency* (Oxford: Oxford University Press, 2006), 9.

useful in underscoring that the balance between liberty and safety must be struck at the margin. One is not to ask whether liberty is more or less important than safety. One is to ask whether a particular security measure harms liberty more or less than it promotes safety.[87]

And he further considers the matter from a different angle:

> Civil liberties depend on national security in a broader sense. Because they are the point of balance between security and liberty, a decline in security causes the balance to shift against liberty. An even more basic point is that without physical security there is likely to be very little liberty. Who would dare, without protection against terrorist retaliation, to criticize Islam? Intimidation can stifle liberty as effectively as laws can.[88]

The author closes his book with a sharp statement of David Hume: "The safety of the people is the supreme law. All other particular laws are subordinate to it and dependent on it."[89]

All this concerns civil rights versus public safety within a particular state. However, as the constitution is not a suicide pact, the same applies to international law. This has been clearly emphasized by the Finnish professor Martti Koskenniemi, who wrote the following about the Geneva Conventions:

> Why are the four Geneva Conventions there? Well, as every history of humanitarian law informs us: in order to provide for the security of the occupying power while safeguarding the essential interests of the local

87. Ibid., 31–32. A group of eminent Israeli jurists participated in a symposium on Posner's book, all of them criticizing his approach (*Israel Law Review* 42 [2009]: 225–74). Professor Alon Harel ("Cost-Benefit Analysis and National Emergencies: A Review of Richard Posner's *Not a Suicide Pact*") strikes an interesting note in his last paragraph by saying that "some advocates of balancing may accuse me of being a hopelessly soft, leftist, romanticist, or perhaps, an enemy of numbers or rationality." Actually, the majority of the Israeli legal community, as well as of its intelligentsia in general, follows a tendency of softness, of a highly humanistic approach even to problems that deal with life and death, influenced by their interpretation of the Jewish people as a "light unto the nations," in the prophet Isaiah's words (49:6) – an exemplary society that puts human rights – even of murderous enemies – above all considerations. The Supreme Court of Israel, especially under Judge Aharon Barak, followed the same philosophy. Under the same illusion lives a considerable part of the Israeli press, otherwise of the highest caliber.
88. Ibid., 46–47.
89. Ibid., 158.

population. If some of their provisions go against either of those objectives there is no reason to apply them. Surely, as we have learned to say, international law is no suicide pact. It is followed because it safeguards valuable objectives. If it did not, but instead contributed to undermining those objectives, what possible reason would there be to follow them?[90]

Among other rules, article 28 of the Fourth Geneva Convention of 1949 is a good illustration of this theory, as it provides that "the presence of a protected person [a civilian] may not be used to render certain points or areas immune from military operations." This rule annuls all the complaints of the UN representatives, of the media, of the nongovernmental organizations, of the European statesmen and organizations regarding Israel's measures of defense that victimize Arab civilians, given that missiles against Israel's population are intentionally launched from within Arab civilian populations.

90. Martti Koskenniemi, "Occupied Zone – 'A Zone of Reasonableness'?," *Israel Law Review* 41, nos. 1–2 (2008): 21.

Chapter Eleven
The UN in the Footsteps of Hitler

The Demonization of the State of Israel

Modern antisemitism has taken a new face as its main target has become the State of Israel. UN Watch, a website devoted to tracking the United Nations' actions and exposing its hypocrisy, notes that within just twenty years of having itself created the State of Israel with its General Assembly's Resolution 181, the UN turned tables in what has become a concentrated effort against the Jewish state. The UN engages in a "relentless and virulent propaganda war" against Israel, making the UN into "Ground Zero for today's new antisemitism.".[1]

The policies of the UN against the State of Israel, which have been affecting the security of Jews in Europe, amounts to what I classified in chapter 4 as "complicity after the war." In fact, the world organization's policies amount to the continuation of Hitler's goal: the elimination of the Jewish race from the earth.

On July 15, 2014, Hillel Neuer, the executive director of UN Watch, who has been heroically pointing out the demonization of the State of Israel by the world organization, posted in his Facebook page the following condemnation of the world's "shock" at the events taking place in Gaza when a few hundred civilians (among them Hamas terrorists dressed as civilians) fell victims of Israel's response to the intensive missile attacks it was suffering from the criminal Palestinians:

1. "UN, Israel and Anti-Semitism," UN Watch, http://secure.unwatch.org/site/c.bdK-KISNqEmG/b.1359197/k.6748/UN_Israel__AntiSemitism.htm.

If in the past year you didn't cry out when thousands of protesters were killed and injured by Turkey, Egypt and Libya, when more victims than ever were hanged by Iran, women and children in Afghanistan were bombed, whole communities were massacred in South Sudan, 1800 Palestinians were starved and murdered by Assad in Syria [two hundred thousand Syrians were annihilated, some by chemical weapons], hundreds in Pakistan were killed by jihadist terror attacks, 10,000 Iraqis were killed by terrorists, villagers were slaughtered in Nigeria, but you ONLY cry out for Gaza, then you are not pro HUMAN RIGHTS, you are only ANTI-ISRAEL.[2]

This was very clearly characterized by Canada's prime minister Stephen Harper in his speech to the Israeli parliament in January 2014. He declared:

As once Jewish businesses were boycotted, some civil-society leaders today call for a boycott of Israel. On some campuses, intellectualized arguments against Israeli policies thinly mask the underlying realizations such as the shunning of Israeli academics and the harassment of Jewish students. Most disgracefully of all, some openly call Israel an apartheid state.

Think about that. Think about the twisted logic and outright malice behind that: A state, based on freedom, democracy and the rule of law, that was founded so Jews can flourish as Jews, and seek shelter from the shadow of the worst racist experiment in history, that is condemned, and that condemnation is masked in the language of anti-racism. It is nothing short of sickening.

In much of the Western world, the old hatred, crude anti-Semitism, has been translated into more sophisticated language for use in polite society. People who would never say they hate and blame the Jews for their own failings or the problems of the world, instead declare their hatred of Israel and blame the only Jewish state for the problems of the Middle East.[3]

During the 2014 conflict with Hamas, Turkish prime minister Recep Tayyip Erdogan stated that Israel's defense against Hamas rocket fire is "barbarism

2. Hillel Neuer, "Test Yourself: Are You Pro Human Rights, or Just Anti-Israel?" July 16, 2014, UN Watch, http://blog.unwatch.org/index.php/2014/07/16/test-yourself-are-you-pro-human-rights-or-just-anti-israel/.
3. David M. Weinberg, "Harper's Vital Validation," *Jerusalem Post*, January 24, 2014.

that surpasses Hitler," which led the US House of Representatives to consider condemnation of the Turkish premier's antisemitism. A bipartisan resolution asserted that Erdogan's statement "sparks unwarranted anger towards Jews and endangers the Turkish Jewish community and Jews around the world." The resolution proposed to "decry and condemn Erdogan's comparison as an insult to the memory of those who perished in the Holocaust and an affront to those who survived, and their children and grandchildren, the righteous gentiles who saved Jewish lives at peril to their own lives and to those who bravely fought to defeat the Nazis."[4]

On September 8, 2014, a symposium on "Global Anti-Semitism: A Threat to International Peace and Security" was held at the United Nations. The keynote speech was given by Brigitte Gabriel, a Christian Lebanese woman who has become known as an advocate for the case of Israel. She began with a reference to the 3D Test of Antisemitism proposed by former Soviet refusenik and current Israeli politician and human rights activist (as well as chairman of the Executive of the Jewish Agency) Natan Sharansky.[5] The three Ds of Sharansky's test are demonization, double standards, and delegitimization applied to the State of Israel. This litmus test is being employed by all who deal with the many problems that Israel faces in the international arena as the perfect way to characterize modern antisemitism, turned against the state of the Jews. After describing Sharansky's test and her own qualification for discussing these issues based on her family's persecution at the hands of Islamists when she was a child, she pointed out, "If Israel has been committing genocide against the Palestinians, then why has the population of Palestinians increased more than 600 percent since 1948? Israel must be the most incompetent mass murderer in the history of the world."[6]

Israel, she continued, is "held to a standard that no other country in the world would be expected to meet," in and of itself an antisemitic attitude. While "Israel is a vibrant democracy where human rights are protected and respected," she pointed out, "the United Nations' so-called Human Rights

4. Michael Wilner, "House to Consider Condemnation of Erdogan for Anti-Semitism," *Jerusalem Post*, July 31, 2014, http://www.jpost.com/Operation-Protective-Edge/House -to-consider-condemnation-of-Erdogan-for-anti-Semitism-369647.
5. Natan Sharansky, "Foreword," *Jewish Political Studies Review* 16, nos. 3–4 (Fall 2004): 5–8.
6. Brigitte Gabriel, "Tolerating Hate Is Not an Option."

Commission spends most of its time and effort investigating and condemning Israel, while they gloss over or ignore the massive and continuing human rights violations that occur in Iran, Cuba, China and many other brutal repressive autocracies."

After describing the use of human shields by Hamas in its agenda to impose Islam on Israel and the world, Gabriel noted that "Israelis have learned from history that if someone repeatedly says they're going to kill you, *they mean it*. A lesson the world is only now learning."

Gabriel stands with the Middle East's only democracy and urges the rest of the world to do so as well, "to ensure that people of all faiths can live in peace and harmony and that Jews are never persecuted and victimized by barbaric, murderous ideologies ever again. That Jews can walk in any street in the world with their head held high and safe. That Israel, the Jewish state, the only democracy in the Middle East, continues to shine as a beacon of light in the darkest region in the world."[7]

The UN's Hypocritical Attitude from Day One

The UN's negative attitude toward the State of Israel essentially began at the time of its creation. After the 1948–49 war between the newly proclaimed State of Israel and the attacking armies of five Arab states, the United Nations created the United Nations Relief and Works Agency for Palestinian Refugees in the Near East (UNRWA). The intention was to assist more than half a million Arab refugees who had (depending on whom one asks) voluntarily fled or been expelled from their villages as a result of the war (itself a result of the Arab countries' immediate aggression on the fledgling State of Israel).

In fact, the exodus of the majority of the Palestinian Arabs resulted from the warnings that they received from the attacking Arab armies, urging that they abandon their homes and move out of the Israeli territory, in order not to be harmed by the imminent attack and planned annihilation of the Israeli population. The Arabs are therefore the ones who caused the resulting refugee problem.[8]

---

7. Ibid.

8. Two weeks before the invasion, on May 1, 1948, the Arab League secretary-general Abdul-Rahman Azzam Pasha declared: "If the Zionists dare establish a state, the massacres we would unleash would dwarf anything which Genghis Khan and Hitler perpetrated." Azzam reiterated his message the day the Arab armies attacked: "This will be a war of extermination

Israel managed to defend herself at the cost of some six thousand lives – exactly one percent of its Jewish population at that time. Yet once an armistice was signed, UNRWA was created to deal with the Palestine refugees, defined as "persons whose normal place of residence was Palestine during the period of 1 June 1946 to 15 May 1948, and who lost both home and means of livelihood as a result of the 1948 conflict."

UNRWA's process includes a built-in heritage of refugee status, as children (even adopted ones) of men certified as Palestine refugees also receive refugee status and services from UNRWA. In 1950 the agency served some 750,000 Palestinian refugees. The number of eligible people with refugee status today exceeds five million.

At the very same time when Arabs left the nascent Jewish state, over six hundred thousand Jews came to Israel from Iraq, Syria, Lebanon, and other Middle East countries from which they had to escape. They were forced to leave all their belongings in their country of origin, where their families had lived for centuries. Israel facilitated their adaptation in the new environment and after a few years those refugees became integrated in the country's economy and slowly they also integrated in the country's culture. Israel never made an issue of this great event, which began tragically and ended happily.

This is not what happened to the Arab refugees who were sent to fifty-nine refugee camps in Jordan, Lebanon, Syria, the West Bank, and the Gaza Strip. The Arab countries refused to grant them nationality or to integrate them in their economies and societies; the refugees were forced to remain as refugees, living in the UNRWA camps in hopeless poverty.

UNRWA itself continues to grow and flourish; it is actually the single largest UN agency. It has more than twenty-five thousand employees, nearly all of whom are Arabs living in the agency's service area.

The maintenance of the status of refugees and the continuous growth of their number is one of the main factors for the animosity toward Israel not only of the so-called refugees themselves, but also of the Arab states that house their camps. The Palestinian refugees were treated in a totally different manner from the refugees of the world wars and local conflicts. These are taken care of

and a momentous massacre which will be spoken of like the Mongolian massacres and the Crusades." Sarah Honig, "Another Tack: Cluing Condi in," *Jerusalem Post*, August 9, 2007, http://www.jpost.com/Opinion/Columnists/Another-Tack-Cluing-Condi-in.

by the United Nations High Commissioner for Refugees (UNHCR), known as the UN Refugee Agency; the agency protects and supports refugees at the request of a government or of the UN itself and assists in their voluntary repatriation, local integration, or resettlement in a third country. A few years after World War II there were practically no more refugees from the millions who had been left in that status at the end of the conflict. Within a few years all those Germans, Hungarians, Poles, Ukrainians, Turks, Greeks, Bulgarians, Rumanians, Indians, Pakistanis, and more had been integrated into their new settings, and so there were no further consequences.

Only for Palestinian refugees did the UN create a separate agency that has persistently followed a policy that perpetuates the refugee status, which exacerbates the refugees' animosity against the State of Israel. The Arab refugee problem feeds the tension and the state of belligerence, idealized and maintained by the UN – the leading enemy of the State of Israel.

The UN's agency for Palestinian refugees is actually the main factor in the maintenance of the Arab-Israeli conflict, as the Arab leaders insist on their right of return to Israel, which would guarantee them a majority and consequently the elimination of the Jewish state. Even if there were a possibility of agreement as far as territories and Jerusalem are concerned, the insistent demand for the return of the refugees ensures that no agreement will ever be possible.

In recent years UNRWA has become a real and effective accomplice to Palestinian terrorism, keeping its offices side by side with known terrorists (for example in the Second Lebanon War in 2006) and doing nothing about it.

In the Protective Edge Operation of July-August 2014, when Israel finally reacted to the continuous rocket launching that Hamas was directing at Israeli's population, UNRWA set up a shelter right in the vicinity of a Hamas launch site. This was an obvious act of complicity in a war crime: exploiting civilians as human shields. It was also discovered that UNRWA facilities were used to stockpile weapons.

Despite all these shocking collaborations of UNRWA with the terrorist group Hamas, the UN kept quiet. It is logical and legitimate to establish that the UN itself has become an accomplice to Hamas in moments of violent conflict between a democratic state and that declared and recognized terrorist organization.

And in "normal" times – in the absence of open conflict – UNRWA supports schools that inculcate in their charges outright hatred of Jews and Israel.[9]

And so the United Nations is an active enemy of the State of Israel.

The UN as a Tool for Discrimination: "Zionism Is Racism"

The Armistice Agreement signed by Israel and the attacking Arab states (after Israel's War of Independence) was immediately violated. Syrian snipers would shoot at Israeli civilians near the border and shell Israeli villages. And Egypt and Jordan provided tactical support to terrorist attacks launched from their territory (in flagrant violation of the Armistice Agreement). Yet the Security Council condemned *Israel* – for defending herself.

When Egypt blocked the Straits of Tiran (which effectively squashed all Israeli shipping activity based in its southern port city of Eilat), the United Nations said nothing. Israel was forced to undertake the 1956 Sinai Campaign (in concert with Britain and France). Israel then held the Sinai until the United Nations Emergency Force (UNEF) stepped in.

And then came November 10, 1975, when the United Nations General Assembly passed Resolution 3379, which declared that "Zionism is a form of racism and racial discrimination." A total of 72 delegates voted yes, 35 opposed, 32 abstained, and 3 were absent.

Among the yes votes were Iraq (murderer of its Kurd population), Saudi Arabia (which does not allow churches of any religion in its territory and treats women as inferior human beings), Congo (where millions of people were murdered in the major genocide after World War II), Rwanda (where the lack of any notion of respect for human life led to the murder of eight hundred thousand human beings in the course of a few weeks), and many other states with serious records of discrimination, racism, and atrocities of all kinds. Naturally, the yes votes included the Islamic-Arab group and most of the third-world states. Brazil, at the time under a severe military dictatorship that had revoked all political rights and tortured and killed the young people who opposed their regime, joined the yes vote.

Resolution 3379 was a terribly hypocritical deed. It condemned the Zionist movement that had tried to avoid the Holocaust and saved many of the potential victims of this most egregious human persecution, that led to the

9. Moshe Dann, "Who Support UNRWA – and Why?," *Jerusalem Post*, August 29, 2014.

creation of the State of Israel which received hundreds of thousands of Jews interned in the postwar camps in Europe and saved another few hundred thousand who were in imminent danger in the Arab countries. This evil resolution was approved by the organization that pretends to respect, stimulate, and defend human rights.

Saad Eddin Ibrahim is an Egyptian intellectual who was incarcerated by the Mubarak regime from 2000 to 2003 and managed to move to the United States, where he became a visiting professor at Harvard University. Ibrahim published an article in the *Wall Street Journal* in which he dealt with the states that condemn the State of Israel in the United Nations. The article helps to understand how the "Zionism is racism" proposition gained acceptance by the majority in the UN:

> Most of the governments that pile on to condemn Israel and the so-called "neocolonial" West have terrible human-rights records. These include tyrannical regimes such as Zimbabwe, Myanmar, Libya, Iran, Syria and Egypt (my home country). Their atrocious violations have been widely reported by organizations like Amnesty International and Human Rights Watch....
>
> But members of like-minded voting blocs – such as the Organization of the African Unity and the League of Arab States – comprise more than two-thirds of the U.N. membership votes.[10] Together they can railroad through any resolution, no matter how absurd. It was this Afro-Islamic-Arab bloc that made sure Iranian President Mahmoud Ahmadinejad would be the keynote speaker in the opening session of this year's U.N. World Conference Against Racism, Racial Discrimination, Xenophobia, and Related Intolerance.[11]

The United Nations became a hostage of these states that do not respect life, do not respect human rights, do not respect other peoples, and do not respect their own people. These barbaric regimes have become the commanding group of the world organization.

The delegate of the United States, Ambassador Daniel Patrick Moynihan,

---

10. In 1948, when the State of Israel was created, there were around ten Arab and Islamic states in the United Nations. Today there are fifty-six (Anav Silverman, "Watching the UN," *Jerusalem Post Magazine*, December 28, 2012, 10).

11. Saad Eddin Ibrahim, "Tyrants Get Another U.N. Platform," *Wall Street Journal*, April 24, 2009.

spoke after the vote, saying that "the United States rises to declare before the General Assembly and before the world, that it does not acknowledge, it will not abide by, it will never acquiesce in this infamous act."[12]

Leonard Garment, the US representative to the UN Human Rights Commission, declared that to equate Zionism with racism was "to completely distort the history of the Zionist movement, born of the centuries of oppression suffered by the Jewish people in the Western world and designed to liberate an oppressed people by returning them to the land of their fathers."[13]

On the day the resolution was passed, the Israeli ambassador, Chaim Herzog, who later became president of the Jewish state, made the following declaration:

> I can point with pride to the Arab ministers who have served in my government; to the Arab deputy speaker of Parliament, to Arab officers and men serving of their own volition in our border and police defense forces, frequently commanding Jewish troops, to the thousands of Arabs from all over the Middle East coming for medical treatment to Israel, to the fact that Arabic is an official language in Israel on par with Hebrew, to the fact that it is as natural for an Arab to serve in public office in Israel as it is incongruous to think of a Jew serving in any public office in an Arab country. Is that racism? It is not. That…is Zionism. This Resolution is another manifestation of the bitter anti-Semitic, anti-Jewish hatred which animates Arab society. Who would have believed that in the year 1975, the malicious falsehoods of the "Elders of Zion" would be distributed officially by Arab governments? Who would have believed that we would today contemplate an Arab society which teaches the vilest anti-Jewish hate in the kindergartens? We are being attacked by a society which is motivated by the most extreme form of racism known in the world today.
>
> For us, the Jewish people, this resolution based on hatred, falsehood and arrogance, is devoid of any moral or legal value. For us this is no more than a piece of paper and we shall treat it as such.[14]

---

12. Cited in Gil Troy's book *Moynihan's Moment: America's Fight against Zionism as Racism* (New York: Oxford University Press, 2013), 275.

13. Cited in ibid., 123.

14. http://en.wikipedia.org/wiki/United_Nations_General_Assembly_Resolution_3379, accessed August 9, 2014.

And with that he ripped a copy of the resolution in half.

President George H.W. Bush introduced the motion to revoke Resolution 3379. He stated:

> UNGA Resolution 3379, the so-called "Zionism is racism" resolution, mocks this pledge and the principles upon which the United Nations was founded. And I call now for its repeal. Zionism is not a policy; it is the idea that led to the creation of a home for the Jewish people, to the State of Israel. And to equate Zionism with the intolerable sin of racism is to twist history and forget the terrible plight of Jews in World War II and, indeed, throughout history. To equate Zionism with racism is to reject Israel itself, a member of good standing of the United Nations.
>
> This body cannot claim to seek peace and at the same time challenge Israel's right to exist. By repealing this resolution unconditionally, the United Nations will enhance its credibility and serve the cause of peace.[15]

Gil Troy narrates Moynihan's fight to have the resolution repealed, which he finally achieved in 1991. The author adds: "And yet, even though the Soviet manipulators behind the resolution saw the Soviet Union fall, the lie had entered into international discourse – and still distorts discussions about Israel and the Middle East, especially since the 2001 United Nations Conference against racism in Durban."

The repeal of the resolution on Zionism did not change much. On the contrary. As time goes by, as the Muslim-Arab world persistently attacks the State of Israel in various forms and as Israel manages to neutralize the dangers – sometimes beating the enemy, sometimes paralyzing him for some time – the hatred and persecution of the Jewish state has kept growing, reaching absurd, obscene levels. It has created a negative attitude toward Israel within the populations of democratic countries, to the point that speculations about the dangers of a new Holocaust have been growing and spreading among observers, thinkers, and serious journalists.

This trend keeps growing within the United Nations. Hillel Neuer, executive director of UN Watch, reports:

15. President Bush's address to the UN General Assembly, New York, September 23, 1991, www.presidency.ucsb.edu/ws/index.php?pid=20012.

On December 18, 2012, the General Assembly adopted nine resolutions against Israel, specifically on the Palestinians, with one demanding that Israel hand over the Golan Heights to Syria. None of the resolutions referred to the Syrian war plans that had fired missiles at a refugee camp two days earlier and killed 20 Palestinians near Damascus.

The UN automatic majority has no interest in truly helping Palestinians, nor in protecting anyone's human rights; the goal of these ritual, one-sided condemnations remains the scapegoating of Israel.[16]

Neuer went on to point out that in 2012, the UN General Assembly passed twenty-two resolutions against Israel, while only four other resolutions were aimed at specific countries (Burma, North Korea, Syria, and Iran, none of which are democracies as Israel is). Meanwhile, countries such as Syria and Libya have been appointed to committees on human rights (in Libya's case even being named chair of the UN Human Rights Council!).[17] Although the resolution equating Zionism with racism was revoked in 1991, the UN's discriminatory attitude toward Israel has been cemented.

The hypocritical United Nations policy against the State of Israel has been increasing from year to year. At its twenty-fifth session, held in Geneva in March 2014, the Human Rights Council approved five anti-Israel resolutions. The council's agenda item 7 mandates that Israel must be debated at every session of the council, the Jewish state being the only country with such a standing agenda item.

Paula Schriefer, head of the US Delegation to the Council, charged that this behavior damaged the peace process, declaring that

16. Cited in Anav Silverman, "Watching the UN," *The Jerusalem Post Magazine*, December 28, 2012, 10. The Human Rights Council was created in 2005 during the World Summit held that year at the General Assembly of the United Nations. In the "outcome" of that grand meeting, paragraphs 157 and 158 stated: "Pursuant to our commitment to further strengthen the United Nations human rights machinery, we resolve to create a Human Rights Council. The Council will be responsible for promoting universal respect for the protection of all human rights and fundamental freedoms for all, without distinction of any kind and in a fair and equal manner." In reality, the council is nothing more than a continuation of the Human Rights Commission, which drafted the Universal Declaration of Human Rights and not much later started to persecute the State of Israel.
17. Ibid.

her country remains deeply troubled by the Council's agenda item directed against Israel and by the many repetitive and one-sided resolutions under this agenda item, which have become an obstacle to any progress in the peace negotiations. None of the world's worst human rights violators, some of whom are the object of resolutions at this session, have their own stand-alone agenda item at this Council. Only Israel, a vibrant and open democracy, receives such treatment. I would also highlight that country after country that spoke so passionately against country-specific mandates this morning, have no difficulty supporting this single-country mandate. Unfortunately, not only are the resolutions under this agenda item biased, but they work against our collective efforts to advance a peaceful resolution of the Arab-Israeli conflict. We are disappointed that this Council continually singles out Israel for criticism without acknowledging the violent attacks directed at its people. Especially disturbing is this Council's complacency with the repeated introduction of a resolution focusing on the Golan Heights. To consider such a resolution while the Syrian regime continues to slaughter its own citizens by the tens of thousands exemplifies the absurdity of this agenda item.[18]

How can any decent human being sent by his or her government as a delegate to the United Nations tolerate so many lies? How can he participate in the cynical, shameful theater of the absurd performed by the United Nations General Assembly, the Security Council, the Council on Human Rights, and UNESCO, with their false policies, inconsistencies, and cruel injustices against one particular state?

The obscenity of UNESCO reached the point where in 2012 it condemned Israel for designating Rachel's Tomb in Bethlehem and the Patriarch's Tomb in Hebron as National Heritage Sites. Instead, UNESCO declared that the tombs of the biblical Jewish patriarchs and matriarchs were mosques.

The organization had issued a report in 2006 in which it said that the greatest Jewish theologian and legal authority in history, Rabbi Moses Maimonides

---

18. Item 7: Resolutions A/HRC/25L.36, A/HRC/25/L37, A/HRC/25/L.38, A/HRC/25/L.39, A/HRC/25/L.40. Explanation of Position by the Delegation of the United States of America, delivered by Paula G. Schriefer, Human Rights Council 25th Session, Geneva, March 27, 2014, https://geneva.usmission.gov/2014/03/28/us-remains-deeply-troubled-by-hrcs-stand-alone-agenda-item-directed-against-israel.

(the Rambam), was a Muslim. In 2009 the agency labeled Jerusalem as "a capital of Arab culture."[19]

Professor Alan Dershowitz's Condemnation of the UN

On September 22, 2011, Harvard professor of criminal law Alan Dershowitz exposed the falsity inherent in the "Zionism is racism" libel and, more generally, in the UN stance on Israel. Professor Dershowitz's remarks, delivered at the Hudson Institute in New York, across the street from UN headquarters, touch the heart of internationalized human rights matters as advocated by the United Nations.[20] The most relevant of his remarks are here summarized:

- The UN facilitated terrorism, stood idly by genocide, gave a platform to Holocaust deniers, and did not give any incentive to the Palestinians for negotiating a reasonable two-state solution.
- In the dramatic year of 1975 when between two and three million Cambodians were being murdered by Pol Pot, the United Nations devoted all of its time to debating whether Zionism was racism and did not spend one single session trying to stop the bloodshed in Cambodia.
- Years later, genocides were taking place in Rwanda and Darfur, but the United Nations was debating the building of houses on the West Bank of the Jordan River.
- How many times have the rights of women, the rights of gays, and the rights of minorities been ignored because the United Nations had no time for these "minor" rights as they had to focus on the "major oppressor of the world," namely Israel.
- The official, open policy of the Palestine Liberation Organization, of Fatah, and of Hamas is to murder Israelis, as well as Jews wherever found. This violates the UN charter, yet the UN gradually implemented important steps in favor of the Palestinians.
- You cannot even get into the UN if you are representing some oppressed group, whether it be the Tibetans, the Kurds, the Armenians, or the Chechens.

19. See Glick, *The Israeli Solution*, 180.
20. Professor Dershowitz's speech was delivered at the conference The Perils of Global Intolerance: The United Nations and Durban III, the Hudson Institute, New York, September 22, 2011, https://www.youtube.com/watch?v=DDOA3_vZIzc.

- The United Nations has become the main advocacy arm for one group of people, the Palestinians.
- Regarding the "two-state solution," those countries that do not recognize the right of Israel's existence should not be allowed to vote. Their vote is an exercise in hypocrisy since they are actually voting for one state only – the Palestinian one.
- The United Nations, while making a long series of demands on Israel, never made any demand on the other side. "I challenge you to find any document of the United Nations which demands of Palestine to do A, B, C, or D. They simply do not exist."
- The undemocratic Palestinian Constitution calls for one official established religion – Islam – and states that the primary source of legislation will be sharia law. What will be with the rights of the Christians?
- The Palestinians affirm that their state will not allow any Jew in its territory, by which it will become the first officially *judenrein* state since the end of Nazi Germany. Why should the Palestinians change this policy if the United Nations does not demand it?
- How dare states such as Saudi Arabia, Cuba, Venezuela, Zimbabwe, Iran, Bahrain, Syria, Belarus and other tyrannies lecture Israel about human rights? How dare Turkey, which has attacked its own Kurdish and Armenian minorities, and Russia, which has attacked its own Chechen minority, or so many other states that have brutally repressed their minorities, lecture Israel?
- The United Nations has become the main advocacy arm for one group of people, the Palestinians, and thereby neglected the rights of so many other peoples, such as the Kurds, Armenians, and Chechens.
- Does no one recognize the need for a single neutral standard of human rights? Have human rights now become the permanent weapon of choice for those who practice human wrongs?

And the illustrious Harvard law professor concluded his condemnation with the following words:

Tiny Israel has contributed more to the progress of the world, more to the welfare of the world, more to the hope for peace than almost all of the nations combined that sit in that building. Think of how many lives Israel has saved through its medical technology, how many Arab and Muslim lives have been saved through Israel's medical technology. How much benefit has been achieved by Israel's environmental breakthroughs, how much Israel has done to feed the hungry with its agricultural development which it exports to the world. How much Israel has done to help those afflicted by natural disasters, as Israel is always the first to be there.... And Israel has done more, contributed more to the world in teaching them how to fight terrorism within the rule of law.

To Professor Dershowitz's heavy accusations and hearty message, let's add that one and a half million Arabs live in Israel as citizens of the state. They vote and are voted for, with thirteen members in parliament, as well as eminent judges in all courts, including in the Supreme Court. Israeli hospitals treat all their patients – Jews, Christians, and Muslims – with the same care, and these institutions have many Arab doctors and nurses that treat Jews and Christians in the most natural way. Israel's universities are open to Arab students. Twenty percent of Haifa University's students are Israeli Arabs. Arabs have begun to enter the Israeli diplomatic service. Private companies and the public sector contract Arab workers on all levels.

Various studies have demonstrated that no Arab citizen of Israel would want to move to any Arab country, since in Israel they enjoy absolute religious and political freedom, in addition to a reasonable-to-good standard of living, and they benefit from the state's medical assistance and social security, on the very same level as the state's Jewish citizens. On any day of the week the malls of the cities in the vicinity of Arab villages are full of Arab families busy shopping or sitting in the restaurants and coffee shops. They live a normal life and are treated by the government, the enterprises, and the Jewish population in the most natural and friendly manner. They practice their religion in Israel in accordance with their own wishes: some are very orthodox, following all Muslim religious prescriptions, others totally liberal, a freedom they do not enjoy in the majority of the Arab states.

As Gabriela Shalev, ambassador of Israel to the United Nations, stated:

Victims of the most severe violations of their most basic rights in the Democratic Republic of the Congo, Sudan, North Korea, Afghanistan, Somalia, Iran, Myanmar, Zimbabwe and elsewhere cry out for their plight to be heard, for their suffering to be redressed by the international community.

Still the United Nations reserve the overwhelming majority of its condemnation for Israel. This can only be interpreted as politically correct modern anti-Semitism.[21]

The Palestinian National Charter: The Annihilation of Israel

Seven years before the "Zionism is racism" resolution of the General Assembly of the United Nations – in July 1968 – the Palestine National Council approved the "Palestinian National Charter," which vehemently sets out its anti-Zionist philosophy. Its most important points are reproduced here:

> Article 9 – Armed struggle is the only way to liberate Palestine. Thus it is the overall strategy, not merely a tactical phase. The Palestinian Arab people assert their absolute determination and firm resolution to continue their armed struggle and to work for an armed popular revolution for the liberation of their country and their return to it. They also assert their right to normal life in Palestine and to exercise their right to self-determination and sovereignty over it.

> Article 19 – The partition of Palestine in 1947 and the establishment of the state of Israel are entirely illegal, regardless of the passage of time, because they were contrary to the will of the Palestinian people and to their natural right in their homeland, and inconsistent with the principles embodied in the Charter of the United Nations, particularly the right to self-determination.

> Article 20 – The Balfour Declaration, the Mandate for Palestine, and every-thing that has been based upon them, are deemed null and void. Claims of historical or religious ties of Jews with Palestine are incompatible with the fact of history and the true conception of what constitutes statehood. Judaism, being a religion, is not an independent nationality. Nor do Jews constitute a single nation with an identity of its own; they are citizens of the states to which they belong.[22]

21. *Jerusalem Post*, November 15, 2013, 20. Shalev's speech was delivered at the College of International Affairs, National Cheng Chin University, Taiwan.
22. The Arabs insist on denying the millenary ties of the Jews to Holy Land, to Jerusalem, to the Temple Mount, to the First and Second Holy Temples. By that – as already pointed out in an earlier chapter – they are also denying the history of Christianity which started with Jesus Christ and his visits to the Temple in Jerusalem, as described in various passages of the New Testament (for example, Luke 2 and Mark 11:15).

Article 22 – Zionism is a political movement organically associated with international imperialism and antagonistic to all action for liberation and to progressive movements in the world. It is racist and fanatic in its nature, aggressive, expansionist, and colonial in its aims, and fascist in its methods. Israel is the instrument of the Zionist movement, and geographical base for world imperialism placed strategically in the midst of the Arab homeland to combat the hopes of the Arab nation for liberation, unity and progress. Israel is a constant source of threat vis-à-vis peace in the Middle East and the whole world. Since the liberation of Palestine will destroy the Zionist and imperialist presence and will contribute to the establishment of peace in the Middle East, the Palestinian people look for the support of all the progressive and peaceful forces and urge them all, irrespective of their affiliation and beliefs, to offer the Palestinian people all aid and support in their just struggle for the liberation of their homeland.

Article 23 – The demand of security and peace, as well as the demand of right and justice, require all states to consider Zionism an illegitimate movement, to outlaw its existence, and to ban its operations, in order that friendly relations among peoples may be preserved, and the loyalty of citizens to their respective homelands safeguarded.[23]

This was followed by the Palestinian 1974 Political Program which states, among its ten articles, the following:

Article 1 – To reaffirm the Palestine Liberation Organization's previous attitude to Resolution 242, which obliterates the national right of our people and deals with the cause of our people as a problem of refugees. The Council therefore refuses to have anything to do with this resolution at any level, Arab or international, including the Geneva Conference.

Article 2 – The Liberation Organization will employ all means, and first and foremost armed struggle, to liberate Palestinian territory and to establish the independent combatant national authority for the people over every part of Palestinian territory that is liberated. This will require

23. "The PLO Charter," http://www.iris.org.il/plochart.htm. See also http://avalon.law .yale.edu/20th_century/plocov.asp.

further changes being effected in the balance of power in favor of our people and their struggle.

Article 3 – The Liberation Organization will struggle against any proposal for a Palestinian entity the price of which is recognition, peace, secure frontiers, renunciation of national rights and the deprival of our people of their right to return and their right to self-determination on the soil of their homeland.[24]

From the principles established in these proclamations it is clear and undeniable that the basic, fundamental intention of the Palestinian National Charter is the elimination of the State of Israel.

All Arab promises of revoking the charter and substituting it with a new one have never been implemented. No new charter has been drawn up, nor has a legal committee been set up to rewrite one. In fact, very much to the contrary, statements by Arab leaders indicate that the PLO Charter remains in force. At the Sixth General Conference of the PLO in 2009, Abu Mazen (aka Mahmoud Abbas) declared that the PLO Charter of 1968 constituted part of the identity of the Palestine Liberation Organization and formed the basis of the organization's political program.[25]

The support that the Palestinian Charter requested from the world community in 1968 came in the form of the November 1975 "Zionism is racism" Resolution of the UN General Assembly, and though the resolution was revoked in 1991, the anti-Zionist, anti-Israel syndrome has been growing more malevolent from year to year.

The actual implementation of the murderous Palestinian approach to Israel and its citizens is nurtured from three sources – the schools, the mosques, and the Arab media. In these three frameworks Palestinians are constantly indoctrinated with hatred for Israel and urged to eliminate the state and its people.

As Caroline Glick, prominent Israeli journalist and author, has declared, Israel could take action to punish the Palestinians for their unlawful behavior, thereby preventing them from proceeding. "We can arrest their imams for

---

24. "The PLO's 'Phased Plan,'" IRIS, http://www.iris.org.il/plophase.htm.
25. Einhorn, "The Status of Judea and Samaria (The West Bank)," 23–24.

soliciting murder. We can close their schools and shutter their television stations for the same reason. But we have done none of these things."[26]

Abbas seeks to turn the West Bank into an Islamist state.[27]

The World Organization versus the State of Israel

In its inception, the UN demonstrated recognition and sympathy for the Jewish tragedy in the Nazi era, as demonstrated by the debates of the Human Rights Commission when it was drafting the Universal Declaration of Human Rights and the Convention on Genocide (1946–48), followed by Resolution 181 – the partition plan that made possible the proclamation of the Jewish state (1947). Yet just one generation later (1975) the United Nations made a 180-degree turn and established an entirely biased policy regarding the Jewish State of Israel. The UN betrayed its original positions, proclamations, and resolutions by supporting the determination of the Arabs who call themselves "Palestinians" to destroy the State of Israel and annihilate the survivors of the Holocaust.

That is what the United Nations General Assembly endorsed in 1975 by approving the "Zionism is racism" racist resolution.

Notwithstanding the revocation of the calumny in 1991, the United Nations, through its General Assembly, the Security Council and the Council (formerly Commission) on Human Rights, has grown into the great enemy of the State of Israel – the headquarters of the libel against the Jewish state (and consequently of the Jewish people). This was again demonstrated in the 2014 Gaza war, when rockets were found in a UN school and returned by the international organization to the terrorists, while at the same time the Human Rights Council decided to establish a commission to investigate "Israel's war crimes in Gaza" – meaning that the council concluded that Israel had perpetrated war crimes before any investigation began. The council had done the same in the past, notably when Israel defended itself from Hamas rockets in 2009, through Operation Cast Lead. To preside over the commission on the 2014 Operation Protective Edge, the council nominated a known Israel basher,

26. Caroline Glick, "The Names of the Victims," *Jerusalem Post*, June 27, 2014.
27. Khaled Abu Toameh, an Arab Israeli journalist, writes that Abbas has chosen to align himself with Hamas and Islamic Jihad. "Abbas Paving the Way to Turn West Bank into an Islamist State," Gatestone Institute, March 20, 2015, http://www.gatestoneinstitute .org/5419/west-bank-islamist-state.

Professor William Schabas, who in a recent statement had advocated bringing Israel's Prime Minister Netanyahu to the International Criminal Court.

Aryeh Neier, founding director of Human Rights Watch and a colleague of Schabas's in the Paris School of International Affairs, declared that Schabas should recuse himself, adding that "any judge who had previously called for the indictment of the defendant would recuse himself."[28]

Hamas commits two war crimes concomitantly: Hamas launches rockets on populated areas of Israel and does it from populated areas in Gaza, so that when Israel defends itself by hitting the sources of the rocket launching, it ends up causing civilian casualties. Hamas could launch its rockets from sparsely populated areas, but then the Hamas members would suffer the consequences and practically no Gaza civilians would be victimized. As was widely observed by Israeli prime minister Benjamin Netanyahu and others during the war, while Israel uses missiles to protect its civilians, Hamas uses its civilians to protect its missiles.

Alan Dershowitz reminds the world community that "when a criminal takes a hostage and uses him as a shield from behind whom he fires at civilians or at the police, and if a policeman fires back and kills the hostage, it is the criminal and not the policeman who is guilty of murder. So too with Hamas: when it uses human shields and the Israeli army fires back and kills some of the shields, it is Hamas that is responsible for their deaths."[29]

Similarly, Dershowitz lays blame at the United Nations' feet for setting up shelters for civilians right in the middle of areas that are being used to launch rockets, rather than evacuating civilians to safer, less populated areas. This is overt complicity of the world organization with the Hamas terrorists.[30]

In the 1930s and '40s, Franklin Delano Roosevelt's government and the British Foreign Office became accomplices to Hitler, as demonstrated in chapters 2–4 above. By 2014, everyone who has eyes to see, ears to hear, and

28. "Exclusive: Schabas' Own Colleague, Human Rights Icon Aryeh Neier, Calls for Him to Quit UN Gaza Probe Due to Prior Statements," October 1, 2014, UN Watch, http://www .unwatch.org/exclusive-schabas-own-colleague-human-rights-icon-aryeh-neier-calls-for-him-to-leave-un-gaza-probe/. Professor Schabas eventually resigned from the commission when it was revealed that he had received payment from Hamas for a legal opinion.
29. Alan Dershowitz, "The Empty Spaces in Gaza," *Jerusalem Post*, August 6, 2014, http:// www.jpost.com/LandedPages/PrintArticle.aspx?id=370210.
30. Ibid.

a little common sense will realize that the United Nations has become a full-fledged accomplice of the Palestinian terrorist. They are followed by the media, which corrupts the description of what goes on in the defensive war of Israel against the cowardly attacks of the Hamas terrorist and obfuscates about the multiple problems occurring in the West Bank, stemming from the Palestinian terrorist activities. Their allegation concerning Israel's occupation has no basis, as explained in chapter 10. Yet these lies generate anti-Israel sentiment and lead to the demonization of the Jewish state and the growth of world antisemitism.

On November 14, 2013, the General Assembly of the United Nations once again voted on nine separate resolutions condemning Israel while ignoring every other conflict, every other tragedy going on throughout the globe, all of which involve far greater numbers of people and far more serious human suffering.

At one point during the course of the voting, one of the translators was accidentally caught on a hot mic saying what she really thought about what was going on: "I think when you have ... like a total of ten resolutions on Israel and Palestine, there's gotta be something, *c'est un peu trop, non?* [It's a bit much, no?] I mean, I know ... there's other really bad s**t happening but no one says anything about the other stuff."

When the translator realized that this "unscheduled bout of candor," as Jonathan S. Tobin referred to it in *Commentary* magazine, was being broadcast, she immediately apologized, and an official announcement was made that there was "a problem with the interpretation." As Tobin quips, "Never have truer words been spoken at the United Nations."[31]

This demonization of the State of Israel, of its institutions, of its army, has been spreading all over Europe. In Belgium a government-funded website was discovered hosting lesson plans comparing Israelis to Nazis, including cartoon images of Gazans as concentration camp inmates. The Simon Wiesenthal Center identified this as "a classic example of Holocaust inversion," portraying the Israelis as the new Nazis.[32]

31. Jonathan S. Tobin, "Correct Translation? The UN Is a Joke," *Commentary*, http://www.commentarymagazine.com/2013/11/15/correct-translation-the-united-nations-i., accessed on July 31, 2014.

32. Sam Sokol, "Anti-Semitism in the Guise of Holocaust Education?" *Jerusalem Post*,

Palestinian Terrorism

The territory that has been causing continuous problems for the last century is the land that was under Jewish sovereignty two thousand years ago. We refer to the territory that today constitutes the State of Israel, the territories of Samaria and Judea (the "West Bank"), the territory of Gaza, and the territory of the present Hashemite Kingdom of Jordan. This is also the land where Christianity was born, the land that was invaded by the Greeks and then by the Romans, who expelled the Jews from their homeland and brought about the Diaspora.

The Arabs, on the other hand, are latecomers. As Rabbi Stewart Weiss observes:

> Despite [the Arabs'] attempt to fabricate history and claim they are an "ancient, indigenous" people with a distinct culture, language, dress, etc., the facts prove clearly otherwise. In 1857, British Consul James Finn observed that "the country is, in a considerable degree, empty of its inhabitants." A decade later, in 1867, the president of Harvard University, Charles W. Eliot, visited [the Holy Land] and noted: "A beautiful sea lies unbosomed among the Galilean hills, in the midst of the land once possessed by Zebulun, Naftali, Asher and Dan. Life here was once idyllic; now it is a scene of desolation and misery." And in the same year, the famous American author Mark Twain also visited the Holy Land and testified: "This is a desolate country, a silent mournful expanse. There are two or three small clusters of Beduin tents, but not a single permanent habitation. One may ride 10 miles and not see 10 human beings."
>
> But then, when the Jews began to return to Zion in the beginning of the 20th century [small groups arrived at the end of the nineteenth century] and bring the long-dormant land back to life, the surrounding Arabs decided to jump on the bandwagon and get in on a good thing. There was massive Arab immigration during the British Mandate and, while England turned a blind eye to this influx – illegal, by their own admission – it severely limited Jewish immigration....
>
> The Palestinians themselves, in rare moments of candor, acknowledge the charade of a Palestinian "people." Walid Shoebat, an Arab terrorist,

September 18, 2013, http://www.jpost.com/Jewish-World/Jewish-News/Report-Belgian-government-website-compares-Israel-to-Nazi-Germany-326501.

makes it clear: "Today's Palestinians are immigrants from throughout the region – Yemen, Saudi Arabia, Morocco, the Jordanians next door. My grandfather in Bethlehem told me his village of Beit Sahur was empty before his father settled there with six families." And PLO official Zahir Muhsein, in a 1977 interview with Dutch newspaper *Trouw*, admitted: "A Palestine 'people' does not exist. The creation of a Palestinian state is only a means of continuing our struggle against the State of Israel. There is just one people – the Arab nation – and only for political and tactical reasons do we speak today about the existence of a 'Palestinian people.'"[33]

This reality of the Arab presence in the Holy Land is the theme of a very important book by Joan Peters, *From Time Immemorial*, in which the author, after painstaking research in the Foreign Offices of England and France as well as many other sources, demonstrates how the territory that eventually became the State of Israel was a wasteland in the 1880s and an insignificant number of Arabs were living there. When Jews began coming from Europe to work on the land, Arabs from different parts of the Middle East arrived, attracted by the possibilities of working and earning a living from the Jewish settlers. The Ottomans welcomed this Arab immigration, which grew even more in the period of the British, who stimulated their coming while raising difficulties to Jewish immigration. And so the "Palestinian" narrative of Arabs living "from time immemorial in the Palestine that became Israel" is totally devoid of truth.[34]

Many violent eruptions have occurred in this land in the last hundred years: the Arab attacks against the Jewish population in the early years of the twentieth century, especially in the 1920s and 1930s; the 1948 onslaught of five Arab armies immediately after the proclamation of the Jewish state, which has become known as the War of Independence; the constant terrorist invasions of the 1950s and 1960s; the 1956 Sinai Campaign; the Six-Day War; the Yom Kippur War; the two wars in Lebanon; the two Intifadas; and the wars in Gaza.

The last of these occurrences have again raised the matter of civilian deaths

33. Stewart Weiss, "In Plain Language: In Place of a Jewish State," *Jerusalem Post Magazine*, November 28, 2014, 37, http://www.jpost.com/Opinion/In-Plain-Language-In-place-of -a-Jewish-state-383040.

34. Peters, *From Time Immemorial*, especially pages 240–45, 250–51, and 262.

during fighting, which has become one of the outstanding factors of the anti-Israeli policies of the United Nations, of the European Union, and of most of the democracies of the world. This is partly due to ignorance of the facts on the ground and partly to a bigoted narrative of the Arab propaganda blindly accepted by international organizations. These factors are aggravated by a highly prejudiced world media that does know the truth, but has become an accomplice to the murderous terrorism of the "Palestinians." Above all, the campaign against Israel regarding civilian deaths among the Arabs derives from traditional antisemitism.

As already observed above, when an enemy sends missiles from within its citizens' private homes, from its hospitals and schools, the other side reciprocates defensively by targeting the source of the attacks and, in consequence, civilians are killed. Who is to blame – the side that protects itself behind human shields, or the side that defends itself by responding to the enemy fire? If one doesn't return fire, there is no alternative but to let yourself be destroyed.

How is a country to fight against an enemy that does not observe human rights?

As Professor Yaffa Zilbershats of Bar-Ilan University affirms:

> There should be new rules to deal with issues such as reciprocity – whether one side has to observe international law restrictions if the other side does not, situations in which civilians attack civilians and commit their actions from civilian centers against other civilian centers.[35]

As already pointed out in an earlier chapter, the Fourth Geneva Convention of 1949 on the Protection of Civilians in Time of War provides that "the presence of a protected person may not be used to render certain points or areas immune from military operations." In the case of a protective measure against missile attacks, the rule is all the more applicable. And furthermore, there is no applicability of the Geneva Conventions to the case of the West Bank and Gaza Strip since the convention "is based on the assumption that

---

35. Dan Izenberg, "Dershowitz: 'International Court Doesn't Give Just Rulings,'" *Jerusalem Post*, March 19, 2008, http://www.jpost.com/International/Dershowitz-Intl-Court-doesnt-give-just-rulings.

there had been a sovereign who was ousted and that he had been a legitimate sovereign," which is not the case here, as explained above.[36]

The international entities have created a new, spurious international law that follows their abject political agenda. The European Union, for example, issued a statement on March 2, 2008 – when Israel was defending itself from a continuous rain of missiles coming from Gaza – urging Israel to "refrain from all activities that endanger civilians as such activities are contrary to international law." When thousands of missiles were being launched by Hamas on the south of Israel, the European Union did not utter a word of condemnation against Hamas, nor a word of support for the State of Israel. Only when Israel began defending itself, the union started lecturing Israel about how not to defend itself. This reveals blatant complicity with Israel's attackers.[37]

After Israel's defensive operation against Hamas, in 2009, the Human Rights Council of the UN ordered a report that accused Israel of war crimes and possible crimes against humanity. The author of the report, former judge Richard Goldstone, recanted his conclusions a few months later, declaring that "we know a lot more today about what happened in the Gaza war of 2008–09 than we did when I chaired the fact-finding mission appointed by the UN Human Rights Council that produced what has come to be known as the Goldstone Report. If I had known then what I know now, the Goldstone Report would have been a different document."[38] However, the damage the report had caused to Israel's reputation and the increase of bad will among the nations of the world and in the UN had been done.

On October 16, 2009, Colonel Richard Kemp appeared before the UN Human Rights Council to give his testimony on the military operations of the Israel Defense Forces in Gaza against Hamas. A former commander of British forces in Afghanistan, Colonel Kemp had served with NATO and with the

36. See former ICJ president Stephen Schwebel's editorial comment in chapter 10.
37. "The Law and Gaza," *Jerusalem Post*, March 6, 2008, internet edition.
38. Richard Goldstone, "Reconsidering the Goldstone Report on Israel and War Crimes," *Washington Post*, April 1, 20111, https://www.washingtonpost.com/opinions/reconsidering -the-goldstone-report-on-israel-and-war-crimes/2011/04/01/AFg111JC_story.html. It is very strange to have a man who spent his professional life judging declare that he signed a report to the United Nations without full knowledge of the facts and circumstances!

UN, having commanded military operations in North Ireland, Bosnia, and Macedonia and participated in the Gulf War.

Colonel Kemp listed some of the steps taken by Israel, such as dropping two million leaflets and making over one hundred thousand phone calls to warn civilians of the areas where military operations would have to be performed; he pointed out that the Israeli army had aborted missions that had been prepared to take out Hamas military capability, in order to prevent civilian casualties; he further noted that Israel had allowed humanitarian aid into Gaza during the conflict.

Kemp acknowledged that "of course innocent civilians were killed, war is chaos and full of mistakes. There have been mistakes by the British, Americans and other forces in Afghanistan and in Iraq, many of which can be put down to human error. But mistakes are not war crimes."

"More than anything," Kemp declared, "the civilian casualties were a consequence of Hamas' way of fighting. Hamas deliberately tried to sacrifice their own civilians."

And he concluded with the following statement: "Based on my knowledge and experience, I can say this: during Operation Cast Lead, the Israeli Defense Forces did more to safeguard the rights of civilians in the combat zones than any other army in the history of warfare."[39]

In 2014, the Israeli government decided to go back to a former practice that had been abandoned – the demolition of the terrorist's family's house in cases where the terrorist died. Beyond that, the government is considering the cancellation of Israeli citizenship of the terrorist's families, who would consequently lose their medical care and other privileges of social security.

Naturally, the permanent criticizers of Israeli's policies immediately condemned this practice as collective punishment, forbidden by the Fourth Geneva Convention on Protection of Civilians in Times of War (1949). Article 33 of the convention states that "no persons may be punished for an offense he or she has not personally committed. Collective penalties and likewise all measures of intimidation or of terrorism are prohibited." It also states that "reprisals against persons and their property are prohibited." Of course no

---

39. Col. Richard Kemp, testimony to UN Human Rights Council Special Session on behalf of UN Watch, October 16, 2009, https://www.youtube.com/watch?v=JMofTssoUX4.

critique was addressed at Egypt for destroying hundreds of home along the Rafah border to prevent Hamas from digging smuggling tunnels.

It so happens that Israel has established that if a Palestinian terrorist, ready to commit a murderous act, knew that his family would suffer as a consequence of his act, he would likely refrain from his criminal intent. So the measures taken against the family of a deceased terrorist serve as a deterrent to the next terrorist's criminal acts and ultimately result in saving lives.

As argued in chapters 6 and 10, the right to life stands above all other human rights. In this spirit, the right to life of future victims of terrorists stands higher than the property rights and social benefits of a terrorist's family. In addition, the Palestinian family is responsible for the hate education the terrorist received at home and so its members are accomplices to the terror act.

But article 33 also states that "all measures of intimidation or of terrorism are prohibited." Has this prohibition been raised in the halls of the United Nations, in the international media, in the work of the human rights organizations that are so keen on defending the families of terrorists from collective punishment? Has article 33 been invoked to condemn the continuous chain of terrorist acts against the civilian population of Israel?

Interestingly enough, the next article in the Geneva Convention – article 34 – determines that "the taking of hostages is prohibited." Has anybody heard any reference to this rule in the successive taking of hostages by the various Palestinian terrorist organizations, mainly Hamas and Hezbollah? Did any nongovernmental organization, any human rights institution raise this rule when Gilad Schalit was kept hostage by Hamas for over five years from 2006 to 2011?

The incoherence, the inconsistencies, the cynicism, the hypocrisy, the falsity of all those who criticize Israel's policies is so clearly evident that it is nothing more than the demonization of the Jewish state – the modern version of antisemitism.

The One-Sidedness of Certain Legal Literature

The American scholar's mode of publishing "Legal Texts and Materials" – collections of all kinds of texts published in different sources – is an easy endeavor, as it does not necessarily require the author or authors to take a position on the matters that the publication deals with; it is simply a matter of choosing and copying texts from other authors and different kinds of sources – from legal literature to newspaper materials to statements of private organizations. At most, at the end the editors will provide questions related to the materials published.

Naturally, the choice of the materials can indicate the position of the authors of the collected materials. Such is the case with the over fifteen-hundred-page collection on international human rights by Philip Alston and Ryan Goodman. The editors inserted a few short materials on Israel's 2009 reaction to Hamas's continuous bombarding of civil targets in the south of Israel, practically all of which derive from official reports that criticize and condemn Israel for its military reactions against Gaza and for the deaths of Gazan civilians during these operations. The editors bring almost none of the various available materials demonstrating that Hamas utilizes its civilians as shields to protect themselves and forces civilians to stay in the locations from which they launch rockets on Israeli territory. There are only a few lines from the Israel Ministry of Foreign Affairs as an "Initial Response to the Fact Find-ing Mission on Gaza." The materials naturally include Human Rights Council decisions on the deaths of civilians as well as on the "Occupied Palestinian Territory, including East Jerusalem and the Occupied Syrian Golan." But not a word on the crimes against humanity by Hamas in its constant attacks against the civilian populations of the south of Israel.[40]

As a matter of fact, the book does not include materials on Hamas and Hezbollah, the two organizations that plan and execute terrorist acts against the State of Israel. It also does not deal with the charter of the Palestine Liberation Organization (PLO) and its murderous contents regarding the Jewish state. Not even the serious violations of human rights of members of its own communities – executed without trial – are dealt with in the long collection of texts and materials.

However, the authors could not avoid reporting that the Western Group in the UN consider that the existence of a separate item of the Human Rights Council dedicated exclusively to Israel is discriminatory and evidence of a double standard that singles out Israel and downplays other situations of grave concern. In this spirit the authors refer to the UN secretary-general's expression of concern at the council's "disproportionate focus on violations by Israel. Not that Israel should be given a free pass. Absolutely not. But the

---

40. Alston and Goodman, *International Human Rights*, 720–28.

Council should give the same attention to grave violations committed by other states as well."[41]

Another concession the authors make is when they refer to the internal situation of the State of Israel, on which they report that "in terms of Israel's domestic human rights situation, the relationship with the relevant UN treaty bodies has been consistently positive."[42]

The UN as Accomplice to Terrorists

In chapter 9 I dealt with the UN's position on terrorism, a subject that must be further elaborated upon. On March 23, 2007, John Dugard, a UN "special rapporteur" on human rights, delivered to the Council on Human Rights an "analysis" of Israel's "colonialism and apartheid," denouncing the purported way in which the Palestinians are "brutally subjugated by a Western-affiliated regime." The envoy was given shows of support from the likes of council members Cuba and Pakistan, as well as the "observer" states Sudan, Syria, and Iran. The latter accused Israel of "terrorist activities."[43]

Dugard's statement received a strong rebuttal from Hillel Neuer, the courageous and valiant executive director of the NGO UN Watch, who spoke thus:

> Mr. President
>
> Six decades ago, in the aftermath of the Nazi horrors, Eleanor Roosevelt, René Cassin and other eminent figures gathered here, on the banks of Lake Geneva, to reaffirm the principle of human dignity. They created the Commission on Human Rights. Today, we ask: What has become of their noble dream?
>
> In this session we see the answer. Faced with compelling reports from around the world of torture, persecution and violence against women, what has the Council pronounced, and what has it decided?
>
> Nothing. Its response has been silence. Its response has been indifference. Its response has been criminal.

41. Ibid., 720.
42. Ibid., 727.
43. "Your U.N. at Work," *Wall Street Journal*, March 30, 2007.

One might say, in Harry Truman's words, that this has become a Do-Nothing, Good-for-Nothing Council.

But that would be inaccurate. This Council has, after all, done something.

It has enacted one resolution after another condemning one single state: Israel. In eight pronouncements – and there will be three more this session – Hamas and Hizbullah have been granted impunity. The entire rest of the world – millions upon millions of victims in 191 countries – continues to be ignored. So yes, the Council is doing something. And the Middle East dictators who orchestrate this campaign will tell you it is a very good thing. That they seek to protect human rights. Palestinian rights.

So too, the racist murderers and rapists of Darfur women tell us they care about the rights of the Palestinian women; the occupiers of Tibet care about the occupied; and the butchers of Muslims in Chechnya care about Muslims.

But do these self-proclaimed defenders truly care about Palestinian rights?

Let us consider the past four months. More than 130 Palestinians were killed by Palestinian forces. This is three times the combined total that was the pretext for calling special sessions against Israel in July and November. The champions of Palestinian rights – Ahmadinejad, Assad, Khaddafi, John Dugard – they say nothing. Little 3-year-old boy Salam Balousha and his two brothers were murdered in their car by [Palestinian National Authority] Prime Minister Haniyeh's troops. Why has this Council chosen silence?

Because Israel could not be blamed, because, in truth, the despots who run this Council couldn't care less about Palestinians or about any human rights.

They seek to demonize Israeli democracy, to delegitimize the Jewish state, to scapegoat the Jewish people. They also seek something else. To distort and pervert the very language and idea of human rights.

You ask: What has become of the founders' dream? Of Eleanor Roosevelt, of René Cassin, of John Humphrey, P.C. Chang, Charles Malik, who assembled here in Geneva sixty years ago? With terrible lies and moral inversion, it is being turned into a nightmare. Thank you, Mr. President.[44]

44. Hillel Neuer, "Human Rights Nightmare," speech before UN Human Rights Council

The Human Rights Council president Mr. Luis Alfonse de Alba, of Mexico, reacted in the following manner:

> For the first time in this session I will not express thanks for that statement. I shall point out to the distinguished representative of the organization that just spoke, the distinguished representative of United Nations Watch, if you'd kindly listen to me. I am sorry that I'm not in a position to thank you for your statement. I should mention that I will not tolerate any similar statements in the Council. The way in which members of this Council were referred to, and indeed the way in which the council itself was referred to, all of this is inadmissible. In the memory of the persons that you referred to, founders of the Human Rights Commission, and for the good of human rights, I would urge you in any future statements to observe some minimum proper conduct and language. Otherwise, any statement you make in similar tones to those used today will be taken out of the records.[45]

In its edition of March 30 of the same year (2007), the *New York Sun* referred to a collection of clips organized by UN Watch:

> One can watch and hear an envoy from Nigeria assert that "stoning under Sharia law for unnatural sexual acts... should not be equated with extrajudicial killings..." Or watch an envoy from Iran defend the Holocaust denial conference. Or watch a defense of the Hezbollah terrorist organization. Or speaker after speaker liken Israel to the Nazis, only to get thanked by Mr. de Alba or whoever is presiding.[46]

The next day, in its March 31 edition, the *National Post* reports that on Friday, the council wrapped up its fourth session since its inception. Despite evidence from its own investigator that the genocide in the Darfur region of Sudan was being perpetrated by that country's dictatorial Islamist government, the council was unable even to call the mass killings a genocide, much less pin blame on Khartoum. Muslim and African representatives would permit only an expression of "deep concern" for the murder of hundreds of thousands,

4th Session, March 23, 2007, UN Watch, http://secure.unwatch.org/site/apps/nlnet
/content2.aspx?c=bdKKISNqEmG&b=1313923&ct=3698367&printmode=1.
45. Ibid.
46. Ibid.

the displacement of two million or more, and the systematic rape of women and girls.

On July 16, 2014, the UN Office for the Coordination of Humanitarian Affairs (OCHA) issued a report stating that "the Israeli military delivered text messages to virtually all the residents of Ash Shuja'iyya and Az Zaitun neighborhoods in eastern Gaza city, approximately 100,000 people, warning them to leave their homes by 8 am, ahead of attacks to be launched in the area." The Israel Defense Forces also made phone calls and distributed leaflets.

The OCHA then describes what came next: "Subsequently, the Palestinian Ministry of Interior in Gaza reportedly instructed the residents to...not flee the area." As a result, OCHA admits that the vast majority decided to stay.

This report indicates two important points: that Israel adhered to the Geneva Convention demand of providing "effective advance warning" to civilians and that Hamas violated the rule forbidding parties to "direct the movement of civilians in order to shield military objectives from attack."

What was Hamas trying to protect when it used Palestinians as human shields?

The IDF refers to Shuja'iyya as the Hamas "terror fortress" in the Gaza Strip, having found there more than ten openings to tunnels and since July (2014) Hamas fired over 140 rockets at Israel from this neighborhood alone. The IDF chief of general staff Benny Gantz declared that Hamas has built a war machine in residential areas.

Four days later, on July 20, came the outrageous reaction of UN secretary-general Ban Ki-moon, as he declared that "dozens more civilians, including children, have been killed in Israeli military strikes in the Shuja'iyya neighborhood in Gaza. I condemn this atrocious action. Israel must exercise maximum restraint and do far more to protect civilians."

Ban Ki-moon said nothing about Hamas having failed to protect Gazan civilians. He said nothing about Hamas having put civilians directly in harm's way. In fact he said nothing about any "atrocious action" by Hamas. He also made no demand that Hamas "restrain" itself from fulfilling its stated goal, namely the destruction of the State of Israel. And, of course, he did not mention a word about all the efforts by the Israeli army to move Arab civilians out of harm's way, as recognized by a UN body.

The secretary-general of the UN said nothing about UNRWA discovering rockets in one of its schools and promptly giving them back to the rocketeers – or as the UNRWA spokesman Chris Gunness delicately called them, "the local authorities."

These attitudes of Ban Ki-moon and of the UNRWA amount to outright complicity with the Hamas terrorists.[47]

Israel has repeatedly warned that rockets were being launched from schools, clinics, hospitals, mosques, humanitarian facilities, and other civilian localities. Israel urged the UN to handle this issue, warning that terrorists were hiding missiles within classrooms and storerooms. The UN did not even bother to check and certainly did nothing to clear those facilities. And then the organization has the chutzpah to criticize Israel when it tries to destroy the sources of the thousands of rockets that had been launched against its civilians.

The United Nations Commissioner for Human Rights from 2008 to 2014, South African Navi Pillay, constantly criticized Israel for "excessive use of force" and never had a word of critique for the Hamas terrorists. At the 2009 Durban III conference, held in Geneva and convened to "strengthen political commitment to fight racism," Mahmoud Ahmadinejad, at the time president of Iran, delivered a condemnation of Israel as "totally racist." Sitting right behind Ahmadinejad, Mrs. Pillay did not utter a word of protest about his noxious speech or about those who would applaud such hate, but she did criticize Canada and others for not sitting in on the session. The Durban III conference was chaired by Libya, Iran, and Cuba – three of the most prominent violators of human rights; on that occasion the West was lectured for not doing enough about human rights abuses by none other than Zimbabwe's Robert Mugabe, the great violator.[48]

On July 23, 2014, at a UN Human Rights Council emergency session on the situation in Gaza, Hillel Neuer made another important intervention regarding Israel's defensive reaction to a constant shower of rockets that Hamas was sending over practically the entire territory of Israel. He declared:

47. These points are contained in a report on the UN's bigoted attitude toward Israel's Operation Pillar of Defense: Anne Bayefsky, "Ban Ki-moon's Shameful Message in Israel's Hour of Need," *Jerusalem Post*, July 22, 2014. http://www.jpost.com/LandedPages /PrintArticle.aspx?id=368415.
48. David Akin, "UN's a Massive Joke," *Toronto Sun*, September 25, 2011, http://www .torontosun.com/2011/09/23/uns-a-massive-joke.

An entire nation – towns, villages and cities, from the Negev Desert up to the Galilee, from the Judean hills of Jerusalem to the Tel Aviv seashore – has been under brutal and relentless attack, from more than two thousand mortars, rockets and long-range missiles, fired from Gaza toward civilians in every part of the Holy Land.

Never before, in the modern history of nations, has a free and democratic society come under such sustained bombardment from a terrorist organization, one that openly strives for and celebrates the murder of civilians, and that, as its general worldview, glorifies death.

I turn now to the resolution upon which this Council will soon vote. The text before us denounces Israel, denies its right to self-defense, and disregards Hamas war crimes.

We ask: why does this Council refuse to say that which was said only two weeks ago by the Palestinian ambassador himself? In an extraordinary moment of candor, Palestinian Ambassador Ibrahim Khraishi admitted, on Palestinian TV, that "each and every Palestinian missile launched against Israel civilians constitutes a crime against humanity."

Can any UN entity, or any individual, be truly for human rights when they refuse to say that which was said by the Palestinian ambassador himself?

Is it possible that the true purpose of this session is to silence the true victims and voices of human rights around the world by deflecting attention from the world's worst abuses?

We ask all those who embrace hypocrisy and double standards: if in the past year you didn't cry out when thousands of protesters were killed and injured by Turkey, Egypt and Libya; when more victims than ever were hanged by Iran; women and children in Afghanistan were bombed; whole communities were massacred in South Sudan; hundreds in Pakistan were killed by jihadist terror attacks; 10,000 Iraqis were killed by terrorists –

At this point of the exposition by the UN Watch, Egypt's ambassador interrupted Mr. Neuer to raise a point of order, saying that "I think we are meeting today for the special session to discuss the current crisis in Gaza and the violations committed within this crisis, so I don't see why we have a reason to discuss other issues relating to human rights situations on other countries."

The ambassadors of the United States, of Canada, and of Israel urged the president of the council to allow Mr. Neuer to proceed, as the cases that occurred in other countries were relevant to the subject.

This was opposed by the representatives of the great democracies of Venezuela, Iran, and Cuba, which opposed further references foreign to the subject matter under consideration.

The president of the session returned the floor to UN Watch, requesting that he adhere to the matter under discussion.

As he got the floor again, Mr. Neuer observed that the Palestinian ambassador, who had also intervened, did not deny the remarks he had made on TV regarding the crimes against humanity perpetrated by Hamas.

And he closed his intervention with the following remarks:

> Finally, we ask: If those who refuse to speak out for Palestinians – 1800 Palestinians, if not more – who were starved to death, murdered by Assad in Syria, but you only cry out when Israel can be blamed, then you are not pro human rights, you are only anti-Israel.

As the ambassador of Syria again raised an objection, Mr. Hillel Neuer concluded:

> Let the world note that in a session purportedly on Palestinian human rights, the government of Syria objected to us mentioning the 1800 Palestinians that they starved and murdered.[49]

After that the UN Human Rights Council had no problem in approving an international inquiry into Israel's violation during Operation Pillar of Defense and, as already noted, nominating as its president the bigoted anti-Israel professor William Schabas.

The Malignant International Red Cross

Consistent with the anti-Jewish policy it followed during the Second World War, the International Committee of the Red Cross has been the initiator of condemnations against the State of Israel's presence in the West Bank, denominating it as the Occupied Palestinian Territories and applying to them

---

49. Hillel Neuer, testimony at the UN Human Rights Council Emergency Session on Gaza, July 23, 2014, UN Watch, http://www.unwatch.org/unw-testimony-at-unhrc-urgent-session-on-gaza/.

the Fourth Geneva Convention of 1949, of which the entity is the "official guardian."

Using this exclusive position it turned the convention –which was intended to ensure protection of civilians threatened by war – into a political hammer against Israel.

The territory of the West Bank is at best a disputed territory – actually it is the territory where the Jews lived and created their rich legal literature until the Romans' expulsion of its legitimate occupiers – and so it was destined to become the modern Jewish state by the Balfour Declaration and the British Mandate of Palestine. It was never under Arab rule and, as exposed in chapter 10, the Palestinians have absolutely no rights over it since their repudiation of the Partition Plan contained in UN Resolution 181, but the Red Cross insists not only on calling it occupied territory but also determining that it is under "illegal occupation." The Geneva Convention is concerned with humanitarian issues, the rights of protected persons, and has no mandate to designate new states.

The illegality of the International Red Cross's position is to refer to a territory as occupied, when this term only applies to a sovereign territory of another state. This is absolutely not the case with the West Bank, as it had not been under any state's sovereignty.

From "illegal occupation" the Red Cross jumped to the accusation that Israel commits "war crimes," "crimes against humanity," and "violations of international humanitarian law." Evidently this institution ignores all of the renowned public international law scholars who consider Israel's defensive occupation as perfectly legal. But the International Red Cross does not care about legal opinions as it proceeds with its persecutory policy against the Jews in the tradition it established during the Second World War.

In 2002, the International Red Cross was part of the international community that falsely accused Israel of committing a massacre in Jenin during Operation Defensive Shield. When it was finally proven that only terrorists had been targeted and that no civilian had died, the malignant institution did not retract its original accusation. Cornelio Sumaruga, former president of the International Red Cross, was part of a biased UN commission that was appointed to investigate the charges. He called the Star of David – symbol of the Magen David Adom – "a swastika."

In 2009, the International Red Cross accused Israel of killing 1,380 civilians and wounding 5,640 others, of attacking medical staff and ambulances during the IDF's incursion into Gaza to stop the rocket attacks, all based on Hamas reports. The institution made no distinction between terrorists and civilians, nor did it mention Hamas's use of civilians as human shields, or recognize Israel's right to self-defense.

The label "illegal occupation" has been repeatedly employed by the United Nations despite the fact that Resolution 242 (after the Six-Day War), when referring to "territories occupied in the recent conflict," does not specify which territories and, as explained in chapter 10, the resolution deals with states' territories and not with nonsovereign territories.

The Foul Media

Regarding the 2014 Gaza conflict, an American journalist, after criticizing Obama's policies toward Israel and the corruption prevalent in the UN, turned to the media and accused it of reporting casualty numbers, including the number of civilians killed, without a caveat that these numbers came from Hamas or their UN minions, or that terrorists don't wear uniforms and hence are counted as civilians. The media does not employ its critical faculties despite the Palestinian Arabs' long history of exaggerating statistics, faking photogenic atrocities like the "Jenin massacre" and the IDF's supposed killing of Muhammad al-Durrah (both found to be completely false), and tweeting gruesome images of dead women and children killed in other conflicts like Syria. The Palestinian Arabs have even taken scenes from horror movies and claimed that they happened in Gaza. It is incredible that the media, presumably dedicated to getting the story right and distrustful of information they can't confirm themselves, repeat as fact what is actually propaganda and do not bother to even preface such information with a statement such as "according to Hamas spokesmen" when repeating casualty numbers.[50]

A vehement accusation by the BBC and CNN was the subject of an advertisement published numerous times by the American Friends of Women for Israel's Tomorrow (Women in Green) at the time when Arafat was conducting a terrorist war against the citizens of Israel with daily suicide attacks. The ad said that these two TV stations were conducting an apparent war against

---

50. Bruce S. Thornton, "Obama and the U.N.'s Alternate Universe," August 1, 2014, *Frontpage Magazine*, http://victorhanson.com/wordpress/?p=7728.

the Jewish state and were indirectly encouraging Arafat to proceed with his terrorist war against Israel's civilian population. The text concludes by saying that "the almost daily Jewish deaths are attributable to the encouragement given Arafat by the unfair, uncritical, slanted and prejudicial news reporting of the BBC and CNN. Their behavior is immoral. The management of these TV stations should be held responsible for the mounting Jewish casualties."[51]

These two TV channels as well as various others have become addicted to lying, to misrepresenting, to inverting the facts – in sum, to accepting the Arab propaganda as facts on the ground and leading the world to a permanent state of abhorrence toward the State of Israel. This is classic complicity with war crimes, crimes against humanity, and atrocities of the worst kind.

On October 22, 2014, a Palestinian driver with a terrorist background (he had spent time in an Israeli jail for terrorism and was a family relation of a former head of Hamas's military wing) plowed into a group of innocent pedestrians at a light-rail stop, killing a three-month-old baby and a twenty-two-year-old woman and wounding six other people. When the terrorist tried to escape, he was shot and killed by police. The initial Associated Press headline was "Israeli Police Shoot Man in East Jerusalem." That he had intentionally run over people, killing two and wounding several others very seriously, that he was a known terrorist – all that was not relevant. Later, after an outcry, AP relented and revised the headline. And yet the URL of its post – news.yahoo. com/Israeli-police-shoot-man-east-jerusalem-153643679.html – retained the original headline for a while, even after the text had been revised.

On the same terrorist attack, *The Guardian* headline read: "Jerusalem Car Crash Funerals held." Under the headline, the newspaper noted that the victims were killed "when a car driven by a Palestinian man veered onto a Jerusalem pavement crowded with pedestrians."[52]

Another illustration of the maliciousness of the "foul press" (as Emile Zola referred to the French newspapers on the eve of the twentieth century regarding their antisemitic campaign with reference to the Dreyfus Affair): On the morning of November 18, 2014, two Palestinian terrorists marched into a synagogue in Jerusalem, in the neighborhood of Har Nof, and murdered

---

51. Ad published in *Jerusalem Post* of May 11, 2001, and in previous and subsequent editions.
52. Daniel Gordis, "Can We Please Stop Talking about 'Hasbara'?" *Jerusalem Post Magazine*, November 7, 2014, 34.

four eminent rabbis who were dressed in their ritual shawls, wearing their phylacteries, and reciting the morning prayers. Subsequently, the terrorists were killed. CNN advertised to the whole world that two Palestinians were killed by Israelis in Jerusalem. Only hours later, it adds that four Israeli Jews were also killed.

The perversion is manifest, and it repeats itself at every murderous event.

The anti-Israel attitude is a constant in the majority of the newspapers, television channels, news agencies, and other sources of public information all over the world. When it concerns the Jewish state, negative news is the basic orientation. The news about Israel has stopped having any semblance of journalism; it has become pure Arab propaganda.

The media has turned into a major accomplice of the Arab terrorist organizations, as these are encouraged to proceed with their murderous acts by the approval received from the foul press. The men and women responsible for this journalistic policy should know that they are partners to the murder of civilians, to the unprovoked attacks of Hamas, Hezbollah, and the other terrorist organizations in their campaign to destroy the Jewish state and annihilate its Jewish population. The owners and directors of these TV channels, news agencies, and newspapers, as well as their correspondents, should be tried for their participation in war crimes, crimes against humanity, and in the attempt to commit genocide.

In May 2015, Colonel Richard Kemp received an honorary doctorate from Bar-Ilan University. He delivered a lecture at the Begin-Sadat Center for Strategic Studies in which he reported on the consequences he had been suffering because of his testimony at the Human Rights Council in favor of the IDF's defensive campaign that it launched against Hamas in 2009. And thus he spoke:

> In social media I have been the subject of sustained assaults by particularly virulent anti-Israel and antisemitic networks. In universities I have been the subject of demonstrations that have sought to silence me. I have been accused of corruption and being in the pay of the Zionist entity. I have been deliberately denied business opportunities. I have been placed on a terrorist death list.
>
> That is not because I speak out against the moral bankruptcy, corruption, incitement to terrorism or oppression of the Palestinian Authority;

or the murder, brutality and terrorist violence of Hamas, Hezbollah, or the Palestinian Islamic Jihad. I have spoken out at least as much against al-Qaeda, the Taliban, the Iranian regime, the IRGC and many other sponsors of terror and terrorist groups without anything like this level of attempted intimidation.

Rather it is for one reason, and that is because I fail to falsely condemn Israel in circumstances where to even be neutral on the subject is itself a crime in the eyes of so many. It is because I have gone further, and used my military experience and my objective view to explain and defend Israel's legitimate military actions.

Consider: Hamas and other Palestinian terror groups use human shields in the hope that Israel will attack and kill their people. They do this for one purpose: to gain the global condemnation of the State of Israel. Their particular target is the media, which they know will magnify and intensify their message to the world and force national governments, the UN, human rights groups and other international organizations to bring down unbearable pressure onto Israel.... The terrorist strategy is executed through a conspiracy with a compliant and complicit media.

The media turn a blind eye to wrong-doing, corruption, law-breaking and immorality of one side; while exaggerating, falsifying, distorting and over-emphasizing allegations of wrong-doing against the other.[53]

Here we have complicity once again playing the role that leads to the impunity of the evildoer and the persecution of the victim. Then the complicity of England and America with the Nazis, now the complicity of the UN and the media with the Islamist terrorists; then at the cost of the Jewish people in Europe, now sacrificing the Jewish state in the Middle East.

The Collaboration of NGOs with Arab Terrorism

Immediately following the October 22, 2014, terrorist attack in Jerusalem (which killed a three-month-old baby and a young woman and injured several people), Human Rights Watch tweeted: "Palestinian deadly crash into train stop. Israel calls it 'terrorist attack... typical of Hamas.'" Days later, when the

---

53. David M. Weinberg, "British Commander Provides Hope to Turn Back the Tide against Israel," *Jerusalem Post*, May 22, 2015.

second victim died, more of the same: "Second fatality from Palestinian who drove car into Jerusalem train stop. Police treating it as a 'purposeful attack.'"

That is the constant policy of practically all nongovernmental organizations – accepting Arab propaganda, negatively advertising Israel's defense measures against terrorist attacks, and never referring to those as such. These organizations became spokesmen of the Palestinians, following the policy of the media.

They advocate free speech, excepting when it concerns Israeli representatives or their friends. A characteristic example is Amnesty International's behavior. The Columbia University chapter of this organization invited Professor Alan Dershowitz to deliver a talk on human rights in the Middle East. After he had accepted the invitation, the national office of Amnesty International demanded that the Columbia chapter of the organization disinvite the Harvard law professor, an expert on human rights who is a moderate on issues of the Arab-Israeli conflict. As the disinvited guest writes, the reasons Amnesty International censored his speech to its members is because he has been

> somewhat critical of Amnesty International's one-sided approach to the Israeli-Palestinian conflict. For example, I wrote an article criticizing Amnesty International's report on honor killings in the West Bank. An honor killing occurs when a woman has been raped and her family then kills her because of the shame her victimization has brought. Despite massive evidence to the contrary, Amnesty International mendaciously claimed that honor killings had increased in the West Bank since the Israel occupation and that the fault for this increase in Arab men killing Arab women lies with Israel. The reality is that there are far fewer honor killings in the West Bank than there are in adjoining Jordan, which is not under Israeli occupation, and that the number of honor killings in the West Bank has been reduced dramatically during the Israeli occupation.
>
> Facts mean little to Amnesty International when Israel is involved and they were afraid to have their members hear the truth. They feared an open marketplace of ideas, so they tried to shut me down.
>
> Amnesty International, especially its European branch, located in London, has abandoned its commitment to human rights in preference for an overtly political and ideological agenda. Its position on the Israeli-Palestinian conflict has become particularly troubling. It has demonized

Israel for its attempts to protect its citizens from Hamas war crimes. In a recent report, it condemned Israel for its military actions in Gaza without even mentioning the Hamas terror tunnels that provoked Israel's defensive actions – the tunnels that were built for one purpose – to kill and kidnap Israeli citizens. But Amnesty International never mentioned the tunnels and made it seem that Israel sent troops into Gaza simply to kill as many Palestinians as possible.

Professor Dershowitz sums up his view on this "human rights" organization:

> Amnesty International has become an apologist for terrorism and an enemy of democracy. Its failed effort to stifle my free speech and the rights of Columbia students to listen to me is symbolic of what a once great organization has become – a cheerleader for human wrongs rather than human rights.[54]

So we have Amnesty International, Human Rights Watch, and a series of nongovernmental organizations following the same line as the majority of the media – the demonization and delegitimization of the State of Israel.

The BDS Movement

It is called Boycott, Divestment and Sanctions – a movement that has infiltrated itself into American and British universities, for the purpose of fighting against the State of Israel, in the name of Arab human rights, claiming that Israel conducts an apartheid state policy.

This is a wicked movement based on a false analysis of the reality of life in Israel and of the circumstances that brought about what is commonly called the occupation of the Palestinian land. In the various parts of this book in which the situation of the Israeli Arabs is dealt with, it has been demonstrated how they are treated on the highest levels of equality, as they participate in all sectors of the country's economy, culture, education, and health and judicial systems. BDS proponents often focus on the condition of the Palestinian Arabs living in the West Bank. Yet considering that Israel has not annexed the so-called "occupied territories," considering that these territories are classified by the Israeli Supreme Court as under "belligerent occupation," and considering that the

54. "How Amnesty International Suppresses Free Speech," November 10, 2014, http://www.gatestoneinstitute.org/4863/amnesty-international-free-speech.

UN has classified Israel's presence there as "illegal occupation," it is clear that the West Bank is under a different status than the State of Israel proper. One cannot claim that Israel is an apartheid state because of certain special rules affecting the population of those territories, established for security reasons in defense against terrorism that has lasted for many decades. What occurs in a territory outside the official borders of a state cannot characterize the nature of the state itself. So to call Israel an "apartheid state" due to defensive measures in territories outside the state amounts to defamation.

Besides the falsity of the accusation itself, there is further evidence of the bigotry of the BDS movement. And that is because no human rights movement can be considered honest if it concentrates on one situation, against one state, in favor of one people, not considering all other suffering minorities around the world. If it does not expand its views but concentrates on one case only, it is not seriously interested in human rights but is instead based on political interests.

BDS only seeks to damage Israel, and if possible, destroy it. If BDS were interested in Palestinian rights, it would be boycotting Egypt for destroying hundreds of Palestinian homes on the Gaza border in October 2014 in order to stop Hamas from smuggling weapons. If BDS were interested in protecting Arab life, it would be boycotting Syria for murdering hundreds of thousands of Arabs. If BDS had an interest in protesting an occupation, it would be boycotting China for occupying Tibet since 1950. If BDS cared about Arab human rights, it would be divesting from Saudi Arabia, Jordan, Egypt, Qatar, Syria, Lebanon, and every other Arab country where citizens are denied the most basic rights, such as freedom of the press, freedom to protest against their governments, freedom to vote, the woman's freedom to love the person of her choice, and freedom to practice other religions – all of which are guaranteed to Arabs only in the State of Israel.[55]

Globalized Antisemitism

What happens in the halls of the United Nations, its General Assembly, and the Human Rights Council regarding the State of Israel and the coverage of the Arab-Israeli conflict by the perverted press influences public opinion

---

55. On the comparisons with other situations of human rights violations see Shmuley Boteach, "Six Ways to Fight BDS Lies on Campus," *Jerusalem Post*, December 12, 2014.

in the streets and homes of Europe and of other parts of the world, turning condemnations of Israel into overt antisemitism.

In the last years, antisemitic manifestations have been growing in number and violence in France, Belgium, Holland, England, Sweden, Hungary, and elsewhere. In some cities, Jews have been warned not to go out wearing kippot (skullcaps) on their heads or carrying any other sign of their Jewishness. The situation has been deteriorating from year to year.

Recall the murderous attack at the Jewish school in Toulouse in March 2012; the attack at the Jewish museum in Brussels in May 2014; the wild, threatening riots in front of Parisian synagogues; the vandalism of Jewish stores in the French capital; the anti-Israel demonstrations in many European capitals, with calls of "murder the Jews" led by Muslims fueled by a hateful education and upbringing; and the attack on the kosher market of Paris, in early 2015. European Jews are once again insecure, feeling endangered on the streets and even in their own institutions.

Are we facing the possibility of a new Kristallnacht?

France's interior minister Bernard Cazeneuve promised to crack down on antisemitism after the capital witnessed violence caused by pro-Palestinian rallies to protest Israel's role in the July 2014 fighting in Gaza. Parisian mayor François Pupponi said that "we never saw such hatred and violence as we witnessed in Sarcelles; people are astonished and the Jews are frightened."[56]

An English columnist for the *Times of London* has written that "when London demonstrators and British intellectuals declare that Israelis are the new Nazis, colonizing land to which they have no historic connection and which they have stolen from the Palestinians, they make themselves accessories to an infernal creed which is inciting violence and murder against Jews."[57]

On July 22, 2014, the foreign ministers of Germany, France, and Italy issued a joint statement in Brussels condemning the antisemitism, racism, and xenophobia that marred rallies against Israel's role in its conflict with Hamas. The statement read: "Anti-Semitic incitement and hostility against Jews, attacks on people of Jewish faith and synagogues have no place in our societies."[58]

56. Joseph Strich, "France Slams Anti-Semitic Violence Spilling Over at Pro-Gaza Rallies," *Jerusalem Post*, July 22, 2014.
57. Melanie Phillips, "How the West Is Complicit in Islamic Jew-Hatred," *Jerusalem Post*, July 18, 2014.
58. Reuters, "Germany, France, Italy Condemn Anti-Semitism in Anti-Israel Protests,"

What the foreign ministers missed is that the "rallies against Israel," in response to its defense from the Hamas attacks, are in themselves antisemitism in its modern version. They do not realize, or do not want to recognize, that there is no distinction between antisemitism and anti-Zionism, between anti-Judaism and the wild attacks against the defense policies of the State of Israel.

An important reply to the European foreign ministers is contained in an article published in the *Wall Street Journal* by Rabbi Jonathan Sacks, former chief rabbi of the British Commonwealth, in which he makes the following statements:

> In France, worshipers in a synagogue were surrounded by a howling mob claiming to protest Israel policy. In Brussels, four people were murdered in the Jewish museum and a synagogue was firebombed. In London, a major supermarket said that it felt forced to remove kosher food from its shelves for fear that it would incite a riot. A London theater refused to stage a Jewish film festival because the event had received a small grant from the Israeli embassy.
>
> And Jews are leaving. A survey in 2013 by the European Union Agency for Fundamental Rights showed that almost a third of Europe's Jews have considered emigrating because of anti-Semitism, with numbers as high as 46 percent in France and 48 percent in Hungary. Quietly, many Jews are asking whether they have a future in Europe.
>
> Some of what we are seeing in Europe is the old anti-Semitism of the far right and the radical left, which never went away and merely lay dormant during the years when attacks on Jews were considered unacceptable in polite society. This taboo is now well and truly broken. Anti-Semitism has returned to Europe within living memory of the Holocaust. Never again has become ever again.
>
> But the driving thrust of the assault on Jews is new. Today's anti-Semitism differs from the old in three ways. First, its pretext. In the Middle Ages, Jews were hated for their religion. In the 19th and 20th centuries, they were hated for their race. Today, they are hated for their nation state. Israel, now 66 years old, still finds itself the only country among the 193

Jerusalem Post, July 22, 2014, http://www.jpost.com/Breaking-News/Germany-France-Italy-condemn-anti-Semitism-in-anti-Israel-protests-368490.

in the United Nations whose right to exist is routinely challenged and in many quarters denied.

There are 102 nations in the world where Christians predominate, and there are 56 Islamic states. But a single Jewish state is deemed one too many. And the targets of terror in Europe are all too often not Israeli government offices, but synagogues, Jewish schools and museums – places not of Israeli policy-making but of ordinary Jewish life.[59]

An outstanding analysis of antisemitism from a historical perspective is contained in *Constantine's Sword: The Church and the Jews*, authored by James Carroll, a former priest and a profound expert on the history and philosophy of the Catholic Church. Among many others in his book, here is an important lesson that stretches from the fifteenth to the twentieth centuries:

> Actually Catholic racial anti-Semitism started in 1449 when the city council of Toledo passed an ordinance decreeing that "no *converso* of Jewish descent may have or hold any office or benefice in the city." And although Pope Nicholas v reacted against this, the king of Castile formally approved the regulation. Jews would be legally defined now in Spain not by religion but by blood.[60]
>
> In 1546, Pope Paul III had appointed a *converso* priest to a clerical position at the cathedral in Toledo. The archbishop of Toledo defied the pope by rejecting the appointed priest on the grounds that he had impure blood. Paul III withdrew the appointment. The next year the archbishop issued the Statute of Toledo, called *limpieza de sangre* or blood purity, according to which no one of Jewish blood could hold office in the cathedral. Though the pope and other prelates of the Church did not approve the decree, the Inquisition began extending such *limpieza* statutes to other institutions – people of Jewish ancestry were banned from holding office in Iberian universities, in religious orders, in various guilds and in some municipalities. In 1555 Gian Pietro Caraffa, the grand inquisitor, became Pope Paul iv, and he immediately ratified the blood purity statute of Toledo.[61]
>
> So German racial anti-Semitism has its origin in the Catholic Church,

59. Jonathan Sacks, "Europe's Alarming New Anti-Semitism," *Wall Street Journal*, Oct. 2, 2014.

60. Carroll, *Constantine's Sword*, 347.

61. Ibid., 374–75.

as Rosemary Radfort Ruether reports that even in the twentieth century, Catholics up for appointment to "offices entrusted with the care of souls" were at times required to "display their genealogical charts," to show that there were no Jews among their ancestors. Blood purity regulations, Ruether asserts, "remained on the books in Catholic religious orders, such as the Jesuits, until the twentieth century. They are the ancestor of the Nazi Nuremberg Laws."[62]

Cardinal Cassidy, a friend of the Jews, declared to James Carroll that the Church-enforced ghetto was the "antechamber of Nazi death camps."[63]

After the religious, and then the racial, antisemitism, arose the political antisemitism, which is represented by anti-Zionism. It started overtly in 1975 with the UN resolution that "Zionism is racism." Today, any effort Israel expends in order to defend itself from the missile attacks of Hamas results in "rallies against Israel." This amounts to negation of Israel's right to defend itself, its right to exist.

But the European foreign ministers, the prime ministers, and the majority of members of the national parliaments, as well as the European intelligentsia, the university professors, the journalists and, above all, the European Union's leaders, do not want to recognize that the anti-Israel manifestations of all sorts are the modern face of the hatred of the Jew. Many of them may actually be real antisemites who express their feelings by criticizing and combating the Jewish state.

Are we facing a new Holocaust?

Holocaust denial has become irrelevant, to the point that a great American scholar compared it to the sport that has been made from time to time of the Muslim prophet. Claiming religious defamation, Ronald Dworkin has compared the Danish cartoons that defamed the Muslim religion, which caused the protest of millions of Muslims in 2006, to denial of the Holocaust. Under the title "Even Bigots and Holocaust Deniers Must Have Their Say," we read in the British *Guardian* the following pearl:

Muslims who are outraged by the Danish cartoons point out that in several European countries it is a crime publicly to deny, as the president of Iran

---

62. Ibid., 382.
63. Ibid., 381.

has denied, that the Holocaust ever took place. They say that western concern for free speech is therefore only self-serving hypocrisy, and they have a point. But of course the remedy is not to make the compromise of democratic legitimacy even greater than it already is but to work toward a new understanding of the European convention on human rights that would strike down the Holocaust-denial law and similar laws across Europe for what they are: violations of the freedom of speech that that convention demands.[64]

Dworkin further writes that "we cannot also forbid people from . . . claiming, in cartoons or otherwise, that Islam is committed to terrorism, however silly we think that opinion is."[65]

A few remarks are in place. The first consideration is that there are no laws that forbid insults to other religions (though Britain has retained the crime of blasphemy, but only for insults to Christianity, as Dworkin notes), but it so happens that there are express, clear legal rules, national and conventional, forbidding Holocaust denial. So we should not equate an action that is legally forbidden with a legally permissible action.

A second aspect to be reckoned with is that religious defamation is an act without further consequences, beyond the pain it causes to the affected people, whereas denial of the Holocaust is hate speech – more than that – incitement, and many times clear incitement to go ahead with a new Holocaust. Ahmanidejad has denied the Holocaust and immediately thereafter advocated the destruction of the State of Israel.

Abbas wrote his doctoral thesis on denying the Holocaust. His speeches and the honors that he bestows on Palestinian terrorists that kill Jews, added to the contents of the charter of his Palestinian Liberation Organization as well as his partnership with Hamas, clearly add up to a genocidal intent.

There is a great difference between defamation and insult, on the one hand, and genocide propaganda on the other.

And above all there is the "right to truth," also referred as the "right to know." Every society is entitled to have the crimes committed against it officially recognized, in respect for its dignity and in order to prevent future recurrence

64. "Even Bigots and Holocaust Deniers Must Have Their Say," *The Guardian*, February 14, 2006, in Alston and Goodman, *International Human Rights*, 679.
65. Ibid.

of such crimes.[66] Various principles have been established in favor of the right to truth, such as the Joinet-Orentlicher Principles which provide that

> every people has the inalienable right to know the truth about past events concerning the perpetration of heinous crimes and about the circumstances and reasons that led, through massive or systematic violations, to the perpetration of those crimes. Full and effective exercise of the right to the truth provides a vital safeguard against the recurrence of violations.

The Van Boven-Bassiouni Principles recognized the same right to truth as an integral part of the wider issue of reparation for gross violations of human rights and humanitarian law.[67]

The Inter-American Commission on Human Rights stated:

> The right to truth constitutes ... a right of a collective nature. ... Allowing society as a whole to have access to essential information. ... Every society has the inalienable right to know the truth about past events, as well as the motives and circumstances in which aberrant crimes came to be committed, in order to prevent repetitions of such acts in the future.[68]

The rules, national and international, that forbid denial of the Holocaust fit perfectly into the right to truth – the right to know, which is characterized as a legitimate, fundamental human right. Those who deny the Holocaust are committing a clear violation of the human right that seeks to protect civilization against the repetition of the heinous crimes committed by the Third Reich under the command of Hitler and the complicity of those who were referred to in chapters 2 and 3.

Another consideration is that denial of the Holocaust amounts to denying the basis of the first and most important work of the UN Commission on Human Rights in its good days, when delegates from the United States, the

---

66. Yasmin Naqvi, "Right to Truth of International Law: Fact or Fiction," *International Review of the Red Cross* 88 (2006): 245–6, as quoted in Pok Yin S. Chow, "Memory Denied: A Commentary on the Reports of the UN Special Rapporteur in the Field of Cultural Rights on Historical and Memorial Narratives in Divided Societies," *The International Lawyer* 48, no. 3 (2015): 199.
67. The Joinet-Orentlicher Principles and the Van Boven-Bassiouni Principles are cited from Pok Yin S. Chow's article, referred to in the previous note, at 201.
68. Ibid., 200.

United Kingdom, Russia, France, and a few other countries, as well as many delegates from state members in different organs of the UN, worked tirelessly for two years to draft the Universal Declaration of Human Rights, inspired by the unanimous theory that the Holocaust of the Jews by Hitler was the fundamental reason to create such a document, in order to protect humanity in the future from the repetition of such barbarism. Deny the Holocaust and you deny the inspiration and the meaning of the UDHR, as far as the UN Commission on Human Rights is concerned. Deny the Holocaust and you belittle the importance and the legal basis of human rights, as far as the United Nations is concerned.

The real meaning and purpose of Holocaust denial laws has not been well understood even by the German Constitutional Court, as can be seen in the *Holocaust Denial Case* which upheld a decision of the state government in Munich to the effect that at a meeting of the National Democratic Party at which the Holocaust denier David Irving was due to speak, the so-called "Auschwitz Hoax" theory must not be promoted, holding that this theory "was an insult to a group, which meant that the personal dignity and honour of 'today's Jews' (as distinct from the Jews who died in the Holocaust) would be undermined."[69]

The prohibition of denying the Holocaust is not a matter of anybody's honor; rather it is one of the component factors necessary to avoid the repetition of history, which goes together with educating the younger generations about the horrors of those catastrophic years. Denying the Holocaust makes a farce of this education and destroys the whole strategy of guaranteeing a humane future not only for Germany and the other European countries, but for the whole world.

To maintain an alert remembrance of the Holocaust, as well as of the Armenian Genocide, and now also of the disasters that fell upon so many peoples in the post–World War II world, is the highest obligation that governments have, to be honored by maintaining these memories as a fundamental factor in education and culture, to reach not only the schoolchildren but the mature populations as well.

69. Auschwitz Lie Case (Holocaust Denial Case), Bundesverfassungsgericht (BVerfGE) [Federal Constitutional Court] April 13, 1994, 90 BVerfGE 241, as reported by Neville Cox, "Blasphemy, Holocaust Denial, and the Control of Profoundly Unacceptable Speech," *The American Journal of Comparative Law* 62, no. 3 (2014): 751–52.

The extent of the line defended by Dworkin that we should strike out the prohibition on Holocaust denial reveals an absolute lack of understanding of what the Holocaust was, what it meant, and what it continues to mean in the perverse minds of antisemites all over the world, who are not willing to rest until the final destruction of the Jewish people is realized. To compare this with regular freedom of speech reveals a false understanding of free speech, on the one hand, and allows active incitement to collective murder, on the other hand.

The Holocaust followed a psychological process. This was articulated by Bach-Zelewski, one of the witnesses at Nuremberg who explained how another Nazi, Ohlendorf, could admit the murder of ninety thousand people: "I am of the opinion that when – for years, for decades, the doctrine is preached that the Slav race is an inferior race and Jews not even human, then such an outcome is inevitable. *The Sturmer* and other publications were allowed to disseminate hatred of the Jews and in the speeches and public declarations of the Nazi leaders, the Jews were held up to public ridicule and contempt."[70]

Denying the Holocaust eliminates the moral considerations it evokes. Holocaust denial brings back the whole weight of the German anti-Jewish propaganda and of the Church's racist dogma, easily directed to a new wave of wild antisemitic feelings and expressions, and ultimately, to the road leading to a repetition of history.

The Western world, most especially the European countries, have produced a bizarre method of camouflaging the ongoing, growing antisemitism by proclaiming that Islamophobia represents the greatest threat to human rights in the world! In Europe, synagogues and not mosques are being desecrated; Jews and not Muslims are being persecuted; the media is promoting antisemitic propaganda by demonizing the State of Israel while keeping as quiet as possible about the terrible violations of human rights that go on in the Muslim states. The continuous campaign against Islamophobia is the height of hypocritical falsity.

In England this hypocrisy has reached to extreme levels, to the point that "any attempt by British society to defend itself or its values, either through antiterrorist laws or the reaffirmation of the supremacy of Western values,

70. Alston and Goodman, *International Human Rights*, 658.

is denounced as Islamophobia. Even use of the term 'Islamic terrorism' is regarded as 'Islamophobic.'"[71]

A "Legal" Pogrom of the UN against Israel

On September 8, 2014, at UN headquarters, Ugoji Adanma Eze of the Eng Aja Eze Foundation and the government of Palau convened a conference on the threat that global antisemitism poses to international peace and security. Upon taking the podium, Anne Bayefsky accused the UN of having launched a "legal" pogrom against the Jewish state. A "legal" pogrom, she added, is a license to kill.

> Why couldn't the UN, founded on the ashes of the Jewish people, and presently witnessing a widespread resurgence in antisemitism, sponsor a conference on combating global antisemitism?
>
> The answer is clear. Because the United Nations itself is the leading global purveyor of antisemitism.
>
> Photo-ops of the UN Secretary-General and the UN High Commissioner for Human Rights at the gates of Auschwitz are not an alibi.
>
> One does not honor the memory of Jews murdered by intolerance six decades ago by inciting murderous intolerance towards the remnant of the Jewish people in the here and now.
>
> Incitement to hate, like declaring Israel to be racist – as does the UN Durban Declaration – is the flagship of the UN's racist anti-racism program of action. In theory, the UN Charter demands equality both of individual men and women and of nations large and small. In reality, the UN mass-produces inequality for Jews and the Jewish nation....
>
> Modern anti-Semitism targets Israel's exercise of the right of self-defense because self-defense is the essence of sovereignty. Demonize and delegitimize self-defense, the plan is, and the viability of the Jewish state will be degraded....
>
> Today, UN antisemitism has taken yet one more treacherous turn. The UN has launched a legal pogrom against the Jewish state.
>
> Hired guns, posing as independent arbiters, such as William Schabas are appointed to discover what they've already found. Guilty!

71. Melanie Phillips, *Londonistan*, xxi.

Phony legal rules misinterpret proportionality to favor a "more even number" of dead Israelis. The Iron Dome worked too well!

And the International Criminal Court is poised to pounce.

Serious about "never again"? Then never forget that the perversion of the legal system is how genocide begins.[72]

News broke out at the end of February 2015 that William Schabas resigned his position as head of the committee investigating the role of Israel in the 2014 conflict with Gaza. His decision to resign came following a decision by the council to open an investigation regarding a conflict of interest on his part, when it was discovered that he had received payment from the Palestinians in return for a legal opinion regarding issues that the committee was responsible for.[73]

His resignation was tardy, as for months the committee had already been investigating and drawing conclusions, all under Schabas's directions. The Legal Forum for Israel wrote to the UN Human Rights Council demanding that all the committee's work product be discarded, since it was directed by someone with a clear conflict of interest.

The committee accused Israel of employing disproportionate measures in its fight against Hamas. This argument is one of the most hypocritical attitudes of Israel's enemies. Anyone who complains about "disproportionality" must explain exactly what the Israel Defense Forces should have done to neutralize the terrorist threat from Hamas while causing less destruction than what occurred, taking into consideration that the civilian victims were caused by Hamas's murderous strategy of forcing them to stay in the most dangerous places, from where the missiles against Israel were launched.[74]

Whenever the Israel Defense Forces finally react to the constant attacks of

72. "The United Nations: World's Leading Purveyor of Antisemitism," September 16, 2014, http://www.gatestoneinstitute.org/4708/united-nations-antisemitism.

73. Ron Prosor, Israeli ambassador to the UN, published an article in the *New York Times* on April 2, 2015, in which he wrote: "Mr. Schabas was forced to resign after documents came to light revealing that, in 2012, he had done consulting work for the Palestine Liberation Organization. Surprisingly, this fact slipped Mr. Schabas's mind during his vetting process." http://mobile.nytimes.com/2015/04/010pinon/united-in-ignomin.

74. Dore Gold, former ambassador of Israel to the United Nations, narrates the measures taken by Israel to save civilians from any harm, before it launched its 2014 attack against Hamas. He further narrates how the Hamas leadership sabotaged those measures and kept civilians in the exact locations where Israel's defensive attack was going to take place.

Hamas, the honorable secretary-general of the United Nations Ban Ki-moon only has words of critique to the victim, such as the ones he launched against Israel on July 20, 2014, quoted above.

For the UN, no move that Israel makes, short of surrender to the Palestinian mob, will ever be sufficient.[75]

The Israeli Ambassador at the UN Accuses

In November 2014, the Israel ambassador to the UN, Mr. Ron Prosor, addressed the General Assembly of the United Nations; in an extraordinary exposition he showed the terrible hypocrisy that pervades the United Nations and the extreme cynicism that guides the European countries in their treatment of the Arab-Israeli conflict. His speech constitutes a frontal accusation against the falsity of the world organization toward the State of Israel.

This is the full content of his speech:

Mr. President,

I stand before the world as a proud representative of the State of Israel and the Jewish people. I stand tall before you knowing that truth and morality are on my side. And yet, I stand here knowing that today in this Assembly, truth will be turned on its head and morality cast aside.

The fact of the matter is that when members of the international community speak about the Israeli-Palestinian conflict, a fog descends to cloud all logic and moral clarity. The result isn't realpolitik, its surrealpolitik.

The world's unrelenting focus on the Israeli-Palestinian conflict is an injustice to tens of millions of victims of tyranny and terrorism in the Middle East. As we speak, Yazidis, Bahai, Kurds, Christians and Muslims are being executed and expelled by radical extremists at a rate of 1,000 people per month.

How many resolutions did you pass last week to address this crisis? And how many special sessions did you call for? The answer is zero. What does this say about international concern for human life? Not much, but it speaks volumes about the hypocrisy of the international community.

"Israel's Doctrine of Proportionality in Gaza," *Los Angeles Times*, July 31, 2014, http://www .latimes.com/nation/la-oe-gold-israel-gaza-proportional-force-20140801-story.html.
75. Anne Bayefsky, "Ban Ki-moon's Shameful Message in Israel's Hour of Need," *Jerusalem Post*, July 22, 2014, http://www.jpost.com/LandedPages/PrintArticle.aspx?id=368415.

I stand before you to speak the truth. Of the 300 million Arabs in the Middle East and North Africa, less than half a percent are truly free – and they are all citizens of Israel.

Israeli Arabs are some of the most educated Arabs in the world. They are our leading physicians and surgeons, they are elected to our parliament, and they serve as judges on our Supreme Court. Millions of men and women in the Middle East would welcome these opportunities and freedoms.

Nonetheless, nation after nation, will stand at this podium today and criticize Israel – the small island of democracy in a region plagued by tyranny and oppression.

Mr. President,

Our conflict has never been about the establishment of a Palestinian state. It has always been about the existence of the Jewish state.

Sixty-seven years ago this week, on November 29, 1947, the United Nations voted to partition the land into a Jewish state and an Arab state. Simple. The Jews said yes. The Arabs said no. But they didn't just say no. Egypt, Jordan, Syria, Iraq, Saudi Arabia and Lebanon launched a war of annihilation against our newborn state.

This is the historical truth that the Arabs are trying to distort. The Arabs' historic mistake continues to be felt – in lives lost in war, lives lost to terrorism, and lives scarred by the Arabs' narrow political interests.

According to the United Nations, about 700,000 Palestinians were displaced in the war initiated by the Arabs themselves. At the same time, some 850,000 Jews were forced to flee from Arab countries.

Why is it, that 67 years later, the displacement of the Jews has been completely forgotten by this institution while the displacement of the Palestinians is the subject of an annual debate?

The difference is that Israel did its utmost to integrate the Jewish refugees into society. The Arabs did just the opposite.

The worst oppression of the Palestinian people takes place in Arab nations. In most of the Arab world, Palestinians are denied citizenship and are aggressively discriminated against. They are barred from owning land and prevented from entering certain professions.

And yet none – not one – of these crimes are mentioned in the resolutions before you.

If you were truly concerned about the plight of the Palestinian people there would be one, just one, resolution to address the thousands of Palestinians killed in Syria. And if you were so truly concerned about the Palestinians there would be at least one resolution to denounce the treatment of Palestinians in Lebanese refugee camps.

But there isn't. The reason is that today's debate is not about speaking for peace or speaking for the Palestinian people – it is about speaking against Israel. It is nothing but a hate and bashing festival against Israel.

Mr. President,

The European nations claim to stand for Liberté, Égalité, Fraternité – freedom, equality, and brotherhood – but nothing could be farther from the truth.

I often hear European leaders proclaim that Israel has the right to exist in secure borders. That's very nice. But I have to say – it makes about as much sense as me standing here and proclaiming Sweden's right to exist in secure borders.

When it comes to matters of security, Israel learned the hard way that we cannot rely on others – certainly not Europe.

In 1973, on Yom Kippur – the holiest day on the Jewish calendar – the surrounding Arab nations launched an attack against Israel. In the hours before the war began, Golda Meir, our Prime Minister then, made the difficult decision not to launch a preemptive strike. The Israeli Government understood that if we launched a preemptive strike, we would lose the support of the international community.

As the Arab armies advanced on every front, the situation in Israel grew dire. Our casualty count was growing and we were running dangerously low on weapons and ammunition. In this, our hour of need, President Nixon and Secretary of State Henry Kissinger, agreed to send Galaxy planes loaded with tanks and ammunition to resupply our troops. The only problem was that the Galaxy planes needed to refuel on route to Israel.

The Arab States were closing in and our very existence was threatened – and yet, Europe was not even willing to let the planes refuel. The United States stepped in once again and negotiated that the planes be allowed to refuel in the Azores.

The government and people of Israel will never forget that when our very existence was at stake, only one country came to our aid – the United States of America.

Israel is tired of hollow promises from European leaders. The Jewish people have a long memory. We will never ever forget that you failed us in the 1940s. You failed us in 1973. And you are failing us again today.

Every European parliament that voted to prematurely and unilaterally recognize a Palestinian state is giving the Palestinians exactly what they want – statehood without peace. By handing them a state on a silver platter, you are rewarding unilateral actions and taking away any incentive for the Palestinians to negotiate or compromise or renounce violence. You are sending the message that the Palestinian Authority can sit in a government with terrorists and incite violence against Israel without paying any price.

The first E.U. member to officially recognize a Palestinian state was Sweden. One has to wonder why the Swedish Government was so anxious to take this step. When it comes to other conflicts in our region, the Swedish Government calls for direct negotiations between the parties – but for the Palestinians, surprise, surprise, they roll out the red carpet.

State Secretary Söder may think she is here to celebrate her government's so-called historic recognition, when in reality it's nothing more than an historic mistake.

The Swedish Government may host the Nobel Prize ceremony, but there is nothing noble about their cynical political campaign to appease the Arabs in order to get a seat on the Security Council. Nations on the Security Council should have sense, sensitivity, and sensibility. Well, the Swedish Government has shown no sense, no sensitivity, and no sensibility. Just nonsense.

Israel learned the hard way that listening to the international community can bring about devastating consequences. In 2005, we unilaterally dismantled every settlement and removed every citizen from the Gaza Strip. Did this bring us any closer to peace? Not at all. It paved the way for Iran to send its terrorist proxies to establish a terror stronghold on our doorstep.

I can assure you that we won't make the same mistake again. When it comes to our security, we cannot and will not rely on others – Israel must be able to defend itself by itself.

Mr. President,

The State of Israel is the land of our forefathers – Abraham, Isaac, and Jacob. It is the land where Moses led the Jewish people, where David built his palace, where Solomon built the Jewish Temple, and where Isaiah saw a vision of eternal peace.

For thousands of years, Jews have lived continuously in the land of Israel. We endured through the rise and fall of the Assyrian, Babylonian, Greek and Roman Empires. And we endured through thousands of years of persecution, expulsions and crusades. The bond between the Jewish people and the Jewish land is unbreakable.

Nothing can change one simple truth – Israel is our home and Jerusalem is our eternal capital.

At the same time, we recognize that Jerusalem has special meaning for other faiths. Under Israeli sovereignty, all people – and I will repeat that, all people – regardless of religion and nationality can visit the city's holy sites. And we intend to keep it this way. The only ones trying to change the status quo on the Temple Mount are Palestinian leaders.

President Abbas is telling his people that Jews are contaminating the Temple Mount. He has called for days of rage and urged Palestinians to prevent Jews from visiting the Temple Mount using (quote) "all means" necessary. These words are as irresponsible as they are unacceptable.

You don't have to be Catholic to visit the Vatican, you don't have to be Jewish to visit the Western Wall, but some Palestinians would like to see the day when only Muslims can visit the Temple Mount.

You, the international community, are lending a hand to extremists and fanatics. You, who preach tolerance and religious freedom, should be ashamed. Israel will never let this happen. We will make sure that the holy places remain open to all people of all faiths for all time.

Mr. President,

No one wants peace more than Israel. No one needs to explain the importance of peace to parents who have sent their child to defend our homeland. No one knows the stakes of success or failure better than we Israelis do. The people of Israel have shed too many tears and buried too many sons and daughters.

We are ready for peace, but we are not naïve. Israel's security is paramount. Only a strong and secure Israel can achieve a comprehensive peace.

The past month should make it clear to anyone that Israel has immediate and pressing security needs. In recent weeks, Palestinian terrorists have shot and stabbed our citizens and twice driven their cars into crowds of pedestrians. Just a few days ago, terrorists armed with axes and a gun savagely attacked Jewish worshipers during morning prayers. We have reached the point when Israelis can't even find sanctuary from terrorism in the sanctuary of a synagogue.

These attacks didn't emerge out of a vacuum. They are the results of years of indoctrination and incitement. A Jewish proverb teaches: "The instruments of both death and life are in the power of the tongue."

As a Jew and as an Israeli, I know with utter certainly that when our enemies say they want to attack us, they mean it.

Hamas's genocidal charter calls for the destruction of Israel and the murder of Jews worldwide. For years, Hamas and other terrorist groups have sent suicide bombers into our cities, launched rockets into our towns, and sent terrorists to kidnap and murder our citizens.

And what about the Palestinian Authority? It is leading a systemic campaign of incitement. In schools, children are being taught that 'Palestine' will stretch from the Jordan River to the Mediterranean Sea. In mosques, religious leaders are spreading vicious libels accusing Jews of destroying Muslim holy sites. In sports stadiums, teams are named after terrorists. And in newspapers, cartoons urge Palestinians to commit terror attacks against Israelis.

Children in most of the world grow up watching cartoons of Mickey Mouse singing and dancing. Palestinian children also grow up watching Mickey Mouse, but on Palestinians national television, a twisted figure dressed as Mickey Mouse dances in an explosive belt and chants "Death to America and death to the Jews."

I challenge you to stand up here today and do something constructive for a change. Publically denounce the violence, denounce the incitement, and denounce the culture of hate.

Most people believe that at its core, the conflict is a battle between Jews and Arabs or Israelis and Palestinians. They are wrong. The battle that we are witnessing is a battle between those who sanctify life and those who celebrate death.

Following the savage attack in a Jerusalem synagogue, celebrations erupted in Palestinian towns and villages. People were dancing in the streets and distributing candy. Young men posed with axes, loudspeakers at mosques called out congratulations, and the terrorists were hailed as "martyrs" and "heroes."

This isn't the first time that we saw the Palestinians celebrate the murder of innocent civilians. We saw them rejoice after every terrorist attack on Israeli civilians and they even took to the streets to celebrate the September 11 attack on the World Trade Center right here in New York City.

Imagine the type of state this society would produce. Does the Middle East really need another terror-cracy? Some members of the international community are aiding and abetting its creation.

Mr. President,

As we came into the United Nations, we passed the flags of all 193 member states. If you take the time to count, you will discover that there are 15 flags with a crescent and 25 flags with a cross. And then there is one flag with a Jewish Star of David. Amidst all the nations of the world there is one state – just one small nation state for the Jewish people.

And for some people, that is one too many.

As I stand before you today I am reminded of all the years when Jewish people paid for the world's ignorance and indifference in blood. Those days are no more.

We will never apologize for being a free and independent people in our sovereign state. And we will never apologize for defending ourselves.

To the nations that continue to allow prejudice to prevail over truth, I say "J'accuse."

I accuse you of hypocrisy. I accuse you of duplicity.

I accuse you of lending legitimacy to those who seek to destroy our State.

I accuse you of speaking about Israel's right of self-defense in theory, but denying it in practice.

And I accuse you of demanding concessions from Israel, but asking nothing of the Palestinians.

In the face of these offenses, the verdict is clear. You are not for peace and you are not for the Palestinian people. You are simply against Israel.

Members of the international community have a choice to make.

You can recognize Israel as the nation-state of the Jewish people, or permit the Palestinian leadership to deny our history without consequence.

You can publically proclaim that the so-called "claim of return" is a non-starter, or you can allow this claim to remain the major obstacle to any peace agreement.

You can work to end Palestinian incitement, or stand by as hatred and extremism take root for generations to come.

You can prematurely recognize a Palestinian state, or you can encourage the Palestinian Authority to break its pact with Hamas and return to direct negotiations.

The choice is yours. You can continue to steer the Palestinians off course or pave the way to real and lasting peace.

Thank you, Mr. President.[76]

The UN Complicity with Hitler

The UN's insistence that Israel return the "occupied territories including East Jerusalem"[77] has to be seen in light of the facts on the ground. A withdrawal of Israel from East Jerusalem would immediately introduce there the most militant of the Arab terrorist groups. That does not mean Hamas – which would be disastrous enough, based on the sad experience of the withdrawal from Gaza. It would mean also al-Qaeda, ISIS, and other such groups with their murderous policies and capabilities.

Dore Gold exposes that a withdrawal from Jerusalem would inspire jihadist forces from South Asia to the Middle East as well as their offshoots living in the heart of Europe, creating enormous new energy for their global campaign. A new, Clinton-style agreement to divide Jerusalem would surely reignite the global jihad, even if the deal were conceived for the express purpose of containing it. Mishandling the Jerusalem issue could have disastrous worldwide consequences.[78]

The highly populated Jerusalem would be an ideal target for the rockets and missiles of the terrorists that would easily occupy the strategic points of the Old City. The old and new buildings of the ancient-modern capital of the Jews would be an easy prey for the barbarians of the twenty-first century, out

76. "Amb Prosor addresses UNGA on the Question of Palestine, 24 Nov 2014," Israel Ministry of Foreign Affairs, http://mfa.gov.il/MFA/InternatlOrgs/Speeches/Pages/Amb-Prosor-addresses-UNGA-on-the-Question-of-Palestine-24-Nov-2014.aspx.
77. A position many times defended by the European Union, which follows the UN in many of its anti-Israeli policies.
78. Gold, *The Fight for Jerusalem*, 27.

to destroy the City of David and annihilate its Jews. One can only imagine the consequences of such a tragedy for the rest of the state and its population.

Based on all the above considerations, it is perfectly valid to say that the United Nations has become the posthumous accomplice to Hitler in the criminal enterprise to liquidate the Jewish people. At the same time, the world organization is blind to the mortal dangers that the community of nations faces if strong measures are not taken to neutralize the jihadists everywhere, anywhere.

Obama – The Advocate of Islamic Terror?

As if the discriminatory practices by the UN, the European Union, and the various other propaganda machines were not enough, this generation was blessed with a handsome American president, whose verbosity is the opposite of Franklin Delano Roosevelt's discretion, and who is creating situations that may be destroying the Western world.

Obama is correct that Islam was once a civilization rich in philosophy, astronomy, science, and medicine, as he mentioned in his speech in Cairo in 2010. But what the Obama administration does not consider is that Islam's dedication to knowledge came to a halt. While the Christian peoples around the world dedicated themselves more and more to all fields of knowledge and art, the Muslims closed themselves in their own communities, abandoned learning, and consequently stopped participating in the progress and development of civilization.

A few points in that 2010 speech, however, indicate that the president does not have a clear picture of certain very important world problems, beginning with the situation of the Palestinian people. President Obama stated that

> for more than sixty years they have endured the pain of dislocation. Many wait in refugee camps in the West Bank, Gaza and neighboring lands for a life of peace and security that they have never been able to lead. They endure the daily humiliations – large and small – that come with occupation. So let there be no doubt: the situation for the Palestinian people is intolerable. America will not turn our backs on the legitimate Palestinian aspiration for dignity, opportunity and a state of their own.[79]

79. Remarks by the President at Cairo University, June 4, 2009, https://www.whitehouse .gov/the-press-office/remarks-president-cairo-university-6-04-09.

Well, to begin with, if part of the Palestinians live in other lands, their situation has no connection with what the president called "occupation." Those and all the others who live in refugee camps are in this situation thanks to the UN policies (applied through UNRWA) that have been forcefully keeping them in camps, instead of giving them the chance to develop a normal life. The main supporter of UNRWA is the government of the United States, the major participant of the UN budget. Hundreds of thousands of Arabs could have lived in the West Bank, in Syria, in Lebanon, and in other Arab countries as free and enterprising citizens, but they were turned into prisoners of the cruel UN system, to which the Arab countries allied themselves, denying citizenship to their Arab brothers. And Mr. Obama's country is the main contributor to this unfortunate situation.

Regarding "occupation," Obama knows very well how much effort President Clinton invested with the help of Israeli prime minister Ehud Barak to reach a peace agreement and give the Arabs back the "occupied territories." He knows that it was the Arab leadership of the arch-terrorist Arafat that did not accept any agreement, launching the aggressive, cruel Intifada and refusing further peace offers in the following years.

Years later the same happened with Prime Minister Ehud Olmert and President Abbas: gracious, advantageous offers from Israel, total refusal from Abbas.

President Obama knows very well that the "occupation" is a consequence of the 1967 war that the Arabs launched against the State of Israel with the intention of eliminating the Jewish state from the map. And that instead of moving toward peace, the Arabs approved genocide charters against the Jews of Israel – both the PLO and Hamas charters. The "lack of opportunity in the West Bank," which President Obama referred to, has been reinforced – after UNRWA's policies – by the Arab states that have cooperated in worsening the situation between Israel and the Palestinian leadership. And of course with the complicity of the United Nations' one-sided resolutions against Israel and of all those states that bow to the malignant organs of the world organization. So, before Obama asserted in Cairo that "Israel must live up to its obligations to ensure that Palestinians can live and work and develop their society," he should have done his homework and realized that the United States' support of the UN's policies regarding the refugees is actually the major cause of their fate. It is the United States and not Israel that is responsible for the unhappiness of so many Arabs known erroneously as "Palestinians."

Obama spoke then of the tradition of tolerance he saw in Indonesia as a child, and from there he jumped to welcome "efforts like Saudi Arabian King Abdullah's interfaith dialogue." Interfaith dialogue in Saudi Arabia? What was the president of the United States referring to? To the absolute lack of religious freedom in that kingdom? To the absence of one synagogue, of one church in the whole country? To the people who have been jailed, tortured, and killed for embracing another faith? A few years later Obama visits Saudi Arabia and bows to the king. And then again, in 2015, comes to his funeral. What does this sequence of submissive attitudes amount to?

An important aspect of Saudi Arabia's position in the world was noted back in 2004, when Lee Kaplan of *Frontpage Magazine* wrote:

> Over the last 30 years, the Saudi royal family has contributed upwards of $70 billion to spread its anti-American and anti-Israel propaganda....
>
> By creating new Middle East Studies Centers and such endowed chairs on campuses across the nation, the Saudis are able to influence the curriculum taught to the next generation of Americans. That curriculum is decidedly anti-Western, anti- Christian and anti-Jewish.[80]

This tortuous way of falsifying realities has been a constant in Obama's pronunciations. Five years later, in 2015, as the world faced a mega-avalanche of Muslim jihadist acts of terrorism of the greatest barbarity – and the president of the United States, when asked about terrorism, answers that terrorism is overrated; and when asked about the tragic events in Paris, he said that the massacres there were committed by a "bunch of violent, vicious zealots who ... randomly shot a bunch of folks in a deli in Paris."[81]

In other words, as Caroline Glick writes in the *Jerusalem Post*, Amedy Coulibaly, the terrorist at Hyper Cacher, the kosher supermarket he targeted, was just some zealot. The Jews he murdered while they were shopping for Shabbat were just a "bunch of folks in a deli." No matter that Coulibaly called a French TV station from the kosher supermarket and said he was an al-Qaeda terrorist, that he chose the kosher supermarket because he wanted to kill Jews. And so Barak Obama pretended that Jews are not specifically targeted

80. Lee Kaplan, "The Saudi Fifth Column on Our Nation's Campuses," *Frontpage Magazine*, April 5, 2004, http://archive.frontpagemag.com/Printable.aspx?ArtId=13551.
81. Interview with Matthew Yglesias, *Vox*, http://www.vox.com/a/barack-obama-interview -vox-conversation/obama-foreign-policy-transcript.

for murder simply because they are Jews, dismissing the legitimate concern Jews harbor for their safety, whether in Diaspora communities or in Israel.[82]

Obama compared the jihadists to the Crusaders of a millennium ago in his effort to whitewash Islam from any blame for the insecurity that prevails in the world.

This return to the Crusades brought journalist Sarah Honig to comment that "by resonating prevalent Muslim apologetics, Obama effectively tells Muslims that they have a valid gripe. Wittingly or unwittingly, he signals all Muslims – even within the mainstream of purportedly pacifist Muslims – that they are justified to pursue their jihad against all the many national categories currently demonized as Crusaders."[83]

Ms. Honig further argues:

> Obama has just given voice to the terrorists' grievances and perhaps convinced a few more impressionable members of the much vaunted silent Muslim majority to join the jihad and to wreak vengeance against latter-day Crusaders. The thrust of his argument is that Christians and Jews today should not condemn those who burn captives alive, decapitate others, stone women, sell small girls into slavery, toss gays off high rises, bury children alive and actually crucify "infidel" boys – to say nothing of holding hostages to ransom, skyjacking, flying planes into skyscrapers, setting off explosive devices in busy marketplaces, firebombing busses or rocketing civilians in their homes.[84]

Should we admit that Obama's assistants do not follow the Arab press? Otherwise they would have read the following article, which appeared in *Asharq Al-Awsat*, published in London, on February 5, 2015:

> We were all shocked by how Islamic State burned to death Jordanian pilot Muath al-Kasasbeh earlier this month. But we are reacting as if we were suddenly awakened one bright morning to the brutality of this organization – as if we did not know; as if Islamic State's extreme actions stand

82. Caroline Glick, "Mainstreaming Jew Hatred in America," *Jerusalem Post*, February 12, 2015.

83. Sarah Honig, "Another Tack: The Crusades Aren't Our Problem," *Jerusalem Post*, February 12, 2015, http://www.jpost.com/Opinion/Another-Tack-The-Crusades-arent -our-problem-390884.

84. Ibid.

in complete contrast to its guidelines and ethics. Sadly, we are getting it all wrong. What should surprise us is not the organization's barbarism, but rather that we had an unspoken expectation it would act within the boundaries of logic and humanity.

Islamic State is a movement that believes in sadism and brutality – not only to outsiders, but also to its own people. Hundreds of its members have been brutally murdered for being "disloyal," via methods that were not much more humane than burning. In Syria, thousands of Muslims were tortured and killed by the organization and its competitor, Jahbat al Nusra.

Meanwhile, in the West, people continue to regard this war as one waged by Islam on the infidels. They fail to understand that, in the eyes of Islamic State, almost all Muslims deserve a death sentence. Many governments refuse to intervene, employing the excuse of "leaving room for diplomacy."

Sooner rather than later, we will all be burned by the fire we are playing with. The world is procrastinating and delaying its response, and time is working against us.[85]

A week later, following the decapitation of twenty-one Coptic Christians by Islamic State, the White House stood alone in its refusal to note that the victims were murdered because they were Christians.

Obama denies Islamic terror against Jews, Islamic terror against Christians, and Islamic terror against Muslims. Above all, the president continues in his blind policy that can easily lead Iran to acquire nuclear arms, despite the obvious existential risk – mainly for the State of Israel, but also for a few Middle East countries, not to speak about a direct danger to the United States.

On October 26, 2005, Ahmadinejad made his famous reference about the need to "wipe Israel off the map." What did not receive the same attention was another part of his speech in which he said: "We are now in the process of an historical war between the World of Arrogance [i.e., the West] and the Islamic world."[86] And he added that a "world without America and Zionism is attainable."[87]

85. Cited in "Hot off the Arab Press," *Jerusalem Post*, February 12, 2015, http://www.jpost.com/Magazine/Hot-off-the-Arab-press-390832.
86. "Iranian President at Tehran Conference: 'Very Soon, This Stain of Disgrace [i.e. Israel] Will Be Purged from the Center of the Islamic World – and This Is Attainable,'" MEMRI Special Dispatch no. 1013, October 28, 2005.
87. Ibid.

Not to stop Iran's nuclear plans is equivalent to creating conditions for a new Holocaust, actually for a world Holocaust.

Are we facing a new case of complicity with Hitler's "Final Solution"? Will historians one day draw a bridge between Roosevelt and Obama regarding the survival of the Jewish people? Do we have a mysterious personality sitting in the White House who may become dangerous to the whole of humanity?[88] Is there some connection between Roosevelt's and Obama's attitudes toward the Islamic world? Any connection between the submissive attitude of the two American presidents to the king of the Saudis?

---

88. As Caroline Glick writes: "Iran's single-minded dedication to its goal of becoming a regional hegemon and its commitment to its ultimate goal of destroying the US is being enabled by Obama's policies of accommodation." "In Israel's Hour of Need," *Jerusalem Post*, February 27, 2015.

Chapter Twelve
A New World Organization

Islamist Terrorism

In the first part of the twentieth century, terrorism was concentrated in the murderous activities of the Arabs in the Holy Land. It started in the second and third decades of the century and developed after the proclamation of the State of Israel. We referred to it in chapter 11 as "Palestinian Terrorism."

In the second part of the century there appeared international terrorism, proceeding from Islamist organizations. New York, London, Paris, Buenos Aires, Jerusalem, and other locales throughout the world were hit by terrorist acts that caused the deaths of innocent civilians. These locations were targeted by the international Muslim campaign that originates in various geographical points and aims at the conquest of the world through terror.

Al-Qaeda, Hamas, Hezbollah, ISIS, Boko Haram, and the many other groups that follow the murderous jihad philosophy, whether working independently or in coordination, have become the great danger of the present times, and the danger has been growing from year to year. The UN is hostage to the member states that, one way or another, support terrorism. Besides this aspect of international politics, the UN has adopted a philosophy that terrorists' human rights must be taken into the highest consideration and thereby has aided their progress, as we have seen in chapter 9.

Iran and its subsidiary Hezbollah have amplified their terrorist activities in various parts of the world; their operatives have been caught in the involvement of terrorist activities in different countries.

In Argentina, Special Prosecutor Alberto Nisman spent eight years investigating the bombing of the Jewish cultural center in Buenos Aires in 1994, which killed eighty-seven people and injured more than three hundred. Nisman released a five-hundred-page report documenting the Iranian-Hezbollah penetration of Latin America. He found that the 1994 terrorist bombing had been entirely orchestrated by "the highest echelons in the government of the Islamic Republic of Iran."[1]

Nisman wanted arrest warrants for former Iranian president Hashemi Rafsanjani and members of his government such as the ministers of intelligence and security, the foreign minister, and the then general commander of the Iranian Revolutionary Guard. The prosecutor detailed Hezbollah's involvement in the attack and showed that the suicide bomber himself was an agent of Hezbollah, the "terrorist proxy of the Iranian regime." Nisman pointed out that the Iranian ambassadors in Argentina, Chile, and Uruguay all left several days before the attack.

One day after his report became known, the prosecutor was killed in his home. Apparently the *longa manus* of terrorism was there in Buenos Aires to stop the prosecution.

In view of the revelations in the Argentinian prosecutor's report and everything that is known regarding the other terrorist attacks, Irwin Cotler asks: "What can the international community do to combat this dangerous wave of international terror? What must be done to bring the perpetrators to justice, lest a culture of impunity continues to encourage terrorist acts?"[2]

The sad reality is that one cannot expect the United Nations to undertake any measure to combat this spreading international war for the reason that follows.

The United Nations: Hostage to Terrorist Member States

As seen in chapter 11, the United Nations, which created the Universal Declaration of Human Rights in response to the atrocities committed during the Second World War, most especially against the Jewish people, has become the great promoter of contemporary antisemitism through its unrelenting anti-Israel policies. This began at virtually the same time as the declaration's approval and in the ensuing years has acquired colossal dimensions.

The hypocritical behavior of the UN reached levels that could never have

---

1. Cited in Irwin Cotler, "The Iran-Hezbollah Terror Connection: What Must Be Done?" *Jerusalem Post*, July 12, 2013.
2. Ibid.

been foreseen. The first grand manifestation of the hypocrisy that took over the United Nations occurred in October 1, 1975, when Idi Amin, as chairman of the Organization of African Union – known as a major violator of human rights to his people in Uganda – addressed the General Assembly in a rabid speech, which denounced the "Zionist-US conspiracy" and called for the expulsion of Israel and also for its extinction – a typically genocidal speech. The assembly gave him a standing ovation when he arrived, applauded him throughout, and again rose to its feet when he left. In those years the Afro-Asian-Arab and Soviet bloc already made up the majority of the General Assembly. (Today this majority may have lost some of the republics of the Soviet bloc but gained European and Latin American partners. And so the hypocrisy proceeds.) The day after his speech, the UN secretary-general and the president of the General Assembly offered a public dinner in Amin's honor.[3] By doing so the UN gave support to the murderer of his own people and the proponent of the genocide of another people.

Another major enemy of human rights and advocate of the extinction of a member state of the UN is the former president of Iran, Mahmoud Ahmadinejad. Speaking to the General Assembly of the United Nations on September 24, 2012, he said that Israel had no roots in the Middle East and would be "eliminated."[4] This was a categorically genocidal speech at the site of the world organization that claims as its mission to combat human rights violations, and above all genocide.

This was made possible by members of like-minded voting blocs, such as the Organization of the Islamic Conference, the Organization of African Unity, and the League of Arab States, which comprise more than two-thirds of the UN membership. Together they can railroad through any resolution, no matter how absurd.[5] The United Nations is a permanent hostage to these blocs of nondemocratic states that are mega-violators of human rights.

---

3. Johnson, *Modern Times*, 536. The author refers to Daniel Patrick Moynihan, *A Dangerous Place* (Boston: Little Brown, 1978), 154–55.

4. Matt Spetalnick and Mark Felsenthal, "Obama Warns Iran on Nuclear Bid; Containment 'No Option,'" Reuters, http://www.reuters.com/article/us-un-assembly-obama-excerpts-idUSBRE88O0F520120925. The United States dismissed the Iranian president's comments as "disgusting, offensive and outrageous" (*Jerusalem Post*, internet edition).

5. Saad Eddin Ibrahim, "Tyrants Get Another UN Platform," *Wall Street Journal*, April 24, 2009.

Some commentators have no problem in picturing the UN in the most horrible colors. An American classicist at the California State University has written that

the U.N. is a morally bankrupt, corrupt congeries of international thugs and creeps, along with invertebrate Western states who mask their fear and appeasement with the Kabuki dance of international diplomacy. But only in an alternate universe does the U.S. spend one minute on a nakedly ideological outfit like the UNHRC, or give half a billion dollars a year to an organization like the U.N., the purpose of which is to damage America's security and interests at every turn.[6]

Anne Bayefsky, who has been waging a constant war at the United Nations, has defined the organization as "neither redeemable nor reformable" and accused it of corrupting its most important mission – human rights.

It is therefore a joyless task to have to announce that the image of the UN as human rights leader or the centerpiece of the effective promotion and protection of human rights is a delusion. It is not redeemable, reformable or entitled to an inevitable role as the only game in town. But that is not the worst of it. Not only is the organization inept, inefficient, wasteful, neglectful, cumbersome and unable to fix itself. The UN has taken our dearest values and corrupted them utterly. It has turned human rights victim into villain and villain into victim. It has trashed the sacred trust of universal values and replaced them with phony particularities. It has provided a platform for anti-Semites and abusers and silenced the voice of the tortured and abused.[7]

Bayefsky characterizes the UN as follows:

The UN is an organization owned and operated by non-democracies. It pushes democracies within the organization apart in the pathetic struggle for a very small piece of the pie. And in the dust-up the bits left on the floor are the cries of the real victims of human rights.[8]

---

6. Bruce S. Thornton, "Obama and the U.N.'s Alternate Universe," *Frontpage Magazine*, July 31, 2104, http://www.frontpagemag.com/fpm/237215/obama-and-uns-alternate-universe-bruce-thornton.

7. Bayefsky, "Neither Redeemable nor Reformable," *Justice* 45 (spring 2008): 29.

8. Ibid., 34.

The League of Nations and United Nations

The League of Nations was described as "a chimera, a hall of empty mirrors and empty people."[9]

In 1931, when Japan invaded Manchuria, the League of Nations responded to China's appeal for help by calling for countries to stop trading with Japan, but because of the Depression, many countries refused to abide. So the league called for Japan to withdraw from Manchuria; Japan's response was to leave the League of Nations.

In 1935, Italy invaded Abyssinia. The Abyssinians did not have the strength to withstand, so they appealed to the league for help. The league condemned the invasion and called upon member states to impose trade restrictions with Italy. The trade restrictions were not carried out because they would have little effect, as Italy would be able to trade with nonmember states, particularly the United States.

In 1938 the league stopped functioning and in 1946 its assets were transferred to the United Nations.

The historian of the Universal Declaration of Human Rights, Johannes Morsink, writes that "after the repeated condemnations by the Allies of the Nazi violations of human rights and fundamental freedoms, many countries had come to look upon the United Nations as the new world organization that was to have some teeth in it. They did not want an organization that would be as impotent as the League of Nations had been, failing in the 1930s to prevent Italy's conquest of Ethiopia and Hitler's taking of the Rhineland. Hence the strong desire to see to it that human rights talk was not just talk, but coupled with the necessary machinery of implementation and realization."[10]

As we approach the seventieth anniversary of the creation of the United Nations, it has become evident to any informed member of the international community that the organization has failed miserably to protect the fundamental right to "life, liberty and security of person," as set in article 3 of the Universal Declaration of Human Rights.

In the United Nations, as opposed to the League of Nations, all existing states are members. No state was refused membership, in direct violation of article 4 of the organization's charter, which states that "membership in

---

9. Albert Cohen, cited in Winter and Prost, *René Cassin*, 80.
10. Morsink, *Universal Declaration*, 12.

the United Nations is open to all other peace-loving states which accept the obligations contained in the present Charter and, in the judgement of the Organization, are able and willing to carry out these obligations."[11]

The disrespect of this basic rule for acceptance of new member states and the lack of expulsion of the worst violators has brought about the incoherence of the UN's policies, the hypocrisy of its resolutions, the domination of the General Assembly by a majority of nondemocratic states, and the subservience of the so-called third-world countries (and many times even of the advanced countries) to the whims of the undemocratic, violent human rights violators. Besides that, the strictly political and nonlegal orientation of the Security Council – controlled by the five veto-holding states, which are very frequently in disagreement – as well as the politicization of the International Court of Justice have betrayed the purposes of the organization. And so, we witness the abandonment of the suffering populations of Asia and Africa, the lack of enforcement of the human rights proclaimed in the Universal Declaration, the impunity of the great genocidaires, responsible for the most terrible atrocities against millions of human beings, the impotence (or unwillingness) to fight international terrorism – all indications that the organization marches to a point of strangulation.

On April 29, 1946, the first meeting of the Commission on Human Rights of the Economic and Social Council was held. Henri Laugier (Canada), the assistant secretary-general of the UN in charge of social affairs, opened the meeting, in the presence of Professor René Cassin (France), Dr. L. Hsia (China), Mr. K.C. Neogi (India), Mr. Dusan Brkish (Yugoslavia), Mr. Nicolai Kiukev (USSR), and Mrs. Eleanor Roosevelt (USA). On that momentous occasion, Laugier stated: "You will have to look for a basis for a fundamental declaration on human rights, acceptable to all the United Nations, *the acceptance of which will become the essential condition of the admission in the international community.*"[12]

---

11. The free acceptance and maintenance of all states invalidates article 6 of the UN charter, which states: "A Member of the United Nations which has persistently violated the Principles contained in the present Charter may be expelled from the Organization by the General Assembly upon the recommendation of the Security Council."
12. Max Beer, "Can We Save the Bill of Human Rights? Opportunity for a New Start," *Commentary*, October 1, 1953, https://www.commentarymagazine.com/?s= Can+We+Save+the+Bill+of+Human+Rights, and Allida M. Black, "Eleanor Roosevelt and

No such condition was ever implemented, as the new member states of the United Nations were accepted into the organization without any checking into whether they accepted the principles established in the UDHR. In truth, Laugier suggested acceptance, which is not enough; the necessary condition should have been the actual observance of human rights.

And so the world is "blessed" with a monumental organization, with an annual budget of billions of dollars, that has no capability to stem the two great ongoing tragedies, capable of destroying the world – terrorism and genocide.

A Bill of Human Rights outside the United Nations

The idea of creating an entity outside the United Nations is not new.

Back in 1948, Professor Hersch Lauterpacht, judge of the International Court of Justice, maintained that "there is no decisive reason why an International Bill of Human Rights between states genuinely resolved to place the rights of man under safeguards independent of their own will and power should not effectively come into being outside the United Nations." He explained that this could materialize between members of a regional association of states linked together by a common heritage of respect for the rule of law and rights of man as the most precious asset.[13]

This initiative is all the more necessary in a world that, since the time Lauterpacht expressed his vision, has gone through and continues to suffer so many catastrophic violations of the rights of man. The materialization of Lauterpacht's vision requires an organization composed of a group of nations that would set human rights above all aims and undertake to protect their own populations from any harm, and also, whenever feasible, to intervene in third-party states – not members of their organization – in order to save human beings from destruction.

A "League of Democracies"

In Eric Posner's *The Twilight of Human Rights Law* we read the following idea about replacing the UN's Security Council:

the Universal Declaration of Human Rights," *OAH Magazine of History* 22, no. 2 (April 2008): 34–37, www.jstor.org/stable/pdfplus/25162170. Emphasis mine.
13. Lauterpacht, "The Universal Declaration of Human Rights," 377.

A number of commentators and politicians have proposed that liberal democracies should form a "league" or "concert" that would put steady pressure on non-democracies to change their systems. In its most radical vision, the league would replace the United Nations Security Council, depriving China and Russia of the power to deny legal authority to military interventions against dictatorships. Just such a proposal was made by interventionists frustrated by China's and Russia's refusal to condemn the Syrian government's massacres of civilians in the Syrian civil war.

The League of Democracies is a radical idea from the standpoint of international law, since it would exist in defiance of many countries, including several of the most powerful. It is driven by frustration with a state of affairs in which nearly all countries give their consent to human rights treaties but many countries refuse to comply with them, and nearly all countries refuse to enforce them against each other. But if one accepts human rights treaties as law, the League of Democracies is a logical implication of it. The problem is enforcement, and since only liberal democracies take human rights seriously, only liberal democracies can be depended on to enforce them.

The League of Democracies is driven by a vision of a world in which all countries respect human rights and are at peace with each other. It is an appealing vision, but the problem is getting from here to there. Countries excluded from the League of Democracies will be more reluctant than ever to cooperate with members in areas such as trade and security where there are shared interests. Thus, a League of Democracies, by further institutionalizing and promoting the idea that states that violate human rights lack legitimacy, would contribute to international polarization and disorder, and for the sake of a utopian goal – a world of human rights respecting and peaceful states – that is unlikely to be realized.[14]

The proposition is utopian and could not be implemented, as the replacement of the Security Council would depend on the consent of the United Nations General Assembly, where a majority stands firm on the side of Russia and China in everything that concerns the denials of human rights. How could a human rights–violating community elect a human rights–observant body? Another problem with the proposition is that there is really no way

14. Posner, *Twilight of Human Rights Law*, 135–36.

of enforcing or even of exercising pressure on states to comply with human rights observance.

The only solution is the total disengagement from the United Nations by all liberal democracies and by states wishing to cooperate with human rights observance, peace, and security, as will be elaborated on below.

Eric Stein left his native Czechoslovakia in 1939 and succeeded in coming to the United States, where he became a very prestigious Michigan Law School professor. In 2003 he wrote that he had become deeply disillusioned by the shortcomings of the United Nations, which by then had proved incapable of unifying the world under the rule of law. "In postwar Washington, I was entirely swept up by the vision of a new world order based on international law and universal institutions, with the United Nations at the center. This vision, however, faded quickly."[15]

Emile Zola and the Dreyfus Affair, 1894–1906

L'affaire Dreyfus, as it is known in France, is seen as a symbol of the willful miscarriage of justice. It resulted in a vehement manifestation of antisemitism on the part of the French people, demonstrating how the alleged misdeed of a single Jew can overflow into a wild campaign against the Jewish people as a whole.

On the other hand, the *affaire* touched the Jews of Europe and their friends so deeply that it ended up resulting in *Der Judenstaat*, the book in which journalist Theodor Herzl launched the idea of the creation of a Jewish state. Herzl had been profoundly affected by the dangers that Jews continued to confront in Europe despite all the proclamations and declarations about human dignity, liberty, equality, fraternity, and full rights for people of all origins. The ideas articulated in his book gave birth to the Zionist movement, which resulted in the return of Jewish sovereignty in its land, after almost two thousand years of Diaspora.

The *affaire* that so motivated Herzl was an 1894 incident in which Captain Alfred Dreyfus, an artillery officer in the French army, was framed and convicted of treason in order to protect the actual traitor. Dreyfus made a convenient scapegoat because he was Jewish. He was given a life sentence,

---

15. Anne Boerger, "At the Cradle of Legal Scholarship on the European Union: The Life and Early Work of Eric Stein," *American Journal of Comparative Law* 62, no. 4 (2014): 869.

of which he served five years before social pressure forced a new trial. In this trial as well, Dreyfus was convicted, but the trial was so obviously unfair and the conviction so baseless that the president of the republic gave Dreyfus a pardon and he was set free. In the end it became clear that Dreyfus was in fact completely innocent.

Indeed, in 1931, German documents confirmed that Esterhazy had really been the spy; even so, the French army was not ready to recognize the truth about its crime against Dreyfus. As late as 1994, it published a study to mark the centennial of Dreyfus imprisonment in which the army presented itself as a victim of the *dreyfusards* (the defenders of the captain), who were described as socialists, republicans, and radicals, opponents of the military class. Regarding Dreyfus himself, the most that the military publication was able to state was that "his innocence is the theory generally accepted by the historians."[16]

The antisemitic wave that accompanied the affair expressed itself in the press, in the streets, and in parliament.

The leader of this campaign was the arch-antisemite Eduard Drumont, author of *La France juive*, the main theme of which was that the Jews not only crucified Christ in the past, but were continuing to crucify Him in France. The book ran into 121 editions. After the success of the book, Drumont founded a successful antisemitic daily newspaper, *La libre parole*, which led the campaign against Dreyfus and the Jews. The paper would proclaim *"Le juif, voilà l'ennemi"* (The Jew – there is the enemy).[17]

When Dreyfus was convicted, Drumont wrote in his paper that "Dreyfus committed no crime against his fatherland," and then explained, *"Pour trahir sa patrie, il faut en avoir une"* (To betray one's fatherland, one must first have one).

The majority of the French intelligentsia sided against Dreyfus. Known as the *antidreyfusards*, they established the League of the French Fatherland, made up of intellectuals, students, lawyers, doctors, and university professors. Included in the league were eighty-seven members of the Collège de France and the Institut and twenty-six of the forty members of the French Academy.

This league kept on functioning after the close of the Dreyfus affair as an

---

16. Carroll, *Constantine's Sword*, 453–56.
17. O'Brien, *The Siege*, 62–64.

organization dedicated to antisemitism. Years later, it was integrated into the French Vichy regime that collaborated in sending hundreds of thousands of French Jews and refugees from other countries to their deaths in the concentration camps.[18]

On the other hand, among the *dreyfusards* – those who defended Dreyfus's innocence – were personalities like Marcel Proust, Anatole France, Henri Poincaré, Georges Clemenceau, and other intellectuals. The leader of Dreyfus's defenders was Emile Zola, France's most popular writer at the time. He investigated the case and wrote a long letter to the president of the French Republic, Monsieur M. Félix Faure, in defense of Dreyfus. Zola gave the letter to Clemenceau, who published it on the front page of the daily *L'Aurore* on January 13, 1898, under the headline *J'Accuse*. The piece describes in all its details the libel against Captain Alfred Dreyfus.

The letter ends with accusations against a series of military authorities – hence the title *J'Accuse*. It became the most famous piece of journalism in any language, in any country, at any time.

It is a long piece, in which the author accuses the officers who took part in the Dreyfus trial of miscarrying justice. Zola shows how after it had been so discovered, those officers continued defending their position through "the most preposterous and blameworthy machinations." He likewise accused the War Office of having conducted an abominable campaign in the press (especially in *L'Éclair* and *L'Écho de Paris*) in order to cover up its misdeeds and lead public opinion astray. Zola concluded the letter by challenging the authorities to sue him for libel for having insulted the honor of public officials.

The effect of this piece was tremendous. All day long, the street vendors in Paris shouted *"L'Aurore"* at the top of their lungs, ran about with huge bundles of the paper under their arms, and thrust copies at eager buyers. In hoarse but triumphant voices, the fine name of this newspaper rose above the feverish activity in the streets. The impact was so stunning that Paris was nearly turned upside down. *L'Aurore* sold between two hundred thousand and three hundred thousand copies, ten times the normal number. Léon Blum was to recall, in his *Souvenirs*, that *"J'Accuse* overwhelmed Paris in a single day. The Dreyfus cause was given a new lease of life. We regained confidence;

18. Johnson, *History of the Jews*, 390.

we could feel it flooding through us, while our furious adversaries staggered under the blow."[19]

Emile Zola published various other pieces in French newspapers, a few of them containing strong attacks on what he called the "foul press." In 1897, the Chamber of Deputies voted to side with the injustice that had been done by the judiciary in the Dreyfus affair. In an interview published on December 6, 1897, by *L'Aurore*, Zola expressed his wrath. He concluded his declaration to the journalist by saying: "These votes will have only one result: they will give an instant's satisfaction to the foul-smelling, scandal-mongering press that is concerned only with circulation figures, not with moral convictions. That press is making France lose its wits and fall apart."[20]

Zola published a "Letter to France" on January 7, 1898, in which he referred to "the lies in the press, the diet of inept farce, low insults and moral depravity that it feeds you every morning.... How could you possibly demand truth and justice when they are doing so much to denature your legendary virtues, the clarity of your intelligence and the sturdiness of your reasoning?"[21]

He considered the Dreyfus Affair to be a "crime against society perpetrated by antisemitism, by saturating the public with lies and calumny."[22]

In "Letter to the Senate," published by *L'Aurore* on May 29, 1900, Zola attacked the press again, saying: "But that is not all. The worst part and the most painful part is that the foul press was allowed to poison the country, to feed it the most brazen diet of lies, slander, trash and outrageous nonsense and so make the country lose its head."[23]

At the official ceremony in which Dreyfus's rank was degraded, an immense and excited crowd, hearing Dreyfus's cries of innocence, began to whistle and chant such slogans as "Death to Dreyfus! Death to the Jews!" As the affair developed, the antisemitic campaign grew in intensity. Zola dedicated his mind, soul, and pen to fight the return in France to open antisemitism. In his "Letter to the Young People" of December 14, 1897, he screamed out:

19. Emile Zola, *The Dreyfus Affair: "J'Accuse" and Other Writings*, ed. Alain Pagès, trans. Eleanor Levieux (New Haven: Yale University Press, 1998), xviii.
20. Ibid., 27, 29.
21. Ibid., 35, 37–38.
22. Ibid., 41.
23. Ibid., 158.

Can young people be anti-Semites? Is that possible? Can it be that their fresh new brains and souls have already been deranged by that idiotic poison? How very sad, how disturbing a prospect for the twentieth century that is about to begin! One hundred years after the Declaration of the Rights of Man, one hundred years after that supreme act of tolerance and emancipation, we are reverting to wars of religion, to the most obnoxious and inane type of fanaticism! It may be understandable in certain men who have their role to play, an attitude to keep up and an all-devouring ambition to satisfy. But in the young! In those who are born and who grow so that all the rights and freedoms we dreamt the coming century would be resplendent with can flourish! They are the long-awaited architects of that dream – and what do they do but proclaim their anti-Semitism! They will begin the century by massacring all the Jews, their fellow citizens, because they are of a different race and a different faith! Is this the way to take possession of the City of our dreams, the City of equality and fraternity? If youth had really come to that, it would be enough to make a man weep, enough to make him deny all hope and human happiness.[24]

The *Figaro* of December 5, 1897, published a piece by Emile Zola, in which he stressed the underlying antisemitism of the Dreyfus affair, saying:

And this whole lamentable Dreyfus Affair is the work of anti-Semitism: it and it alone made the miscarriage of justice possible; it and it alone is driving the public to hysteria; it and it alone is preventing that miscarriage from being quietly, nobly acknowledged, in the interest of this country's health and good name. Could anything have been simpler or more natural than to seek out the truth as soon as the first serious doubts set in? Surely it is obvious that if we have come to this pass, to this degree of raging folly, it must be due to some concealed poison that is making us all delirious.

Today, since we began demanding that the truth be brought to light, the anti-Semitism has become still more violent and instructive. It is anti-Semitism itself that is on trial – and if the innocence of a Jew were to be revealed, what a slap in the face that would be for the anti-Semites! Could there possibly be such a thing as an innocent Jew? The whole carefully constructed scheme of lies would collapse. A whiff of fresh air would be

24. Ibid., 33.

let in: good faith and fairness would then spell the ruin of a sect that only manages to hold sway over simple minds by brandishing the crudest insults and most bare-faced slander.[25]

In the "Letter to France" already referred to, Zola attaches antisemitism to the Catholic Church. He writes:

> And do you know where else you are headed, France? To the Church. You are going back to the past, the past filled with intolerance and theocracy that your most illustrious children wrestled with and thought they had slain by sacrificing their intelligence and their blood. What a triumph it would be if a religious war could be unleashed! No, no, the people are not believers anymore; but isn't this the first step towards making believers of them – starting the old medieval intolerance all over again, burning Jews in public? Anyhow, the poison has been found; and once the people of France have been turned into fanatics and executioners, once their generosity and their love for the hard-won rights of man have been wrenched out of their hearts, God no doubt will do the rest.[26]

In the same piece he predicts that eventually the public will turn against the "foul press":

> One of these days the public will suddenly gag on all the filth it has been fed. It is bound to happen. . . . The public will bring its weight to bear. In an outpouring of sovereign generosity, the public will decide there are to be no more traitors; it will call for truth and justice. Thus, anti-Semitism will be tried and sentenced for evil deeds, for the loss of dignity and health this country has suffered as a result.[27]

Zola was tried for libel and condemned to a year's imprisonment. He went into exile in England where he remained for almost a year. Ultimately he was the victor in his war against the French army and the French press.

Dreyfus's rehabilitation was the work of a few intellectuals dedicated to truth and justice, who valiantly fought the corrupt military system and the bigoted intellectual leadership of the French people. The great victor of this

25. Ibid., 24.
26. Ibid., 39.
27. Ibid., 41.

war was the heroic Emile Zola, whose honest, straightforward campaign in favor of human rights, of the real equality and liberty for all humans, echoes till the present day, over a century later.

From Emile Zola we should learn that resolutions, declarations, proclamations, conventions, covenants, and all such documents are not worth the paper they are written on if peoples and nations are not ready to go out to fight the good fight – to support minorities; to protect the weak, the underprivileged, women, and children; to wage war against oppressors and dictators of all kinds, even on the other side of our planet; to honor with deeds the dignity of every human being; to fight the press when it commits the sin of bigotry through lies and calumnies; and to abolish the venom of antisemitism.

Zola tirelessly campaigned in defense of the fundamental rights of every person. He did it as the nineteenth century was closing; his splendorous lesson echoes in our hearts in this tragic second decade of the twenty-first century.

New Year, 2017: Emile Zola on the Eiffel Tower

Emile Zola died in 1902. At the time of his death, he was recognized not only as one of the greatest novelists in Europe, but also as a man of action – a defender of truth and justice, a champion of the poor and the persecuted. At his funeral he was eulogized by Anatole France as having been not just a great man, but "a moment in the human conscience." Crowds of mourners, prominent and poor alike, lined the streets to salute the passing casket. In 1908, Zola's remains were transferred to the Pantheon and placed alongside those of Voltaire, Jean-Jacques Rousseau, and Victor Hugo.

Zola's works and deeds influenced the course of French history; his daring spirit and inspiring courage remained alive throughout these 120 years to all lovers of liberty, equality, and fraternity within the human race.

At midnight of December 31, 2016, as the New Year 2017 strikes out in Paris, Zola suddenly appears, standing on the Eiffel Tower. He is wrapped in a big black scarf, his beard has grown, he looks up to heaven and recites the second verse of King Solomon's Ecclesiastes: "Futility of futilities! Futility of futilities! All is futile!" He stops, stares into heaven, and with his deep insight looks back upon the world events of the past hundred years. He begins to bemoan the state of the world, his voice shaken and frightening. Thousands of Parisians and tourists run to the tower to witness the phenomenon of resurrection, to hear the voice of this heroic fighter for human dignity, to learn what he has to say on the world of yesterday, on the world of today.[28]

And this is what they hear:

I ACCUSE the governments of all states, including of those known as liberal democracies, that have not expressly and officially recognized the historical fact of the Armenian genocide and the continuing cultural genocide of that persecuted people by the Turkish authorities till the present times;

I ACCUSE the American government for not having recognized the terrible complicity of the White House and the State Department with Hitler's quasi-total annihilation of the European Jewish people, as diagnosed by the Treasury Department of the same US government at the time of the Second World War;

I ACCUSE the British government for having submitted itself to Arab-Muslim pressure during the World War II years, closing the doors of Palestine to Jewish refugees and then supporting the Arab invasion of the newly born State of Israel; the present ambivalence of the British government in relation to the Arab-Israeli conflict maintains and aggravates its failure to comply with the obligations it received from the League of Nations with the Mandate for Palestine;

I ACCUSE Belgium, France, England, and Italy for the tragic events that have been occurring in their former colonies in Africa, which are mostly due to the fact that the colonizers exploited the colonies and – when they finally departed – left them totally unprepared in all fields of economic and democratic development;

I ACCUSE those European states that considered above everything else their own economic interests in moments of murderous conflicts that convulsed the African countries; I ACCUSE them for not coming to save

---

28. This was originally delivered by me in Portuguese at a conference on October 6, 2010, under the title "*O Caso Dreyfus e a Dramática Ressureição de Emile Zola*" (The Dreyfus case and the dramatic resurrection of Emile Zola), at the Centro de História e Cultura Judaica, Rio de Janeiro. It was published by the center in *Humanismo Judaico na Literatura na História e na Ciência*, vol. 2 (Rio de Janeiro: Verve, 2013), 21–34.

persecuted masses and sometimes even supporting the murderers, such as France did in Rwanda;

I ACCUSE the European states that put their interests above the survival of those peoples who were caught in an interethnic war in the former Yugoslavia;

I ACCUSE the European states for wanting to force Israel into making any and all concessions to the Palestinians, who are sworn to destroy the Jewish state, as clearly stated in their charter;

I ACCUSE the Obama administration of following the same policy, which would lead to the destruction of the State of Israel;

I ACCUSE the governments of Saudi Arabia, Iran, and Qatar for financing terrorist organizations that have returned to the most barbaric times of history, committing atrocious acts against civilians all over the world;

I ACCUSE Saudi Arabia and all the other Muslim states for their tyrannical regimes, total lack of liberty, discrimination against women, lack of justice, and murderous reactions against any opposition;

I ACCUSE the European governments for not dealing with the problems posed by their aggressive Muslim terrorists with severe, energetic measures and instead allowing, out of cowardice, an old religious fanaticism to gradually take over and bring instability in the heart of the continent;

I ACCUSE the human rights nongovernmental organizations for not promoting the needed campaign to fight all terrorist organizations and their war crimes against humanity;

I ACCUSE Amnesty International and similar organizations that deplore Palestinian civilian victims without considering that these fatalities occur because the terrorist organizations send their missiles from residential buildings and from hospitals and put their children in front of the terrorists as human shields;

I ACCUSE the United Nations, especially the so-called states of the third world, of having adhered to the noxious campaigns of the Muslim-Arab-African bloc against democracy, against human rights, and against the State of Israel, the only democracy in the Middle East;

I ACCUSE the organs of the United Nations – the General Assembly, the Security Council, the Council for Human Rights, and UNESCO – for having ignored the principles established in the Charter of the United Nations, in the Universal Declaration of Human Rights, in the Convention on Genocide, and in all the other basic international declarations, thereby abandoning suffering and persecuted populations and strengthening the hands of criminal despots;

I ACCUSE the United Nations for having created and maintained for seven decades the UNRWA, which was supposed to take care of the so-called Palestinian refugees but did nothing to integrate them in the Arab countries where they live, but, on the contrary, kept them as refugees in order to maintain this hypocritical card against the State of Israel, and handed the administration of this false refugee organization to Arabs who have used it as a basis for terrorism against Israel;

I ACCUSE the United Nations Council for Human Rights for inverting the realities of the Israel-Palestinian conflicts, protecting the aggressor and accusing the victim, and presiding over investigatory commissions composed of "experts" known as enemies of Israel, which did nothing other than blindly accept the complaints, false versions, and falsified pictures manufactured by the Palestinians;

I ACCUSE the Vatican for its lack of courage to face the enemies of all peoples – the jihad terrorists who have been killing Christians and kidnapping Christian girls, raping them, and then selling them into slavery; I ACCUSE the Vatican for abstaining from the necessary good fight against the present destroyers of humanity;

I ACCUSE the International Red Cross which, after having cooperated with the Nazis during the Second World War, proceeds with its antisemitic policies and unjustly condemns the State of Israel based on a false interpretation of the Geneva Conventions;

I ACCUSE the foul international media for perverting and corrupting the truth, turning victim into perpetrator and criminal into victim and becoming a real accomplice to the murderous terrorist organizations;

I ACCUSE the major international TV channels and newspapers for keeping silent about the Palestinians' constant attacks on the Israeli civilian population and their open determination to destroy the State of Israel; I ACCUSE them for not missing an opportunity to condemn Israel's legitimate defensive actions, thereby joining the club of accomplices to the anti-Israel and anti-Jewish jihad;

I ACCUSE the International Court of Justice for getting involved in the political machinations of the Security Council and reaching a decision without any factual basis and without any recourse to legal sources, but instead in accordance with the interests of the stronger parties and of the governments of their home countries;

I ACCUSE those of the Western intelligentsia and those universities in Europe and in the United States that advocate a boycott of Israeli scholars and Israeli products, justifying their attitudes on entirely false reports regarding the events of the Arab-Israeli conflict; they accuse the most democratic country in the Middle East of apartheid – exactly the great crime perpetrated by Israel's accusers, the Arab states and the Palestinian institutions;

I ACCUSE the leftist political movements around the world for the cynical campaigns they have been moving against the State of Israel, accusing Israel of being an apartheid state despite the fact that this goes against all the evidence of life in Israel, where Arabs have the same rights as Jews and where Arabs live freely and with all opportunities of economic and cultural development;

I ACCUSE the same movements of keeping absolute silence about the repeated declarations of the Palestinian leadership that they will not accept one Jew living in their planned Palestinian Muslim state – which they insist will be *judenrein* – that being the highest level of apartheid;

I ACCUSE the International Criminal Court for its inoperativeness in bringing to trial and condemning the great genocidaires who travel freely around the world, some of them having been received festively by the General Assembly of the United Nations, where they get the attention and the applause of the majority of member states;

I ACCUSE the European states of the crime of malicious and hypocritical modern anti-Semitism, veiled in their negative attitudes toward the State of Israel;

I SUFFER to see that the anti-Semitism that I fought during the Dreyfus Affair, 120 years ago, which affected life in Paris and in the whole of France, has been spreading throughout the world community of nations, which hides its evil anti-Semitism under the cover of demonization and delegitimization of the state created on the millenary land of the descendants of the biblical fathers;

I ACCUSE the successive governments of the State of Israel for not responding adequately to the Arab propaganda, by not taking advantage of the help of non-Jews who have declared their willingness to participate in the defense of the Jewish state's good name, by not reminding the world of the historical background of the Arab-Israeli conflict, by not showing the world the ugly, bigoted education given to the Palestinian children and the hateful propaganda of the Muslim imams in their mosques, both of which incite to hate and murder Israelis as well as Jews anywhere.

I ACCUSE the Jewish community of the United States for not coming down to Washington and standing in front of the White House in the thousands, in the tens of thousands, to demand the freedom of Jonathan Pollard, condemned for life in a hateful judgment that did not take into consideration the agreement made with the accused that if he gave up on a trial, he would be given a light sentence, whereas others who spied for real enemies of the United States received much lighter sentences;[29]

I ACCUSE the Jewish community of the United States and of Europe for not doing enough to support the State of Israel in the critical situation it faces under the pressures from the Palestinian terrorists, the Arab states,

---

29. Jonathan Pollard was finally paroled in November 20, 2015, but to onerous parole conditions that impede his religious observance and prevent him from being gainfully employed. See Gil Hoffman, "Jonathan Pollard Job in Limbo Due to Parole Conditions," *Jerusalem Post*, December 2, 2015, http://www.jpost.com/Diaspora/Jonathan-Pollard-job -in-limbo-due-to-parole-conditions-436110; Sam Gluck, "Pollard: Parole Terms Violate Religion," JP Updates, December 15, 2015, http://jpupdates.com/2015/12/15/pollard- parole-terms-violate-religion/.

the UN organs, the media, and the nongovernmental organizations; the foul Arab propaganda should receive the answer it deserves through a systematic worldwide counter-propaganda, for which many non-Jewish personalities have expressed readiness to lend their support.[30]

And finally, with the greatest pain, I ACCUSE my country and my countrymen – France and the French – for going back to their miserable anti-Dreyfus campaign when they turned against all French Jews; for never really regretting their active collaboration with the Nazi invaders, helping them in locating and sending Jews of all ages to Auschwitz; and for conducting in the current days the most fascistic policies against the State of Israel, a manifest attitude of the ugliest, most cruel antisemitism.

Exhausted, Zola closes his eyes and slowly disappears from the view of the enormous crowds that ended up surrounding the Eiffel Tower, and from the millions all over the world who succeeded in listening to his words through the TV channels that rushed to the Eiffel Tower as soon as the great fighter for human rights appeared.

And silence descends upon Paris, upon all Europe, and upon the United States – traumatized by the voice of conscience.

Disengaging from the United Nations

In a speech delivered at a Chinese university, former Israeli ambassador to the UN Gabriela Shalev exposed the constant, growing, hypocritical policies of the United Nations. She referred to "voices that call for us to disengage, to walk out from the UN," since the automatic majority against Israel renders the UN a lost cause for this country. The former ambassador disagreed with these voices and concluded in a manner contradicting the strong critique she had raised, saying: "The United Nations is a parliament of the world. All nations are represented in it. But as the world is not a perfect place, the parliament cannot be perfect. The UN is – as Ambassador Susan Rice said – imperfect but indispensable."[31]

Susan Rice and Gabriela Shalev are wrong. The UN was not created to

---

30. See former prime minister of Spain José María Aznar's vehement article in the *Times of London* of June 17, 2010, reproduced in chapter 4.

31. Gabriela Shalev, "Representing Israel at the UN," *Jerusalem Post*, November 15, 2013.

represent the world but to improve the world, to avoid the tragedies that occurred in the First World War and more so in the Second World War, "to save succeeding generations from the scourge of war, to establish conditions under which justice can be maintained, to practice tolerance and live together in peace with one another, to maintain international peace and security, to ensure that armed forces shall not be used," as solemnly proclaimed in the preamble of its charter and detailed in its text.

The UN established in the Universal Declaration of Human Rights that "the inherent dignity and equal and inalienable rights of all members of the human family is the foundation of freedom, justice and peace in the world" and that "all human beings are born free and equal in dignity and rights, endowed with reason and conscience and should act towards one another in a spirit of brotherhood."

The UN promised in its official program to bring peace to the world and to protect victims of the worst human rights violations by approving the Genocide Convention, with the purpose of preventing and punishing the major crime committed by Nazi Germany against the Jewish people. And then the world organization approved two covenants and one protocol to the same tune of protecting each and every human being as well as minorities of all kinds in the civil, political, economic, and cultural fields. And then hundreds of international agreements followed, all dealing with security, peace, and human rights.

Technically, the fundamental documents were wrongly worded, as demonstrated in earlier chapters of this book. But the ultimate purpose, the fundamental objectives for the creation of the United Nations were clearly set to protect humanity from disaster, from war, from atrocities, from genocide.

The United Nations has failed completely in the accomplishment of its own goals. Viewing the United Nations as a "parliament" is an illusion, a false illusion. The hypocritical, cynical world organization cannot be considered "indispensable," when it is there only to aggravate the problems through toleration of the worst atrocities and complicity in the major crimes against humanity.

The idea of disengagement from the UN coupled with a suggestion to create a new organization, composed exclusively of democratic states, has been coming up discretely. Isi Leibler, a distinguished Israeli journalist, wrote the following in the *Jerusalem Post*:

Hopefully, as US public opinion becomes increasingly disillusioned and angered with the hypocrisy and double standards employed by the immoral, tyrannical forces dominating the current United Nations, President Obama may be persuaded to act. Alternatively, Congress could employ its own clout and if necessary deny funding in order to stem the UN's obscene activities. It if fails to do so, it may even ultimately decide to encourage the creation of a new global association of democratic states.[32]

Another proposition was put forth by prestigious American journalist Charles Krauthammer, who wrote that

[the UN is] inherently a corrupt organization because it's a sandbox of dictators. It began as something essentially run by the Western democracies and it ran somewhat efficiently the first decade or so. Then you had decolonization. You ended up with 100, 150 countries, very few of whom are democratic. It is a playpen of dictators. And they run it that way. And the idea that they would use it for anything other than to promote authoritarianism and to attack the West is a fiction.

It will always be that way because it's a universal organization. The alternative is to form a league of democracies... which over a generation or two would take over the functions and the stature of the UN.[33]

The UN cannot be redeemed nor reformed because the majority of its members will not allow it. As we saw, the idea of creating a close-knit organization of states, obligatorily including only democratic regimes, appeared very early in the life of the UN, proposed by one of the most distinguished legal scholars in the field of international law – Professor Hersch Lauterpacht – and has been coming up here and there in recent editorials.

When we consider the sources of the UN's budget, disengaging from the UN becomes a viable plan. From 193 members of the United Nations, 90 are considered "free" countries, according to a report of "Freedom House."[34] The budget of the world organization for the year 2013 was over two and a half

32. Isi Leibler, "United Nations: Convergence of Hypocrisy, Deceit And Evil," *Jerusalem Post*, February 4, 2013.

33. "Krauthammer's Take," *National Review Online*, July 5, 2012, http://www.nationalreview.com/corner/304894/krauthammers-take-nro-staff.

34. Freedom House report for the year 2015. Posner (*Twilight of Human Rights Law*, 4) refers to a Freedom House report for 2013 with practically the same result.

billion dollars.[35] Fourteen of the richest democratic states contribute over 72 percent of the budget contributions, whereas five of those states contribute close to 51 percent of the total.[36] That means that a small group of states, anywhere between five and fourteen countries, could bring the United Nations to a standstill were they to decide to withdraw from the organization.

Interfaith Cooperation

Lord Jonathan Sacks, philosophy professor and former chief rabbi of the British Commonwealth, published in 2002 *The Dignity of Difference*,[37] a warm call for tolerance and reciprocal respect, based on the central idea of human dignity.

The author describes two unusual events that brought together representatives of all faiths. The first took place in the United Nations building on August 28, 2000, reuniting Tibetan monks, Japanese Shinto priests, Sufis, Sikhs, imams, Native Americans, African priests, and Anglicans. "Being there was like walking into a living lexicon of the religious heritage of mankind. Never before had there been such a gathering at the UN."[38] The United Nations had designated 2001 as the International Year of Dialogue between Civilizations. The new world order following the end of the Cold War was rapidly turning into a new world disorder. The end of a single overarching confrontation between Soviet Communism and the West had given rise not to peace but to a proliferating number of local conflicts between peoples who had previously lived together, if not in peace, then at least without bloodshed. The gathering of religious leaders was a prelude to the assembly of 159 heads of state a week later. It was heralded as the Millennium World Peace Summit.[39]

Lord Sacks explains that the aim was to enlist leaders of every major faith community to the cause of global peace. He reports that the degree of convergence was surprising, that there was a significant measure of consensus

35. This does not include the special peace and security budget for the peacekeeping missions, which for the 2013–14 fiscal year amounted to 7.54 billion dollars.
36. The five states United States, Japan, Germany, France, and the United Kingdom made up a total of 50.746 percent of the 2013 budget. Those five plus Italy, Canada, Spain, Brazil, Australia, South Korea, Mexico, Netherlands, and Switzerland complete the fourteen states that contributed together 72.696 percent of that year's budget.
37. *The Dignity of Difference: How to Avoid the Clash of Civilizations* (London: Continuum, 2002).
38. Ibid., 5.
39. Ibid., 5–6.

on the need for mutual respect and nonviolent methods of conflict resolution, on shared responsibility for the future of the planet, on obligations to the poor and duties to protect the environment. At the end of four days of deliberations the delegates signed a joint declaration of commitment to peace in its many dimensions.[40]

The author describes another extraordinary event that took place in January 2002 at Ground Zero, site of the destruction of the World Trade Center on September 11, 2001.

> Standing beside me were representatives of the world's faiths, brought together by their participation in the World Economic Forum, which had moved from Davos, Switzerland, to New York, as a gesture of solidarity to a city which had suffered so much trauma and loss. The archbishop of Canterbury said a prayer. So did a Muslim iman. A hindu guru from India recited a meditation and sprinkled rose petals on the site, together with holy water from the Ganges. The Chief Rabbi of Israel read a reflection he had written for the occasion. Another rabbi said kaddish, the traditional Jewish prayer for the dead. It was a rare moment of togetherness in the face of mankind's awesome powers of destruction. I found myself wondering at the contrast between the religious fervour of the hijackers and the no less intense longing for peace among the religious leaders who were there. The juxtaposition of good and evil, harmony and conflict, global peace and holy war, seemed to me a fitting metaphor for the century we have just begun. We have acquired fateful powers. We can heal or harm, mend or destroy on a scale unimaginable to previous generations. The stakes have never been higher, and the choice is ours.[41]

Rabbi Sacks distinguishes politicians, who have power, from religions, who have something stronger – namely, influence. He reminds us how superpowers rise and fall: Spain in the fifteenth century, Venice in the sixteenth century, Netherlands in the seventeenth, France in the eighteenth, Britain in the nineteenth, and the United States in the twentieth. By contrast, the great religions survive: Islam is fifteen hundred years old, Christianity two thousand,

40. Ibid., 6.
41. Ibid., 1–2.

and Judaism four thousand;[42] he tells of his friendship with leaders of other faiths, including Islam – not only from Britain, but also from the Middle East. And then comes his final question: Can we make place for each other?

In his more recent book, entitled *The Great Partnership: God, Science and the Search for Meaning*, Rabbi Jonathan Sacks refers to a study conducted throughout the United States between 2004 and 2006 by sociologist Robert D. Putnam, referred to in Putnam's book *American Grace*,[43] which showed that those who frequently go to church or synagogue are more likely to make donations to charity, for any purpose, than their secular counterparts, as well as more likely to volunteer their time for a cause or even on an individual level to help another person. Not only are religious service-goers more likely to offer assistance to other individuals, but they are also more likely – by a wide margin – than secular people to give of themselves to society in the form of involvement with civic organizations and the political process.[44]

The research concluded that religion creates community, community creates altruism, and altruism turns us away from self and toward the common good.

Regarding the international suffering that is going on, it is known that the majority of the Muslims in the world do not support jihad – they simply refrain from involvement out of apathy and/or fright. It is also known that a substantial number – possibly the majority – of the religious Muslim leaders favors mutual tolerance and peace. A way must be found – organized by all Christian denominations and the democratic governments – to empower these leaders to turn the Muslim masses against the jihadists and to support by all means the fight that must be waged by all nations to eliminate this curse from the earth.

La Convivencia

In his master opus, James Carroll describes the friendly coexistence of Jews, Christians, and Muslims in the Iberian Peninsula of the early medieval age. His description of the history of those times reveals a completely different picture

---

42. Ibid., 195, and Sacks, *The Great Partnership*, 176–67.
43. Robert D. Putnam and David E. Campbell, *American Grace: How Religion Divides and Unites Us* (Simon and Schuster, 2012).
44. Rabbi Jonathan Sacks, *The Great Partnership: God, Science and the Search for Meaning* (London: Hodder and Stoughton, 2011), 277–78.

from that reflected in the events of later times. Some of his descriptions on the subject are as follows:

> In Cordoba, for example, under the rule of the Islamic caliphate, Christians were welcome to hold their worship services in the Great Mosque, and they did so. It was one of the grand building complexes in Europe dating to the eighth century, proudly situated by a noble river, above an ancient Roman bridge.... [45]
>
> Jews were taught Arabic by Muslim scholars, and they mastered the Koran as well as Hebrew Scriptures.... The most familiar such figure is the Cordoba native Moses ben Maimon, whose writing proves the point: perhaps the most revered of all Jewish sages, Maimonides wrote in Arabic, not Hebrew.... Because his creativity and intelligence were nurtured by the richest diversity of influences in the world – among the richest in history – Maimonides became "the greatest genius ever produced by the Jewish people." ... So Maimonides is a kind of measure of the value of *convivencia* [coexistence]. And as Muslims were the teachers of Jews, so Jews were schoolmasters to Christians, particularly in Castile and Catalonia.... [46]
>
> Yet *convivencia*, that it existed at all, establishes that there is nothing monolithic about the history of Jewish-Christian relations, and nothing fated to lead inexorably to disaster. That Jews and Christians, together with Muslims, can live in amity, respecting differences while honoring commonalities – that this is no pipe dream – is proven by the fact that, for centuries, they did just that.... [47]

There is no reason why the religions of the world should not be able to establish a *convivencia* in the twenty-first century and together cooperate with a new world organization.

Once the United Nations suffered the same fate as the League of Nations, a group of democratic states could form together. Convinced that an organized community of nations must be based on the premise that human rights are respected in the internal regimes of each state, this being a condition sine qua non for belonging to the new organization, they would draft a program based

45. Carroll, *Constantine's Sword*, 322.
46. Ibid., 323.
47. Ibid., 323–24.

on the principles established in the three historical precedents of the UDHR, as described in chapter 6. The program would be adapted to the contemporary realities, taking into consideration the tragic world events that occurred from the beginning of the twentieth century to the present.

Besides the state delegations to the drafting committee, a number of representatives of the great world religions would participate, in order to cooperate with the aim that the ethical fundaments inherent in all faiths will be duly considered and respected in the structure and working of the new league of nations.

The organization would set in its agenda the obligation of mutual respect and reciprocal support and establish a series of economic rules to be followed in international trade as well as regarding support extended to nonmember states and their communities.

All the sincere and inspiring declarations that were heard at the time of the preparation of the Universal Declaration of Human Rights would be duly considered, but the documents to be drafted for the new organization would keep in mind the failures of the past and of present times so that the program can be structured in accordance with the realities of the world community.

Each of the participating states would agree up front that in case of grave internal turmoil that could endanger its population, the other participating states would be entitled to intervene in order to protect endangered people and reestablish internal peace. This would establish a precedent for any state that would later apply for membership in the new world organization. In this way, the principle of sovereignty would be clearly established, but alongside that would be the authorization for intervention in case a qualified majority of members agreed on the need for doing so.

The acceptance of membership of other states would be strictly conditioned on their being governed according to democratic rules, on their manifesting absolute respect for all human rights, and on their readiness to submit to the decisions of the majority of the member states.

This system would lead to a very slow growth of the entity's membership, and so for a long time the world would be divided between member states and other states not integrated in the organization.

After submitting itself to the conditions established for membership, the candidate-state would be accepted on an experimental basis in order to ascertain the stability of its democratic regime and its respect for human rights.

Most importantly, the so-considered liberal democratic states would have to eliminate their traditional attitudes of putting their economic and/or political interests above all considerations when dealing with the crisis and sufferings of other peoples. Above all else must stand the respect of the democracy of other states and the prohibition against any kind of involvement in the healthy development of their political and economic progress. The United States, England, France, and other states considered liberal democracies would have to recognize their past sins toward weaker states and take upon themselves the compromise never again to export terror, but instead to respect the dignity of other peoples as they respect that of their own. By so doing they would be setting an honorable example to the rest of the community of nations.

The new organization would not be a hostage of the states that support terrorism, as is the present reality of the United Nations. It would have a free hand to fight this murderous evil that grows exponentially. The war on terror would not be restricted by the UN's hypocritical theories regarding the human rights of the terrorist. It would be a long and difficult war but, as more and more states realized the need to destroy this dangerous enemy of civilization and accepted cooperation with the new organization, a future of peace and tranquility could be envisaged.

As long as the world remained divided between state members of the new world order and states that did not submit to the principles of equality of all human beings, difficulties would arise in the field of international market economy. To deal with this we would need great economists who are also intelligent statesmen, conscious of the political implications. They would establish a system that would maintain the free flow of international commerce to whatever extent possible, without damaging the basic philosophy of the new organization.

The Contribution of Great Religious Leaders

The new world organization would gain inspiration and orientation if the great leaders of all religions united in its support. Religious leaders could help create a system in which ethics and morality would control and direct international economy and politics, for "an ethical norm is a common denominator in all religious systems."[48]

---

48. Rabbi Joseph B. Soloveitchik, *The Halakhic Mind: An Essay on Jewish Tradition and Modern Thought* (Philadelphia: Jewish Publication Society of America, 1983), 70.

The alliance of all religions would be the strong and determinant influence over the state members composing the new organization. Once the representatives of the willing democracies agreed on a certain policy, the religious leaders would be there to give support and advice, as the power of ethos would be the fundamental philosophy of the new organization. And through its fairness, correctness, and coherence, the organization would gain respect from the non-associated states. In such a system, the ideals that were just a dream in the post–World War II era could become a reality as peoples in danger would be saved, peoples in need would be supported, and help would be extended to reorganize and bring peace to failed states. The world would march toward the reign of peace on the planet as the rights of every human being would be respected, in the spirit of the dignity of difference and the nobility of cooperation.

Rabbi Sacks shows how religion teaches us that humanity as a whole is above any political entity and that the realm of faith is where the peoples of the world can unite and cooperate.

The philosopher-rabbi's basic theory is that if we believe in God, then we have to recognize that the one Divinity has created many religions and we must make place for all of them.

Can we expect a similar attitude from leaders of the other great religions? Could they come together, not for an afternoon on the site of the world organization, but to steadfastly work out a scheme of cooperation based on tolerance and reciprocal goodwill, and under this ideal, plan how to help the establishment of a new world organization based on justice and freedom?

And how will the world religions be represented? Will their most representative authorities cooperate?

A Dream That May Still Materialize

The records of the first meeting of the Commission on Human Rights of the Economic and Social Council registers the presentation of Mr. Henri Laugier, assistant secretary-general of the UN in charge of social affairs, whose statement was referred to in chapter 6 and above in this chapter in an abbreviated form and is now quoted in its full text:

You will have to look for a basis for a fundamental declaration on human rights acceptable to all the UN. The acceptance of which will become the essential condition of the admission in the international community. You will have before you the difficult but essential problem to define the violation of human rights within a nation, which would constitute a menace to the security and peace of the world and the existence of which is sufficient to put in movement the mechanism of the UN for the maintenance of peace and security. You will have to suggest the establishment of machinery of observation which will find and denounce the violations of the rights of man all over the world. Let us remember that if this machinery had existed a few years ago, if it had been powerful and if the universal support of public opinion had given it authority, international action would have been mobilized immediately against the first authors and supporters of fascism and Nazism. The human community would have been able to stop those who started the war at the moment when they were still weak and the world catastrophe would have been avoided.[49]

The mission described by Monsieur Laugier was not accomplished by the United Nations for the reasons that have been explained in the course of this book. A new world organization, set up and conducted with strict adherence to respect for human rights, individually and collectively, could materialize the dream that inspired the world in the aftermath of World War II.

Closing the United Nations through the disengagement of a number of relevant state members would open a new chapter in the history of world cooperation that might be able to lead to peace and security for humanity.

49. Max Beer, "Can We Save the Bill of Human Rights? Opportunity for a New Start," *Commentary*, October 1, 1953, https://www.commentarymagazine.com/?s=Can+We+Save+the+Bill+of+Human+Rights, and Allida M. Black, "Eleanor Roosevelt and the Universal Declaration of Human Rights," *OAH Magazine of History* 22, no. 2 (April 2008): 34–37, www.jstor.org/stable/pdfplus/25162170.

Bibliography

Abella, Irving, and Harold Troper. *None Is Too Many: Canada and the Jews of Europe, 1933–1948*. Toronto: Lester and Orpen Dennys, 1983.

Alston, Philip. "The Universal Declaration at 35." *Review of the International Commission of Jurists* 31 (1983): 60–70.

Alston, Philip, and Ryan Goodman. *International Human Rights: The Successor to International Human Rights in Context*. Oxford: Oxford University Press, 2012.

Alvarez, Jose E. "Note from the President." *American Society of International Law Newsletter* 23, no. 2 (spring 2007): 1, 7.

Amann, Diane Marie. "International Decisions: Prosecutor v. Lubanga." *American Journal of International Law* 106, no. 4 (October 2012): 809–17.

Ancel, Bertrand, and Yves Lequette. *Grands arrêts de la jurisprudence française de droit international privé*. 3rd ed. Paris: Dalloz, 1998.

Aristotle. *Nicomachean Ethics*. Translated by W.D. Ross. In vol. 9 of Hutchins, *Great Books*.

Ascensio, Hervé, Emmanuel Decaux, and Alain Pellet, eds. *Droit international penal*. Paris: Pedone, 2000.

Barak, Aharon. *The Judge in a Democracy*. Princeton, NJ: Princeton University Press, 2006.

Bayefsky, Anne. "Ban Ki-moon's Shameful Message in Israel's Hour of Need." *Jerusalem Post*, July 22, 2014. http://www.jpost.com/LandedPages/PrintArticle.aspx?id=368415.

———. "Europe, US pressuring Israel to endure discrimination at UN Human Rights Council." *Jerusalem Post*, October 27, 2013. http://www.jpost.com/LandedPages/PrintArticle.aspx?id=329832.

———. "Neither Redeemable nor Reformable." *Justice: The International Association of Jewish Lawyers and Jurists* 45 (spring 2008): 29–35.

———. "The United Nations: World's Leading Purveyor of Antisemitism." Gatestone Institute, September 16, 2014. http://www.gatestoneinstitute.org/4708 /united-nations-antisemitism.

Baynes, Norman H. *The Speeches of Adolph Hitler, April 1922–August 1939.* Vol. 1. London: Oxford University Press, 1942.

Beit Sourik Village Council v. The Government of Israel, HCJ 2056/04, Israel: Supreme Court, 30 May 2004. In *Israel Law Review* 38, nos. 1–2 (winter/spring 2005): 83–133.

Beitz, Charles R. *The Idea of Human Rights.* Oxford: Oxford University Press, 2009.

Bellamy, Alex J. "Military Intervention." In Bloxham and Moses, *Oxford Handbook of Genocide Studies,* 597–616.

Bennoune, Karima. Review of *Enforcing International Law Norms against Terrorism,* edited by Andrea Bianchi. *American Journal of International Law* 100, no. 2 (April 2006): 507–13.

Beres, Louis René. "Terrorists are not 'Freedom Fighters.'" News with Views, March 13, 2002. http://www.newswithviews.com/israel/israel15.htm.

Birnbaum, Ervin. "Évian: The Most Fateful Conference of All Times in Jewish History," part 2. *Nativ,* February 2009.

Black, Allida M. "Eleanor Roosevelt and the Universal Declaration of Human Rights." *OAH Magazine of History* 22, no. 2 (April 2008): 34–37.

Bloxham, Donald, and A. Dirk Moses, eds. *The Oxford Handbook of Genocide Studies.* New York: Oxford University Press, 2013.

Bloxham, Donald, and Devin O. Pendas. "Punishment as Prevention? The Politics of Punishing Génocidaires." In Bloxham and Moses, *Oxford Handbook of Genocide Studies,* 617–37.

Boerger, Anne. "At the Cradle of Legal Scholarship on the European Union: The Life and Early Work of Eric Stein." *American Journal of Comparative Law* 62, no. 4 (2014): 859–92.

Bonell, M.J. *An International Restatement of Contract Law.* 2nd ed. New York: Transnational, 1997.

Boyle, Kevin. "Stock Taking on Human Rights: The World Conference on Human Rights, Vienna 1993." *Political Studies* 43, no. 1 (August 1995): 79–95.

Brownlie, Ian. *Principles of Public International Law.* 2nd ed. Oxford: Clarendon Press, 1973.

Buergenthal, Thomas. "The Evolving International Human Rights System." *American Journal of International Law* 100, no. 4 (October 2006): 783–807.

———. *International Human Rights in a Nutshell.* Nutshell Series. St. Paul, MN: West Publishing, 1988.

Bulag, Uradyn E. "Twentieth-Century China: Ethnic Assimilation and Intergroup Violence." In Bloxham and Moses, *Oxford Handbook of Genocide Studies*, 426–44.

Calvo-Goller, Karin. "More Than a Huge Imbalance: The ICJ's Advisory Opinion on the Legal Consequences of the Construction of the Barrier." *Israel Law Review* 38, nos. 1–2 (winter/spring 2005): 165–88.

Carnegie, A.R. "Jurisdiction over Violations of the Laws and Customs of War." *British Yearbook of International Law* 39 (1963): 402–24.

Carreau, Dominique. *Droit International*. 5th ed. Paris: Pedone, 1997.

Carroll, James. *Constantine's Sword: The Church and the Jews*. Boston: Mariner, 2001.

Cassel, Doug. Review of *All the Missing Souls: A Personal History of the War Crimes Tribunals*, by David Scheffer. *American Journal of International Law* 107, no. 1 (January 2013): 252–59.

Chow, Pok Yin S. "Memory Denied: A Commentary on the Reports of the UN Special Rapporteur in the Field of Cultural Rights on Historical and Memorial Narratives in Divided Societies." *International Lawyer* 48, no. 3 (2015): 191–213.

Cohen, Amichai. "Rules and Applications of International Humanitarian Law." *Israel Law Review* 41, nos. 1–2 (2008): 41–67.

Cohen, G. Daniel. "The Holocaust and the 'Human Rights Revolution.'" In Iriye, Goedde, and Hitchcock, *Human Rights Revolution*, 53–71.

Cohn, Haim. *Human Rights in Jewish Law*. Hoboken, NJ: Ktav, 1984.

Cornwell, John. *Hitler's Pope: The Secret History of Pius xii*. New York: Viking, 1999.

Cotler, Irvin. "The Iran-Hezbollah Terror Connection: What Must Be Done?" *Jerusalem Post*, July 12, 2013.

———. "The Universal Lessons of the Holocaust." *Jerusalem Post*, January 24, 2014.

Cox, Neville. "Blasphemy, Holocaust Denial, and the Control of Profoundly Unacceptable Speech." *American Journal of Comparative Law* 62, no. 3 (2014): 739–74.

Cretella Neto, José. "Dos Fundamentos Jurídicos do Combate ao Terrorismo." Thesis, University of São Paulo Law School, 2006.

Cribb, Robert. "Political Genocides in Postcolonial Asia." In Bloxham and Moses, *Oxford Handbook of Genocide Studies*, 445–65.

Crook, John R., ed. "Contemporary Practice of the United States Relating to International Law." *American Journal of International Law* 106, no. 4 (October 2012): 843–84.

———. "Contemporary Practice of the United States Relating to International Law: State Department Hails U.S. Accomplishments in UN Human Rights Council; United States to Seek Election to Another Council Term." *American Journal of International Law* 105, no. 3 (July 2011): 592–94.

———. "Contemporary Practice of the United States Relating to International Law:

United States Criticizes ASEAN Human Rights Declaration." *American Journal of International Law* 107, no. 1 (January 2013): 237–39.

―――. "Contemporary Practice of the United States Relating to International Law: U.S. Official Describes U.S. Policy toward International Criminal Court." *American Journal of International Law* 106, no. 2 (April 2012): 384–86.

―――. "Contemporary Practice of the United States Relating to International Law: U.S. Special Operation Personnel Raid Compound in Pakistan, Kill Osama bin Laden." *American Journal of International Law* 105, no. 3 (July 2011): 602–5.

―――. Review of *Evidence Before the International Court of Justice*, by Anna Riedel and Brendan Plant. *American Journal of International Law* 107, no. 1 (January 2013): 259–65.

Curran, Vivian Grosswald. Review of *Grands Systèmes de droit contemporains*, by Gilles Cuniberti. *American Journal of Comparative Law* (2013): 721–26.

D'Amato, Anthony, and Mary Ellen O'Connell. "United States Experience at the International Court of Justice." In *The International Court of Justice at a Crossroads*, edited by Lori Fisler Damrosch, 403–22. Dobbs Ferry, NY: Transnational, 1987.

Dershowitz, Alan. "How Amnesty International Suppresses Free Speech." November 10, 2014. http://www.gatestoneinstitute.org/4863/amnesty-international-free-speech.

―――. "Israel Follows Its Own Law, Not Bigoted Hague Decision." *Jerusalem Post*, July 11, 2004. Internet edition.

―――. Speech delivered at conference The Perils of Global Intolerance: The United Nations and Durban III. The Hudson Institute, New York, September 22, 2011. https://www.youtube.com/watch?v=DDOA3_vZIzc.

Dicey and Morris on the Conflict of Laws. Edited by Lawrence Collins. 12th ed. London: Sweet and Maxwell, 1993.

Dixon, Martin, and Robert McCorquodale. *Cases and Materials on International Law*. London: Blackstone Press, 1995.

Dolinger, Jacob. "*O Caso Dreyfus e a Dramática Ressureição de Emile Zola*" (The Dreyfus case and the dramatic resurrection of Emile Zola). In *Humanismo Judaico na Literatura na História e na Ciência*, vol. 2, edited by Centro de História e Cultura Judaica, 21–34. Rio de Janeiro: Verve, 2013.

―――. *Direito e Amor*. Rio de Janeiro: Editora Renovar, 2009.

Donovan, Donald Francis. "Responding to Mass Atrocities: The Challenge and Promise of International Law." *American Society of International Law Newsletter*, January–March 2014.

Duffett, John, ed. *Against the Crime of Silence: Proceedings of the Russell International War Crimes Tribunal*. New Jersey: O'Hare Books, 1968.

Dumas, Jacques. "La Sauvegarde Internationale des Droits de L'Homme." *Recueil des Cours de l'Academie de Droit International à la Haye* 59 (1937): 5–95.

Einhorn, Talia. "The Status of Judea and Samaria (the West Bank) and Gaza and the Settlements in International Law." Jerusalem Center for Public Affairs, 2014. http://jcpa.org/article/status-of-settlements-in-international-law/.

———. "The Status of Palestine/Land of Israel and Its Settlement Under Public International Law." *Nativ Online: A Journal of Politics and the Arts* 1 (2003). http://www.acpr.org.il/english-nativ/issue1/einhorn-1.htm.

Feierstein, Daniel. "National Security Doctrine in Latin America: The Genocide Question." In Bloxham and Moses, *Oxford Handbook of Genocide Studies*, 489–508.

Feinberg, Nathan. *Studies in International Law with Special Reference to the Arab-Israel Conflict.* Jerusalem: Magnes Press, Hebrew University, 1979.

Feingold, Henri L. *The Politics of Rescue: The Roosevelt Administration and the Holocaust, 1938–1945.* New Brunswick, NJ: Rutgers University Press, 1970.

Flusser, David. *Jewish Sources in Early Christianity.* Translated by John Glucker. Tel Aviv: Mod Books, 1993.

Friedenson, Joseph, and David Kranzler. *Heroine of Rescue: The Incredible Story of Recha Sternbuch Who Saved Thousands from the Holocaust.* New York: Mesorah Publications, 1984.

Friedman, Thomas L. *From Beirut to Jerusalem.* New York: Doubleday, 1989.

Friedmann, Wolfgang. *The Changing Structure of International Law.* New York: Columbia University Press, 1964.

Gabriel, Brigitte. "Tolerating Hate Is Not an Option." *Frontpage Magazine,* September 10, 2014. http://www.frontpagemag.com/2014/brigitte-gabriel/tolerating-hate-is-not-an-option.

Gaudemet, Jean. *Les sources du droit de l'église en occident du IIᵉ au VIIᵉ siècle.* Paris: Cerf, 1985.

Gilbert, Martin. *The Holocaust: The Jewish Tragedy.* New York: Collins, 1986.

Glaser, Stefan. *Droit International Pénal Conventionnel.* Brussels: Établissements Émile Bruylant, 1970.

Glendon, Mary Ann. *A World Made New: Eleanor Roosevelt and the Universal Declaration of Human Rights.* New York: Random House, 2002.

Glick, Caroline B. *The Israeli Solution: One-State Plan for Peace in the Middle East.* New York: Crown Forum, 2014.

Gold, Dore. *The Fight for Jerusalem: Radical Islam, the West, and the Future of the Holy City.* Washington: Regnery Publishing, 2007.

Goldhagen, Daniel Jonah. *Hitler's Willing Executioners: Ordinary Germans and the Holocaust*. New York: Vintage, 1997.

Goldsmith, Jack L., and Eric A. Posner. *The Limits of International Law*. Oxford: Oxford University Press, 2005.

Goodwin, Doris Kearns. *No Ordinary Time: Franklin and Eleanor Roosevelt; The Home Front in World War II*. New York: Simon and Schuster, 1994.

Green, Leslie C. *International Law through the Cases*. 4th ed. Toronto: Carswell, 1978.

Greenawalt, Alexander K.A. Review of *Genocide: A Normative Account*, by Larry May. *American Journal of International Law* 105, no. 4 (October 2011): 852–58.

Greig, Donald W. *International Law*. London: Butterworths, 1970.

Grotius, Hugo. *The Rights of War and Peace*. Book 1. Edited by Richard Tuck. Based on the French edition by Jean Barbeyrac. Natural Law and Enlightenment Classics. Indianapolis, IN: Liberty Fund, 2005.

Guggenheim, Paul. *Traité de Droit International Public*. Vol. 2. Geneva: Georg, 1954.

Guillaume, Gilbert. "O Estado de Israel e a Questão Palestina." In *Terrorismo e direito: Os impactos do terrorismo na comunidade internacional e no Brasil. Perspectivas politico-jurídicas*, edited by Leonardo Nemer Caldeira Brant, 69–102.

Harris, David John. *Cases and Materials on International Law*. 5th ed. London: Sweet and Maxwell, 1998.

Harris, Grant T. "Human Rights, Israel and the Political Realities of Occupation." Israel Ministry of Foreign Affairs. *Israel Law Review* 41 (2008): 87–174.

Hegel, Georg Wilhelm Friedrich. *Philosophy of History*. Translated by J. Sibree. In vol. 46 of Hutchins, *Great Books*.

———. *Philosophy of Right*. Translated by T.M. Knox. In vol. 46 of Hutchins, *Great Books*.

Henkin, Louis. "International Law: Politics, Values, and Functions." *Hague Academy of International Law* 216 (1989): 13–416.

Henkin, Louis, Richard Crawford Pugh, Oscar Schachter, and Hans Smit. *International Law: Cases and Materials*. 3d ed. St. Paul, MN: West Publishing, 1993.

Higgins, Rosalyn. "The June War: The United Nations and Legal Background." *Journal of Contemporary History* 3 (1968): 253–73.

Hirsch, Moshe. "The Legal Status of Jerusalem Following the ICJD Advisory Opinion on the Separation Barrier." *Israel Law Review* 38, nos. 1–2 (winter/spring 2005): 298–315.

Hobbes, Thomas. *Leviathan*. In vol. 23 of Hutchins, *Great Books*.

Holman, Melissa. "The Modern-Day Slave Trade." *Texas International Law Journal* 44 (fall/winter 2008): 99–121.

Horovitz, Sigal. "How International Courts Shape Domestic Justice: Lessons from Rwanda and Sierra Leone." *Israel Law Review* 46, no. 3 (November 2013): 339–67.

Huneeus, Alexandra. "International Criminal Law by Other Means: The Quasi-Criminal Jurisdiction of the Human Rights Courts." *American Journal of International Law* 107, no. 1 (January 2013): 1–44.

Hutchins, Robert Maynard, ed. *Great Books of the Western World.* 54 vol. Chicago: Encyclopedia Britannica, 1952.

International Legal Materials. American Society of International Law.

Iriye, Akira, and Petra Goedde. "Introduction: Human Rights as History." In Iriye, Goedde, and Hitchcock, *Human Rights Revolution*, 3–24.

Iriye, Akira, Petra Goedde, and William I. Hitchcock, eds. *The Human Rights Revolution: An International History.* New York: Oxford University Press, 2012.

Ishay, Micheline R. *The History of Human Rights: From Ancient Times to the Globalization Era.* Berkeley: University of California Press, 2004.

Jitta, Josephus. *Metodo del Derecho Internacional Privado.* Translated by J.F. Prida. Madrid: La Espana Moderna.

Johnson, Paul. *A History of the Jews.* New York: Harper and Row, 1988.

———. *Modern Times: The World from the Twenties to the Eighties.* New York: Harper and Row, 1985.

Kaiser, Hilmar. "Genocide at the Twilight of the Ottoman Empire." In Bloxham and Moses, *Oxford Handbook of Genocide Studies*, 365–85.

Kant, Immanuel. *Critique of Practical Reason.* Translated by Thomas Kingsmill Abbott. In vol. 42 of Hutchins, *Great Books.*

———. *Fundamental Principles of the Metaphysic of Morals.* Translated by Thomas Kingsmill Abbott. In vol. 42 of Hutchins, *Great Books.*

Kelsen, Hans. *Principles of International Law.* 2nd ed. Revised and edited by Robert W. Tucker. New York: Holt, Rinehart and Winston, 1966.

Kemp, Richard. Statement to the UN Human Rights Council Special Session. October 16, 2009. UN Watch. https://www.youtube.com/watch?v=JMofTssoUX4.

Kertzer, David I. *The Popes against the Jews: The Vatican's Role in the Rise of Modern Anti-Semitism.* New York: Alfred A. Knopf, 2001.

Kirgis, Frederic L. Review of *The United Nations Secretariat and the Use of Force in a Unipolar World: Power v. Principle*, by Ralph Zacklin. *American Journal of International Law* 105, no. 3 (July 2011): 619–22.

Koskenniemi, Martti. "Occupied Zone – 'A Zone of Reasonableness'?" *Israel Law Review* 41, nos. 1–2 (2008): 13–40.

Krauthammer, Charles. "Krauthammer's Take." *National Review Online*, July 5,

2012. http://www.nationalreview.com/corner/304894/krauthammers-take-nro
-staff.

Kretzmer, David. Introduction. *Israel Law Review* 38, nos. 1–2 (winter/spring 2005): 6–16.

Kunz, Josef L. "The United Nations Declaration of Human Rights." *American Journal of International Law* 43, no. 2 (April 1949): 316–23.

Laqueur, Walter. *The Terrible Secret: Suppression of the Truth about Hitler's "Final Solution."* New York: Henry Holt Books (Owl Books), 1998.

Lauren, Paul Gordon. *The Evolution of International Human Rights: Visions Seen.* Philadelphia: University of Pennsylvania Press, 1998.

Lauterpacht, Elihu. *Jerusalem and the Holy Places.* London: Anglo-Israel Association, 1968.

Lauterpacht, Hersch. "The Universal Declaration of Human Rights." *British Yearbook of International Law* 25 (1948): 354–77.

Leibler, Isi. "United Nations: Convergence of Hypocrisy, Deceit And Evil." *Jerusalem Post*, February 4, 2013.

Levin, Nora. *The Holocaust: The Destruction of European Jewry, 1933–1945.* New York: Schocken, 1973.

Locke, John. "A Letter Concerning Tolerance." In vol. 35 of Hutchins, *Great Books.*

Loftus, John, and Mark Aarons. *The Secret War against the Jews: How Western Espionage Betrayed the Jewish People.* New York: St. Martin's Press, 1994.

London, Louise. *Whitehall and the Jews, 1933–1948: British Immigration Policy and the Holocaust.* Cambridge: Cambridge University Press, 2000.

Lopes Cardozo, Nathan. *Crisis, Covenant and Creativity: Jewish Thoughts for a Complex World.* New York: Urim, 2005.

Maine, Sir Henry Sumner. *Ancient Law.* London: Oxford University Press, 1959.

Mann, F.A. "The Protection of Shareholder's Interests in the Light of the Barcelona Traction Case." *American Journal of International Law* 67, no. 2 (April 1973): 259–74.

McDougal, Myres S., and W. Michael Reisman. *International Law in Contemporary Perspective: The Public Order of the World Community.* Mineola, NY: Foundation Press, 1981.

Medoff, Rafael. *FDR and the Holocaust: A Breach of Faith.* Washington: The David S. Wyman Institute for Holocaust Studies, 2013.

Mendelssohn, Moses. *Jerusalem, or On Religious Power and Judaism.* Translated by Allan Arkush. Hanover: Brandeis University Press, 1983.

Meron, Theodor. *Human Rights Law-Making in the United Nations: A Critique of Instruments and Process.* Oxford: Clarendon Press, 1986.

————. "On a Hierarchy of International Human Rights." *American Journal of International Law* 80, no. 1 (January 1986): 1–23.

————. "Reflection on the Prosecution of War Crimes by International Tribunals." *American Journal of International Law* 100, no. 3 (July 2006): 551–79.

Mill, John Stuart. *On Liberty*. In vol. 42 of Hutchins, *Great Books*.

Montesquieu. *The Spirit of Laws*. Translated by Thomas Nugent. In vol. 38 of Hutchins, *Great Books*.

Morgenthau, Henry. *Ambassador Morgenthau's Story: A Personal Account of the Armenian Genocide*. 1918. Reprint, New York: Cosimo, 2010.

Morse, Arthur D. *While Six Million Died: A Chronicle of American Apathy*. 1967. Reprint, New York: Overlook Press, 1998.

Morsink, Johannes. *The Universal Declaration of Human Rights: Origins, Drafting and Intent*. Philadelphia: University of Pennsylvania Press, 1999.

Murphy, Sean D., ed. "Contemporary Practice of the United States Relating to International Law: Terrorist Attacks on the World Trade Center and Pentagon." *American Journal of International Law* 96, no. 1 (January 2002): 237–63.

Musmanno, Michael. "The Objections in Limine to the Eichmann Trial." *Temple Law Quarterly* 35, no. 1 (fall 1961): 1–22.

Neuer, Hillel. "Human Rights Nightmare." Speech before UN Human Rights Council 4th Session, March 23, 2007. UN Watch. http://secure.unwatch.org/site/apps/nlnet/content2.aspx?c=bdKKISNqEmG&b=1313923&ct=3698367&printmode=1.

————. Statement to UN Human Rights Council Emergency Session on Gaza. July 23, 2014. UN Watch. http://www.unwatch.org/unw-testimony-at-unhrc-urgent-session-on-gaza/.

————. "Test Yourself: Are You Pro Human Rights, or Just Anti-Israel?" July 16, 2014. UN Watch. http://blog.unwatch.org/index.php/2014/07/16/test-yourself-are-you-pro-human-rights-or-just-anti-israel/.

Novick, Peter. *The Holocaust in American Life*. New York: Houghton Mifflin, 2000.

O'Brien, Conor Cruise. *The Siege: The Saga of Israel and Zionism*. New York: Simon and Schuster, 1986.

Oppenheim, L.F.L. *International Law*. 9th ed. Vol. 1, *Peace*. Edited by Sir Robert Jennings and Sir Arthur Watts. London: Longman, 1997.

Palazzi, Abdul Hadi. "Jerusalem: Three-Fold Religious Heritage for a Contemporary Single Administration." In *Jerusalem: City of Law and Justice*, edited by Nahum Rakover, 77–83. Jerusalem: Library of Jewish Law, 1998.

Pascal, Blaise. *Pensés*. Translated by W.F. Trotter. In vol. 33 of Hutchins, *Great Books*.

Pattison, James. *Humanitarian Intervention and the Responsibility to Protect: Who Should Intervene?* Oxford: Oxford University Press, 2012.

Peixoto, Jose Carlos de Matos. *Curso de Direito Romano.* Vol. 1. 2nd ed. Rio de Janeiro: Fortaleza, 1950.

Perl, William R. *The Holocaust Conspiracy: An International Policy of Genocide.* New York: Shapolsky, 1989.

Persky, Anna Stolley. "The Capital of Rape: Fighting Widespread Sexual Violence in the Democratic Republic of the Congo." *American Bar Association Journal* 98, no. 2 (February 2012): 59–60.

Peters, Joan. *From Time Immemorial: The Origins of the Arab-Jewish Conflict over Palestine.* USA: Harper Torchbooks, 1988.

Phillips, Melanie. *Londonistan: How Britain Is Creating a Terror State Within.* New York: Encounter Books, 2006.

Pillet, Antoine. *Principes de droit international privé.* Paris: Pedone, 1903.

Plawski, Stanislaw. *Étude des principes fondamentaux du droit international pénal.* Paris: Librairie Générale de Droit et de Jurisprudence, 1972.

Podgers, James. "1985–1994: The Legacy of Nuremberg." *American Bar Association Journal* 101, no. 1 (January 2015): 55.

Pomerance, Michla. "A Court of UN Law." *Israel Law Review* 38, nos. 1–2 (winter/spring 2005): 134–64.

Posner, Eric A. *The Twilight of Human Rights Law.* Inalienable Rights Series. Oxford: Oxford University Press, 2014.

Posner, Richard A. *Not a Suicide Pact: The Constitution in a Time of National Emergency.* Oxford: Oxford University Press, 2006.

Pufendorf, Samuel von. *The Whole Duty of Man According to the Law of Nature.* Translated by Andrew Tooke. Natural Law and Enlightenment Classics. Indianapolis, IN: Liberty Fund, 2003.

Pusey, Allen. "Aug. 12, 1998: Swiss Banks Settle Holocaust Claims." *American Bar Association Journal* 100, no. 8 (August 2014): 72.

———. "Students Spark Civil Rights Sit-Ins." *American Bar Association Journal* 100, no. 2 (February 2014): 72.

Rakover, Nahum, ed. *Jerusalem: City of Law and Justice.* Jerusalem: Library of Jewish Law, 1998.

Ratner, R. Steven, Jason S. Abrams, and James L. Bischoff. *Accountability for Human Rights Atrocities in International Law: Beyond the Nuremberg Legacy.* 3rd ed. Oxford: Oxford University Press, 2009.

Report of the Harvard University School of Law. Supplement of the *American Journal of International Law* 29 (1935): 1–1240.

Restatement of the Law, Third: The Foreign Relation Law of the United States. 2 vols. St. Paul, MN: American Law Institute, 1987.

Robinson, Geoffrey. "State-Sponsored Violence and Secessionist Rebellions in Asia." In Bloxham and Moses, *Oxford Handbook of Genocide Studies*, 466–88.

Roscini, Marco. "The United Nations Security Council and the Enforcement of International Humanitarian Law." *Israel Law Review* 43 (2010): 330–59.

Rosenberg, Shimon, and Yaakov Astor. "The Dark Side of FDR and the American Jewish 'leaders' Who Advised Him." *Zman*, August 2011.

Roth, Cecil. *A Short History of the Jewish People.* London: East and West Library, 1953.

Rousseau, Jean Jacques. *On the Origin of Inequality.* Translated by G.D.H. Cole. In vol. 38 of Hutchins, *Great Books*.

———. *The Social Contract.* Translated by G.D.H. Cole. In vol. 38 of Hutchins, *Great Books*.

Sacks, Jonathan. *The Dignity of Difference: How to Avoid the Clash of Civilizations.* London: Continuum, 2002.

———. *The Great Partnership: God, Science and the Search for Meaning.* London: Hodder and Stoughton, 2012.

———. *A Letter in the Scroll: Understanding Our Jewish Identity and Exploring the Legacy of the World's Oldest Religion.* New York: Free Press, 2000.

Sartre, Jean-Paul. *Anti-Semite and Jew: An Exploration of the Etiology of Hate.* New York: Schocken Books, 1948.

Schabas, William A. "The Law and Genocide." In Bloxham and Moses, *Oxford Handbook of Genocide Studies*, 123–41.

———. *Unimaginable Atrocities: Justice, Politics, and Rights at the Crimes Tribunals.* Oxford: Oxford University Press, 2012.

Scheffer, David. *All the Missing Souls: A Personal History of the War Crimes Tribunals.* Princeton and Oxford: Princeton University Press, 2012.

Schwebel, Stephen. "Editorial Comment: What Weight to Conquest?" *American Journal of International Law* 64, no. 2 (April 1970): 344–47.

Seidenberg, Steven. "A Law with Bite." *American Bar Association Journal* 99, no. 12 (December 2013): 58–59.

———. "Of Human Bondage." *American Bar Association Journal* 99, no. 4 (April 2013): 51–57.

Seiff, Abby. "Seeking Justice in the Killing Fields: For a War Crimes Tribunal in Cambodia, Successful Prosecution of Khmer Rouge Leaders Is No Sure Thing." *American Bar Association Journal* 99, no. 3 (March 2013): 50–57.

Sharansky, Natan. "Foreword." *Jewish Political Studies Review* 16, nos. 3–4 (Fall 2004): 5–8.

Sloss, David. Review of *Socializing States: Promoting Human Rights through International Law*, by Ryan Goodman and Derek Jinks. *American Journal of International Law* 108, no. 3 (July 2014): 576–82.

Sohn, Louis B., and Thomas Buergenthal, eds. *The International Protection of Human Rights*. Indianapolis, Indiana: Bobbs Merrill, 1972.

Soloveitchik, Joseph B. *The Halakhic Mind: An Essay on Jewish Tradition and Modern Thought*. Philadelphia: Jewish Publication Society of America, 1983.

Sorensen, Max, ed. *Manual of Public International Law*. New York: St. Martin's Press, 1968.

Spinoza, Baruch. *Ethics*. Translated by W.H. White. In vol. 31 of Hutchins, *Great Books*.

Steiner, Henry J., and Detlev F. Vagts. *Transnational Legal Problems*. 3rd ed. New York: Foundation Press, 1986.

Sweeney, Joseph Modeste, Covey T. Oliver, and Noyes E. Leech. *The International Legal System: Cases and Materials*. 3rd ed. Westbury, NY: Foundation Press, 1988.

Talbot, Ian, and Gurharpal Singh. *The Partition of India*. Cambridge: Cambridge University Press, 2009.

Tardif, Adolphe. *Histoire des sources du droit canonique*. Paris, 1887. Reprint, Aalen: Scientia Verlag, 1974.

Templeman, Lord, and Robert MacLean. *Public International Law*. London: Old Bailey, 1997.

Tiburcio, Carmen. *The Human Rights of Aliens under International and Comparative Law*. The Hague, Netherlands: Martinus Nijhoff, 2001.

Tribunal permanent des peuples. *Le crime de silence: Le génocide des Arméniens*. Paris: Flammarion, 1984.

Troy, Gil. *Moynihan's Moment: America's Fight against Zionism as Racism*. New York: Oxford University Press, 2013.

Tusa, Ann, and John Tusa. *The Nuremberg Trial*. New York: Atheneum, 1986.

Ussher, Clarence D. *An American Physician in Turkey: A Narrative of Adventures in Peace and War*. 1917. Reprint, London: Sterndale Classics, 2002.

Vieira, Manuel A. *Derecho Penal Internacional y derecho internacional penal*. Montevideo, Uruguay: Fundacion de Cultura Universitaria, 1969.

Vincent, Nicholas. *Magna Carta: A Very Short Introduction*. Oxford: Oxford University Press, 2012.

Weiss, Stewart. "In Plain Language: In Place of a Jewish State." *Jerusalem Post*

Magazine. November 28, 2014, 37. http://www.jpost.com/Opinion/In-Plain-Language-In-place-of-a-Jewish-state-383040.

Weston, Burns H., Richard Falk, and Anthony D'Amato. *International Law and World Order: A Problem-Oriented Course.* 2nd ed. St. Paul, MN: West Publishing, 1990.

Wiesel, Elie. *And the Sea Is Never Full: Memoirs, 1969– .* New York: Alfred A. Knopf, 1999.

Winter, Jay, and Antoine Prost. *René Cassin and Human Rights: From the Great War to the Universal Declaration.* Human Rights in History. New York: Cambridge University Press, 2013.

Wyman, David S. *The Abandonment of the Jews: America and the Holocaust, 1941–1945.* 1984. Reprint, New York: The New Press, 2007.

Yahil, Leni. *The Holocaust: The Fate of European Jewry.* Oxford: Oxford University Press, 1990.

Zola, Emile. *The Dreyfus Affair: "J'Accuse" and Other Writings.* Edited by Alain Pagès. Translated by Eleanor Levieux. New Haven: Yale University Press, 1998.

Zumrut, Osman. "The Influence of Jewish Law on Islamic Legal Practice." In *Jerusalem: City of Law and Justice,* edited by Nahum Rakover, 475–83. Jerusalem: Library of Jewish Law, 1998.

▌Index